1 MONTH OF
FREE
READING

at

www.ForgottenBooks.com

By purchasing this book you are eligible for one month membership to ForgottenBooks.com, giving you unlimited access to our entire collection of over 700,000 titles via our web site and mobile apps.

To claim your free month visit:
www.forgottenbooks.com/free62549

ISBN 978-0-483-71160-0
PIBN 10062549

THE

ART OF BEAUTIFYING

SUBURBAN HOME GROUNDS

OF SMALL EXTENT.

ILLUSTRATED BY UPWARD OF TWO HUNDRED

PLATES AND ENGRAVINGS

OF PLANS FOR RESIDENCES AND THEIR GROUNDS, OF TREES AND SHRUBS, AND
GARDEN EMBELLISHMENTS;

WITH DESCRIPTIONS OF THE BEAUTIFUL AND HARDY

TREES AND SHRUBS

GROWN IN THE UNITED STATES.

BY

FRANK J. SCOTT.

NEW YORK:
AMERICAN BOOK EXCHANGE,
TRIBUNE BUILDING.
1881.

To the memory of A. J. Downing, his friend and instructor, this book is dedicated, with affectionate remembrance, by the author.

TABLE OF CONTENTS.

PART I.

SUBURBAN HOME GROUNDS.

PART II.

TREES, SHRUBS AND VINES.

CHAPTER IV.

CHAPTER V.

CHAPTER VI.

A KEY TO THE SYMBOLS USED IN THE FOLLOWING
DESIGNS

_____ Open fence on street lines

_____ Close high fence, or wall

.... Light wire fence, or no fence at all

_____ Road and Walk lines

Beds of quite low annuals or perennials

Flowering plants, *18 inches high and upwards*

Rose beds

Tilled ground for Vegetables

× Pillar Roses

Street trees   Vase with base   Rustic Vase

Deciduous trees *branching high enough to allow a clear view under their branches*

Pine tree

Arbor Vitaes and Cedars

Spruce Firs Hemlocks &c.

Small deciduous trees

Shrubbery

A   Apple tree

C   Cherry tree

Standard Pear tree   [△ Dwarf Pear tree]

Y   Peach tree

O   Plum tree

Q   Quince tree

Grape tree, or vine on stake

PART I.

SUBURBAN HOME GROUNDS.

INTRODUCTION.

"The landscape, forever consoling and kind,
Pours her wine and her oil on the smarts of the mind."

LOWELL.

THE aim of this work is to aid persons of moderate income, who know little of the arts of decorative gardening, to beautify their homes ; to suggest and illustrate the simple means with which beautiful home-surroundings may be realized on small grounds, and with little cost ; and thus to assist in giving an intelligent direction to the desires, and a satisfactory result for the labors of those who are engaged in embellishing homes, as well as those whose imaginations are warm with the hopes of homes that are yet to be.

It is more than twenty years since the poetical life and pen of

A. J. Downing warmed the hearts of his countrymen to a new love and zest for rural culture. In the department of suburban architecture, the work so charmingly begun by him has been carried forward by Vaux and a host of others, whose works are constantly appearing. But in the specialty of decorative gardening, adapted to the small grounds of most suburban homes, there is much need of other works than have yet appeared. Downing had begun in the books entitled "Cottage Residences and Cottage Grounds" and "Country Houses," to cover this subject in his peculiarly graceful as well as sensible style; but death robbed us of his pleasant genius in the prime of its usefulness. Since his time many useful works have appeared on one or another branch of gardening art; but not one has been devoted entirely to the arts of *suburban-home* embellishment. The subject is usually approached, as it were, sideways—as a branch of other subjects, architectural, agricultural, and horticultural—and not as an art distinct from great landscape-gardening, and not embraced in flori-culture, vegetable gardening, and pomology. The busy pen of the accomplished Donald G. Mitchell has treated of farm embellish-ment with an admirable blending of farmer-experience and a poet's culture; but he has given the farm, more than the citizen's subur-ban lot, the benefit of his suggestions. Copeland's "Country Life" is a hand-book grown almost into an encyclopædia of garden and farm work, full of matter giving it great value to the farmer and horticulturist. Other works, too numerous to mention, of special horticultural studies, as well as valuable horticultural an-nuals, have served to whet a taste for the arts of planning as well as planting. Some of them cover interesting specialties of decorative gardening. It is a hopeful sign of intelligence when any art or science divides into many branches, and each becomes a subject for special treatises. But books which treat, each, of some one department of decorative gardening, should follow, rather than precede, a knowledge of the arts of *arrangement*, by which, alone, all are combined to produce harmonious home-pictures; and for precisely the same reason that it is always best to plan one's house before selecting the furniture—which, however good in itself, may not otherwise suit the place where it must be used.

The term landscape-gardening is misapplied when used in connection with the improvement of a few roods of suburban ground ; and we disavow any claim, for this work, to treat of landscape-gardening on that large scale, or in the thorough and exhaustive manner in which it is handled by the masters of the art in England, and by Downing for this country. Compared with the English we are yet novices in the fine arts of gardening, and the exquisite rural taste even among the poorer classes of England, which inspired glowing eulogiums from the pen of Washington Irving thirty years ago, is still as far in advance of our own as at that time. British literature abounds in admirable works on all branches of gardening arts. LOUDON's energy and exhaustive industry seem to have collected, digested, and illustrated, almost everything worth knowing in the arts of gardening. But his works are too voluminous, too thorough, too English, to meet the needs of American suburban life. Kemp, in a complete little volume entitled "How to lay out a Garden," has condensed all that is most essential on the subject *for England.* But the arrangements of American suburban homes of the average character differ so widely from those of the English, and our climate also varies so essentially from theirs, that plans of houses and grounds suitable there are not often adapted to our wants. There is an extent and thoroughness in their out-buildings, and arrangements for man-servants and maid-servants and domestic animals, which the great cost of labor in this country forces us to condense or dispense with. Public and private examples of landscape-gardening on a grand scale begin to familiarize Americans with the art. The best cemeteries of our great cities are renowned even in Europe for their tasteful keeping. But more than all other causes, that wonderful creation, the New York Central Park, has illustrated the power of public money in the hands of men of tasteful genius to reproduce, as if by magic, the gardening glories of older lands. But public parks, however desirable and charming, are not substitutes for beautiful HOMES ; and with observation of such public works, and of examples of tasteful but very costly private grounds in many parts of the country, there comes an increasing need of practical works to epitomize and Americanize the principles of decorative gardening, *to illustrate their application to small grounds, and to effect in miniature, and around ordinary homes,* some of their loveliest results. Some of the most prized pictures of great landscape painters are scenes that lie close to the eye ; which derive little of their beauty from breadth of view, or variety of objects ; and yet they may be marvels of lovely or picturesque beauty. The half-acre of a suburban cottage (if the house itself is what it should be) may be as perfect a work of art, and as well worth transferring to canvas as any part of the great Chatsworth of the Duke of Devonshire.

Of the millions of America's busy men and women, a large proportion desire around their homes the greatest amount of beauty which their means will enable them to maintain; and the minimum of expense and care that will secure it. It is for these that this work has been prepared. It is not designed for the very wealthy, nor for the poor, but principally for that great class of towns-people whose daily business away from their homes is a necessity, and who appreciate more than the very rich, or the poor, all the heart's cheer, the refined pleasures, and the beauty that should attach to a suburban home.

In planning home-grounds, a familiarity with the materials from which the planter must choose is requisite to success in producing a desired effect. This work, therefore, embraces descriptions and many illustrations of trees and shrubs ; and is intended to be full in those matters which are of most interest to unscientific lovers of nature and rural art, in their efforts to create home beauty ;—such as the *expression* of trees and shrubs, as produced by their sizes, forms, colors, leaves, flowers, and general structure, quite independent of their characteristics as noted by the botanist. The botanical information incidentally conveyed in the names and descriptions of trees, shrubs, and flowers, has been drawn, it is hoped, from the best authorities ; but, for any errors that may be found in them, the author asks the kind indulgence of the more scientific reader.

CHAPTER I

ART AND NATURE.

"All nature is but art unknown to thee;
All chance, direction which thou canst not see.
POPE.

THE prevalent idea that the best decorative gardening is simply an imitation of pleasing natural scenery, is partially incorrect. If an imitation of Nature were the only aim, if she were simply to be let alone, or repeated, then a prairie, a wild forest, an oak-opening, a jungle, or a rocky scene, would only need to be inclosed to seem a perfect example of landscape gardening. All these forms of Nature have their peculiar beauties, and yet these very beauties, when brought into connection with our dwellings, are as incongruous as the picturesqueness of savage human life in streets or parlors. All civilization is marked by the touch of the arts which have subjugated the ruder elements in human and vegetable nature to mould and re-arrange them. We are not made to be content on nature's lower levels; for that spark of divinity within us—Imagination—suggests to us progress and improvement, and these are no less natural than existence. The arts which make life beautiful are those that graft upon the wildings of nature the refinements and harmonies which the Deity through the imagination is ever suggesting to us.

Decorative gardening had reached a high degree of perfection among ancient nations before the art now known as Landscape Gardening had its origin, or rather the beautiful development which it has reached in England within the last three centuries. The art which reproduces the wildness of rude nature, and that which softens the rudeness and creates polished beauty in its place, are equally arts of gardening. So too are the further arts by which plants and trees are moulded into unusual forms, and blended by studied symmetries with the purely artificial works of architecture. All are legitimate, and no one style may say to another, "Thou art false because thou hast no prototype in nature," since our dwellings and all the conveniences of civilized life would be equally false if judged by that standard. However diverse the modes of decorative gardening in different countries, all represent some ideal form of beauty, and illustrate that diversity of human tastes which is not less admirable than the diversity of productions in vegetable nature.

That may be considered good gardening around suburban homes which renders the dwelling the central interest of a picture, which suggests an intention to produce a certain type of embellishment, and which harmoniously realizes the type intended, whether it be a tree-flecked meadow, a forest glade, a copse belted lawn, a formal old French garden, a brilliant parterre, or a general blending of artfully grown sylvan and floral vegetation with architectural forms.

Not to reproduce the rudeness of Nature, therefore, but to adapt her to our civilized necessities, to idealize and improve, to condense and appropriate her beauties, to eliminate the dross from her vegetable jewels, and give them worthy setting—these are the aims of Decorative Gardening.

CHAPTER II.

DECORATIVE PLANTING—WHAT CONSTITUTES IT?

"He who sees my park, sees into my heart!"—PRINCE PUCKLER TO BETTINA VON ARNIM.

THE objects sought in Decorative Planting are various. The simple pleasure of working among and developing beautiful natural productions is one; the desire to make one's place elegant and attractive to other's eyes, and therefore a source of pride to the possessor, is also one of the strongest objects with many. To have a notably large variety of flowers, shrubs, or trees, is a very common form of planting enthusiasm; and the passion for some special and complete display of certain species of flowers (florists' hobbies) is another. Finally, and highest of all, *is the appreciation of, and desire to create with verdant Nature, charming effects of sunlight and shadow, or lovely exam-*

2

ples, in miniature, of what we call landscapes. Decorative Planting should have for its highest aim the beautifying of HOME. In combination with domestic architecture, it should make every man's home a beautiful picture. As skillful stonecutting, or bricklaying, or working in wood, does not make of the artisan an architect, or his work a fine art, so the love of trees, shrubs, and flowers, and their skillful cultivation, is but handling the tools of the landscape gardener—it is not gardening, in its most beautiful meaning. The garden of the slothful, overgrown with weeds and brambles, could not have been much more ugly to look upon than many flower-gardens, in which the whole area is a wilderness of annuals and perennials, of all sorts and sizes and conditions of life, full of beautiful bloom if we examine them in detail, and yet, as a whole, repulsive to refined eyes as a cob-webbed old furniture museum, crammed with heterogeneous beauties and utilities. Such gardens cannot be called decorative planting. They are merely bouquet nurseries of the lowest class, or botanical museums. Neither the loveliness of flowers, nor the beauties of trees and shrubs, alone, will make a truly beautiful place, unless arranged so that the special beauty of trees, plants, and flowers is subordinated to the general effect. An attempt to make good pictures by hap-hazard applications to the canvas of the finest paint colors, is not much more sure to result in failure than the usual mode of filling yards with choice trees, shrubs, and flowers. It is as easy to spoil a place with too many flowers as to mar good food with a superfluity of condiments. The same may be said of a medley plantation of the finest trees or shrubs. Numbers will not make great beauty or variety; on the contrary, they will often destroy both. That is the best art which produces the most pleasing pictures with the fewest materials. Milton, in two short lines, thus paints a home:

> "Hard by a cottage chimney smokes,
> From between two aged oaks."

Here is a picture ; two trees, a cottage, and green sward—these are all the materials. Unfortunately the "two aged oaks," or their equivalents, are not at hand for all our homes.

Has the reader ever noticed some remarkably pleasant old

home, where little care seemed taken to make it so; and yet with an air of comfort, and even elegance, that others, with wealth lavished upon them, and a professional gardener in constant employ, with flowers, and shrubs, and trees in profusion, yet all failing to convey the same impression of a pleasant home? Be assured that the former (though by accident it may be) is the better model of the two. A well-cut lawn, a few fine trees, a shady back-ground with comfortable-looking out-buildings, are the essentials; and walks, shrubs, and flowers, only the embellishments and finishing touches of the picture. Only the finishing touches—but what a charm of added expression and beauty there may be in those perfecting strokes! How a verdant gate-way arch frames the common walk into a picture view; how a long opening of lawn gives play room for the sunlight to smile and hide among the shadows of bordering shrubs and trees; how an opening here, in the shrubs, reveals a pretty neighborhood vista: how a flower-bed there, brightens the lawn like a smile on the face of beauty; how a swing suspended from the strong, outstretched arm of a noble tree attracts the children, whose ever-changing groups engage the eye and interest the heart; how a delicate foliaged tree, planted on yonder margin, glows with the light of the afternoon sun, or with airy undulations trembles against the twilight sky, till it seems neither of the earth or the sky, but a spirit of life wavering between earth and heaven!

Let us, then, define Decorative Planting to be the art of picture making and picture framing, by means of the varied forms of vegetable growth.

CHAPTER III

WHAT KIND OF HOME GROUNDS WILL BEST SUIT BUSINESS MEN, AND THEIR COST.

"Nature is immovable and yet mobile; that is her eternal charm. Her unwearied activity, her ever-shifting phantasmagoria. do not weary, do not disturb; this harmonious motion bears in itself a profound repose."—MADAME MICHELET.

IT is always a difficult matter to keep the happy medium between extravagance and parsimony. This uncertainty will be felt by every business man of moderate means who begins.

the expenditures about a suburban home. All men, who are not either devoid of fine tastes, or miserly, desire to have as much beauty around them as they can pay for and maintain; but few persons are familiar with the means which will gratify this desire with least strain on the purse. Two men of equal means, with similar houses and grounds to begin with, will often show most diverse results for their expenditures; one place soon becoming home-like, quiet, and elegant in its expression, and the other fussy, cluttered, and unsatisfactory. The latter has probably cost the most money; it may have the most trees, and the rarest flowers; more rustic work, and vases, and statuary; but the true effect of all is wanting. The difference between the two places is like that between the sketch of a trained artist, who has his work distinctly in his mind before attempting to represent it, and then sketches it in simple, clear outlines; and the untutored beginner, whose abundance of ideas are of so little service to him that he draws, and re-draws, and rubs out again, till it can hardly be told whether it is a horse or a cloud that is attempted. If the reader has any doubt of his own ability to arrange his home grounds with the least waste expenditure, he should ask some friend, whose good taste has been proved by trial, to commend him to some sensible and experienced designer of home-grounds.

It may be set down as a fair approximation of the expense of good ground improvements, that they will require about one-tenth of the whole cost of the buildings. Premising that the erection of the dwelling generally precedes the principal expenses of beautifying the grounds, this amount will be required during the two years following the completion of the house. If the land must be cleared of rocks, or much graded, or should require an unusually thorough system of tile-drainage, that proportion might be insufficient; but if the ground to be improved is in good shape, well drained, rich, and furnished with trees, a very much smaller proportion might be enough; and almost the only needful expense, would be that which would procure the advice and direction of some judicious landscape gardener. As a good lawyer often best earns his retainer by advising against litigation, so a master of gardenesque art may often save a proprietor enough, to pay for all that will be needed, by advising him what *not* to attempt.

But it is on bare, new grounds, that there will be most room for doubt of what to attempt. The man who must leave his home after an early breakfast to attend to his office or store business, and who only returns to dinner and tea, must not be beguiled into paying for the floral and arboricultural rarities that professional florists and tree-growers grow enthusiastic over, unless the home members of his family are appreciative amateurs in such things. Tired with town labor, his home must be to him a haven of repose. Gardeners' bills are no pleasanter to pay than butchers' and tailors' bills, and the satisfaction of paying either depends on the amount of pleasure received, or hoped to be received, from the things paid for. A velvety lawn, flecked with sunlight and the shadows of common trees, is a very inexpensive, and may be a very elegant refreshment for the business-wearied eye; and the manner in which it is kept will affect the mind in the same way as the ill or well-ordered house-keeping of the wife. But the beauties and varied peculiarities of a fine collection of trees, shrubs, and flowers require a higher culture of the taste, and more leisure for observation, than most business men have. All women are lovers of flowers, but few American ladies are yet educated in that higher garden culture—*the art of making pictures with trees, lawn, and flowers.* Without this culture, or a strong desire for it, it is best that the more elegant forms of gardening art should be dispensed with, and only simple effects attempted. Now a freshly mown meadow is always beautiful, and a well-kept lawn alone produces that kind of beauty. But the meadow or lawn, without a tree, is tame and monotonous. Large trees are necessary to enliven their beauty. A well-built house, with broad porch or veranda, may enable one to get along very comfortably without the shade of trees to protect its inmates from the excessive heat of the sun; but the play of light and shade in the foliage of trees, and upon the lawn, is as needful food for the eye as the sunny gayety of children is to the heart. These two things, then, are the most essential to the business man's home—a fine lawn and large trees. The former may be produced in a year; the latter must be bought ready grown on the ground. No amount of money spent at nurseries will give, in twenty years, the dignified beauty of effect that a few fine old trees will realize as soon as your house and lawn are completed.

But, unfortunately, the mass of men are obliged by business necessities, or other circumstances which are imperative, to build on sites not blessed with large trees. To enable them to make the most of such places, it is hoped that the succeeding chapters will point the way.

There is one hobby connected with removing from a city house to one "with some ground around it," which has been happily caricatured by some modern authors. We refer to the enthusiastic longing for fresh vegetables "of our own raising." A wealthy citizen, who had been severely seized with some of these horticultural fevers, invited friends to dine with him at his country-seat. The friends complimented his delicious green corn. "It *is* capital, I'm glad you appreciate it," said he; "it is from my own grounds, and by a calculation made a few days since I find that the season's crop will cost me only ten dollars an ear." Certainly this is an extreme case; but among the expensive luxuries for a business man's home a large kitchen garden is one of the most costly. Grass, and trees, and flowers, give daily returns in food for our eyes, seven months of the year, and cost less; yet many good housewives and masters spend more in growing radishes, lettuce, peas, beans, and even such cheap things as cabbages and potatoes, than it would cost to buy just as good articles, and maintain, besides, a lawn full of beauties. Vegetable gardening is a good and profitable business on a large scale, but on a small scale is not often made so, except by the good Dutch women, who can plant, hoe, and market their own productions, and live on the remainders. The kitchen garden does more to support the family of the gardener than the family of the proprietor, and it is respectfully suggested that the satisfaction of having one's table provided with our Patrick's" peas and beans is not a high order of family pride. The professional gardener, who does the same business on a much larger scale, and vends his vegetables at our doors, is likely to grow them cheaper and just as good as we can grow them.

But in the matter of fruit, it is different. There are some fruits

that can only be had in perfection ripened on the spot where they
are to be eaten.   All market fruit-growers are obliged to pick fruit
before it is ripe, in order to have it bear transportation and keep
well.   We cannot, therefore, get luscious ripe fruit except by growing it; and we advise business men of small means and small
grounds to patronize the market for vegetables, but to grow their
own strawberries, raspberries, peaches, and pears; at least so far
as they may without making the beauty of their grounds subordi-
nate to the pleasures of the palate.   The eye is a constant feeder,
that never sates with beauty, and is ever refining the mind by the
influence of its hunger; but even luscious fruits give but a momen-
tary pleasure, and that not seldom unalloyed by excess and cloying
satiety.   Nature is more lavish of her luxuries for the eye than of
those for the stomach, and, in an economic point of view, it will be
wise to take advantage of her generosity.   To this end, it may be
profitably borne in mind that pleasing distant or near views of
country or city, of trees or houses, of sea or stream, which cost
nothing to preserve or keep in order, are the best picture investments that can be made; and to make charming verdant frames
for these pictures as well as little " cabinet pieces " of your own
for your neighbors to look in upon, will call into play the best skill
in gardenesque designing.

To make the most of common and inexpensive materials requires the same culture of the eye and the mind, as the manipulation
of the rarest.   To produce an effective picture with a single color
requires the same talent that would produce only more brilliant
effects with all the colors of the palette.   The most needed advice
to novices in suburban home-making is this: if you can afford to
spend but little on your grounds, study with the greater care what
beauty outside of them can be made a part of the outlook from
them; do not introduce anything which will convey the impression
that you desire to have anything look more expensive than it
really is; dispense with walks and drives except where they are
required for the daily comfort of your family; eschew rustic ornaments, unless of the most substantial and un-showy character, *and
in shadowy locations;* avoid spotting your lawn with garish carpentry, or plaster or marble images of any kind, or those lilliputian

caricatures on Nature and Art called rock-work; and, finally, by the exquisite keeping of what you have, endeavor to create an atmosphere of refinement about your place, such as a thorough lady housekeeper will always throw around her house, however small or plain it may be.

As the wife and family are the home-bodies of a residence, the business man of a city who chooses a home out of it should feel that he is not depriving them of the pleasures incident to good neighborly society. During his daily absence, while his mind is kept in constant activity by hourly contact with his acquaintances, the family at home also need some of the enlivening influences of easy intercourse with their equals, and should not be expected to find entire contentment in their household duties, with no other society day after day than that of their own little circle, and the voiceless beauty of grass, flowers, and trees. A throng of arguments for and against what is vaguely called country life suggest themselves in this connection, some of which are treated of in the following chapter, in which suburban and country homes are contrasted. The former, as we would have them, involve no banishment from all that is good in city life, but are rather the elegant culmination of refined tastes, which cannot be gratified in the city; the proper field for the growth of that higher culture which finds in art, nature, and congenial society combined, a greater variety of pleasures than can be found in the most luxurious homes between the high walls of city houses; a step in advance of the Indian-like craving for beads, jewelry, and feathers, which distinguishes the city civilization of the present day. Choosing a home out of the city simply because it can be secured more cheaply than in it, is not the kind of plea for a suburban life which we would present, yet we urge that at a given cost of home and living it yields a far greater variety of healthful pleasures, and a fuller, freer, happier life for man, woman, and child, than a home in the city.

CHAPTER IV

SUBURBAN NEIGHBORHOODS COMPARED WITH COUNTRY PLACES.

" 'Twas town, yet country too; you felt the warmth
Of clustering houses in the wintry time."—GEO. ELIOT.

LANDSCAPE GARDENING, on a grand scale, in this country, is only to be accomplished in public parks and cemeteries. Parks of considerable extent, as private property, are impracticable, by reason of the transient nature of family wealth, in a republic where both the laws and the industrial customs favor rapid divisions and new distributions.

Attempts to makc and keep great private parks are generally conspicuous failures. Some of the old family parks on the Hudson River, and a few in other parts of the country, may be thought of as exceptions, but they are exceptions which rather prove the rule ; for most of them are on portions of manorial grants, held under almost feudal titles, which have remained in the same families through several generations, simply because they are held under laws which present a jarring contrast with the general laws of property which now govern in most of the States. Great fortunes cannot be lavished perennially for half a century to keep them up, where fortunes are so seldom made or kept in families of high cultivation—the only ones which are likely to be led by their tastes, or qualified by their education, to direct such improvements successfully. It is from this lack of cultivation, and from sheer ignorance of the fine arts, the great expenditures and the generations of patient waiting for results, which are all necessary to produce such works, that so many wealthy men stumble and break their fortunes in ridiculous attempts to improvise parks. It would be well for our progress in Landscape Gardening that this word park, as applied to private grounds, should be struck out of use, and that those parts of our grounds which are devoted to what feeds the eye and the heart, rather than the stomach, should be called simply HOME-GROUNDS ; and that the ambition of private wealth in our republic should be to make gems of home beauty on a small scale, rather than fine examples of failures on a large scale. A township of land, with streets, and roads, and streams, dotted with a thousand suburban homes peeping from their groves ; with school-house towers and gleaming spires among them ; with farm fields, pastures, woodlands, and bounding hills or boundless prairies stretched around ;—these, altogether, form our suburban parks, which all of us may ride in, and walk in, and enjoy ; and the most lavish expenditures of private wealth on private grounds can never equal their extent, beauty, or variety.

A serious inconvenience of extensive private grounds, or parks, is the isolation and loneliness of the habitual inmates of the house— the ladies. Few, even of those who have a native love for rural life, can long live contented without pleasant near neighbors. A

large family may feel this less than a small one.   Those who have
the means, the health, and the disposition to entertain much company at home, will escape the feeling of loneliness.   But much
company brings much care.   It is paying a high price for company
when one must keep a free hotel to secure it.   To do without it,
however, soon suggests to the ladies that fewer acres, and more
friends near by, would be a desirable change ; and not knowing the
facility with which the happy medium may be reached, they are apt
to jump at the conclusion that, of the two privations—life in the
country without neighborly society, or life in the city without the
charms of Nature—the latter is the least.   Thousands of beautiful
homes are every year offered for sale, on which the owners have
often crippled their fortunes by covering too much ground with
their expenditures.   Instead of retiring to the country for rest and
strengthening recreation, they have added a full assortment of
losing and vexatious employments in the country to their already
wearisome but profitable business in the city.   It is the ambition
to have "parks" (young Chatsworths!)—to be model farmers and
famous gardeners ; to be pomologists, with all the fruits of the
nursery catalogues on their lists : in short, to add to the burden of
their town business the cares of half a dozen other laborious professions, that finally sickens so many of their country places after a
few years' experience with them.   There is another large class of
prosperous city men who have spent their early years on farms,
and who cherish a deep love of the country through all their de-
cennial rounds of city life ; who have no fanciful ambitions for
parks ; whose dreams are of hospitable halls, broad pastures, and
sweet meadows, fine cattle and horses.   It is a less vexatious mesh
of ambitions than the preceding, but one that requires a very
thoughtful examination of the resources of the purse and the calls
that will be made upon it, before purchasing the model farm that
is to be.   And we beg leave to intrude a little into the privacy of
the family circle, to inquire how long will the wife and daughters
be contented with isolation on ever so beautiful a farm ; how long
before the boys will leave home for business or homes of their
own ; and how long, if these are dissatisfied, or absent, will the
"fine mansion" and broad fields, in a lonely locality, bring peace

and comfort to the owner? That there are men and families that
truly fill, enjoy, and honor such life, it is good to know; but they
are cluster-jewels of great rarity.

Our panacea for the town-sick business man who longs for a
rural home, whether from ennui of the monotonousness of business
life, or from the higher nature-loving soul that is in him, is to take
country life as a famishing man should take food—in very small
quantities. *From a half acre to four or five acres will afford ground
enough to give all the finer pleasures of rural life.* The suburbs of
most cities, of from five to fifty thousand people, will have sites at
reasonable prices, within easy walking distance of business, where
men of congenial tastes and friendly families may make purchases,
and cluster their improvements so as to obtain all the benefits of
rural pleasures, and many of the beauties of park scenery, without
relinquishing the luxuries of town life.

In the neighborhood of large cities, horse and steam railways,
and steamers, transport in a few minutes their thousands of tired
workers to cheerful villages, or neighborly suburban homes, environed with green fields and loveable trees. To be thus transported
from barren city streets to the verdant country is a privilege for
which we cannot be too grateful. But, if we are to choose a suburban residence for the whole year (not migrating to a city home
or hotel with the first chills of November), it is a serious matter to
know whether there is a good hard road and sidewalk to the home.
City life, with its flagging, and gas lights, and pavements, comes
back to the imagination *couleur de rose* when your horses or your
boots are toiling through deep mud on country roads. This is bad
enough by daylight; at night you might feel like stopping to bestow a benediction on a post that would sparkle gas-light across
your path. Now the moral which we would suggest by thus presenting the most disagreeable feature of suburban life, is this: to go
no farther into the country than where good roads have already
been made, and where good sidewalks have either been made, or,
from the character or growth of the neighborhood, are pretty sure
to be made within a short time. Some persons must, of course, be
pioneers. Those who locate in a new suburban neighborhood
expect to buy their lots enough cheaper than the later comers to

compensate for the inconveniences of a sparse neighborhood. But, in playing pioneer, one must be pretty sure that followers are on the track, for "hope deferred maketh the heart sick." One of the greatest drawbacks to the improvement of suburban neighbor-hoods is the fact that many persons own long fronts on the roads who are not able to make the thorough improvement of roads and sidewalks in front of their grounds which the new-comers, located beyond them, require. This should have been foreseen by the new-comers. Having chosen their homes with the facts before them, they must not complain if some poor farmer or "land-poor" proprietor is unable to improve for their benefit, and unwilling to sell at their desire. In choosing a suburban home, the character of the ownerships between a proposed location and the main street or railroad station should be known, and influence to some extent one's choice.

The advantages cannot be too strongly urged, of forming com-panics of congenial gentlemen to buy land enough for all. Select a promising locality, divide the property into deep narrow strips, if the form of the ground will admit of it, having frontages of one, two, or three hundred feet each, according to the means respec-tively of the partitioners, and as much depth as possible. A depth four times as great as the frontage is the best form of subur-ban lots for improvement in connection with adjoining neighbors. Lots of these proportions insure near neighbors, and good walks and roads in their fronts, at least. Acting together, the little com munity can create a local pressure for good improvements that will have its effect on the entire street and neighborhood. In subse quent chapters we propose to show how such neighbors may im prove their grounds in connection with each other, so as to realize some pleasing effects of artistic scenerv at a comparatively small expense to each owner. Even the luxury of gas in our suburban houses and roads is quite practicable in the mode of dividing and improving property which we have recommended; and with good roads, sidewalks, and gas, added to the delightfulness of rural homes, no healthy-hearted family would wish to have their perma-nent home in a dark and narrow city house. Our cities would gradually become great working-hives, but not homes, for a majority of their people. It may be said that such homes as we speak of, in the suburbs of great cities, would be simply village resideuces. It is true; but they would be villages of a broader, more generous, and cosmopolitan character than old-fashioned villages. Post-offices, shops and groceries, butchers, bakers, blacksmiths, shoemakers, and laborers of all kinds must be near by, and a part of our community, or there would be no living at all; but where a large, and probably the most wealthy, part of the inhabitants go daily to the city centre to transact business, the amount of traffic carried on in the village or suburban centre will not be large enough to seriously injure the general rural character of the vicinity. The stir of thrifty industry is in itself refreshing, and the attractions of lecture, concert, and dancing halls, and ice-cream resorts, cannot be dispensed with.

We believe this kind of half-country, half-town life, is the happy medium, and the realizable ideal for the great majority of well-to-do Americans. The few families who have a unanimity of warm and long-continued love for more isolated and more picturesquely rural, or more practically rural homes, are exceptions. The mass of men and women are more gregarious. Very poetical or reflective minds, or persons absorbed in mutual domestic loves, find some of their deepest pleasure in seclusion with Nature. But the zest even of their calm pleasures in the country is greatly heightened by frequent contrasts with city excitements, and by the company of sympathetic minds, who enjoy what they enjoy. A philosophic Frenchman, who lived much alone, was once asked by a lady if he did not find solitude very sweet. He replied, " Indeed, madam, when you have some pleasant friend to whom you can say ' Oh, how sweet is solitude.' " A *suburban* home, therefore, meets the wants of refined and cultivated people more than any other.

CHAPTER V

BUILDING SITES AND GROUND SURFACES.

HAVING, in the chapter on "Suburban Neighborhoods compared with Country Places," suggested the most desirable proportions for suburban lots, we propose in this to consider building sites with reference to their tree-furniture, their natural surfaces, and the better ways of improving them. But it may not be superfluous to repeat, that where the form of the lot can be determined by the purchaser, a proportion where the depth is from three to four times as great as the frontage is usually the most desirable.

A varied surface is, of course, a great desideratum; yet, for quite small grounds, abruptness or picturesqueness is seldom compatible with the high keeping that is essential near the dwelling.

Occasionally, in rocky situations, or on the border of a running brook, such sites may be charmingly harmonized with the practical requirements of the dwelling and outbuildings; but they are exceptional. The great mass of house sites are smooth swells or levels.

Trees already grown are invaluable. To have them, or not to have them, is, to speak in business phrase, to begin with capital or without it. As capital draws to itself capital, so trees are magnets of home beauty, towards which domestic architecture, the gardener's arts, and varied family enjoyments are most naturally attracted. But there are trees whose age and habits of growth are not such as to give them high value. Forest trees, which have attained a lofty height, are not only dangerous in proximity to a dwelling, but are also likely to maintain a sort of living death when their contemporary trees are cut from around them—putting forth their leaves annually, it is true, but dying limb by limb at their summits, and scattering on the ground their dead twigs and branches. No grandeur of lofty trunk can mitigate the danger from spring winds or summer tempests that may bring its crushing weight upon the house and its inmates. But trees which have grown broadly in open ground, and lashed their arms and toughened their fibres in the gales of half a century, may be relied on to brood protectingly over a home; and few among these are more loveable in blossom, shade, and fruit, than fine old apple-trees. There is another class of trees which have little beauty as environments of a dwelling. We refer to " second-growth " trees, which have grown thickly together, and which, though valuable for their shade, form rather a nursery of rough poles, with a valuable mass of foliage over them, than an ornamental grove. Rough woods are quite too common in this country, and too rude in all their looks and ways, to be welcomed to our cultivated homes as we welcome the civilized and polished members of the tree family. But such dense groves of second-growth trees usually have many specimens among them well worth preserving, and which, if twenty feet high or upwards, will better repay good nursing and care than any young trees that can be planted to fill their places. The proprietor of such a building site is much more likely to err, however, in leaving too many than too few; and the thorough cutting out of the grove, which a landscape artist will insist on, may seem like wholesale slaughter to the owner.

Trees which have grown up singly, or in groups of a few only, exposed on all sides to the full glow of the sun and air, are worth more than a whole catalogue of nursery stuff for immediate and permanent adornment. It is surprising how little additional price most purchasers are willing to pay for lots that are enriched by such native trees, while they willingly expend ten times their cost in the little beginnings of trees procured from nurseries. *One* fine-spreading tree, of almost any native variety, is of inestimable value in home adornment. Few exotic trees are so beautiful as our finest natives, and nothing that we can plant will so well repay the most lavish enrichment of the soil to promote its growth as one of these trees "to the manor born." In locating a house with reference to fine trees already growing, it is much better to have them behind, or overhanging the sides, than to have them in front; the object being to make them a setting, or frame-work, for the house ; to have the house embowered in them, rather than shut out behind them.

Let us now consider some different forms of *ground surfaces.*

FIG. 1.

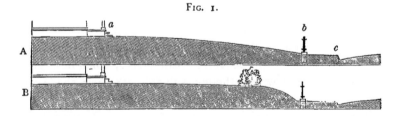

Ground which rises from the street, so that where it meets the house it is about on a level with the top of an ordinary fence at the street line, is a good form of surface. This rise should not, however, be on a plane from the street boundary to the dwelling. The lawn, and whatever is planted, will show to much better advantage if the rise takes the form of the arc of a circle, as shown in Fig. 1, section A, on which the front steps of the house are indicated at *a*, the front fence at *b*, and the street sidewalk at *c.*

Or, for increasing the apparent extent of the ground, the curve rising more rapidly near the fence may be an improvement, as shown in section B, of the same cut.

FIG. 2.

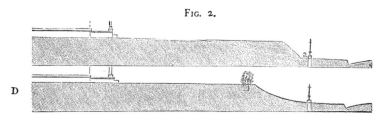

D

Sections C and D, of Fig. 2, illustrate three less common, and perhaps more elegant forms for ground surfaces next to the street. Back of the fence, at *a*, is a strip of ground, level with the sidewalk, not more than a foot wide, which should be kept free from grass by the hoe. The grass at the bottom of the terrace slope can then be trimmed to a line parallel with the fence. The effect is very pretty; and as it would be difficult to keep grass neatly cut at the bottom of such a slope so near the fence, this plan saves labor. The lower line on section C, of the same cut, shows a form that may be substituted for the terrace slope ; and at D is another form more gardenesque than either.

It is surprising how much larger grounds look which show such surfaces than those which are on a plane, level with the street. A quick rise from the street has the disadvantage, when the distance from the house to the gate is short, of requiring steps to gain the rise near the gate. Though no serious objection in summer, they are often dangerous in winter, especially to old people. In towns, a choice between such surfaces is frequently necessitated by the grading of a street a few feet below the level of adjacent lots. These should never be walled next to the street the full height of the excavation. The cuts just described illustrate appropriate modes of shaping the surface of the ground next to the street where the grade has not cut more than four feet below the general level at the street line. Grass slopes, behind light fences, are not only much cheaper than stone walls, but add more to the beauty of the grounds.

Fig. 3 shows a more elegant treatment of the same sort of surface for a deeper and larger lot. Here a space, at least wide enough to swing a scythe easily, is left between the fence and the first grass terrace. It must not be less than six feet wide, nor more than one-sixth of the distance from the fence to the house steps. Another grass terrace around the house is shown at C.

FIG. 3.

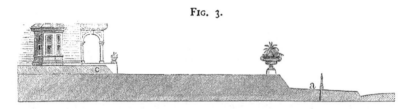

Two terraces of this kind are as many as any ordinary place will bear. To break a small lawn into a multiplicity of terraces is a sure means of spoiling it. This form of surface is well adapted to be carried around three sides of a block embracing several residences, the fronts of which should be from 80 to 150 feet from the street, and the lower grass plat at *a* from 10 to 20 feet wide.

Fig. 4 shows two forms of treating a bank made by a deeper street-cut—say from six to eight feet. Owners frequently wall

FIG. 4.

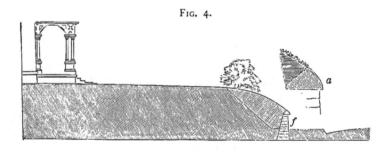

such street lines the whole height of the cut. No more foolish expenditure can be incurred, both in an economic and artistic point of view. It is difficult to make such a wall that will resist the enormous pressure of the earth when frosts disintegrate, and heavy rains soften it. If constructed so that it can resist for years this interior pressure, it must be by the expenditure of a sum of money that might create ten times the beauty if expended in other ways.

A solid wall from two to three feet above the sidewalk level is as high as we would advise on street lines from which it is intended that grounds shall show their beauty. On Fig. 2, sections C and D, where the street cut is three or four feet, the ground-slope down to the sidewalk, as shown by the formal terraces, and the lower line, on section C, is more pleasing than any wall.

But for the deep cut illustrated by Fig. 4, it is an open question whether, as some kind of fence will be necessary, a partial wall, as at *f*, may not effect that object, and produce the best form of ground surface. It will be seen by the enlarged section *a* that the coping of the low wall (say 3 feet) is to be cut so as to make its outer surface a continuation of the sloping bank above. This will make a pretty effect, and no other fence will be required ; but the wall must be of great strength. The lower line being merely a sloping bank of grass, would require another kind of fence, and to be treated as at *a*, Fig. 2.

Fig. 5 is intended to illustrate the prettier effect that may be produced by making use of small inequalities of the ground, instead

FIG. 5.

of grading to a uniform slope. It does not show just the surface it was intended to show, but will suggest to the observer the greater possibility of pleasing effects than on a uniform plane.

Where a natural elevation for a house occurs a few rods from the street, with an intervening level between it and the street, it is usually better to preserve its form, than to grade down and fill up to bring the whole lot to what some persons are pleased to term "a correct grade." Fig. 6 illustrates what is meant ; the natural surface is a graceful form, and the most capable of decorative effect.

Though rising ground is usually more valued than that which

is below the level of the road, it is not always more desirable.   If
a dwelling-site has its main walks to the doors on a level with the
street, and a part of the ground lower, but relatively higher than

FIG. 6.

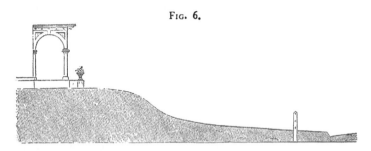

other grounds farther back, the location may be capable of more
beautiful effects than a plain swell.   A bird's-eye view over small
grounds is so rare that any approach to it is a pleasing novelty,
and the opportunities to obtain such effects should be made the
most of   The most lovely views the world can boast are narrow
valleys seen from adjacent hills.   Figs. 7 and 8 are sections showing pleasing forms of surfaces below the level of the street, but
overlooking lower ground farther back.

A building site may even be much lower than its street entrance, as in Figs. 7 and 8, where the level of the road is shown

FIG. 7.

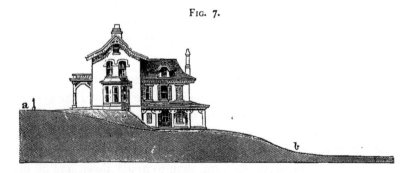

at *a*, on the condition already . named, *that the ground in its
rear be still lower relatively.*   A cottage in the spirit of the Swiss
style, in such a locality, would be quite appropriate, or, indeed,
any style in which the roof lines are both prominent and grace-

ful. It is essential, however, that the house site should not have the appearance of being in a basin, much less be so in fact; for the latter would be a miserable inconvenience in wet weather, and the mere supposition of such a situation would make the site seem undesirable even if the soil and drainage were perfect. Such locations should not be basins with reference to the surrounding land, however dry the soil, as in that case the damp evening and morning air would settle in them. But if the rear ground, as shown in Figs. 7 and 8, is the bank of a stream or valley, down to which the damp cool air will flow, then such sites may really be freer from morning and evening damps than much higher ground which is not high relatively to other ground near by.

A form of ground surface is especially desirable, for small lots, on which side-hill houses, blending the character of city basements and village cottages, will look well. Fig. 7 represents one form

Fig. 8

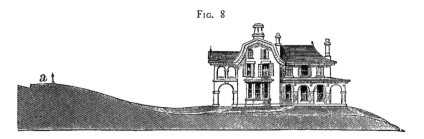

that might be suggested for such a site, and Fig. 9 a mode of treating the ground of a town lot which is below the street level.

In Fig. 7, nearly all of the lot is supposed to be behind the house, the front being connected by a short, straight walk with the street, and by a diverging curved walk with the basement entrance on the rear plateau, where it is supposed the kitchen and dining-room are located.

Fig. 9 illustrates the treatment of a corner lot, around which the streets have been graded considerably *above* the lot surface. Instead of filling the lot to the street level, it should be treated as here shown; and there is no question that the house is not only better, but the ground improvement is far more pleasing than it could have been made on a level with the street.

After all, the vast majority of building sites are pretty nearly level surfaces, and if we will but learn to develop all the beauty that such are capable of, there will be little cause to envy the

FIG. 9.

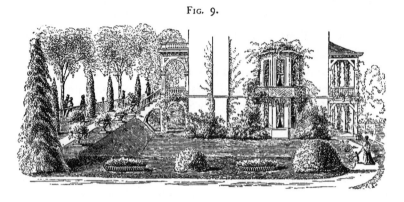

possession of more varied surfaces. Most of the designs which follow will be for such places, as they can be planned with more certainty of being useful to a great number of persons. Varied surfaces require such thorough knowledge of each peculiarity of the ground, the drainage required, the difference of levels, the nature of the trees, or rocks, or water, that may be upon it, that their features must not only be seen, but carefully surveyed and platted, in order to be planned to advantage ; and even then the skill of an artist-gardener will be essential to their judicious improvement, unless the proprietor is a person of unusual taste in such matters. Many persons involve themselves in useless expenditures on such sites from misdirected zeal for improvement, and ignorance of *what not to attempt.* Uneven sites also necessitate greater skill in the architect, in adapting the house to the ground.   It is by such adaptations, happily executed, that the difference between architects of fine native taste and culture, and mere routine designers, is occasionally illustrated. · And the same faculty for the happy adaptation of one mode of planting or another to suit different ground surfaces, to develop the best effects of existing trees, to turn a rock or a brook to the best account, is that which distinguishes the artistic from the commonplace planter.

Drainage.

The absolute necessity of deep *sub-soil* drainage is known to all intelligent agriculturists and gardeners ; but on the supposition that among our readers are town-bred people who have not had occasion to become well-informed in even the rudiments of horticulture, we will state broadly, that deep and thorough sub-soil drainage is the most essential of all preparations for the growth of trees and shrubs ; without which neither care nor surface enrichment of the soil will develop their greatest beauty. Many valuable shrubs cannot survive the winters of the middle States in imperfectly drained soils, which in those deeply drained and cultivated are hardy and healthy. In Chapter XVIII, on the philosophy of deep drainage and cultivation, and the treatment of half-hardy trees and shrubs, to which, in this connection, the reader's attention is earnestly invited, the results of drainage are more fully treated. The same causes which make the most thorough drainage of the soil a *pre*-requisite to success in growing half-hardy trees, act with equal efficiency to give fuller health and greater vigor to those which are hardy. The white oak may continue to grow, in a slow and meagre way, in a soil filled during most of the year with superfluous moisture ; but if that same soil were deeply and completely drained the annual growth would be doubled, and the increased abundance and finer color of the foliage becomes as marked as the difference between an uncultivated and a well-tilled field of corn. A lilac bush growing in a soil cold with constant moisture a little below the surface, will develop only surface roots ; and having no deep hold in the soil, its main stems will hang to one side or another with a sort of inebriate weakness. But if the soil is dry, deep, and porous, when the plant is set out, the roots strike down deep and strong, the stem will exhibit a sturdy vigor, and the top a well-balanced, low-spreading luxuriance, never seen in cold undrained soils. Even willows, much as they love a moist soil, are much more healthy and symmetrical when planted in well-drained than in wet places ;—their peculiarity being to flourish best where their roots can find water by seeking it, as an animal goes to a stream and stoops to drink, but not by standing in it perpetually.

Trees requiring much moisture, which grow close to streams or wet places, usually have their finest development when standing several feet above the level of the water *in ground that is perfectly drained by the proximity of a watercourse,* and which at the same time affords the roots an opportunity to drink at will when deep enough.

No thorough gardener, or intelligent planter, is content with surface or *open-ditch* drainage. It is always insufficient, bungling, and untidy. The most perfect drainage is that formed by a gravelly soil underlaid with coarser gravel to a considerable depth. This is Nature's sub-soil drainage; and it is a well-known fact that soils but meagrely supplied with vegetable and mineral food for plants—"poor soils" as they are often called, when judged by their appearance rather than their results—will yield better annual returns in crops than the richest undrained lands. Where Nature has provided this sub-soil drainage, other drains may not be necessary; but there are few localities where the sub-soil is so perfect as to render artificial drainage superfluous. Where cellars are found to be always dry, though not provided with drains, the natural drainage may be considered perfect; but it will not do to infer that because one spot is dry, without drains, that another a hundred feet from it, on a different altitude or exposure, is equally favored; though large districts of country are occasionally found where good natural drainage is the rule, and springy sub-soils the exception. The writer has observed some very suggestive phenomena illustrating the relative efficiency of sub-soil and surface drainage. On the same slope of one large field, where the soil is a friable clay, one half the field had been sub-drained with lines of tile thirty feet apart and three feet deep, and the surface left level between them; the other half was plowed into "lands," or ridges of the same width, sloping down to ditches in the middle which were two feet below the level of the highest ground between them. After heavy rains the surface of the open-ditch part of the lot always glistened with moisture and was sticky for several days, although the descent was so rapid that the water seemed to run off immediately. On the sub-drained part, level as it was, the surface always had a dry spongy appearance, was free from superfluous moisture, and ready to be worked and pleasant to be walked upon

in half the time required to dry the sticky surface of the other part
of the field. The advantage did not stop here. The porous character given to the soil by the formation of innumerable and invisible channels in a vertical direction down through the earth to the
drains below, had such a tendency to lighten the ground that it
became much more capable than the harder-surfaced soil to resist
drouth; and was just as much moister in very dry weather as it
was dryer in wet weather. This is in consequence of the fact,
well known to cultivators, that the more porous and deeply worked
a soil is, the greater is its power of absorbing moisture from the
atmosphere in times of drouth. In sandy ·soils with clay substratum the effect of drainage is quite as striking in its effect on
the growth of plants and trees as in clayey lands, though not so
necessary for comfort in walking upon, or working the soil. A
wet sandy soil is more apt to be cold and sour than a clayey soil,
notwithstanding its·more comfortable surface; and the sandy loams
known as "springy," which have veins of quicksand not far below
the surface, are those which most need drainage, and which are
most difficult to drain well.

The top of a hill, or a steep hill-side, is as likely to need sub-
soil drainage as the bottom of a valley. It is the nature of the sub-
soil in each case, that renders drains necessary or superfluous, and
not the relative altitude of the location. Land surveyors are
familiar with the fact that swamps are most numerous in the
neighborhood of summit-levels.

Tile and other earthernware pipes are the best materials
for common drains; and for garden and suburban lot drainage,
should be put down from three to four feet below the surface.
Professional drainers, or tilers, who use long narrow spades and
hoes can put down drains four or five feet deep with a small dis-
placement of soil, and so rapidly that it is not an expensive operation to drain thoroughly a half acre or acre suburban lot by a
series of drains not more than twenty feet apart, provided there is
a sewer or other good outlet near by. Persons who are about to
build on suburban lots which require drainage, should have the
work done in connection with the house main drain, which is
usually deep enough to be used as a trunk drain for the land; and

all the needful connections can be made to better advantage when
planned and executed at one time, than when pipes must be
found and tapped for subsequent connections. When the work
is done, the exact locality of the main drain, and all its connections, should be marked with blue ink on a general plan of the
house and grounds.

Rats, mice, and moles frequently make their nests in tile-drains
when there is no water in them, and may stop them completely.
If the mouths of drains are always immersed in water, or if there
is a constant flow of water through them, there will be little danger
from this cause. But the best precaution is to fill one-third or one-
half the depth of the ditch above the tile with coarse gravel around
the tile, and broken stone, brick, or coal-clinkers above, putting
a layer of sod over all. The deeper drains are located, the less
danger there is of their becoming nests for these animals ; and the
greater the fall, and the amount of running water, the more certain
will they be to keep clean and serviceable.

Where tile is used in a soil that has veins of quicksand opening in the sides of the ditch, it should be laid on a board bed, and
surrounded and covered with straight straw, and then with coarse
sand (which is not quicksand) or gravel, on top of the straw ;
otherwise the quicksand will get into, and clog the drain.

There is considerable choice in tiles. One should be willing
to pay a little extra for those which are unusually straight and
smooth, as well as hard. In good clay-beds the round tile, which
are a trifle the cheapest, answer very well, but the " sole-tile "—
those which have a flat bottom and a round or egg-shaped tube—
are better for most kind of works, the latter being the most
perfect form of all. For house-drains of considerable importance,
glazed pipes, which fit into each other with collars around the
joints, are preferable. These, however, are not used so much for
land drainage as for conduits of waste water from the house. Where
it can be done so as not to create any offensive odor, all the
water wastage from the house which contains fertilizing ingredients
should be conducted to some reservoir, where, by mixing it with
dry earth, or diluting it with pure water, it may be returned to
the land.

CHAPTER VI

DWELLINGS, OUTBUILDINGS, AND FENCES.

* * "You shall see a man,
Who never drew a line or struck an arc,
Direct an Architect and spoil his work,
Because, forsooth, he likes a tasteful house !
He likes a muffin, but he does not go
Into his kitchen to instruct his cook ;

Nay, that were insult ! He admires fine clothes,
But trusts his tailor ! Only in those arts
Which issue from creative potencies
Does his conceit engage him."

HOLLAND'S KATRINA.

SO many excellent works have been published of late years on cottage and villa architecture, and so many competent architects are to be found in our large towns and cities, that it seems almost an unpardonable offence against propriety in our day for any one to build an unsightly cottage or mansion. If the reader contemplates building a house, we pray him to lose no time in obtaining and carefully reading some of these works; and if he finds in them a plan and exterior that meet his wants, let him entrust no illiterate carpenter with their execution, but employ some competent architect, who will furnish all the drawings, not only of the dwelling itself, but of the stable and all the outbuildings. There is no better evidence of a vulgar taste, or an exhausted purse, than to see dwellings of some architectural pretension and expensive finish, with rude outbuildings, having no resemblance in style to the house, and seeming, by their incongruity, to say to every passer—"You see we are but poor relations." Decorating the street-front of the house only, or robbing the outbuildings to add finery to the dwelling, belongs to the same class of mistakes as that of the ostrich, which, in flying from danger, seeks a place in which to thrust its head only, and there thinks itself safe and unseen. Do not our friends, who think their outbuildings of little importance, reveal their foolishness in the same way?

There is an unfortunate tendency among our countrymen who are building houses, to be willing victims of some fashionable mania pertaining to architectural styles; so that different eras of style in domestic architecture can be distinctly traced throughout our country by a multitude of examples of what were, in their day, called houses in "the classic styles," and their Doric, Ionic, and Corinthian varieties; houses in "the Gothic style," with its rustic Norman, Tudor, Elizabethan, and Castellated varieties; houses in "the Italian style," with bracketed, Romanesque, Lombard and Swiss varieties; and lastly, those least grotesque, but often clumsy forms for small houses, "the French or Mansard-roof style;"—a title that does not even assume to designate a style of architecture for an entire house, but fore-dooms a dwelling to be designed for the purpose of sustaining a certain fashionable hood of roofs. Hardly do we begin to adapt one style or another to our needs in building, with a tolerable degree of fitness and good taste, before some supposed new style, or novel feature of an old style, intrudes itself as "the fashion," and straightway builders throughout the breadth of our land vie with each other in numberless caricatures of it. That new, or rather unfamiliar old styles are constantly being made known to us by beautiful photographic prints and engravings of the most remarkable existing architecture, is certainly cause for congratulation ; but the misfortune is that we use them as if their mere novelty, in whatever form adopted, and the fact of their being the latest mode, were alone sufficient evidence of their fitness and tastefulness. We forget the vast difference there is between obeying the behests of fashion in those things which pertain to articles of apparel that are usually worn out by the time the fashion changes, and building houses that must stand for many years, and which, if not designed so as to be truly and pleasingly adapted to the use intended, without any reference to the prevailing mode, will remain objects of ridicule for all the period of their duration after their style has ceased to be fashionable.

There is no style the mere adoption of which will secure a tasteful house ; while a truly competent architect may design admirable houses with entire disregard of the formulas of established styles, as well as by the careful study and adaptation of them. The style should be in the brain and culture of the designer, and not in the age or associations of certain imported forms, which he may be requested to duplicate. But architects usually have their preferences in styles. They will be likely to succeed best in those which they like best. One will study Gothic more thoroughly than Italian forms, and will therefore design more tastefully in the spirit of the former. Another will excel in Italian, or classic forms ; and another still, with more cosmopolitan culture and creative art, with the taste to produce harmonious proportions, and with care to make a thorough adaptation of the means to the end, may develop most tasteful and appropriate designs with little reference to set forms.

The persons for whom a house is to be designed are usually the best judges of their own domestic wants, and will generally furnish an architect with the rough floor plans of what they desire. Good architects will studiously conform to their wishes pertaining to the distribution of interior comforts, in such plans ; but when it comes to the matter of choosing a style, they should be as little trammeled as possible, save in its expense. That architects occasionally mislead those who are about to build, by lower estimates of the cost of executing their designs than what proves to be the actual cost, may be true ; but we have found that such complaints are apt to come from those who had not given the architect a full and frank statement of their wants and their limitations ; and oftener still from those who have merely consulted with an architect, obtained a few sketches, and his rough *guess* of the cost of what the proprietor says he wants, and endeavored to save the further cost of full sets of drawings and specifications, from which alone an architect can make a true estimate.   Then, after working up their plans with builders to whom the work is intrusted or contracted, and altering and adding as the work progresses, if they find the total cost to be much greater than the cost suggested by the architect, the latter is charged with the fault.   The fact is, that when a man fancies he can be his own architect, his imagination is excited by the possibility of achieving a great many pleasant results by his own peculiarly fortunate talents ; and in endeavoring to realize one after another of his desires, the building enthusiasm draws him so gradually, and by so many unseen currents into the maelstrom of expense, that he rarely realizes, until too late, the quality of his conceit and extravagance.   We believe that the employment of an honest and qualified architect will always be an economy to the employer, and that to dictate to him the adoption of any particular style because just then it happens to be the rage, is a pretty sure way to secure his poorest, instead of his best designing.

Another matter that we would most earnestly impress on all persons about to build is this : that, when it is the intention to employ an architect, he should be given months, instead of days, to mature his designs.   We would always doubt the competence of that architect who prides himself on throwing off designs in a hurry. Long practice, and plethoric portfolios, may greatly facilitate the rapidity with which good designs can be matured, but it is nevertheless true that all designs which are at all original in character, and at the same time tasteful and harmonious, are the result of many sketches, and careful comparisons, corrections and eliminations, which can only be made when ample time is given.   Dwelling-houses of moderate cost are the most difficult, in proportion to their cost, of all forms of architectural designing ; and specifications for them the most tedious and embarrassing. A court-house, or city-hall, that costs a hundred thousand dollars, will give an architect no more thought, nor tax his creative faculties so much, as the designing of an original and tasteful suburban dwelling costing not more than one-tenth that sum. It is therefore very desirable that those who wish to have houses of enduring beauty should give themselves and their architects ample time to mature the plans.

There is a world of expression in the character of outbuildings that is little thought of or understood in this country, notwithstanding their mere conveniences are carefully considered. A stable and carriage-house should be one of the attractive, home-looking features of every place large enough to require them ; and, if properly built and taken care of, no more to be shut out of sight than your house chimneys. What more pleasing sight than to glance over a smooth lawn, under trees, or through vistas of shrubbery, to the sunlit open space around the carriage-house door, where the horse in the brightly-polished " buggy" stands neighing for you, or the children are clustered around "our pony"—while doves are cooing in their little house above, and martins and swallows twitter about the eaves, up to which luxuriant grape-vines clamber. Ah, the children are at home there ! One has not learned the art of enjoying home till he knows how much of beauty and delight there may be in the domestic work-places, and buildings set apart for the animals that serve us. The English are much more generous in their tastes in this respect than we. An English lady shows her stable, her horses, cows, pigs, and poultry, with the same pride and affection for her animal retinue that she has in leading you through the beauties of her lawn and flowers.

The stable, the wood-shed, the well-house, the tool-room, and all needful back buildings, should be made with as much reference to good taste in their design as the dwelling, and should all have the same general architectural character. The style and keeping of all these will have more to do with the home-look and general elegance of a suburban residence than any amount of ponderous or super-fine carpentry, masonry, or interior decoration.

4

COLOR.

The color of houses and outbuildings is a subject in which
fashion has ranged widely in different directions.   Twenty-five
years ago, white, white, white, everywhere and for everything, was
"the American taste."   Suddenly the absurdity of being always
dressed in white struck the great public, and parrots of fashion
everywhere echoed remarks about "garish white," "neutral tints,"
"subdued tones," till a mania seized whole communities to paint
wooden houses, cottages and all, "to imitate brown stone!"   Everything of wood was dismally darkened and sanded, and brick som-
brely stuccoed and "blocked off," as if we were ashamed of our
best materials, and must needs conceal them.   Our homes, before
sepulchrally white, and garishly brilliant, were then crocked and
blackened with bogus stone colors.   The most beautiful and necessarily most pleasing of all colors for window-blinds, which barmo-
nizes with nearly every neutral tint, and with all natural objects—
ever-beautiful green—the tenderest and most welcome of all colors
to the delicate eye, was thrust aside even by the cultivated taste
of Downing; and in its place dull brown blinds, and yellow blinds,
and verdigris-bronze blinds, were the fashion and "in taste."
Common sense and common eyesight have been too strong for
such a fashion to endure long, and green again greets our grateful
eyes on cottage, villa, and mansion windows.   After the rage for
dark colors, the reaction carried many back to white again, but
on the whole the color of our houses is greatly improving.

In choosing colors, the proprietor needs to guard himself from
himself.   If he desires some color different from any which the
neighborhood affords an example of, let him beware of trusting
to his own selection of paints in the pot, or from a specimen patch
on the house.   Both will deceive him.   Colors which appear to
have no character at all on small surfaces, are often beautiful when
applied to an entire building; while the tints which please us best
in samples may be rank and vulgar on broad surfaces.   After
giving a general idea of what is wanted, to a skillful painter, it
is better to leave the exact, shade to him, or to your architect.
They may fail to meet your wishes exactly, but console yourself

with the reflection that had you made the selections, the result might have been worse ! Between dwelling, outbuildings, fences, garden decorations, &c., there should be a strong similarity of tone, though the depth of color may differ materially. A gray or cool drab-colored house should not have a warm brown color for its outbuildings. A cream-colored house should have its outbuildings of some darker shade, in which yellow is just perceptible as one of its constituent parts. In places where they are much shaded by trees, the outbuildings may, without impropriety, be the color of the dwelling, provided the latter is some un-showy neutral tint. Shading parts of the buildings with different colors is practiced with beautiful effect by good painters, but the proprietor is here again warned not to trust to his own skill in choosing colors.

FENCES.

We are at a loss how to convey just ideas of the choice that should be made among the infinite variety of fences in our country without writing an illustrated essay. For country, or large suburban grounds, it is safe to say, except where hedges are maintained, that *that kind of fence is best which is least seen, and best seen through.* But in towns our fences must harmonize with the architecture and more elegant finish of the street, and therefore be sufficiently well-designed and constructed to be in themselves pleasing objects to the passer-by. The great desideratum is to answer this requirement, and at the same time to adopt some design that will least conceal the lawn and other beauties beyond or behind it. Our fences should be, to speak figuratively, *transparent.* Now what will make a comparatively transparent fence is a matter much more difficult to decide than the reader will suppose. Where iron fences can be afforded, it is easy to effect the desired result ; but they are so expensive that wood will long continue to be the main fence material even in towns. Where something really elegant can be afforded, an architect's services should be called into requisition as much as for the residence design. A fence may be as fine a work of art as any other construction, but the architect ought to bear in mind that it should not unnecessarily conceal the beauty it encloses. Among the less expensive kinds of fencing, we will mention a few of the forms generally used. First, and most common of all fences claiming to be ornamental, is the plain picket fence, made of strips set vertically the whole height of the fence, and from one and a half inches square to one inch by three. All picket fences shut out a view of the ground behind them until one is nearly opposite the pickets, as completely as a tight board fence of the same height. An old and ornamental form of picket fence is that composed of three horizontal rails, with two equal spaces between ; one set of pickets being short, and terminated in points above the middle rail, while every other one rises through the top rail in the same way. This gives double the space between the pickets on the upper half of the fence, where a transparent fence is most indispensable. It is the best, and also one of the most expensive of the old forms of wooden fences, and the only kind of picket fencing that should be tolerated for enclosing ornamented grounds.

Fences formed of horizontal rather than vertical pieces are preferable ; and the openings between the bars should be as wide as insurance against animals will permit. A substitute for the old-style of picket fences, now much used, is composed of boards sawed so that their openings form ornamental designs. These are adopted from German designs for cheap balconies and veranda guards, for which purposes they are well adapted and beautiful ; but for front fences they are even more objectionable than pickets, because they bar more completely the view of what is behind. To unite strength, beauty, and " transparency," is the object to be gained. What wooden fences will best do this, we must leave to the reader's ingenuity and good sense to decide. Those who build most expensively do not necessarily secure the most tasteful places, and in fencing there is much opportunity to let thought balance money. Some very pretty rod-iron fences are now made, both vertical and horizontal, which are much cheaper than woven wire or cast-iron ; but both of the latter being always at hand or ready made for those who have the means to use them, will probably continue to increase in use. The tasteful forms in which iron fences are generally made, together with their indestructible character, will continue to make them more and more desirable. Were it not for the shameful freedom given to animals in many town and village streets, such fences might be made so much lower and more open than now, as materially to lessen their cost. If the reader will turn to the vignette at the head of this chapter, he will see a form of iron posts and rods well adapted to a suburban place.

We would suggest that all fences, not of a massive character, should have an open space under them, so that a scythe may pass clear through. No person should consider his grounds well kept unless the sidewalk in front or around his premises, is as neatly kept as the part within the enclosure. An open space under the fence, through which the blade of a scythe may glide, greatly facilitates the mowing of the lawn on both sides of the line.

For large suburban places, we would suggest that a sod fence, with light posts, and one or two horizontal bars above it, may be made both elegant and sufficient as a street protection. Fig. 10 represents a section of the fence proposed, the dotted line *a a* being the natural surface. The sod should be laid with a slight inclination downwards towards the centre of the fence, so that rains striking the sides will have a tendency to soak into, instead of being shed from them. If the sods are of a soil retentive of moisture (and most soils which grow a good sod are), the sides of the fence, if kept well mowed, will make a beautiful low green hedge. In very dry weather, of course, such fences would suffer and turn brown, though even then they will not be unsightly if their form is good. If water and watering facilities are at hand, they may be kept bright at all seasons. The little hollows at either side must also be kept shaved close, and will add to the beauty of the yard by giving a slight roll in the surface all around the outside boundary. The bottom and sides of the hollows should be made so that a hand mowing-machine can run upon them easily. The right side of the section was intended to represent a single slope, and the left side a hollow with a level bottom, and the slope carried farther off. The latter is the better manner. On Fig. 11, several bottom-lines are shown to suit different requirements in making

Fig. 10.

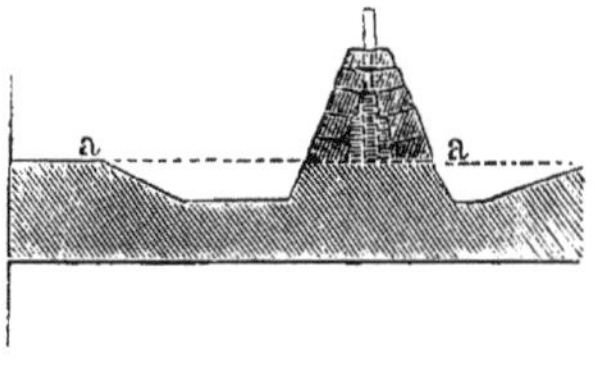

fences of this kind. The sod fence may be made altogether on top of the natural surface, but as its height would be greater, it might be too serious an obstruction to views of the grounds. Lowering the ground on both sides will generally give the earth and sod required for such a fence, and make the needful height for protection against animals without barring a view of the grounds. If jumping animals are to be guarded against, it may be well to insert posts at regular distances for bars across their tops, as shown in the

FIG. II.

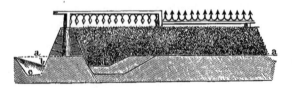

same cut, and to use vertical pickets, say a foot or more long, through the bars. A picket line is more of a terror to animals than a horizontal fence of the same height, and the pickets may be so small and wide apart as not to intercept views upon the lawn within. Where cattle are not allowed in the street, a single bar or rail, running from post to post, within three or four inches of the top of the sod, with ornamental iron points screwed to the top, will make a pleasing enclosure. There is a great variety of such castings to choose from. Some of the narrower patterns of woven-wire fencing would have an admirable effect on low sod fences. The reader's ingenuity will doubtless suggest various ways of improving these hints concerning sod fencing ; but it must be borne in mind that fences of this character are unsuited to the use of those who do not feel disposed to give them the constant care which is required to keep a lawn in order ; and in those semi-civilized towns where hogs are allowed at large, they are of course impracticable. Where it is desired to have the sod fence sufficiently high to be a good protection against cattle, without any posts or bars above them, it is best to make the additional height by larger and deeper excavations on each side, or on the side on which the height is most needed. A straight slope like that at *b,*

Fig. 11, is easily made and kept clean with a scythe or machine; but the lower double lines can be used, where a higher fence is needed, provided the level on the bottom is wide enough to allow the use of a scythe or hand-mowing machine. As such ridges of turf are peculiarly exposed to injury from excessive cold, it is recommended, in districts where evergreen boughs, especially hemlock, can be procured, that the top of the turf be covered late in the fall. Such twigs can be neatly interlaced, with little trouble, under the bar above the turf, so as to form an evergreen hedge through the winter, and the snow that will lodge in them will proteet the bank from constant heaving by freezing and thawing in the winter and early spring, and give the grass additional vigor when the time comes to uncover it.

These sod enclosures are illy suited to form front fences in village neighborhoods, and are suggested solely for places of large extent, and with rural surroundings.

With regard to live hedges, some cautions are needed. The practice of hedging one's ground so that the passer-by cannot enjoy its beauty, is one of the barbarisms of old gardening, as absurd and unchristian in our day as the walled courts and barred windows of a Spanish cloister, and as needlessly aggravating as the close veil of Egyptian women. It is not well, generally, to plant live hedges on the street fronts of a town or suburban residence. On larger places they are very useful and beautiful as separating screens between the decorated ground and the vegetable garden, or hiding

FIG. 12.

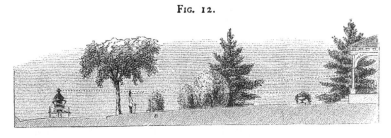

portions of outbuildings, or as a protection for fruit yards against injurious winds; but as a street fence for town or suburban resi dences they should be made use of but rarely. There are other

places enough where we may avail of all their beauties. Fig. 12
shows a section of front grounds and street with a hedge on the
street line.   It will be seen that the line of view from the eye of a
man on the sidewalk, over the top of the hedge, isolates him as completely from the view of the grounds as a jail wall; and even from
a carriage, in the middle of the street, one can see but little more.

A word, in conclusion, about gateways and gate-posts. Showy
posts of carpentry or masonry, which are not of solid wood or solid
stone, or which are made higher than the general character of the
fence calls for, are apt to seem pretentious.   A gateway, whether
for a carriage road or a walk, should always be marked in some
way, so that one will know at a glance, and at some distance, just
where the entrance is. This is generally and properly done by
making the gate-posts conspicuous, either by their size or their
finish.   But it is easy to overdo, by giving them a cheap showiness
or massiveness disproportionate to their importance.   Stone is far
more beautiful than any other material for posts, and for the gateways of walks should be used in simple forms and of single
blocks, if it can be afforded.   Or, after making a suitable foundation of cheaper stone, the part above ground may be a single block
of sufficient weight not to be jarred on its foundation by the ordinary
use of the gates.   It is not necessary that the two gate-posts be alike.
The one upon which a gate is swung requires to be far heavier than
the one into which it latches, and it will not be "out of taste" to
make the size of each conform to its use, and to economize by
making one heavy post instead of two.   Children will swing on
gates in spite of all warnings, and the gates must be hung so that
they will bear the strain.   To insure this solidity, great weight
is required, or else the post must be very thoroughly bedded in
the ground.   There is much less strain on the post into which
the gate catches, and therefore no need of making it of the same
weight and expense.   In making the suggestion that it is not necessary to have the opposite posts of the gateway fac-similes of
each other, it must not be understood that there is any impropriety
in it, but only that the means are best adapted to the end when the
one which is most heavily taxed shall be provided first to meet the
calls upon it.   For gateways on drives it is not always practicable

to obtain single blocks of sufficient weight to resist the constant strain of a long gate. Single gates being preferable to double ones for this purpose, the posts to which such gates are hung should have marked importance, and may, with propriety, be of block masonry, or of brick, with stone caps and binding layers ; and it must not be forgotten that mere height and size, for the purpose of rendering them conspicuous, is not the true object, but that weight and tasteful forms are required. The facility with which slender wood posts can be encased with heavy shells of carpentry, has had a bad influence in substituting showiness for solidity ; yet it is also true that much real beauty of form and effect is obtained by casing posts with joiner's work, at a small expense compared with what is required by the use of heavy timber or stone. Each man's necessities and culture must be the law to himself in this matter. The post in the vignette at the head of this Chapter is a fair example of a simple and unpretending form of stone post. There are few matters in which the taste of the proprietor, or his architect, may be more pleasingly illustrated than in the designs for stone gate-posts. In putting in posts of wood or single blocks of stone deep in the ground, the hole around them should be filled with sand, and especial care should be used to have the bottom firm and solidly bedded before filling more than a few inches ; the top of the stone should then be fastened in place by braces until the filling is completed. It is desirable that the part of a stone below the surface of the ground increase in size like a wedge, with the largest end down, for if the stone is the reverse in form, that is to say, a wedge with the point down, it then forms a shoulder against which the earth in swelling, as it does by freezing, will inevitably heave the post upwards. Iron gate-posts, arched over like those shown by Fig. 184, and covered with wire, are charming for village-lot entrances, though less expressive of solidity and homeliness than stone. Even for an iron fence, the contrast between the low massiveness of well-designed stone gateways, and the lightness of iron work, is quite pleasing. And if these stone posts are used *only* for gateways (and we think it better not to use them anywhere on a front except for gateways and street corners), they become the most prominent feature of the street front. There is no end to

FIG. 13.

charming architectural combinations for gateways, but it will not do on a place which has not otherwise a highly architect ural character, to "make it up" on the gate way.

On places where solid constructive dec orations cannot be afforded, we advise the use of topiary work, by which is meant the fanciful forms sometimes given, by cutting and trimming, to verdant arbors, thickets, trees, and hedges. There are many species of evergreens which may be planted on each side of the gateways of ordinary foot-walks so as to be made into charming arches over the entrance. With patience and annual care, these can be perfected within about ten years, but they will also afford most pleasing labor from the beginning ; and the infantile graces of the trees, which are year by year to be developed into verdant arches, will probably afford quite as much pleasure in their early growth as in their perfected forms. In the descriptions of the trees which are suitable for this kind of topiary work, the mode of managing them will be noted in detail. We here introduce the same cuts to give a hint of the effect intended, though, when well grown, such arches are far more beautiful than our engraving can even suggest. Fig. 13 shows a pair of hemlocks planted inside of a gateway, and grown to a height of 10 to 12 feet, and only trimmed on the inside. Fig. 14 shows the effect at the end of ten years—the tops of the two trees having been twisted together so as to grow as one tree over the centre of the arch, and all parts trimmed year by year to the form illustrated. Fig. 15 shows the effect

FIG. 14.

FIG. 15.

that may be produced from the same trees by permitting the main stems to keep their upright direction, and forming the arch by encouraging and uniting the growth of the inner branches at the proper height. Where evergreens are to be planted for this purpose, the fence should curve inwards to the gate, as shown by the transverse section (Fig. 16), so that trees designed to form the arch can be planted on

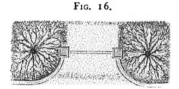

FIG. 16.

a line with the posts, and two or three feet from them. All this topiary work may be a substitute for expensive gateways, or it may, with equal propriety, be introduced as an accessory decoration, where the posts are not of a massive, or highly ornate character. In the latter case, whatever beauty of design and workmanship has been wrought out in stone should not be deliberately concealed by such forms of verdure.

CHAPTER VII.

NEIGHBORING IMPROVEMENTS.

Small is the worth of beauty from the light retired."—TENNYSON.

THERE is no way in which men deprive themselves of what costs them nothing and profits them much, more than by dividing their improved grounds from their neighbors, and from the view of passers on the road, by fences and hedges. The beauty obtained by throwing front grounds open together, is of that excellent quality which enriches

all who take part in the exchange, and makes no man poorer.
As a merely business matter it is simply stupid to shut out,
voluntarily, a pleasant lookout through a neighbor's ornamental
grounds. If, on the other hand, such opportunities are improved,
and made the most of, no gentleman would hesitate to make
return for the privilege by arranging his own ground so as to
give the neighbor equally pleasing vistas into or across it. It
is unchristian to hedge from the sight of others the beauties of
nature which it has been our good fortune to create or secure;
and all the walls, high fences, hedge screens and belts of trees
and shrubbery *which are used for that purpose only*, are so many
means by which we show how unchristian and unneighborly we
can be. It is true these things are not usually done in any
mere spirit of selfishness : they are the conventional forms of
planting that come down to us from feudal times, or that were
necessary in gardens near cities, and in close proximity to populous
neighborhoods with rude improvements and ruder people. It is a
peculiarity of English gardens, which it is as unfortunate to follow
as it would be to imitate the surly self-assertion of English travel-
ling-manners. An English garden is "a love of a place" to get
into, and an Englishman's heart is warm and hospitable at his own
fire-side ; but these facts do not make it less uncivil to bristle in
strangers' company, or to wall and hedge a lovely garden against
the longing eyes of the outside world. To hedge out deformities
is well ; but to narrow our own or our neighbor's views of the free
graces of Nature by our own volition, is quite another thing. We
have seen high arbor-vitæ hedges between the decorated front
grounds of members of the same family, each of whose places was
well kept, and necessary to complete the beauty of the other and
to secure to both extensive prospects ! It seems as if such persons
wish to advertise to every passer, "my lot begins here, sir, and
ends there, sir," and might be unhappy if the dividing lines were
not accurately known. "High fences make good neighbors," is a
saying often repeated by persons about walling themselves in.
The saying has some foundation in fact. Vinegar and soda, both
good in their way, are better kept in separate vessels. If a man
believes himself and his family to be bad neighbors, certainly they

ought to fence themselves in, thoroughly. Or if they have reason
to believe their neighbors are of the same sort, they may well be
sure of the height and strength of the divisions between them.
But we prefer to imagine the case reversed; and that our neighbors are kindly gentlemen and women, with well-bred families, who
can enjoy the views across others' grounds without trespassing upon
them. These remarks are intended to apply to those decorative
portions of home-grounds which, in this country, and especially in
suburban neighborhoods, are usually in front of the domestic offices
of the house. The latter must necessarily be made private and
distinct from each other. One of the most fertile sources of disa-
greements between families having grounds opening together, are
incursions of boisterous children from one to another. Now it is
suggested that children may be trained to respect and stop at a
thread drawn across a lawn to represent a boundary, just as well as
at a stone wall. Every strong high barrier challenges a spirited
boy's opposition and enterprise, but what costs no courage or
strength to pass, and a consciousness of being where he don't belong, generally makes him ashamed to transgress in such directions.
A well-defined line will, in most cases, be all that is necessary.
This may be simply a sunk line in the grass, as shown at *a*, Fig. 17,

FIG. 17.

or it may be a row of low, small cedar or iron posts, with a chain or
wires running from one to another, or some very low, open, and light
design of woven-wire fencing; anything, in short, which will leave
the eye an unbroken range of view, and still say to the children,
"thus far shalt thou go, and no farther." If parents on both sides
of the line do their duty in instructing the children not to trespass
on contiguous lawns, less trouble will result from that cause than
from the bad feelings engendered by high outside boundary walls,
that so often become convenient shields to hide unclean rubbish
and to foster weeds.

An interesting result, that may be reached by joining neighboring improvements, is in equalizing the beauties of old and new
places. Suppose B. has bought an open lot between A. and C.,
who have old places. The grounds of A., we will suppose, are

filled, in old village style, with big cherry trees, maples, lilacs, spruce trees, roses, and annuals; and C.'s grounds may have a growth of noble old trees, which had invited a house to make its home there. Between the two is Mr. B.'s bare lot, on which he builds a "modern house," which is, of course, the envy of the older places. But Mr. B. and his family sigh for the old forest trees on the right, and the flowers, and verdure, and fruit trees on the left. Not having them to begin with, we advise him to make a virtue of necessity, and cause his neighbors to envy him the superior openness and polish of his own grounds. A. has a yard cluttered with the valuable accumulations of years; a fine variety of trees, shrubs, and flowers; yet nothing shows to advantage. The shade, the multiplicity of bushes, the general intertanglement of all, make it very difficult to grow a close turf, and keep it mown as a lawn. Mr. B., on the other hand, can begin, as soon as his ground is enriched and set to grass, to perfect it by constant cutting and rolling till it is a sheet of green velvet. Cut in the lawn, here and there near his walks, small beds for low and brilliant flowers may sparkle with sunny gayety; at the intersection of walks, or flanking or fronting the entrances, low broad-top vases (rustic or classic, as the character of the house or their position may require) may be placed, filled with a variety of graceful and brilliant plants. In two or three years, if Mr. B. shall thus have made the most of his open ground, ten chances to one both of the neighbors will be envying the superior beauty of the new place. It will, probably, really be the most charming of the three; not, however, by virtue of its open lawn alone, but by the contrast which his neighbor's crowded yard on one side, and the forest trees on the other, serve to produce. Each of their places forms a back-ground for his lawn; while, if the three places are allowed to open together, his lawn is a charming outlook from the shades of theirs. *Neither one of these places would, alone, make landscape beauty; yet the three may make charming combinations from every point of view.* Every home needs some fruit trees, and a shadowy back-ground, or flanking, of noble forest trees, which Mr. B. would desire to have started as soon as possible; but with such adjoining improvements as we have described, he should preserve the distinctive elegance of his front grounds, and leave them as open and sunny as possible. If, however, B.'s bare lot stood unflanked by old trees or old places, then his aim should be materially changed, and a few large trees, and some shrubbery, would enter into his designs for planting. Though farther on we shall endeavor to impress again the necessity of restraint in choosing but few among the thousands of trees, shrubs, and flowers that are offered to every planter, it is appropriate that, in this chapter on Neighboring Improvements, we should also suggest to planters how very few of all the sylvan and floral treasures that beautify the surface of the globe, each one's half acre or five acres can comfortably accommodate. As every city has its hundreds or thousands of good and charming people, whose acquaintance we may never have time to make, we very sensibly confine our companionship to a few congenial families, in whose intimate friendliness we have much more pleasure than if we were to "spread too thin" in efforts to embrace an entire community. Just so with the populous best society in the community of trees, to whose members the citizen is about to be introduced. He had better abandon the idea of domesticating them all into his home circle. He may even leave scores of the best families out entirely, and still have all that he can well entertain and cultivate. But by means of neighborhood association in improvements, the neighborhood, as a whole, may furnish examples of almost every kind of vegetable beauty that the climate admits of. Suppose, for instance, that a dozen neighbors, known as A. to L. respectively, have each an acre to devote to decorative planting. Laid out in the old way, with the stereotype allowance of evergreens, deciduous trees, and shrubs, they would, as plantations, have but little more interest after one was seen than duplicate copies of a book that we have done with. But if A. shall conclude to make the pines and birches his specialty, and procure all the varieties that are pleasing to the eye, which grow well in our climate, and arrange them around his home under the direction of some intelligent planter who knows the best locations for each, he will find, at the end of ten years, that his place will be a distinguished one. He will have about fifty varieties of hardy pines to choose from, among which from ten to twenty are trees of great beauty; and the beautiful birches will sparkle among them as well set jewels. The pines will embrace a variety of sizes and forms, from the graceful and lofty white pine of our forests, and the much larger pines of California and Oregon, down to interesting bushy dwarfs, which do not exceed the lilac in size. Making a specialty of the pine and the birch families will not prevent A. from having a due proportion of open lawn, and a small variety of the finest flowering shrubs and flowers, proportioned to the size of his lawn.

Now we will suppose Mr. B. is his next neighbor, and that he chooses to make the maple tree his specialty. No one familiar with the almost endless number of varieties of the maple, foreign as well as native, with all their diversity of growth and wealth of foliage, with their spring loveliness and autumn glories, their cleanliness and their thrift, can for a moment doubt the beauty that might be produced under proper management on Mr. B.'s acre. A few trees, but a few, of more irregular outlines, should be admitted as a foil to the compacter maples.

Next Mr. C. must choose his favorites. Supposing his house to be of some unpicturesque style, he may take the different species and varieties of the horse-chestnut, *Æsculus*, and the common chestnut, *Castanea*. At certain seasons of the year his place would be unrivalled in display of flowers and foliage.

If D. will take the oak, he will not find his acre large enough to accommodate one-half of the hardy and beautiful varieties which are natives of his own country alone. But as the oak is rather slow in developing its best traits, Mr. D. would be wise to find a site for his specialty on which some varieties of oak have already attained good size.

The elms, with some other trees that contrast well with them, will furnish a beautiful variety for E.

Mr. F. may make trees of gorgeous autumn foliage his specialty, and, while surrounded by some of the loveliest of spring and summer trees, may have his place all aglow in September and October with the dogwood, the liquidamber, the pepperidge or tupelo, the sassafras, the sugar, scarlet, and Norway maples, the scarlet oak, and many others.

If G. will make a specialty of lawn, shrubs, and flowers alone, among a thousand beauties he can hardly fail to make an interesting collection.

H. may have a predilection for spruces, hemlocks, and spiry-top trees, and make the evergreens of those forms, and the deciduous trees that harmonize with them, his specialty.* But care must be used not to render the place gloomy with their too great abundance.

I. will not have any species in particular, but loves those trees, of whatever species, which spread low and broadly, but clear above the lawn; like the apple-tree, the mulberry, the horse-chestnut, the catalpas and paulonias, the white oak, the beech, and some varieties of the thorn.

J. admires the classic formalities of the old French style of gardening, and prefers trees and shrubs that will bear clipping well, and grow naturally or artificially into symmetric and formal shapes; with straight walks and architectural decorations. In close neighborhoods, and on well-improved streets, architectural gardening is the most elegant of all, but requires much money for constructions, which, if not thorough and tastefully complete, were better not attempted.

K. wishes a place full of graceful forms, and will use those trees which will best carry out his idea. His walks must be serpentine; his trees weeping varieties, both deciduous and evergreen, of which the variety in form and character is such as to enable him to make a most picturesque as well as graceful collection.

L. has a special admiration for trees of exotic or tropical appearance, and *if his soil is deeply drained,*† *rich, and warm,* the mag-

---

* Spiry-topped evergreens, like the balsam fir or Norway spruce, are rather impracticable to make entire plantations of on any place. Their forms are too monotonous, and their shadows too meagre, to be used with the same careless profusion near a dwelling that we may employ broadly-overhanging trees, like the elms, oaks, pines, and maples. Such evergreens are planted quite too much already; many fine places having been rendered most gloomy by their great abundance. A specialty of this kind would, therefore, be "stale and unprofitable," unless made with great skill.

† By deeply-drained, we do not mean the draining of a foot below the surface, but at least four feet, so that the large roots of trees will be invited to penetrate into the substratum, which is never cold to the freezing point, and from which the roots of trees form conductors to the branches above, and thus serve to modify the rigors of the upper air by the warmth of the earth below the frost. If one will but think of the difference in winters' coldest days, between riding all day with warm blocks to the feet, or without them, he can appreciate the argument for inviting trees to root deeply in the earth's warm substratum.

nolias, catalpas, paulonia, mulberries, and ailanthus, with some evergreens of rounded forms, will make an interesting collection.

We have here named a dozen places, with each a specialty. Now, it is to be clearly understood that the nature of the locality, the form of the ground, the peculiarities of the soil, and the architecture of the house, are all to be taken into consideration before deciding what species of planting to make the specialty of any one home. It would be ridiculous to plant weeping willows on a dry, bald site, or gloomy balsam firs on a sunny slope, or a collection of spiry evergreens alone on a level lawn, or in juxtaposition with masses of round-headed trees, like maples and horse-chestnuts. All the surrounding circumstances must govern the choice ; and neighbors should consult together with competent advisers, as far as practicable, before determining what each will plant, so as to make contiguous grounds harmonize, as well as add to the variety of each other's grounds.

To be repeating the same round of common favorite trees in one place after another, on a fine suburban street, is to lose much of the varied beauty which would result from each planter making thorough work in some one specialty of arboriculture. To employ an artist in landscape gardening to design all the places that adjoin each other, with reference to a distinctive characteristic for each, and a happy blending of the beauty of all, would, of course, be the most certain way to secure satisfactory results. It will be found, as we grow more intelligent in such matters, that it is quite as essential to the beauty of our home-grounds to commit their general arrangement to professional artists, and to be as absolutely restricted to their plans, as it has been in the management of cemeteries. So long as each lot-owner can plant and form his lot to suit himself alone, whatever his taste may be, such grounds will be but a medley of deformities. To insure a high order of beauty in neighboring improvements, all planting must be done under some one competent direction. The result of this is seen in our beauti ful modern cemeteries. A similar subordination of individual fan cies to a general plan, in a community of neighboring grounds, may develop like results.

STREET TREES.

The subject of street trees comes properly under the head of neighboring improvements. It might be inferred, from the modes of planting recommended in the preceding pages, that a variety of trees will be recommended for one street in preference to a single sort. On the contrary, the effect is much better, on a straight street or road, to have an avenue composed of a single species of tree only. To attempt the varieties of park scenery on an avenue is as much out of place as to compose a park of straight rows of trees. There ought to be but one variety of street tree on the same block, at least, and the longer the continuity is kept up the nobler will be the effect. Street trees are usually planted quite too close together. For wide avenues (where alone such great spreading trees as the elm, sycamore, silver maple, and silver poplar should be planted), from thirty to fifty feet apart is near enough, and thirty feet is the least distance that any street trees should be planted from each other. The finest deciduous trees are those already most commonly planted—elms, maples, and horse-chestnuts. The white pine is a noble street tree, very little used. It deserves to be; but as it must be planted of smaller size than the deciduous trees, in order to do well, and therefore requires box protection during a greater number of years, it should only be planted where such protection is sure to be given. No trees should be planted, in streets, which do not come early into leaf, or which have disagreeable blossoms, or which bear nuts or eatable fruit, or the leaves of which are subject to worms, or do not drop promptly and dry after the first severe autumn frosts. The different varieties of the maple, the horse-chestnut, the weeping elm, and the English and Scotch elms, all unite to a great extent the best qualities for street trees. The linden is peculiarly subject to worms, and should not, therefore, be planted in streets. The elm, near the sea-coast, is also infested by a species of worm, which does not, however, seem to be very annoying in the interior. The tulip tree, or white wood, is rather difficult to transplant, and not adapted to any but a rich warm soil; but, once established in such a soil, it makes an elegant street tree. The oaks grow too slowly to be popular; and many of them have not a cheerful expression in winter. The willows generally have thin leaves, which rot where they fall, and therefore make the walks filthy under them in autumn. The poplars all have blossoms, or cottony seeds, that are annoying. Among the foreign maples, the Norway and the sycamore maples are well adapted to street planting, but not superior to the sugar maple. If we were to name six species of trees to choose from for the street, they would be the American weeping elm, the Scotch or Wych elm, the horse-chestnut, the sugar, Norway, or sycamore maples, the weeping white birch, and, in light, warm soils, the white pine.

Charming effects may be produced by planting such trees as the weeping birch at long intervals, to break the monotony of heavier formed trees by the delicate sprightliness of their foliage in summer, and their brilliant white-barked spray when the trees are leafless. We know no reason why several varieties of the birch would not make admirable avenues for streets which are too narrow for elms, and in which maples and chestnuts make too deep a shade.

In conclusion, we will venture to suggest an innovation for town streets which are occupied for residences alone, and upon which there is little travel in vehicles. The roadway on such streets is often needlessly wide, and trees planted on the sidewalk on both sides of the road, expand their tops so as to obstruct a view of the street, and so close to the house that their beauty cannot be seen. It is recommended that such streets have but one row of trees, and that in the middle of the road, where a strip of grass, six feet wide or more, would give them a pleasing setting. As this width of grass cannot be spared from many town sidewalks, but can be from the roadways, the plan **may** occasionally be used to advantage.

HARLEY.

CHAPTER VIII

MATERIALS USED IN DECORATIVE PLANTING.

THERE are no vegetable productions in Nature which, when thoroughly observed and understood, are not beautiful. Few plants are more beautiful than the thistle. Most weeds will elicit our admiration if their forms, growth, and structure are carefully noticed. Even bare rocks give pleasure to the eye, and their vastness and ruggedness awaken emotions of sublimity, as sun, moon, or darkness light and shadow them. A lightning-shivered pine, projecting from a mountain side, makes a striking point in a painter's landscape, and serves to heighten, by contrast, the smooth-featured loveliness of a valley below it.

Yet the thistle would give more pain than pleasure as a pot or border plant. What we call weeds are only so because some other plants unite more beauties, or give more pleasurable returns for cultivation. We reject the former, because we cannot have all, and therefore choose their betters. The shivered pine, though pleasingly picturesque up among the rocks, would give more pleasure added to the wood-pile than to the front yard of the citizen; and the rocky beauties of mountain scenery are sometimes those of which the poet says—

" 'Tis distance lends enchantment to the view."

The noble exhilaration of climbing and roaming over mountain scenery is a charm not so much of their beauties, seen near by, as of the tonic air, and tonic exercise, and bounding blood, and glow of pride to be above some part of the world and to look down upon it.

Tennyson thus nobly contrasts the mountain with the valley

" Come down, O maid, from yonder mountain height :
What pleasure lives in height (the shepherd sang),
In height and cold, the pleasure of the hills ?
But cease to move so near the heavens, and cease
To glide a sunbeam by the blasted pine,
To sit a star upon the sparkling spire,
And come ! for Love is of the valley ; * * *
* * * * let the torrent dance thee down,
To find him in the valley ; let the wild
Lean-headed eagles yelp alone, and leave
The monstrous ledges there to slope, and spill
Their thousand wreaths of dangling water-smoke, ·
That like a broken purpose waste in air :
So waste not thou : but come ; for all the vales
Await thee ; azure pillars of the hearth
Arise to thee : the children call, and I,
Thy shepherd, pipe ; and sweet is every sound,
Sweeter thy voice, but every sound is sweet ;
Myriads of rivulets hurrying through the lawn,
The moan of doves in immemorial elms,
And murmuring of innumerable bees."

We turn from where we stand upon the mountain, not so much to look at the vast and rugged forms around us, as upon the lovely scenery at its base ; scenes where the hand of Art has set its impress on the works of Nature, and added human interests to their normal beauty.

Mountain and picturesque scenery is something which can neither be transplanted nor successfully imitated, and is, therefore, rarely within the pale of decorative gardening, as applied to the grounds of towns-people. Great mossy boulders, little ledges, and stony brooks, are now and then natural features of suburban sites, and should be prized for the picturesque effects and variety of interest that may be made with them. The paltry artificial rock-works that mar so many otherwise pretty grounds, need scarcely be mentioned, as the sight of them must necessarily make their proprietors feel as dissatisfied with their effect as the animal who essayed to don the garb and imitate the roar of the lion was with his success. It is not intended, however, to condemn those rock-works which are *unobtrusively placed*, for the purpose of growing to better advantage certain favorite plants, but only "rock-work" which is built for exhibition.

What, then, are the materials which every one may command, and which can be combined in town and village grounds to realize the greatest and most permanent pleasure? We will name these:

Of Nature's gifts—Earth, Grass, Trees, Shrubs, Flowers, Vines, and Water; of Art's productions—Houses, Walks, Roads, Fences, and all the needful accessories of dwellings for cultivated people. Let us briefly sketch what are the essential characteristics of Na ture's materials.

EARTH.—Of the Earth we demand, for decorative planting, that she shall be rich, and her bosom smooth and flowing; that, whether varied in surface by billowy inequalities, or formed to less interesting slopes or levels, the surface lines shall always be smooth, and free from all rough irregularities.

GRASS.—This is the most lowly, the simplest, and the loveliest element to be used in the adornment of home. A chapter will hereafter be devoted to it under the head of *The Lawn*. Here its essential use and beauty is defined to be—a close-fitting green robe thrown over the smooth form of the earth, through which every undulation is revealed, and over which the sunlight will play as upon velvet, and the shadows of environing objects be clearly outlined as upon a floor.

TREES.—The beauty of trees is in the endless variety of their forms, their coloring, the contrasts of light and shade in the depths of their foliage, and their shadows, which play with the sunlight and moonlight on the grass beneath them. The latter is one of their greatest charms, but one which the smoothness of the ground and grass has much to do in developing. There is also a noble fascination in viewing the grand trunks of large trees towering over our heads, their rough branches projected in bold defiance of gravitation, swaying listlessly in quiet air, toying with gentle breezes, or lashing the air in proud defiance of its ruder gales.

SHRUBS.—These are to small places the lowly representatives of what trees are to the park; and more: for there are few trees which we value for their flowers, while most ornamental shrubs are covered at some season with a bloom of glowing colors, and adorned with the same luxuriance of leafage that clothes the best trees. They are the main-stay after grass for the adornment of pleasure grounds of small extent. The variety to choose from is large, and a study of the peculiar beauty of each, and the position for which it is best adapted, is one to which we ask the marked attention of the reader. Their appropriate or improper placement will make or mar the beauty of the grounds.

VINES, though in some respects classed with shrubs, have so distinct a beauty of their own that they constitute a separate element of embellishment. Their proper places are so evident, and generally so well understood, that fewer mistakes are made in placing them than any other class of plants. Housekeepers differ widely whether to have or not to have their interlacing foliage on porch and verandas, or embowering their windows. Of their loveliness to the eye in those situations there is no question. Whether their beauty compensates for the occasional inconvenience of the insects they harbor, is to be decided by each lady housekeeper for herself. It is a clear case for toleration and Christian forbearance, if we would retain these most winsome features of cottage decoration. Of vines on ornamental frames we will treat further on, here remarking, that, as usually placed, on garish white frames, in the most conspicuous positions, they are much like graceful and beautiful girls—less lovely when thus thrust forward to attract attention, than when, in more modest positions, their grace and beauty draw one to them.

FLOWERS.—So beautiful and varied are they, that a thousand life-times of study could not learn all their infinite varieties. Henry Coleman, the distinguished agriculturist of Massachusetts, once naively wrote: "When I hear a man ask, 'What's the use of flowers?' I am always tempted to lift his hat and see the length of his ears !" All civilized beings love flowers, and ladies often " not wisely, but too well." We will endeavor to show, hereafter, how they may be wisely cherished.

WATER.—Of`water, we can only require that it be pure and clear, and *in motion*. The scope of this work is too limited to deal much with the capabilities of this lovely element in the hands of the landscape gardener. Only in large and expensive places can artificial ponds or lakes be introduced to advantage as a decorative element. But we protest against all those abominations made with water, called fish-ponds ; or indeed any ponds at all where the surrounding earth, or the earth beneath them, is rich enough to cause water-vegetation, or scum, in them. To invite a clear rippling brook to spread itself out into a stagnant pool, is as bad as to inveigle your most entertaining friend into " a dead-drunk." It is an outrage on nature and decency. But a brook may be made doubly interesting, sometimes, by obstructing it with stones ; by creating cascades ; by forcing it to rush and hide in narrow crevices, to emerge foaming with excitement ; and, finally, to spread over a shallow bed of bright pebbles, and sparkle leisurely in the sun. Such brooks can be made a perpetual charm. All their beauties may be heightened by art, but not the art of the mill-dam, or fish-pond maker. The fish and fevers bred in such places are not of sufficient value to the producer to warrant the outlay

The needful works of art—houses, walls, fences, and decorative constructions—belong more to the architect than to the landscape gardener, and the employment of only architects of thorough education and culture, is the policy of the citizen who wishes to make a permanently pleasing home, and no foolish expenditures. The building of expensive summer-houses and arbors in ordinary suburban places is rarely necessary. Where grounds are large enough to make them *real conveniences*, the strong rustic cedar constructions much used of late years (of which admirable examples are to be seen in the New York Central Park), are well adapted for shady places away from the house and the street.

CHAPTER IX.

R IGID self-denial, in dispensing with many things that seem desirable, will be found essential to the best effect and enjoyment of those home-adornments which we can afford. Limited as most men are in income; circumscribed as their building lots usually are, and fixed by circumstances quite different from those which would influence a choice for landscape gardening alone, one of the most difficult lessons to learn is, to proportion planting and expenditures to the lot and the income. And not this alone, but to the demands of a refined taste; which is intolerant of excesses and vulgarity even in garden ing. To build a larger house than the owner can use or furnish, or to lay out grounds on a more costly scale than his means will enable him to keep in good order, is a waste, and may result in making his place unsightly rather than a beautiful improvement. We doubt the good taste of a man, whose enthusiastic love of company induces him to invite to his house such incongruous numbers that they crowd and jostle each other at table, and must be lodged uncomfortably on floors and in out-buildings. But it is just this kind of over-doing which is the stumbling-block of many who are embellishing their homes. The cost of superfluous walks, if they are well made, is apt to suggest an early inquiry into their needfulness ; but trees and shrubs are so cheap, *and so small, at*

first, that excessive planting is almost as certain to be indulged
in, as excessive eating by one who has long fasted. A dozen
varieties of trees, and scores of shrubs, each of which has a special
and familiar beauty, call winningly to the planter, "choose me!"
If he good-naturedly yields to every beauty's beckoning, he finds,
too late, that in trying to please all he has satisfied none, and
perhaps done injustice to all. Crowded together more and more
as they grow, each will hide the beauty of the other, and only
darken the ground they were intended to adorn. A single native
tree, growing alone, or, if the ground be very small, a single full-
grown shrub, with room and soil enough to give luxuriant development of all its beauty, will do more, far more, to beautify one's
home, than the finest variety of trees, growing together like an
overgrown nursery. Yet, in planting a small lot, where no trees
are already grown, those who love variety must be chary of planting even one full-sized tree. Eugene Baumann, of Rahway, N. J.,
one of the few thoroughly cultivated garden artists in this country,
in alluding to the folly of planting large trees at all in small lots,
very happily illustrates its absurdity by likening it to the choice of a
table for a small drawing-room, the four corners of which would
touch the four walls. Few persons realize the rapidity with which
trees grow and time flies ; and in planting are pretty sure, after a
few years, like the Vicar of Wakefield, to find their sylvan family-
pictures too big for the room.

Let it, then, be borne in mind that *the smaller the lot, the
smaller should be the materials used to adorn it.* For city fronts of
from 10 x 20 feet to a few rods in area, the arts of gardening will
take an architectural direction, so that cut-stone walks, bordered
with bedding plants and low annuals, and well-placed and well-
filled vases, will be the only form in which vegetable beauties can
be introduced. For places of a rood in extent, (we mean only
the space devoted to decorative planting), a lawn will be essential ; and there may be introduced many shrubs as well as flowers ;
but trees sparingly, if at all. Of architectural or constructive
decorations, there will be room for considerable expenditure, and
more discretion. Only on places having upwards of half an acre
devoted to ornamental keeping, ought trees which attain large size

to be planted. If, however, there are fine trees already growing on any lot, all the arrangements of walks and plantings should be made to avail of their beauty, and to heighten it.

Kemp's observations on this subject are so pertinent that we shall quote them; premising that *garden* as here used by him, means the pleasure-ground of a place.

"Possibly the greatest and most prevalent error of those who lay out gardens for themselves is, *attempting too much*. A mind unaccustomed to generalize, or to take in a number of leading objects at a glance, finds out the different points embraced in landscape gardening one by one, and, unable to decide which of them can most suitably be applied, determines on trying to compass more than can readily be attained. One thing after another is, at different times, observed and liked, in some similar place that is visited, and each is successively wished to be transferred to the observer's own garden, without regard to its fitness for the locality, or its relation to what has previously been done. A neighbor or a friend has a place in which certain features are exquisitely developed, and these are at once sought to be copied. The practice of cutting up a ground into mere fragments is the natural result of such a state of things.

"There are several ways in which a place may be frittered away, so as to be wholly deficient in character and beauty. It may be too much broken up in its *general arrangement;* and this is the worst variety of the fault, because least easily mended and most conspicuous. To aim at comprising the principal features proper to the largest gardens, in those of the most limited size, is surely not a worthy species of imitation, and one which can only excite ridicule and end in disappointment. * * * *

"A place may likewise, and easily, be too much carved up into detached portions, or overshadowed, or reduced in apparent size, by *planting too largely*. Trees and shrubs constitute the greatest ornaments of a garden ; but they soon become disagreeable when a place is overrun with them, by contracting the space, and shutting out light, and rendering the grass imperfect and the walks mossy. Nothing could be more damp, and gloomy, and confined, than a small place too much cumbered with plantations. Nor is

the consideration of its influences on the health of the occupants
at all unimportant; for where sun and wind cannot get free play,
a moist and stagnant air, injurious to all animal life, is necessarily
occasioned.   *   *   *   *   *   *   *   *   *

"In the immediate neighborhood of the house, moreover, it is
particularly desirable that trees and large shrubs should not
abound.   Independently of darkening the windows, they communicate great dampness to the walls, and prevent that action of the wind
upon the building which alone can keep it dry, comfortable, and
consequently healthy.

"Another mode in which the effect of a garden may be marred
by too much being aimed at, is *in the formation of numerous flower
beds*, or groups of mixed shrubs and flowers on the lawn.   This is
a very common failing, and one which greatly disfigures a place;
especially as, when intended only for flowers, such beds usually
remain vacant and naked for several months in the year."

The necessity of avoiding to shade a house with trees, or
shrubs against its walls, is doubtless much greater in Great Britain
than in our much dryer and hotter climate; still, it is certain that
the suggestions of the author just quoted are quite too much dis
regarded in this country; so much so, that some of our highest
medical authorities, of late, attribute much of the consumption so
fatal in New England families, to the want of sun, the damp air,
and the tree and shrub-embowered and shutter-closed houses peculiar to its villages and farms.

A common error in fitting up a home is the idea, apparently
acted upon by the owner, that his own place "is all the world to
him."   Now, a glimpse of a near or distant mountain, river, pond,
or lake; of a single beautiful tree, or a church spire, or a neighbor's pretty house and lawn, or a distant field-chequered farm, are
all our own if we choose to make them so.   As H. W. Beecher
pithily puts it: "Men's eyes make finer pictures, when they know
how to use them, than anybody's hands can."   To shut one's place
out of view of one or all of these things, by planting it full of little trees and little bushes, to be admired principally because they
are "my" little trees and bushes, is surely a sad weakness; yet
how many homes are seen, commanding pictures of great interest

or beauty, which have been completely shut out of view by plantations of trees and shrubs, in consequence of the ill-directed zeal
of the master or mistress of the house
to fill "our yard" with beautiful things.

FIG. 18

Fig. 18 is a view out of the narrow side-
light of a friend's bay-window. It scarcely
takes in more than an eighth of a rood
of his own ground, and yet makes a
charming outlook, over an animated river,
to distant fields, and homes, and fine
trees, of which the engraving gives but a
bare suggestion. A single tree, or a
group of shrubs planted in the wrong
place, would have shut out, completely,
this pleasant picture.

It cannot be too strongly impressed
on the reader's mind, that most grounds, *and all that are nearly
level, can be much better arranged on paper, where all parts are under the eye at the same moment, than upon the ground, while planting.*
Beginning to erect a house before a plan has been made, is not
more sure of begetting blunders, than beginning to plant in the
same way; and though the blunders of misplanting may not be
so costly, they are certain in the end to be quite as unsightly.

We would by no means recommend every man to be the plan-
ner of his own grounds, if competent garden artists are to be had;
but in the absence of such, and on the supposition that we are
addressing men and women studious of culture in the art, who
may, by dint of such study, and pondering over their own dear
home-plan, do something better for themselves than the common
run of such vegetable gardeners as they can find can do for them,
we would only endeavor to aid them in the attempt. And we
firmly believe that a knowledge of the best arts of gardening will
be increased by recommending, to educated men and women, the
careful study and maturing of their own plans. The first result of
such labor will be to elevate their conceptions of the range of gardening art, to impress them with their own ignorance, and to
enable them to better appreciate, and therefore set a higher value

on the professional services of educated gardeners. It would be as absurd for the mass of men, engrossed in active business, to devote a large amount of time to the study of the mere rudiments of gardenesque art, simply to enable them to lay out a half acre or acre of land, as it would be for the same business man to pore over an architect's library and pictures to enable him to design his own house—*provided* skillful planters were as easily found as competent architects. Twenty years ago there was the same dearth of architects of culture as there now is of educated gardeners. The general study of domestic architecture, which Downing's works then aided to make a fashion, produced, at first, an astonishing fermentation and rising of architectural crudities; but it also produced, afterwards, a crop of architects. If we can induce every family who have a home to adorn, to study the art of planning and arranging their own grounds, the seed will be planted that will germinate, in another generation, in a crop of art-gardeners of such high culture, and of such necessity to the educated community, that it will be one of the honored professions of our best collegiates. Now, however, the number of such men, devoted to this profession, is so small, that we have not heard even of more than half a dozen skilled, professional gardeners among our thirty millions of native Americans; and not greatly more than double that number of educated foreigners, who have established a deserved fame among us as men of culture in their art. Even these men, with few exceptions, are little known outside the wealthy circles of the great cities, nor half appreciated where they are known. Until employers are themselves persons of culture, artists, even when employed, are regarded as a kind of dilettanti, whom it is necessary to employ rather to conform to "the fashion," than for such service as the employer is competent to appreciate, and really enjoy the results of. We know of nothing that will at the same time cultivate a taste for the fascinating art of gardenesque designing, and produce a quick return of pleasure for the time spent, as the study of paper plans for one's own grounds.

Ignorant gardeners, and self-sufficient business men who know nothing about gardening, are apt to indulge in ridicule of this paper gardening, but it is the ridicule only which is ridiculous.

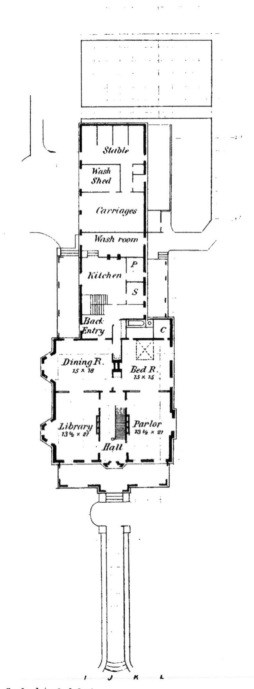

Stable

Wash
Shed

Carriages

Wash room

Kitchen

P

S

Back
Entry

C

Dining R.
15 × 18

Bed R.
15 × 15

Library
13½ × 27

Parlor
13½ × 21

Hall

Scale ⅛ inch-1 foot.

Architecture, in execution, becomes a matter of stone, brick, mortar, wood, and iron; but who, except an ignoramus, would expect the skillful architect to devote himself to the handling of these materials, instead of to his books, his pictures, and his drawing-board? Good garden designs necessitate the same kind of thought, and taste, and careful comparison of different plans, and consideration of expense, before commencing to handle the materials, that are to be used to carry out the design. The plan must be complete before commencing work on the foundations, whether for architecture or for decorative gardening. The time to do this can best be given during the days and long winter evenings preceding the season for work; and cannot be in those few lovely days of swelling buds, into which so many kinds of spring work are necessarily crowded. If, however, there is any skillful garden designer within reach, we advise, unhesitatingly, his employment. He will do the planning in one-tenth the time that an amateur can, and probably a great deal better; and his services should be paid for as for those of other professional men of education and culture.

If the reader will be governed by our advice, we shall insist on his having a correct map made of the lot upon which he has built, or proposes to build, and plant; showing accurately the location and plan of the house, and all the outbuildings, and the position of every tree or large shrub already growing. Such trees or shrubs should have the breadth of their tops lightly sketched in. Rock boulders, or ledges, which are not to be removed, should also be distinctly platted. The map should be drawn on a scale that will permit of its being pasted on a drawing-board not larger than two feet by three. The best of drawing-paper should be used. It should be moistened, and put on by some draughtsman familiar with the mode of doing it. If a lot 100 × 300 is to be platted on a scale of one-eighth of an inch to a foot, it will cover $12\frac{1}{2}$ × $37\frac{1}{2}$ inches of paper. Scaled one-twelfth of an inch to a foot, the same lot would cover $8\frac{1}{3}$ × 25 inches of paper, which would be the best scale for a lot of that length. For a larger lot it would be advisable to reduce the scale to one-sixteenth of an inch to the foot (or sixteen feet to one inch); and for a lot not more than a hundred feet long, or where not more than one hun-

dred feet need be planned for planting, a scale of four feet to the
inch ($\frac{1}{4}$ of an inch to the foot) may be used. It is best to have
the scale fourths, eighths, twelfths, or sixteenths of an inch, as
these divisions of a foot come on all ordinary measuring-rules.
There should be a clear margin of at least two inches of paper
outside the lot lines; the outer inch to paste the paper to the
board, and the inner inch for a margin, when it becomes necessary to cut the paper from the board. A duplicate should be
made of this skeleton map, as first made, to keep safely in the
house; and as the plans for planting are matured and carried out
from the board, or "field map," the house map should have such
work platted upon it, in duplicate. The map which is pasted to
the board may be materially protected from damage by rain, wet
grass, or dirt, to which it may be exposed during the planting
season, by covering it with ordinary transparent tracing linen.

To facilitate the planning or arrangement of the various things
to be planted on different parts of the lot, as well as to make the
plan more easy to work from in planting, the map should be divided into one-inch squares by ordinary blue lines, and these subdivided into eighth-inch squares by very faint blue lines. Each side
of these inch squares will then represent four, eight, twelve, or
sixteen feet, according to the scale chosen. One accustomed to
the use of a decimal scale, may have the squares made one and
one-fourth inches on each side, and then subdivided into tenths,
each one of which will then be an eighth-inch. Paper thus ruled
for the use of civil-engineers and architects, may be procured at
most large stationers. These squares, when the distances they
represent are borne in mind, serve as a substitute for measurements on the map. Plate I, which is on a scale of 32 feet to one
inch, (our page being too small to admit any larger scale), illustrates the mode in which a map should be made. It will be seen
that the intersections of the square lines with the exterior boundaries of the lot are numbered on one side and lettered on
another, from the same point, marked *o.* This is to facilitate
measurements and references to the intersections. Before proceeding to lay out walks, or to plant from the plan, it will be
necessary to have the fence measured and marked in the same

way, 1, 2, 3, 4, etc., on two opposite sides of the lot, and A, B, C on the other sides. These marks may be made distinct on the inside of the fence, in some inconspicuous place where they will not mar it.

Now let us suppose that the house and out-buildings have been correctly platted on the map of the lot, as shown on Plate I, and that the walks, trees, shrubs, and flower-beds have been planned and drawn as shown thereon. The first out-door work to be done is to lay out the walks on the ground in conformity to the plan. The front walk is six feet wide. This will be laid out simply by making its center on the center line of the main hall, extended to the front fence, or by taking for the center, at the street, a point two feet to the right of J, (looking towards the house.) This walk is here supposed to be made with a stone coping at the sides, (after the manner shown in the vignette of Chapter IV,) terminating eight feet from the front steps, with low pedestals and vases, and a circular stone or gravel area, as shown on the plate. The plan supposes the lot to have a street on the side as well as in front, and that its· surface is elevated from two to four feet above the front street.

The rear walk and carriage-road are combined in a roadway eight feet wide, four feet on each side of station 17, which is 136 feet (17 × 8=136) from the front corner. By counting the squares (each four feet), the size and form of the graveled space in front of the carriage-house will be readily ascertained. The curves may be made by little stakes or shingle splinters stuck until they are satisfactory. The grape walk, which is eight feet between the outside of the trellised posts, is on a right line with the rear part of the house, so that no mistake can be made in its location. The walk at the left is four feet from the trellis, and four feet wide, with a rose or other vine trellis, or a low flower vase, facing its extremity. The walks for the vegetable garden are too simple in their character to need more than mention. They open at three points into the grape walk, by openings or arches under the top slat of the trellis. It will be observed that the carriage-house, stable, and kitchen department of the house are under a continuous roof; a plan that we commend for those gentlemen who keep all things

tidy on all parts of their home-grounds, as economical, exceedingly convenient, cleanly, and, in the hands of a good architect,
effective in adding to the apparent extent and home-look of the
place. But for persons unaccustomed to maintain the same cleanliness around the outbuildings as in the "front yard," it may not
do so well.

The walks being disposed of, let us attend to the planting; and
begin with the front. Further on we may describe in detail *what*
trees and shrubs may be especially adapted to the different places
here marked; our object now being only to allude to the manner
in which the plan, that has been completed on paper, may be
worked out on the ground. At *a*, *b*, and *c* are three pairs of trees,
intended to form a short umbrageous approach-avenue to the
house. They are all seven feet from the walk; *a a* are two
squares, or eight feet from the front; *b b*, five squares, or twenty
feet; *c c* are eight squares, or thirty-two feet. Flanking these, on
the left, is a mass of evergreens, several of which are on the line
H, and others on the intersections of squares to the left, as shown
by the plan. At the intersection of the lines 2 and A, or sixteen
feet from the front, and eight feet from the side fence, is the
small tree *f*; at the intersection of 2 and D is a small tree or
shrub *e*; and four feet farther right, and four feet nearer the front
street, is its companion shrub *e*. The small tree or large shrub *d*,
is shown by the squares to be eight feet from the front, and twenty
feet from the side street, on the line 1. The intelligent reader
will see how easily the plan for the arrangement of trees and
shrubs may be worked out in this manner throughout; and, after
a few years' growth *and good care* of his plantings, ought to realize
plainly the superior beauty of a well-considered plan.

CHAPTER X.

IF, as we have insisted, a correct map has been made of the grounds, with all the buildings, and the trees already growing, marked thereon, the next work is to lay out roads or walks upon this map. First, question your wants as to where the street entrances or gates had better be made. This is to be decided principally by the direction of daily travel over them. They should always be in the directions that the family go oftenest, and should be laid out so as to connect most conveniently the street or streets with the entrance doors of the dwelling and outbuildings. *No more walks should be made than are wanted for daily use, either for business or pleasure.* In small grounds, walks made merely for the purpose of having "pretty walks" meandering among suppositional flower-beds, convey the impression of a desire for show disproportionate to the means of gratifying it. Where there is an acre, or more, of ground devoted to decorative gardening, and it is intended to keep a gardener in constant employ in the care of it, then walks conducting to retired seats, or summer-houses, or made for the purpose of revealing pleasing vistas, or intricacies in the shrubbery, or charming surprises in flowers that may be arranged upon their borders, may add greatly to the beauty of the place. We would not advise having any carriage-way to the front entrance of a house, unless the distance is from eighty to one hundred feet between the steps and the street, and on a lot at least one hundred and fifty feet in width. For most residences the front street is near enough for a carriage to approach with visitors and callers, who generally choose fair weather; and the family can go to and from their own vehicles by some of the rear entrances of the house, past which the road from the street to the carriage-house should lead. Where houses are designed so that their main entrance is on the side, then a carriage-road may pass it properly, though the lot should be narrower than the size just mentioned. For lots having such narrow street fronts in proportion to their depth, this is the best arrangement for the house, as it leaves the finest rooms adjoining each other in the front. See Plates XIII, XXV, and XXVII.

In laying out a carriage-drive avoid sharp turns, and, as far as possible, the segments of circles reversed against each other, as in a geometric letter S. Such parts of circles, though graceful on paper, give the effect of crooked lines, as seen in perspective. A line that will enable the driver to approach the main steps most conveniently is the true line, unless trees or shrubs already growing prevent, in which case the same rule must be followed as nearly as practicable. By the most convenient approach is meant that which a skillful driver would make if he were driving over an unbroken lawn from the entrance-gate to the porch.

Nearly all amateur landscape-gardeners will blunder in their first attempts to lay out roads or walks, by making the curves too decided. The lines most graceful on paper will not appear so in perspective, as we walk along them; and it will not do, therefore, in laying them out on a paper plat, to suppose they will appear the same on the ground. If grounds were to be seen from a balloon the effect would be the same as upon your plan; but as we are all destined to look along the ground, instead of vertically down upon it, it will be seen why curves that look graceful on paper are likely to be too abrupt and crooked in perspective. If the reader will place the paper plan nearly on a level with his eye, and glance along the line of the proposed road or walk, he will be able to judge how his curves will seem as seen when walking towards or upon them; supposing, of course, that the ground to be platted has a tolerably level surface. There are several of the plans which follow whereon the walks will have the appearance, at first sight, of being awkwardly direct, having neither the simplicity of a straight line, nor the grace of Hogarth's line of beauty; but if the hint just given about glancing along the line of the walk with the eye nearly on a level with the paper is followed, they will be found more pleasing.

There are many places where the house is large compared with the size of the lot, on which straight walks are not only admissible, but where to attempt curved walks would be ridiculous. Some of the succeeding plans will illustrate such. The vignette of Chapter IV illustrates an elegant approach of this kind, over which trees have formed a noble arch. Steps and copings of cut stone, with pedestals and vases, may be designed to make such entrances as beautiful architecturally as the means of the proprietor will justify. The mere platting of walks on such places is too simple a matter to require any suggestions here. All foot-walks should approach the entrance steps either at right angles or parallel with them; and in all cases should start at right angles with the line of the entrance gate.

The width of roads and walks must vary according to the extent of the grounds and the character of the house. For a cottage with small grounds, make the walks narrow rather than wide. The apparent size of the ground will be diminished by too ambitious walks. But there are limits of convenience. A broad walk always gives one a sense of freedom and ease, which is wanting when we must keep our eyes down to avoid straying from the narrow way. For small places, therefore, we must compromise between the prettier external effect of narrow walks and the greater convenience of wide ones. Four feet is the least width appropriate for a cottage main walk, and two feet for the rear walks. But for most town or suburban places, from four to six feet for the main walk and three feet for the rear walks, are appropriate widths. It is essential, however, that no shrubbery or flower-beds approach nearer than two feet from them. A walk three feet wide, with two feet of closely-shaven lawn on each side of it, is really just as commodious as a walk six feet wide closely bordered or overhung by rank annuals or gross shrubs. At the foot of the

steps it is desirable to have greater width than in other parts of
the walk.

The width of carriage-drives should be governed by the same
considerations as the walks. Eight feet is the least width, and
fourteen feet the greatest, that will be appropriate to the class of
places for which this book is designed; and whatever the width
elsewhere, it should not be less than twelve feet opposite the main
entrance steps, unless it traverses a porte-cochere. The turnway in
front of the main entrance should be on a radius of not less than
ten feet to the inner line of the road, and more if space permits;
but not to exceed a radius of twenty feet, unless the location of
trees or the shape of the ground make it specially desirable to turn
a larger circuit.

Opportunities to make or lose pleasing effects are always presented where there are trees or shrubs already grown. To conduct
walks or roads so as to make them seem to have grown there; to
arrange a gateway under branches of trees or between old shrubs,
or leading around or between them; to have walks divide so that a
tree shall mark their intersection; to weave a turnway smoothly
among old tree trunks—all such arts as these are precisely the
small things which prove the taste, or lack of it, in the designer.

In making the carriage-road and the walks, there is an immense
difference in expense between excessive thoroughness and the
"good enough" style. Digging out from a foot and a half to two
feet of the soil the whole width of the road or walk, tile-draining
on each side, then filling up with broken stone or seoriæ, and
finally covering the surface with several inches of pure gravel,
and paving the gutters with pebbles, is the thorough style. But
on sandy and gravelly soils we have seen excellent walks and
roads (for light carriages) made by simply covering the ground
with from two to three inches of good gravel or slate. The preparation necessary for this kind of road-making being to excavate
below the level of the
border, so as to leave a
rounded surface with tile
of three to four inches
diameter, placed in the

FIG. 19.

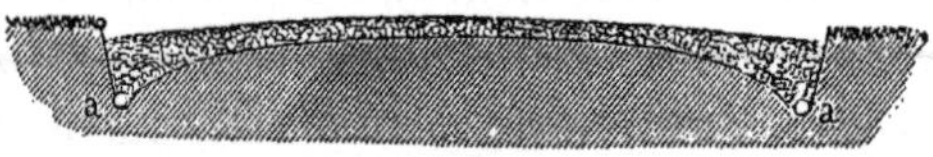

bottom of trenches on
each side, as shown by
the accompanying sketch.
Four inches thickness of
gravel on a road thus pre

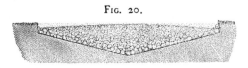

Fig. 20.

pared will, with proper care, make an excellent road. On clay,
roads can be made with no more additional preparation than to
provide for a few more inches of gravel. Fig. 20 shows a suitable
form for such a roadway. Of course the grades of the roads
lengthwise must be such as to carry the water in the gutters and
drains to proper outlets. We suggest this method of road-making
for those sections of the country where stone is costly, and for
those improvers who cannot afford to use a large amount of money
in road foundations.

The main thing to secure good walks or roads is *constant care.*
Weeds and grass must be kept from encroaching by the use of the
hoe and edging-spade ; the gravel must be kept in place by the use
of the rake and roller. No thoroughness of construction will make
such care needless, and by it the least expensive walks and roads
may be kept in excellent condition at small cost.

Solid stone flagging, if neatly dressed, is of course preferable
for walks to gravel, and will be used where it can be afforded.
Where the asphaltum or coal-tar composition, now used with great
success for walks in the Central Park, can be put down by some
one thoroughly conversant with the mode of doing it well, it will
be found a very fine material ; but while green it involves much
risk to carpets. Where the soil is clay, and good gravel or composition not easily obtained, (as in many parts of the western
states,) and flagging is too expensive, seasoned white pine board
or plank walks may be substituted. These, if carefully laid, (across
the line of the walk,) and the edges sawed to the requisite curves
or straight lines, make very comfortable walks. The main difficulty is to find mechanics who will have skill and patience to put
them down in the graceful curved lines that are desired. Inch
lumber, daubed on the *under side* with hot coal-tar to postpone
rotting, will answer very well for walks from two to three feet
wide. For wider ones two-inch plank is recommended.

Pine walks, if made of good stuff, and tarred as suggested, will last from eight to ten years; and if sufficient care is used in their construction, will be found very satisfactory substitutes for stone or gravel, even for curved lines. For straight walks they are always satisfactory as long as sound. In districts where stone and gravel are scarce and dear, they must long continue in use; and there is no reason why they should not be shaped into graceful forms, since wood is so much more facile to work than stone. Several methods of preserving wood from decay are now attracting great attention, and it is believed that some of them will be effectual to so increase the durability of wood that its use for walks will be far more desirable than heretofore. It is essential in all walks that the sod shall be about an inch above the outer surface of the walk, so that a scythe or rolling mower may do its work unobstructed in passing near or over them.

To lay out the carriage-drive and the walks in conformity to the paper plat that has been made, is a work requiring some patience and skill. There are persons whose love for beautiful effects in landscape-gardening is evident, who are so wanting in what is called a mechanical eye, as to be incompetent to lay out their own grounds, even with a plat before them. If you, kind reader, are one of those, send for the nearest good gardener to do the work for you; or invite some friend or neighbor, who has given evidence of this talent by the making of his own place, to come and help you. He will not be likely to turn away from your appreciation of his taste and skill. If, however, your ground is large enough to admit of much length of walks, the labor of laying them out would more properly devolve upon a professional gardener—if such there be in your neighborhood. It will not, however, be advisable to listen to all the suggestions of improvements that any "professional gardener" may volunteer for your guidance. Genuine landscape-gardeners are rare everywhere, and bear about the same proportion to good common gardeners that accomplished landscape-painters do to house-painters. The probabilities are that your neighborhood has some gardener competent to plat walks, lay turf, cut your shrubbery-beds, and do your planting; but, ten chances to one, he will lay more stress on the form of some curlecue of a flower-bed than on those beautiful effects of rich foliage and open glades—of shadow and sunlight—that are often produced with the simplest means by Dame Nature or the true landscape-artist. If, therefore, you have a well-matured plan, and the gardener is competent to study it intelligently, let him make suggestions of changes before the work on the ground commences ; but thereafter oblige him either to work faithfully to your plan, or else furnish you with a better one ; and do not let him bluff you into an entire surrender by his professional sneers at paper plans. Of course these remarks are intended to apply to the common run of illiterate gardeners, who have happened to make a trade of this species of labor, and not to another class who may have chosen the profession from a love for it, and who have intelligence or imagination enough to understand something of the art of arranging their sylvan and floral materials so as to make pictures with them.

Almost every neighborhood has a few gentlemen of superior taste in such matters, whose dictums will, perforce, help to educate the common run of self-sufficient gardeners ; and it is hoped that so promising a field of labor will soon attract the attention of Americans of the highest culture, to whom we can turn for professional work in ground designs ; who, as Pope describes one—

> "Consults the genius of the place in all
> That tells the waters or to rise or fall ;
> Or helps the ambitious hill the heavens to scale,
> Or scoops in circling theatres the vale :
> Calls in the country, catches opening glades,
> Joins willing woods, and varies shades from shades ;
> Now breaks or now directs the intending lines,
> *Paints as you plant, and, as you work, designs !*"

CHAPTER XI.

ARRANGEMENT IN PLANTING.

THOUGH set rules, in matters of art, are sometimes "more honored in the breach than in the observance," it is also true that every art has certain general prin- ciples, the observance of which will rarely lead to great faults, while their violations may. We therefore hope that the following suggestions or rules, drawn to meet the requirements of small suburban grounds, will be of some use, and serve as a starting-point for that higher culture which educates the intuitive perceptions of the artist to dispense with rules, or rather, perhaps, *to work intuitively by rule,* as an æsthetic instinct.

I. *Preserve in one or more places* (according to the size and form of the lot) *the greatest length of unbroken lawn that the space will admit of.*

II. *Plant between radiating lines from the house to the outside of the lot, so as to leave open lines of view from the principal windows and entrance porches ; also find where, without injuring the views to and from the house, the best vistas may be left from the street into the lot, and from one point to another across the grounds, or to points of interest beyond.*

III. *Plant the larger trees and shrubs farthest from the centre of the lawn, so that the smaller may be seen to advantage in front of them.*

IV. *On small lots plant no trees which quickly attain great size, if it is intended to have a variety of shrubs or flowers.*

V. *In adding to belts or groups of trees or shrubs, plant near the salient points, rather than in bays or openings.*

VI. *Shrubs which rest upon the lawn should not be planted nearer than from six to ten feet from the front fence, except where intended to form a continuous screen of foliage.*

Rule I.

Preserve in one or more places (according to the size and form of the lot) *the greatest length of unbroken lawn that the space will admit of*

To illustrate this rule we ask the reader's attention to some of the plates. Plate No. IV represents in the simplest manner one mode of observing it. It is a lot of fifty feet front, and considerable depth, isolated from the adjoining properties on both sides by a close fence or hedge. On it is a small compact house, thrown back so as to leave about eighty feet depth between it and the street. Each bay-window of the principal rooms has a look-out upon all the beauty that may be created on this small space. To economize ground for the greatest extent of lawn possible on this lot, the main walk to the house is entirely on one side of it and of the line of view out of the bay-windows over the lawn ; and leads directly to the main veranda entrance. From the bay-windows to the street, in a right line between them, not a tree, shrub, or flower is to be planted. If the grounds were of greater extent, it would be desirable to have the views out of each of these windows different from the other, so that in going from one room to the other, and looking out upon the lawn, it would exhibit a fresh picture. But to attempt to divide this lawn into two by a middle line of shrubbery would belittle both, and crowd the shrub-bery so that nothing could be seen to advantage. The lot is quite too small to attempt a variety of views, and the lawn is made to look as large as possible by placing all trees and shrubbery on the margin ; in short, the greatest length and breadth of lawn that the lot will admit of is preserved.   Plate VII shows a village lot of the same frontage as the preceding, but on which the house is only twenty-five feet from the street.   There can be no good breadth of lawn on this lot, since the house occupies the ground that forms the lawn on Plate No. IV.   But a peculiar little vista over narrow strips of lawn skirting the walk is obtained on entering the front gate.   This is upwards of one hundred feet in length, and widens out around the flower-bed S, so that in perspective, and contrasted with the length and narrowness of the strips of lawn near the house, it will give the effect of greater distance and width than it has.   Such a plan as this requires the most skillful planting and high keeping.   Indeed, there is more need of skill to make this narrow strip a pretty work of art than on the larger lots that are planned for this work.   Plates XIV and XV show corner lots also of fifty feet front, with houses entirely on one side of the lot, and lawns as long as the depth will admit of, margined by assorted small shrubs and clipped trees.   On the former the house is placed against the side street, leaving the lawn on the inside, and a pleasing vista over it to an archway that opens into a long grape arbor. This will make a lengthened perspective of lawn and garden as great as the size of the lot will allow.   On Plate XV the house is placed so as to leave the lawn space between it and the side street, and the main garden walk is arranged so that from the back veranda and the library windows it will form a little perspective. The latter plan, it will be seen, is for a city basement-house, while the former has a kitchen on the main floor.   Plates Nos. V and VI are of lots 60 × 150 feet, where the lawns occupy as great a length as can be spared for decorative purposes.   These side lawns are no wider than those of Plates XIV and XV, as the additional ten feet width of lot, on the right, is shut out of view, and devoted to small fruits.   This strip in the hands of a garden artist might be made very charming in itself, but where one man would make it so, a thousand would fail.   We therefore advise in general not to plant anything against the walls of the house in such narrow strips as these, unless they have the most sunny exposure.   In towns, where lots of this size are built on, other houses are usually so near such improvements, as to darken the ground with their shade. The degree of exposure to the sun and air in these places must govern their use, but in general it is better to have either grass or pavement in them, or a paved walk and bedding plants, that may be renewed from a green-house. Plate XIII shows a lot of one hundred and sixty feet front by three hundred feet deep, on which a vista of unbroken lawn, the entire depth of the lot, is obtained from the main entrance. This place is supposed to adjoin lots whose fronts are improved in common, so that each of the principal windows of the house is provided with a distinct foreground for a picture, the middle distance of which will have such character as the neighboring improvements make. Were the ground improved to conform to this plan the effect would be much finer than the rather formal character of the trees in the design would indicate.

Plates X and XI are of lots two hundred feet front by three hundred feet deep. On the former, the rule we are endeavoring to illustrate is sacrificed in a measure to the requirements of an orchard and kitchen-garden; on the latter, the orchard is given up to secure the beauty of a more extended lawn and more elaborate plantation.

On Plate XXVII are some good illustrations of this rule applied to the laying out of what are usually considered awkward forms of lots to improve. It will be seen that the views from the street-corner, at the point A, on the right-hand plan looking towards the house, and in other directions, are long, open, and well varied, in the grouping of trees, shrubs, and flowers. As one walks along to B and C, at each opening between groups of shrubs the views are over the longest stretch of lawn that the size of the lot will admit of; while the views from the main windows of the house, and from the front and rear verandas, are as extended as possible.

Plate XXII, which is designed to illustrate the advantage of joining neighboring improvements, however cheap or simple their character, is an excellent illustration of the beauty and garden-esque effect that may be secured by leaving an unbroken vista of lawn and low flowers from one side of a block to the other, as shown on the line B C, though the block is covered by five inexpensive residences. The vignette of Chapter IV is a view taken from the point A, and gives but two-thirds of the length of view that is seen from either of the side streets. Of course the flowers to be planted in the beds on the lawn in the above line of view, should be only those which grow within a few inches of the ground; otherwise the effect intended would be marred.

Plate XXIX is a good example, on a larger scale, of long and open views.

Plate XXI is an illustration of the rule to which we ask the reader's attention, as an example of triple vistas on a lot only one hundred feet wide; first, that formed by the small shrubs and flowers bordering the main walk, with the terrace steps and the house bounding the view at one end, and a hemlock archway at the other. From the bay-windows of the house the two other divisions of the lawn are designed to show to the best advantage, and over the low clipped parts of the front hedge, at *a a*, made low for this purpose, their beauty can also be seen by passers on the street.

Rule II.

Fig. 21.

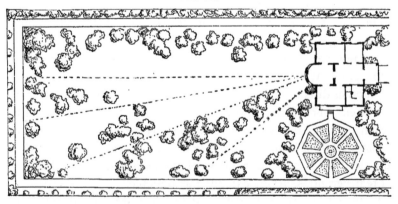

Plant between radiating lines from the house to the outside of the lot, so as to leave open lines of view from the principal windows and entrance porches; also find where, without injuring the views to and from the house, the best vistas may be left from the street into the lot, and from one point to another across the grounds, or to points of interest beyond.

The accompanying plan, adapted from Loudon, gives a good illustration of the observance of the second rule. The plan represents the part of a lot in the rear of the dwelling, all of which is devoted to lawn and decorative planting ; the entrance-front being close to the street. The plantation is supposed to be entirely secluded from the street and from contiguous properties by walls. The space covered is about 150 × 300 feet. 'The dotted lines radiating from the bow-window show the apparently loose, but really well studied distribution of groups of trees and shrubs in radiating lines. On the right, one of these groups forms a screen of shrubbery to divide the lawn from the elaborate flower-garden which forms the distinctive feature of the view from the dining-room window. On smaller lots the first part of the second rule cannot be illustrated with so much effect, but a general conformity to it may be observed in many of our larger plans.

Plate II represents a lot one hundred and fifty feet front by two hundred and fifty deep, where the house is placed much nearer the front of the lot, and nearly in the centre. So placed, the longest views over its lawn cannot be obtained from the house in any direction, but from many points in the front street, and within the grounds, the lines of view are as long and unbroken as the size of the lot will admit of ; while a partial privacy is given to the space between the bay-windows and the side street, by a close plantation of hedge and shrubbery. Openness, rather than privacy, is the characteristic of this plan, however, and its best views are obtained on entering or passing it. Yet the lawn, as seen from the bay-windows, will be broken by shrubs and trees into a much greater variety of views than a careless examination of the plan would lead one to suppose. From o, at the intersection of the two streets, the eye ranges between two near groups of shrubbery, which frame the view over the lawn to the bay-windows ; and on the right, in front of the back veranda, between slender conical trees, a flower-bed and a pyramid of roses, under the shade of fruit trees in the back yard, to the carriage-house front:—a distance equal to the entire length of the lot. From the point marked 2, the view changes ; the croquet-ground, and the intervening compact shrubs and flower-beds, and an evergreen group at *g*, come into view.

Or the eye rests on the near group of shrubs opposite Fig. 3 ;
or to the left, ranges to the various groups on that side of the
grounds.   At Fig. 5 the view on the right, of the trees, hedge, and
shrubbery, from *g* to *w*, together with pleasing views in other directions, make this point the one from which the whole place is seen
to the best advantage.   The views through the archway of trees
over the front gateway are pleasing in every direction ; and in the
line towards *u*, extend nearly the entire length of the lot.   This
form of lot, when the house is so near the centre, is less adapted to
illustrate the rule under consideration than most others, and we
have pointed out its peculiarities in this connection to show the
effort to conform to the rule under adverse circumstances.   The
reader will please to observe on this plan a dotted line from *d* to
the left, parallel with the front street.   This is forty feet from the
front.   Within a distance from ten to fifty feet from such fronts is
usually the part which should be left unplanted, in order that all
the places in the block may, on that line, form a continuous
lawn of such park-like character as no one lot could furnish.   Most
of our plans are designed in this manner to secure the advantages
of associate improvements, and " views from one point to another
across the grounds, or to some point of interest beyond the
grounds."

Rule III.

*Plant the larger trees and shrubs farthest from the centre of the
lawn, so that the smaller may be seen to advantage in front of them.*

The necessity of observing the third rule, in small places, is so
obvious, and it is so easy to follow, if one but knows the character
of the trees and shrubs he is using, that few remarks upon it
are necessary.   The vignette at the head of this chapter is intended
as an illustration of the great number and variety of shrubs and
small trees which may be exhibited in a single group, in such a
manner that each may show its peculiar beauty without concealing
any of the others, and at the same time form a harmonious collection.   Not less than twenty species of trees and shrubs may be
seen at once in such a group, each growing to a perfect develop-

ment of its best form; while by a different arrangement in planting, the beauties of all the smaller shrubs might be lost to the eye, and their growth marred by the domineering habits of the larger ones. It will be noticed that in this vignette the weeping elm forms the centre of the group. Close to it may be planted some of the large shrubs which flourish in partial shade and under the drip of trees. Outside of these a few of the smallest class of trees, of peculiar and diverse forms, and then the smaller and finer shrubbery arranged to carry out the spirit of the rule. No engraving, however, can do justice to the variety of character in foliage, flowers, forms, and colors, that such a group may be made to exhibit.

Rule IV.

On small lots plant no trees which quickly attain great size, if it is intended to have a variety of shrubs or flowers.

The fourth rule is somewhat difficult to illustrate, because of the frequency with which good taste may insist on exceptions to it. Few suburban places are so small that one or two large trees, not far from the house, will not add greatly to their home-look and summer comfort. Trees which overhang the house and form a background, or vernal frame-work for it, are the crowning beauty of a home picture. But, in planting small lots, the need of a few fruit trees, such as cherries and pears, which one cannot well do without, and which, for the safety of the fruit, must be near or behind the house, is a necessity that obliges us to dispense with the grandeur of great trees where their beauty is most effective and to endeavor to develop another type of beauty for small places, viz.: that of artistic elegance in the treatment of small things. And it is some satisfaction to know that, with the latter, what we attempt may be achieved in a few years, while, if we set about planting to secure the nobler effect of large trees, a life-time will be required to see its consummation. Where any large tree is already growing, the style of planting must conform to its position, size, and character; but where the plantation is on a bare site, the rule is a proper one to follow. In the former case the fine tree is to be considered "master of the situation," and all things are to be arranged with due regard to it; but in the latter there is an open field for the taste and judgment.

RULE V.

In adding to belts or groups of trees or shrubs, plant near the salient points, rather than in bays or openings.

The fifth rule is one which novices in planting are always violating. It is such a temptation to plant a tree or shrub "where there is most room for it," and "where it will show handsomely," that the ignorant planter at once selects some clear place on his lawn, or some open bay, for the new comer; quite forgetful that a few such plantings will break the prettiest of lawns into insignificant fragments, and change the sunny projections and shadowy bays of a shrubbery border into a lumpish wall of verdure.

The placement of large and showy bedding plants or annuals and perennials must be made on the same principle. They are to be regarded as shrubs, and the places for them must be determined by their usual size at midsummer.

Low-growing flowers, or brilliant-leaved and bushy plants, may occasionally be relieved to advantage in the shady bays of a shrubbery border, especially if a walk leads near them; but in general, flower-beds (except such as are formed into artistic groups as a special feature of a window-view), should be either near walks or the points of shrubbery projections. Like gay flags on a parade ground, they show to best advantage in the van of the advanced columns.

RULE VI.

Shrubs which rest upon the lawn should not be planted nearer than from six to ten feet from the front fence, except where intended to form a continuous screen of foliage.

The sixth rule is one which may not be practicable to follow on very small lots, or where the space is narrow between the house and the street; but there would be a marked improvement in the appearance of most places by its observance. In the first place, the shrubs themselves, which, it must be supposed, are only planted because they are beautiful, will show to much better ad vantage with this introductory lawn or foreground to spread upon. To crowd against a fence groups of shrubs which will bend grace fully to the lawn on every side if room is given them, is much like the misplacement of elegant robes in a crowd, where they may be injured, but can never be seen to advantage. Such a strip of introductory lawn is to the ground what a broad threshold stone is to the house entrance, giving the place a generous air, and seeming to say that the proprietor is not so stinted for room that he must needs crowd his sylvan company into the street. Yet it must frequently happen that the exigencies of small or peculiarly shaped lots, require a violation of this rule, in order to secure sufficient breadth of lawn within, to present a good appearance from the house. The plans on Plates XXII, XXIII, XXIV, and XXVII, are examples of this necessity. Plates II, XII, XIII, and XVIII, on the other hand, show a general attention to the rule ; while in the other plans it is kept in view more or less, as the circumstances of each case seem to require.

There is another matter which can hardly be made the subject of any rules, but yet demands the attention of every planter. Nearly all trees and shrubs are more beautiful on their southerly than on their northerly sides, and some trees which glow with beauty towards the sun are meagre and unsightly towards the north. This fact must therefore be borne in mind in deciding where to plant favorite trees or shrubs, so that their fairest sides may be towards those points from which they will be most seen ; and as there are a few varieties and species of trees which are beautiful on all sides—the box and hemlock, for instance—they may be placed in locations where the others will not show to advantage.

CHAPTER XII

RELATIVE BEAUTY OF *LAWN*, TREES, SHRUBS, AND
FLOWERS.

THE true lover of nature is so omnivorous in his tastes, that for him to classify her family into different grades of usefulness or beauty, is about as difficult a task as to name which of her vegetable productions is the best food. But though a variety is better than any one, there is, in both cases, strong ground for a decided choice; and we repeat what has already been suggested, that, of all the external decorations of a home, a well kept LAWN is the most essential. Imagine the finest trees environing a dwelling, but everywhere beneath them only bare ground: then picture the same dwelling with a velvet greensward spreading away from it on all sides, without a tree or shrub upon it, and choose which is the most pleasing to the eye. The question of value is not to be considered, but simply which, in connection with the dwelling, will make the most satis⁻factory impression on the mind. The fine trees are vastly the more valuable, because it requires half a life-time to obtain them, while the lawn may be perfected in two or three years.

The comparative value of trees and shrubs depends much on the extent of the ground and the taste of the occupants. If the lot is small, and the family has a decided appreciation of the varied characteristics of different shrubs, they will have much more pleasure from a fine collection of them than from the few trees which their lot could accommodate. But if the occupants are not particularly appreciative of the varied beauties of smaller vegetation, then a few trees and a good lawn only, will be more appropriate for their home. Larger lots can have both, but the foregoing consideration may govern the preponderance of one or the other. When once the planting fever is awakened, *too many of both are likely to be planted*, and grounds will be stuffed rather than beautified.

One full grown oak, elm, maple, chestnut, beech, or sycamore will cover with its branches nearly a quarter of an acre. Allowing seventy feet square for the spread of each tree (all the above varieties being occasionally much larger), nine such trees would completely cover an acre. But as we plant for ourselves, instead of for our children, it will be sufficient in most suburban planting to allow for half-grown, rather than full-grown trees. Grounds, however, which are blessed with grand old trees should have them cherished lovingly—they are treasures that money cannot buy— and should be guarded with jealous care against the admission of little evergreens and nursery trees, which new planters are apt to huddle under and around them, to the entire destruction of the broad stretches of lawn which large trees require in order to reveal the changing beauty of their shadows. Where such trees exist, if you would make the most of the ground, lavish your care in enriching the soil over their vast roots, and perfecting the lawn around them; and then arrange for shrubs and flowers away from their mid-day shadows. Even fine old fruit trees, if standing well apart on a lawn, will often give a dignity and a comfortable home-look to a place that is wanting in places which are surrounded only with new plantings.

But it is an unfortunate fact that nine-tenths of all the town and suburban lots built on are bare of trees, and therefore, after the attainment of a fine lawn, the lowly beauties of shrubs and flowers, with all their varied luxuriance of foliage and fragrant bloom, must be the main features of the place, while the trees are also growing in their midst which may eventually over-top and supersede them. If one could imagine Americans to live their married lives, each pair in one home, what a pleasing variety might the changing years bring them. An unbroken lawn around the dwelling should typify the unwritten page in the opening book of earnest life. Young trees planted here and there upon it would suggest looking forward to the time when, under their grand shadows, the declining years of the twain may be spent in dignity and repose. Flowers and shrubs meanwhile repay with grateful beauty all their care, until, over-shadowed by the nobler growth, they are removed as cumberers of the ground, and give way to the simplicity that becomes " a fine old home."

Most small places can be much more charmingly planted with shrubs alone, than with trees and shrubs mingled. Indeed, it is one of the greatest blunders of inexperienced planters to put in trees where there is only room enough for shrubs. A small yard may be made quite attractive by the artistic management of shrubs and flowers whose size is adapted to the contracted ground; but the same place would be so filled up by the planting of a cherry tree or a horse-chestnut, that no such effect could be produced.

Where the decorative portion of the grounds do not exceed a half acre, there can be little question of the superior beauty of shrubberies to the very small collection of trees that such narrow limits can accommodate. The greatly increased beauty of shrubs when seen upon a lawn without any shadowing of trees, nor crowded one side or another " to fill-up," can only be appreciated by those who have seen the elegance of a tastefully arranged place planted with shrubs alone.

The part which annuals and low growing flowers should have in home surroundings may be compared with the lace, linen, and ribbon decorations of a lady's dress—being essential ornaments, and yet to be introduced sparingly. Walks may be bordered, and groups pointed, and bays in the shrubbery brightened by them;

or geometrically arranged groups of flower-beds may be introduced in the foreground of important window views ; but beware of frequently breaking open stretches of lawn for them. Imagine bits of lace or bows of ribbon stuck promiscuously over the body and skirt of a lady's dress. " How vulgar !" you exclaim. Put them in their appropriate places and what charming points they make! Let your lawn be your home's velvet robe, and your flowers its not too promiscuous decorations.

Of constructive garden decorations (in which are included pillars and trellises for vines, screens, arbors, summer-houses, seats, rockwork, terraces, vases, fountains, and statuary), and their comparative value, we will merely say that really tasteful and *durable* ornamentation of that kind is rather expensive, and therefore to be weighed well in the balance with expenditures of the same money for other modes of embellishment before ordering such work.

The following remarks from Kemp's admirable little work on Landscape Gardening* express our views so fully that we will give them entire :

" A garden may also be overloaded with a variety of things which, though ornamental in themselves, and not at all out of keeping with the house, or the principal elements of the landscape, may yet impart to it an affected or ostentatious character. An undue introduction of sculptured or other figures, vases, seats, and arbors, baskets for plants, and such like objects, will come within the limits of this description. And there is nothing of which people in general are so intolerant in others, as the attempt, when glaringly and injudiciously made, to crowd within a confined space the appropriate adornments of the most ample garden. It is invariably taken as evidence of a desire to appear to be and to possess that which the reality of the case will not warrant, and is visited with the reprobation and contempt commonly awarded to

---

* This is an English work entitled " How to lay out a Garden," a work so complete and well condensed, that were it not for the difference in the climate, and in the style of living (and consequently of the plans of dwellings, and their outbuildings and garden connections), which English thoroughness and cheaper labor make practicable, there had been no need of this book.

ill-grounded assumption. An unpresuming garden, like a modest individual, may have great defects without challenging criticism; and will even be liked and praised because of its very unobtrusive ness. But where a great deal is attempted, and there is much of pretension, whether in persons or things, scrutiny seems invited, incongruities are magnified, and actual merits are passed by un-noticed, or distorted into something quite ridiculous."

The improver must decide, before he begins to plan for plant-ing, what the size and features of his lot, and his own circum-stances, will enable him to accomplish *most perfectly.*

If there are trees or shrubs already of good size growing on the lot, the first study should be to develop and exhibit all their traits to the best advantage; and to this end a rich soil and a perfected lawn are the most essential.

If the lot is bare of trees, a smooth surface and fine lawn are still ground-works precedent to planting, whether the lot be large or small. If large enough, choose among large trees the principal features of its embellishment; if less than an acre, plant sparingly trees of the first class; if a rood, or but little more, then lawn, shrubs and flowers should be its only verdant furniture.

We class among shrubs many dwarf evergreens, which, be-cause they belong to species which usually attain large size, are included in nursery catalogues under the head of trees. They will be found classified in our Appendix. We also regard as shrubs, in effect, those vigorous growing annuals or perennials like the ricinus, cannas, dahlias, and hollyhocks, which grow *too high to be seen over,* and which cast shadows on the lawn near them.

CHAPTER XIII.

THE LAWN.

"Whether we look, or whether we listen,
We hear life murmur, or see it glisten;
Every clod feels a stir of might,
    An instinct within it that reaches and towers,
And, groping blindly above it for light,
    Climbs to a soul in grass and flowers."

LOWELL.

"On each side shrinks the bowery shade,
Before me spreads an emerald glade;
The sunshine steeps its grass and moss,
That couch my footsteps as I cross."

ALFRED B. STREET.

A SMOOTH, closely shaven surface of grass is by far the most essential element of beauty on the grounds of a suburban home. Dwellings, all the rooms of which may be filled with elegant furniture, but with rough uncarpeted floors, are no more incongruous, or in ruder taste, than the shrub and tree and flower-sprinkled yards of most home-grounds, where shrubs and flowers mingle in confusion with tall grass, or ill-defined borders of cultivated ground. Neatness and order are as essential to the pleasing effect of ground furniture as of house furniture. No matter how elegant or appropriate the latter may be, it will never look well in the home of a slattern. And however choice the variety of shrubs and flowers, if they occupy the ground so that there is no pleasant expanse of close-cut grass to relieve them, they cannot make a pretty place. The long grass allowed to grow in town and suburban grounds, after the spring gardening fever is over, neutralizes to a certain degree all attempts of the lady or gentleman of the house to beautify them, though they spend ever so much in obtaining the best shrubs, trees, or flowers the neighbors or the nurseries can furnish. It is not necessary to have an acre of pleasure ground to secure a charming lawn. Its extent may always be proportioned to the size of the place; and if the selection of flowers and shrubs and their arrangement is properly made, it is surprising how small a lawn will realize some of the most pleasing effects of larger ones. A strip twenty feet wide and a hundred feet long may be rendered, proportionally, as artistic as the landscape vistas of a park.

And it needs but little more to have room to realize by art, and with shadowing trees, the sparkling picture that the poet, Alfred B. Street, thus presents in his " Forest Walk."

> " A narrow vista, carpeted
> With rich green grass, invites my tread:
> Here showers the light in golden dots,
> There sleeps the shade in ebon spots,
> So blended that the very air
> Seems net-work as I enter there."

To secure a good lawn, a rich soil is as essential as for the kitchen garden. On small grounds the quickest and best way of making a lawn is by turfing. There are few neighborhoods where good turf cannot be obtained in pastures or by road-sides. No better varieties of grass for lawns can be found than those that form the turf of old and closely fed pastures. Blue-grass and white clover are the staple grasses in them, though many other varieties are usually found with these, in smaller proportions.

The ground should be brought to as smooth slopes or levels as possible before laying the turf, as much of the polished beauty of a perfected lawn will depend on this precaution. If the ground has been recently spaded or manured, it should be heavily tramped or rolled before turfing, to guard against uneven settling. A tolerably compact soil makes a closer turf than a light one. Marly clay is probably the best soil for grass, though far less agreeable for gardening operations generally than a sandy loam. After compacting the soil to prevent uneven settling, a few inches on top must be lightly raked to facilitate laying the turf, and the striking of new roots. Before winter begins all newly laid turf should be covered with a few inches of manure. After the ground settles in the spring this should be raked off with a fine-toothed rake, and the lawn then well rolled. The manure will have protected the grass from the injurious effect of sudden freezing and thawing in the winter and early spring, and the rich washings from it gives additional color and vigor to the lawn the whole season. The manure raked from the grass is just what is needed to dig into the beds for flowers and shrubs, or for mulching trees. This fall manuring is essential to newly set turf, and is scarcely less bene ficial if repeated every year. Cold soap-suds applied from a sprink ling-pot or garden-hose when rains are abundant, is the finest of summer manure for grass. If applied in dry weather it should be diluted with much additional water. The old rhyme—

> "Clay on sand manures the land,
> Sand on clay is thrown away"

is eminently true in relation to the growth of grass. The clay should always be applied late in autumn.

If grounds are so large that turfing is too expensive, the soil should be prepared as recommended above for turfing, and seeded as early in the spring as the ground can be thoroughly prepared and settled. If the surface has been prepared the preceding autumn, then it will be found a good practice to sow the grass seed upon a thin coating of snow which falls frequently early in March. Seed can be sown more evenly on snow, because better seen, than on the ground.

A variety of opinions prevail concerning the best grasses for seeding. It will be safe to say that for lawns timothy and red clover are totally unsuited, and that the grasses which make the best pastures in the neighborhood, will make the best lawns. The following mixture for one bushel of seed is recommended in Henderson's Manual of Floriculture, viz :

> 12 quarts Rhode Island Bent **Grass.**
> 4 quarts creeping Bent Grass.
> 10 quarts Red-top.
> 3 quarts Sweet Vernal Grass.
> 2 quarts Kentucky Blue Grass.
> 1 quart White Clover.

We have seen very successful lawns made with equal parts, *by weight*, of Kentucky blue grass, red-top, and white clover seed. The quantity required is about a half bushel to each one hundred feet square.

When rains are frequent, *no lawn can be brought to perfection if cut less often than once a week,* and two weeks is the longest time a lawn should remain uncut, except in periods of total suspension of growth by severe drouth. Where shrubs and flowers are placed properly, there will always be clear space enough to swing a lawn scythe or roll a lawn machine. Only in the most contracted yards should there be nooks and corners, or strips of grass, that an ordinary mower cannot get at easily, and without endangering either the plants or his temper. Places that are so cluttered with flowers, trees, and shrubs that it becomes a vexatious labor for a good mower to get in among them, are certainly not well planted. Good taste, therefore, in arrangement, will have for its first and durable fruits, *economy*, a product of excellent flavor for all who desire to create beauty around their homes, but who can illy afford to spend much money to effect it, or to waste any in failing to effect it. The advice to plant so as to leave sufficient breadth to swing a scythe wherever there is any lawn at all, is none the less useful, though the admirable little hand-mowing machines take the place of the scythe ; for a piece of lawn in a place where a scythe cannot be swung, is not worth maintaining.

Rolling mowers by horse or hand power have been principally employed on large grounds; but the hand machines are now so simplified and cheapened that they are coming into general use on small pleasure grounds, and proprietors may have the pleasure of doing their own mowing without the wearisome bending of the back, incident to the use of the scythe. Whoever spends the early hours of one summer, while the dew spangles the grass, in pushing these grass-cutters over a velvety lawn, breathing the fresh sweetness of the morning air and the perfume of new mown hay, will never rest contented again in the city. It is likely that professional garden laborers will buy these machines and contract cheaply for the periodical mowing of a neighborhood of yards, so that those who cannot or do not desire to do it for themselves may have it done cheaply. The roller is an essential implement in keeping the lawn to a fine surface, and should be thoroughly used as soon as the frost is out of the ground; for it will then be most effective to level the uneven heaving and settling of the earth. After heavy rains it is also useful, not only in preserving a smooth surface, but in breaking down and checking the vertical tendency of grass that is too succulent.

The season after seeding many persons are discouraged by the luxuriance of the weeds, and the apparent faint-heartedness of the grass. They must keep on mowing and rolling patiently. Most of these forward weeds are of sorts that do not survive having their heads cut off half a dozen times; while good lawn grasses fairly laugh and grow fat with decapitation. Weeds of certain species, however, will persist in thrusting their uninvited heads through the best kept lawns. These are to be dealt with like cancers. A long sharp knife, and busy fingers, **are the** only cure for them.

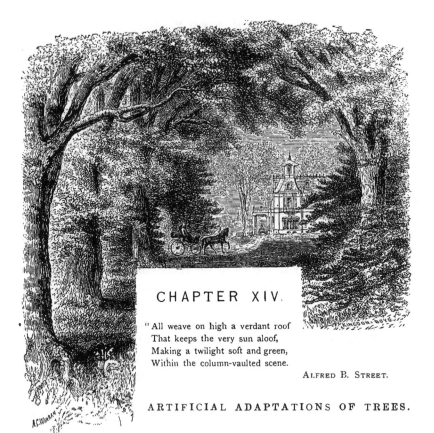

CHAPTER XIV.

"All weave on high a verdant roof
That keeps the very sun aloof,
Making a twilight soft and green,
Within the column-vaulted scene.

ALFRED B. STREET.

ARTIFICIAL ADAPTATIONS OF TREES.

ALL modes of growing trees for decorative or business purposes may be considered artificial, but what is here
meant by artificial adaptations are those less common
forms of culture, by which shrubs and trees are brought
by skill, or persistent manipulation, into unusual forms for special
purposes. Hedges, screens, verdant arches, arbors, dwarfed trees,
and all sorts of topiary work, are examples of such arts. It is
sometimes objected to these formally cut trees, that they are unnatural, and therefore inadmissible in good decorative gardening.
But houses, fences, and walks are not natural productions, nor are
lawns or flower-beds. All our home environments are artificial,
and it is absurd to try to make them seem otherwise. The objection arises from a common misunderstanding that all decorative

gardening is included in, and subject to the rules of landscape-gardening : an unfortunate error. The word landscape conveys an idea of breadth and extent of view, so that landscape-gardening means gardening on a great scale, in imitation of natural scenery. All the effects that can be produced artificially with small trees, by topiary arts, may seem puerile as parts of a landscape ; but in the dimensions of a small lot, where each feature of the place needs to be made as full of interest as possible, no such idea is conveyed. On the contrary, whatever little arts will render single sylvan objects more curious and attractive, or more useful for special purposes, may with propriety be availed of. It is as absurd to apply all the rules of grand landscape-gardening to small places, as to imitate in ordinary suburban dwellings the models of palaces. The only limit to the use of topiary work of the character we are about to treat of is, that whatever is done shall be subsidiary to a general and harmonious plan of embellishment, and *that the forms employed shall have some useful significance.* To shape trees into the forms of animals, or to resemble urns or vases, or into ungraceful forms suggestive of no use or beauty, are farcical freaks of gardening art to be played very rarely and unobtrusively. As one of Walter Scott's famed Scotch Judges, when caught in the act of playing king in a court of buffoons, is made to say that it takes a wise man to know when and where to play the fool, so in such freaks of art as those just named, great prudence is necessary. The safest course is not to worry or coax nature into such caricatures. But hedges, arches, arbors, and bowers of verdure are all useful, and the tribute that nature renders to art in such forms is as proper and sensible as the modes by which her grains and vegetables are improved on farms and in gardens.

HEDGES AND SCREENS.—These are· usually made of shrubs or trees which naturally take a dense low growth, and, if for barriers against animals, of those which are thorny. The wild thorns, and other trees clipped by browsing cattle and sheep until they seem condensed into solid masses of leaves and thorns, doubtless suggested the use of hedges, which has become more general in England than in any other country ; and there the climate and the high rural tastes of the people continue to produce their greatest variety and perfection. With us they are never likely to be used to so great an extent for fences owing to the cost of maintaining them ; but as ornamental and useful screens, and for other decorative purposes, there need be no limit to their variety. For these purposes some of the evergreens are best.

The arbor-vitæs are peculiarly adapted for hedges and screens ; especially for those of medium height, which are not intended to turn animals. The species and varieties of arbor-vitæ are numerous, but it is doubtful if there is one among them all more valuable for this purpose than the indigenous American species which is found wild on the banks of the Hudson, and other eastern rivers ; though it is claimed for the Siberian arbor-vitæ, and with truth, that its foliage has a richer shade of green.

Fig. 22.

There is a material difference in the value of different forms for hedges ; and the kind of tree used, the purpose for which the hedge is intended, and the exposure it is to have, must influence the choice of one form rather than another.

Fig. 22 represents a hedge-plant of the arbor-vitæ as grown, say the third year after planting. It must now be decided what form the hedge is to have. Fig. 23 is a section of the most common, and, for the arbor-vitæ and hemlock, in open exposures, a good form. But it is evi-dent that a hedge of this form gets less sun at the bottom than near the top, and the natural result is to produce the weakest growth at the bottom, and finally that the lowest branches die out. The shaded parts

Fig. 23.

Fig. 24.

of hemlocks, if contiguous to moisture, do not seem to suffer for want of the direct rays of the sun, but a majority of hedge-plants need a full and even light upon them. It is not merely the direct rays of the sun which are essential, but that constant light from the sky which, with or without the sun, always rests upon the top of a hedge. If the top be broad as in Fig. 24, it receives nearly all the direct light from above, and shades the

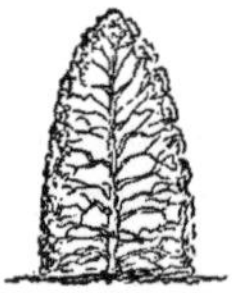

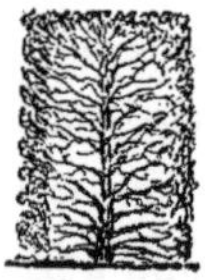

FIG. 25.

FIG. 26.

part below, and if one side of the hedge is towards the north, that side will be deficient in sunlight also. A form where the top is as broad as the bottom is therefore bad. Besides, a flat top with vertical sides is a clumsy form, and even were it not liable to lose its foliage at the bottom, would not be desirable. It is difficult to keep a full and healthy growth at the base of such hedges after the first five years of their growth, though the hemlock and arbor-vitæs are more manageable in this respect than many other hedge-plants. The best form for a hedge is the pyramidal, as in Fig. 25. This has the benefit of an equal distribution of light from all directions on the two sides of the hedge. It is also the simplest form to make and keep in order ; and is recommended for evergreen hedges or screens in ordinary exposures. But the thin sharp points at the top, and at the bottom on each side, are much more liable to injury, and thus mar the continuity of the hedge lines, than the rounded form of Fig. 23. This objection may be remedied by cutting off the top so as to leave a thickness of about six inches of level surface there, and the same of vertical surface at the sides, as in the section Fig. 26. And as a graceful concave surface is prettier than a straight one, the sides above may be hollowed slightly, as shown in the same cut. This form tends to give strength and density of foliage to the bottom of the hedge, by exposing it more fully to the light from above. Fig. 27 shows the same principle applied to a tall hedge-screen, such as may be made with the Norway spruce. Very perfect high hedges may be made with this tree in the simple cone form with less labor than the form indicated by Fig. 27 will require, but the latter is the best in principle, as well as the most beautiful. The different lights and shadows which fall on contiguous curved surfaces, or different planes, may be studied with good effect in forming hedges. Fig. 28 is a very pretty and practicable form which we suggest for those who are willing to take the trouble to perfect it.

Where one side of a hedge has a northern exposure, or is much shaded by trees, it may be well to vary the form so that that side shall present a broader surface to the vertical light to compensate for the lesser sunlight, as shown by Figs. 29

Fig. 27.

and 30. The two sides of a hedge are rarely seen at one view, so that its apparent symmetry will not be marred ; and this difference of form may be recommended as a pleasing variety—giving the beauty of two forms of hedge in one—as well as for the purpose of equalizing the vigor of the two sides.

Arbor-vitæ and hemlock hedges may be made of any height, from three to fifteen feet. Those which are to be kept of the minimum size will require almost as much time to perfect them as the taller ones, as they must be cut back frequently from the start, to force the plants into a dwarf habit, and ought to be grown to the required breadth at the bottom before they are of full height.

Fig. 28.

For a height of three feet, let the hedge be two feet wide at the bottom. As the height is increased the base need not increase proportionally. A hedge six feet high may have a base of three and a half feet, one ten feet high five feet, and so on ; remembering to give the side which is to have the least light the greatest expansion at the bottom.

We consider the tree box, where hardy, the best of all evergreen trees for low hedges, and though its growth is slow compared with that of the trees already named, we would use it in preference to anything else for hedges not designed to be more than three feet high. But it may

Fig. 29.

not be hardy enough to be reliable in a climate more severe than that of the city of New York ; and as it does best in partially shaded places, it is less beautiful in open, dry, and sunny exposures. For such places

Fig. 30.

the arbor-vitæ is better.

For topiary screens of great height the hemlock and Norway spruce, both of which bear cutting well, are very beautiful. More care is required in making hemlock, than arbor-vitæ hedges, as they are not so tenacious of life, and require a soil of greater moisture.

There should be a small reserve of trees kept in one's own garden for the purpose of filling the gaps the next season following the planting. It is desirable to obtain plants not more than one foot high which have been twice transplanted in the nursery. They may be planted from one to two feet apart, according to the size of the hedge intended. The larger the hedge is to be, the greater the distance that may be allowed between the trees. The hemlock loves a cool, as well as moist soil, and does well in partial shade, though *if the roots be in cool, moist soil,* its greatest luxuriance and beauty is developed in the most sunny exposure; that is to say, it should have its roots in the shade and the top in the sun. Its own boughs trail naturally on the ground to make such a protection for the roots, and in forcing the tree into a hedge form it should be allowed, and even forced, to make the greater part of its growth laterally. For some years after planting, the top growth should be continually cut back, and the side branches allowed full license. At the end of three years the hedge should be pyramidal, and not more than three feet high, and the same width at the bottom. For a hedge from five to eight feet high, a width of four feet is sufficient, and the top should not be allowed to increase faster than six inches a year till the required height is attained. Where a hedge of greater altitude is desired, we would allow the hemlock to attain the full breadth required for the perfected hedge before permitting much increase in height. If, for instance, a screen fifteen feet high is wanted, then the trees that compose the hedge-row should be allowed to grow until they cover five feet in breadth, while the top should be kept back, so that in four years after planting its section will present the form of an equilateral triangle. Thereafter the bottom should be kept nearly the same width, and the top allowed to increase in height at the rate of not more than a foot a year until the required height is attained. The hemlock and arbor-vitæ may be trimmed at any time from the middle of June to the first of October. June and September are, however, the best periods. The soil along young hedge-rows should be cleanly cul-

tivated as for a row of garden vegetables. The arbor-vitæs grow
so naturally into a hedge-form, that little skill is required to shape
them. The hemlock and other evergreens require much more
attention.

Where it is necessary to have a high screen without delay, we
would plant the Norway spruce, and let it grow pretty nearly in a
natural way, until it reaches the height needed. The plants need
not be nearer than two feet apart, and are apt to grow more evenly
when small trees—say from one to two feet high—are planted.
Those which grow fastest must be kept back to the same rate of
growth as the weakest, or the former will in a few years over-top
and kill out the latter. Further than for this purpose, the lower
branches should not be cut back unless the top is also cut. A verdant wall of Norway spruce twelve feet high may be grown in six
years from the time of planting, and must be allowed three or four
feet on each side of the stems for the lateral extension of the lower
branches. When the required height is attained, the tops can be
kept cut to it, and both sides clipt back to the form of the section
of a cone, the base of which is equal to half its height. The screen
can thereafter be cut late every June, so as to leave but an inch or
two of the last growth, and again in September if a second growth
has pushed strongly.

It is seldom desirable to make topiary screens more than ten
or twelve feet high, as the trouble and expense of clipping them
from a movable scaffold is considerable. Where there is need,
and room, for higher screens, the object may be attained less
expensively and less formally with groups and belts of pines and
firs. But it happens sometimes that a screen of considerable
height is required where there is not ground to spare for the
growth of trees in a natural way; and in such cases it is practicable to form Norway spruce hedges to any height at which they
can be clipped, and without occupying for the base of the hedge
more than from six to ten feet in width.

In general, hedges should be within a height that a man
on the ground, with the proper instrument, can cut any part of
them.

For evergreen hedges of a defensive character, that is to say, which have the strength, or the thorns, to prevent animals from going through them, we know of none that have been proved. What is called the Evergreen thorn, *Crætegus pyracanthus*, is an admirable thorny hedge-tree, but not truly an evergreen. It may, perhaps, rank as a sub-evergreen. The Menzies fir, *Abies menziesii*, seems to be peculiarly fitted for such a hedge, its leaves being sharp and stiff as needles, the growth compact, the foliage dense, and pointing in all directions. It is now a high-priced tree. When it becomes cheap we hope to see it tried for hedges. Like the hemlock and the balsam fir, it does best in a warm, humid soil, and it is possible that in the exposures required for hedges, it may not prove hardy enough to resist both the sun and the cold. The Cephalonia fir, *Picea cephalonica*, though its leaves are less cutting than those of the Menzies fir, are still somewhat formidable ; and as its growth is vigorous, healthy, and compact, it may prove valuable for large hedges.

There are some dwarf species of white pine which will make exquisite low hedges of a broader and rounder form than is recommended for any of the foregoing trees ; but they are not yet furnished at such rates as to make their use practicable ; and the common white pine may be clipped into hedge forms.

The American holly, *Ilex opaca*, has stiff glossy leaves armed with spines on their scolloped edges, and will probably make the most formidable of evergreen hedges for this country.

The yews, much employed in England for hedges, are not hardy enough to be used north of Philadelphia.

Among deciduous trees and shrubs the number adapted to hedges is much larger than most persons suppose. Almost the whole family of thorns, natives of this country, as well as of Europe, besides the fragrant hawthorn, are easily made into excellent hedges. Our wild crab-apple tree can be trimmed into a compact form of superlative beauty and fragrance in the blooming season, and sufficiently offensive by its thorns to turn trespassers. The mere capability of any tree or shrub to become a strong, dense, and handsome wall of foliage, if kept down to a hedge form, is not a sufficient recommendation. It is not so much a question of what trees and shrubs *can* be made into hedges, as which of them can be grown for that purpose, and kept in hand-some and serviceable shape with the least annual expense and liability to accidents or diseases. Hedges may be made of the honey locust, but the labor of restraining their sprouts and suckers is about as profitable as that of training a Bengal tiger to do the work of an ox. The beautiful osage orange partakes somewhat of the same wild character, but has been subdued with great success, and is likely to prove the most valuable of live fencing in the Middle and Western States. But we see no advantage for merely decorative purposes on suburban grounds in confining a deciduous tree of such erratic luxuriance within monotonous hedge-limits, while evergreen trees of greater beauty, which naturally assume formal contours, can be more easily grown and kept in order for the same purpose.

Hedges, formidable by reason of their thorns, are only re-quired for suburban places, on boundary lines contiguous to alleys or streets, where trespassers are to be guarded against. In such localities there is probably nothing better than the osage orange.

The beautiful English hawthorns, with their variety of many-colored blossoms, will develop their greatest beauty and bloom in other than hedge-forms. The buckthorn so much lauded twenty years ago for a hedge-plant, is one of the poorest and homeliest of all. The Fiery or Evergreen thorn, *Cratægus pyracanthus*, is a variety with very small leaves, almost evergreen, which assumes a hedge-form naturally, is formidable with thorns to resist intrusion, and covered with red berries in autumn. It grows slowly, and will make a charming low hedge. The Japan quince will also form a fine hedge with sufficient patience and labor. Its growth is ex-ceedingly straggling, and the wood so hard to cut that it is expen-sive to keep in shape ; but when grown to the proper size and form, its showy early bloom and glossy leaves, hanging late, make it one of the prettiest. The common privet belongs to a differ-ent class. It is a natural hedge-plant ; strikes root freely from cuttings, grows quickly, and its wood cuts easily. The leaves appear early and hang late, and though not of the most pleasing color, they form a fine compact wall of verdure. It is, therefore, natural that the privet should long have been a favorite for garden hedges. The wax-leaved privet, *Ligustrum lucidum*, and the California privet, *L. californica*, are shrubs of larger and more glossy foliage, and probably hardy in most parts of the country. The lilacs, bush honeysuckles, syringas, altheas, weigelias, and some wild roses, may all be grown as hedges with pleasing effect where deciduous plants are used. In short, good hedges are much more the result of the patience and persistent care of the gardener than of the natural tendencies of certain shrubs or trees.

FIG. 31.

VERDANT ARCHES AND BOWERS. — In Chapter VI some allusion was made to the pretty effect of verdant gateway arches. There is no limit to the charming variety of effects that can be produced by training and pruning trees and large shrubs, both evergreen and deciduous, into fanciful forms for gateway and garden arches, verdant pavilions, and bowers. As evergreens are most constantly beautiful for such purposes, we will first call attention to a few forms in which they may be used. The hemlock can be treated as illustrated by Figs. 31, 32, and 33, which we here repeat. The first represents two hemlocks which have been planted two feet away from, and on each side of an ordinary gateway. After five or six years' growth they may be high enough to begin work upon. A crotched stick about two feet shorter than the distance of the trees apart, is stretched from one

FIG. 32.

to another, from six to seven feet from the ground, and fixed there to keep the tops apart up to that point. Above the stick, the tops (supposing that they are tall enough to admit of it) are to be bent towards each other until they join, then twisted together, and tied so that they cannot untwist. To do this so as to form a graceful arch, the trees must be about eleven or twelve feet high. After they are firmly intertwined at the top, which is usually in about two years growth, the clipping of the sides and tops can be going on to bring the arch to a form like that of

Fig. 33.

Fig. 32, or to any similar design the proprietor may desire. An arch like the latter figure may be brought to considerable perfection in the course of ten years. Fig. 33 shows the probable appearance that a hemlock archway would present in twenty years after planting, supposing the trees were allowed to develop more naturally after their artificial character was well established. Such arches increase in quaint beauty as they grow old, and after the first ten years will need but little care. Fig. 34, as we have already mentioned in Chapter VI, is intended to show another effect, which may be produced with the same side trees, by joining and twisting together two side branches to form the arch, leaving the main stems to form two spiry sides, and trim-

Fig. 34.

ming to produce this form. Another mode that, if well executed, would produce a curious effect, is to unite the main stems as in the first mode, but instead of twisting them to grow vertically over the middle of the gate, the twist should be made horizontally, so that the tops would project sideways, as shown farther on for elm-tree arches. This in time would develop into a wide crescent, inverted over the arch, or it might be likened to a pair of huge horns guarding the arch. The variety of novel forms that such trees can be made to assume after ten or twelve years' growth will surprise most persons. The same kind of arches on a smaller scale can be made with the arbor-vitæ, but the branches are not so pliable. It may be used to advantage for narrower and lower arches.

For arbors or bowers the hemlock is equally well adapted. We would suggest as the simplest form to begin with, that four hemlocks be planted at the intersection of two walks, say five or six feet apart. By cutting back the side branches to within one foot of the trunk, the growth at the tops will be increased so that in five or six years they may be tall enough to allow the opposite diagonal corners to be twisted together. If the trees are all thrifty, the twist will become fixed in two years. The fragrant and graceful foliage of the hemlock can thus be made to embower retired seats, or make quaint openings for diverging paths. Such arbors or arches can be made much more quickly with carpentry and lovely vines, but the permanent and more unusual structures made with living trees must nevertheless be more interesting.

The hemlock may be used to make artificial pavilions of a still larger kind if trained through a period of ten or fifteen years. Suppose six trees to be planted at the corners of a hexagon ten or twelve feet in diameter. Let them feather naturally to the ground on the outside of the group, and trim to within one or two feet of the trunks on the inside. When twelve feet high, pass a rope around the circle, on a level, two or three feet below their tops, so as to draw them towards the centre of the circle as far as the main stems may be safely bent, which will probably be about three feet inside of the perpendicular. If the circle is twelve feet in diameter, this will still leave six feet uninclosed at the top. The rope is to be left around them until the trees have grown five to six feet higher, when another binding will bring their tops together, and if

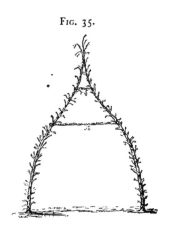

Fig. 35.

they are long enough they may be twisted together. Fig. 35 is a section of the stems alone, to illustrate the general form intended. When the six trees are together at the centre they should be made to grow like one, and the branches that grow from the upper sides of the curved stems must be cut back to prevent them from becoming leaders. Fig. 36 shows one development of this mode of training; the sides and top having been trimmed in mosque dome form, the curve of the living frame of the pavilion being well adapted to produce it. It will require from twelve to fifteen years to perfect such a pavilion, but the group will be pretty, and interesting at every stage of its growth. In this, as in most other things in life, it is well to remember Shakespeare's lines—

"*What's won is done ;—joy's soul lies in the doing.*"

A pretty variation of the above plan, for larger verdant pavilions, may be created by simply bending the tree-tops towards the centre in the manner above described, but not close together, leaving a circular opening six feet wide over the centre, in the manner of a dome sky-light.

FIG. 36.

The fir trees, though fine for lofty screens or hedges, have more rigid wood, and do not bear so much bending; still very beautiful results of a similar kind may be produced with the Norway spruce, which is the best of the firs for this purpose. It bears cutting quite as well as the hemlock.

The *Cypressus Lawsoniana* which combines a rapid growth, and the freedom of the hemlock, with arbor-vitæ-like foliage, will be an admirable tree for large works of this kind, if it continues to prove hardy.

The pines are mostly disposed to drop their lower limbs as they increase in height, and this peculiarity may be availed of in producing other forms of growth. If, for instance, it is desired to make an evergreen umbrage in which to take tea out of doors in summer, it may be provided by planting four white pines, say twelve feet apart each way; and when they are from eight to ten feet high, cutting their leaders out so as to leave a tier of branches as nearly as possible at the same height on the four trees. The following year see to it that none of these upper branches turn up to make leaders, and if necessary tie them down to a horizontal direction. By attending to this for two years the top tier of shoots will make a horizontal growth, which will meet in a few years over head, and form a table-like top of foliage. But to insure this effect, the tree must be watched for some years to prevent any strong shoots from taking an upward lead, and thus draw the sap away from the horizontal branches. After these have met over head, and form a sufficient shade, the part above may be allowed to grow as it will. The check and change in the growth of the trees by such manipulation, carried on for several years, insures a novel and picturesque form for the group that will be permanent. As the white pine attains great size at maturity, it is not well to attempt such an arbor on quite small grounds.

Deciduous trees being more subject to insects on their foliage, are less desirable than evergreens for these uses, but they spread at the top more rapidly, can be more quickly grown to the re quired forms, and are covered at certain seasons with beautiful and fragrant blossoms ; so that in *variety* of attractions some of them are unequalled by any evergreens. The latter wear through out the year the beauty of constant cheerfulness, while the former, with the changing seasons, are alternately barren of graces, or bending with foliage and glowing with blossoms.

For archways there are no finer deciduous trees than the English hawthorns, and the double flowering scarlet thorn, *Cræte-gus coccinnea flore plena*. They can be planted at the sides of foot-path gates, in the same manner as recommended for the hemlock, and it will only be necessary to trim them on the inside, so as to keep the opening unincumbered ; as the hawthorns bloom best on their extended garland-like branches. But they should be trimmed enough to prevent any decidedly straggling outline, to show that they are intended as artificial adaptations for a purpose. Fig. 37 shows a suitable form for a hawthorn arch.

For bowers, or umbrageous groups surrounded by open sunny

ground, the same form suggested for hemlocks and pines is adapted to the hawthorns; viz., planting in a square or circle so that the interior can be used for a cool summer resort for smoking or reading, a place to take tea, or a children's play-house. A dense canopy of leaves forms the coolest of shades in the hot hours of summer days. To form such a canopy with hawthorns will require about ten years, and may be made by planting six trees in a hexagonal form. All our readers may not remember that if they make a circle of any radius, that radius applied from point to point on the circle will mark the six points of a hexa-gon. The following varieties of hawthorn are recommended for five of these places, viz.: the common white, *Cratægus oxycantha*, the pink flowered, *C. o. rosea*, the dark red, *C. o. punicea*, the double red, *C. o. punicea flore plena,* the double white, *C. o. multiplex*, and for the sixth the double scarlet thorn, *C. coccinnea flore plena*. These will in time make a bower of exquisite beauty in the time of bloom, and of such full and glossy foliage that it will have great beauty during all the leafy season. After such bowers are well thickened overhead by the annual cutting back of the rankest upright growth, they are interesting objects even in winter, by the masses of snow borne on their flat tops, and the contrast presented between the deep shadows under them, and the brightness of the snow around.

Fig. 37.

Some gardeners object to the use of the hawthorn in this coun-try, on account of its alleged liability to the attacks of a borer that injures the trunk, and the aphis which attacks the leaves. We shall not advise to refrain from planting it on this account, believ-ing that if planted in deep good soils, and the ground beneath kept clean, it will usually make so vigorous a growth as to repel the attacks of these insects, which usually choose feeble and stunted trees to work in. The hawthorns are all bushy when young, and their development into overarching trees will be somewhat slower than that of the following deciduous trees.

The sassafras is eminently adapted to form a useful bower of the kind above described, as it naturally assumes a parasol-like top, grows rapidly, and dispenses with its bottom limbs quickly. Being disposed to form crooked stems, some care must be used in choosing straight-bodied thrifty nursery trees, and pro-teeting the trunks until they are large enough not to need it. Six thrifty trees will grow into a perfect canopy, of the size suggested, within five years, if their central stems are cut back, and kept to a height of about eight feet. For the next five years all the upright growth at their tops should be annually cut back, so that the trees will not exceed twelve feet in height. Afterwards they may be allowed to grow naturally; but their greatest beauty will not be attained in less than fifteen or twenty years.

Fig. 38 shows the appearance they should make in ten or twelve years after planting.

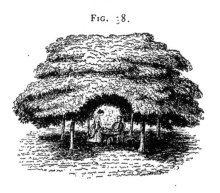

Fig. 38.

Next to the sassafras, probably the judas or red-bud trees, *Cercis canadensis* and *C. siliquastrum*, form most naturally into this kind of flat-roofed bower. The White-flowered dogwood, *Cornus flori-da*, is also adapted to the same use. Both spread lower than the sassafras, but do not grow so rapidly when young. The moose-wood or striped-barked maple, on the other hand, attains the height required in a single season, and its green and yellow-striped bark is ornamental. The branches, after the trunk has attained the height of ten or fifteen feet, radiate naturally to form a flat-arched head, and grow much slower than the first vigorous growth of the stem would lead one to suppose. The foliage is large and coarse, but the form of the tree is suited to the purpose under consideration. Its large racemes of winged seeds, of a pinkish color, are very showy in August. The paper mulberry is also a valuable tree for such uses, and attains the required size and density of head in less time than any of the others. The foliage is unusually abundant and of a dark green color.

Perhaps the most beautiful of all small trees for such purposes is the weeping Japan sophora.   It is grafted from seven to ten feet high on other stocks, and for many years its growth is slow ; but if one will have the patience to wait, a more charming and curious bower can be made with a circle of sophoras than of any tree we know of.   An engraving of this variety may be found in the description of the species, Part II, Chapter III.

We have named only a few of the trees which may be made use of for growing these artificial bowers.   For very small grounds there are many arboreous shrubs which may be used to produce similar effects on the inside, and appear as naturally grown groups on the outside.

Single apple trees sometimes form great bowers with their own branches alone.   There is a beautiful specimen of this kind in the grounds of W. S. Little, Esq., of Rochester, N. Y.   It is an old tree of the twenty ounce pippin variety.   At the height of seven or eight feet its branches spread horizontally, and finally bend to the ground on all sides, enclosing in deep shadow a circular space forty feet wide ; an arched opening is made on one side.   A sketch of this tree is given in the engraving at the end of this chapter.

Elms may be used with good effect for arches of a larger growth than those already suggested.   The adjoining sketch, Fig. 39, will illustrate one mode of procedure, where there is room for large trees. Two common weeping elms are to be chosen, each having two diverging branches at the height of six to eight feet from the ground, and to be so planted that the extension of these branches will be parallel with the fence. · For a foot-walk gate-way, plant them about two feet back from the fence-line, and the same distance, or less, from the walk.   After the trees have grown so that the branches towards the gate are long enough to be connected, as shown in Fig. 39, and upwards of half an inch in diameter, they

FIG. 39.

may be brought together and twisted round and round each other vertically, and tied together so that they cannot untwist; or they may be grafted together as shown on the sketch at *l.* The twist will, however, be the strongest and simplest mode. The branches that proceed fròm the twisted ones below the union, must be kept cut back to within two or three feet, so as to éncourage the strongest growth in the part above the twist. The next sprıng, if these[l] united branches have done well, the outer branches of both trees may be cut off at *a, a,* and grafted with scions of the Scamston elm. If the grafts take, and the growth and trimming of all parts are properly attended to, the lower growth forming the gateway arch should be all Scamston elm, crowned over the centre with the loftier common elm, presenting an appearance in the course of ten years something like the accompanying engraving.

FIG. 40.

The Scamston elm grows with great vigor in a horizontal and downward direction only, and its long annual shoots, and dark glossy leaves overlap each other so closely that an arch cut in one side has the appearance of being cut through a mound of solid verdure. Their tops are flatly rounded, like unfinished hay-stacks.

9

and the common elm emerging from the centre (as shown in the engraving), and bending its long arms over the former with a freer growth, might, we think, present a combination of grotesque grace less formal in expression than our illustration.

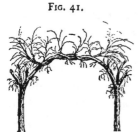

FIG. 41.

A broad flat-topped arch of a similar character may be made by grafting all four of the branches with the Scamston elm at *a*, *a*, Fig. 39, and the points opposite. This may be perfected more quickly.

For an archway over a carriage entrance two common elms may be planted by the sides of the gateway, and when their side branches are long enough, may be twisted round and round each other, and tied together, and the other parts of the tree trimmed to develop the best growth of the branches depended on to form the arch. Fig. 41 illustrates the appearance of the trees without their leaves a year or two after the twist has been made.

CHAPTER XV

BEFORE proceeding to examine the plans, the reader is requested to observe the symbols used, as shown on the preceding page.

We desire also to offer a few preliminary explanations. First, every intelligent reader knows that no two building lots are often exactly alike in any respect. Not only in size and form, but in elevation, in shape of surface, in the exposure of the front to the north, east, south, or west, or intermediate points; in the presence and location of growing trees, large or small; in the nature of the improvements to the right or left, in front or rear; in the aspect of the surrounding country or city; in the connections with adjacent streets or roads; in the prospective changes that time is likely to bring which will affect their improvement for good or ill;—all these things are external conditions as similar in the main as the colors of the kaleidoscope, *and as invariably different from each other in their combinations.* Not only these external conditions, but an equally numerous throng of circumstantial conditions connected with the tastes, the means, the number, and the business of the occupants, tend to render the diversities of our homes and home-grounds still more innumerable. It is, therefore, improbable that any one of the plans here presented for the reader's study will *precisely* suit any one's wants; but that their careful examination and comparison will be of service in planning houses and laying out lots of a somewhat similar character, we earnestly hope. We furnish them as a good musical professor does his instrumental studies, not to be used as show-pieces, but to be studied as steps and *points-d'appuis* for one's own culture.

In naming the selection of trees and shrubs for many of the smaller places, we have endeavored to be as careful in their selection as if each place were an actual one, and our own ;—leaning, however, in most cases, to that style of planting which will have the best permanent effect, rather than to an immediate but ephemeral display ; and fully conscious that a skillful gardener may name many other and quite different selections for the same places, that will be equally adapted to them ; and that in carrying out such plans on the ground, the insufficiency of designs on so small a scale to present all the finishing small features that make up the beauty of a complete place, will be very evident. The choice of trees and shrubs for locations otherwise similar, must be influenced by a consideration of the climate. Many which do well near the sea-coast are not hardy on more elevated ground in the same latitude ; while others are healthy in the high lands that prove sickly in more southern and alluvial valleys. A selection for a lot near New York should not be altogether the same as for Saratoga or St. Pauls, Richmond or Louisville ; and for the Gulf States (except in the most elevated regions) it would be totally unsuited. Southward from the latitude of New York, each degree (except so far as the influence of latitude is counteracted by that of altitude) will enable the planter to grow some tree or shrub not safe to plant, under ordinary conditions, any further north. As the latitude and climate of New York city represent the average requirements of a greater population than any other, in this country, our selection for the places described in this chapter are generally suited to such a climate ; and in planting, the reader must be directed by his own study as to what substitutions are necessary in latitudes north or south of it.

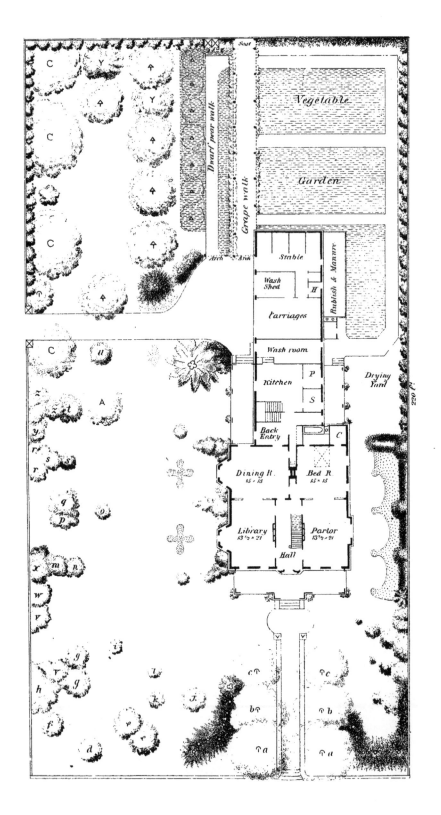

Vegetable

Garden

Dwarf pear walk

Grape walk

Seat

Arch Arch

Stable

Wash Shed

H

Rubbish & Manure

Carriages

Wash room

Kitchen

P

Drying Yard

S

Back Entry

C

Dining R.
15 × 13

Bed R.
15 × 15

Library
13½ × 21

Parlor
13½ × 21

Hall

220 ft.

C Y
Y
C

C

C u

z
z t
y
r
r
s
q
p o
x m n
w
v
i
g
r
g
h
f
k J.
p
c
b
a
d

c
b
a

We have remarked in a preceding chapter on the impractica-
bility of furnishing plans for grounds of uneven surfaces, or for
those which have trees growing on them, without an accurate
survey of all these features. The plans which follow, therefore,
pre-suppose bare sites, and rather level ones ; but the study of
arrangement on these will be found to embrace most of the ques-
tions that interest those who are forming or expecting to form
suburban homes.

PLATE I.—B.

Plan for a Compact House and Stable on a Corner Lot 128 x 220 *feet.*

Reference has been made to this plate in Chapter IX for
the purpose of illustrating a mode of planning the grounds on
paper, and working from the paper plan. The lot has an
area of less than two-thirds of an acre. The main house is
thirty-six feet square, with a kitchen-wing twenty-two feet wide,
carried back under a continuous roof to form the carriage-house,
wash-shed, and stable,—in all sixty-four feet in length. We believe that it is rarely that so many of the requirements of a
pleasant house are brought within so small an area. Doubtless
most lady-housekeepers will rebel against the thought of having
the carriage-house and stable in such close proximity to the
dwelling. It is the only plan in this work thus arranged ; but in
our north-border States we believe it to be a wise arrangement ;
not only vastly more economical in construction, and convenient
for the family and their servants, but also, in the hands of a good
architect, capable of adding greatly to the attractiveness of the
house by giving it an air of extent and domesticity that so many of
the box-like suburban houses of the day are totally wanting in. We
do not believe there is any more need of being annoyed by flies or
smells from a stable than from a kitchen ; and if the latter can be
kept so that it is a pleasant room to have within ten feet of living-
rooms, where doors open directly from one to another, we know no
reason why the stable may not be within fifty feet, where there are
no direct connections, and four or five intervening partitions. One

only needs to see how pleasantly it looks and works in the keeping
of a neat family, to be surprised that this system has not long ago
been adopted at the north. It is not only a great economy in the
first cost of the house and stable, but an equal economy of lot-
room. Here is a lot of but little more than half an acre, with the
apparent ground-room for a mansion ; with a lawn two hundred
and twenty feet in length, a large variety of trees and shrubbery,
an abundance of summer fruits, and a sufficient kitchen-garden for
the use of one family ; and yet nothing is crowded. This economy
of space is in part attributable to the compact unity of the dwelling
and domestic offices.

Let us now examine the ground-plan. The street in front is
supposed to be two feet and a half below the ground-level on that
front, and to have a wall with a stone coping level with the
grass ;—the side-street rising so that where the carriage-road
enters it, the two are on the same level. The coping of the
front wall is carried around and continued up the sides of the
main entrance-walk in a style similar to, but not quite so
costly, as that illustrated in the vignette of Chapter IV. This
walk is six feet wide. Street trees, if any are planted in
front, should be placed so that the middle of the space between
them is on the line of the middle of the walk continued, and
should be the same distance apart as the trees of the short avenue
on each side of the walk ; that is, twenty feet. Supposing the
street trees are elms, we would plant at *a, a,* weeping Scotch elms,
Ulmus montana pendula; at *b, b,* weeping beeches ; at *c, c,* cut-
leaved weeping birches. The evergreen screens on the right and
left are to be composed principally of hemlocks. That on the
right is intended to make an impervious screen so that the yard
behind it on that side cannot be seen from the street. The
flower-beds on the parlor side of the lot are designed to be the
especial charge of the lady-florist of the house, and these evergreen screens will give a partial privacy to that section of the lot.
The screens also act as boundaries of the avenue, making the
entrance-walk a distinct and isolated feature—a shadowy arbor of
the overarching foliage of deciduous trees, with a back-ground on
each side of evergreen verdure. The depth of shadow in passing

through such an approach will serve to bring into bright relief the unshadowed front of the house, and the open expanse of sunny lawn around it. The evergreen trees that are within fifteen feet of the deciduous trees which form the avenue should not be allowed to make their full natural growth upwards, but be topped irregularly so that the latter may not be obstructed in their natural expansion. The avenue trees are to be considered the rightful owners of all the space they can grow to fill, and the evergreens only tenants at will so far as they occupy places which the branches of the deciduous trees will eventually overgrow. But for many years both may grow unharmful to the other.

In the back part of the lot let us take an inventory of the utilitarian features of the plan, and then of their connection with the decorative effect. The grape-walk, it will be seen, is on a right line with the length of the side veranda. A double arch marks the entrance to this and the dwarf pear walk. Arch openings in the grape-trellis give access to the walks of the kitchen-garden for the family, while for work and for servants' use, another walk leads from the wash-room and the back veranda. The vegetable garden is thus entirely out of sight from the house, and from every part of the grounds, and yet has a sufficiently open exposure, and the most convenient proximity to the kitchen. The long grape-walk trellis will have a good exposure, to whatever point of the compass its length tends. The same may be said of the dwarf pear border. There are six standard pear trees, four cherry, two peach, and one apple tree marked on the plan. Other peach trees may be planted in between the cherries and pears if the owner will be sure to cut them out as soon as the cherry and pear trees need all the room. Few persons are aware how much healthier and more productive fruit trees are which are allowed to grow low, and with unlimited expansion from the beginning. Therefore we warn against planting permanent trees too thickly, and against leaving short-lived trees, like the peach, too long in the way of the permanencies. There are, however, some dry clay soils where the peach tree does not quickly become decrepit—as it is pretty sure to do in a light sand or rich loam—and there it may be well to allow it the necessary room for mature growth, independent of the growth of other trees. It will be seen that the borders of the lot offer ample room for the growth of small fruits for one family. Strawberries may be grown in cultivated strips under the standard pear trees.   •

From the dining-room window which opens upon the veranda, pleasing vistas down the grape-walks and the pear-walks will be seen through the vine-covered parts of the veranda, and the arches that mark the entrances to those walks. The height of the veranda floor will conceal one-third of the gravel space in front of the carriage-house from the eye of a person sitting in the dining-room, so that the vines that should wreath the end-opening of the veranda and the arches beyond, and their interior perspective, will be the principal objects in view. Between the row of dwarf pears and the side-street the arrangement of fruit trees is such that, seen from the front, the open lawn space surrounded by them will have quite as elegant an air as any other portion of the ground. The large fir tree at the end of the row of pear trees, and the arbor-vitæ hedge between it and the arch, are intended to shut from view the tilled ground under the pear trees, and, together with the large pine tree nearer the house and its subjacent evergreen shrubs, to give a cheerful winter tone to this most used portion of the "back-yard."

On the front portion of the lot, the trees indicated by letters on the plan are intended to be the following—the list being made for a climate like that near the city of New York.

At *d*, the dwarf white-pine, *P. strobus compacta;* at *e, e,* a pair of Japan weeping sophoras ; at *f,* Parson's American arbor-vitæ, *Thuja occidentalis compacta;* at *g, g,* the American and European Judas trees ; at *h,* the *Kolreuteria paniculata;* at *i,* the golden arbor-vitæ ; at *j,* the Indian catalpa ; at *k,* the erect yew, *Taxus erecta;* at *l,* the golden yew, *Taxus aurea;* at *m* and *n, Weigelas amabilis* and *rosea;* at *o,* the new weeping juniper, *J. oblonga pendula; p* and *g,* the weeping silver-fir and the weeping Norway spruce ; *r, r, y,* and *z, z,* an irregular belt of Siberian and other arbor-vitæs ; *s, s,* weeping arbor-vitæs, *Thuja pendula;* at *t,* Sargent's hemlock ; at *u,* a cherry tree (this in lieu of the cherry tree near the carriage-road gate, where, if the soil is congenial, we

would plant a pair of white-pines, one on each side of the gateway, and not far from the posts). Under and between the trees *h*,
and *g, g*, we would have a mass of rhododendrons; or, if cheaper
and more rapid growing materials for a group are preferred, the
space may be filled with the variegated-leaved and wax-leaved
privets and low-spreading spireas; at *v, w*, and *x*, in the next
group, may be planted a choice of deutzias, honeysuckles, syringas,
lilacs, and snow-balls—one of each. Around the firs at *p* and *q*,
while they are small, a group of rhododendrons may be planted.
The single small shrubs (or trees) opposite the front corner of the
house, may be single well-grown bushes of *Deutzia gracilis;* or
the double flowering-plum, *Prunus sinensis;* or the purple-leaved
berberry; or, if dwarf evergreens are preferred, the Irish and
Swedish junipers, the Japan podocarpus, the tree-box (for clipping), the golden arbor-vitæ, the golden yew, or the erect yew,
Taxus erecta, may all be rivals for these places. With constant
care to keep them to their most slender form, those beautiful
novelties, the weeping Norway spruce and silver firs, *Abies excelsa
inverta* and *Picea pectinata pendula*, might grace this place better
than anything else, though they may in time grow to great height.

In the four inner angles of the two bay-windows, unless the exposure is to the south or southwest, we would plant rhododendrons
of medium size, and fill the corner-beds with the same, graded
down to the smallest varieties at the points. In the middle,
between the bay-windows, two feet from the house, plant the
Cephalotaxus fortunii mascula, and beyond it, to complete the
group, three flowering deciduous shrubs graded in height as follows: Six feet from the house the double-flowered pink deutzia;
two feet further out the *Deutzia gracilis;* and two feet from that,
on the point, the *Daphne creorum*. While these shrubs are small,
use the ground between them for annuals and bulbous flowers.

The group under the pine tree, and between it and the rear
veranda steps, may be composed of two varieties of the tree-box
near the steps—the common and the gold-edged leaved—Sargent's
hemlock near the corner of the road, and the variegated-leaved
privet, the purple berberry, the variegated-leaved elder, and some
kalmias to complete the bed. It is essential that there should be

a sufficient mass of evergreen verdure around the pine to shut the carriage-yard out of view from the front.

The border near the right-hand fence, in front, is a hemlock, or an arbor-vitæ screen; with single specimens standing in front of it, of any of the choice varieties of common deciduous flowering shrubs. The plan fails to show the continuity of the evergreen screen along that side of the lot, and consequently some of the deciduous shrubs are too near the fence. The hedge back of the large flower-bed should also occupy double the width shown on the plan. The isolated, very small shrub-marks, represent slender junipers, or single brilliant-leaved plants.

The few flower-beds that are shown on the lawn-side of the house can probably be filled by most ladies quite as tastefully as we could suggest. The continuous bed opposite the large window of the parlor will demand much skill in arrangement, if filled with annuals and perennials. But as these are likely to be changed every year, and as skill in such matters is the result of experience alone, it is needless to specify any one list of varieties, or order of arrangement for them. In case the occupants of the place prefer not to take care of a great bed of annuals, the entire bed may be devoted to the culture of roses; and if these also involve too great an annual outlay of time and money, the ground may be left in lawn alone, and the border broken by a few fine shrubs upon it.

The location of the parlor on this plan, with its principal window looking out on the shortest and most unsatisfactory view of the place, may be open to criticism. But it must be borne in mind that, on small lots, all the sides of a dwelling cannot have park-like exposures; and the room that is least used, and least looked out of, is the one that should have the least interesting exposure. Parlors are principally used by day as reception rooms for casual callers, and in the *evenings* for sociable gatherings. In neither case are the guests, or the family, in the habit of paying much attention to out-of-door views. The furniture of a parlor is likely to be scrutinized more than that of other rooms, but the out-looks from it are of less importance than from those rooms which the family and their intimate friends frequent.

Plate II.

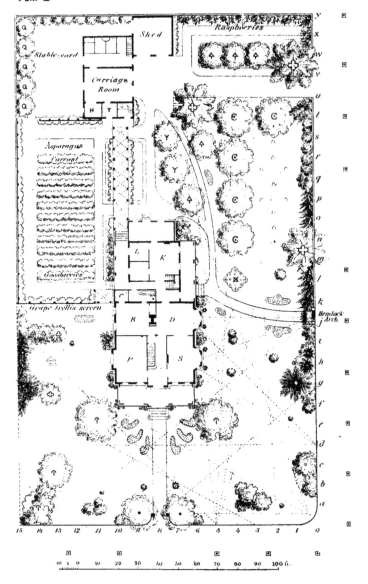

Raspberries

Shed

Stable-yard

Carriage Room

Asparagus

Currant

Gooseberries

Grape trellis screen

Hemlock Arch

Plate II

A Corner Lot having one hundred and fifty feet front on one street, and two hundred and fifty feet on another.

The figures at the bottom, and the letters on the side of the plate, represent spaces of ten feet each. The house is commodious, and its form the most simple and compact. The fronts (veranda lines) are sixty feet from the two streets respectively. A carriage-house of suitable size occupies the rear corner of the lot, with a stable-yard behind it, and a passage-way for a cart around it. A straight walk to the front door, and a straight road to the carriage-house, are the most appropriate ways to each ; while the side-entrance walk, being prolonged to form the walks to the kitchen, the garden, and the stable, is laid down in a curved form to make it most convenient for these purposes. A covered trellis or arbor forms a continuation of the back veranda, and a dry passage from the back hall to the out-buildings. This is designed for grape vines. The kitchen-garden occupies a space about 45 × 90 feet, including the walks. The side fence or wall of the garden, if the exposure is to the east, south, or southwest, may be covered with grapes ; if to the north, with currants or raspberries. The main square of the kitchen-garden is drawn as if covered with small fruits. It may be so used, or filled with vegetables alone. A row of fine cherry trees are set forty feet from the side fence, starting ten feet from the carriage road, and twenty feet apart, and a sixth at the same distance from the first, on the line towards *t.* The plan indicates the locations for five pear trees, two peach trees, quinces, raspberries, etc. A greater number *may* be planted in these spaces, but not without eventual injury to the appearance of the grounds. Peach trees are short-lived, and usually scrawny and ill-favored after the first five years of their growth. We would place them reluctantly in any part of grounds that may be seen in connection with other parts which are occupied by lawn-trees and flowers under high keeping. But a place for a few trees having been indicated, it may be as well to put out four or five there as two. They will soon crowd each other too closely, but they pay for themselves quickly, and die early. There is no question of the great superiority of peaches grown to ripeness on one's own trees, over the half-ripe beauties of the markets; and if the proprietor, to have their fruit. is willing to guard their health, he must also be willing to bear with their mature ugliness.

We will now describe the plan with reference to those things which are planted for their decorative effect alone; premising, however, that walks, arbors, and fruit trees, are quite as much a part of the embellishments of the ground as evergreens or flowering shrubs: and are all placed with reference to their effect in connection with the latter. .

The plan supposes a slight downward slope of the ground from the house to the outside street boundaries; the floor of the house being about four feet above the lawn adjoining it, and the latter unbroken by terraces or architectural forms of any kind. It is intended as a plain example of conformity to good taste in arrangement, rather than of any great art in gardening; and combines as much length of open lawn, with as great a variety of trees, shrubs, and flowers as the size will admit of, without making it an expensive place to keep.

The front walk is six feet wide. The gate posts are set back five feet from the street line. On a line with the posts, and from two to five feet from them, a pair of trees are to be planted to form an arch over the gate. If large trees like elms or pines are used, let them be planted at the greater distance; if small trees like the sassafras, the nettle tree, or the red-bud or Judas tree (*cercis*) are employed, two feet from the posts will be enough. If a more artificial form of verdant arch is desired, the proprietor can choose some of the trees and forms recommended in Chapter XIV. The American weeping elm or the Scotch elm, arch a gateway quickly and nobly, but will eventually be so large as to shade the whole of that part of the yard. A pair of sassafras trees, planted within two or three feet of the walk, would make one of the richest natural canopies over the gate, but perhaps too much like a parasol, and not enclosing the way sufficiently on the sides; but by planting beneath them, in the inner curve of the fence, the tree-box, which does well in partial shade, and surrounding the trunks on the other sides with some low-growing shrubs that also do not suffer by shade, the arch may be made complete with a variety of surroundings. Just beyond, say fifteen feet from the gate, are two Irish junipers. The lawn between these and the steps is unbroken save by six beds for very low flowers, as shown on and near the dotted line ending at *d*, and between it and the veranda. The line *d* is intended to designate a strip upon and near which nothing should be planted; so that a continuous open lawn-view may be had across this place to the places on the left of it, and from them back to the street on the right at *d*. The group above Figs. 11 and 12 may be composed of dwarf evergreens as follows: on the right, the dwarf white pine, *P. strobus compacta;* on the left, six feet from it, the golden arbor-vitæ; in the middle above them, four feet from each, the yew, *Taxus erecta*, the foliage of which is very dark; and above, close to it, the golden yew, with leaves and twigs, as its name imports, prettily tinged with a golden hue; next above, as shown by the speck on the plan, a plant of the dwarf fir, *Abies gregoriana* or the *Andromeda floribunda*, either of which is exceedingly dwarf. These would in time make a charming small evergreen group, but the dwarf trees which compose it grow slowly, so that it is necessary to keep the ground cultivated between the trees, and filled with bulbs, annuals, or perennials, until the evergreens are large enough to meet. Fig. 42 is a sketch made in the home-grounds of Mr. S. B. Parsons, at Flushing, L. I., showing an actual group somewhat similar to the one just suggested, composed of but four trees or shrubs, and three species. The low one in front is the *Andromeda floribunda*, the next the golden arbor-vitæ, and the two behind it the Irish yew, *Taxus baccata*. An engraving can scarcely suggest the beautiful contrasts of colors and surfaces that these present. On either side of the veranda, and about twelve feet in a diagonal line from its corners, two large

Fig. 42.

trees are indicated. The choice of these may safely be left to the reader. They should be of hardy, healthy, thrifty sorts. Horse-chestnuts, maples, and elms are usually the most beautiful rivals for such places. Of horse-chestnuts we would recommend the common white for one side, and for the other side the double white flowering, which blooms several weeks later than the common sorts, and forms a taller tree in proportion to its breadth. The red-flowering horse-chestnuts are lower and rounder-headed trees, of slower growth, and would not pair so well with either of the sorts named, but would be very appropriate if used on both sides. Of a totally different character from any of these named, is the cut-leaved weeping birch, of rapid growth, elegant at all seasons, and also adapted to these positions.

Opposite *g*, ten feet from the fence, is a Norway spruce, or, if the location and latitude are not too cold for it, the Nordmanns fir, *Picea nordmaniana*, which, in rich soils, has foliage of unusual beauty. Back of it towards the fence, fill in with hemlocks, arborvitæs, and yews, which grow to the ground and make an impenetrable mass of evergreen foliage. The side gateway is intended to be covered with a hemlock-arch of· some of the forms suggested in Chapter XIV, which should connect with a continuous hedge, broken at *m, n*, by one or two pines, and varied from the pines to the carriage-way gate with a belt of many kinds of shrubs. At *c*, five feet from the fence, plant the *Kolreuteria paniculata*, and at *b*, near the fence, a bed of low-growing spireas. The group between 2 and 4 may be composed of bush honeysuckles or of shrubby evergreens. The small shrub nearly over 2 may be an *Abies gregoriana*, or a golden yew. The group in the left-hand corner may be composed of good old shrubs like lilacs, the purple berberry, weigelas, deutzias, and the purple-leaved filbert; and for the two trees we would suggest the common catalpa for the place ten feet from the fence, and the *Magnolia machrophylla* for the one nearer the house. On the left, on the line of the middle of the front veranda, and twenty feet from the left side of the lot, a single specimen of the Bhotan pine, *P. excelsa*, or the two weeping firs, *Abies inverta* and *Picea pectinata pendula;* just behind them some of the yews of the podocarpus or cephalotaxus tribe; back of these, along the fence, a dense mass of hemlocks, with now and then some light-colored or variegated-leaved small plants or shrubs on the border in front of them. The group beyond, projecting towards the house, is supposed to be composed of a variety of the best arbor-vitæs broken in color by some of the dark yews,—the little out-lying member of the group to be the Irish juniper.

It is impracticable to trace through all the details. The reader must observe that the very small shrubs which are indicated in isolated positions on the lawn are intended for very compact evergreen or other shrubs, which take up but little room and are pleasing objects at all seasons of the year. At the four outer corners of the two bays may be planted, in pairs, specimens of the Irish and Swedish junipers, or some of the slender yews. At the corner of the open space in front of the carriage-house is a horse-block, to be shaded by a white pine. Nearly in front of the side entrance to the house is a rosary, for which may be substituted with good effect a Bhotan pine, with a cut-leaved weeping birch close behind it, if the proprietor does not wish to make and keep up the rose-bed with the expense and care which it annually requires. If the birch just named has been selected for the tree near the corners of the front veranda, it need not be repeated.

These grounds, with no other plantings than are indicated, would doubtless look bare for some years. The places which the trees and shrubs are ultimately to cover, must be filled, in the intervening time, with annuals and bedding-plants which will make the best substitutes for them. We would decidedly advise *not* to plant trees or large shrubs any nearer together than they ought to be when full grown, on the tempting plea that when they crowd each other some of them may be removed. Nine persons out of ten will not have the nerve to remove the surplusage so soon as it ought to be done, and when they do see the unsightly result of a crowded plantation, there will be one good excuse for not doing it, viz.: that trees which have grown up together have mis-shaped each other, so that when one is cut away those that remain show one-sided, and naked in parts. It is better to have patience while little trees slowly rise to the size we would have them ; and, while watching and waiting on them, let the ground they are eventually to cover be made bright with ephemeral flowers and shrubs. When the trees approach maturity they will have developed beauties that crowd'ed trees never show.

PLATE III.

Crowded and Open Grounds Compared, on a Cottage Lot of fifty feet front.

Here we have two lots 50 × 200 each.   The plan and position for a small cottage-house, and the walks, are the same on both. The plan on the right is intended to show the common mode of cluttering the yard so full of good things that, like an overloaded table, it lessens the appetite it is intended to gratify.   Let us picture Mr. and Mrs. A., master and mistress of the house, unskillful but enthusiastic, engaged in their first plantings.   The lot is a bare one.   Fruit trees are the first necessities ; places are therefore found for four cherry, and five pear trees, without trespassing much on the "front yard," which is sacred, in true American homes, to floral and sylvan embellishments.   It is to fill this ground that our proprietors are now to make choice of trees and shrubs. Mr. A. and wife are agreed that evergreens are indispensable, and that the balsam fir and the Norway spruce are the prettiest of evergreens—for "everybody plants *them*."   Accordingly a couple of Norway spruces flank the gate at a little distance inside, and a pair of balsam firs (prettiest of trees as they emerge, fragrant, from the nurserymen's bundles) are placed conspicuously not far from the house-steps, on each side the main-walk.   Mrs. A. suggests that the weeping-willow is the most graceful of all trees.   Who can gainsay that?   Mr. A. does not, and in go two willows in the two front corners of the yard.   Then there's the mountain ash with a "form as perfect as a top, and such showy clusters of red fruit," suggests Mrs. A., "and everybody plants them."   Of course this tree is planted, one on each side of the yard, midway between the walk and sides of the lot, in that open space above the willows. Then the walk is bordered from the gate towards the house with rose-bushes of all sorts, while lilacs, honeysuckles, spireas,

Plate III.

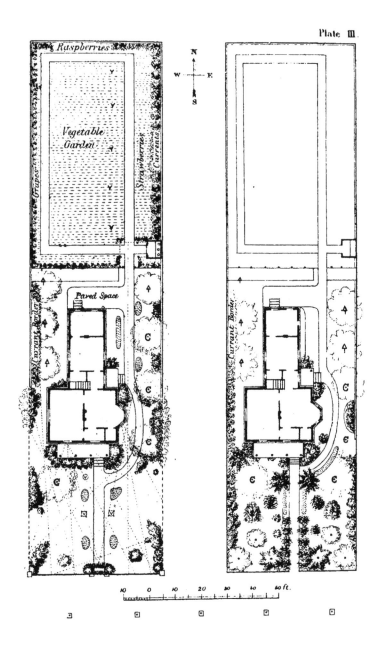

Raspberries

Vegetable
Garden

Grapes
Strawberries
Currants

N
W — E
S

Currant Border

Currant Border

Paved Space

10 0 10 20 30 40 50 ft.

syringas, and whatever else is known to be beautiful and easily obtained, are crowded along the side fences. Mrs. A. insists that a
space shall be left on both sides of the main-walk for *her* flowers.
Accordingly the beds are formed as shown on the plan, and planted
with all the fine flowering bulbs and annuals that she can get
plants or seeds of. There is still wanting a feature that some
neighboring place has, viz.: one or more fanciful trellises—master-
pieces of delicate carpentry, brilliant with white paint—upon which
to train pillar roses. "There's just the place for them," says Mrs.
A., "just in the middle of the yard, on each side," and there they
are placed.

We need not follow their planting further. The plan (on the
right) shows how the place will be filled in two or three years.
Each latest planting is put in the most convenient open space, and
every spring brings some new candidate for a place. At the end
of eight or ten years let us look in upon the ground and see the
result. There *should* be a home-picture, with its encircling fore-
ground, its open middle distance, its vine-clad cottage centre,
smiling like a speaking portrait well framed. What will it be, if it
has been planted and kept in this mode, still so common in
suburban places? A mass of agglomerated and tangled verdure.
Pass along the street, and the lovely foliage of the two willows
marks the spot, but beneath their overshadowing foliage the evergreens and other trees have a feeble existence, and their spindling
forms as they essay, with prim pertness, to stretch above the
crowding shrubs and tangled grass around them to maintain their
individuality, are met by a wet blanket of the willow's shade in
summer, and her damp old clothes in the autumn. Straggling
rose-bushes and overgrown shrubs elbow each other over the walk,
and quarrel for space with the grass and old annuals that try in
vain to get their share of room and light. As some English re-
viewer says of the bedrooms of little gothic cottages—"somewhere
around among the gables"—may be observed of all the pretty
things that have with so much care been planted on this place—
they are to be found somewhere among the bushes; and behind
all, as if the one great object of planting were to hide it out of
sight, is a cottage.

10

Happily such modes of planting are becoming rarer, but they are still quite too common.

Now we do not mean to convey the idea that this little piece of ground might be made into a little park by judicious planting, or that all of what has been crowded into it might have been put in differently, without crowding it.   It is a small lot on which it is not possible to have a great variety of trees and shrubs without cluttering it, and losing all appearance of a lawn.   Our plan on the left of the same plate is not designed to show the most artistic way of treating this small yard, but to show the most simple way of not overdoing by *mis*-planting.   The fruit trees are introduced in about the same places as in the other plan, but in front of them no overshadowing trees are planted.   At the sides, other yards are supposed to connect with this lot, and openings are left in the border shrubbery to avail of whatever pleasant lookouts may thus be obtained.   All the middle portion of the yard is unbroken by shrubbery, which is arranged in groups near the corners, and around the house.   The entrance gateway should be embellished with a verdant arch of hemlock ; the front corners of the lot may be marked by carefully grown specimens of arbor-vitæs or slender junipers ; the small trees standing alone, about seven feet from the front, should be choice specimens, either evergreen or deciduous, similar in form, and as dissimilar as possible in color and foliage. Among evergreens we would name for these places the two weeping firs—*Abies inverta pendula* and *Picea pectinata pendula*—as the most appropriate of all ; or, for one side the yew *Taxus stricta* or *erecta*, and on the other the yew *Taxas aurea ;* or the weeping arbor-vitæ for one side, and the weeping juniper for the other ; or with dwarfs, of the dwarf pine *P. strobus compacta* on one side, and the mugho pine on the other.   With deciduous arboreous shrubs or small trees, the variety to choose from is very great.   We will suggest for one side the weeping Japan sophora, grafted not more than seven feet high, and for the other the double scarlet hawthorn, *C. coccinnea flore plena*, cut to resemble the sophora in outline ; or for one side the Indian catalpa (see Fig. 129), and for the other a sassafras or a white dogwood, *Cornus florida*, kept clipped down at the top so that it shall not exceed eight feet in height or

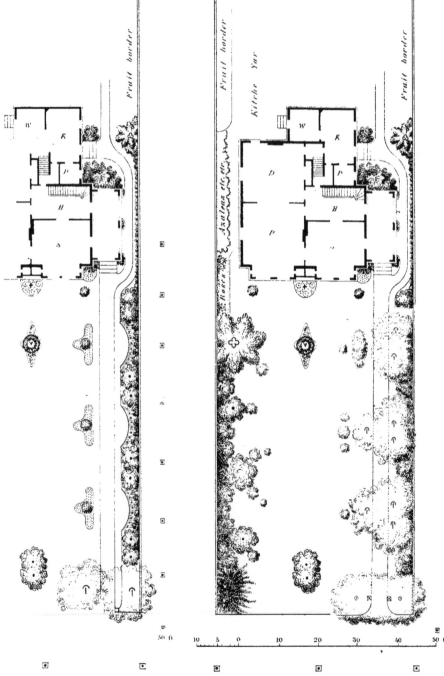

breadth of top. In selecting some deciduous miniature trees for these places we would choose those that have low, parasol forms, and clean, tree-like, but very short stems. The common orange quince tree, if planted in a deep moist soil, grown thriftily, and *treated with the same attention that we would bestow on a valuable exotic,* is one of the most beautiful of very low spreading-topped shrubby trees, and well adapted to the places under consideration. The kilmarnock willow, though it has neither the beauty of blossom, leaf, or fruit, that distinguish a well-grown quince tree, is certainly a sort of model of formal grace and symmetry, and might be used on one side and balanced on the other with a low-grown ever-flowering weeping cherry, *Cerasus semperfloreus.* Or luxuriantly grown single bushes of the common fragrant syringa, tartarian bush honeysuckle, rose weigela, or lilac *rothmagensis,* will be appropriate for the same place.

The plan in general is too simple to require explanation, and is introduced to call attention to the superior beauty of simplicity, compared with complexity of planting, on small places.

PLATE IV, A AND B.

Designs for a Lawn on a Lot of fifty feet front with considerable depth.

This design has already been alluded to in Chapter XI, on Arrangement in Planting, in illustrating the application of Rule I to small places. The lot has a front of fifty feet, and an indefinite extension in the rear. The plan is designed to show the pretty space of lawn that can be kept on a quite small lot, provided the latter has depth enough, by placing the house well back. The lot is supposed to be between side properties which it is impracticable to connect with, and therefore isolated by close fences and border shrubbery from them. The distance from the street to the bay-windows is eighty feet. The compact house plan is adapted to the position by having its entrance on the side, so that the best window-views possible under the circumstances will be secured from the bays of the two principal rooms. The walk, as we have previously observed, is made near one side, to leave all the central portion of the lot in open lawn. It is not possible to keep this openness of expression, and at the same time have large trees on the lot. They must be dispensed with; and in stocking the borders to make a rich environment of verdure for the lawn, the choice must be exclusively among small trees and shrubs. Let us begin at the gate. Here we would set out to have a hemlock arch;—though the trees as shown on the plan erroneously symbolize deciduous trees. At the opposite front corner we would plant the two slender weeping firs, *Abies excelsa inverta* and *Picea p. pendula.* But as their growth is slow compared with that of many fine deciduous shrubs, a mass of the latter may be planted near the firs, to fill that corner with foliage until the latter are from twelve to twenty years old, when the weeping firs will be large enough to fill it beautifully without support. The border on the left should be made up of evergreen shrubs or trees, as varied in foliage as possible, and of those sorts which do not exceed six or seven feet in height and breadth. The iso lated small trees or shrubs which stand out from this border are designed to be of deciduous sorts, the most charming for their forms, foliage, or flowers; the largest of which should not, within ten years, exceed ten feet in breadth. These, and the dwarf shrubs which flank them, can be selected from the lists to be found in the Appendix. As some of those which are in time the most interesting are of exceedingly slow growth, bedding plants and annuals which will preserve the same form for the groups by their proportioned sizes may be substituted. But there is no question of the superior beauty, in the end, of the place which is largely composed of trees and shrubs that make it charming in winter and early spring as well as in summer. The quick and brilliant effects that may be produced with bedding-plants can, however, be combined somewhat with more permanent plantings, if the planter will be watchful not to let his vigorous but ephemeral summer-plants smother the slower growing dwarfs. The latter will not long survive being thus deprived of sun and air in summer, and then left bare in the bleak winter, while their summer companions which lorded over them have been carefully removed to the cellar or the green-house. A pine tree is shown on the left near the house. This is exceptionally large. It is intended for a white pine, which grows rapidly in breadth as well as height, and might soon cover half the width of the lot with its branches. But it is readily "drawn up," as foresters say,—that is, it is easily reconciled to the loss of its lower limbs, and sends its vigor to the upper ones; so that it naturally becomes an over-arching tree. In time it will over-top, and form an evergreen frame for that side of the house, while the lawn under it will be unbroken. The small round shrubs near the outside corners of the bay-windows may be, one, a golden arbor-vitæ, and the other the golden yew, both rather dwarf evergreens, of pleasing form, and warm-toned verdure. Between the bay-windows, and near the house, is a suitable place for an elegant rose-pillar or trellis, and a bed of roses. Directly in front of it, and sixteen feet from the house, is a good position for a fine vase, or a basket in a bed of flowers, as shown on the plan. The pair of trees nearly in the middle of the front, near the street, we would have the weeping Japan sophora, on a line with the middle of the house, and not more than four feet apart. The main walk is represented on the plan by two modes of planting; the one, marked A, characterized by an alternation of shrubs and bedding-plants on the right, and beds of flowers on the left; the other, marked B, by a symmetric disposition of three groups of trees crossing and arching over the walk, and a belt of shrubs against the fence.

For the first, or shrub and flower-border plan, the following selection of shrubs is recommended on the fence-border. All the way from the street, to opposite the house, we would plant the Irish and English ivy close to the bottom of the fence, and would endeavor to make it cover the latter completely. Supposing the fence not to be more than four or five feet high, these ivies can generally be made to effect this, and although the growth near the top may often be winter-killed, the plants, if taken care of, will finally make a rich wall of verdure. If there is no probability of eventually joining, by openings on that side, with neighbors' improvements, it will be a great addition to the beauty of this border to have the fence a well-made stone wall, upon which the ivy is always most beautiful. From the hemlock arch to a point twenty feet from the fence, plant with tree-box, mahonias, and rhododendrons, set two and a half feet from the fence ; ·then a concave bed ten feet long is devoted to bulbous flowering-plants and annuals ; the next ten feet to be occupied by the pink and the red-flowered tree honeysuckles six feet apart, with the fragrant jasmine between them ; the next ten feet in flowers as before ; the next to be occupied by the *Deutzia crenata alba* and the *Deutzia crenata rubra flore plena*, six feet apart, with the *Deutzia gracilis* between them ; the next, flowers ; and the last group of shrubs to be the *Lilac rothmagensis* and the *Weigela rosea* six feet apart, with the *Spirea calosa alba* between and the golden yew, *Taxus aurea*, beyond ;—closing the planting on that side. On the veranda-posts five different vines may be trained ; on the fence in front of them nothing better can be done than to cover it with Irish ivy, or such low-growing annual vines, on cords or wires, as will make the best wall of leaves and flowers during the summer, and which can be readily cleared away before winter. Beyond the veranda, on the left, is a place for a group of shrubs of anything that the lady of the house fancies. The evergreen at the end of the narrow walk around the veranda should be some tall and handsome tree. If the soil is sandy, the white-pine kept well trimmed will make a fine mass of evergreen verdure the most quickly. In a climate not more rigorous than that of Philadelphia, the Lawson cypress, *C. lawsoniana*, is a good tree for the place ; further north, the pyramidal spruce, *Abies excelsa pyramidata*, a slender, vigorous, and peculiar variety of the Norway spruce, will answer well ; and so will a Bartlett or Seckel pear tree, or any good cherry tree. The evergreen, however, makes the best back-ground setting for the house. By planting an evergreen on each side the walk, at that point, an arch may eventually be cut under them to form a vista from the veranda into the garden. This purpose may be most quickly effected with white-pines or hemlocks.

The embellishment of the walk-border by the other mode, as shown on the plan B, may be done as follows : the border of ivy along the fence or wall, and the principal shrubs for twenty feet next the front, may be the same as on the first plan ; but all the flower-beds are to be omitted. Twenty-three feet from the street, and two feet from the walk on the right, plant an American Judas tree, *Cercis canadensis;* four feet further, on the same side, the European Judas tree, *Cercis siliquastrum;* opposite to them, on the left side of the walk, a clean stemmed white-flowering dogwood, *Cornus florida.* Sixteen feet from the upper Judas tree, plant a pair of sassafras trees four feet apart in the same relative positions as the Judas trees in the first group ; opposite to them, on the left of the walk, the Scamston weeping-elm, grafted eight feet high on a common elm stock. The next group, sixteen feet further on, is made with a pair of *Kolreuteria paniculata* on the right, and a narrow group of low choice shrubs on the left of the walk. ·*Very dwarf* evergreens, or deciduous shrubs, may be planted to the left of each of these groups, as indicated on the plan, or those places may be filled with single plants of rich and abundant foliage, like the more robust geraniums, the *Colleus verschafelti,* cannas, little circles of salvias, etc., etc.

It is intended that the groups of low-growing trees which border this walk shall form flat arches over head, not more than eight feet over the walk ; and the trees must be reared and pruned to effect this object. The Judas trees and the dogwood naturally spread quite low. The study with them will be, how to draw them up so that they will not be in the way over head. The sassafras, though a flat-topped tree, sometimes gets too high before beginning to spread. If it keeps a strong centre-stem it should be topped at eight feet high to hasten its spreading. The *Kolreuterias* are rather too large for their place, but are low-spreading trees of great delicacy of foliage and warmth of color ; and even if they finally extend their branches far towards the bay-windows, the view under them will be the more pleasing.

PLATES V AND VI.

Designs for Village Lots 60 × 150 *feet: one an In-Lot, and the other a Corner Lot.*

These designs are very simple and inexpensive in their character, and have been partially described in Chapter XI. The house-plan is the same in both; not compact, but rather stretched along the side of the lot farthest from the street so as to leave a fair space on the other side, upon which the best rooms and the verandas (which may be considered the pleasantest summer rooms of a house) are located. The house-fronts are each forty feet from the main street. Both ground-plans are supposed to open into other yards adjoining, on a line from ten to twenty five feet from the street; on that line they are, therefore, left unplanted with anything that will obstruct views across the lawn. On Plate V the walks are made in right lines; while, on Plate VI, the entrance being at the corner, convenience dictates curved lines as the most desirable. If, on the latter, the gateway were in the same place as in the former, the straight-line walk would be preferable, as there would be no object in making it otherwise.

PLATE V.—The front gate is to be arched over in some of the modes suggested in Chapter XIV, and on the left a dense screen to the corner is to be made with evergreen shrubs or shrubby trees. Twenty feet from the front, and five feet from the left side, a tree of medium size is represented. It may be any one of the following: a *Magnolia machrophylla*, catalpa, double white or red-flowering horse-chestnut, bird cherry (*Prunus padus*), a cut-leaved weeping birch, purple-beech, *Kolreuteria*, *Virgilia*, red-twigged linden, grape-leaved linden, scarlet maple, purple-leaved maple, *Salisburia* or ginkgo tree (if cut back at the top), or a sassafras. Any handsome tree will do which branches low, but still high enough to allow a person to walk under its branches after it has been planted five or six years, and which does not quickly become a great tree. Five feet from the fence,

Plate V

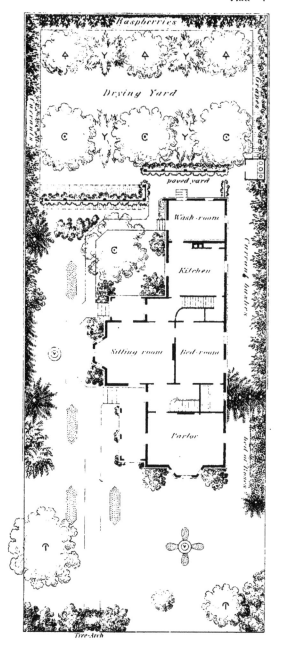

Raspberries

Drying Yard

paved yard

Wash-room

Kitchen

Sitting room | Bed-room

Parlor

Tree-Arch

10   20   40   50 ft.

facing the main entrance steps, we would plant the pendulous Norway spruce, *Abies excelsa inverta;* along the fence towards the front, a dense mass of low-growing evergreens ; along the fence on the other side of the spruce (opposite the bay-window), a hemlock hedge, merging as it recedes from the front to the grape-trellis into a belt of evergreens.   The groups of shrubs indicated in many places against the house, must be of the best species, which grow from two to seven feet in height ; and ought to embrace in each group one or more shrubs with fragrant flowers, so that there shall be no summer month when the windows will not be perfumed from them. It is becoming a fashion to decry the planting of shrubs in contact with dwelling houses.   This fashion is a part of an extreme reaction that possesses the public mind against the old and un-healthy mode of embowering houses so completely under trees, and packing yards so densely with shrubs, that many homes were made dark and damp enough to induce consumption and other diseases ; and physicians have been obliged to protest against their injurious effects on the health of the inmates.   But low-growing shrubs planted against the basement-walls of suburban houses, and rising only a few feet higher than the first floor, are not open to any such objections.   A house that is *nested* in shrubs which seem to spring out of its nooks and corners with some-thing of the freedom that characterizes similar vegetation spring-ing naturally along stone walls and fences, seems to express the mutual recognition and dependence of nature and art ; the shrubs loving the warmth of the house-walls, and the house glad to be made more charming in the setting of their ver-dure and blossoms.   Many pleasing shrubs will do well where their roots can feel the warmth that foundation-walls retain in winter, which will not flourish in open exposed ground.   Some will do well in shady nooks and northern exposures which cannot be grown in sunny projections ; others need all the sun of the latter exposures, and are grateful in addition for all the reflected heat from the house-walls.   The foundations (provided of course that they are of a deep and substantial character) thus become protect-ing walls that offer to the skillful planter many studies in the selection and arrangement of small shrubs.   No well-constructed house will be dampened, or have the sunlight excluded from its windows, by such shrubs as we would recommend for planting in the groups indicated against the houses in Plates V and VI. Small as they are, each one of these little places for shrubs are studies. Whether to plant a single robust shrub in each place, which will spread to fill it, or to form a collection of lilliputian shrubs around some taller one, is for the planter to decide. We cannot here indicate, in detail, the plantings for all these places. It will be observed that the right-hand front corner of the lot is filled with shrubs, supposed to be but a part of a group, the other part of which is on the lot of the adjoining neighbor. This may be composed of large shrubs, such as altheas, deutzias, lilacs, etc., for the interior, and weigelas, bush honeysuckles, Gordon's currants, berberries, and low spireas of graceful growth for the outside. The tree ten feet from the right-hand corner should be one of the smallest class. The weeping Japan sophora grafted not more than six feet high, the ever-flowering weeping cherry, the new weeping thorn, the double scarlet thorn (*Coccinnea flore plena*) will make pretty trees for such a place. If something to produce a quick, luxuriant growth is preferred, the Judas tree, *Cercis canadensis*, or the Scamston weeping-elm, grafted on another stock seven or eight feet high, will do ; though the latter will eventually become a wide-spreading tree too large for the place.

The isolated small tree, or large shrub, about seven feet from the fence near the middle of the front, may be an *Andromeda arborea*, or the Indian catalpa (the hardiness of which is not fully tested north of Philadelphia), the purple-fringe (grown low as a tree), the tree honeysuckle, *Lonicera grandiflora*, grown low on a single stem, the *Weigela amabilis*, also in tree-form ; Josikia or chionanthus-leaved lilac, the dwarf weeping cherry (a very slow grower), the *Chionanthus virginica* (a little tender north of Philadelphia), the rose acacia grown over an iron frame, or any outarching, low, small tree, weeping or otherwise, the foliage of which is pleasing throughout the season. Or, if a single evergreen is preferred, any one of the following will do : the dwarf white-pine, *P. strobus compacta*, the golden yew, *Taxus aurea*, the weeping silver-fir, *Picea pectinata pendula*, the golden arbor-vitæ, or the weeping arbor-vitæ. None of these will grow to greater size than the place requires, but they grow slowly. A pretty effect may be produced here by planting the erect yew, *Taxus erecta*, where the centre of the tree is indicated on the plan, with a golden arbor-vitæ in front and a golden yew behind it. The erect yew is taller than the others, and very dark, so that if the three are planted not more than one or two feet apart, they will grow into a beautiful compact mass made up of three quite distinct tones of foliage. Or another pretty substitute for the one small tree, as shown on the plan, may be made by using the excessively slender Irish juniper for a centre 1, and grouping *close* around it the golden arbor-vitæ 2, the *Podocarpus* (or *Taxus*) *japonica* 3, the dwarf silver-fir, *Picea compacta*, 6, the pigmy spruce, *Abies excelsa pygmæa*, 4, the dwarf hemlock, *Abies canadensis parsoni*, 5, and the creeping euonymus, *Japonicus radicans marginatus*. This will in time make an irregular pyramid composed of an interesting variety of foliage and color, and easily protected in winter, if the plants are of doubtful hardiness or vigor

The vase and flower-beds in front of the bay-window need no explanation. All the flower-beds shown on this plan, except the one opposite the back-porch, should be filled only with flowering-plants of the lowest growth : the bed excepted, and the place behind it, shown as shrubbery, may be occupied by taller plants, which are showy in leaves or flowers : but we think the effect will be more constantly pleasing if the latter is filled with evergreen shrubs from two to seven feet in height, mostly rhododendrons.

At the front end of the bed of roses, on the right, we would plant the Nordmans fir, *Picea Nordmaniana*, an evergreen tree of superior foliage, and believed hardy in most parts of the country It eventually becomes a large tree, but will bear trimming when it begins to encroach too much upon the lawn.

The hemlock screen represented opposite the bath-room window should be thrown back to the end of the wash-room if the owner prefers to have that strip of ground in lawn, rather than under culture. We ask the reader to excuse us for having placed it where it is, for the space between the house and the currant-bushes allows of a pretty strip of lawn six feet wide, from which narrow beds may be cut adjoining the foundation-walls, for beds of low or slender annuals, which will not sprawl too far away from the house. The space will certainly be more profitable to the eye in this way than it can be in fruits and vegetables.

PLATE VI.—This plan is so similar to the preceding, and both are of so simple a character, that the intelligent reader will learn by an examination of the plate what manner of planting is intended. This plate differs principally from Plate V in having four pine trees of conspicuous size on the street margin of the lot. This pre-supposes a well-drained sandy soil, for without a congenial soil the pines will not develop great beauty. Supposing this condition to be satisfied, evergreens may be made a specialty of this place, and used as follows: Close by the left-hand gate-post (entering from the street), plant a bunch of the common border-box ; a foot from it, and midway between the walk and side fence, a plant of the broad-leaved tree-box ; a foot further, on the same mid-line, a plant of the gold or silver striped-leaved tree-box ; then fill in with hemlocks a foot apart, and a foot from the fence, as far as the group is designated. Four feet from the same gate-post, and two feet from the walk, plant a *Podocarpus japonica;* eight feet from the gate, and three from the walk, the *Cephalo-taxus fortunii mascula;* four feet beyond, and four feet from the walk, the golden arbor-vitæ. Between the right-hand gate-post and the pine tree, fill next to the gate with the common English ivy, to trail on the ground and form a bush; next, midway between the fence and walk, and four feet from the post, the golden yew (*Taxus baccata aurea*) ; next, same distance from the walk, Sargent's hemlock (*A. canadensis inverta*) ; and between the pine and the fence, fill in with mahonias (*aquifolium* and *japonicum*). The pine here alluded to, to be the common white pine. The dwarf trees shown on the plan, twenty feet from the gate, are the *Abies gregoriana* on one side the walk, and on the other the *Picea hudsonica*, or the *Picea pectinata compacta*. These, and the gateway groups, form an entrance through evergreens alone. In climates more severe than that of New York city, substi-tute the *Pinus strobus compacta* for the *Cephalotaxus fortunii*

Plate VI.

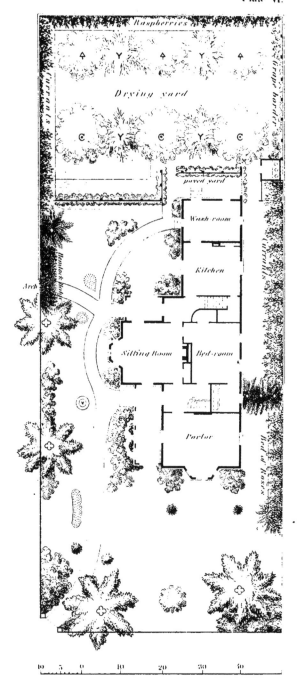

Raspberries

Grape border

Currants

Drying yard

paved yard

Wash room

Kitchen

Hedge box

Currants

Arch

Sitting Room

Bed room

Parlor

Bed of Roses

10 5 0 10 20 30 40

mascula. The pine tree in the right-hand corner may be an Austrian, taking care to select one of short dense growth. Between it and the corner fill in with a mass of assorted rhodo dendrons, or with such shrubs as bush honeysuckles, deutzias of the smaller sorts, the common syringa, purple berberry, variegated elder, etc. The single tree in the middle of the front may be the weeping Japan sophora, the Judas tree (*Cercis canadensis*), or a neatly grown specimen of the white-flowering dogwood (*Cornus florida*). The two small trees marked on the plan 10 feet in front of each front corner of the house should be the two slender weeping firs, the *Abies excelsa inverta* and the *Picea pectinata pendula*, which will in time form a graceful flanking for the bay-window, and point the two groups of fragrant-blossomed deciduous shrubs shown on each side of it. The shrubbery shown between the walk and the main side veranda and its column vines should be entirely composed of bedding plants of rich foliage and successive bloom, which can be cleared away late in autumn. The remainder of the plan is so like that for Plate V, that no further designation of trees and shrubs need be made. A planter who is familiar with the dimensions and qualities of trees and shrubs may make a different choice, perhaps improve on those here named, and give another character to the place. The gateway entrance, for instance, may be bordered by low-growing umbelliferous trees like the Judas tree, the weeping sophora, the Scamston elm, the sassafras, or the *Kolreuteria paniculata,* of which any two would soon grow to form a natural arch. The use of any of these trees will not prevent the planting, under them, of those small evergreens like the ivy, the box-wood, and some others which flourish in partial shade. Or, some of the trees mentioned in Chapter XIV for artificial arches, may be employed in the same place instead of the groups of low evergreen shrubs, or the trees just named. The pine trees which are shown on the plan (if, as before remarked, the soil is congenial to them), in connection with the other evergreens, in the course of ten years would give an evergreen character to the outer limits of the lot without trespassing too much on the lawn space ; and although a repetition of the same species of tree is not usually desirable on a small lot, the white pine unites so many more qualities which suit it for the places indicated, than any other evergreen, that we would make its use a specialty of the plan. The exquisite Bhotan pine is still of doubtful longevity with us ; that is to say, it occasionally dies out after eight or ten years of healthy growth, just when its fountain-like tufts of drooping foliage have become so conspicuously beautiful as to endear it greatly to the owner. The same may be said of the long-leaved Pyrrenean pine. Neither the Austrian or the Scotch pines drop their lower limbs with so little injury to their symmetry as the white pine, nor have either of them so fine a texture of foliage or wood when seen near by. On small lots, ground-room cannot well be afforded for that extension of the branches of evergreens upon a lawn, which constitutes one of their greatest beauties where there is space enough around to allow them to be seen to advantage. Therefore trees which develop their beauty overhead, and permit the lawn to be used and seen under their boughs, are more desirable.

Plate VII.

A long, narrow House, with Front near the Street, on an In-Lot sixty feet wide, and of considerable depth.

We have here an inside lot of sixty feet front, occupied to the depth of one hundred and thirty feet by the house, the walks and the ground embellishments. The kitchen-garden is back of the grape trellis, which should be of an ornamental character. The house is stretched out to correspond with the form of the lot, which is supposed to have no desirable ground connections with the adjoining lots, yet not so disagreeably surrounded as to make it necessary to shut out by trees and shrubs the out-look over the fences from the side-windows of the bay. The style of planting here shown is such as would suit only a person or family of decided taste for flowers, and the choicest selections of small shrubs. In the rear left-hand corner is room enough for two cherry trees, under which the lawn forms a sufficient drying-yard, and a convenient currant-border utilizes a space next the fence. Besides

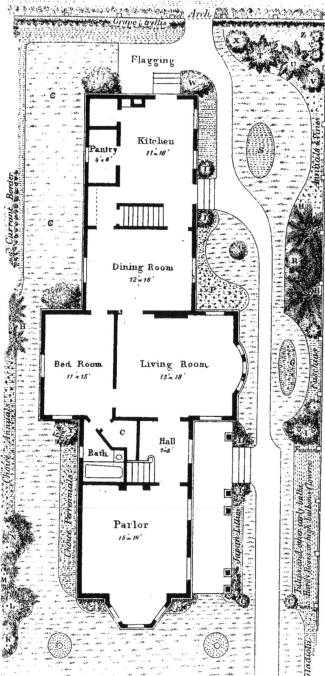

Plate VII.

Kitchen Garden

Arch

Grape trellis

Flagging

Kitchen
11 x 16'

Pantry
4 x 8'

Dining Room
12 x 16'

Bed Room
11 x 15'

Living Room
15 x 18'

Bath

C

Hall
7 x 8'

Parlor
15 x 16'

Currant Border

Choice Annuals

Choice Perennials

Various Shrubs

the cherries, no large trees are to be planted except hemlocks (marked H), which are gracefully shrubby in their early growth, and can be so easily kept within proper bounds by pruning, that they are introduced to form 'an evergreen flanking' for the rear of the house, and back-ground for the narrow strips of lawn on either side of it. In time they will overarch the walk, and under their dark shadows the glimpse of the bit of lawn beyond, with its bright flowers, will be brought into pretty relief. Our engraver has been somewhat unfortunate in the *extreme* rigidity of outline given to all the trees and shrubs shown on this plan, yet precision and formality are peculiarities which the narrow limits of the lot render necessary, and the completeness with which this specialty is carried out will constitute its merit. Nearly all the shrub and tree embellishment is with small evergreens, flowers of annuals, and bedding plants. Flowers are always relieved with good effect when seen against a back-ground of evergreens. It will be observed that the close side-fences are, much of their length, uncovered by shrubbery. They must, therefore, be very neatly, even elegantly made, if the proprietor can afford it. They then become a suitable backing for the flowers that may be made to form a sloping bank of bloom against them. By finishing the inside of the fence *en espalier*, it may be covered all over with delicate summer vines whose roots, growing under it, will interfere little with planting and transplanting seeds, roots, and bulbs in front of them. In naming the trees intended for this plan, it must not be supposed that other selections equally good, or better, may not be made by a good gardener. The following is suggested as one of many that will be appropriate to the place :

A, A. Two hemlocks planted two feet from the fence and from the walk to form an arch over the gate when large enough, as shown in Chapter XIV.

B. Parson's dwarf hemlock two feet from the walk and six feet from the fence.

C, C, C, C. Irish junipers two feet from the walk.

D. Space between juniper and corner post on the right may be filled with mahonias, English ivy, and azalias that love shade.

E (next to the fence). Dwarf weeping juniper, *J. oblonga pendula.*

E (in the centre of front group). The pendulous Norway spruce, *Abies excelsa inverta,* the central stem of which must be kept erect by tying to a stake until it is from six to eight feet high.

F, F. One, the dwarf Norway spruce, *Abies gregoriana,* and the other the dwarf silver-fir, *Picea pectinata compacta.*

G (in the front group). Golden arbor-vitæ.

G (opposite bow-window of living-room). A bed of assorted geraniums.

G (opposite dining-room). A single plant of *Colleus verschafelti.*

H, H, H. Hemlocks; for the left-hand front corner use Sargent's hemlock, *Abies canadensis inverta;*—its main stem to be kept tied to a stake until it has a firm growth six feet high.

I, I, I (on the left side of walk). Dwarf-box for clipping.

I (on right side of walk). The weeping arbor-vitæ and the dwarf weeping juniper, *J. oblonga pendula.*

J. *Podocarpus japonica,* if protected in winter.

K. Parson's arbor-vitæ, *Thuja occidentalis compacta,* two feet from the fence. Between K and L plant a golden arbor-vitæ.

L. The pendulous silver-fir, *Picea pectinata pendula,* four feet from the fence. Directly back of it, midway between it and the fence, the erect yew, *Taxus erecta,* whose deep green foliage will contrast well with the golden arbor-vitæs near it, and as its hardiness in all localities is not so well proved as that of the other trees near it, its placement back of them, and near to the fence, will serve to insure its safety from cold.

M. Irish and Swedish junipers near the fence.

N. The dwarf white-pine, *P. strobus compacta,* four feet from the fence; and behind, on each side, small rhododendrons. Four feet above the pine, near the fence, plant a common hemlock, and when it is large enough to form a back-ground for the dwarf pine—say from eight to ten feet high—keep it well clipped back to prevent it from spreading over the dwarfs, and taking up too much of the lawn.

O, O. Round beds for verbenas or other creeping flowers of constant brilliancy.

P.   Bed for favorite fragrant annuals or low shrubs.

Q (by the side of the kitchen).   Bed for flowering-vines to train on the house, or, if the exposure be southerly, or southeasterly, some good variety of grape-vine.   Whichever side of the rear part of the house has the proper exposure to ripen grapes well, cannot be more pleasingly covered than with neatly kept grape-vines ; which should not be fastened directly to thé house, but on horizontal slats from six inches to a foot from the house ; and these should be so strongly put up that they may be used instead of a ladder to stand upon to trim the vines and gather the fruit.

R.   Rhododendrons.

S.   Bed of cannas, or assorted smaller plants with brilliant leaves of various colors.

T, U, V, X, Z.   A bed of rhododendrons.

W W, W.   May be common deciduous shrubs of any favorite full foliaged sort.

Y.   Rhododendrons and azalias.

Opposite the corner of the veranda where fuschias are indicated, the space should be filled between the Irish juniper and the fence with the golden arbor-vitæ and the *Podocarpus japonica*, planted side by side.

The foregoing list for planting is made on the assumption that the owner is, or desires to be, an amateur in the choicest varieties of small evergreens, as well as in flowers, and willing to watch with patience their slow development ; for there is no doubt that with deciduous shrubs a showy growth of considerable beauty can be secured in much less time.   Yet the type of embellishment made with such a collection of evergreens as have been named for this place, is so much rarer, and has so greatly the advantage in its autumn, winter, and sprıng beauty, that we would have little hesitation in adopting it.

For the benefit, however, of those who wish a quicker display of verdure in return for their expense and labor in planting, wc subjoin an essentially different list of trees and shrubs for the same plan, viz

11

A, A.　Two Scamston elms (planted two feet from fence and walk) grafted on straight stocks eight feet from the ground, to form a tabular topped arch over the gateway, by interweaving the side branches which are nearest to each other.　These grow so rapidly that all the space within ten feet from the centre of the gate will in six years be deeply shaded by them, so that only those plants which are known to flourish in deep shade should be planted near the gate.　Among these the English ivy may occupy the same place in the corner as before.

B.　May be the *Cephalotaxus fortunii mascula*, or purple magnolia.

C, C (nearest the gate).　*Daphne cneorum.*　C, C (near the veranda).　Should be Irish juniper as in the first plan, and the space marked *fuschias* to be filled as before recommended ; C on left-hand front of lot to be an Irish or Swedish juniper.

D.　Box-wood, spurge laurel, hypericum, purple magnolia, or rhododendrons.

E (middle group).　*Andromeda arborea,* or, south of Philadelphia, the Indian catalpa, *C. himalayensis.*

F, F.　*Spirea reevesii flore plena* and *Spirea fortunii alba.*　G (of same group).　*Spirea Van Houtti.*　In the spaces between G and F the *Deutzia gracilis* and the *Andromeda floribunda* may be planted within two feet of the stem of the. *Andromeda arborea.*

H (in left-hand corner).　Two deutzias, the white and red, *D. crenata alba* and *D. crenata rubra flore plena*, planted side by side.　The other H's to be hemlocks as in the other plan.

I, I, I, I.　Tree-box on left of walk, Siberian arbor-vitæ on the right.

J.　*Deutzia gracilis.*

K.　Purple berberry two feet from fence.　Above it, the same distance from the fence, the variegated-leaved althea.

L.　Common red Tartarian honeysuckle, four feet from fence. Behind it, next to the fence, the spurge laurel, *Daphne laureola.*

M.　Two Swedish junipers one foot from fence.

N. *Weigela rosea* three feet from fence. Close to fence, on each side of it, the English ivy.
O. Beds for creeping flowers as in previous plan.
P. Bed for annuals or low shrubs.
Q. Same as in former list.
R. A bed of salvias, to fill in between the hemlocks.
S. Cannas, or some lower bedding annuals.
T. The lilac, *Rothmagensis rubra.*
U. Gordon's flowering currant.
V. Two dwarf rhododendrons, *roseum elegans* and *album candidissima,* and behind them towards the grape trellis and next the fence, the taller rhododendrons, *grandiflorum* and *album elegans.* These will fill as near to the trellis as anything should be planted.
X. Rhododendrons, *grandiflorum* and *candidissima* planted together.

Shrubs shown at the house-corners should be selected from those whose branches droop toward the ground, well covered with foliage, and whose flowers are fragrant ; such as the common syringa, bush honeysuckles, jasmines, wild roses, purple magnolia, etc., etc. ; the beauty and abundance of the foliage throughout the season being of more importance than the blossoms. But there are shrubs which combine nearly every merit of foliage, bloom, and fragrance, and these are often the common sorts best known.

It is not practicable to name in detail everything which may be planted on a lot of this size, and the two lists just given will form a ground-work into which may be interwoven a great variety of quite small shrubs without breaking the arrangement intended.

In whatever way this place is planted, the area in lawn is so narrow that it can only be made to look well by the nicest keeping.

PLATE VIII.

A simple Plan for a Corner Lot one hundred by one hundred and seventy feet, with Stable and Carriage-house accommodations.

By referring to Plates IX and XII, and comparing them with the one now under consideration, it will be seen that there is a similarity in the forms and sizes of the lots and the house-plans. A comparison of their differences will be interesting. Plates VIII and IX represent corner lots 100 × 170 feet, having stable and carriage-house accommodations, while Plate XII is an in-lot 100 × 160 feet, without those luxuries, but with convenience for keeping a cow. Plan VIII is designed to illustrate the utmost simplicity of style, requiring the minimum of trouble and expense in its maintenance. In both plans the nearest part of the house stands thirty feet from the side street, and eighty-two feet from the street upon which the bay-windows look out. On this plan the short straight walk from the side street to the veranda is the only one that requires to be carefully made, and is but twenty-seven feet in length from the street to the steps ; while on Plate IX there is an entrance from both streets, connected by a curving walk with the main house entrance, and other walks to the kitchen entrances and carriage-house. This difference in the walks is suggestive of the greater embellishment of the latter plan in all other respects, and, with its vases, flower-beds, and more numerous groups of shrubbery, indicates the necessity for the constant services of a gardener. Plan VIII, on the other hand, with its plain lawn, and groups of trees which require but little care, and its few plain flower-beds, may easily be taken care of by any industrious pro-. prietor, before and after the hours devoted to town business— especially if the wife will assume the care of the flowers—and if the lawn is in high condition, and the trees are kept growing luxuriantly, the simplicity of the planting will not result in any lack of that air of elegance which most persons desire to have their places express ; for it is not so much costliness and elaborateness that challenges the admiration of cultivated people as the uncon-

Plate VII.

Raspberry Border

Cow s d & Manure

Carriages

Grape Border

Currants

Currants

Hemlocks

Drying Yard

S. K

K

D

C

P

P

S. H

S

Sycamore
Maple

Sycamore
Maple

Arbor
Vitae
plicata

Hemlocks

Sassafras

Sassafras Liquidamber
w Bignonia

scious grace with which a plain dress may be worn, so as to appear elegant notwithstanding its simplicity. It will be observed that there is no vegetable garden on either plan, but a good number of cherry, pear, and other fruit trees, as well as an abundance of grapes, currants, raspberries, and strawberries are provided for. Yet in the neighborhood of the carriage-house, the ground in cultivation under the trees may serve to produce a small quantity of those low vegetables which take but little room, and are wanted in small quantities only

Supposing the walks to be laid out as shown on the plan, the first things to be planted are the fruit trees. Three cherry trees— say the mayduke, black tartarian, and late-duke ; seven pear trees (not dwarfs)—say one Madeleine, one Dearborn's seedling, one Bloodgood, two Seckels, and two Bartletts ; two peach trees, the George the Fourth or Haine's early, and Crawford's early ; and a few orange-quinces near the stable, are all the fruit trees there is room for. The sides of the carriage-house and stable will afford the best of places for the growth of grapes ; the vines, however, should not be fastened directly to the wall, but on a trellis six inches or a foot from it, to allow a circulation of air through the foliage. Besides these, a few vines may be grown to advantage on a trellis back of the kitchen, and on a circular trellis around the gravelled space in front of the carriage-house,* and also on the back fence, marked raspberry border, if preferred. Currant bushes and raspberries do well in partially shaded situations, while grape vines need the most sunny exposure. The places for one or the other must therefore be chosen with reference to the light and shade adjacent to buildings, fences, and trees.

The fruit trees being disposed of, let us turn to the lawn-ground. The front gate recedes from the street four feet, forming a bay from the side-walk. On the left, as one enters, the view is all open across the lawn. On the right of the gate, along the fence, there is a heavy mass of shrubbery, to be composed of lilacs, honeysuckles, weigelas, or any of the thrifty common shrubs which

---

* The carriage turn-way is represented a little broader than it need be. There should be ten feet space between it and the back fence to make room for the trellis for grapes.

do not grow bare of leaves at the bottom. Or, if an evergreen screen is preferred to these blossoming shrubs, the border may be planted irregularly with the American and Siberian arbor-vitæs. On the left, next to the fence, and close against it, we would plant English ivy, tree-box, periwinkle, or myrtle for the first ten feet, and hardy dwarf arbor-vitæs, hemlocks, and yews on the next ten feet. On the right of the walk, and two feet from it, is a straight bed for annual and bulbous flowers, which is backed by a bed of shrubbery running parallel with the walk, designed to shut from view the kitchen drying-yard, under the cherry and pear trees. This screen should be composed entirely of evergreens which can be kept within seven feet in height. In the front, next to the flower-bed, may be a collection, in a row, of the finest very small dwarfs, of as many species as the owner desires to procure, backed by a dense mass of arbor-vitæs and hardy yews intermingled. The row of dwarf evergreens should in time occupy the space which is marked as a bed for annuals, while the former are too small to fill it. The masses of shrubs shown against the house may be of common sorts which are favorites with the proprietor or his family, and that do not exceed seven feet in height. On the left of the walk the flower-beds 1, 2, and 3 may be filled, each, with one species of low flowers not exceeding nine inches in height, so as to make brilliant contrasts of colors. Beds 4 and 6 may be filled with bulbous flowers in the spring, and later, with geraniums, lantanas, or salvias. Bed 5 admits of some skill in arrangement. In its centre, next to the house, we would try the Japanese striped maize ; next to it a half circle of salvias ; outside of these a half circle of mountain-of-snow geranium ; next, a circle of *Colleus ver-schafelti*, and, next the grassy margin, the Mrs. Pollock geranium. Another season the same bed might be splendid with cannas alone, as follows : for the centre, one plant of the blood-red canna, *C. san-guinea chatei*, six feet high ; one foot from it, three plants of the *C. sellowi*, four to five feet high ; next, a circle of the *C. flaccida*, three feet ; and for the outer circle the *C. compacta elegantissima*, two feet high, alternated with the *C. augustifolia nana pallida*. If the occupant of the house does not wish to obtain plants from the green-house to stock these beds, they may be cheaply and prettily filled by annuals graded in size in the same manner as above indicated for a bed of cannas. The circular border of cultivated ground be- tween the dining-room bay-window and the hemlock border may also be filled with annuals, graded from those that grow only a few inches high next the grass, to an outer circle made with flowering plants from four to six feet high. Bed 7 is intended for an assort- ment of geraniums. At 8 is a good place for the pendulous silver- fir; and at 9 for Sargent's hemlock, *Abies canadensis inverta,* trained to a straight stick, and kept small by pruning.

On a line with the side-walls of the house, and twenty feet in front, two sycamore maples are designated. We do not intend to recommend this variety as any better or more beautiful than the sugar, red-bud, or Norway maples, or than the horse-chestnut, but it represents a type of trees with formal outlines, and rich masses of foliage, which are appropriate for such places ;—unless the style of the house is picturesque ; in which case elms, birches, and other loose growing trees would be more appropriate. The centre group of evergreens is mostly composed of common and well-known sorts, the points being representations of the arbor-vitæ family, and the centre of the taller hemlocks. Lawson's cypress is still a rare tree, and its hardiness is doubtful north of Philadelphia. Where it may not be safely used, a full-foliaged specimen of the Norway spruce may be substituted. South of New York, near the sea-coast, we would also substitute the *Glypto-strobus sinensis pendula* for the arbor-vitæ *plicata.* While these trees are small they will appear insignificant in so large a bed ; but we advise no one to trust himself to plant trees more thickly than they should eventually grow, on the plea that when they crowd each other a part may be removed ; for however sound the theory, it is rarely carried out in practice. Besides, no trees are so beautiful as those which have an unchecked expansion from the beginning ; and this is especially the case with evergreens, some of which never recover from the malformations produced by being crowded during the first ten or fifteen years of their growth. Therefore, let the open spaces between the permanent trees, in the beds which are out- lined for cultivation, be filled during their minority with showy annuals or bedding plants ;—taking care not to plant so near to the young trees as to smother or weaken them by the luxuriant growth of the former.

The evergreen group on the right is intended to be made up entirely of firs—hemlocks, Norway and black spruces—mixed indiscriminately, to show as a mass, and not as single specimens. If the proprietor has a desire for rarities in this family, they can be substituted.

The group on the left, as its symbols show, is intended to be entirely of pines. In the centre, plant a white pine and a Bhotan pine side by side and close together, the former on the south side of the latter. Fifteen feet back of them put in an Austrian pine · towards the front the cembran pine ; to the extreme right, the dwarf white pine, *P. strobus compacta*, and in the spaces between fill with the varieties of the mugho or mountain pine, or with rhododendrons.

The deciduous group lightly outlined near the right hand corner explains itself. If thriftily grown, the trees there marked should make a beautiful group in summer, and a brilliant one in autumn.

The pair of trees near the left-hand corner we would have the *Kolreuteria paniculata*.

The hemlock border on the left, opposite the dining-room bay window, is intended to form a close screen, to grow naturally till the trees occupy from seven to ten feet in width from the fence, when they are to be kept within bounds by pruning. They should be planted about two feet apart.

PLATE IX.

Plan for a Corner Lot 100 × 170 feet, planted in a more elaborate style than the preceding plan.

In describing the preceding plate, allusion was made to the greater expensiveness of this plan. Premising, therefore, that it is intended for a person who loves his trees and plants, and who can afford to keep a gardener in constant employ, we will

Plate IX.

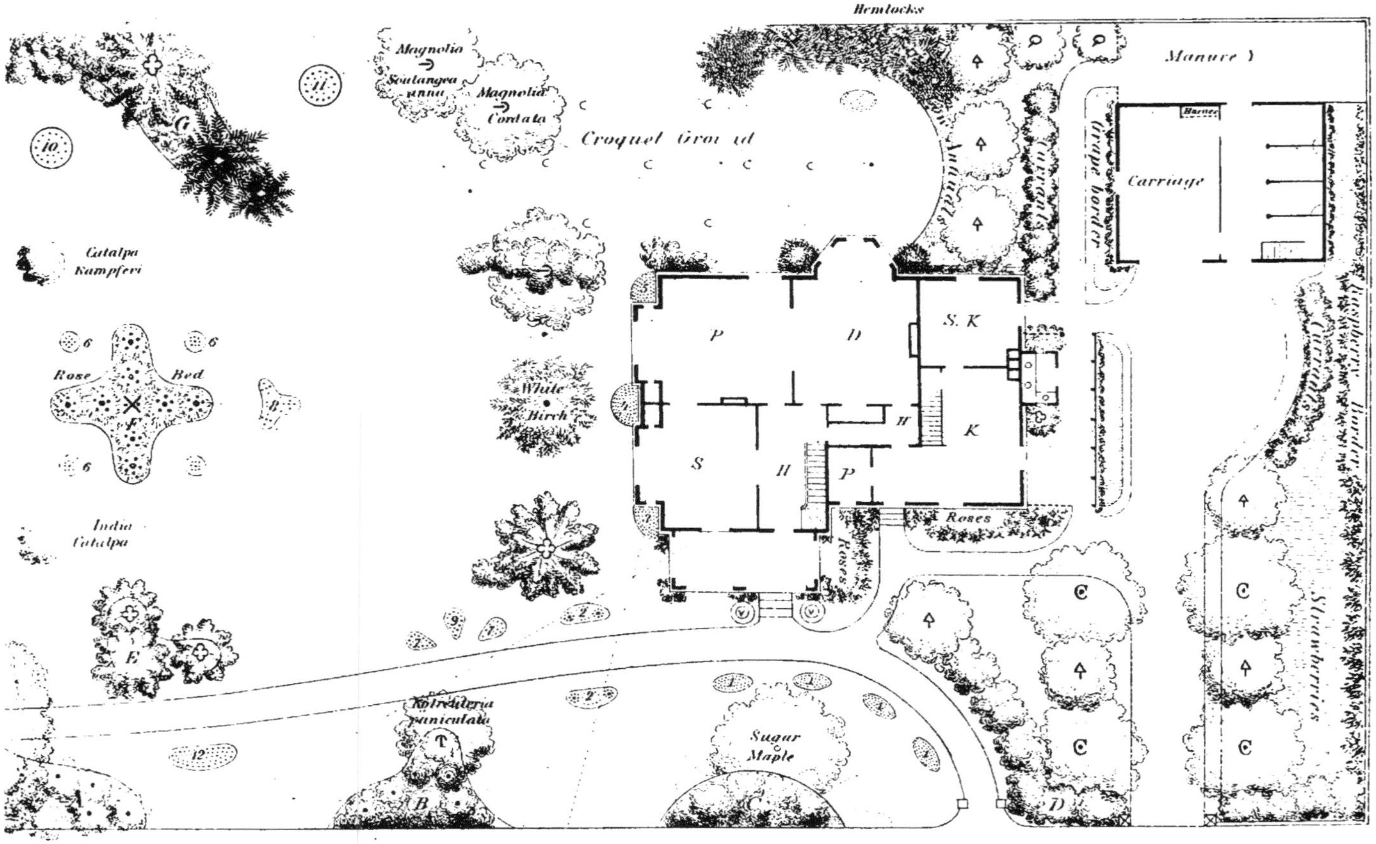

Raspberry Border
Currants
Strawberries
Manure
Carriage
Grape border
Currants
New Annuals
Hemlocks
S. K.
K.
Roses
Roses
D
H
P
Roses
S H
P
S
Croquet Ground
Magnolia
Soulangea purpurea
Magnolia Contata
White Birch
Sugar Maple
Hibiscus paniculata
B
Rose Bed
Catalpa Kampferi
India Catalpa
E

briefly describe those features of the place which need explanation.

The front entrance of the place (the one at the bottom of the page on the plate) is designed to have an elm tree arch over it, similar to that shown by Fig. 40 in Chapter XIV. The group A, on the right near the gate, may be entirely composed of rhodo dendrons.

The group E is composed of a pair of weeping silver-firs (nearest the gate), the mugho pine on the left, and the dwarf white pine, *P. compacta*, farthest from the gate.

Group B, on the right, will shade the walk with the low and broadly spreading top of the *Kolreuteria paniculata* at its point, behind which may be another group of rhododendrons, and close to the fence a compact border of hemlocks, which must be allowed to spread well upon the ground, and mingle their boughs with the rhododendrons, but not to exceed eight or ten feet in height.

The group C, with a sugar maple (in the place of which a pair of *Magnolia machrophyllas*, planted close together, might be substituted with good effect) in front of it, is to be composed of a circle of choice dwarf evergreens on the side next the house, backed by a hemlock border along the fence, as described for the preceding group.

From the following list a choice of dwarf evergreen trees or shrubs can be made : *Pinus strobus compacta, Pinus strobus pumila, Pinus sylvestris pumila, Pinus mughus, Picea pectinata compacta, Picea pectinata pendula, Picea hudsonica, Abies nigra pumila, Abies nigra pendula, Abies excelsa gregoriana, Abies excelsa inverta, Abies e. conica, Abies canadensis inverta, Abies canadensis parsoni, Andromeda floribunda,* tree-box, *Buxus arborea, Hypericum kalmianum* and *H. prolificum,* the kalmias, the creeping junipers *Juniperus repens, Juniperus repanda densa, J. succica, J. succica nana, J. hibernica, J. oblonga pendula, J. spæroides, Thuja aurea, Thuja occidentalis compacta, Taxus baccata aurea, Taxus erecta, Taxus baccata elegantissima, Cephalotaxus fortunii mascula, Taxus* or *Podocarpus japonica,* the rhododendrons, and the mahonias. For the sizes and characteristics of all these, we must refer the reader to the descriptions of

evergreen trees in Part II. By selecting the smallest evergreens
for the front of the group, and placing the larger ones behind, even
a small bed like this will accommodate a large number of specimens. The side towards the veranda is laid out in a formal
circle for convenience in first laying it out, but as the planting
progresses, and as it becomes desirable to add one small thing
after another to the group, this, as well as some of the other
groups, may be enlarged in the manner shown by the dotted lines ;
or, it can be laid out in that manner at first, if the list of small
choice evergreens to be purchased is large enough to fill it. Most
of the finer dwarf evergreens are rare and costly compared with
common sorts, so that the lists must be made with prudence, in
order that these, together with other more indispensable purchases
from the nurseries, shall not amount to so large a sum as to surprise and discourage the planter. Where the resources of the
proprietor will not permit him to procure at once everything that
can be advantageously used on the place, it is best to plant, the
first season, all the larger (which are usually the commoner and
cheaper) trees and shrubs, keeping the beds filled with showy
annuals, while acquiring, year by year, choice additional collections
of permanencies. But it is quite essential to the formation of
tasteful grounds that all the large permanent trees and shrubs be
placed properly in the beginning, so that whatever is afterwards
added will be of such subsidiary character as will group with and
around the former.

The group D, from the gate to the pear tree, should be composed of a mass of low evergreen trees or shrubs planted about six
feet from the walk ; and from the foot-walk gate to the carriage
gate with a hedge of Siberia arbor-vitæ planted two feet from the
fence. Between this hedge and the pear tree, at the intersection
of the walks, there will be room enough for the following : mugho
pine (*P. mughus*), the dwarf white pine (*P. s. compacta*), the *Cephalotaxus fortunii mascula*, the conical yew (*Taxus erecta*), the
golden yew (*Taxus aurea*), the golden arbor-vitæ (*Thuja aurea*),
Sargent's hemlock (*Abies canadensis inverta*), and the weeping
juniper (*J. oblonga pendula*). By alternating the dark and light
colored foliage of these evergreen shrubs, placing the dark ones

farther from the walk than the light ones, they will form an in.
teresting border, and in time a dense screen.

Fifteen feet from the end of the veranda towards the front
street, and twelve feet from the walk, a pine tree is indicated.
This may be either the common white pine, or the more beautiful
Bhotan pine, if one is willing to risk the permanence of the latter ;
—unless the soil of the locality is such that neither of these pines
will develop its beauty—in which case we would substitute either
Nordmanns fir (*Picea nordmaniana*), or some deciduous tree which
branches low. This tree is placed for the purpose of breaking
the view from the street to the veranda, so that persons sitting in
the latter will have a partial privacy from the street passers. If
the soil is deeply fertile, and not too dry, the *Magnolia soulangeana*
may be substituted for the pine, in climates not more severe than
that of New York city ; while further north the double white-flowering horse-chestnut, allowed to branch low, is admirably adapted to
the position. The white birch, in front of the centre line of the
house, should be the cut-leaved weeping variety, which is too
beautiful and appropriate to the place to allow anything else to be
substituted for it. The tree in front of the other corner of the
house, in the climate just mentioned, may be the *Magnolia
machrophylla;* in the northern States, any one of the following :
the red-flowering, or double white-flowering horse-chestnut, purple-
leaved beech, grape-leaved linden, the sugar, red-bud, Norway or
sycamore maple (especially the gold-leaved variety of the latter),
the oak-leaved mountain ash, or the tulip tree. While the tree is
young a group of shrubs may be planted on an irregular line with
the side of the house, so that the tree will form its centre, as shown
on the plan. The position of two magnolias on the left may be
determined by reference to the scale. In a region too cold, or a
soil too thin or dry for the magnolias, we would substitute a
group of three beeches—the weeping beech in the centre, the cut-
leaved nearest the house, and the purple-leaved nearest the street.
It will be observed that this side of the lot connects quite openly
with the adjoining lot—having few trees or shrubs on the margin.
If there is no division fence, or only a light and nearly invisible
one, and that lot is pleasingly improved, the views across it from

the parlor and dining-room windows will exhibit a generous expansion of lawn which it is desirable to secure ; and it will probably include in the view from them some embellishments which this place has not. If, however, there is anything unsightly in the neighbor lot, or any unfriendly disposition on the part of its owner that induces him to ignore the advantage of mutual views over each other's lawns, and to fence or plant to prevent it, that side may then be filled with masses of shrubbery in a manner similar to that shown on the left of Plate IV.

The group G, at the left, may be planted from the street to the pine with the strong growing old shrubs—lilacs, weigelas, honeysuckles, syringas, deutzias, etc., etc. Under, or rather near, the white or Austrian pine (the former pine if the soil is sandy, the latter if it is clayey), plant almost any of the yews, the Sargent hemlock, the *Hypericum kalmianum* and *H. prolificum*, the tree-box variety *angustifolia*, and the variegated-leaved elder, all of which flourish in the shade of other trees. At the upper extreme of the group plant the pendulous Norway spruce, *Abies excelsa inverta;* eight feet behind it the common Norway spruce, and between this and the pine the Chinese cypress, *Glypto-strobus sinensis pendula*, and some of the evergreen shrubs just named.

The belt of hemlocks against the fence, opposite the dining-room bay-window, is to be terminated at the front by a slender weeping silver-fir, *Picea pectinata pendula*. The trees at the two corners of the dining-room bay are intended for Irish junipers, or the weeping juniper, *J. oblonga pendula*. Other trees and shrubs are designated on the plan, and need no explanation.

There are many small flower-beds on the plan, and one quite large rose-bed in the middle of the front at F. The latter is to have an elegant rose-pillar, or a substantial trellis in the centre, with groups of roses of varieties graded to diminish in size to the points. Or, if preferred, this may be a group of evergreens with the slender weeping silver-fir for a centre, and lower trees and dwarfs around it, so as to form the same figure of a cross. This will, in time, be more beautiful throughout the greater part of the year than the rose-bed, but the latter can be made far more brilliant in summer. Yet the rude, briary appearance of rose-

Plate X.

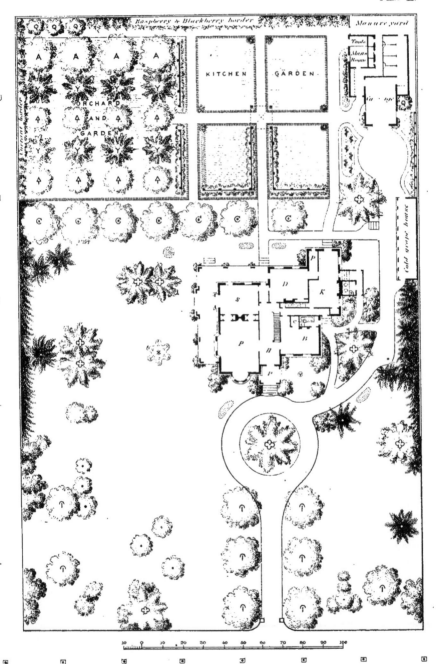

Raspberry & Blackberry border

Manure yard

KITCHEN GARDEN

ORCHARD AND GARDEN

Currant border

Cold grape house

Tools
Ahaux
Room

10 0 10 20 30 40 50 60 70 80 90 100

bushes, after the leaves fall, is a serious objection to them when compared with the cheerful elegance of a well-formed evergreen group at all seasons of the year. The other flower-beds are small, and of the simplest forms. Beds 1, 1, 1, 1 should be filled in spring with bulbous flowers, and later with verbenas, portulaccas, *Phlox drummondi*, escholtzias, or similar low plants. Beds 2, 2 may have three geraniums in each, the largest variety in the middle. Beds 3 and 5, in the wall-corners, should have some little evergreen vines, say English or Irish ivies, planted in the extreme corner, with heliotrope and mignonette around them. Bed 4 may be planted as suggested in the description of Plate VIII. Beds 6, 6, 6, 6 may be filled with four varieties of cannas of about equal height; 7, 7, and 9 with low bulbs in spring, and later with gladiolii in the centre and petunias or other flowers of similarly brilliant and abundant bloom, around them. Bed 8 to have a mountain-of-snow geranium, or a *Wigandia caracasana* in the centre, and three robust plants of *Colleus verschafelti* on the points ; 10 is a mass of cannas ; 11 may be a bed of hollyhocks, with a tall sort in the centre, and low varieties around it. We have merely suggested the flowers for the various beds as a starting-point for persons unfamiliar with flowers. Most intelligent ladies, as well as gardeners, are more familiar with flower culture than with any other gardening art, and will be able to vary the beds from year to year, and to improve on the selections here given. They will also learn by experiment, better than they can be told, the best materials to use in embellishing with flowers and wreathing leaves, the vases near the entrance steps.

PLATE X.

A Simple Plan for Planting an Interior Lot two hundred feet front and three hundred feet deep.

This plan represents a large mansion on an in-lot two hundred feet front by three hundred feet deep. Plate XI is the same house and lot treated more elaborately. The same differences, carried out on a larger scale, may be observed between these two plans of

grounds, as between those of Plates VIII and IX ; the one here
described having a less extent of drive, walks, and ornamental
plantations than the plan shown by Plate XI.   All the surroundings are supposed to be the same, and the different modes of laying
out the grounds are meant to represent simply the different tastes
or means of occupants.   Here the proprietor is supposed to desire
grounds of the most simple character, which will be at the same
time suitable to the mansion and the lot.   The entrance road,
turnway, and drive to the stable are the most direct and simple
that can be made ; and they constitute also the only entrance
walks to the house.   Ninety feet of the rear of the lot is devoted
to utilities, viz.: to carriage-house conveniences, to a kitchen-
garden, and an orchard ; the ground in the latter being also devoted to culture for small fruits and vegetables until the fruit trees
are large enough to shadow the whole ground.   The front two
hundred and ten feet, is all devoted to the house and its ground
embellishments.   The drive is ten feet in width ; the circle around
which it turns is thirty feet in diameter.   An avenue of three elm
trees on each side of the entrance-drive are its only decorations,
though the street-trees in a line with them will give it the appearance of an avenue of eight instead of six trees.   In the centre of
the circle a pine tree is designated—to be a white pine if the soil
is sandy, otherwise an Austrian.   These trees are chosen because
they are of rapid and healthy growth, and cast their lower branches
as they grow large, so that the lawn beneath them, while it is
deeply shadowed, is not destroyed, and the view under the
branches is unobstructed.   This will be rather an objection than
a merit with those persons who desire the main entrance to be
quite secluded and concealed from view.   We would recommend
for them that the circle be planted with a group of firs, whose
branches rest upon the ground during all stages of their growth,
and would eventually cover the whole circle with an impenetrable mass of foliage.   A single Norway spruce planted in
the centre will do this.   So, probably, would a Nordmanns fir,
Picea nordmaniana.   While these trees are small, the borders of
the circle (supposing it to be desirable to shut out the view of the
approach road from the porch) may be planted, four feet from the

road, with quick growing deciduous shrubs, such as bush honeysuckles, lilacs, weigelas, deutzias, etc., which can be removed when
the centre tree begins to crowd them. Or, with one of the same
large evergreens in the centre, a gardenesque border may be
formed around the circle with single specimens of rare dwarf
evergreens, planted four feet from the road. Doubtless the noblest
feature of such a turn circle is a single great spreading tree
like a mature white oak or American chestnut, and if the proprietor appreciates the pleasures of hope, and desires the greatest
simplicity of effect, he had better plant the latter. We have seen
specimens of the American chestnut of colossal size, which men
now living remember as sprouts.

A lot so large as this must needs have a ground-plan of the
planting made on a large scale, and as it is extremely difficult to
carry out any system of planting for such a place from a verbal
description, we shall not attempt to describe in detail all the
materials that form the plantation, but make merely a rough
inventory of its properties. Though it is an in-lot, and in the
main designed without connection with adjoining lots, from which
it is shown to be separated by high fences or walls and shrubbery
to within sixty or seventy feet of the street, yet on this front space
we have left openings on each side for connections with adjoining
grounds. Back of this, each side of the lot is bounded by screens
of evergreens. On the right of the drive to the carriage-house is
a cold grape-house. The house-front is supposed to be to the
east, so that this grapery has a southern exposure. It may seem
to have no border for the roots of the grape vines, if it is supposed
that the road in its front has been made by excavating all the
good soil and substituting broken stone and gravel only. But we
would not have this done. For a road-bed, or for a grape border,
the drainage must be equally deep and effective. That being
secured we would make the road-bed of the best grape soil, and
pave over it with stone, after the "Belgian" and "Medina" pavement manner, at least as far as the length of the grape house ;
using no more sand or gravel than is necessary to bed or fill in
between the stone. Of course this bed will rise and fall by the
freezing and thawing of the soil beneath, but this will do no

harm. The rich soil of the pavement-bed will also start vegetation between the stones, but on so narrow a road, in constant use, the extra labor required to keep the surface clean is inconsiderable. On the other hand the pavement acts as a cooling mulch in summer and the contrary in winter—it equalizes both the temperature and moisture of the roots, and by the reflection of heat from its surface, adds to the heating power of the sun's rays in maturing the grapes within. Were the road-bed not made suitable feeding ground for the roots of the vines within, such a position for a grapery would of course be impracticable; but when thus prepared it becomes the most advantageous for the production of good grapes, as well as convenient of access. Beyond the cold grape-house the fence is made use of for training hardy grape vines. On the left is a bed designed for growing Delaware grapes on stakes, at first, with the intention of making them eventually into self-sustaining low trees. On and near the garden-walk from the back veranda are also trellises and an arbor for hardy grapes. A row of seven cherry trees planted one hundred feet from the back line of the lot forms a sort of dividing line between the decorative and the utilitarian parts of the lot. The orchard-rows back of it, when the trees are well-grown, will, however, add much to the pleasant character of the vistas from the front street, and need not be out of harmony with the groupings on the lawn in front of them. While the trees are small, and the ground cultivated in garden crops, it may be desirable to have a grape-trellis or an arbor-vitæ hedge-screen midway between the rows of cherry and pear trees, or a bed of tall and massy annuals; but after ten years the effect will be better if there is no division between the lawn and the orchard.

PLATE XI.

A Plan for a First Class Suburban Home on a Lot two hundred feet front and three hundred feet deep.

This plan differs from the *country* residence of a retired citizen in this, that it is a home which does not include orchards, pastures, and meadows, but is devoted to the development of sylvan beauty

Plate XI.

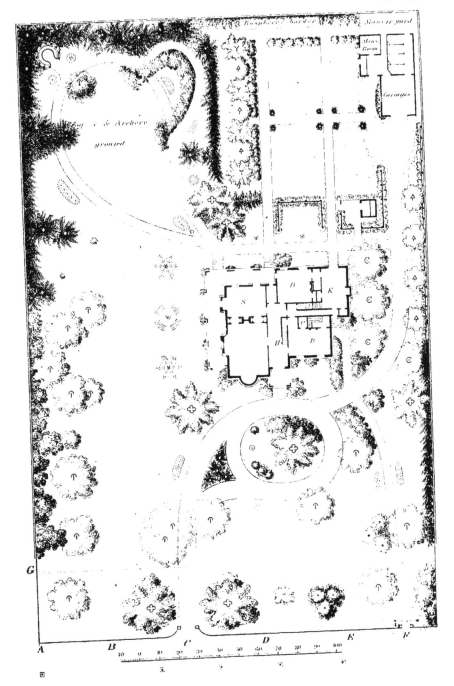

rather than pecuniary utilities, or farm conveniences. It is a suitable home for a family of cultivated people, with ample means, and rural tastes.

The orchard which takes an important place in the preceding plan is here omitted, to make a more extensive lawn and a fine pleasure-walk. The entrance-drive is more expensive than in the preceding plan, and a side entrance walk is added. In dispensing with an orchard we have endeavored to introduce in other places enough fruit trees to supply the family with those kinds of fruit which it is most indispensable to have on one's own place. It will be seen that there are four cherry trees on the north (right) side of the house; four pear trees along the border leading to the carriage house, three more on the left-hand border of the kitchen-garden, and four peach trees. Some of the groups in other parts of the grounds may now and then include a fruit tree. Apple and pear trees, Siberian crabs and quinces, which harmonize well with some of the purely ornamental trees, may be introduced in sufficient numbers in this way to furnish a good supply of summer fruits. The north fence back of the evergreen-screen is a continuous trellis for hardy grapes. Grape trellises also occupy the ends of two divisions of the kitchen-garden back of the house. If a grape-house is added, it may occupy either the place indicated on the preceding plan, or be built with its back to the walk on the left of the garden, and facing the left. In this case a few of the trees there would be omitted, and a slight change made in the arrangement beyond. Raspberries can be grown in abundance on the border next the back fence, strawberries under the growing fruit trees, and currants on the walks where designated. The kitchen-garden is certainly small for so fine a place, being but 60 × 80 feet, including the central-walks; but this space, if well used for those things only which can be better grown than bought, will produce a greater amount of vegetables than many persons suppose; and in addition to this space permanently dedicated to such things, room will be found for many years on the borders and among the young trees of a plantation to grow many vegetables which are by no means unsightly. In fact, such plants as beets, carrots, parsnips, cabbages, and sea-kale, all of which have foliage

12

of great· beauty and are of low growth, can occasionally be grown
to advantage, to cover ground which needs cultivation, in places
where they will fill in with as good effect as flowering annuals.   A
good gardener can also grow strawberries with profit in young
shrubbery plantations, where their presence will not be noticed.

Let us now suppose ourselves in the street on the side-walk
at A.   From that corner the house and grounds will be seen to
good advantage, but the finest lines of view on the latter will be
obtained further to the right.   At the point B, the whole length of
the lawn to the evergreen boundaries and shrubby groups of the
croquet and archery ground is an unbroken expanse, margined
on the left by varied groups of trees with clear stems, whose
shadows fleck, but do not interrupt the view ; behind these, masses
of large flowering shrubs form continuous bays and projections of
foliage that rest upon the lawn ; while on the right, in the distance,
glimpses of the pleasure-walk, now open, now lost to sight behind
verdant arches and projecting groups, and nearer, the long vine-
covered front of the veranda, and the light colors of many flower-
beds in dark bays or on open lawn—altogether, will give from
this point of view an impression of beauty and extent not often
realized on less than an acre and a half.   Nor will the view be less
pleasing from the main entrance at C, for from this point the trees
and the shrubbery on the left are seen to better advantage, and
the evergreen groups, summer-house, and flower-beds of the far
corner come into view.   From D and E the views are shorter, but
take in a variety of groups and single trees which will be more or
less interesting according to the choice of materials in planting,
and the luxuriance with which they are grown.   Glimpses may
also be seen from these points of the long lawn and the flower-
beds on the south side of the house.   At F, over the gateway, we
would have a hemlock arch like some of those shown in Chapter
XIV.   Standing under this arch, narrow openings between shrubs
and trees give a glimpse directly in front, margined by low beds of
flowers, of the fruit trees and vines that border the drive down to
the carriage-house front ; which should, of course, be designed to
form a pleasing centre of this vista.   The views will also be pleasing in every direction as one walks along towards the house.   On

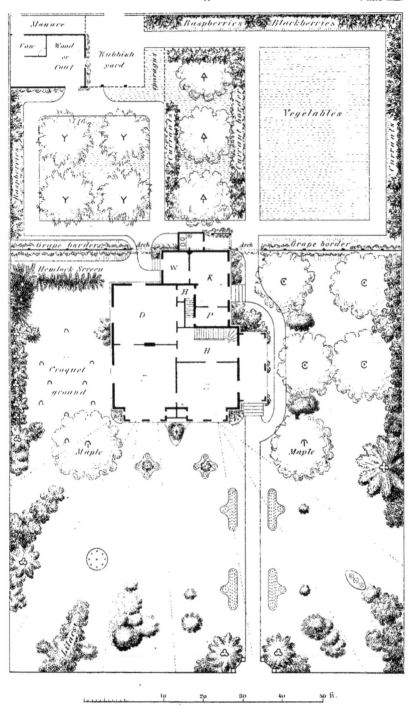

Manure

Cow | Wood or Coal

Rubbish yard

Raspberries

Currant border

Currant border

Raspberries & Blackberries

Vegetables

Currants

Currants

Grape border

Arch

Arch

Grape border

Hemlock Screen

W

K

H

D

H

P

H

C

C

C

C

Croquet ground

Maple

Maple

Lilacs

10   20   30   40   50 ft.

the line G, H, between thirty and forty feet from the street, an open line of lawn is maintained with a view to reciprocity of vistas with the smaller front grounds of adjoining neighbors.

As remarked of the preceding plan, this design embraces too much for verbal description, and should be planted after a well-considered working plan. But there is one small feature to which we would call attention, viz.: the triangular piece between the entrance-road and turn-ways. This is marked to be planted with fir trees, to grow into a dense mass, in order to counteract as far as possible, by its shadows and the depth of its verdure, the bare exposure of the surrounding roads. The centre tree should be the Norway spruce, and the others surrounding it, hemlocks.

A careful examination of the plan will, we trust, supersede the necessity of any further description.

PLATE XII.

An Inside Lot one hundred feet front, and one hundred and sixty feet deep.

Reference was made to this plate in descriptions of Plates VIII and IX, the house-plan and the lot, in form and size, being nearly the same ; this plan being an in-lot with no carriage-house and stable, and the others being corner lots with these conveniences. The lot here represented is supposed to have an alley on the rear end, and to front on the south side of an east and west street. This gives the bay-window front of the house a northern exposure. A great advantage, in the outlook from the windows, results from this exposure, viz.: that one sees the sunny-side of all the shrubbery in the front grounds, and thus has the satisfaction of finding his verdant pets always in a smiling humor. The house is sixty feet from the front street, and about the same depth in the rear end of the lot is devoted to the kitchen-garden, fruits, and cow, wood and coal-house ; this part being separated from the part devoted to lawn by a grape-trellis and border. Near the street the neighbors' lots are supposed to offer satisfactory openings where indicated by the upper dotted lines on each side. The groups of shrubbery are placed so as to illustrate many of the suggestions of the rules given in Chapter XI. No long vista of lawn is possible, but the groups and single specimens of shrubs or dwarf trees, with a few bedding-plants and flower-beds, if properly chosen, and planted in conformity with the plan, and well grown, will hardly fail to make a yard of superior attractiveness; especially pleasing as seen from the bay-windows;—the arrangement having been made with reference to the effect from them.

Description.—Let us begin at the front-entrance gate, from which a walk four feet wide leads straight to the veranda entrance, and a walk three feet in width to the kitchen entrance. On each side the front gate arbor-vitæ trees (the Siberian) are designated, with low masses of evergreen shrubs between them and the fence. An opening to a straight walk like this is especially appropriate for a verdant arch, and if the proprietor has the patience to grow one, the substitution of the hemlock for the arbor-vitæ is recommended. For an arch, the trees should not be planted more than two feet away from the walk.

The only large trees on this plan are a pair of maples, about twelve feet, diagonally, from the corners of the veranda and main house respectively; a white or Austrian pine on the right border, four cherry trees in the right-side yard, and the pear trees in the kitchen-garden department. The maples may be the purple-leaved, and the golden-leaved varieties of the sycamore maple. A hemlock screen or hedge bounds the croquet ground on the south; at the corner are a few Norway spruces; next, in front, a group of arbor-vitæs; then a continuous hedge of the same for twenty feet, terminated by a group of arbor-vitæs and yews chosen to exhibit contrasts of color.

The group on the left, between the upper dotted lines, is to be composed of a variety of strong growing common shrubs, with a Lawson's cypress or a Nordmanns fir, or the Chinese cypress, *Glypto-strobus sinensis,* where the symbol of the arbor-vitæ is shown. Towards the street from that tree we would put in ever-green shrubs only.

The lilac group in front may embrace all the finest varieties of that family—the common white and Charles the Tenth varieties near the centre; the chionanthus-leaved next towards the house; the Chinese red, *Rothamagensis rubra*, next; the Persian white, *Persica alba*, next; the dwarf, *Syringa nana*, at the point; and the Chinese purple and white for the two wings of the group. Near the fence we would plant a few common bush honeysuckles, as the dust from the street has a less injurious effect on their foliage than on that of the lilacs.

The central front group, to the right of the lilac group, may be:—a purple fringe tree nine feet from the fence, and in succession from it, towards the house, the pink-flowering honeysuckle, *Lonicera grandiflora*, five feet from the fringe tree; the *Deutzia crenata rubra*, four feet further; and at the point, the *Deutzia gracilis*, four feet from the latter. The shrub on the right may be Gordon's flowering currant.

The single small trees on each side the entrance, twelve feet from the front, and fifteen feet from the middle of the walk, may be, one the weeping silver-fir, and the other the weeping Norway spruce, grown as slenderly as possible. The shrubs towards the fence, under and next to the fir tree on the right, may be hardy varieties of dwarf evergreens or a bed of mahonias.

The group in the right-hand corner may have at its point towards the house a bed for cannas, or other showy-leaved plants; next to it the Chinese purple magnolia; back of that the *Magnolia soulangeana*, grown low, or a weeping Japan sophora, and between it and the front, a bed of rhododendrons, or two or three mugho pines; the projecting shrub on the left to be the dwarf white pine, *P. strobus compacta*.

The side border, under and near to the large pine, we would have a bed of rhododendrons; next to these, towards the street, the evergreen shrub, *Cephalotaxus fortunii mascula*, and for the point in front of it, the golden yew. Along the fence, above the pine, the border may be composed of the finest collection of hardy evergreen shrubs that the proprietor can afford; or, if they are too expensive, or too long in developing their beauties, the border may be made almost as satisfactory with common deciduous shrubs.

The groups in front of the veranda, between the cherry trees, and those against the house, may be composed of shrubs which are family favorites, or with annual and perennial flowering plants of graded sizes. The flower-beds adjacent to the main walk are for low-growing plants only. The two small bushes behind the flower-beds nearest the gate are to be, one the golden arbor-vitæ, and the other the golden yew ; and in the rear of the next flower-bed on the right, an Irish juniper is intended. Between the bay-windows a weeping juniper, *J. oblonga pendula*, or the weeping Norway spruce, *Abies e. inverta*, may be planted, or the bed may be occupied as described for Plate VIII. The beds directly in front of the bay-windows can be different each year, with such plants as some of the medium-sized cannas, the *Wigandia caracasana*, the *Nicoteana atropurpurea grandiflora*, and the Japanese maize for the centre plant, and round, bushy-headed plants, like the geraniums and the *Colleus verschafelti*, for the projecting parts of the beds.

Since the engraving has been completed, we perceive that the kitchen department of this lot—that back of the grape-trellis—might be more advantageously planned, but as we cannot now correct it, the reader's ingenuity must be exercised to improve it.

Plate XIII.

A Plan of the Grounds for a Commodious House with a side-entrance porch, on an Inside Lot having a front of one hundred and sixty feet on the street, and a depth of three hundred and eight feet.

The front of the main veranda of the house is seventy feet from the street ; the distance from the porch-front to the side of the lot is sixty-five feet, and the space between the house and the right-hand side of the lot is forty feet. This is a very desirable form of lot. It allows of a long reach of lawn on the entrance-side, and sufficient openness on all sides to be in keeping with so large a house ; while there is ample room for stable and carriage-house conveniences, fruit trees, and a vegetable garden.

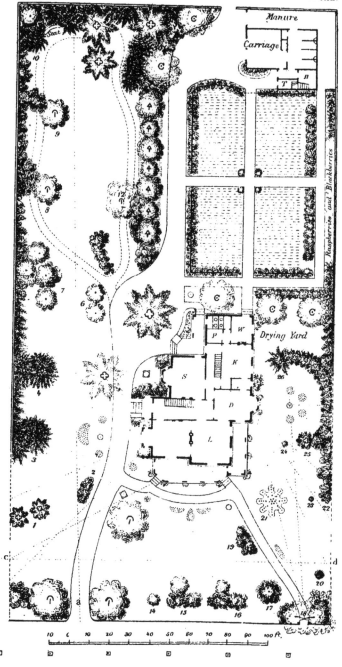

Plate XIII.

This is the first plan that shows a residence with its carriage-porch and main entrance on the side—an arrangement that economizes space to great advantage on narrow lots, and enables the architect to have more liberty in the arrangement and exposure of the principal rooms, and to make more pleasing views from their windows over the grounds.* It will be seen that the turn-way of the carriage-road is partly back of the house, around a circular grass plat twenty feet in diameter, in the centre of which is a pine tree. The drive turns close to the back veranda, where a platform-step is provided for easy ingress and egress from carriages. This is likely to be the carriage-porch of the family when unaccompanied by friends. Beyond the turn, the road is straight along the trellised boundary of the kitchen-garden, and widens with abundant space in front of the carriage-house. Near the rear of the lot. are a few cherry and peach trees ; back of the drying-yard and kitchen are others. A row of pear trees on the left of the main drive are enough to furnish a summer and autumn supply of this delicious fruit ; while in other portions of the grounds, apples and crab apple trees may be introduced as parts of groups. Of the small fruits the garden plan shows an ample provision.

The purely decorative portion of the place may be in part described as follows :—beginning at the carriage-entrance. This starts from the middle of the opening between two street trees, and is flanked on either side simply by a pair of trees of any fine variety of elms or maples, chestnuts, horse-chestnuts, oaks or beeches, to be planted ten feet from the fence, and the same distance from the drive. While they are young the ground for a radius of six feet around them should be kept in cultivation, and planted on its outer margin with such deciduous shrubs as flowering-currants, purple berberries, variegated-leaved elder, privet, glossy-leaved viburnum, common bush honeysuckles, or whatever else will grow in partial shade, not exceeding six or seven feet in height, and with branches bending to the grass. When the trees are ten or fifteen years

---

* We cannot commend this house plan as particularly adapted to the lot. *The plan for the grounds grew up around the house as a thing already fixed.* The latter is designed to meet the wants of a man of " bookish " tastes, as well as wealth, who needs a fine library-room separate from the family room.

planted, all these must be removed.   Or the groups of shrubbery
around these trees may be composed entirely of rhododendrons if
the proprietor can afford it.   The group to the left, adjoining the
neighbor-lot, is intended as a continuation of the group around the
left-hand gateway tree, and may be composed of similar shrubs of
larger growth.   The two small pine trees farther up on the left,
marked 1, are to be the mugho and dwarf white pines—the latter
towards the house.   The group of shrubs (2) between these and
the carriage-way, and near the latter, should be choice small hardy
evergreens—say, for the centre, the weeping juniper, *J. oblonga
pendula*, or the erect yew, *Taxus erecta;* each side of this, on a line
parallel with the road, and three feet from the centre, the golden
arbor-vitæ, and the golden yew ; at the ends, and three feet from
the latter, plant the dwarf silver-fir, *Picea pectinata compacta*, and
the dwarf spruce, *Abies gregoriana.* · Outside the line of these,
and midway of the spaces between them, plant the pygmy spruce,
the dwarf black spruce, the dwarf Swedish juniper, the juniper
repanda densa, the trailing juniper *repens*, and the *Daphne
cneorum*.   The first pair of fir trees on the left, next the fence (3),
may be, one the Norway, and the other the oriental spruce.   The
border along the fence is to be of hemlocks ; the next pair of firs
(4) may be the cephalonian fir, nearest the fence, and the Nordmanns fir ten feet in advance of it.   The pine tree (5) opposite the
bay-window of the room marked S, is improperly placed there.   It
should be fifteen feet further towards the front of the lot ; and is
intended for the Bhotan pine.   The two small trees on the left (6),
opposite the turn-circle, are a pair of Judas trees.   The group of
four trees next the fence (7) may be a pair of sassafras in the
middle ; a weeping Japan sophora nearest the house, and the
white-flowering dogwood farthest from the house.   An under-
growth nearest to the fence may be made with the red-twigged dogwood, *Cornus alba*, the flowering-currants, and the variegated-leaved
elder ; and the border continued to the rear corner with common
and well-known shrubs.   No. 8 is for a *Kolreuteria paniculata*,
connected by overarching shrubs with the side-border ; 9 is a
weeping beech ; 10, 10, masses of hemlocks ; the tree in the far
corner an Austrian pine ; 11 a white pine, and behind it an

Austrian pine ; and hemlocks and white pines fill the border towards the carriage-house.

On the right of the lawn the fruit trees are sufficiently symbolized. At 12, a purple beech ; at 13, a group of the choicest shrubs increasing in size as they recede from the house. For the point nearest the carriage-road the *Andromeda floribunda* is well suited ; eighteen inches behind it the *Deutzia gracilis;* the same distance from that, two plants side by side and one foot apart from the *Rhododendron roseum elegans;* then pairs of plants of rhododendrons in the following order, *R. album candidissima, R. grandiflorum gloriosum;* and beyond them, for the end of the bed, Sargent's hemlock, or the pendulous Norway spruce, *A. e. inverta;* or, the weeping silver-fir, *Picea p. pendula.* The group at the turn of the carriage-road, and on a line with the pear trees, may be composed of any good common shrubs of large size, being careful to place those which grow bare at the bottom in the rear of those whose foliage bends gracefully to the ground. The bed adjoining the rear veranda is for the choice small pet-flowers of the lady of the house, whatever they may be.

On the front, the large tree to the right of the carriage-road, nearest the house, is intended for the cut-leaved weeping birch, or a pair of them planted but a few feet apart. At 14 may be a single plant of the old red tartarian honeysuckle, grown in rich ground and allowed to spread upon the lawn. At 15, on the end towards the house, a Japan weeping sophora grafted not more than seven feet high ; in the middle, on the side towards the street, the *Andromeda arborea;* and on either side of that the *Deutzias crenata alba,* and *Crenata rubra.* At 16, towards the house, the broad-leaved strawberry tree *Enonymus latifolius;* on the left of the group the *Weigela rosea;* four feet to the right of it the *Weigela amabalis;* four feet to the right again, the *Weigela arborea grandiflora;* and at the right end of the group, the great-leaved snow-ball, *Viburnum machrophyllum;* and between these and the strawberry tree, the dwarf snow-ball, *Viburnum anglicum.* At 17 plant the great-leaved magnolia, *M. machrophyllum.* At 18 we would make a flat pine tree arch over the gateway, as suggested in Chapter XIV. At 19 is a bed of

shrubs that should be always in high condition, as it is conspicuous from every point of view. We will suggest for its point
nearest the house the *Spirea callosa alba;* then the *Deutzia gracilis;* next, two feet from the former, the *Spirea reevesi flore plena;*
next (in the middle line of the bed), the *Spirea callosa fortunii,* with
a *Daphne cneorum* on each side of it to cover its nakedness near
the ground ; and for the end of the bed nearest the entrance-gate,
the Chinese red, or the Chinese purple magnolia. Or this bed
may be filled with evergreen shrubs or shrubby trees alone, as
follows: for the point nearest the house, the *Daphne cneorum;* near,
and behind it, the *Andromeda floribunda;* next, two feet from the
former, a pair of rhododendrons, *Roseum elegans* and *Album candidissima;* next, in the middle, a single rhododendron, *gloriosum,*
with a rhododendron, *everestianum,* on each side of it ; next, in the
centre line of the bed, the *Cephalotaxus fortunii mascula;* and for
the end of the bed next the street the golden yew, or the. golden
arbor-vitæ. No. 20 is the weeping juniper, *Oblonga pendula* ; 21 is
a grand rose-bed ; 22, a belt of common shrubs ; 23, an Irish
juniper; •24, a Swedish juniper ; 25, Siberian arbor-vitæs, continued as a high hedge around to 26, where it is terminated by a
Nordmanns fir. In the centre of the semicircle which this hedge
is intended to describe, and on a line with the centre of the dining-
room, is to be an elegant vase for flowers ; and four circular beds
for low brilliant flowers are intended to make the view from the
bay-window more pleasing. The very small shrubs at the corners
of that bay-window represent Irish junipers.

The flower-beds in this plan need not be described in detail
Quite a number of vases are marked on the plan, but they are not
essential to the good effect of the planting, though pleasing additions if well chosen and well filled.

Fig. 43 is a view of the house on this plan, taken from a point
on the street line fifty or sixty feet to the left of this lot, looking
across a portion of the neighbor-lot, and its light division fence.
The architect having kindly furnished a sketch of the house without any reference to the grounds, we have endeavored to sketch
the sylvan features as shown on the ground-plan, from the same
point of view ; but it is quite impossible in small engravings to do

FIG. 43.

HARLEY SC.

justice to the pleasing effects of such plantations. Photographic
views occasionally give exquisite effects of parts of embellished
grounds, but even these fail to convey a correct impression of the
accessories of the central point of view.   It is quite certain that a
place planted (and well kept) in the manner indicated by this plate
and description, will be far prettier than any picture of it that can
be engraved.

PLATES XIV AND XV.

Two Methods of Planting a small Corner-Lot.

In these two plates we desire to illustrate two modes of treating a village corner lot of fifty feet front, where the small depth of
the lot, or other circumstances, requires the house to be placed
quite near the front street.   The house plans resemble each other
in form, though it will be seen that the one on Plate XIV is set
but five steps above the level of the ground, and has its kitchen
and dining-room on the main floor, while the plan on Plate XV
is a city basement house, with kitchen and dining-room under the
bed-room and parlor, the main floor being raised ten steps above
the street.   The two ground plans (by which we mean plans of
the grounds) differ essentially in this, that the first has one side-
wall of the house directly on the street, so as to throw its narrow
strip of lawn, and embellishments, on the inside of the lot, away
from the side-street ; while on Plate XV the entire length of the
house on that side is supposed to be a party-wall, as if it were
part of a block, or one of a pair of houses.

GROUND PLAN OF PLATE XIV.—The veranda front is but
eight feet from the street.   Unless the approach-steps are of a
character less plain than those shown on the plan, little can be
done to decorate this narrow space.   The veranda can be covered
with vines, and a strip three feet wide in front of it may be devoted to choice flowers ; but we would advise to have nothing
there but the vines and the lawn.   On each the steps we
would plant either the tree-box, the golden yew, the golden arbor-

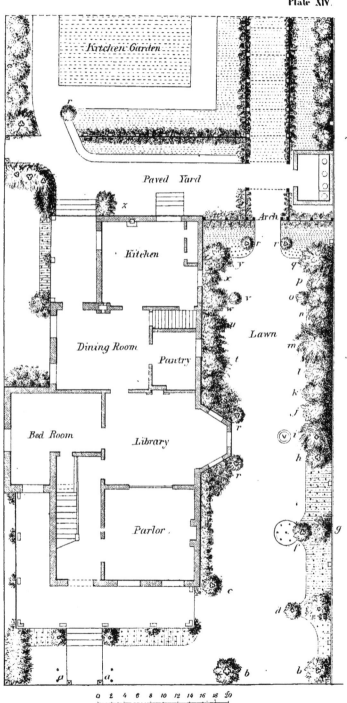

Plate XIV.

Kitchen Garden

Paved Yard

Arch

SIDE STREET.

Kitchen

Dining Room

Pantry

Lawn

Bed Room

Library

Parlor

Scale 16 feet 1 Inch.

vitæ, or the arborescent English ivy. If the front were to the north or east, and the soil a moist, friable loam, a very elegant sylvan arch might be made in time by planting six hemlock trees; two in the corners just described, and four inside the gate—two on each side, and but a foot apart, as shown by the dots at *a, a.* Two of these could be made to grow into an arch over the gate, and the others to form two arches at right angles to the first, on each side of the walk. This would only be practicable, however, in case the town authorities will allow the trees nearest the gate to develop into the street; but with four feet additional width in front of the veranda, it would be feasible without such privilege. In the left corner of the front, a Siberian arbor-vitæ screen is intended. The veranda on the left is intended to be partially inclosed between the posts with lattice-work, and covered with vines—there being just room enough between the veranda-foundation and the street line for the protection of their roots.

Let us now turn to the narrow lawn-strip on the right; a space but twenty feet wide and seventy feet deep to the arch-entrance of the grape-arbor and kitchen-garden on a line with the rear of the house. Midway of this strip the bay-window projects. The two objects to be kept in view in laying out this bit of a lawn are, first, to make the most pleasing out-look from the bay-window; and, second, the most pleasing in-look from the street. It is assumed that there is no desirable connection to be made with the lot on the right, so that a fence necessarily bounds the view on that side. We must suppose also that there is no house built, or likely to be built, up to that line, otherwise it would not be sensible to place the house on the street-side of the lot, but rather in the manner shown by Plate XV.

The close fence, back to opposite the bay-window, should be covered with English ivy if it can be made to grow there. Unless the exposure is due south, there ought to be little difficulty in getting the ivy to cover the fence if the owner will take the trouble to have it thatched over with straw on the approach of winter, and the base well mulched. A fence in such a place, if of wood, must be a neat piece of work, and well painted. Ivy will not creep up painted wood. We would therefore make a kind of trellis from post to post on the inside of the fence, and put down small sticks with the bark on, by the side of the ivy roots. These should be inside the trellis-bars, and reach nearly to the top of the fence, and be fastened there. The plants will readily climb these sticks and soon hide them from sight. In a few seasons, if they have been safely preserved through the first winter,* the branching arms of the ivy will extend over the bars of the trellis, and by their radiating growth soon weave a self-sustaining wall of verdure. By the time the barky sticks decay, the ivy will have no need of their support. This ivy-wall being the right flank of our little lawn, it is essential that it be well planted.

At the street front of this lawn are two Siberian arbor-vitæs *b, b,* shown on the plan of a size they are likely to attain in about five years after planting. Doubtless at first these alone will leave the front too open, but in ten years they will be all this part of the place will require.

To return to the lawn : *c* is the weeping juniper, *J. oblonga pendula; d,* an Irish juniper ; *e,* a pendulous Norway spruce, *Abies e. inverta; f,* a golden arbor-vitæ ; *g,* the weeping silver-fir, *Picea pectinata pendula ;* on one side of the latter may be planted the dwarf silver-fir, *Picea pectinata compacta,* and on the other the *Picea hudsonica.* The dotted circle projecting into the lawn in front of the arbor-vitæ is for any showy bulbous or bedding-plants which will not spread much beyond the limits of the bed. At *h,* plant Parson's American arbor-vitæ, *Thuja occidentalis compacta ;* at *i,* another pendulous Norway spruce ; in front of it a vase ; at *j, k,* and *l,* three bushy rhododendrons ; or, the golden yew, *Taxus aurea,* the erect yew, *Taxus erecta,* and the juniper, *Repanda densa.* At *m,* Sargent's hemlock, *Abies canadensis inverta ; n, Andromeda floribunda* and *Daphne cneorum.* At *o* and *v,* plant a pair of *Deutzia gracilis,* or showy bedding plants; or fine conservatory plants in boxes, buried ;—plants of gorgeous foliage to be preferred : back of *o,* the weeping arbor-vitæ ; at *p,* the purple-leaved berberry ; *q, Weigela amabalis ; r, r, r, r,* Irish or Swedish junipers.

---

* The first winter or two, these sticks may be turned down along the fence with the ivy upon them for greater ease in protecting the latter.

Near the arch entering the garden, two Bartlett pear trees may be substituted for them; but in this case the grape vines on the trellis will be rendered barren as soon as the trees grow to shade them. As the pear trees will probably furnish the most valuable crop and form a not inappropriate feature, there will be no impropriety in using them. The plants for the side of the house will depend somewhat on its exposure. The following list will do for any but a north exposure. From *c*, back to the bay-window, a selection of the finest low-growing monthly roses, alternated with *Salvia fulgens* or *splendens*, or with any of a thousand beautiful annuals or perennials of low compact growth. At the inner angle of the bay-window a group of five rhododendrons; *R. grandiflorum* in the corner, and four of the best dwarf sorts around it, will be appropriate. If the exposure of this wall is to the north, we would cover it with the superb native of our woods, the Virginia creeper or American ivy. At *s*, the old bush honeysuckle, *Lonicera tartarica*. Under the middle window of the bay make a narrow bed for mignonette and heliotrope. At *t*, the *Deutzia crenata alba* and *crenata rubra flore plena* planted side by side so as to intermingle their growth; at *u*, the lilac *S. rothmagensis;* at *w*, the variegated-leaved tree-box; at *x*, *Spireas reevesi flore plena* and *callosa*, together; at *y*, the *Weigela rosea.* This completes a selection for this lawn-border. Different selections as good or better may doubtless be made by persons versed in such matters. While the evergreens recommended for the right-hand border are small, tall gay-blossomed plants may be used to fill the bed. If the occupant desires a quick and showy return for his planting, the evergreen shrubs which we have named for this fence-border may be too slow in their growth to suit; and the fine varieties of lilacs, honeysuckles, weigelas, deutzias, spireas, syringas, and snow-balls may be substituted.

The veranda that opens from the dining-room has some flowers at its base, vines on its posts, a lilac-bush at *z* on the right of the steps, and a compact hedge of Siberian arbor-vitæs on the left to screen the kitchen-yard from observation. The trees near the gate may in time be made to overarch it. The grape-trellis should finish with an arch over this entrance to the garden. The tree *r*, in the garden, is an Irish juniper, which is so slender that its shade is not likely to injure the grape vines.

We have considered these grounds too small to introduce any trees, not even fruit trees ; but of small fruits the garden may have a good supply.

PLATE XV.—There being no bed-room projection on the side of the house, the lawn is seven feet wider than on the preceding design. The house being a city basement plan, with a high porch, the entrance is designed with more architectural completeness. The street margin of the lot is supposed to stand twenty-one inches above the level of the sidewalk, with a stone wall all around, the coping of which is to have its upper side level with the lawn next to it, and to be surmounted by a low iron fence. The front porch (designed for iron) is approached by three stone steps on the street line, landing on a stone platform 4 × 6. The side walls of the steps to the porch form vase pedestals. The walk to the basement is fourteen inches below the level of the lawn, and seven inches above the street sidewalk. At the angles of the basement area wall, the copings are squared for the reception of vases. The rear walk, from the side street, rises by two steps on the street line, so that it will be below the level of the lawn for ten or fifteen feet from the gate. The ground should rise about one foot from the fence to the house.

For the benefit of readers not very familiar with the study of house-plans, some explanation may be necessary to an understanding of the back-stair arrangement on this plan, which will be found quite simple and convenient. The dining-room being in the basement, broad stairs lead down to it from the main hall. Servants may come up these stairs from the basement, and go into the second story by the back stairs from the passage (which also opens into the library-room) without entering the hall or the living-rooms of the main floor. If it is considered essential to have a direct communication between the bed-room and the basement, a private stairway may be made from the closet, under the back stairway.

The library is to have a glazed door (glazed low) to enter the

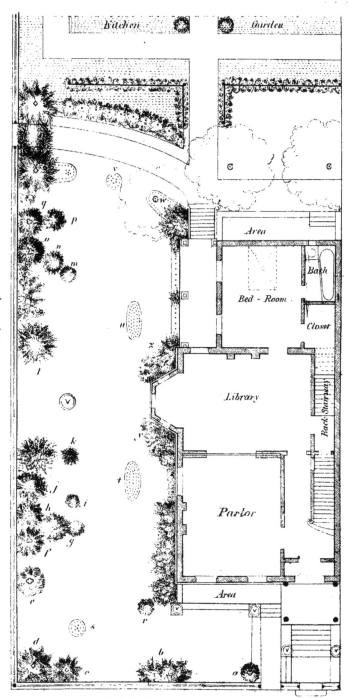

Kitchen Garden

IDE STREET

c c

Area

Bath

Bed - Room

Closet

Library

Back Stairway

Parlor

Area

Scale 16 feet, 1 inch.

side veranda. Through this a pretty perspective down the garden-walk will be seen. More space being devoted to lawn in the rear of this house than on the preceding plan, three cherry trees are introduced there.

The best frontage for this place would be to the north, giving the open side of the house an eastern exposure. A front to the east or the south would not be objectionable, as the side lawn and lookout from the house would still be sunny ; but if the house were to front to the west, then the open side would be to the north— an uncheerful exposure, that ought to be avoided where possible.

The verdant embellishment for the ground may be as follows : first, four vases filled with flowers, two by the side of the main steps, and two on the area coping. The former should be the more elegant forms. At *a*, is an Irish juniper (which should be set a foot or two farther from the walk) ; at *b*, a group consisting of a *Lilac rothamagensis* in the middle, and the double white and double pink-flowering deutzias on each side of it; or of the *Weigela amabalis* in the centre, with the common tartarian bush honey suckle on one side, and the .pink-flowering deutzia on the other. These are expected to expand freely over the fence and sidewalk. At *c*, Sargent's hemlock ; at *d*, a weeping Norway spruce (*inverta*) ; at *e*, a dwarf white pine (*compacta*) ; at *f*, the erect yew, *Taxus erecta ; g, g,* Parson's arbor-vitæ and the golden yew ; at *h*, the weeping silver-fir, *Picea p. pendula ;* at *i*, the Japan podocarpus, in the climate of Cincinnati, and the golden arbor-vitæ farther north. At *j*, another weeping Norway spruce ; at *k*, the *Cephalotaxus fortunii mascula* nearest the street, and the weeping arbor-vitæ on the side towards the house. At *l*, Nordmanns fir, *Picea nordmaniana ;* from *l* to *o*, a screen of Sargent's hemlock ; *m*, weeping juniper, *J. oblonga pendula; n,* Siberian arbor-vitæ ; *o.* the pendulous red-cedar, *J. virginiana pendula; p,* the weeping silver-fir ; *q*, the weeping Norway spruce, *Abies e. inverta.* A hemlock screen to be continued along the street line from *q* across the walk, so that the two trees nearest the gate may in time form an arch over it. At *r*, near the front of the house, may be the dwarf Hudson's Bay fir, *Picea hudsonica,* or the low dwarf silver-fir, *Picea pectinata compacta,* or the slender Irish juniper. The shrubs near

the house-wall may be low-growing roses, or rhododendrons alternated with the scarlet salvia among them. In the inner angles of the
bay-window, if of brick, we would have the English ivy, or the
Virginia creeper ; if of wood, then some rhododendron of medium
height, and around them at *y* and *z*, compact masses of the smallest
sorts ; or one side may be more quickly filled with a single pink
deutzia, and the other with a tartarian bush honeysuckle. The
shrubs at the corner of the rear veranda may be the Chinese sub-
evergreen honeysuckle on the post ; a Swedish juniper next to it';
and the erect yew, the golden yew, and the golden arbor-vitæ
around the juniper.

The materials for the flower-beds *s, t, u, v, w, x*, need not be
specified in detail.

The border back of the rear walk represents current bushes.
It might better be a grape-trellis.

PLATE XVI.

*A large Mansion on an In-Lot of two hundred feet front by three
hundred and forty feet deep.*

This house is, in size, much above the average of suburban
homes, and the area of the lot is sufficient to harmonize with the
mansion-character of the house.* The arrangement of the drive-
way is quite simple. The house being placed nearly in the middle
of the width of the lot, and the stable, vegetable-garden, and
orchard, occupying the rear third of the length of it, there is not an'
extent of lawn in proportion to the depth of the lot ; the ground
design being in this respect inferior to that of Plate XI, where a
lot forty feet shorter has a lawn much longer. The difference is
mainly in the greater extent of the orchard, the vegetable-garden
and the stable yard on the plan now under consideration ; and the
different positions of the mansion and the stable on the respective

---

* The vignette at the head of Chapter VI is from a drawing of this house, kindly furnished
by the architect, R. W. Bunnell, Esq., of Bridgeport, Conn., but the grounds as there shown are
not intended to illustrate this plan.

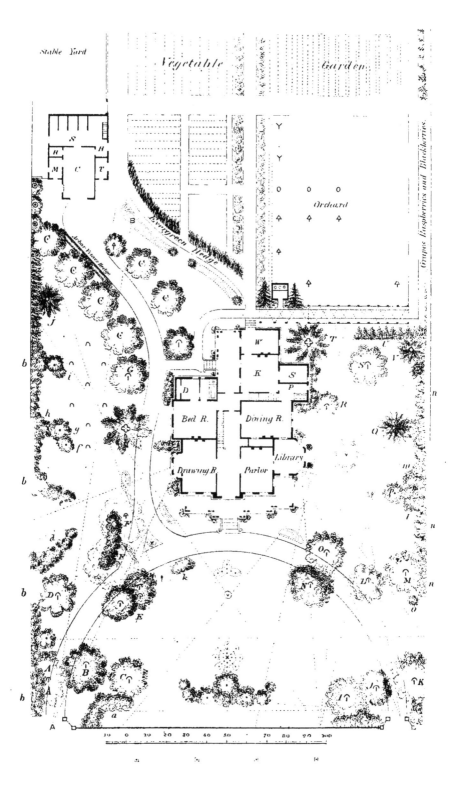

lots. The design of Plate XI is for a front to the east; the house is therefore placed near the north side of the lot, the exposures of the principal rooms are to the east, south, and west, and the views out of them are made longer and nobler by thus crowding the house and all its utilitarian appendages towards that side. The present plan is suited to a lot having a frontage to the south, and the plan calls for an equally good exposure for the rooms on both sides of the house. The liberal space allowed for orchard, vegetable-garden and stable-yard necessarily deprives the ground of the fine air that longer and broader stretches of unbroken lawn produce; but each of the principal rooms having exposures differing essentially from the others, the variety of views must atone for their want of extent.

The carriage-entrances to this place are shown nearer to the corners than they should be. On so broad a front there should be twenty feet instead of ten, between the drive at the entrances and the nearest part of the adjacent lots. Premising this alteration to be made in the plan, the only change in the planting would be that the trees B, C, and I, J, shall be planted nearer together, and more nearly at right-angles, than parallel, with the front of the lot. The capital letters on the plan are used to designate the larger class of trees of a permanent character, and the small letters, the shrubs and very small trees.

Though this is an in-lot, and generally margined by high fences and close plantations, one opening on each side has been left to give views across neighbor-lots which are supposed to warrant it. If the reader will follow on the plan we will select trees and shrubs as follows: on the left of the left-hand gate as we enter may be a weeping willow, midway between the drive and the adjoining lot line, and ten feet from the front. The margin, *b, b*, is to be planted with a dense mass of fine common shrubs, or left more open, accordingly as the neighbor-lot at that point is pleasing or the reverse. B, is a golden willow; and C, a weeping birch. All these trees grow with great rapidity. D, may be a weeping beech; E, a group of three sassafras trees; F (nearest the house), the *Kolreuteria paniculata;* F (nearest the street), the purple-leaved sycamore maple; G (northwest of the bed-room), the golden-leaved

sycamore maple ; H (though it is not so marked), we would prefer to make a pair of pines, the Austrian and the white, the former
in the rear of the latter.   The pine tree directly west of the bed-
room may be either the white, Austrian, Bhotan, or Pyrenean,
the two latter being the most interesting, but of uncertain longevity.   Beginning at the right-hand front entrance, J, K, may be
Scotch weeping elms, and I, the Scamston elm.   The shrubbery at
and near the entrance is for effect during the first ten years after
planting, and to be removed when the elms shadow that entrance
sufficiently.   At L, plant a *Kolreuteria paniculata ;* at M, the
paulonia ; at N and O, weeping birches ; at P, the *Magnolia
machrophylla ;* at Q, Nordmanns fir ; at R, a *Magnolia tripctata ;*
at S, the weeping beech ; at T, a white or Austrian pine ; at U, a
hemlock screen ; at V, a group of Norway spruces.   The fruit trees
on the plan may be known by their symbols.

Of shrubbery and shrubby trees the middle group (unlettered)
near the front is the most important, as it is visible from almost
every point of view in and near the grounds.   Measured on the
curved line of its centre, it is fifty feet in length, and may be made
an artistic miniature arboretum of choice things, either evergreens
or deciduous ; but should be all one or the other, on its upper
outline ; though the *under-shrubs* may be deciduous and evergreen
mingled.   In either case its arrangement should be planned, and
its materials selected by a skillful gardener.   It is impracticable, in
the limits of this work, to present the working details for such
groups on a scale that can be readily followed ; we therefore
merely suggest that the centre should be made with something
that will not exceed twenty feet in height at maturity, and the
group should diminish in height at the sides, so that the points
may be occupied by interesting dwarfs that may be overlooked by
persons passing on the sidewalk.

The shrubberies at *a*, and *b, b, b, b, d*, and *e*, are simply masses
of the good old syringas, lilacs, honeysuckles, snow-balls, currants,
altheas, and the newer weigelas, deutzias, spireas, and other shrubs,
which may be arranged in a hundred different ways to give the
foliage and forms of each a good setting.

The small tree at *c*, may be the American red-bud or Judas tree,

Cercis . canadensis ; at *f, Magnolia conspicua ;* at *g, Magnolia machrophylla ;* at *h,* a mass of hemlocks ; at *i,* a pair. of weeping Japan sophoras ; and behind them the white-flowering dogwood, the broad-leaved euonymus, and the variegated-leaved elder ; at *j,* a Norway spruce in front of a hemlock hedge ; at *k* (near the front veranda), a dwarf white pine in the centre, the Hudson's Bay fir on, one side, and the dwarf silver-fir, *Picea pectinata compacta,* on the other. While these are small, fill in between them with low compact rhododendrons. At *l* and *m,* Austrian pines headed back from time to time to force a dense growth ; at *n, n, n,* a belt of hemlocks and arbor-vitæs ; *o,* Sargent's hemlock ; *p,* the weeping juniper, *J. oblonga pendula,* or the Indian catalpa. The shrubbery adjoining the house on the east side may be composed largely of rhododendrons ; on the west side, of shrubs and bedding-plants that flourish in great light and heat.

The rose-bed adjoining the front middle group may be omitted without detriment to the plan, and a smaller rose-bed made in the triangle formed by the intersecting branches of the carriage-road, where a vase is marked, for which a rose-post may be substituted. Besides the climbing roses to be planted one on each side of the post, there will be room in this triangle for three compact rose-bushes.

The flower-beds and vases shown on the plan need no explanation to the intelligent reader.

We desire to call the reader's attention to the fact that this house-plan, and the size and form of the lot, are precisely the same as in Plate XVII, following ; but the lots have different exposures, the houses are placed quite differently on them, and the ground designs are totally changed to suit the circumstances. A comparison of the **two** is a good study.

PLATE XVII.

A large Mansion occupying one end of a Block, with streets on three sides, and an alley on the fourth.

Having already called the reader's attention to the identity of this house-plan with that of Plate XVI, and to the fact that the lots are of the same size and form, but otherwise differently circumstanced, we will briefly sketch the peculiarities of this design. The lot is 200 × 340 feet. It is supposed to be desirable that the house should front on the street that occupies the long side of the lot. The house and stable conveniences occupy so much room, that if the house were thrown back to introduce a carriage-road to the front steps, it would be crowded close to the alley; and even then the drive would be so short as to belittle the noble character of the house and lot. The mansion is, therefore, placed so far towards the front that its entrance porch is but forty feet from the street; a carriage-road to the front is dispensed with, and a broad straight foot-walk alone conducts to the front steps. The private carriage-entrance is by a straight road from the side street to the steps of the back veranda, and the coach-yard; and the family can get into their vehicles there, or in front, at their option. For visitors, a landing on the side-walk is quite convenient enough to the front door for all ordinary occasions.

It will be seen at a glance that the distribution and arrangement of the useful and the decorative parts of this plan are unusually convenient and beautiful; and that a place carried out in conformity to it would produce a more elegant effect, with the same materials and expense, than the plan of Plate XVI. This difference is not to be attributed to the greater street exposure of this plan, or to the different position of the house on the lot, which the surrounding streets necessitate; but is principally the result of a more happy distribution of the several parts. It would be difficult to plan with greater economy in the use of space. But the form and exposure of the lot on the plate alluded to, will

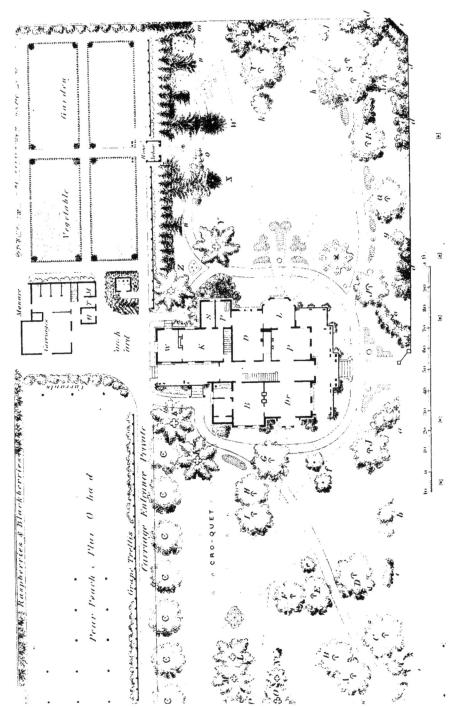

permit of modifications in the arrangement of its parts that for some persons might prove improvements.

To offset the greater length of carriage-road which the lot as planned on Plate XVI exhibits, this plan calls for a much greater length of foot-walks. In vegetable garden and orchard ground, the two plans are nearly equal. This one, however, lacks a stable-yard, that is shown in the former ; which may be provided, if needed, by placing the carriage-house directly in the rear of the residence, and enclosing a space between the former and the vegetable-garden. If this were done, however, it would be necessary to cut off a view of the coach-yard from the main hall looking through the back veranda.

A peculiar arrangement of shrubbery will be observed in front of the house. The latter being close to the street, it is desirable to cover it from too close and continuous observation of the passer-by, as far as can be done without belittling the main entrance way, or crowding shrubbery close to the veranda. The walk opening, on the street line, is sixteen feet wide—the gate being in a bay. For this distance the entire front of the house, as well as charming vistas of the lawns on each side, are in full view ; and the impression of the place obtained here would be the finest. But passing either way, beyond this opening, along the sidewalk, the lower part of the house is entirely concealed by the two diverging masses of shrubbery, *a, a,* which, while they thus act as a partial screen of the veranda and lower windows, open out so as to leave a fine expanse in front of the house in lawn, vases, and flowers. Two horse-chestnut trees at the points of these groups will make an appropriate flanking for the front entrance.

Though this plan may not be impracticable whatever the point of the compass its front faces, yet the most beautiful interior effects—that is, as seen from the house, and within the grounds—will be realized by a frontage to the north ; while the best effect as seen from the streets will be produced by a frontage to the south—either a north or south front being better for this plan than one to the east or west.

The following is one selection of trees and shrubs for the place—the capital letters indicating the large trees, and the small letters the inferior trees and shrubbery. A and B are the purple-leaved and the golden-leaved sycamore maples; C, the weeping willow; D, the weeping beech; E and F, the common and the cut-leaved weeping birches; G, the ginkgo or Salisburia tree; H, the purple-leaved beech; I, the *Kolreuteria paniculata;* J, J, the red-flowering, and the double white-flowering horse-chestnuts; K, K, a pair of pines in each place—the Bhotan (*excelsa*) and white pine in one, and the Bhotan and Austrian in the other—to be planted six feet apart, the Bhotan on the north side in both cases; L, white pine; M, Austrian pine; on the right of N, the weeping Norway spruce; and on the left, the Cembran pine, or (south of New York and near the sea) the cypress, *Glypto-strobus sinensis;* O, the white or the Austrian pine, as the soil may be better for one or the other; P, a mass and belt of hemlocks; Q, a weeping Scotch elm; R, the grape-leaved linden; S, nearest the intersection of the walks, the sugar maple, and to the right of it the purple-leaved sycamore maple; T and V a mass of Austrian pines, with an undergrowth of hemlocks; U, catalpa; W, a pair of weeping Norway spruces, with hemlocks behind them; X, the weeping silver-fir backed by hemlocks and flanked with a group of rhododendrons; Y, a pair of pines, the white and the Pyrenean, six feet apart; Z, the Austrian and the Bhotan pines, the same distance apart.

Of the shrubbery we can indicate only the general character of the groups, and name specimens only when standing singly, or a few in a group. The masses *a, a,* may be shrubs of fine common sorts, the taller in the centre line of the group, and the margins filled in with rhododendrons; or may be composed entirely of evergreens, such as the arbor-vitæs, yews, dwarf firs, junipers, and pines, with rhododendrons and azalias among them. The deciduous shrubs, however, would make a fine border in much less time, and at less expense than the latter. At *b,* a *Weigela amabilis* in the centre, and on each side the weigelas *rosea* and *hortensia nivea;* at *c,* the two deutzias *crenata alba* and *crenata rubra flore plena;* at *d, d, d, d, d,* masses of common shrubs, not allowed to exceed seven feet in height, forced to make a dense mass at the bottom, and planted to form an irregular outline next to the lawn;

at *e*, the oblong weeping juniper, *J. oblonga pendula ; f*, a pair of weeping Japan sophoras grafted nine feet high, and . planted ten feet apart ; *g*, the Chinese white magnolia ; *h*, a mass of rhododendrons and purple magnolias ; *i, i*, hemlock gateway arches—the hemlocks to form a dense screen for ten or fifteen feet on each side of the arch ; *j*, the Hudson's Bay fir ; *k*, the *Magnolia machrophylla ; l* (adjoining the house), a mass of evergreens of dwarf character, including rhododendrons, kalmias, and azalias ; *m* and *n*, hemlock screens ; *o*, a mass of rhododendrons. The small group under the corners of the drawing-room bay-windows may be composed of the English or Irish ivys in the corners, and low varieties of rhododendrons ; or, of brilliant bedding-plants alone.

This place is large enough to make a conservatory a desirable feature. If wanted in connection with the house, by using the room marked P as a library-room, the room L (if that side of the house has an east exposure) would be an admirable place for it. If a distinct structure is preferred, a good place would be on a line with the carriage-road, and ten feet from it, in the corner of the orchard nearest the house.

The large flower-bed near L is intended for large bedding plants. The great rose-bed at the intersection of the walks on the right would require to be filled with uncommon skill to make it pleasing throughout the summer season, though it may be superbly beautiful in June, and interesting under ordinary treatment, with partial bloom, until frosts. In winter and early spring, however, it can hardly be otherwise than unsightly. A group for that place, of more continuous beauty, which will cost less labor in its maintenance, may be composed of the following evergreens:—for the centre the weeping Norway spruce (*inverta*) ; around it the following, the positions for which must be determined by a study of their characters : the Sargent hemlock, Parson's dwarf hemlock, variegated-leaved tree-box, golden and weeping arbor-vitæs, the erect yew (*erecta*), the golden yew, the *Cephalotaxus fortunii mascula*, the *Podocarpus japonica*, the creeping juniper (*repens*), the juniper *repanda densa*, the juniper *oblonga pendula*, the juniper *spæroides*, the Hudson's Bay fir *hudsonica*, and the dwarf firs, *Picea pectinata compacta* and *Abies gregoriana*.

The group of large flower-beds opposite the library window, with a vase in the centre, should be filled with rather low flowers, and made as continuously brilliant as possible. Forming the fore-ground of a fine stretch of lawn beyond them, the view as seen from the main window of this room may be made quite elegant and park-like in its effect.

PLATE XVIII.

Plan for a Residence of Medium Size, with Stable and Carriage-house, Orchard, and Vegetable-garden, on a Corner-Lot 200 × 300 *feet.*

Here we have a house of moderate size on a lot which gives ample space around it, and which is provided with length of carriage-road disproportioned to the size of the house. It is suited to the use of a small family, who entertain much company, and keep horses and carriages.

The location of a large kitchen-garden in the southwest corner of the lot, where the lawn might be extended with fine effect, as in Plates XI and XIII, was made in order to place the orchard away from the side street, and the enterprise of bad boys. The vegeta-ble-garden offers few temptations for moonlight poachers over a street-fence, but an orchard in the same place is almost irresisti-ble. By interposing the kitchen-garden between it and the street, the fruit is safer. Were it not for this reason we would decidedly prefer to have the kitchen-garden back of the house, the orchard on the south side of the lot, and so arranged that the ground under the trees should appear to be a prolongation of the south lawn. The plan being made with reference to the protection of the orchard, sacrifices to this object Rule I, of Chapter XI—there being no length of lawn on the lot commensurate with its size. Yet the manner of grouping, in those portions of the lot which are in lawn, is such as to conceal this defect in a great degree from the eye of an observer in the street, or in the house ; though it is evi-dent enough on the paper plan.

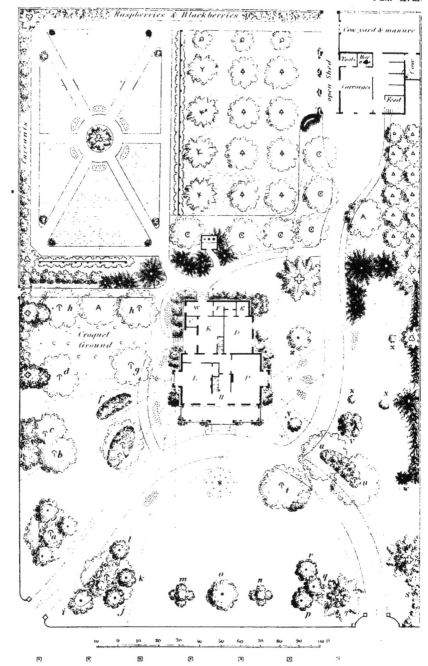

Plate XVIII.

Raspberries & Blackberries

Currants

Cow yard & manure

Tools

Hay

Carriages

Feed

Cow

open Shed

Croquet
Ground

10 0 10 20 30 40 50 60 70 80 90 100 ft

We have alluded to the length of carriage-road on this lot as disproportioned to the size of the residence. This is so decided that we must consider the plan as an example of a fault to be avoided, rather than a plan to be followed. Not only the length of the drive is objectionable for a residence of this simple character, but also the corner entrance, which is usually the least convenient point for crossing the street-gutters and the side-walks. Plate X shows a much more sensible entrance and carriage-way.

In other respects this plan is better ; the grouping being such as would give very pleasing effects, whether looking towards the house or from it. On the south are several openings to the street, and on the north one only, connecting with private grounds on that side.

Supposing the roads, walks, orchard, and garden to have been laid out as shown by the plan, the following trees and shrubs are suggested for some of the principal plạces. The lines conforming in part to the forms of the groups of shrubs are intended to show the form of beds to be enriched and prepared for them.

The group at *a*, on the left of the corner entrance-way, to be composed of a weeping willow or a weeping Scotch elm in the centre, and the three best varieties of dogwood on the three points of the group ;—the bed to be filled, while these are growing, with spreading shrubs of low growth. The group, on the right of the same entrance, to have an American weeping elm in the centre, and at *i, j, k*, and *l*, the American and European Judas trees, the broad-leaved strawberry tree (*Enonymus latifolius*), and the dogwood (*Cornus florida*) ; and between them the syringas, weigelas, variegated elder, flowering currants, etc., etc.

The trees at *b* and *c* may be the double-flowering white and the red-flowering horse-chestnuts ; between them and the fence a mass of large shrubs. At *d*, a weeping beech ; between it and the fence plant shrubs, to be removed when the beech needs all the space ; near the fence Siberian arbor-vitæs to form a concave hedge to, and across, (overarching) the side-entrance gate. At *e*, ten feet from both the walk and the drive, a pair of sassafras trees four feet apart, with an oval mass of low spreading shrubs—spireas, flowering-currants, berberries, deutzias, red-twigged dogwoods, and honey-suckles around them.　At *f*, a choice selection of the most pleasing shrubs, either deciduous or evergreen ; of the latter an assortment of the best rhododendrons will make a superb group.　At *g*, a *Magnolia machrophylla;　h*, nearest the house, the *Kolreuteria paniculata; h*, near the gate, the osage orange.　At *o*, in the centre of the front, a purple beech ; at *m* and *n*, groups composed of the weeping Norway spruce (*inverta*) for the centres, and the golden arbor-vitæ, and the erect yew (*Taxus stricta* or *erecta*), the golden yew and the *Podocarpus japonica*, on opposite sides of them. If for this central space it is desired to make a quick mass of foliage in the place of these small groups, a weeping willow, or a group of two or three osage orange trees planted at *o*, a group of deutzias at *m*, and of weigelas or bush honeysuckles at *n*, will quickly effect it.　At the left of the gateway on the right, a pair of pines, the white and Austrian ; *p* and *q*, the dwarf mountain pine (*P. pumila*) and the mugho pine (*P. mugho*) ; *r*, the dwarf white pine ; and between these, while small, plant evergreen shrubs.　At *s*, is a belt of shrubs terminated by a pair of pines, the Austrian and the Bhotan.　At *t*, a pair of weeping birches ; at *u, u*, two pairs of trees, the purple-leaved and the gold-leaved sycamore-maples at one end, and the sugar and scarlet-maples at the other, each pair near together ; and between the trees, while they are young, a group of deciduous shrubbery.　At *v*, a *Magnolia soulan-geana;* at *w*, the weeping silver-fir (*Picea pectinata pendula*) ; along the boundary of the lot in the rear of *w*, a belt of hemlocks broken by an occasional spur of spruce or pine trees ; *x, x, x*, weeping arbor-vitæs, junipers, or other elegant slender evergreens ; and at *z*, another *Magnolia machrophylla*.　On so large a place there will be room around the house, and in the various groups, and along the marginal belts of trees and shrubs, to introduce a hundred things which we have not named ; and a reference to the plate of symbols in connection with the ground-plan will explain what we have not touched upon.

Plate XIX.

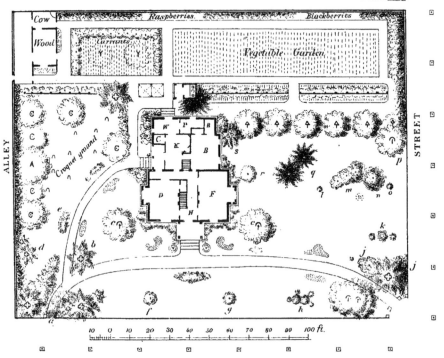

Plate XIX.

Plan for a Residence of Medium Size on a Corner Lot 150 × 200 *feet, with no provision for keeping a horse or carriage.*

This house-plan is the same as that on Plate XVIII, but the lot is only one-half the depth of that one, though the frontage is the same. The street on the longer side being supposed the most desirable to front upon, the division of the lot in lawn, fruit, and vegetable-garden, resembles, on a smaller scale, that of Plate XVII; though on this the direct walk to the front door is dispensed with, and only the entrances at the two front corners of the lot are used. This is rarely a desirable arrangement, but the expression aimed at in the design of this lot is extreme openness and breadth of lawn, in proportion to the size of the lot. To dispense with a walk directly from the street to the front door increases this expression, but it is not essential to it. If the members of the family who occupy the house rarely use a carriage, it is not a matter of much importance to have a direct front walk; especially if all the travel to and from the house is along the street, so that one corner gate or the other makes a nearer approach than a walk in the centre only. But if the family have often occasion to ride, the side-entrances will seem an awkward detour; and we would then by all means dispense with the walk which runs nearly parallel with the street, and have a broad straight walk to the front porch, and a smaller walk to the rear of the house, nearly as here represented. This would, of course, involve considerable changes in the plan for planting.

An alley is supposed to bound the lot on the left; a shed and cow-house* and small cow-yard are therefore represented in the rear corner on that side, and an arbor-vitæ hedge is to be planted inside the fence along the alley. Ten feet from the alley, and

---

* The grass from the lawn, on such a place as this, if fed as cut, is more than enough to supply one cow with green food for seven months of the year;—probably, together with the pail-feed from the house, enough to keep two cows.

back of the front line of the house, is a row of four cherry trees, and two others are indicated on the rear part of the croquet-ground. Six standard pear trees, on the other side of the house, form a row parallel with a continuous grape-trellis which divides the lawn from the vegetable-garden. Some peach trees may be planted in the garden-square next the cow-house. The borders by the fences around the bǎck of the lot furnish ample room for currants, raspberries, and blackberries.

The decorative planting of the lawn-ground may be as follows : on each side of the gateway, at *a*, plant a group of pines, white, Austrian, and Bhotan, to be clipped when they begin to trespass on the walk, and to overarch it when large enough. The group on the left of the walk, directly in front of the same entrance, should be composed of shrubby evergreen trees or shrubs, diminishing to those of small size at the point. At *b*, the weeping silver-fir. At *c, c*, fifteen feet from the front corners of the house, a pair of *either* of the following species, of the varieties named :—of beeches, the purple-leaved and the fern-leaved ; of birches, the old weeping and the cut-leaved weeping ; of horse-chestnuts, the double-white and the red-flowering ; of lindens, the American basswood and the grape-leaved ; of magnolias, the *machrophylla* and the *cordata ;* of mountain ashes, the oak-leaved ; of maples, the purple-leaved and the gold-leaved sycamore ; of oaks, the scarlet (*coccinea*) on both sides ; of tulip trees (whitewood), there being no distinct varieties, the same on both sides, or a tulip tree on one side, and a virgilia or *Magnolia cordata* on the other. Our own choice among these would be of birches, maples, or horse-chestnuts.

At *d*, the face of the hedge may be broken by a projecting group of yews and arbor-vitæs. At *e*, a group of rhododendrons. At *f* and *g* any one of the following deciduous species of small low trees, if grown with care and symmetry, viz.: the Indian catalpa (*C. himalayensis*) south of Philadelphia ; the Chinese cypress (*Glypto-strobus sinensis*) ; the silver-bell (*Halesia tetraptera*) ; the sassafras (although rather large for the place) ; the dwarf horse-chestnuts, *Pavia coccinea, P. pumila pendula*, and *P. cornea superba ;* the European bird cherry, *Prunus padus ;* the American white-flowering and the Cornelian cherry dogwoods, *C. florida* and *C. mas ;* the

American and the European Judas trees ; the magnolias, Chinese white (*conspicua*), and the showy-flowered (*speciosa*) ; the dwarf profuse-flowering mountain ash (*nana floribunda*) ; the weeping Japan sophora ; the double scarlet-thorn (*coccinea flore plena*) · the weeping larch ; the Kilmarnock willow ; the large-flowered rose-acacia (*grandiflora*), if trained and carefully supported when young ; the American and the broad-leaved strawberry trees ; the largest and most tree-like lilacs ; the purple-fringe ; the syringa, *zcyheri ;* and the new snow-ball or viburnum, *V. machrophylium,* are all pleasing small trees, or tree-like shrubs, any two of which will be appropriate for these two places. Our preference among them would be the weeping Japan sophoras grafted from seven to eight feet high. If evergreens are desired for these two places, we would certainly select the weeping Norway spruce (*inverta*) and the weeping silver-fir. The small group *h,* should be made up of choice small evergreens, yews, arbor-vitæs, and dwarf firs. The pair of deciduous trees at *i,* on the right, may be a catalpa and a pau- lonia for places south of New York ; and northward, a pair of sassafras and a dogwood (*C. florida*), to make a group of three, or a pair of *Kolreuteria paniculata* only. The group *j,* on the upper side of the walk, is intended to be filled by an Austrian pine, sur- rounded by evergreen shrubs that will form a dense mass. At *k,* a Siberian arbor-vitæ, with the erect yew, on one side, and the golden arbor-vitæ on the other. At *l,* an Irish juniper. At *m,* a collec- tion of magnolias, beginning with the purple-magnolia nearest the house, next to it the Chinese white, then the *M. soulangeana,* and at *n,* the *M. machrophylla,*—all to be encouraged to branch as close to the ground as they will grow. At *o,* the arbor-vitæ *compacta,* or another purple magnolia. At *p,* the weeping beech ; at *q,* a group of the following firs, beginning nearest the house with Nord- manns fir, next the Cephalonian, and last the Norway spruce. At *r,* another *Magnolia machrophylla.* At *s,* a Bhotan pine if on the north or east side, and an Austrian pine if on the south or west side of the house. The shrubbery adjoining the house may be composed of a great variety of common species ; but none that attain a height of more than six feet should be planted under or in front of windows where they might eventually obstruct the views.

PLATE XX.

A Compact House, on an In-Lot of ninety-six feet front, with ample depth, and a Lawn connecting with adjoining neighbors.

The main house is here 36 × 40, and the rear part 20 × 32 feet. The front veranda is ten feet in width, and between it and the street the distance is ninety-six feet. The lot is one hundred and ninety-six feet in depth back to the grape-trellis that divides the lawn from the garden, and is supposed to have ample room back of this for vegetables and small fruits.

Whether or not the occupants of this place keep horse and carriage, the front and sides of the lot are designed without any reference to them.

Floral embellishment is a prominent feature of this design, and this is nearly all in front of the house. The walk with two street-entrances encloses a circle seventy-two feet in diameter, on the margin of which the flower-beds 'are arranged, leaving the interior of the circle in lawn, unbroken save by a large low vase for flowers in the centre. Most of the interest of the place being thus between the house and the street, where exposure to passers on the street might annoy the occupants in the care and enjoyment of their flowers and plants, it is essential that this circle should be hidden from the street except at the gateways. The reader already knows that we have no sympathy with that churlish spirit which would shut a pleasing picture out of sight from the sheer love of exclusive possession ; but we have respect for that repugnance which most persons, and especially ladies, feel against a peering curiosity in their domestic enjoyments ; and as the care of one's flowers and trees is one of the sweetest of domestic labors, we would protect the privacy of working hours among them to an extent· that may not degenerate into a selfish exclusiveness. In this plan, as engraved, the mass of screening foliage is not as large as would be necessary, but the trees as there placed will form a sufficient protection after ten years growth to insure a reasonable privacy for the floral lawn. It will be observed that this is not effected by a

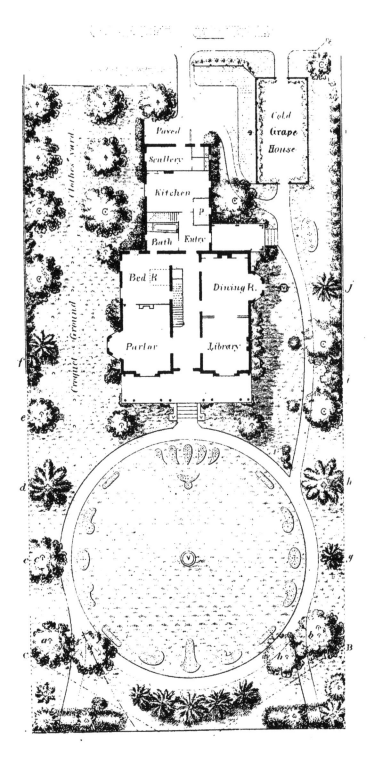

hedge· on the street line, but on the contrary the lawn is open except at the entrances ; and one standing on the sidewalk at A, though barred from all view of the circle by the mass of evergreens opposite, may have pleasing glimpses into the place on the lines A B, A C, and across these corners into the adjoining lot lawns.

The two front gateways should be overarched with evergreen topiary arches—one side with arbor-vitæ, and the other with hemlocks, firs, or pines, as the soil and exposure may make one or the other preferable. The glimpses into the grounds from under either of these arches will extend the whole length of the lawn back to the cold grape-house on the right, and from the left, back to the grape-trellis that separates the vegetable-garden from the lawn. A still longer vista may be· made from the left-hand gateway by making a decorative arch in the grape-trellis at the end of the garden-walk which corresponds with the one at the end of the cold grape-house.

The evergreen group in the middle of the lot near the street may be composed as follows : in the centre two Nordmanns firs, four feet apart, on a line at right angles with the street ; on each side of these a mass of hemlocks (say four on each side) for a distance of sixteen feet each way ; and at each point of the group single specimens of the weeping silver-fir and the weeping Norway spruce. This will make the group about forty feet from point to point, measuring from the stems of the last-named trees.

The trees which arch the intersections of the entrance-walks with the circular-walk, may be double pairs of sassafras on one side, and one pair of kolreuterias on the other. At *c*, a weeping beech ; at *g*, the Chinese cypress (*Glypto-strobus sinensis pendula*) ˙south of New York, and north of it a group composed of the weeping Norway spruce in the centre, and the following junipers around it : the *J. repanda densa, J. oblonga pendula, J. succica nana, J. spæroides ;* or, instead of the junipers, the following dwarf firs, viz. : the *Abies nigra pumila, A. gregoriana, A. conica, A. canadensis inverta* (Sargent's hemlock), *A. canadensis Parsoni* (Parson's hemlock), the *Picea pectinata compacta,* and the *Picea hudsonica.* At *d* and *h*, the finest pines for which the soil and location are suited ; at *e*, the *Magnolia cordata ;* at *f*, a group of evergreen shrubs next the fence,

14

and a weeping silver-fir in front of them, opposite the parlor bay-window.   Two small trees are indicated in front of the corners of the veranda.   If small trees are used in these places, they may be of species like the *Magnolia machrophylla,* the double white-flowering horse-chestnut, and the virgilia, which develop most beautifully when branching near the ground, or, like the weeping sophora, trailing to the ground ; but if large trees are chosen, they should be of sorts which lift their heads on clean stems, so that their lower branches will be above the line of view of persons standing on the floor of the house.

At the point formed by the intersection of the sidewalk with the circular-walk there should be an interesting collection of ever-greens of very slender, or very dwarf character.   Near the point, and two feet from both walks, plant the *Abies excelsa pygmæ ;* three feet from both walks, and back of the former, the *Picea pectinata compacta ;* back of these, and equidistant between the walks, the *Taxus erecta ;* then, a little nearer to each walk than the latter, put in a golden arbor-vitæ and a golden yew, so as to make the group in the form of a Y.   If the proprietor prefers to have something new and striking in this location every year, instead of waiting patiently the interesting development of these dwarfs, this point will be an appropriate place for a skillful arrangement of showy-leaved bedding-plants ; but as there is ample space for these elsewhere, we would much prefer marking the intersection of the two walks with some permanent objects that may be seen in winter and summer, and which, by living and growing year after year, will at length have associations and a little history of their own, and become monumental evidences of past labors.   It is well always to mark the divergence of two walks by some permanent tree or group near the inner angle of intersection, and in the case under consideration, if the group of lilliputian evergreens should seem too insignificant and tardy in their development, or (being rarities) too expensive, we would plant some spreading tree at this intersection, and recommend for that purpose the weeping birch.

From *i* and *f,* on opposite sides of the lot, the side fences should be bordered with evergreen shrubs as far as the back line of the main house, and thence to the garden may be covered

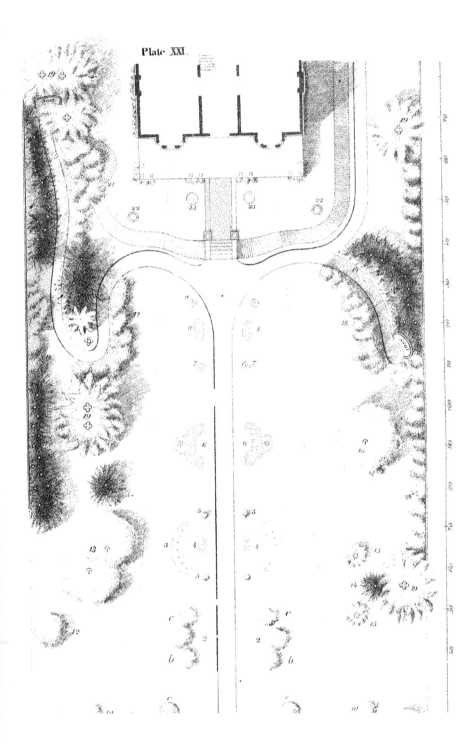
Plate XXI.

with grape-vines or other small fruits, or with a continuous belt of common deciduous shrubs.   Against the foundation-walls of the house we would plant a continuous line of varieties of the English ivy, even if they creep permanently no higher than the water-table. Up to that height they often make a shrubby mass of evergreen foliage, and form a pleasing back-ground for the finer shrubs that may be grown near the house in front of them.   For a running vine on brick and stone walls, and for draping windows and cornices with foliage, the American ivy or Virginia creeper is greatly superior in this country to the English ivy.   We can go no further in designating the shrubs to plant near the house-walls than to merely reiterate that they should be of those flowering and fragrant varieties which are usually full-foliaged, not apt to get bare of leaves at the bottom, and which do not exceed six feet in height ; in short, low, compact, or spreading shrubs.

The fruit-tree features of this place are sufficiently designated by the symbols.

There being a cold grape-house indicated, it is natural to suppose that flowers and bulbs may be forced in it, and that the care of these, together with grounds embellished with so many flowers, will involve the employment of a gardener ; to whom, or to the lady of the house, we leave the selection of the flowers to be used in filling the beds on the margin of the circle, and the vase or basket in its centre.

Plate XXI.

A Plan for a Deep Front Yard, on an In-Lot one hundred feet wide, with the House on a terrace plateau ; designed to harmonize architectural and gardenesque forms.

This plan is a peculiar study in many respects.   All the decorative portion of the grounds is in front of the house, and the depth from the street to the house-front is even greater in proportion to the width of the lot than in the preceding plan.   The arrangement at the street-front is also more simple and more formal ; for here we have a hedge close to the street line, a single entrance, and a long straight walk in the middle of the lot. To this extent the plan is simpler than the preceding one ; but on approaching the house the style becomes more ornate and costly. The house is elevated on a wide terrace, and the steps to reach the terrace-level are fifteen feet in front of the veranda. These steps should be of stone, not less than twelve inches wide, nor more than seven inches rise, and of a length equal to the width of the main walk. Low stone copings at the side of the steps expand at the top into square pedestals for vases, and thence are continued to meet the veranda. Such copings should, where practicable, be of some warm colored stone. It will be observed that the walk at the foot of these stone steps widens out into quite an area, and at this point the design varies by an easy transition from the formal to the graceful style ; the form of the front of the terrace conforming to the curves of the walks. The walks to the left and right diverge first by geometric curves, and then enter, by more path-like lines, dense masses of shrubbery, ending at seats embowered in foliage. From these, vistas open to the most pleasing features of the ground.

The house is supposed to be designed in a half city-style, with a basement-kitchen, and all the principal windows in the front and rear only. The blank sidewalks, if of unpainted brick or stone, may be covered with the Virginia creeper, and on the side-ground back of the points shown on the plate, fruit trees may be planted. If the lot is three hundred feet deep, there will be room back of the house for the needful kitchen-yard and a pretty little vegetable-garden, or a stable and carriage-space ; but hardly for both. A lot of four hundred feet in depth would be more suitable for a house thrown back so far from the front street as this, unless space were obtained in the rear of the house by a latitudinal development of the lot in the rear of other lots.

As the entire embellishment of this place lies in front of the house, and as its features are of that gardenesque character which presuppose a decided love of horticultural art in the occupants, and therefore the necessity of constant labors to be done near the street, some thorough protection of their privacy is essential ; and we have here first introduced a hedge on the street line. The gate-way should be rather larger than is common on foot-walks, and covered with a carefully grown hemlock arch. The hedge may be of hemlock or of Siberian arbor-vitæ, and not more than six feet in height. At *a, a,* it is designed to be hollowed by a concave cut on the sides and top, so that the latter will not be more than three and a half feet high in the middle. With this arrangement there will be three glimpses into the place from the street; one under the gateway arch, and the others over the concave cuts in the hedge. The buttresses on the inside are intended to give variety in the line, and in the lights and shadows of the hedge. They are easily made with the hedge by placing two or three hedge-plants at right angles with the line of the hedge at the points where wanted.

We have called attention in another place to a peculiarity of the arrangement of shrubs and trees on this place. There are three long lines of view, each of pre-eminent interest from the different points where each is likely to be most observed. First the walk-view, as seen from the gateway looking towards the house, or from the terrace steps looking towards the gateway; the second and third, on the lines between the bay-windows and the scollops in the front hedge, ranging the whole distance over an unbroken lawn elegantly margined on both sides with flowers, shrubs, and trees. If the reader will raise this plate nearly level with the eye, and glance along the lines indicated, he will appreciate better than we can explain what we have endeavored to accomplish in this plan. It is desirable, in order to achieve the best result of this arrange-ment, that the character of the foliage on the two sides of the lot should be so different as to give a distinct effect to the views out of the two bay-windows. In addition to these three prominent lines of view, charming long narrow vistas may be made to give interest to the seats at the ends of the walks.

One selection of trees and shrubs for the most prominent places on this plan may be the following:

Group 1, on the left: at *a*, the weeping juniper (*oblonga pendula*); at *b*, the erect yew (*Taxus erecta*); at *c*, the golden yew (*Taxus aurea*); at *d*, the weeping Indian juniper (*J.*

repanda densa); at *e*, the dwarf Swedish juniper (*J. suecica nana*).

Group 1, on the right: at *a*, the Siberian arbor-vitæ; at *b*, Parson's arbor-vitæ (*Thuja occidentalis compacta*); at *c*, the Nootka Sound arbor-vitæ (*Thuja plicata*); at *d*, the erect yew (*Taxus erecta*); and at *e*, the dwarf silver-fir (*Picea pectinata compacta*).

Groups 2, 2, may be composed of evergreens as follows: at *a, a*, the mugho and mountain pines (*P. mugho* and *P. pumila*); at *b* and *c*, in one group, dwarf white pines (*P. strobus compacta*); and on the other the Chinese yews, *Cephalotaxus fortunii mascula* and *C. drupacæ*. Or, of deciduous shrubs, the group may be as follows: at *a*, on the left, the *Weigela amabalis;* and at *b* and *c*, the deutzias *crenata alba* and *crenata rubra flore plena*. At *a*, on the right, the great-leaved snow-ball (*Viburnum machrophyllum*); and at *b* and *c*, the red-tartarian honeysuckle and the lilac *rothmagensis*.

Groups 3, 3, are for showy-leaved bedding-plants or roses; 4, 4, may be filled with choice geraniums.

Figures 5, 5, 5, 5, represent a pair each of Irish and Swedish junipers.

Beds 6, 6, are for roses or showy annuals, perennials, and bulbous flowers; 7, 7, and 9, 9, represent single plants remarkable for beautiful or showy foliage; and 8, 8, are for brilliant low-blooming flowers.

Figures 10, 10, on the left of the walk, may be, one the golden arbor-vitæ, and the other the *Podocarpus japonica;* or the rhododendrons *album elegans* and *gloriosum*. If of deciduous shrubs, one the purple-leaved berberry, and the other Gordon's flowering-currant; or, one the dwarf snow-ball (*Viburnum anglicum*), and the other the variegated Cornelian cherry or dogwood (*Cornus mascula variegata*); or the Chinese purple and the Chinese red magnolias; or the dwarf catalpas *himalayensis* and *kœmpferi*, or any other compact shrubs or dwarf trees of constant beauty of foliage and annual blossoms; 10, 10, on the right, may be, one the weeping arbor-vitæ, and the other the common tree-box.

Figure 11, on the left, the Japan weeping sophora, or the *Magnolia cordata;* 11, on the right, the Chinese cypress (*Glypto-strobus*

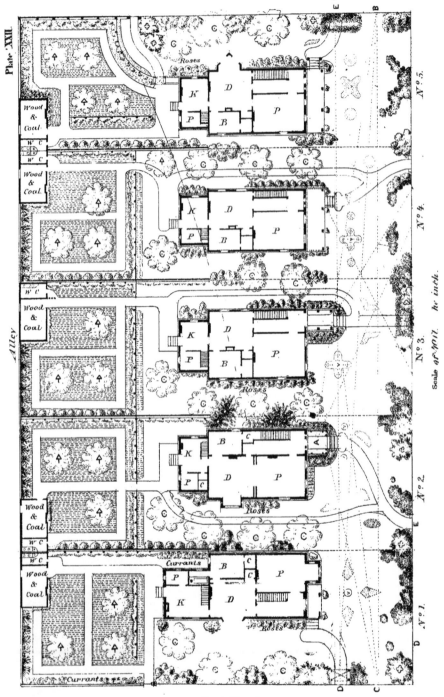

Plate XXII.

Alley

Roses

Wood
&
Coal

W C
W C

Wood
&
Coal

W C

Wood
&
Coal

Wood
&
Coal

W C
W C

Wood
&
Coal

Currants

Currants

Roses

Roses

Roses

East Street

Scale of 90ft. he inch.

N° 1.   N° 2.   N° 3.   N° 4.   N° 5.

K D P B P
K D P B P
K D P B P
B C K P D A P
P B C K D

sinensis pendula) ; 12, the *Magnolia machrophylla;* 13, a pair of *Kolreuterias.*

Figure 14, wherever it occurs, suggests a weeping silver-fir (*Picea pectinata pendula*), a weeping Norway spruce (*inverta*), or some other evergreen of slender or peculiar habit ; 15, 15, the golden yew and golden arbor-vitæ ; 16, the weeping beech, or a pair of them ; 17 and 18, rhododendrons along the walks, and robust shrubs on the outside—either evergreen or deciduous ; 19, 19, 19, hardy pines best suited to the locality ; 20, 20, 20, borders of the finest shrubs ; 21, a heavy mass of evergreens not more than eight to twelve feet high, covering and concealing the slope of the terrace, with a brilliant flower-bed on its upper or terrace level ; 22, 22, suggest large low basket forms for flowers ; 23, 23, are circular beds for tall flowers. The pedestals at the top of the steps to the terrace should have elegant low vases appropriately filled with beautiful plants.

The masses of dark-toned evergreens not numbered represent close plantations of hemlocks and Norway spruce, with such other evergreen trees as may best break the monotony of their colors.

PLATE XXII.

Designs for Neighboring Homes with connecting Grounds.

In the chapter on Neighboring Improvements we have endeavored to call attention to the great advantage that improvers of small lots may gain by planting on some common plan, so that all the improvements of the fronts of adjoining lots may be arranged to allow each of the neighbors a view of the best features of all. This plate is intended to illustrate one of the simplest forms of such neighboring improvements.

The houses themselves are such as proprietors often build in rows for the purpose of adding to the value, and increasing the sale of adjacent property ; but the connection of all the fronts into one long lawn is yet seldom practiced. The elegant effect, however, which this mode of improvement lends to places which, without it, were small and cheap-looking, will add thousands of dollars to their saleable value. It gives a genteel air to the neighborhood that five times the expenditure in buildings would fail to produce, and serves by this fact alone to attract a class of refined people of small means, who might not find the common run of houses, of the cost of these, sufficiently attractive to induce them to select homes there.

Though these five houses are quite similar in size and plan, an inspection of them will show that only Nos. 3 and 4 are alike. The others all differ in some respects; the corner houses especially being adapted to their superior locations and double fronts, and therefore needing to be somewhat more expensive. The main part of each is 25 × 38 feet, and the kitchen part 12 × 20, except on lot number one, where it is larger. There is an alley in the rear, upon which outbuildings are located.

The essential feature of the planting on this neighborhood plan is this: that *back of a line ten or twelve feet from the front street, to the foot-step of the porches, there shall be no shrub or tree planted on any of the fronts;* and only those species of flowers which do not exceed six to nine inches in height. This secures a belt of lawn varying from fifteen to forty feet in width, the entire length of the block, and leaves ample space on each lot for a good selection and arrangement of shrubs and flowers. The light dotted lines on the plan show the leading ranges of view over this common lawn. Of course only the lightest of wire fences are to be used between the lots, if any such divisions are required; and none at all ought to be necessary.

Lot 1 is entered from the side-street, under a gateway arbor. From this entrance the whole length of the block to B and E, two hundred and fifty feet, is a lawn, broken only by beds for low flowers, margined one side by the choicest groups of shrubbery, and on the other by the various architectural features of the steps, vases, porches, and verandas of the five houses, and their flowers and vines. Nothing can more strikingly illustrate the advantage of such neighboring improvements than the view from this point, embracing as it does, under one glance, all the beauty that may be created in the "front yards" of five distinct homes, all forming parts of a

Plate XXIII.

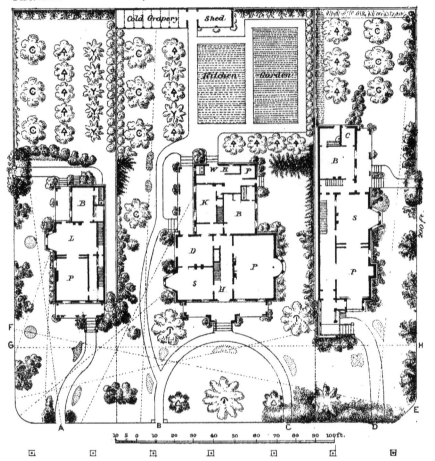

single picture. Similar effects are obtained on entering the verdant gateway arch at E, on lot 5; and also from the side-streets at the points B and C. The shorter views, from the porches and best windows of each house, are all made vastly more pleasing than would be possible on a single lot. The vignette of Chapter IV is a suppositional view from the porch (A) of the house-plan 2, looking towards B.

From the front street, the in-look between the groups that border the front, is such as to make each place when opposite to it, appear to be the most important one.

Only shrubs, or shrubby trees, are to be admitted on the fronts; but on the sides, between the houses, cherry and pear trees may be planted. The flower-beds are all shown somewhat larger on these plans than they should be.

The selections of shrubs, and their arrangement in the many groups adjacent to the front street, will require a thorough familiarity with the characteristics of shrubs, and should therefore be done by an experienced gardener. Our plate is drawn on too small a scale to enable us to designate in detail the composition of all the groups and single specimens indicated on the plan, and as such groups of places must of necessity, at first, be all arranged under the direction of one gardener, it is not desirable that we should make a suppositional list of shrubs and trees for each lot.

PLATE XXIII.

Three Residences occupying the end of a Block two hundred feet in width, on Lots two hundred feet deep.

Here the end of the block is supposed to have been divided into four lots, each 50 x 200 feet; the middle two lots being first occupied by a commodious double-house, and each of the side-lots subsequently improved with basement-kitchen houses, of half city, half suburban character, and the fronts of the three places kept by agreement for mutual advantage.

The house on the left the reader may recognize as similar to

the one shown on Plate XV, on a lot of the same width ; but it is
somewhat differently placed on the lot, and the ground arrangements
are different in front and rear.   One plan provides for a kitchen-
garden, and the other for a fruit-yard only.   It will be observed
that this house, and the basement-house on the other corner, have
blank walls adjoining the neighbor-lots, which are not built up
to the line of the fence, but leave a space, one of five feet and the
other of two feet, between the wall and the lot-line.   This is almost
useless for planting ; but we deem it essential to give the owner no
excuse for that miserable shoddy architecture which constructs a
cornice on one or two sides of a building, and leaves it off on sides
that are equally conspicuous ; on the plea, sometimes, that the
owner who has built up to his line has no right to build a cornice
over his neighbor's property.   Though these houses indicate continuous blank walls on one side, they are not necessarily so, when
this space is preserved ; and if the owner of the middle lot is a
reasonable man, pleasant windows and out-looks may be made
from the halls of both the outer houses, and from the bed-room of
the house on the right.   The arrangement of rooms in the upper
stories is likely also to call for quite a number of windows overlooking the middle lot, and the fact of ownership of even a very
little space in front of them will make it safer for the builder to
plan them.   If the occupants of the three lots are in friendly accord,
the high division fences as shown back of the front lines of the
houses, may be dispensed with back to the rear of the same.   The
blank walls can be covered with the Virginia creeper, and groups of
shrubbery arranged at their base to better advantage than our plan
shows ; the plan supposing a concert of improvements only in
front of the houses.

The house on the right has the form and extent of an unusually commodious and elegant town-house ; the main part being
25 × 50 feet, and the rear 20 × 34.   The front-entrance is quite
peculiar, and, if designed by a good architect, will be an elegant
and uncommon style of porch.   There is a double object in making
it of this form.   It being desirable to have the entrance-gate at D,
where persons passing in will at once have a vista the whole length
of the side-yard to the back corner of the lot (as indicated by the

Plate XXIV.

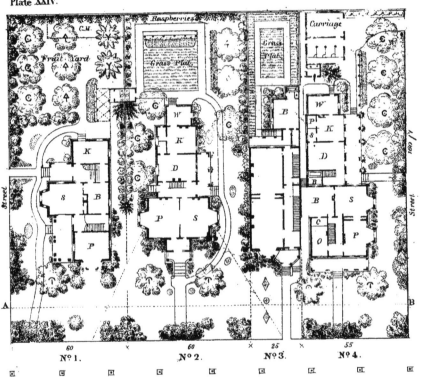

Raspberries. Carriage. Fruit Yard. Grass Plat. Grass Plat.

No 1.   No 2.   No 3.   No 4.

60   60   25   55

10 5 0   10   20   30   40   50   60   70   80   90   100 ft.

dotted line), thus receiving a more favorable impression of the extent and beauty of the ground than if the gate-entrance were directly in front of the front door, this location of the gateway naturally suggests a side approach to the porch. But a porch of this form is of itself desirable in such a location, by permitting a heavy mass of shrubs to be planted directly in its front, leaving the lawn in front unbroken, and making the porch appear more distant and retired from the street than it would were the steps and walk directly in front of it, in the usual mode. It also makes a convenient front-entrance to the basement at the side of the parlor bay-window.

The grounds of this group of places are quite simple in the style of planting; yet, if laid out as here indicated, the materials properly chosen and well kept, they would be noticeable for their elegance. The necessarily small scale on which these groups of houses and lots are planned, makes it impracticable to describe them in detail, especially with reference to the selections of shrubs and trees.

PLATE XXIV.

Four Residences, occupying the end of a Block two hundred feet in width, on Lots one hundred and fifty feet deep, and representing widely different forms of Houses and Lots.

We will here suppose that the two lots on the left, each sixty feet front, were first purchased and improved; and the next twenty-five feet were then purchased by some one who cared little for grounds, and wished merely to provide himself a good town-house; and then the remaining fifty-five feet of the block by some one who could afford a larger style of improvement, including a carriage-house and stable. Also, that numbers one and two having built their house-fronts about forty feet from the street, purchaser number three has the good taste to put his front on the same line; but number four having a much longer house is obliged to crowd forward of the line a little. It is pleasant to observe how, in this group of utterly unlike houses, the peculiarity of each adds to the

beauty of the others; and all succeed, by a harmonious improve
ment of their grounds on a common plan, to realize a great deal of
beauty for which each one pays but a small share. Suppose the
city-house number three were placed twenty feet nearer the street,
it would then destroy the opportunity for the fine lawn on the line
A, B; its blank side-walls would be marplots of the block on both
sides; and its front-porch and bay-window, which now have charming outlooks in each direction, would then have little in view but
the sidewalk and the street. By placing the house back on a line
with the others, the owner has therefore made a great profit for
himself, and conferred an equal one on his neighbors. Let him
carry the same good sense a little farther. He has not cared to
have much ground, but that strip twenty-five feet in width in front
of his house must, in some way, be made creditable to the neighborhood. If it were filled with trees, shrubs, or flowers, these
would destroy his grass-plat and outlooks, and his neighbors would
have no considerable length of grassy ground; it would be selfish,
after securing pleasant views from his bay-window over his neighbors' improvements, to so plant his own lot that their views would
be destroyed. We would therefore suggest to him not to plant a
tree, or a shrub, in front of his steps; but to place in the centre of
the space in front of the bay-window a vase for flowers, of the most
beautiful and substantial form that he can afford, and make it his
"family pride" to see that the filling of the vase and of the small
flower-beds in front and behind it is as perfect a piece of art as
possible. The plain lawn surrounding them, and the absence of
any attempt at rural effect in front of this city-house, will alone
give it an air of distinguished simplicity, while these characteristics
will make its lawn, and vase, and flowers, a harmonious part of the
common improvement of the whole block-front. We thus see how
the owner of the narrowest lot of the group holds, as it were, the
key to the best improvement of the block, and by the use of generous good sense, or the want of it, can consummate or mar the
beauty of a whole neighborhood of grounds.

On lot 1, the house and grounds resemble those shown on
Plate VI, though they are not identical. Besides the fruit trees
in the back-yard it should have no other trees, except one of

small size as shown near the front corner of the veranda ; for which place we recommend the *Magnolia machrophylla.* The two small trees near the corners of the front bay-window, may be the catalpas *himalayensis* and *kœmpferi;* and the isolated tree nearest the street, the white-flowered magnolia (*conspicua*), or a single fine specimen of weigela, deutzia, lilac, viburnum, or honeysuckle. The gateway arch should be of hemlock, with evergreen under-shrubs near it.

On lot 2, but two trees are shown in front of the house. These are twenty feet in front of the main house corners. Of rapid grow-ing deciduous trees for this place, none are better adapted than the weeping birches ; of those of slower growth, the double white-flowered horse-chestnut ; or of evergreens, the weeping Norway spruce and weeping silver-fir. The gateway arch should be made with hem-locks.

Lot 4 has also two trees in front of the corners of the veranda. These being but eight feet from the latter, should be of some species which makes clean stems of sufficient height to carry their branches over its roof, in order not to darken and obstruct the out-look from the veranda. For this the ginkgo tree, most of the birches, and the scarlet oak are well adapted. But if it is desired to have the veranda deeply shaded, and somewhat secluded by foliage in summer, then the magnolias *soulangeana* or *cordata,* or almost any of the hard maples and horse-chestnuts, or the beeches and lindens, will do. We decidedly prefer deciduous trees to ever-greens, in places so near the pleasantest outlooks from the house as these trees are located ; for the reasons that their shadows are broader and more useful in summer, and by dropping their leaves in autumn, they relieve us in winter of a shade that would be needless and sombre.

PLATE XXV.

*Two Suburban Houses with Stables and Gardens, on original Lots
100 × 200 feet, illustrating a mode of embellishment by the addition of a Lot behind other Lots.*

The reader must imagine these two houses originally built on
lots of the same size as that of plan No. 2 of this plate, viz.:
100 × 200 feet, having similar lots behind them, fronting on the
side-street.

.The owner of the corner lot No. 1, having it in his power, and
desiring to enlarge his embellished grounds, buys the lot 100 × 200
feet in the rear of the two lots, first occupied, and thus doubles the
area of his ground. The carriage-house and stable which he may
or may not have had before, can now be located on the part of the
new lot in the rear of the stable on original lot No. 2. Around it,
in the rear of the same lot, is ample room for the vegetable-garden,
and a yard for the horse and cow. This leaves the entire length
of the ground near the side-street clear for decorative improvement.
The outside kitchen-door of the house on lot 1 is through the
laundry W, where the paths connecting it with the stable and outbuildings are entirely disconnected from the pleasure-walks. The
carriage-road which connects with the steps of the back veranda is
for the use of the family and household friends only ; the street on
the main front being the place for casual callers to alight.

Had the house been originally designed for the lot as it now
stands, it could doubtless have had its best rooms arranged to look
out more directly on the best portions of the grounds. As it is, the
parlor gets no part of the benefit of the enlargement of the place
by the addition of the rear lot. But the dining-room D, by a wide
window or low-glazed door opening upon the back veranda, com-
mands a full view of the croquet and archery ground, and its surrounding embellishments ; and the family sitting-room S secures
a similar view with a different fore-ground, by a bay-window projected boldly towards the side-street for that purpose. The outlook
from the unusually large parlor on this plan, depends mostly on the

Plate XXV.

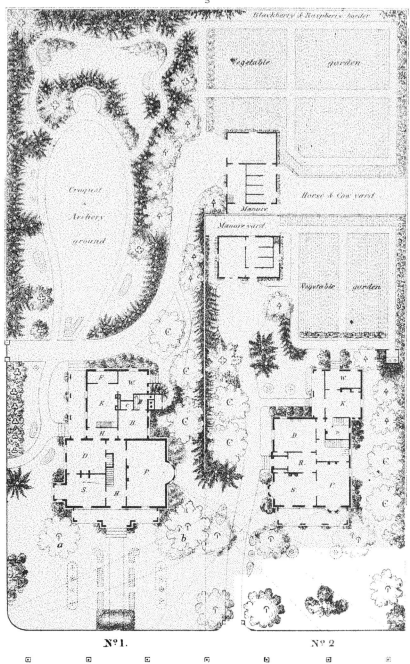

Nº 1.

Nº 2

adjoining place for the fine open lawn that is in view from the bow-window; but as the finest rooms of the house on lot 2 are equally dependent on the outlook across lot 1 for their pleasing views, it is not to be supposed that the occupants of either would wish to interrupt the advantageous exchange. The extreme openness of lawn on the front of both places, and the almost total absence of shrubbery on the front of No. 1, is for the purpose of giving a generous air to both, and to maintain all the advantages of reciprocity. It would be quite natural to suppose that No. 1, which is an old place remodelled, had once had its front yard filled full of shrubs and trees, and that in the formation of the new lawn in the rear the shrubbery was mostly removed to make the lawn more open, and to stock the groups of the new plantation; and then that the flower-beds were planned to relieve its plainness, without obstructing the neighbor's views, as shrubs and trees might.

The house on lot No. 2 is 40 × 44 feet, with a kitchen-wing 18 × 24. Having the main entrance on the side, the carriage-way passes the door, on the way to the stable, without unnecessary detour; and the best rooms of the house occupy the entire front. The house is considerably smaller than that on lot No. 1, though all its rooms are of ample size; the difference between the houses being in the stately parlor and bed-room on the first floor, which the house on lot No. 1 has, and the other has not. The sitting-room and parlor of the latter, however, opening together by sliding doors, will be fully equal in effect to the single parlor in the former plan; and, in proportion to its size, the latter seems to us the best house-plan.

The details of the planting on both places we can follow no further than the plate indicates them, without drawings on a larger scale to refer to. The fronts are simple and open to a degree that may be unsatisfactory to many persons—especially near the street-front of the corner lot; but as that lot is supposed to be richly embellished with shrubbery in the pleasure-ground back of the carriage-entrance, we believe the marked simplicity of the front will tend to make the new portion of the place more interesting by the contrast which its plainness presents to the profusion of sylvan and floral embellishments of the pleasure-ground proper.

PLATE XXVI.

A Village Block of Stores and Residences, illustrating a mode of bringing Grounds back of Alleys into connection, for Decorative Purposes, with the Residences on the Village Street.

We desire to call the reader's attention to this elaborate study of an unusual mode of securing to homes on contracted village lots the delightful appendage of charming little pleasure grounds.

The business of small villages usually clusters on one street, and sometimes occupies but a few stores near "the corners;" and it is a common practice of thrifty and prudent village merchants to have the residence on the same lot with the store, or on an adjoining lot. As the village increases, the lots near the leading merchant's are those earliest occupied by good improvements, in stores or residences. Our plate shows a village or suburban block of two hundred feet front on the principal street, with lots one hundred and fifty feet deep to an alley.

Let us suppose that Mr. Smith, the wealthiest business man of the vicinage, has purchased the one hundred feet front on the right, and erected two fine stores on the corner (one of which he occupies), and a dwelling-house on the balance of the lot. While beginning to amass wealth he was doubtless occupying a much smaller store and house, and has erected these large improvements when his means enabled him to move with considerable strength. Let us further suppose that on the completion of this fine residence, a couple of well-to-do citizens buy two adjoining lots of twenty-five feet front each and put up a pair of city houses; and that the corner fifty feet, on the left, is then improved as shown on the plate.

Mr. Smith, and those who have built after him, have all been intent on getting themselves good houses, and have not had either the leisure or the taste to give much thought to grounds for embellishment. With a business exacting all his time, and a young family to provide for, the business man has looked forward to a new store or a new house as the *ultima thule* of his ambition. But when these are acquired, and larger means and more leisure and observation of

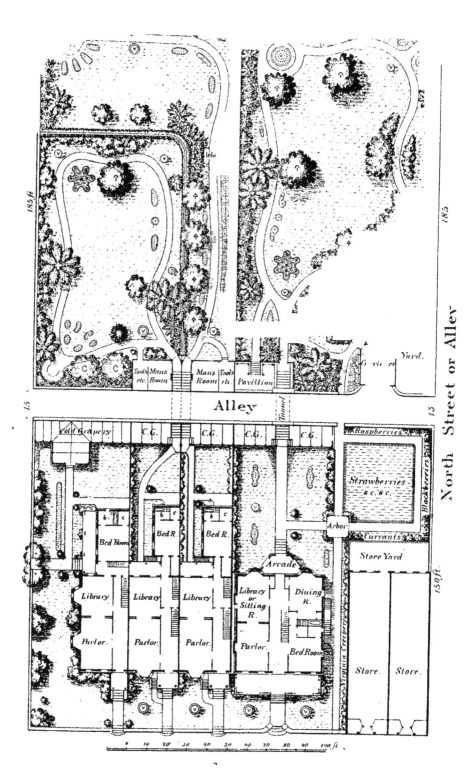

the results of culture and wealth in other places open his eyes to other refined objects of expenditure, he cannot but see, living as he does in the centre of a farming country, with open fields and pleasant shade-trees only a few squares away, how he has cramped his house, like a prisoner, between the walls of his stores and his new neighbors, and has not even play-room for his children. But the fine house is built and cannot be abandoned. The neighbors, with fine, but smaller city-houses, are in the same predicament. They are all persons in good business, with (we will suppose) the average taste of tolerably educated people for a certain degree of elegance outside as well as inside their houses.

We have represented the entire fronts of the lots as bounded by a low stone-wall and coping, making the grounds four steps (twenty-eight inches) above the level of the sidewalks, and the main floors of the houses five steps more, so that the basement-kitchens for which all the houses are planned will be mostly above the level of the ground. In addition to a fine *low* iron fence on the stone coping, and some elegant vases in the centre of each of the front spaces between the walks, and the vines on the porches and veranda, the three places nearest the store can have little more done to them to make them attractive homes exteriorly. The back-yard of the double-house has room for a little decoration, and as the wall next to the alley has an east exposure, it is a good place for a cold grape-house, and is used accordingly. The rear arcade and bay-windows of the library and dining-rooms now have a pleasant look-out on a pretty bit of grass-plat, dotted with a vase and a few beds for low flowers; the grapery bounding the view in front, and a square rose-covered arbor marking the intersections of the walks on two sides of the fruit and vegetable square, behind the store-yards. The other neighbors follow suit with cold grape-houses along the alley; the one on the extreme left improving on the others by adding a decorative gable-entrance fronting the main street, and forming a pleasing termination to the view of the side-yard as seen from the front. These four places now have about all the out-door comforts and beauties that the lots are capable of; but after all they are city houses, on cramped city lots. The pleasures incident to the care of these bits of lawn, the filling of the

15

vases, and the management of the vines and plants in the grape-
houses, all have a tendency to beget a craving for-more room ; for
similar pleasures and more beautiful creations on a larger scale.
Mr. Smith, the owner of the stores and the double-house, has been
obliged to buy the lot back of the alley (100 × 185 feet) to get
room for his stable, vehicle, and man-servant. Not being in a
street where property is used for business, or popular for residences,
he buys it for a small part of what lots on the east street are worth ;
and the lot is first used for a horse and cow pasture, or run-ground,
in connection with the stable. Now let us suppose Mr. Smith is
one of those good specimens of business-men whose refined tastes
develop as their means increase, and that he longs, and that his
good family seconds the longing, for those lovely stretches of lawn
flecked with shadows of trees, margined with shrubberies, and
sparkling with flowers, that some friend's acre has enabled him to
display ; that the family envy the possession of fine croquet grounds
where children, youth, and old people are alike merry in the open
summer air with the excitement of the battles of the balls ; that
they desire some better place than the street to air the little children, and to stroll with family familiarity on fair summer days, and
evenings, and sociable Sundays.

To obtain all these pleasant features of a home without going
into the country, or exchanging the home in the heart of the village
for a new one farther off, or giving up the convenient proximity to
his business which Mr. Smith has always enjoyed, *we propose to
tunnel the alley*, and to convert the cow-pasture-lot into a little
pleasure-ground, as shown on the plan. This project, however, pre-
supposes that the soil is naturally so gravelly as to be self-draining,
so that water might never rest in the tunnel, or else that drainage
for the bottom of the tunnel can be effected by a sewer in the alley
beneath it, or not far off.

It may be asked—"why tunnel rather than bridge the alley?"
The reasons are conclusive in favor of the tunnel. A bridge over
the alley must be high enough to allow a load of hay to pass under.
The great height would make it a laborious ascent and descent.
In going from one piece of embellished ground to the other it is
precisely to avoid the sight of the alley that we want bridge or

tunnel. But by mounting a bridge, although we thus secure clean footing at all times, which might not be the case in crossing on the ground, the alley would be more entirely in sight than if one were to cross it in the usual way; and (if the bridge were uninclosed) persons making use of it would be targets for the eyes of the neighborhood. If inclosed and roofed, its height would make it absurdly conspicuous, expensive, and liable to be carried off by winds. Whether used or not, it would stand obtrusively in sight from all directions, without the excuse for its conspicuousness which attaches to a wind-mill, which, to be useful, must stand on tip-toe to catch each wandering breeze.

The tunnel, on the other hand, is unobtrusive, out of sight of all but those who use it, private, and a cool summer retreat. It forms, when properly constructed, a novel contrast and foil to the sunny garden to which it is designed to introduce the passer. Descending into its vaulted shade, the view on emerging into a sunny pleasure-ground is made doubly charming by the contrast. Its sides should be recessed for seats, which in the hottest days of summer will have a delightful coolness, and in winter form good places for storing half-hardy box plants, bulbs, and small trees. One needs but call to mind the charming tunnels for foot-paths in the New York Central Park to imagine the beauty that may be given to even such small tunnels as the ones here recommended.

If well constructed, such tunnels cannot be done cheaply. But in a case like the one under consideration, where the owner of a fine place must either sell out and improve elsewhere, or else devise some mode of utilizing the lots across the alley, the expense of a tunnel and its appropriate adjuncts, will be very small compared with the sacrifices that would be necessary to secure the same benefits by removal.

The construction of such a tunnel and its approaches requires the employment of a very good architect. To enable the reader to have a better idea of the plan, as indicated on our plate, we will give some explanations in detail. Nine feet below the surface of this alley is supposed to be deep enough for the floor of the tunnel. Seven feet clear will be high enough for the inside passage, which will leave enough earth over the top of a brick arch to protect it;

and six feet will be a sufficient clear width inside. For an alley fifteen feet wide, the arch should be eighteen feet long. The steps down to it, and their flanking walls, would make a length of ten to fifteen feet more on each side—depending on the manner of the descent, and the nature of the superincumbent improvements—and likely in any case to make the entire excavation upwards of forty feet in length, including the slopes for the steps. The side-walls throughout should be double or hollow walls; the inner one of brick, nicely pointed, the outer one of stone, and both made water-tight with water-lime cement. The arch over the tunnel proper should be made with great care to render it perfectly water-tight also; and if the entire filling above the arch, and on the outside of the side-walls, is made with good gravel, broken stone, or, coarse sand, so as to let all surface water soak down directly to the drain below the floor of the tunnel, there will be little liability to excessive dampness or dripping water in the tunnel. The arch for the main tunnel on this plan is to have the springing points five feet from the floor, and to be that segment of a circle which will make the centre seven feet high. For stairs, broad solid stone steps are of course the best in the long run, but some expense for such work may be saved by having the slope down to the tunnel floored with a smooth water-lime cement, and a flight of plank steps put in, supported at the ends only, and high enough above the sloping cement floor to allow the latter to be readily brushed and kept clean under the plank steps. These, having the air circulating freely all around them, will not be liable to quick decay.

In the plan under consideration, the walk leading directly from the rear arcade of the double-house to the grape-house is to descend gradually for about twenty feet, so that at the front line of the latter it will be two feet below the general surface, and a step on the same line will drop eight inches more to a stone landing, from which four steps *up* on each side lead to the two sides of the grape-house, and ten steps *down*,·to the floor of the tunnel. On the side towards the mansion, the inclosed porch and roof of the entrance to the tunnel being made in the construction of the grape-house, cannot be considered a part of the cost of the former, but the flanking walls, the steps, the tunnel itself, and the necessary covered porch over the exit from the tunnel on the farther side of the alley, altogether involve a considerable expenditure. The whole could probably be done in a plain style for about one thousand dollars, including a handsome inclosed porch on the upper side, but not including the pavilion shown on the left of it, which is a separate affair ; though the two may be made together as one construction.

This pavilion will certainly be a desirable feature after the pleasure-ground has become sufficiently complete to make a view over it pleasing. It should have a solid wall on the alley side. The floor is raised five feet above the lawn, and the space beneath (with a floor a foot or two below the lawn and a window on the alley) may be used as the gardener's work-room. Fronting to the west as here shown, the pavilion will be a pleasant place for members of the family to retire on warm summer evenings after tea to observe the warm lights on the trees, the lengthening shadows on the lawn, and all the glories of our American sunsets. Or, if a darker seat in the summer-house in the far corner of the lot be preferred, the light of the sun upon the arches and other features of the pavilion will make a bright addition to the beauty of the view towards it.

Before describing the pleasure-ground upon which the proposed tunnel from the double-house opens, we wish to call attention to what new ambitions the spirit of emulation is likely to produce in the owners of the two city houses on the twenty-five feet lots adjoining. They are much worse off for yard-room than Mr. Smith ever was, and his successful use of the rear lot by means of the tunnel suggests to them the purchase of the equal sized remaining lot back of their own improvements. Both want it, and they compromise by buying it together, with a view of joining in the expense of a tunnel-entrance to it. It will be seen that we have arranged for them a double-tunnel with passages four feet in width.

The new lot must be partitioned between them, so as to give each an equal area, and an equal value. This is done in a peculiar way in order to make the form and consequent effect of the improvements on each lot as different from the other as practicable. Each owner has entrance to his own tunnel through his grape-house, and the exit porches on the opposite side open upon lawns and pleasure walks that can quickly be made interesting. In connection with the double exit porch we have drawn buildings for hired men, including workshops and tool-rooms of the same width, under a roof supposed to be a continuation of the pavilion-structure on Mr. Smith's lot. Many persons who employ men-servants object to lodging them in their residences. As rooms for them may be provided more cheaply in connection with the building of this tunnel porch than if built separately, we have introduced them; but they are not essential to the plan.

We will now sketch the general features of the planting for the first described lot back of the alley. It must be borne in mind, to begin with, that this lot, 100 × 185 feet, is a small area upon which to place all the structures and gardenesque embellishments that the ground-plan indicates; and being surrounded by a high wall or fence to insure its absolute seclusion, its lawn-surface will be still further lessened by the belts of trees and shrubs that must be planted inside the walls to relieve their monotony. This limited area can be planted so as to avoid inelegant crowding only by a selection of trees of secondary size, and a very judicious choice of shrubs. But when such walled grounds are successfully treated, there is an expression of *snugness* and elegant privacy about them that the ladies are apt to speak of as "delicious." Those who have passed through dark houses on some of the narrow streets of old Paris, and emerged suddenly in great gardens behind them, which one could hardly imagine there was vacant room for within a mile of the place; or those who have been equally surprised and delighted with the brilliant gardens behind the dismal street-walls of Spanish American cities, can appreciate fully how charming such grounds as these *may* be made, and how the mere novelty of such a tunnel-entrance to a walled garden will give it a special charm.

We have not hitherto called attention to the path from the kitchen (under the dining-room) directly to and across the alley, to the carriage-house and stable. Between this path and the exit-porch of the tunnel, the space is to be filled with a pine tree and a dense growth of hemlocks, and an impervious screen of the latter is to be continued along the right-hand side of the path issuing from the tunnel;—to be grown to a height that will conceal the stable buildings from view as one passes along by the side of them. The path connecting the stable and the main path, should open from the latter under a narrow hemlock-arch. The group of evergreens on the left of the exit from the tunnel must be those which do not exceed seven feet in height, or which may readily be kept down to that height, and not interfere with the view from the arcade;—say a pair of Sargent's hemlock, next to the arcade, the *Cephalotaxus fortunii mascula* next; the golden arbor-vitæ in front of that; and a bed of flowers diminished to a point as shown on the plan.

At the divergence of the main paths a really elegant flower-vase should be placed; it being the first object that will engage the eye on emerging from the tunnel. Behind it a rose-bed is shown. Perhaps a fine evergreen would be better there, say the weeping silver-fir, on a line with the centre of the tunnel and the vase.

Following the main path to the right, there should be masses of strong-growing shrubs between it and the stable, to prevent the latter from being noticeable in passing. A mass of shrubs eight feet high, within two yards of the walk, will conceal an object twenty-four feet high, twenty-four feet from the walk. Of course all parts of this stable-building should be well finished, as it must be seen from nearly every part of the pleasure-ground, but if the upper parts of it—the roof-lines, cornices and upper windows—are properly designed, a view of them over the shrubs and among the tops of the environing trees will improve, rather than injure, the expression of the place. The three sunny sides of the building are also to be covered with the foliage of grape-vines. In addition to the needful shrubbery to conceal this building from too close inspection, the corner of the lot in its rear is to be stocked with cherry and pear trees. Where the walk turns toward the left, leaving the fruit-tree group, a mass of fine shrubs borders the walk on both sides; then for a short distance the lawn opens on the right to a grape-espalier, and a group of the finest rhododendrons in front of it; on the left, at *a*, is a pair of *Kolreuterias*, and beyond them another group of rhododendrons and azalias. We here come in sight of the summer-house in the corner, with its flanking of hemlocks and bright little flower-beds, and a vase opposite the walk from it. The view of the grounds from this point is intended to

be the best.   Passing along to the left, the tree marked *b*, is intended for the weeping beech ; beyond, the walks form a circle
for a grand mass of bedding-plants, in a bay of evergreens.   The
tree *c*, may be the *Magnolia machrophylla*; at *d*, a pair consisting
of a sassafras and a white-flowering dogwood ; opposite to them a
group of three pines, the Bhotan, Austrian, and white.   On the
right (returning towards the tunnel), the wall between the pines is
to be screened by a collection of small evergreens.   As they will
have only a north exposure until their tops are higher than the
division fences, a hemlock hedge close to the fence, with a formal
collection of rhododendrons and evergreen dwarfs in front of it,
will be best there.   The pine tree at the last turn of the walk is
intended for the dwarf white (*compacta*) ; or, a weeping Japan
sophora would be well placed there.

The suppositional plantings of the other lots back of the alley
we must leave to the reader ; except to mention that the long wall
which divides the place just described from its neighbor, offers on
its south side too good an opportunity for a grape-border to be
lost.   We have therefore used its entire length for that purpose.

The reader will hardly fail to notice that the corner place on
the left, which originally had double the width of lot of its next
neighbors, and that too on a corner where bay-windows, and
ground well improved on the side, gave it many advantages in point
of beauty and comfort, has now no pleasure-ground that deserves
the name compared with those which have been secured by means
of the tunnel, in connection with the houses on the twenty-five
feet lots.

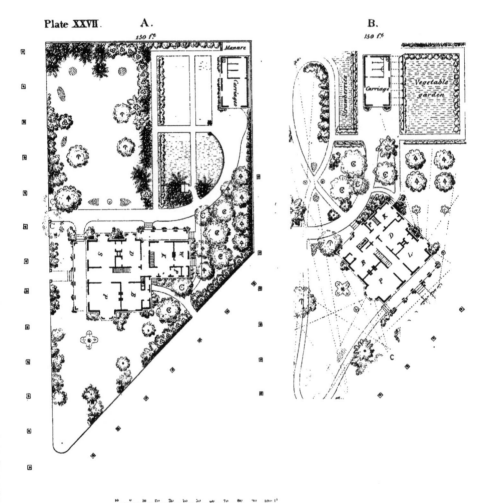

Plate XXVII.

PLATE XXVII, A AND B.

Two Plans for Residences and Grounds on Lots having acute Angles formed by equally important Streets.

These are common forms of town and suburban lots, which puzzle improvers as to how to front the house, to plan it, and to place the outbuildings, and lay out the ground so that the improvements shall look well, and the connections be the most convenient from both streets.

The two ground-plans here given show different modes of fronting a house that is nearly the same in plan on both, on the same lot; the different frontages involving a totally different style of laying out in each case, and some variations in the kitchen part of the house-plans.

The lots are one hundred and fifty feet on each of the shorter sides, and would be three hundred feet in length on the longest side if extended to a sharp point; this makes them equal in area to a parallelogram 150 × 225 feet; a trifle more than three-quarters of an acre.

The carriage-house and road are of similar character in both plans, and enter from the same street. In other respects the ground-plans differ widely, and yet have some points of resemblance which the form of the boundaries renders essential. Both have been designed with care to make them valuable studies for those who have similar lots to improve. Design B has a considerable length of pleasure-walks which may be dispensed with, without marring the design for planting; and design A shows no walks on the pleasure-ground proper, though a walk could be laid out around the lawn above the house, if thought desirable, without changing the plan of its planting. The dotted lines on design B represent some of the open lines of view to and from the principal windows of the house, from the streets, and from one part to another of the grounds.

The extremely small scale of the drawings make it impractica ble to give details for planting.

PLATE XXVIII.

Plans for two Triangular Corner Lots opposite each other.

The upper of these two lots is larger than those of Plate XXVII, and contains an acre and a half, but is of precisely the same form, and supposed to be differently circumstanced in the character of the street on its longest side ; which, though used for the carriage-entrance A, and one foot-path entrance *b*, is not of sufficient importance to make it desirable to leave openings in the shrubbery on that side for views from the street to the house. The residence is more mansion-like than those on the plate referred to, and its carriage-entrance has a much more stately character. The large turn-way in front of the main entrance is larger than necessary for a turn-way merely, in order to make a broader green directly in front of the main entrance, and to give room for a grove of fine trees with which it is to be shaded. The walk from the front street at *c*, with the one before mentioned at *b*, and the kitchen entrance-gate at *d*, give the most convenient access from the streets to the house from whichever direction one comes, and leave a large area between *c* and *b*, unbroken by walks, which the plan shows to be carefully and elegantly improved ; while to the right of the walk from *c*, a heavy mass of shrubbery forms a boundary between the pleasure-ground proper, and a considerable orchard, kitchen grass-plat, and vegetable-ground. The triangular space between the walk-entrance *b*, and the carriage-entrance A, should be filled with evergreens—say a Norway spruce in the centre and hemlocks around it. Between *a* and *d* is room for masses of some of the noblest shrubs. The small scale of the drawing here again forbids a further detailed enumeration of the materials for the plantation.

The lower plan is essentially different in its conditions and treatment from the three that have been noticed, though it resembles plan B, of Plate XXVII in its frontage, if that plan were turned upside down. But on this plan we suppose the lot to be little more than a mere triangle—turning the corner on the left only

200 f.

Manure Yard

Raspberries

Carr- Stable
ages shed

Melon Ground

Vegetable
Garden

Y Y Y

Orchard

and

Garden

d

C C C

D K

C C C

B L

C C C

L

C C C

P

300 f.

210 f.

A

c

b

N

a

C

C

C C C C C C

I

P D

T

B

K P M

Carriages

C'

100

200 ft

forty feet, just far enough to include a row of fruit trees and a private entrance to the stable and carriage-house on that side by a straight road to it. It will be observed that the kitchen, carriage-house, and stable are joined, and turned into the corner of the lot in the most compact arrangement possible; and that the entire house-plan (the main part of which is 33 × 50 feet) is a model of compactness, convenience, and good connections with the several parts of the ground. The latter also affords a rare study of the elegant effect that may be produced on only two-thirds of an acre by skillful arrangement of buildings and plantings, and the abandonment of a vegetable-garden.

In most respects this plan if well studied will explain itself; but there are two inconspicuous features on this drawing which the observer may fail to catch the meaning of. First, the point where the long walk to the kitchen diverges from the one leading to the front, shows what appears like a large tree over it. This is intended to represent five trees (the trunks of which are shown by light dots on the engraving) planted in the form of a pentagon, for the purpose of making an umbrage of the character of some of those described in Chapter XIV. Where the hawthorns flourish we would make the collection of them alone, including among them the new thorn (not a true hawthorn), *Coccinea flore plena.* But the group may be well composed of many other small species of trees— taking care that when more than one species or variety is used all shall be of similar size and form, in order to make a congruous mass when grown. Second, at a point opposite the parlor bay-window a round flower-bed is shown, backed by dense evergreen foliage. On each side of this flower-bed a pair of small trees are indicated, connected by light lines. These are intended for hemlock arches of fanciful forms, to give interest to the place by their own novelty, and the pretty effect of vistas through them. The commonest bit of lawn with a glimpse of bright flowers, when seen through such arch-frames, often has a pretty effect that is quite remarkable considering the meagre materials that produce it.

Plate XXIX.

A first-class Suburban Residence and Plantation on a Corner Lot of 300 × 540 feet, containing $3\frac{71}{100}$ acres.

This is one of those elegant places that requires a large income for its maintenance, and which most Americans who have little idea of the breadth of view that the name park implies, are apt to speak of as a private park. It is by no means a park, but it is a generous pleasure-ground for a retired citizen, with all the elegant appliances that wealth makes practicable. There is room enough here to indulge in a great variety of trees and shrubs without crowding the lawn. The latter opens generously upon the public highway in front, and connects on the right with a supposed good neighbor. The entrance-drive is simple in its character, and from the point **A**, the visitor in entering would command vistas the entire length of the lot over the lawn in front ; and at the right, a view of the elaborate flower-garden that forms the principal feature of interest opposite the parlor bay-window. The plan directly violates one rule that is generally desirable to observe in the arrangement of trees, viz.: to plant so as to make the house the centre of the picture from the most prominent or most natural points of view. But on this plan the trees in front, and near the front of the house, when well grown, will effectually hide it from the entrance at **A**, and leave but partial views open from the highway to the east side of the house ; while from all other points along the street towards which it fronts, it will be completely shut off by trees. This has been done for the following reason. On so large a lot it would savor of selfish exclusiveness not to have the lawn open generously to the street. But many families have a strong desire for a considerable degree of privacy in their front veranda and porch. As in this case they front to the south, not only their free use, unobserved from the street, but their comfort in the face of so much gravelled road, requires a mass of trees to shut off too open a view from the street, and to render the veranda and porch comfortable in hot weather by their cooling shadows. It being desirable for

300 ft

Vegetable

Garden

Stable Yard

Carriages
Shed

Cold grape house

D P K

C

E I

F P

A

100 90 80 70 60 50 40 30 20 10 0

these reasons to violate the usual rule, it is better to do it entirely than by halves ; and by inviting the eye, in entering, away from the front to other views around the house, the latter when seen, as it can be to great advantage from the pavilion and from several points in the pleasure-walk in the rear part of the lawn, will (if in itself pleasing) add the more to the attractions of these walks.

———

In concluding this series of designs, we cannot forbear to call attention again to the great advantage that a neighborhood of homes on deep lots, with narrow fronts, has over one of equal population covering an equal area in lots of less depth and more frontage. Narrow frontages enable a community to keep up fine walks and fences in their fronts with less expense to each owner, and thus to add the comforts of city streets to the rural pleasures that await those who court them in the grounds behind the gate. Depth of lots suggests a deep space between the houses and the street, which, by neighborly agreement, opening from one home to another in continuous lawn, and planted with trees and shrubs for the common benefit of all, becomes a broader expanse of embellished ground than is attainable where shallow lots force proprietors to place their residences closer to the street line. Nothing is lost by having the rear part of one's lot, which is necessarily divided by high fences, or walls, from the neighbors, in a long and narrow, rather than a shallow or squarer form. A space forty feet in width, and one hundred and twenty feet in depth behind the house, is more useful for planting, and for domestic purposes, than an area seventy feet square, though the latter is somewhat the largest. The speculative habit of cutting up suburban lands into narrow city lots 25 × 100 feet, or but little more, destroys all chance of making true suburban improvements. Such lots will only sell to citizens who are either too poor, too cockneyish, or too ignorant of their own needs, to insist on something more ; and cannot be managed so as to attract that class of cultivated and intelligent people who want *rurally* suburban homes, and not city houses and city habits on the margin of the country.

CHAPTER XVI.

THE RENOVATION OF OLD PLACES.

WHATEVER objection may be urged against buying and renovating old houses, will not apply to the purchase of ground stocked with old trees and shrubs. Many a rickety, neglected place, is filled with choice old materials, which, with small expenditures in clearing away the superfluities, and polishing the lawn, will group at once into pleasing pictures. Such neglected places may be compared with a head of luxuriant hair all uncombed and disorderly, which needs but to be clean and arranged with taste to become a crown of beauty to the wearer.

Old yards are generally filled with mature trees of choice species, but so huddled together, and filled in with lank neglected shrubs and tangled grass, that one observes only the shiftlessness and disorder, and turns with greater pleasure to look upon a polished lawn with not a tree upon it:—as in music a single note given purely and clearly is more pleasing than the greatest variety of sounds making discords together. But a week's work among these medleys of trees and shrubs—the bold cutting or digging-out of the poorest trees, the re-arrangement of the shrubbery, so that the sunlight may play with the shadows of those that remain, upon some open breadth of velvety grass—and there will stand revealed a mass of beautiful home adornments that the place bare of large trees and mature shrubs will envy. Sometimes old fruit-trees that have had an air habitually expressive of hard times and low living, with a little pruning, and extra feeding, and the well-to-do air that a new green lawn-carpet gives them, will assume a new dress of foliage, and wear it with such luxuriant grace that they become the most pleasing of trees—scarcely recognizable as the same which so lately wore a dejected air.

In renovating old grounds that are filled with mature trees and shrubs, the first thing to be decided on is the amount of clean cutting-out to be done ;—what had better be entirely removed in order that something better may be developed. " Trimming-up," instead of cutting-out, is the common error of persons ignorant of the arts of sylvan picture-making ; an error invariably defended with the potent plea of—" *I* don't believe in cutting down shade trees." It is the semblance of a good reason, and the best excuse that can be given for ignorance in an art which can only be taught by example to those who are not born with landscape mirrors in their hearts. It is only necessary, however, to show a dense grove of high-trimmed trees on one side, and then a similar grove one-third of which has been cut away to make clear openings of sunny lawn through it, and give the remaining trees room to spread their bending boughs to meet the grass, to feel the difference between art that mars, and art that reveals natural beauty.

Yet in regard to "trimming-up" there may be occasions for some exceptional treatment. Noble growths of evergreens growing to the ground sometimes fill the grounds of a small place, obstructing the views over the lawn to a serious extent ; what they conceal being a more important part of the beauty that may be developed than is their own beauty. To destroy the trees may leave too great a void ; to leave them as they are is to retain the gloomy expression that results from lack of sunny lawn and bright vistas *under* the boughs of trees. In such cases we would trim

Fig. 44.

up old fir trees just high enough to give a clear view of the lawn under them, as shown by Fig. 44. The reader will observe that a glimpse of quite an extent of lawn is suggested under the branches of this tree. If, however, the branches rested upon the ground, the landscape vista would be effectually shut out. The advantage of this mode of treatment is principally on small grounds, for, were there space enough to secure ample lawn-views without it, we would by no means recommend this mode of securing them.

In choosing which to cut out, and which to retain, let it be observed that a large tree of an inferior sort may be better worth preserving than a small or thin specimen of varieties that are otherwise superior. There is no more disagreeable impertinence to the cultivated eye than the growth of slender starved saplings planted under the branches of large trees, and striving to get to the sun and sky by thrusting themselves between the limbs of their superiors. As between a sugar-maple and a black oak, for instance, the former is by far the most beautiful and desirable species in all respects ; but, if you have a well branched large tree of the latter and only young sapling maples, we would sacrifice the sap lings of the better breed for the mature beauty of the inferior oak. There is a dignity in big trunks, and loftiness, for which the prettiness of young trees is an unsatisfactory substitute.

Everybody has heard of the countryman who went to see a city but "could not see the town, there were so many houses !" His quaint speech ludicrously suggests the main fault of most old places ; the multiplicity of their trees and shrubs conceal each other, so that they have little beauty either singly or in the mass ; and they are rarely so arranged as to make the home they surround the centre of a sylvan picture. Wherever there are large trees there must be proportional breadths of unbroken lawn—open spaces from which the trees can be seen, or their beauty is of no avail. A dense forest around a home suggests the rudeness of pioneer life, not the refinement of culture. Forests breed timber, not sylvan beauty. It is the pasture-field, the park, and the brook-space, that give sun and scope and moisture to develop the sylvan pictures that painters love. Therefore in renovating over-grown places, bear in mind that the cutting away of some of your old trees may be necessary to reveal and improve the beauty of the others.

Another and different fault of many old places, resulting from the effort of uneducated planters to avoid the error of over-crowding trees and shrubs, is that of distributing them sparsely but pretty evenly all over the place. This is destructive of all picture-like effects, for it gives neither fine groups, nor open lawn; and even the single trees, however fine they may be, cannot be seen to advantage, because there are no openings large enough to see them from. This must be remedied by clearing out in some places and filling-in in others.

There is one value in the possession of thrifty saplings of sorts not especially desirable, that few persons know, and which is very rarely made use of. We refer to their usefulness as stocks upon which to graft finer varieties, and by the greater strength of their well-established roots producing a growth of the inserted sorts much more luxuriant and showy than could be obtained in twice the time by fresh plantings. The black oak is not worth preserving, unless of large size, but it can be readily grafted with the scarlet oak. White oaks in superfluous number may be grafted with the rare weeping oaks of England, or the Japan purple oak, or some of the peculiar varieties of the Turkey oak. The common chestnut (*castanea*) may be grafted with ornamental varieties of the Spanish chestnut; the common horse-chestnut or buckeye with a number of beautiful and singular varieties; the common "thorn apple" of the woods with exquisite varieties of the English haw-thorns; and the same with maples, elms, and all those trees of which grafts of novel varieties of the same species may be procured. Scions of rare varieties may be procured at our leading nurseries, or by sending through our seedsmen or nurserymen to England or

16

France for them; for which purpose application should of course be made as early as mid-winter. These suggestions about using trees to graft upon, apply only to young trees. Large ones should not have their nobler proportions marred by such work.

Old apple-trees are not appreciated as they should be. No tree of its size has a grander spread. Their horizontal branches often have the majesty of small park-oaks. This look of low breadth and strength is expressive of its domestic character, and makes it peculiarly appropriate in proximity to residences of moderate size and cottage character. Few trees are in leaf earlier; none are more fragrant or beautiful in bloom; none bend with such a ruddy glow of useful fruit. The fall of immature fruit is an objection to all fruit trees on lawns. If the proprietor is not tidy enough to have his lawn always close mowed under them, and all insect-bitten fruit and windfalls picked or raked up as soon as they drop, then he does not deserve to have trees that are at the same time beautiful and useful.* These remarks apply especially to full-grown trees. It is only after the apple-tree is from thirty to forty years old that it attains a noble expression, and its best characteristics, like those of the oak and chestnut, are developed in its old age.

Apple or other low branching trees that have become decrepit from age or insects, can be turned to pleasing use by cutting off their branches several feet from the main trunks and training vines over them. The pipe-vine or birthwort (*Aristolochia sipho*), with its luxuriant mass of large heart-shape leaves, makes a superb show on supports of this kind. Almost any of our twining or creeping vines are beautiful enough in such places, and few more so than the common hop; but running roses, though often used in this way, are the least suitable. Trees whose tops are not sound enough to be thus used, may often be sawed off from one to three feet above the ground, and used for bases of rustic flower-vases or

---

* We protest against doing violence to old apple-trees by cutting them to pieces to *graft* them with better ones. The beauty of a broad old tree is worth more than the additional value of grafted fruit will ever be. One cannot see an old apple-tree near a house thus marred, without thinking that the owner is either beauty-blind, or so penurious that he grudges the old tree its room upon the lawn unless he can make it pay ground-rent.

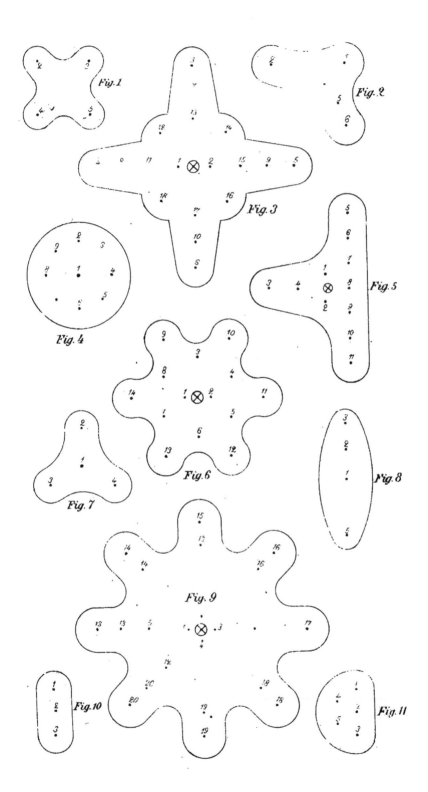

baskets; provided they stand in places where it is appropriate to have flower-vases.

Old shrubs of any of the standard species, if of large size, even though unshapely, may often be turned to good account in the places where they stand, by using them as centres for groups of smaller shrubs. Sometimes their very irregularity of outline will make them picturesque objects to stand conspicuously alone on the lawn. Often a shrub of noble size has been hid by inferior shrubs and trees crowding it, which may all be removed to bring it into full relief. The beauty of full and well grown single specimens of our most common shrubs is as little known as though they were the most recent introductions from Japan. Not one American in a thousand, even among those most observant of sylvan forms, has ever seen a perfectly grown bush-honeysuckle, lilac, snow-ball, or syringa, though every suburban home in the land is filled with them. Growing either in crowded clumps, or under trees, or in poor uncultivated sodden soil, we have learned to love them merely for their lavish beauty of bloom, and have not yet learned what breadth and grace of foliage they develop when allowed to spread from the beginning, on an open lawn.

There are no worse misplantings in most old grounds than old rose-bushes, whose annual sprouts play hide-and-seek with the rank grass they shelter—roses which the occupants from time immemorial have remembered gratefully for their June bloom, till their sweetness and beauty have become associated with the tangled grass they grow in. There is no reason for having a lawn broken by such plants. Rose-bushes do better for occasional transplantings, and their bloom and foliage is always finer in cultivated, than in grassy ground. Mass them where they can be cultivated and enriched together. Plate XXXI shows many forms for rose-beds, and by using care in keeping the strongest growers nearest the centre, varieties enough may be displayed in one snug bed to spoil a quarter-acre lawn planted in the old way—"wherever there is a good open space"—precisely the space that should not be broken by anything, least of all by such straggling growers as roses.

Do not be in haste to decide where the shrubs you dig up shall be planted again.   When the air and sun have been let in to the roots and tops of the best large trees and shrubs, and the lawn is completed about them, it may be that the effect of your lawn, and the trees that shadow it, will be nobler if you omit altogether all the smaller shrubs.   Large trees and shrubs are robbed of half their beauty if they have not a fair expanse of unbroken lawn around them.

VINES ON OLD TREES.—Some evergreens, the balsam-fir for instance, and the hemlock when it is old, become gloomy-looking trees.   The black oak and red oak have also a similar expression, though entirely different in form.   If such trees stand where more cheerful and elegant trees are needed, the desired improvement may be made by enriching the ground near their trunks, and planting at their base, on both sides, such vines as the Chinese wistaria and the trumpet-creeper, which will cover them to their summits in a few years with a mass of graceful spray and luxuriant leafage.*   The Chinese wistaria is probably better adapted to cover lofty trees than other climbers, but the trumpet-creeper, Virginia-creeper, the native varieties of the clematis, and the Japan and Chinese honeysuckles, may all be used.   The wild grape-vine is admirable for filling up trees of thin and straggling growth, such as the oaks before named.   The hardy grape, known as the Clinton, is well adapted to this use, while very good wine can be made of its fruit.   Perhaps no flowering vine excels it in luxuriance of foliage-drapery, but its prolific fruitage renders it necessary to bestow a good deal of time in gathering the clusters scattered among the branches of a lofty tree.   There is no question that the value of the fruit will far more than pay for the labor, but unless picked clean every year it may disfigure both the tree and the lawn. Whether the birds will insure against any damage of this kind we have not had the means of learning.

---

* An exquisite example of the effect of such planting is an old hemlock at "Cottage Place," Germantown, Pa.   The tree is three feet in diameter and eighty feet high.   At a little distance it cannot be recognized as a hemlock, so completely is its lofty summit crowned with a magnificent drapery of the waving foliage of the Chinese wistaria.   A root of the wistaria was planted on each side of the trunk.   Their stems are now from six to eight inches in diameter.

.In conclusion, it may be safely said that new places rarely afford a skillful planter such opportunities for making quick and beautiful effects at small cost as old places of similar extent. Our town suburbs would in a half dozen years be more beautiful than most persons can conceive possible, even without the addition of a single new home, *provided all the old homes could feel the renovating hands of true artists in home-grounds,* and be kept up in the same spirit. The metamorphosis of such places, from cluttered aggregations of superfluities, to gleaming lawns, smilingly introducing the beholder to beautiful trees and flowers that luxuriate in the new-made space and sun around them, is too great not to inspire those who have profited by the change to preserve the beauty that may so easily be brought to light.

OLD HOUSES.—Old places which have houses "just good enough not to move off or tear down," are greatly undervalued by most purchasers. It is not quite in the scope of this work to put in a plea for old houses, but we must confess to a very loving partiality for them when tastefully renovated. No one, however, but an architect who is known to have a tasteful faculty for such adaptations should be employed to direct the work.* There is a thoughtless prejudice in the minds of most Americans against all things which are not span-new; and we have met men of such ludicrous depravity of taste in this respect, as to cut down fine old trees in order to have room to plant some pert and meagre little nurslings of their own buying! Although houses do not grow great by age, like trees, yet, where strongly built at first, and afterwards well occupied, they acquire certain quaint expressions which are the very aroma of pleasing homes; which nothing but age can give a home; and this beauty of some old houses should be as lovingly preserved as that of the aged apple, maple, or elm trees around them.

---

* The attention of the reader is commended to Vaux' "Villas and Cottages," page 205, for some valuable remarks on this subject.

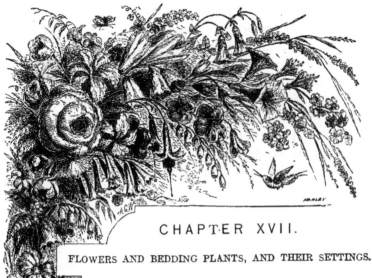

CHAPTER XVII.

FLOWERS AND BEDDING PLANTS, AND THEIR SETTINGS.

We are the sweet flowers
Born of sunny showers,
(Think whene'er you see us, what our beauty saith)
Utterance mute and bright,
Of some unknown delight,
We fill the air with pleasure by our simple breath:
All who see us, love us
We befit our places;
Unto sorrow we give smiles, unto graces—races.

See (and scorn all duller
Taste) how heaven loves color;
How great Nature clearly joys in red and green;
What sweet thoughts she thinks,
Of violets and pinks,
And a thousand flushing hues made solely to be seen;
See her whited lilies
Chill the silver showers,
And what a red mouth is her rose, the woman of her flowers.

Chorus of Flowers, LEIGH HUNT.

A S all vegetable productions, from the greatest trees to the minute mosses, are equally flowering plants, it is to be understood that the subject of flowers, as here treated, is limited to observations on annuals, perennials, and bedding plants.

Considering such flowers as the finishing decorations of a home, as accessory embellishments rather than principal features, it is desired to suggest the places where they may be put with the best effect rather than to give descriptions of even a small number of their almost innumerable variety. The immense collections of our leading seedsmen, and their beautifully illustrated catalogues, give a bewildering sense of the folly of attempting to know, much less to grow, a hundredth part of those which are reputed desirable ; and they also force upon us the wise reflection that the good growth and skilful arrangement of a few species only, will produce effects quite as pleasing as can be attained with the greatest variety.

Annuals, perennials, and bedding plants are used in three tolerably distinct modes, viz. : First, in narrow beds bordering a straight walk to a main entrance, or skirting the main walk of a kitchen-garden. Second, in a variety of beds of more or less symmetrical patterns, grouped to form a flower-garden or parterre, to be an object of interest independent of its surroundings. Third, as adjuncts and embellishments of a lawn, of groups of shrubs, of walks and window views, to be planted with reference to their effect in connection with other things.

On large and expensively kept grounds all these styles may be maintained in appropriate places respectively. But on small lots the first or the last mode should be adopted, though sometimes both may be desirable.

The simplest and rudest mode of planting in the first style, is to border a walk closely with a continuous bed from two to four feet wide, filled with flowering plants of all sizes and shapes and periods of bloom,—here overhanging the walk with unkempt growth, like weeds, there leaving a broad barren spot where spring-flowers have bloomed and withered. Fortunately this mode is becoming less common, and the pretty setting of a margin of well-cut grass is better appreciated than formerly

Flower-beds cut in the grass have a more pleasing effect than when bordered by gravel-walks. When made as marginal embellishments of straight walks, they should rarely be cut nearer than two feet from the side of the walk if they are of much length

parallel with it ; but where the openings between the beds are
frequent, or the beds are in circles or squares with their points
to the walk, one foot of grass between their nearest points and the
walk will answer.   Narrow beds of formal outlines or geometric
forms of a simple character, are preferable to irregular ones.   All
complicated "curlecue" forms should be avoided.   Plate XXX
shows a variety of shapes for flower-beds on straight walks.   Such
beds must, of course, be proportioned in size and form to the
dimensions of the lawn in which they are cut.   They should never
be planted where there is not a space of open lawn back of them
equal at least in average width to the distance across the walk
from one bed to another.   Being close to the eyes of all those who
use the walks, they must be planted and kept with a care that is
less essential in beds seen from a greater distance.   This style of
cultivation necessitates far more labor than the third, which we
have adopted in most of the plans for suburban lots.   To keep a
great number of small beds filled through the summer with low
blooming flowers, and their edges well cut, is expensive ; and, if
they are also planned so that the grass strips between them must
be cut with a sickle, few gentlemen of moderate means will long
have the patience to keep them with the nice care essential to their
good effect.

The border-beds shown on Plate XXX, are all arranged
so that a rolling lawn-cutter may be used easily by hand between them.   These plans are especially adapted to places with
straight main walks, where the gentleman or lady of the house is
an enthusiastic florist.   Walk No. 1 shows a row of round beds
from two to three feet in diameter on each side ; the alternate
circles to be filled with bushy single plants from one and a half to
two feet high, and the others with low bedding flowers that do not
exceed six inches in height.   Nos. 2, 3, and 4 are narrow strips,
and circles or squares alternated.   Such slender evergreens as the
Irish juniper, clipped tree-box, and some of the many dwarf firs,
may be used with good effect in some of these circles, but must
not be too frequent.   The beds at the sides of walks 5 and 6,
require more lawn-room on each side, and will look best filled,
each, with a single color of the lowest bedding-plants.   The

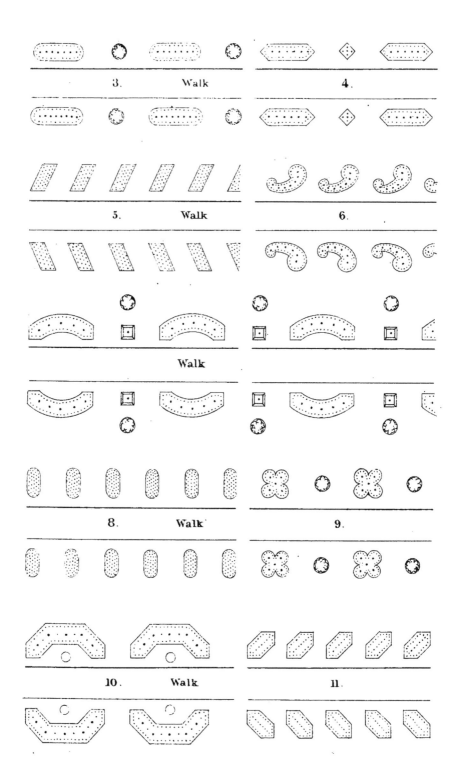

3.   Walk   4.

5.   Walk   6.

Walk

8.   Walk   9.

10.   Walk   11.

same remark will apply to the beds on walks 8 and 11. Walks 7 and 10 have larger beds suitable for filling with plants of different colors and heights. The former is intended to be bordered, between the beds, with square boxes filled with plants from the conservatory, and back of them, in the circles, clipped dwarf evergreens; the latter (10) is to have the small circles next the walk occupied by a succession of pot-plants in bloom, set in larger pots buried in the grass to receive them, so that the former can be taken up and put one side when the grass is to be cut.

Flower-beds which are not more than two feet in width, and on the borders of walks, should have no plants in them more than eighteen inches high, including the height of the flower-stalks, and plants from six to fifteen inches in height have the best effect. In wider beds, by placing the low growing sorts in front, or on the outside edges of the beds, the higher show to good advantage behind them.

In sowing flower-seeds, which are intended to cover a bed, put them in drills across the bed so that a hoe may be used between the plants when they appear.

To make a fine display throughout the season, in beds for low flowers, it is necessary to have at least two sets or crops of plants; one from bulbs, such as snow-drops, crocuses, jonquils, hyacinths, and tulips, all of which may be planted in October, to bloom the following spring; while the bedding-plants for the later bloom, such as verbenas, portulaccas, phlox drummondii, etc., etc., are being started. The bulbs of the former should remain in the ground till June and July to ripen, but the summer blooming plants can be planted between the bulbs, so that the latter can be removed without disarranging the former. Persons having good hot-bed frames, or a green-house to draw from, may make more brilliant beds by more frequent changes, but two crops, if well managed, will be quite satisfactory.

Few persons are aware of the grand displays that may be made in a single season by the use of those annuals, perennials, and bedding-plants which grow quickly to great size. Proprietors commencing with bare grounds can make them very effective temporary substitutes for shrubbery. Many species, especially those half-hardy plants of recent introduction, which are remarkable for the great size, or rich colors of their leaves, are large enough to form, by themselves, groups of considerable size and beauty, from midsummer till frost.   Of these, the different varieties of the ricinus (castor-bean plants) are the most imposing in height, breadth, and size of leaves.   The tree ricinus, *R. borboniensis arboreus*, grows in one season to the height of fifteen feet ; the *R. sanguineous*, ten feet ; the silver-leaved, *R. africanus albidus*, eight feet, and the common castor-oil bean, *R. communis*, five feet. These are all great spreading plants.   The *arunda donax* is a tall plant resembling the sugar-cane, grows rapidly to the height of ten feet, and takes up but little room horizontally.   The magnificent cannas are of all sizes, from two to seven feet in height, and mass well either in beds by themselves, or with low plants of lighter-colored foliage in front of them, and the *arunda donax* or the Japanese striped maize behind them.   The Japanese striped maize is a curiously beautiful species of corn from four to six feet in height, with leaves brightly striped with white and green.   The hollyhocks are noble perennials greatly neglected.   Few plants make so showy a display massed in beds, to be seen at a little distance.   Height, three to six feet.   The *wigandia caracasana* is a very robust bedding-plant which attains the height of six feet, and is remarkable for the size and beauty of its leaves.   The *Nicotea atropurpurea grandiflora* is also noticeable for the robust beauty of its foliage, to which is added the charm of showy dark-red blossoms. The beauty of the gorgeous-leaved *colleus verschafelti* is pretty well known.   In the open sun, and in rich moist soil, each plant will form a compact mass of foliage two feet in height and breadth.   It also makes a brilliant border for the larger plants. The larger geraniums can also be used for the same purpose, and sweet peas, the larger œnotheras, the *lillium giganteum*, and many others, are good taller plants to place behind them.   While masses of shrubs usually display their greatest floral beauty in the spring and early summer, these grand annuals and semi-tropical plants attain their greatest luxuriance of leaf and bloom at the season's close.   The brilliantly-colored or variegated-leaved plants, most of which are half-hardy, require to be propagated and grown in pots in the green-house, but flourish in the open ground during the summer months with great luxuriance, and are among the brightest and most interesting features of suburban lawns. We have named but few out of many of the plants suitable for forming showy masses or conspicuous single specimens. Descriptive lists of all which are valuable may be found in the illustrated catalogues of the great florists and nurserymen.

Fig. 45.

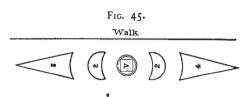

Fig. 45, drawn to the scale of one-sixteenth of an inch to one foot, is a design for a group of small beds to border a straight short walk on each side, and opposite each other. A low broad vase for flowers occupies the centre; the beds 2, 2, to be filled with brilliant bedding bulbs for a spring bloom, and such plants as verbenas, phlox drummondii, and portulaccas for the summer and autumn bloom. The larger beds 3 and 4 (which would be better if finished with a small circle at their points), will have a good effect filled first with bedding-bulbs like the former, and afterwards with a variety of geraniums diminishing in size towards the point of the bed; or roots of the great Japan lily, *Lillium auratum,* may be planted in the widest part of the beds to show their regal flowers above the masses of the geraniums. If such a variety of green-house flowers is greater than the planter wishes to procure, these larger beds, two on each side of the walk, may be filled very showily with petunias in one, dwarf perennial poppies in another, dwarf salvias in another, and coxcombs or pinks in another. The vase, if a broad one, may have a plant of Japanese striped maize for its centre, two *colleus verschafelti,* and two mountain-of-snow geraniums alternated around it, and around the edge of the vase the *vinca elegantissima,* the *lobelia erinus paxtoni,* the *tropæolium,* or some half a dozen other drooping plants of brilliant foliage and blossoms which a florist may name.

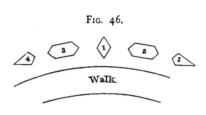

FIG. 46.

Fig. 46 is a group of five small beds on the outside of a circular walk. No. 1 may be filled with four canna plants of sorts from three to four feet high ; the beds 2, and 2, one with Lady Pollock geranium, and the other with some one gorgeous-leaved plant of about the same size ; and beds 3 and 4 with brilliant trailing flowers.

FIG. 47.

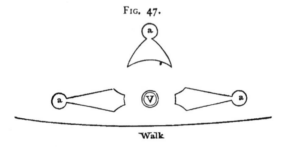

Fig. 47 is a group of beds requiring more space, and adapted to the inner side of a curved walk where there is considerable depth of lawn behind.   V— is a large low vase.   The circular extremities a, a, a, may be filled with compact specimens of curious-leaved plants like the Lady Pollock, or mountain-of-snow geranium, *colleus verschafelti, iresene herbstii,* etc., etc. ; or they may be more permanently occupied by such very dwarf evergreens as the *Abies nigra pumula,* the garden boxwood, or the *Andromeda floribunda.* The narrow parts of the two beds next to the walks should be occupied by some shrubby little annuals or perennials which do not exceed nine inches in height, and the balance of the beds filled with plants increasing in size towards the vase, none of which, however, should be higher than the top of the vase.   The rear bed should be filled in a similar manner, and being further from the walk, may be occupied with showy plants of coarser foliage than the front beds.   By an error in the drawing the circular front of the back bed is made further from the vase than the side ones.   It should be made larger in the direction of the vase, and have its corners truncated like the others.

Fig. 48 is a circular series of eight beds formed on an octagonal plan, with a large vase for flowers in the centre, a width of four feet in lawn around the vase, and the beds, five feet in length, radiating as shown. The plan is suitable for an open space, to give interest to a window view, or to face a porch where the entrance-walk runs parallel with the house. So many different plants may here be used with good effect, that, whichever we may name, may be bettered

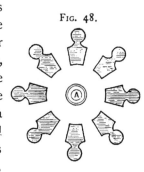

FIG. 48.

by a more skillful florist. Yet we will suggest for the widest part of these beds, stools of the eight finest Japan lilies, to be surrounded by fall planted bulbs that bloom in April and May, which can be removed by the first of June; these to be followed by such plants as gladiolus and tuberoses, on the ends nearest the vase, and by the finest eight varieties of compact geraniums in the outer circles. Or the beds may be planted with an entirely fresh variety of flowers every year.

Fig. 49 is a group of flower-beds suitable to place at the end of a walk or at the intersection of diverging walks. A rustic or other vase is here, also, the centre of the group, with four or five feet of lawn around it. The beds *a*, *a*, should be filled with flowers that do not exceed six or nine inches in height. The beds *b*, *c*, and *d*, are large enough to allow of considerable variety in their composition. The two smaller ones should have no plants that grow higher than two feet, while in the middle of

FIG. 49.

the bed *d*, and in the trefoil end, may be planted those which grow from three to five feet in height.

Fig. 50 (drawn to a scale of one-twelfth of an inch to one foot) requires a larger space such as that made by the turn circle of a roadway, or a place where a walk or road describes the segment of a circle with an open lawn on the inside of the curve. A tree might be planted at the centre, where a vase is designated, and these beds could be formed around it for half a dozen years or more, or until the shade from its branches renders the location unsuitable for

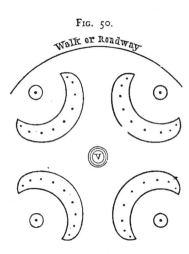

FIG. 50.

the growth of flowers. If a tree be not preferred, then the single vase, or a large basket-vase with a smaller vase rising out of it, would be the most appropriate centre-piece for such a group. The four principal beds are about twelve feet in length on their middle lines, and two and a half feet in greatest diameter. The dots show places for nine robust and compact plants, which may be from four to five feet in height in the centre, and diminish to one foot at each end. Where good plants can be obtained from a green-house, we recommend for the centre of one bed the *Canna coccinea vera*, or the *C. Lindleyana*, which grow to five feet in height, to be flanked with pairs, divided one on each side, of the following varieties, viz.: the *C. limbata major*, four feet high; the *C. bicolor de Java*, three feet; *C. flaccida*, three feet; *C. compacta elegantissima*, two feet; and *C. augustifolia nana pallida*, one foot. Many other varieties will do just as well as the ones named, provided they are of a size to diminish symmetrically from the centre to the ends of the bed. For the centre of another bed the *Nicoteana atro-purpurea grandiflora*, a noble, large-leaved plant, that grows five feet in height, and bears panicles of dark-red blossoms; next to this on either side a plant of *Canna gigantea splendidissima*, three feet; then a pair of *Acanthus mollis*, three feet; next the *Amaranthus bicolor*, two feet; and for the ends, the Lady Pollock geranium, one to two feet. For the centre of a third bed the *Wigandia caracasana* may be used, being another of the splendid leaved plants recently introduced. It grows to the height of six feet. This may be flanked on either side with the *Ricinus communis*, four to five feet high;

next to these a mass of hollyhocks of stocky growth; next the *Mirabilis* (four o'clock), and on the points the *Colleus verschafelti.* In the centre of the fourth bed may be a stool of Japanese striped maize, five to six feet high; next on either side a plant of the striped-leaved *Canna zebrina*, five feet high; next, and in the centre-line of the bed, the *Lillium auratum*, with the *Lillium longiflorum* near the edge of the bed; next the *Salvia argentia*, three feet; and for the ends of the bed the *Amaranthus melancholicus ruber*, one to two feet high. The four outside circles may be filled respectively with the *Colleus verschafelti*, of gorgeous crimson and purple leaves; the mountain-of-snow geranium, with white foliage and scarlet flowers; the *Amaranthus bicolor*, with green and crimson leaves; and the Lady Pollock geranium with variegated leaves. The vase for a group of beds of this size should be large, and well filled in the centre with gay-leaved plants, with more delicate foliage drooping over its sides. If such groups are made without a vase in the centre, we suggest in place of it, the planting of an *Arunda donax* within a circle of Japanese maize, the bed to be about three feet in diameter, and well enriched; or the Irish juniper may be planted as a permanent and more formal centre.

Fig. 51 is a design for a number of beds occupying so great a space that it would constitute a flower-garden. The centre bed is supposed to be cut within a circle of four feet radius, so that it will be eight feet in diameter from point to point. The eight circular beds surrounding it are each three and a half feet in diameter, and laid out so that their centres are on a circle eight feet from the main centre. The inside ends of the outer circle of beds are segments of circles struck from the centres of the small beds, and may be made of any form that the surrounding features of the place suggest. The most elegant feature for the centre of the central bed would be a broad shallow vase two feet in height, and four in breadth, on top, elevated on a pedestal two feet high, which should be concealed by a dense mass of shrubby flowering plants around it; the sides of the vase to be draped with pendulous plants overhanging its sides, and its centre filled with plants of a tropical appearance. Next in elegance to the large vase-centre would be a basket-bed similar to the one shown in the

Fig. 51.

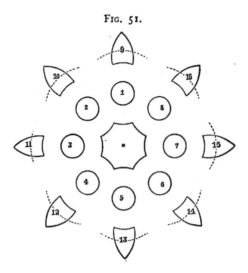

engraving at the end of this chapter.   This would require a different
style of planting.   Supposing its base to be four feet in diameter,
there would be a margin of two feet all around it for low trailing
flowers.   The design for a basket-vase is intended for an open lawn,
and shows a collection of plants quite different from what would be
best for the design under consideration.   Here we would have for
its centre a single group of the *Canna sanguinea chatei*, surrounded
by a circle of Japanese maize ; next a circle of *Salvia argentea*, and
for the outside border the Lady Pollock geranium inter-planted with
some of the slender, drooping, light-leaved plants, named farther on
in this chapter, for the decoration of vases.

If this central bed is to have neither a pedestal-vase nor basket-
vase, it may still be made the most conspicuous point of interest in
the parterre with plants alone.   It is desirable that the lawn should
rise gently towards it on all sides, and that the bed be raised in
the centre as much as may be without making the earth liable to
be washed upon the lawn.   In the centre, *if this flower-garden is
intended to be permanent,* we would plant the remarkable variety of
the European silver fir, known as the *Picea pectinata pendula*, or
the variety of the Norway spruce, known as the *Abies excelsa inverta,* shown in Fig. 52 ; and around it a circle of the tallest Japan
lilies ; next a circle of the mountain-of-snow geranium alternated

with gladiolii ; and for the outside of the same bed, the *Coleus verschafelti,* alternated with the Lady Pollock geranium. Some years will be required to grow the evergreens named to the size that will make them appropriate centres for such a parterre. If a showy bed is required the first season without the use of either vase, basket, or evergreen tree-centre, the following plants may be suggested to effect it, viz. : for the centre, the *Canna gigantea auriantica,* ten feet high ; around it on a circle eighteen inches from the centre, the *Canna sanguinea chatei,* six feet high, to be planted one foot apart in the circle ; next on a circle one foot further out, the *Salvia argentea,* or the mountain-of-snow geranium, to be planted one foot apart in the circle ; for the next circle, one foot from the same, the *Amaranthus melancholicus ruber,* a plant of deep-red foliage from one to two feet high ; and for the edge of the bed the fern-like low white-leaved *Centaurea gymnocarpa ;* or if plants of the latter are too expensive to use freely, make a border of the common Indian pink, or the blue lobelia. These plants, if successfully grown, will make a magnificent bed from midsummer till frost. For a display in the first half of the season, early blooming bulbous flowers must be relied upon. We have thus far considered only the central-bed of the group shown in Fig. 51, and have suggested various modes of treating it which would be equally applicable to a round bed of the size named, were it disconnected with the surrounding beds. For the small circular-beds, each alternate one may have a cluster of the Japanese striped maize in its centre ; the other four beds might have in their centres the *Canna flaccida,* the *Nicotiana atropurpurea grandiflora,* the *Canna gigantea splendidissima,* and the *Wigandia caracasana.* Around their edges may be planted any well-foliaged flowering-plants which do not exceed nine inches in height, and a different species in each bed. The outside tier of beds are for low bedding flowers or annuals, which should not exceed fifteen inches in height for the centres, or more than six inches near the borders.

Fig. 52 represents a circular-bed with one of the pendulous firs mentioned in a preceding page, in its centre, and such tall growing brilliant flowers as the Japan lilies and gladiolii next to it ; a circle of petunias around them ; and creeping plants near the margin.

17

Fig. 52.

The common firs are often planted to form centres for such beds, but they soon grow to such over-shadowing size as to be quite un suitable. The weeping silver fir, and weeping Norway spruce, however, are pendulous to such a degree that they make but slow additions to their breadth. If their central stems or leaders are kept vertical by tying to a stake or straight twig bound to the stem below, and the side branches trimmed back whenever they show a tendency to the normal form, the appearance shown in the cut may be preserved for many years. Where these varieties of the fir are not to be had, the Irish juniper, or the hemlock, may be substituted. The former of those trees is almost monumental in its slender formality, but is pleasing in color and delicate foliage. The latter, if trimmed back every spring in April or May, but not afterwards during that season, will exhibit during the rest of the year the most airy outline of pendulous spray. The trimming in the spring must not be done so as to leave a solidly conical hedge-like form, but with some irregularity, *imitating within slender limits the freedom of outline natural to the hemlock;*—the idea being to produce by artificial means the appearance of one of nature's abnormal varieties or sports, which will bear the same relation to the common form of the hemlock that the pendulous fir in the cut bears to its family.

The last cut of this chapter, already alluded to, is a form of basket-vase now little used, which we recommend as an appro prlate embellishment for a lawn, when filled with suitable plants. Such basket forms may be made either of rustic woodwork, of terra-cotta, or of iron, and need have no bottom; or at least only rims around the bottoms on the inside sufficient to prevent them from settling into the ground unevenly. When filled with earth they form simply raised beds to be planted with such things as the taste of the owner may choose. The basket form simply gives an artistic relief to the bed, and at the same time is so low that it does not obtrusively break the views over a small lawn, like those tall vases of a garish complexion which are often seen in lonely isolation, thrust forward " to show." All vases of classic forms need to be supported by architectural constructions of some kind, near by, which harmonize with them in style; or else to be so embowered with the foliage of the plants they bear, and by which they are surrounded, in the summer months at least, that they will gleam through leaves and flowers like the face of a beautiful woman seen through a veil. The variety of forms and sizes for basket-beds is illimitable; they may be suited to almost any spot where a flowerbed is desirable, and can be made cheaply, or with costly art, as the surroundings may suggest. We venture, however, to warn their makers not to put arch-handles over them. A basket form is chosen because it is pretty and convenient, but it does not follow that the bed of flowers should make any pretence to be in fact a real basket of flowers. The transparency of the deception makes it ridiculous.

Rustic vases made of crooked joints and roots of trees, and twigs with or without their bark, have become quite common, and are often made so strongly and skilfully as to be pleasing works of art. Strength, durability, and firmness on their bases are the essential qualities which they must have. Any construetions of this kind which suggest flimsy wood, or bungling carpentry, or rotting bark, or want of firmness at the base, though they may be planted to give a pretty effect at first, soon become rickety nuisances. But those which are " strongly built, and well," are certainly more likely to have a pleasing effect on common grounds than little plaster, iron, or stone vases, and cannot so easily be used amiss. All rustic constructions of this kind will last much longer, and look cleaner, if the wood is obtained when the bark will peel readily, and made up with no bark upon it. The first effect is certainly less rustic, but sufficiently so to harmonize with the surroundings of a suburban home; and after a few years the advantages of the barkless constructions are very evident.

There is a frequent fault in the use of vases, whether rustic or classic, that mars all their beauty wherever they are placed. We refer to the want of care in keeping their tops level, and their centres vertical. A house "out of plum" is not more unsightly than a vase awry.

The plants used with good effect in rustic vases are those which have large and showy or curiously marked leaves, for the centres, surrounded by delicate-leaved drooping or trailing plants. The gorgeous crimson-leaved *Colleus verschafelti* is a deserved favorite for vases of good size, being a rank grower and developing its greatest beauty in exposures open on all sides to the sun. The following are some of the plants recommended by Henderson, in his book of Practical Floriculture, for the central portions of small baskets, and will answer also for small vases: "The *Centaurea candida,* a plant of white, downy leaves, of compact growth; Tom Thumb geranium, scarlet, dwarf, and compact, blooming all summer; *Sedum sieboldii,* a plant of light glaucus foliage and graceful habit;" and for large baskets the following: "Mrs. Pollock geranium, foliage crimson, yellow and green, flowers bright scarlet; *Centaurea gymnocarpa,* foliage fern-like, whitish gray, of a peculiar graceful habit; *Sedum sieboldii variegatum,* glaucus green, marbled with golden yellow; *Achyranthes gilsonii,* a beautiful shade of carmine foliage and stem; *Alyssum dentatum variegatum,* foliage green and white, with fragrant flowers of pure white; *Altemanthera spathula,* lanceolate leaves of pink and crimson; pyrethrum or golden feather, fern-like foliage, golden yellow." For plants to put around the edge of a small basket or vase, and to fall pendant from its sides, he recommends the following: "*Lobelia erinus paxtoni,* an exquisite blue, drooping eighteen inches; *Tropœolum* (ball of fire), dazzling scarlet, drooping eighteen inches; *Lysimachia numularia,* flowers bright yellow, drooping eighteen inches; *Linaria cymbalaria,* inconspicuous flowers but graceful foliage." For the edging or pendant plants of a large basket he recommends the following, which are also suitable for the edging of a vase: "*Maurandia barclayana*, white or purple flowers; *Vinca elegantissima aurea*, foliage deep green, netted with golden yellow, flowers deep blue; *Cerastium tomentosum*, foliage downy white, flowers white; *Convolvulus mauritanicus*, flowers light blue, profuse; *Solanum jasminoides variegatum*, foliage variegated, flowers white with yellow anthers: *Geranium peltatum elegans*, a variety of the ivy-leaved, with rich glossy foliage and mauve-colored flowers: *Panicum variegatum*, a procumbent grass from New Caledonia, of graceful habit of growth, with beautiful variegated foliage, striped white, carmine, and green." These are mostly half-hardy conservatory plants, and if the proprietor has no conservatory they must be purchased, when wanted, of the florists, or they may be started by a skillful lady-florist in her own window. Nearly every lady of refined taste longs to have a conservatory of her own. But a building, or even an entire room, built for, and devoted to plants alone, is an expensive luxury. Those who have well-built houses heated by steam, or other good furnaces, may easily have a plant-window in a sunny exposure in which the plants required to bed in open ground the following summer may be reared; and beautiful well-grown plants may be obtained from the commercial florists to keep the window gay with blossoms and foliage at a price greatly below the cost for which amateurs can raise them in their own conservatories. These remarks are not designed to discourage the building of private conservatories by *those who can afford them*—far from it—but rather to suggest to those who cannot afford them, not to be envious of those who can.

Roses.—We have not previously mentioned the Rose, among flowers and bedding plants, for the reason that, being the queen of flowers, more than ordinary attention is usually considered due to her. Besides, her royal family are so numerous, so varied and interesting in their characters, and have been the subject of so many compliments from poets, and biographical notices from pens of distinguished horticulturists, that it would be presumption to attempt to describe, in a few brief paragraphs, the peculiar beauties and characteristics of the family; still less of all its thousand members. The mere fact of royalty, however, has attracted such numbers of admirers and chroniclers of their beauty, that, in failing to do justice to them by any observations of our own, there is a satisfaction in knowing that scores of their devoted admirers have written lovingly and sensibly of them ; and from their pages, we may glean and present such general information concerning the relative rank, characters, and habits of the various roses as comes within the scope of a work on the arts of arrangement, rather than a floral manual of classification or culture.

In all the languages of civilized nations volumes have been written on the history, the poetical and legendary associations, the classification, and the culture of the rose ; so that, whoever desires to be especially well informed on any branch of knowledge pertaining to roses will seek among the books in his own language for the special and full information he desires. As roses come properly under the head of shrubs, we shall, under that head, give so much on the subject as may be necessary in connection with the embellishment of suburban places, together with a plate of designs for rose-beds, of a great variety of sizes and forms, with various selections of roses that may be used to advantage in filling them. We will only add here what has before been mentioned in connection with the subject of arrangement, that the planting of rose-bushes, as isolated small shrubs on a lawn, is almost always a misplacement. There are a few sorts, especially some of the wild bush-roses, which form fine compact bushes, sufficiently well foliaged to be pleasing all the summer months when not in bloom ; but the greater part of the finest roses, particularly the perpetuals which make a straggling and unequal growth, produce a far finer effect when planted *pretty snugly* in masses. A practice of planting each root of a sort by itself, like so many hills of potatoes, is quite necessary in commercial gardens where they are grown for sale, and each of a hundred varieties must be kept distinct from every other, so that it may be distinguished readily, and removed for sale without injury to the others; but this is *market*-gardening, not decorative, and the least interesting of all modes of cultivating the rose. Decidedly, the prettier way in small collections is to learn first what is the comparative strength of growth and height of the several plants which are to make up one's collection, and then to distribute the smaller sorts around the larger, so that all may be seen to advantage, and made to appear like a single bush, or symmetric group. As it is desirable to know each sort when out of flower and leaf, labels, fastened with copper wire, can remain attached to the stems near the base as well when in groups as when separate.

It must not be understood that we favor great formality of outlines in a group, or what is called a lumpish mass, but only that the general outline of bush or group shall be symmetrical, and that it shall contain a sufficient mass of foliage in itself to allow the straggling spray, which gives spirit to its outline, to be relieved against a good body of foliage. However formally a rose-bed is laid out, the free rambling growth of the plants will always give a sprightly irregularity of outline sufficient to relieve it from all appearance of primness. It is as unnatural to force the rose into formal outlines as to suppress the frolicksomeness of children; but in both cases the freedom natural to each may be directed, and made to conform, to the proprieties of place and occasion. Allusion has previously been made to the bad taste of conspicuous pieces of white-painted carpentry very generally used as supports for running roses. The simpler and more inconspicuous such supports are made, provided they are substantial, the better.

CHAPTER XVIII.

A LARGE portion of the gross weight of all soils is water. If we dry any soil perfectly, the residuum of weight will bear a very small proportion to the average weight of the soil in its natural condition. Water, therefore, occupies a large part of the texture of what we call solid earth. When we draw the water from any soil by drains, the space occupied by the water in the earth is supplied by air. Thorough draining, therefore, airs the soil to whatever depth it drains off the water. The air transmits heat and cold less rapidly than water by direct conduction, so that, if air occupies the place of water in the interstices of the soil, the latter will feel all changes of temperature more slowly. Deep drainage, therefore, tends to equalize the temperature of the earth's surface, and to neutralize the effect of great and sudden changes in the air above. It is impossible to drain a subsoil too thoroughly from beneath, because the capillary attraction of the earth is always sufficient to draw up from below all the moisture that is essential to most forms of vegetable life; and in addition to the moisture thus drawn from below, the earth, when the air can circulate freely in it, has the power when dry to absorb a vast amount of moisture from the air, as well as to yield it up to the air by evaporation when it holds an excess. To all general observations like these, the reader's intelligence will of course suggest exceptions; as of trees and plants which thrive best where their roots are immersed in water, and which make water their element rather than earth; but the fact holds good as to the great mass of beautiful trees, shrubs, and plants—that they will thrive best, and bear the winter's cold and the summer's heat and drought with least injury, in the most deeply drained soils. If this is true as a general rule, it is plain that for trees which are peculiarly sensitive to either extreme, there is greater need of deep drainage than for any other.

The airing of the soil, which deep draining secures, acts in two ways for the benefit of all vegetation: first, by equalizing the temperature of the soil in consequence of the non-conducting power of air; secondly, by exposing the deeper soil to the contact of air, it becomes changed in character, and undergoes a constant process of fertilization by the action of air upon it. It is being oxygenized. Any one familiar with farming operations in new countries, knows that when virgin soils are first turned over, there are, usually, only a few inches of dark soil on the surface. If the plow turns a furrow five or six inches deep, it will generally show a much lighter color than the surface which is turned under; but in a few years of continued culture this lighter-colored soil becomes as dark as the original surface. By the combined action of the sun and air it has all become equally oxygenized. If such ground were repeatedly plowed without growing a crop from it, and so as to permit no growth of vegetation to be turned under, it would still, for a time, gain rapidly in fertility, by the mere chemical changes produced by the sun and air. What plowing effects quickly by the direct exposure of the upper soil to these elements, deep draining and the consequent airing of the soil effects slowly, and less thoroughly, in subsoils through which the air is induced to permeate. *Imperceptibly, but surely, the earth beneath our feet is being warmed and fertilized by the action of the air upon it, whenever we invite the air in, by drawing the water out.* This increased warmth and richness of the subsoil invites the roots of trees deeper and deeper in proportion as it approximates in character to the warmth and oxygenation of the surface-soil. To have a deeply aired soil, therefore, is to encourage trees to root farther down, and away from the trying changes of winter and spring temperature that weaken or kill semi-tropical trees and shrubs, and often impair the vitality of young trees of hardy species.

Next in importance to deep drainage, therefore, is deep tillage. It supplements drainage by often repeated exposure of a certain depth of soil to the action of the air and sun, by which its oxygenation is carried on more rapidly than it can possibly be when not so exposed.

EARTH HEAT.—The earth grows warmer as we go down. If its temperature were tested in winter, we should find an increasing warmth with each foot of depth below the frost. The more porous and dry the soil, the less depth it will freeze, and the more rapid the increase of temperature below the frost line. This explains why gravelly subsoils make warm soils, and suggests that deep drainage is the most efficient means of providing for trees an equable " bottom heat."

In the northern States the range of earth-freezing is from one to three feet deep. It is not always deepest where the cold is greatest ; for where a considerable altitude makes the winters more severe, the greater snow-falls are likely to husband the earth's warmth as with a feathery blanket, so that the soil may be frozen no deeper at Utica than at Philadelphia. But when the surface protection is the same, altitude and latitude tell quickly on the climate in its effect on trees.

Roots at the surface of the ground are either torpid in their icy encasement, or alternately thawed-out or frozen-in during four or five months. Those a foot below the surface are ice-bound not much more than half this time ; those two feet below, a third ; and those three feet below, not at all. All the roots which are just under the frost-line during any part of the winter, are in no colder soil than the winter surface-soil of the Gulf States. Whether six inches or three feet under the surface, where the ground is not frozen, the roots maintain some action.

The younger and smaller a tree or shrub, the nearer its roots are to the surface, and all its fluctuations and severities of temperature ; and therefore the greater need of guarding against them. The analogy between animals and plants is greater than most persons suppose. "Keep your feet warm and dry, and you will not be likely to take cold," is a trite piece of advice, because it is so true and so useful. Now if we can keep the plants' feet warm and dry, or at least save them from the greatest extremes of cold and wet, we do them the same kindness that we do the children by wrapping their feet in wool and leather protections.

The roots of trees and shrubs during the first five years of their growth are mostly in that part of the soil which is frozen in the northern States from one to three feet deep every winter. Some rapid-growing trees, as the yellow locust and the silver poplar, send down their roots to a great depth very soon after planting. We have seen roots of the locust that had penetrated a marly clay and were as large as pipe-stems at a depth of six feet below the surface, from trees only three years planted. This power of quick and deep rooting in the subsoil is probably the reason why the locust tree, with its tropical luxuriance and extreme delicacy of foliage. is able to endure a degree of cold that many less succulent and hardier looking trees cannot bear.

DEEP ROOTS AS CONDUCTORS OF HEAT TO THE TOPS OF TREES.—The deep roots have an influence in maintaining an equilibrium of temperature in the tree that is little understood. They are direct conductors from the even warmth of the unfrozen subsoil, to the trunk and branches which are battling with frigid air, and winds that strive to rob them of their vital heat. All winter long this current of heat is conducted by the deep roots to the exposed top. The greater the cold, the greater the call on these roots to maintain the equilibrium ; and consequently their usefulness in this respect is in proportion to the extremes of temperature above ground which the tree may be required to resist, and *the proportion of roots which are below the frost-line.* Surface roots are the summer-feeding roots—multiplying their myriads of fibres, each one a greedy mouth, when spring opens and the leaves need them ;—and there is always a perfect proportion between their abundance and vigor, and the luxuriance of the foliage above them. Surface manuring promotes a rank growth of these roots, and of the foliage ; and should only be used for young trees and shrubs which are unquestionably hardy, or for the less hardy which are already deeply rooted ; but not for young trees of doubtful hardiness. These must first be provided with the bottom heat that deep drainage and a well-aired subsoil provides, until they are deeply rooted.

As newly planted trees have not the means of keeping themselves warm in winter by means of their deep roots, it follows that they must be nursed in some way so that they will maintain a vigorous life until they are thus provided.

Trees or shrubs of half-tropical habit, by which we mean those that flourish in our southern States without protection, and which may be so carefully managed as to develop their beauties healthily in the northern States, of course need this careful nursing more than any other; and not only to guard them against winter's excesses, but to give them the most equable ground temperature at all seasons. Most trees in their native localities grow in deep shades, and the soil over their roots is rarely heated by the direct rays of the sun, however powerful its heat upon their tops. The very luxuriance of vegetation forms a bower of shade for the soil; so that in forests the roots of trees are in a soil that is comparatively equable in temperature and moisture. When trees from such localities are grown on open lawns, they are naturally disposed to branch low, in order to cover their roots from the heat of the summer sun by the shade of their own boughs. The magnolias and rhododendrons are marked examples of trees and shrubs which are cultivated most successfully in deeply drained soils, but at the same time are ill-at-ease in ground where the soil over their roots is bared to the scorching summer heat. In the case of evergreen trees, their low-branching keeps the ground under them cool and shady in summer, and also protects the roots in winter—acting as a blanket to hold the radiation of the earth's heat, and to hold the snow which makes another blanket for the same purpose. A well-cut lawn is some protection to the roots of trees, but it interferes with that active oxygenation of the soil which deep culture produces; and while it acts as a shield against the scorching effect of the summer sun on bare earth, and as a mulch to counteract, in a slight degree, the rapid changes of temperature on the surface-roots, it at the same time reduces the vitality and power of resistance to cold in the tree, by preventing the deep soil from becoming well aired and oxygenized, as it is under high culture. Under the sod of a lawn, therefore, the roots of trees will be nearer the surface than in ground under cultivation, and will have less power to resist cold, so far as deep roots enable them to resist it.

If a tree is planted in a thoroughly drained soil which is to be cultivated, instead of one which is to be covered with lawn, it may be set several inches deeper, so that the main roots need not be injured by the spade, while they will be kept in warm soil by the occasional turning under of the surface which has been under the direct action of the sun's rays. The roots at the depth of ten inches, in a soil which is spaded annually, and well cultivated, will be as well aired, and have as warm feeding ground, as in a similar soil two inches below an old sod. This cultivation, therefore, gains for the tree a summer and winter mulching of eight inches in depth above its rootlets; a great gain in winter, and equal to several degrees of more southern latitude.

Half-hardy trees should therefore not only be planted in ground drained most deeply and thoroughly, but also where the ground may be deeply cultivated until they are rooted in a warm subsoil below the action of frosts—say ten years. Trees which eventually grow to considerable size may, when young, be centres or parts of groups of shrubs that also require high culture ; and when the tree begins to over-top the shrubs, the latter should be gradually removed. But it must be constantly borne in mind that all trees, and especially those of doubtful hardiness, need a full development of low side-branches when young, and no shrubbery should remain near enough to them to check this side-growth. When all the excess of shrubbery around the tree is removed, and the latter is supposed to have become sufficiently established to be able to dispense with deep culture, and have the ground under its branches converted into lawn, then two or three inches in depth of fresh soil should be added all around the tree, as far as the roots extend; and for half-hardy trees, an autumn mulching with leaves or evergreen boughs should never be omitted at any age of the tree. The subject of mulching will be treated again in this chapter.

PROTECTION FROM WINDS.—The effect of protection from the winds is nearly the same for delicate trees as for delicate human beings. "Keep out of a strong draught of air" is a common admonition given to those who are healthy, as well as to invalids ; and this, too, when only the pleasant breath of summer is to be guarded against. Now when we reflect that trees have not the power of warming themselves by exercise, but must stand with suffering patience the coldest blasts of winter, with no more covering on body and limbs than sufficed them in genial summer air, how thoughtless and heartless of us to expect any of them, least of all the denizens of semi-tropical forests, to laugh with blossoms, and grow fat with leaves, after being exposed to all the rigors of a northern winter. Ought we not to be most thankful that even the hardened species of northern zones can bear the vicissitudes of our climate? And if semi-tropical trees can also be made to thrive by kindly protection, should we grudge them the care which their delicacy demands?

Much as our horticultural writers have endeavored to impress the importance of protection from winds, by means of walls of hardy evergreen trees, few persons have had the opportunity of observing how great the benefits of such protection. Houses, out-buildings, and high fences may generally be so connected by such hedges and screens as to form warm bays and sheltered nooks where many trees and shrubs of novel beauty may be grown, which, in exposed situations, would either die outright or eke out a diseased and stunted existence. This remark applies with most force to the smaller trees and shrubs for which constructive protections against winds may be erected with no great expense ; or verdant walls may be grown within a few years. Yet larger trees like the *Magnolia machrophylla* and the Bhotan pine (*P. excelsa*) may be so protected in their early growth that the health and vigor acquired during the first ten years of careful attention to their needs will enable them to resist vicissitudes of climate which trees of the same species, less judiciously reared, would die under. Vigor of constitution in animals is not alone a matter of race and family, but also to a considerable degree the result of education and training. Delicate youths who nurse their strength, and battle with their own weakness by obeying the laws of health that intelligence teaches them, often become stronger at middle age than those of robust organization who early waste their vigor by careless disregard of those laws. By studying the nature of trees we may effect similar results with similar care.

Winter protection from winds must be effected principally by hardy evergreens. Of these the Norway spruce is one of the most rapid in its growth. In itself a beautiful object, it may be massed in pleasing groups, or compact belts, or close cut colossal hedges. The white pine in sandy soils has a still more rapid growth, and is, therefore, suited to form the highest screens. The American and the Siberian arbor-vitæs are naturally so hedge-like in form that the sight of them at once suggests their usefulness; while the rambling and graceful young hemlock is readily trained into verdant screens of exquisite beauty.

The relative growth of these trees is about in the following order: The white pine planted from the nursery should attain the height of twenty feet in ten years, and forty feet in twenty years. The Norway spruce grows with about the same rapidity, but its growth being relatively less in breadth at the top, its summit gives less check to winds. The hemlock may attain about two-thirds the size of the pine in the same time ; while the arbor-vitæs just named may be relied on to make about a foot of growth per year. These facts suggest to intelligent planters the service these trees may be made to render in the capacity of protectors of the weaker species of trees and shrubs.

The warming power of evergreen trees in winter is not fully appreciated. They are like living beings, breathing all the time, and keep up, and give off their vital heat in the same manner. In a dense forest the cold is never so intense as on an adjoining prairie ; and the difference between the temperature of even a small grove of evergreens, and open ground near by, is often great enough to decide the life or death of sensitive shrubs and trees. In our chapter on the Characteristics of Trees will be found some interesting facts concerning this quality of trees and plants.

Deep drainage, deep culture, and protection from winds are the three great means to give trees a healthy and rapid development, and to acclimatize those which are not quite hardy. It has also been suggested that certain trees and shrubs need to be protected from the sun, as well as from cold and wind. This fact will be noted in the descriptions of them.

We now come to the *special* treatment of newly planted trees, premising that the general conditions just given have been complied with.

MULCHING. — Mulch signifies any substance which may be strewn upon the ground to retain its moisture for the benefit of the roots which it covers, or to serve as a non-conductor of the coldness or the heat of the air, and to retain the natural warmth of the earth beneath. Mulching may be done in a great variety of ways, and for different purposes. Summer mulching is intended to protect the soil from too rapid drying under the direct rays of the sun. Winter mulching is designed to prevent the sudden and excessive freezing of the earth.

Leaves are the natural mulch for forest trees. At the approach of winter, observe how all the trees disrobe their branches to drop a cover of leaves upon their roots. The winds blow them away from the great trunks which are deep rooted and need them least, to lodge among the stems and roots of the underbrush which need them most. Leaves being the most natural cover for roots are the best. But they cannot be used to advantage in summer in well-kept grounds because of the difficulty of retaining them in place, and their unsightly effect when blown about on a lawn. In autumn, however, they should be gathered, when most abundant, for a winter mulch; and can be retained in place by heavy twigs over them. The twigs and leaves together catch the blowing snow and thus make a warm snow blanket in addition to their own protection. For summer mulching, saw-dust (not too fresh) and "chip-dirt," are good and tidy protections. Old straw is excellent, but is unsightly and too disorderly when blown by winds to be satisfactory in neatly kept places; and when used too freely harbors mice. Tan-bark is a favorite summer mulch, and very good if not put on too thick. Evergreen leaves and twigs are admirable for either summer or winter mulching, but especially for winter, on account of the snow that accumulates in them. Massed to the depth of a foot, the ground beneath them will hardly feel the frosts. Trees or shrubs which are hardy enough to be forced into a rank growth without making their new wood too succulent and tender to bear the following winter, may be mulched with short manure, but trees of doubtful hardiness must not be thus stimulated. If used at all it should be in autumn, for winter service, and raked off in spring, to be replaced by cooler materials during the growing season.

In addition to the mulching required over the roots of young trees and shrubs in winter, it is necessary to cover the trunk, and sometimes the entire tops of those which are half-hardy with some protection. The stems of young trees may be covered with straw bound around them, or with matting, or strong brown paper. Small tree-tops and spreading shrubs may be carefully drawn together with straw cords, and bound up as completely in straw and matting as bundles of trees sent out from a nursery. As such masses are likely to catch the snow, and offer considerable resistance to the wind, it is absolutely necessary in all cases after a subject has been thus bound, that strong stakes be driven near by, and the bound-up branches securely fastened to them until the binding is taken off in the spring. The following cuts, illustrating a mode of protecting peach trees, to secure their fruit-buds from injury in winter, also illustrates the mode of protecting the tops for other purposes. In the case of the peach tree a strong cedar post is supposed to be

| Fig. 53. | Fig. 54. | Fig. 55. |

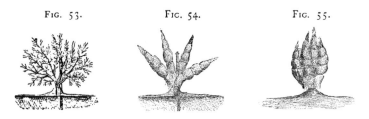

deeply set for a permanent fixture at the same time the tree is planted, and that the latter grows up around it as shown by Fig. 53. At the approach of winter the branches which can be most conveniently bound together are prepared like nursery bundles as

18

shown by Fig. 54; and when done are secured by cords to the central post as shown by Fig 55. In addition to this straw bind ing, earth from beyond the branches is banked up around the stem, as shown in the same cuts. This mode of protection is especially adapted to the fruit-yard.. It would not be admissible to have permanent posts or stakes in the embellished parts of grounds; but a similar mode of protection can be employed by the use of strong stakes to be driven when wanted, and removed in the spring.

Tender vines, and pliable-wooded bushes, may be turned down on the approach of winter, and laid flat upon the ground or lawn, where there is room. If in cultivated ground, there is no better protection than a covering of several inches of earth. If standing upon a lawn they may be either covered with earth in the same way, if it can be brought from a convenient distance, or may be pinned down and covered from four to twelve inches deep with evergreen boughs or twigs.

Very tender plants must of course be covered more deeply than hardier ones, and the cover should be removed gradually in the spring. It is advisable to mark the exact place where each vine or branch is laid, so that in uncovering, in the spring, it may not be injured by the spade.

PART II.

TREES, SHRUBS, AND VINES.

CHAPTER I.

A COMPARISON OF THE CHARACTERISTICS OF TREES.

"I care not how men trace their ancestry,
To Ape or Adam; let them please their whim;
But I in June am midway to believe
A Tree among my far progenitors;
Such sympathy is mine with all the race,
Such mutual recognition vaguely sweet
There is between us. Surely there are times
When they consent to own me of their kin,
And condescend to me, and call me cousin,
Murmuring faint lullabies of eldest time
Forgotten, and yet dumbly felt with thrills
Moving the lips, though fruitless of the words."

LOWELL.

WHEN one reflects that among all the millions of human beings that have existed no two have been alike, and that all their illimitable varieties of expression are produced by the varied combinations of only half a dozen features, within a space of six inches by eight, it ought not to be difficult to conceive the endless diversity of character that may be exhibited among trees, with their multitude of features and forms, their oddities of bark, limb, and twig, their infinitude of leaves and blossoms of all sizes, forms, and shades of color, their towering sky outlines, and their ever-varying lights and shadows. There are subtle expressions in trees, as in the human face, that it is difficult to analyze or account for. A face, no one feature of which is pleasing, often charms us by the expression of an inward spirit which lights it. May we not claim for all living nature, as our great poet Bryant suggests in the following lines, a degree of soul, and for all trees that are loveable at sight a sympathy of soul with the observer which constitutes their pleasing expression?

> " Nay, doubt we not that under the rough rind,
> In the green veins of these fair growths of Earth,
> There dwells a nature that receives delight
> From all the gentle processes of life,
> And shrinks from loss of being.   Dim and faint
> May be the sense of pleasure and of pain,
> As in our dreams ; but haply, real still."

Sunny cheerfulness, gayety, gloom, sprightliness, rudeness, sweetness, gracefulness, awkwardness, ugliness, and eccentricities, are all attributes of trees as well as of human beings. How do trees convey these impressions without suggesting those attributes which we call soul? Some trees look sulky, and repel sympathy—the black oak or an old balsam fir, for instance. People never become greatly attached to such trees. Others are warm, and sunny, and deep bosomed, like the sugar maple ; or voluptuous like magnolias, or wide-winged like the oak and the apple tree—bending down to shade and cover, as mother-birds their nests ;—conveying at once a sense of domestic protection. These are the trees we love. The children will not cry when an old Lombardy poplar or balsam fir is cut down ; but cut away an old apple tree, or oak, or hickory, that they have played under, and their hearts will be quick to feel the difference between trees. Some trees look really motherly in their domestic expression. A large old apple tree,

Fig. 56.
Fig. 56, is a type of such trees. All trees that spread broadly, and grow low, convey this expression. The white birch is a type, on the other hand, of delicate elegance, and is styled by one of our poets

" *   *   * the *lady* of the woods."

There are trees (like those women, who, though brilliant in drawing-rooms, are never less than ladies when busy in domestic labors) which are useful and profitable in orchard and forest, but are doubly beautiful in robes of greater luxuriance upon the carpet of a rich lawn. There are others which no care in culture will make ornaments in "the best society.'

Whoever studies the varied beauties of trees will find that they possess almost a human interest, and their features will reveal varieties of expression, and charms of character, that dull observers cannot imagine.

"The poplars shiver, the pine trees moan.'

The differences between a Lombardy poplar, an oak, and a weeping willow are so striking that the most careless eye cannot mistake one for the other. The poplar, tall, slender, rigid, is a type of formality; the oak, broad, massy, rugged-limbed, has ever been a symbol of strength, majesty, and protection; and the willow, also broad and massy, but so fringed all over with pensile-spray that its majesty is forgotten in the exquisite grace of its movement, is, to the oak, as the fullness and grace of a noble woman to the robust strength of man.

'The more obvious peculiarities and diversities of trees we shall endeavor to present from an æsthetic, rather than a botanist's point of view; not in the interest of science, or of pecuniary utilitarianism, but so as to aid the student of nature to appreciate their beauties; appealing simply to that love of the beautiful in nature which hungers in the eyes of all good people. The delightful science of botany is not likely to be over-estimated, but its study is no more necessary to the appreciation of trees than the study of the chemistry of the air, or the anatomy of the ear, to the lover of music.

What are the essential beauties of trees?

We shall name first that most essential quality of all beauty—

THE BEAUTY OF HEALTH.—No tree has the highest beauty of its type without the appearance, in its whole bearing, of robust vigor. There may be peculiar charms in the decay of an old trunk, or the eccentric habit of some stunted specimen, which ministers to a love of the picturesque; but true beauty and health are as inseparable in trees, as in men and women. Luxuriant vigor is, then, the essential condition of all beautiful trees. Thriftiness cannot make an elm look like an oak, but rather brings into higher relief the distinguishing marks of each, making the elm more graceful, and the oak more majestic. Yet uncommon thriftiness changes the forms of some trees so much that specimens growing in the shade of the forest, stinted by want of sunlight, and crowded by roots of rival trees, are tall, lank, and straggling in limb, with scanty foliage; while the same species grown in rich open ground becomes glorious with its breadth and weighty masses of foliaged boughs. Who would know the common chestnut in the forest by its form, as the same tree that spreads its arms in the open field with all the majesty of the oak? Or the "mast-timber" branchless white pine of a Maine forest as the same tree that forms in open ground a broad-based pyramid of evergreen foliage, and broods with its vast branches like a broad-winged bird upon a meadow-nest? The crooked

Fig. 57.

sassafras of the woods, Fig. 57, running up as if uncertain what point in the heavens to aim at, and at what height to put out its arms, seems as unhappy there as a cultured citizen forced to spend his life among the Camanches. But the same tree, in rich soil in the open sun, expands naturally, as in Fig. 58, into one of the most beautiful heads of foliage among small trees.

Few trees attain a full measure of thrift that are not fully exposed east, south, and west to the sun. We do not mean to assert that trees will not be beautiful without such complete exposure, but that, to realize the highest

Fig. 58.

beauty of which any one specimen is capable, it must be so exposed. A greater variety of beauty is obtained from a group made up of more than one species of tree, thus contrasting several sorts of foliage and form, than from a single tree which might have grown to cover the same space; and we therefore sacrifice the highest type of individual perfection to produce more striking effects with several trees. But the same fact must be observed with reference to the group;—its full beauty can only be realized by having the trees in luxuriant growth; and open, collectively, on all sides to the sun.

BEAUTY OF FORM.—Next to the beauty that comes from vigor of growth, or the glow of high health, is beauty of form. On this matter tastes differ widely. To artists it seems a vulgar uncultivated taste to prefer a solid pumpkin-headed tree, to one of more irregular outline ; but preference is so often expressed for trees of such forms that it may be imprudent to speak disrespectfully of it. Such trees certainly possess the first element of beauty of form, viz., symmetry ; but it is symmetry without variety. They may also have the beauty of thrift and good color. An apple tree from fifteen to twenty years old has this quality of head as shown in Fig. 59. As it grows old, however, its form changes materially, so that its outline is quite irregular and spirited —broader, nobler, and more domestic in expression—as will be seen by comparing Fig. 56 with Fig. 59. Young sugar maples have similar forms slightly elongated, as shown by Fig. 60, though with age they break into outlines less monotonous, as shown by Fig. 61, and their shadows have more character. The same may be said of the horse-chestnuts. The hickories and the white oak, assume more varied outlines while young, without losing that balance of parts which constitutes symmetry. Sugar maples are always symmetric in every stage of their growth ; but their early symmetry is insipid, like that of the human face when unexceptionable in features, but devoid of expression ; or rather like that of the doll-face, which can hardly be said to have either features or expression, but only beauty of color, the semblance of health, and features faintly suggested. The change in forms of many trees which are excessively smooth in their early outlines is towards more and more variety of contour and depth of shadow as they approach maturity, and occasionally in old age they develop into grandly picturesque trees ; as in the case of the white oak and the chestnut among deciduous trees, and the cedar of Lebanon among evergreens.

FIG. 59.

FIG. 60.

FIG. 61.

FIG. 62.

To what extent a tendency to pictur-esqueness may go, without loss of symmetry, it is not easy to say. Fig. 62 is a well-pro-portioned tree of picturesque outline, and symmetrical as to the balance of its parts, but not in the similitude of its opposite halves. It is a form often seen in our native locusts and the Scotch elm. Figs. 63 and 64 are both symmetrical, strikingly pictur-esque in outline, and yet totally unlike each other. The first is a form quite common to young weeping elms ; but with age, unlike most trees, they become more symmetrical and smoothly rounded. A full-grown weep-ing elm is the most perfect example of the union of symmetry, grace, and picturesque-ness, among all the trees of the temperate zone.

FIG. 63.

Tree outlines may be divided into two great classes of forms, which merge into each other in every variety of combination. These are *round-headed* trees, and *conical*, or *pyra-midal* trees.

Fig. 64 is a form characteristic of rapidly grown scarlet oaks or ginkgo trees.

The contrast between this form and that of the young elm above, is very marked ; yet in outline they are almost equally spirited, and in the balance of their oppo-site parts are alike perfect. The elm, how-ever, has the higher type of beauty, by reason of the less mechanical distribution of its weight, and the bolder projection of its branches. All such spirited forms suggest an inherent life and will in the tree, a kind of playful disregard of set forms, a youthful daring and defiance of the laws of gravita-tion that is apt to please persons of imag-inative minds. They are always favorites with artists ; while trees of more compact and methodical arrangement are preferred by

FIG. 64.

persons with whose characters these traits harmonize. These observations refer to outlines only; the expressions of trees produced by other traits often modify óur preferences for trees of favorite forms, by presenting combinations of other kinds of beauty in trees of less interesting outlines.

Fig. 65.

Fig. 66.

Round-Headed Trees.—By *round-headed* is meant simply a general effect of roundness, or of smoothness of outline in the several masses that compose the head of a tree. The young apple tree, Fig. 65, is a perfect type of this form, and may more specifically be called a globular tree, to distinguish the complete roundness of its form from those other round-headed trees which are more nearly hemispherical.

Fig. 67.

Among round-headed trees the different forms of roundness are distinguished by more specific names. The sugar maple usually takes the form of an egg with the small end up, as shown in Fig. 66, and is therefore termed *ovate.* The hickory, Fig. 67, more nearly fills the geometric figure that we call *oval.* The elm, Fig. 68, fills one-half a semicircle or more, with its head, and is of a class of trees appropriately called *umbrella-topped;*—technically they are called *oblate,* or flattened-oval. An old apple tree, Fig. 69, is a good example of this form, and Fig. 58, page 280, of a well grown sassafras, is another.

Fig. 68.

The white oak, Fig. 70, the native chestnut (*castanea*), and the hickories, all have outlines much broken, but the general effect is that of rounded forms.

Fig. 69.

Many of the pines when grown to maturity become round-headed trees, though pyramidal when young.

Fig. 70.   Fig. 71.   Fig. 72.

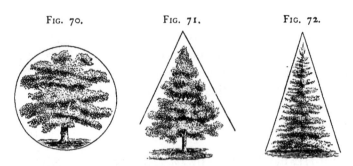

CONICAL TREES.—This term is sufficiently explicit, and includes all those trees of flatly conical form which are usually called pyramidal. The latter term refers to those members of the conical class which have a breadth about equal to their height. The pear tree, Fig. 71, among deciduous trees, is a type of the pyramidal form.

The Norway spruce and hemlocks, Fig. 72, are types of conical forms. Most species of poplar (the Lombardy poplar being an exception) have the pyramidal-conical form while young, but with age they round out into trees of the first class. The Balm of Gilead poplar, and the cucumber tree, are good examples of compact deciduous trees of this class when young, but they all become round-headed trees at maturity.

Nearly all evergreens are conical when young, and very many of deciduous trees also. Few of the latter, however, retain this character after they are full grown. The white pine when quite young is an open-limbed conical tree; but when twenty years old, if it has grown in congenial soil, and an open exposure, it assumes an ovate-pyramidal form, with the rounded masses of foliage that characterize round-headed trees, but retains otherwise the general outlines of the conical class in its after growth. The yellow or northern pitch pine (*P. rigida*) changes from a straggling conical form when young, to an irregularly branched oblate-headed tree in age. The Scotch pine, which is of a rounded conical form when young, becomes, with age, as picturesquely rounded as the oak. The scarlet oak, Fig. 64, is a good example of a straggling conical form when young, though it becomes a loose round-headed tree at maturity.

The balsam fir, the Norway spruce, and the hemlock are conical from first to last,

FIG. 73.

swelling out, however, at maturity, into the ovate-conical form, of which the Swiss or stone pine (*P. cembra*), Fig. 73, is a type in every stage of its growth. The cedar of Lebanon is a distinctly pyramidal-conical tree when young, but widens out as it matures, and finally spreads into an immense

oblate head. The junipers embrace species which are the most slenderly conical of evergreens; the Irish juniper, Fig. 74, having rather the form of a slender club than of a cone. Some varieties of the Norway spruce, and the European silver-fir, are now being propagated, which have branches so pendulous that they are nearly as slenderly conical as these junipers.

Among deciduous trees the Lombardy poplar, Fig. 75, is the type of what are called *fastigiate* trees; *i. e.,* trees of upright and compact growth, being distinguished from other conical trees by a tendency to vertical parallelism of the branches. The balsam fir and the Norway spruce are both conical trees, but having nearly horizontal branches, are not fastigiate; while the Irish juniper, the arbor-vitæs, and the Lombardy poplar, are all fastigiate.

It needs to be impressed on novices in the study of trees that all these various types of trees vary greatly among themselves, so that specimens of any species are often seen quite different from the usual type of that species. These variations are called *varieties*, and when very marked in their character are named, propagated from, and become the curiosities of arboriculture.

PENDULOUS OR WEEPING FORMS.—Of late years, such numbers of new varieties of pendulous trees have been introduced, that they might perhaps be considered as a class; but in a simple classification of trees by their outlines alone, they will be found to group easily with one or another of the classes already described. Pendulous varieties have been found among nearly every species of our hardy trees, both deciduous and evergreen. Many of them are most interesting, curious, and picturesque decorations of small lawns. They include every variety of outline, from the columnar poplar, the slender junipers, and the majestic weeping willow, down to the sorts that creep along the ground. The weeping junipers and arbor-vitæs (*Thuja*) are pensile only at the extremities of their limbs; the new pendulous firs (*Abies excelsa pendula* and *Picea pectinata pendula*) are slenderly conical, but with branches drooping directly and compactly downwards around a central stem. The hemlock and Norway spruce firs belong partly to the class of weeping trees on account of their pendant plumy spray, and the droop of their branches as they grow old, although both are rigidly conical trees in their general outlines. The weeping white birches have upright branches and pendulous spray when young, but as they increase in size the larger branches bend with rambling grace in harmony with their spray, and form picturesquely symmetrical spreading trees; while the weeping beech, assuming every uncouth contortion when young, becomes a tree of noble proportions, magnificently picturesque with age, trailing its slender crooked limbs, covered with a drapery of dark glossy foliage from its summit to the ground. See illustration under head of "The Beech."

FIG. 76.

PICTURESQUE FORMS.—There are trees which cannot easily be classified— trees of straggling or eccentric growth, like the weeping elm, Fig. 76, the honey locust, Fig. 77, and the weeping beech, Fig. 104; diffuse and rambling trees like young scarlet oaks, old larches and pines, and most of the birch family. These highly picturesque forms are exceptional among park-grown trees, and are charming because they are exceptional. Some of the preceding illustrations show how trees may at the same time be symmetrical and picturesque; and we ask the reader to observe how much more interesting a tree is which combines both beauties than the lumpish globular types which are commonly admired. But there are trees which lose, or never have, symmetry of form, and, like some of our other acquaintances, are interesting for their oddities. Look, for instance, at the accompanying cut of the straggling elm, which is a portrait from nature, and the portrait of Parson's weeping beech, on page 328. The latter is a luxuriant mass of pendant branches and foliage, erratic in all directions, and yet one of the most interesting of young trees. It is bizarre, like the expressions of a wit. Its unlikeness to other trees is its superiority; but the exuberant vigor that clothes it with such masses of glossy foliage, adds to picturesqueness the constant loveableness of beautiful health. Of the trees which by nature grow irregularly, the native larch, or hacmatack, is a familiar example, its head generally shooting off to one side after it attains a certain height. The osage orange is so rambling that it suggests a comparison with those eccentric geniuses who, having decided talents in many different directions, attempt to follow them all, and whose successes or failures are equally interesting to observers. Many specimens of the weeping elm, while young, like the wild

FIG. 77.

and not unusual form shown by Fig. 76, are fine examples of erratic luxuriance, but they usually fill up, with age, and finally become models of symmetry. Trees are often made picturesque by accidents, as the breaking of trunks or important branches by summer tornados, or the falling of other trees upon them. Fig. 78 is an example from nature of a white oak upwards of three feet in diameter, which, when young, was bent by the fall of some great tree that rested upon it, until all the fibres of its wood had conformed to the forced position. Fig. 79 is another sketch from nature of an oak that has been robbed of a part of its main trunk, and is picturesque in consequence of it. Advantage should always be taken of the striking effect of such trees by placing gate-ways or conducting walks under them, if practicable; or, if not, then to make them parts of groups in such a way that their picturesqueness may be brought into high relief.

The mere *weight, breadth, and height of the trunk and branches*
of a tree, without reference to its
outlines or foliage, are the principal
sources of *majesty* in trees; and it
is when majesty and picturesqueness
are combined that we realize our
higher ideals of grandeur. A tree
with massive horizontal branches in-
voluntarily impresses us with a sense
of the immense inherent strength

FIG. 78.

that can sustain so great a weight in a position that most squarely
defies the mechanical force of gravity; and therefore conveys the
impression of majesty, though it has no extraordinary height or
dimensions.   On the other hand, the tulip-tree, or the cottonwood,
with a straight and lofty stem from three to six feet in diameter,
is a grand object by virtue of its weight, and loftiness; and the
power that its dimensions express, though its head may not be
proportionally large, nor its bark or branches massive, rough, and
angular, or its outline irregular enough
to be picturesque.   The sycamore, or
buttonball, is a familiar example of a
swelling trunk of majestic size.   Its
bark is as smooth in age as in youth;
but it has a certain picturesqueness
from the contrasts of color caused by
shedding its thin bark laminæ in scales;
and majesty by its size, and the bold-

FIG. 79.

ness of its divergent branches.

Mere size of trunk, and weight of branches, affect us so
powerfully, that when we have lived near a fine old tree, it is not
so much the beauty of its foliage, or the pleasures of its shade, that
produce the reverent love we have for it, but the unconscious
presence of the majesty of Nature impressing us like

"* * * an emanation from the indwelling spirit of the Deity."

By referring to the vignette of the oak at the head of page 302,
the effect produced by mere breadth and weight in producing

majesty, will be readily appreciated. There is neither symmetry nor thrift in its rough trunk and huge gnarled branches; but there is a power and strength there, which represents the history of centuries of growth and battle with the elements. It is a scarred old veteran, a forest Jupiter, "a brave old oak."

Bryant thus apostrophizes one of these old monarchs

> "Ye have no history. I cannot know
> Who, when the hill-side trees were hewn away,
> Haply two centuries since, bade spare this oak
> Leaning to shade with his irregular arms,
> Low-bent and long, the fount that from his roots
> Slips through a bed of cresses toward the bay.
> I know not who, but thank him that he left
> The tree to flourish where the acorn fell,
> And join these later days to that far time
> While yet the Indian hunter drew the bow
> In the dim woods, and the white woodman first
> Opened these fields to sunshine, turned the soil
> And strewed the wheat. An unremembered Past
> Broods like a presence, 'mid the long gray boughs
> Of this old tree, which has outlived so long
> The flitting generations of mankind."

The imagination is stirred to an indescribable affection or reverence for such ancient trunks that it is difficult to account for ;—a something allied to the love or awe with which we regard the Deity.

Among the sources of picturesque effect in old trees are the sharp lights and shades caused by the deep furrows and breaks in their bark,* the abrupt angles of their great limbs, and the broad openings through the masses of their foliage that allow the sun to fleck with bright lights parts of the tree which are surrounded with deep shadows ;—causing what artists call bold effects. These are always inferior in young trees, though there is a vast difference in different species of trees of similar age and size in their tendency to produce these effects.

---

* At Montgomery Place, near Barrytown, on the Hudson, are some old locust trees with bark so deeply furrowed as to make their trunks picturesque to an extraordinary degree, so that this character is a sufficient offset to the meagreness of their stunted tops to save them from destruction. A city visitor there once asked the proprietor why she did not have the bark cut off—"it looks so very rough!"

LIGHTS AND SHADOWS.—The quality of trees, which is least observed except by painters, and yet one which has much to do with their expression, and our preferences for one or another sort, is their manner of reflecting the light in masses, so that it is brought into high relief by the dark shade of openings in the foliage, against which the lights are contrasted. If the reader will study trees, he will see that the lines of light and shade in the Lombardy poplar, Fig. 80, are nearly vertical, and in narrow strips,

FIG. 80. in harmony with the outlines of the tree, while in the

balsam fir and the beech, Fig. 81, they are in nearly horizontal layers, and looking as though the tree had been built up in stratas. .Most of the arbor-vitæ family grow so compact that their shadows, seen at a little distance, are much like those of solid bodies, the openings in their spray being so small, that their surfaces are little broken by shadows. Young apple, maple, and chestnut trees, present, when young, such unbroken surfaces of leaves, that it is proper to say of them, then, that they have insipid or unformed characters. Compare the cut of the young apple, Fig. 82, with an old tree, Fig. 83, or the young maple, Fig. 84, with the mature one, Fig. 85, and it will be seen that not merely their outlines have changed with age, but that there are bolder shadows, and consequently more

FIG. 81. striking lights in the masses of their foliage. The native chestnut (*Castanea vesca*) exhibits a much more radical change from youth to age in its shadows. When young it resembles in form the young apple tree; but when middle-aged, it breaks up into broader masses than any other native tree, except the white oak, which in age it most resembles. Fig. 105 shows its characteristic break of light and shadow. It will be seen that it is neither in vertical nor horizontal lines, but quite irregular, and in large, instead of small masses. Herein consists one of the characteristics that distinguish majestic, or grand, from simply beautiful trees. The sugar maple, as shown in Fig. 85, is broken into

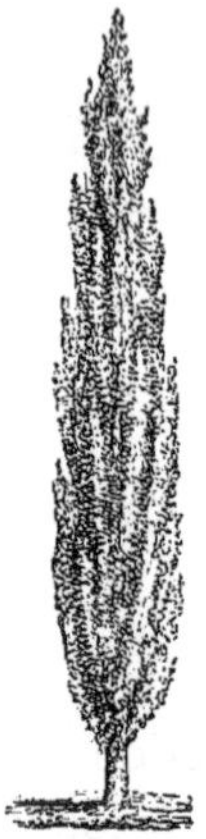

clearly-defined masses of light and shade, but
the masses are small—too narrow and too numerous to produce the grand effects of the
larger openings in the oak and chestnut, though
our cut shows larger lights and shadows than
are usual in the maple. The brighter green
and more abundant foliage of the maple make

FIG. 82.

amends for this inferiority, but it is none the less an inferiority.
An examination of the structure of these trees in winter will show
why the oak and the chestnut mass their foliage
more nobly. It is because they have fewer and
larger branches, not radiating like those of the
maple with uniform divergence, but breaking
out here and there at right angles with the part
from which they issue. The consequence is,

FIG. 83.

that when they are in leaf, the projecting leaf surfaces and the
shadow openings are larger and nobler in expression. The hickories are all observable for the massiveness of their lights and
shadows, and, unlike the chestnut, they assume
this character while yet young. By the shadows
alone it would not be easy to distinguish a
hickory from an oak or chestnut, though they
are readily distinguishable at sight by difference
of contour—the hickory being proportionally
taller and squarer than the others. There is,

FIG. 84.

however, a difference in the shadows that close observers will mark:
the wood being more elastic, the branches of old trees bend to
form curved lines, which give the shadows a similar general di
rection, as will be seen on Fig. 86. This effect
◆may be seen in many other trees, and is more
noticeable in the lower than the upper part of
the tree. There are many species which can be
distinguished readily by this peculiarity in their
shadows in connection with their contours. The
sassafras, Fig. 87, naturally takes an umbrella
form of head, and its foliage divides into curvilinear strata, or rather appears so as seen

FIG. 85.

from the ground.   The linden tree when old, and the common dog-wood (*Cornus florida*), have similar lines of shadows.

If we classify trees by their surface lights and shadows alone, they will divide into three classes, viz: first, those whose lights and shadows fall in lines approaching the vertical ; second, those which divide into strata horizontally ; third, those which break into irregular masses.   The Lombardy poplar will be the type of the former ; the common beech, Fig. 88, of the second : and the white oak of the latter.   Most evergreen trees belong to the second group.   The first class comprises a comparatively small number of trees, but many which belong to one of the last two groups at maturity, are members of the first when young.

FIG. 86.

The cedar of Lebanon is the most remarkable of trees in the second class.   It is the embodiment of majesty in its class, as the oak of the third class.   Of our native trees, the white pine is the grandest type among evergreens east of the Rocky Mountains, of trees with stratified shadows, as the beech is among deciduous trees.   The pin oak is a familiar example of stratified foliage.   Its foliage layers are as distinctly marked as those of the beech, but its branches droop more ; and are so twiggy, thorny, and inter-tangled, that its expression is ruder and its shadows less noble than those of the pine or beech.   The Norway spruce and the hemlock, though the small spray falls with plume-like grace, and the branches droop from the trunk, divide into masses of light and shadow in nearly horizontal lines.   All the trees which maintain this stratified character of shadows have more sameness of outline and monotony of expression than those which break into larger and irregular masses.   The weeping willow, when full grown, with all its delicacy of foliage and

FIG. 87.

FIG. 88.

softness of outline, becomes majestic and noble by the massive irregularity of its shadows; while the Lombardy poplars, Fig. 89, stratified vertically by shadows as of long bundles of foliaged faggots, convey an impression of having all been cast in a common mould. The same effect is produced by the upright junipers, the arbor-vitæs, and other trees of conical outlines and fastigiate shadow lines. Such repetitions of the same formal outlines, how- ever, tend to make them appropriate connecting links between the regularity and symmetry of street improve- ments, of which they form a part, and the wild graces of nature which are in contrast with the repetitions and parallelisms of architectural art. Such trees are, there- fore, used with happy effect in connection with garden walks and terraces, and near buildings. But they must never be seen in numbers together, or they produce the effect of a superfluity of exclamation points in composition. Trees like the Norway spruce, though less formal in outline and shadows than those just named, have still so much of this same uniformity and even rigidity of expression, that they need to be introduced much more sparingly among other trees, near to architecture of any kind, than those of more diversified forms and shadows. One spiry-top tree will serve to give spirit to a whole group of round- headed trees or shrubs, while a group of spiry-top trees with one round-headed tree in it, at once conveys the impression of incon- gruity. Spiry-top trees should be considered as condiments in the landscape—never as main features. Trees and shrubs of formal outlines are the natural adjuncts of grounds arranged on a geometric plan, while those of freer growth are most becoming where geo- metric lines are avoided. In speaking of the "wild graces of nature" as in contrast with architectural art, we do not mean to convey the impression that such a contrast is undesirable. On the contrary, the most perfect works of art in landscape gardening are those in which the free graces of nature are so arranged, that the architectural features of the place will look *as if they had been made for just such a setting.* Contrast does not imply want of harmony; it is a part of harmony; it is rest from monotony; it is as light to shadow.

Fig. 89.

EVERGREEN AND DECIDUOUS TREES AND SHRUBS COM-
PARED.—It is a common complaint among tree-growers that evergreens are neglected more than other trees, considering their
peculiar merits in giving winter as well as summer verdure. We
do not agree with this view. The whole coniferæ or evergreen
tribe were, according to the records of geology, an earlier and (if
the harmony of progress in the development of both the vegetable
and animal worlds is believed) necessarily an inferior order of vegetation to the later forms of deciduous trees. And we think that
those lovers of trees who study them in middle age and maturity,
rather than in their nursery growth and infantile graces, will rank
very few of the evergreens as peers in richness and cheerfulness
of verdure, or grace and variety of expression, with the finest specimens of deciduous trees. During the first twenty years of their
growth, however, their most beautiful characteristics are so conspicuous, and afford to the novice in the study of trees so many
novel graces of form, color and growth—their little pyramids of
verdure gleaming brightly through snows in winter, or resting
lovingly on the lawn and perfuming the air with their balsamic
breath in summer—that they seem to us more like our own children, than those more aspiring trees of deciduous breeds which
stretch away upwards with rambling vigor while young, and whose
beauties begin to multiply only after their branches sway in the
air far over our heads. The very peculiarity which, in youth,
makes the evergreens, as a class, more charming than deciduous
trees, viz: feathery gracefulness of their foliage and outlines, is
reversed at maturity, when most of them become more rigid and
monotonous in outline, and less cheerful in expression, than the
average of deciduous trees. There is a comparative sameness of
form and manner of branching among evergreens, in marked contrast with the infinite variety among deciduous trees.

But though the coniferæ may not take equal rank with deciduous
trees in the variety of their forms or expressions at maturity, they
certainly offer the most pleasing studies for the beginner in gardenesque planting. Many new species of a semi-dwarf character
have been introduced within a few years, and it has also been
found that many of the larger species may, by good trimming, be

kept within a size suited to the limited spaces of suburban lots, either as single specimens, or as hedge screens. For the latter purpose, where it is desirable to break the force of winds, or hide unsightly objects, they may be grown and cut to almost any height and form necessary for the purpose. While deciduous trees and shrubs, which in summer form massy walls of verdure, are all disrobed, and suffer the wintry winds to whistle freely through their bare branches, the evergreen screen is still a thick wall of protection to whatever of less height is under its lee.

One of the most striking beauties of evergreens is the manner in which their branches bear great burdens of snow, and bend under them. The softly-rounded drooping masses of light on the outer boughs, relieved by dark recesses in the foliage, make every tree, at such times, a study for a picture.

The winter color of evergreens is much more affected by the temperature than most persons suppose. In extremely cold weather most evergreens become dull in color, and resume their brightness only with returning warmth. This is always observed in the red cedar, and some of the arbor-vitæs; the former turning to a dingy brown in cold weather; and the latter, though less discolored, are much duller in tone during severe weather; but with the return of the warm days of spring both resume their normal brightness and purity of color. Even the foliage of the white pine shows a very marked change from the effect of cold; often turning to a dull grayish green when the cold is greatest, though with the return of warmth the same leaves regain their warm green color. These facts illustrate that even evergreens are most beautiful in summer, except so far as their masses of foliage afford a resting-place in winter for the snow, and thus create beautiful effects peculiar to themselves which deciduous trees cannot rival.

The beauty of trees, whether deciduous or evergreen, depends very much upon the character of light in the atmosphere. The most beautiful foliage of a deciduous tree, under the leaden sky of a winter day, would be most gloomy and unattractive compared with its expression when bathed in the bright light of a June day, or in the golden air of an August sunset. The summer light with its golden shimmer is essential to the highest charm of trees; and it will be found quite impossible to produce with evergreens, in winter, any of that glow of beauty which makes the heart throb with silent love for verdant nature in summer.

But in the warm days of April and May, when the evergreens have resumed their true colors, and seem by the sudden change from their wintry dullness to fairly smile a welcome to spring, their superiority to deciduous trees is most apparent. Their beauty is then ripe, and grounds that are stocked (not too densely) with them—especially the smaller species and varieties—have a finish that nothing else, at that season, can give. In June and July also, their long plumes and tufts of leaves open and droop with a grace of which there is no counterpart among deciduous trees or shrubbery, superior as the latter are in amplitude of foliage and splendor of blossoms. Evergreens, especially the firs, with age are apt to become gloomy and formal, while deciduous trees are generally improved with age.

The valuable acquisitions from abroad of new species and varieties of evergreens adapted to the embellishment of suburban lots, is very great; and the number growing within the limits of our own country, and still almost unknown except by a few horticultural pioneers, is astonishing. The new varieties of old species, which, by the propagating arts of the nurserymen are multiplied for the public benefit, are also numerous; and the homely adage still holds good when we are searching for novelties among trees that are not natives of our own country, that "we may go further and fare worse." The grandest and most beautiful evergreen that grows in our climate is the white pine; which, to our shame be it said, is little known or appreciated except for its value to cut down, and saw into the lumber used in our houses. The native hemlock, when young, is still the most picturesque in its outline, and delicately graceful in foliage, of all hardy evergreens. The Norway spruce, which is probably the most valuable tree of its type, is not a native; and is largely indebted to its foreign name for its great popularity and universal cultivation; while our native black spruce, very similar, and scarcely inferior to it, is little known.

For elegant *small* pleasure-grounds, however, the newly intro duced dwarf varieties and the curious sports from old species, are novelties which deserve to be studied and planted more than the larger and nobler evergreens.

In conclusion, we hope that in canvassing a few of the qualities of evergreens as compared with deciduous trees and shrubs, we have called attention to the best qualities of both, rather than prejudiced any mind against either

WARMTH OF TREES IN WINTER AND COOLNESS IN SUMMER.— Our clear-headed horticulturist, Thomas Meehan, of Germantown, Pa., has treated this subject so well that we take the liberty of adopting his language.

"We all know that a stove throws out heat by reason of the fuel it consumes, and that in a like manner the food taken by an animal is, as so much fuel to a stove, the source from whence animal heat is derived, and which is given off to the surrounding atmosphere, precisely as heat is given off from the stove; but it is not so well known that trees give off heat in the same way. They feed; their food is decomposed; and during decomposition heat is generated, and the surplus given off to the atmosphere.

"If any one will examine a tree a few hours after the cessation of a snow storm, he will find that the snow for perhaps a quarter of an inch from the stem of the tree, has been thawed away, more or less according to the severity of the cold. This is owing to the waste heat from the tree. If he plants a hyacinth four inches or more under the surface of the earth in November, and it becomes immediately frozen in, and stays frozen solid till March, yet, when it shall then be examined, it will be found that by the aid of its internal heat, *the bud has thawed itself through the frozen soil to the surface of the ground.*

"These facts show the immense power in plants to generate heat, and the more trees there are on a property the warmer a locality becomes.

"Evergreens, besides possessing this heat-dispensing property, have the additional merit of keeping in check cold winds from other quarters, thus filling, as it were, the twofold office of stove and blanket." *

* Am. Hort. Annual, 1867.

The simple facts, as stated by Mr. Meehan, have so great significance that no intelligent man who thinks of them can fail to appreciate the immense influence of trees on climates ; and every suburban home may be made to feel in some degree their ameliorating effect.

· In riding to a suburban home from business in a city, we have felt the effect of mere grass alone, without trees, in cooling the air in hot summer days.   Narrow streets, with high houses, are much cooler at such times than broad streets and open unshaded ground ; and the first feeling in leaving a city office and riding across the bare suburbs that usually intervene between the business part of a city and its pleasant tree-embowered residences, is, that the city street is the most comfortable place.   But when we reach a grass-covered field a trifle less dryness in the air is perceptible ; and when the shadows of trees are reached, there will be a difference of several degrees between the air under them and that in the open highway ; and not merely a difference of temperature as indicated by the thermometer, but also an increased moisture that gives the sensation of a greater difference than the thermometer measures.

CHAPTER II.

DESCRIPTIONS AND ORDER OF ARRANGEMENT.

IN the following descriptions little attention will be paid to the uses of trees in the arts, except only their pleasant usefulness as food for eyes that hunger for all forms of natural beauty. Enjoyment of trees, like enjoyment of sunlight, moonlight, and flowers, is not to be measured by money values, nor to be jostled by statistics of the worth of timber to the artisan, or of shade for the farmer's stock. Yet whoever loves trees will find language inadequate to describe their expressions, or even some of their most common peculiarities, though they be ever so obvious to the admiring eye. We would gladly be able to furnish engravings of every tree and shrub described; but to do this requires the command of artists whose work would involve the expenditure of a small fortune. Few persons are aware of the skill and care required to make a finished drawing on wood of even a single shrub or tree. We do not mean by a shrub or tree such a generic shrub or tree as any good sketcher may easily represent, but *a speaking portrait* of some beautiful specimen, with its animated form, its sunny expression, and its shadowy dimples; with its drapery of peculiar leaves, and all its airy graces. Artists who can thus faithfully portray them are not easily found, or, if found, are usually engaged in larger and more profitable fields of art.

In reading descriptions of trees and shrubs, the reader must bear in mind the great variety of wants and tastes to be provided for. Persons who are enthusiasts for novelties desire to learn as much as possible of the appearance and habits of the latest acquisitions; while a larger class of persons, who need no great number or variety of shrubs or trees, are not less exigent to have pretty full information of just those things which they do happen to grow or to want. It is therefore necessary to give as full descriptions of new things as of old ones of greater value; and to mention, at least, many trees and shrubs which are neither rare nor very valuable, but are often seen and therefore referred to. In the beginning of the chapter on Shrubs, pages 455 to 459, are some remarks on the considerations which influence a choice of shrubs (some of which apply equally to trees), to which the reader's attention is invited.

ORDER OF ARRANGEMENT.—It is extremely difficult to follow any system for the classification of trees and shrubs that will greatly facilitate the reader in finding readily what he wishes to read of, or that will save him constant references to an index. Botanical classifications, when thoroughly made, require quite too much familiarity with botany to give them any value to the mass of readers who know only the a, b, c's of the science; yet they must, after all, be the ground-work of the most convenient arrangement for descriptions. Though the same botanical family—often the same species—has plants of every variety of size, from groundlings to lofty trees, which differ from each other in their larger characteristics as much as from some members of other families with which they have little botanical connection, yet, *in general, it will be found that grouping by botanical relationship brings together those which resemble each other in the greatest number of particulars.*

To classify trees and shrubs by their sizes, would separate family groups, and scatter them promiscuously among each other, while in all respects but size, their similarity of traits make it most easy to describe them by families. Take the oaks, for instance. The different species are numbered by hundreds, all having some marks of consanguinity in their general appearance, but quite diverse in forms and sizes. The immense variety of species of the first differ still more among themselves;—varying in size from lofty trees to pigmy shrubs. If we class them with evergreen trees according to their varying sizes, they would become sadly mixed among the pines, junipers, arbor-vitæs, yews, and a score of newer evergreen families. If classified by forms alone, the same confusion would arise. It is best therefore to keep botanical family groups together. All oaks, for example, large and small, are described consecutively under the head of THE OAK; and as most of them are trees, they are described under the general head of DECIDUOUS TREES; though there are varieties which are really shrubs only.

The lilac family, on the other hand, being *in general* of a shrubby growth, that is, having several stems springing from the base of the trunk to form a top, will all be described under the general head of SHRUBS, although some of them assume a tree-like character. Many of the smaller species of evergreens, like the arbor-vitæs, tree-box, junipers, and yews, are of shrubby, rather than tree-like appearance ; but as they finally tend to make a single stem, they have by long custom been classed with trees, though some of their smaller varieties are quite diminutive by the side of common garden shrubs.

It will be seen by these examples that among descriptions of trees are included many of the smallest materials that enter into the composition of shrubberies ; and among the descriptions of shrubs will be many quite tree-like species and varieties of abnormal vigor, which, if classed by their own characteristics rather than of the family to which they belong, would be described among trees. A copious table of contents giving both the popular and the botanical names for all trees and shrubs described, facilitates better than any new classification, a reference to the subject sought. We shall, however, in an appendix, give some tabular classifications on the basis of sizes and forms, for the convenience of those desiring to make selections, who can by this means compare them in abbreviation.

We shall begin our descriptions of deciduous trees with the oak, and follow with other trees, somewhat in the order of their size and importance in the common estimation, but do not desire the reader to infer that those which happen to be described towards the last, are therefore of less value for decorative purposes than those which precede them.

The descriptions will be made in four classes, as follows :

DECIDUOUS TREES.
DECIDUOUS SHRUBS.
EVERGREEN TREES AND SHRUBS.
VINES AND CREEPERS.

Each of these classes will be the subject of a chapter.

CHAPTER III.

DECIDUOUS TREES.

THE OAK.

Quercus.

HARLEY SC.

> "A little of thy steadfastness,
>   Rounded with leafy gracefulness,
>   Old oak give me ;—
>   That the world's blasts may round me blow,
>   And I yield gently to and fro,
>   While my stout-hearted trunk below,
>   And firm-set roots unshaken be."
>
> LOWELL.

TO convey by words alone an idea of the grand and varied expressions of full-grown oaks would be a task almost as difficult as to impart by description the awful sense of sublimity inspired by rolling thunder. In a country where the oak abounds in all the forests it might seem that it would be sufficiently familiar to most persons ; nevertheless, it is a fact *that not more than one American out of a thousand has ever seen the full expansion of a white oak grown to maturity in open ground!* Downing's excellent description of the forest monarch is so apt that we here transcribe it; premising that such general remarks on the oak usually apply to the white oaks, which at maturity are the noblest of all the species.

"As an ornamental object we consider the oak the most varied in expression, the most beautiful, grand, majestic, and picturesque of all deciduous trees.   *   *   *   When young its fine foliage (singularly varied in many of our native species) and its thrifty form render it a beautiful tree. But it is not till the oak has attained considerable size that it displays its true character, and only when at an age that would terminate the existence of most other trees that it exhibits all its magnificence. Then its deeply-furrowed trunk is covered with mosses; its huge branches, each a tree, spreading horizontally from the trunk with great boldness, its trunk of huge dimension, and 'its high top bald with dry antiquity'— all these, its true characteristics, stamp the oak, as Virgil has expressed it in his Georgics—

> ' Jove's own tree,
> That holds the woods in awful sovereignty.''

While oaks which have already attained great size are the noblest environments of a home, yet for some reasons they are less desirable to plant in small grounds than many other trees which grow to noble size and beautiful proportions in less time, though they may not finally develop so grandly. The finest species of the oak are late in leaf, and of slow growth; are addicted to holding their dry dead leaves upon the branches through the winter and early spring, and then dropping them week after week into the fresh grass of spring lawns just when we want them brightest and cleanest. And the younger and thriftier the tree the greater its tenacity in holding the old leaves. This fault is principally confined to the white and Turkey oaks.

It will surprise most Americans to know the great number of species of oak that are indigenous in this country, and in their own neighborhoods. Loudon in his *Arboretum Brittanicum* enumerates about two hundred species and varieties of oaks known thirty years ago. Nearly one-half of these are natives of our continent. In the following descriptions of a part of them we shall endeavor to name only those which are growing wild in most neighborhoods, and are therefore likely to be objects of study to those interested in trees ; and those foreign sorts which are intrinsically beautiful, and known to be hardy, or nearly so.

There being a great variety of oaks, we hope to facilitate a reference to them by their classification into native and foreign oaks, and subdividing the native oaks into groups, as follows :—

I. The White Oak Group; embracing those trees having lobed leaves with rounded edges and light-colored scaly bark. Leaves dying an ashy or violet brown.

II. The Chestnut Oak Group ; leaves toothed, with rounded edges, dying a dirty white or yellow color. Bark resembling that of the chestnut tree.

III. The Red Oak group ; having deeply-lobed and sharp-pointed leaves, which turn to a deep red, scarlet or purple. Bark smooth when young, and never deeply furrowed. Cup large in proportion to the acorn.

IV. The Black Oak Group ; leaves obtusely lobed, and generally with points. Bark quite dark, and generally much broken by furrows.

V. Willow Oaks ; leaves entire, narrow and small. Sub-evergreen. General appearance of trees when without leaves, like the black oak.

The White Oak Group.

THE WHITE OAK (*Quercus alba*).—This is the grandest, the most common, and the most useful of our northern oaks. Although indigenous, it is almost identical with the British oak *Q. pedunculata* and *Q. sessiflora*. Though we have no such aged and immense trees as can be found of those varieties in Britain, our white oaks may in time become such trees. The great specimens which may have been found growing in open ground in the early settlement of the country while the settlers were compara-

THE VALLEY-ROAD OAK OF ORANGE, N. J.

tively poor, were sadly valuable for ship-timber, and therefore sacrificed on the altars of profit and utility. Trees grown to great size in the forest cannot be preserved when their supporting trees are cut from around them, and we must therefore leave to future centuries to record to what size the trees now growing in open ground may eventually attain. The Wadsworth oak, near Gencsee, N. Y., the valley-road oak of Orange, N. J., of which the above engraving is a portrait, and a few others scattered at rare intervals over the country, are trees of great size, large enough to show that age only is wanting to give them the colossal dimensions of trunk and branches that British oaks have attained, and, compared with which, our largest are mostly but moderate-sized trees. The Wadsworth oak probably comes nearer to the great English exemplars than any other, having a trunk thirty-six feet in circumference. The valley-road oak, just mentioned, has an unusually

20

small trunk (about five feet in diameter) for so great a ramification of branches, which cover a space upwards of ninety feet in breadth; but there is a majestic solidity in the first divergence of the great branches which promises in time to make this an oak of the first magnitude, though it is too rotund to be one of great picturesqueness.   Its height is about eighty feet.   There are some superb specimens in a pasture field near the grounds of Robert Buist, Esq., south of Philadelphia, which measure nearly one hundred feet across the spread of their branches, with trunks about fifteen feet in circumference, exhibiting all the grand characteristics of full grown oaks.   Yet these dimensions are not great compared with those of living British and German oaks, some of which range from forty to sixty feet in circumference of trunk; others from one hundred and twenty to one hundred and eighty feet across the greatest extension of their branches, and from ninety to one hundred and forty feet in height!   One shades an area large enough for two thousand four hundred men to stand in comfortably, and another drips over an area of three thousand square yards, "and would have afforded shelter to a regiment of nearly one thousand horse!"   The trunk of the Cowthorpe oak, which is said to have been the prototype of the Eddystone light-house, exceeds in size, where it meets the earth, the base of that wonderful structure. Many halls in England, of considerable size, are floored with single plank from trees grown on the estates where used.   Even as timber trees, our greatest forest-grown oaks are not equal to their venerable European relatives.   The author has had a

Fig. 92.

forest oak cut from which ten cords of wood were cut, which is about two-thirds the cubic contents of the largest British trees.   This is not an unusual size in our forests; but, alas, very unusual in trees that are rooted, and low spreading enough to resist the gales on open ground. Probably the best exemplars of the oak family in our country are the live oaks of the Gulf States; some of which have been preserved, and rival in the horizontal extension of their branches, the greatest oaks of England.

The accompanying cut, Fig. 92, shows the form of

the leaf of the white oak, and the characteristic form of the · tree when quite young—say from five to ten years after planting from the nursery. In rich and cultivated soil the growth of young white oaks is about two feet a year, but in ordinary soils is not much more than half this. The depth and culture of the soil makes more difference in the rate of growth of the white oak than of the sugar maple or chestnut ; and adds to the beauty of its foliage in the same proportion. The latter trees will often show luxuriant masses of leaves in soils too poor to produce more than a meagre foliage on the oak. When grown in soils that force a rapid growth, it develops early those broad masses of light and shadow which, in its later growth, in connection with the grand horizontal projection and picturesque irregularity of its branches, makes it a favorite tree of most landscape painters. The leaves change in autumn to a dull brown or purple, and hang on thrifty trees till they are fairly pushed off by the growth of new leaves the following May.

THE SWAMP WHITE OAK. *Q. tomentosa.*—This common native oak, one of the most valuable for its timber, is also one of the most beautiful ; and forms a connecting link between the chestnut oaks and the white oak. In form, when young, it closely resembles the burr oak, as shown in Fig. 95 ; but its bark is lighter colored, smoother, and more scaly. The branches are more numerous than those of the white oak, especially the smaller spray, and disposed to droop gracefully as the tree attains a large. size. The leaves, the form ·of which is shown by Fig. 93, are a shining green on the upper surface and whitish on the under side ; occasional specimens displaying leaves so white when turned by the wind, as to be observed among the oaks for this peculiarity. Its growth is a little more rapid than that of the white oak or burr oak, but less rapid, when young, than the red and black oaks. At middle age, however, say from twenty years old and upwards, no oak grows more rapidly. Fig. 94 is a portrait of a beautiful specimen growing on the grounds of T. Van Amringe, near Mamaroneck, N. Y., in a meadow near the waters of Long Island Sound. The

FIG. 93.

FIG. 94

form is more elm-like than the usual character of the tree, but serves to illustrate one form of this species.   It becomes a tree of the largest size, little inferior, in rich cool soils, to the white oak. Though named swamp white oak, it is by no means a swamp tree, but is generally found in such rich moist soils as the whitewood and the magnolias delight in.   We think it the best of all the first family of oaks for decorative planting, because, in a proper soil, it will give the quickest return in beauty. It is reputed the finest of all the northern oaks for *straight* ship timber, and the most durable in the ground.

THE BURR OAK OR OVER-CUP WHITE OAK.   *Quercus macrocarpa.*—The accompanying sketch is characteristic of the burr oak when young ; with age it assumes a spreading form, very similar to, but smaller, than the white oak ; the bark is darker colored, and rougher, and the branches have a corky and ragged look.   The leaf is the largest and most beautiful among oak leaves, and has a form so peculiar as to attract attention, and is admirably adapted to use in architectural designs.   It has been used with beautiful effect as the principal leaf in wrought-stone capitals.   The acorn in its cup is also a picturesque little object, and has given the name of burr to the tree on account of the cup being rough, shaggily fringed, and almost enveloping the acorn like a burr.   Grown in open rich ground it is a decidedly handsome tree in summer, but rude in its winter appearance.   The oak openings in some of the western States are largely composed of this variety.   Nearly every home in beautiful Kalamazoo, Michigan, is surrounded by these trees " to the manor born."   When thus found wild, the tree needs much internal prun-

FIG. 95.

ing of dead branches and twigs, and rarely receives the thorough draining and enrichment of the soil without which few oaks develop a high order of foliage beauty. The rate of growth may be inferred from the growth of one planted by Moses Brown, of Germantown, Pa., a mere whip twenty years ago. It is now forty-five feet high, thirty feet in diameter, and foliaged to the ground ; the form is distinctly conical, but at the same time so irregular in outline as to be quite picturesque.

THE POST OAK. *Q. obtusiloba.*—A dark-leaved spreading oak found generally near the sea. It is not found much north of New York. Its leaf resembles the black oak in color and texture, but the lobes are rounded instead of pointed. The branching of the tree is like that of a rugged white oak. There is a superb specimen growing on the beach at Orienta, in Mamaroneck, N. Y., near the residence of Thomas S. Shepherd, Esq., which measures upwards of ninety feet across the spread of its branches. Usual height and breadth about fifty feet.

FIG. 96.

THE WATER OAK, *Q. aquatica*, is a dwarf species, native of New Jersey and Maryland, which, as far as we are aware, has not been thought worthy of cultivation.

THE HOLLY-LEAVED OR BEAR OAK, *Q. illicifolia*, is a native dwarf, covering vast tracts of barren mountain slopes or table lands where no other tree can resist the winds. In such situations it grows from three to ten feet high. Probably of no value for home-grounds ; but one of those sorts that ought to be experimented with to try the effect upon it of a lowland soil and climate.

THE WATER WHITE OAK OF THE SOUTH, *Q. lyrata*, is a swamp variety, with leaves resembling the burr oak, but smaller and less curiously lobed. It grows principally in the southern States, and there attains a height of eighty feet. Michaux states that plants of it grow finely in a dry soil in the north of France.

THE OLIVE-ACORN OR MOSSY-CUP OAK. *Q. oliveifornus.*—This variety is known by some under the name of mossy-cup oak. As the burr oak has a still mossier cup, it seems to us that the botanical name which Loudon has anglicized, and which is given above, is more appropriate. Its acorn is long, like the olive, and nearly covered by its cup, but not so completely as that of the burr oak. The leaf of this variety is like a white oak leaf, elongated, and more deeply lobed. Its bark is like that of the white oak, but the growth is more slender, and the branches tend to droop gracefully. A native of the northern States.

THE CHESTNUT OAK GROUP.

FIG. 97.

THE CHESTNUT OAK. *Quercus prinus palustris.*—A lofty tree found principally below the latitude of 42°. It is disposed to form a straight trunk, without branches to a considerable height, and then to spread into a broad tufted head. Fig. 97 shows its form of leaf. We have not had the good fortune to see any trees of this variety *grown to maturity* in open ground, and cannot, therefore, speak of its usual character as an ornamental tree; but our impression is that for massy and glossy foliage, and rapidity of growth, it is surpassed by few of the oaks. When young its growth is long-limbed like the red oaks. At all times a cleanly-looking tree.

THE ROCK CHESTNUT OAK. *Q. prinus monticola.*—Downing considers this one of the finest of northern oaks, and states that it grows on the most barren and rocky soils; thus showing its affinity to its namesake and prototype, the chestnut tree. "In open elevated situations it spreads widely, and forms a head like that of an apple tree." The leaves are broader proportionally, and less acutely pointed than those of the preceding variety, by which, and its lower and broader form, it can be recognized. We consider this the finest of the chestnut oak family, and for small grounds the most desirable oak to plant, being more opulent in leaves than any other.

The Yellow Chestnut Oak. *Q. p. accuminata.*—This variety differs little from the *Q. prinus.* The leaves are more pointed, and their petioles are longer. This is not the yellow oak of western woodsmen, which is a variety of the red oak, *Q. rubra.*

The Dwarf Chestnut Oak or Chinquapin. *Q. prinus pumila.*—"A low tree twenty to thirty feet high. Highly ornamental when in full bloom, and most prolific in acorns when but three or four feet high" (Loudon). We have not seen it in rich open ground.

The Red Oak Group.

Fig. 98.

These are all distinguished by a more upright growth of their branches when young than the white oaks; resembling in this quality the chestnut oaks. The branches generally form an acute angle with the main stem, and grow most from their points, so that they are straighter and longer in one direction than those of the white oak group, and consequently form trees more open and straggling. The bark is quite smooth and lighter colored till the tree attains considerable size, and even on full grown trees is never deeply furrowed. Their growth is more rapid than any of the white oak group, and about the same as that of the chestnut oaks. The above cut gives the characteristic form of young trees, and the usual form of the leaf.

The Red Oak. *Quercus rubra.*—A large rapid-growing tree common in all parts of the northern States and Canada. Its early growth is upright but rather straggling. The bark is smooth until the tree is about twenty years old, when it becomes somewhat furrowed, but not deeply, like that of the black oak. The branches are not numerous, but straight and smooth, set at an angle of about 45° with the stem; the foliage tending to their extremities. In color the foliage varies considerably. On the coast of Maine we observed this tree growing in open fields, with a broad flat head, and a golden green tone when the sunlight was upon it that contrasted beautifully with the darker evergreen foliage of that region. But in the neighborhood of the Hudson, and at the west, this fine tone is not common on the red oak, nor is the peculiarly flat top so often seen. It is barely possible that the tree we have seen on the coast of Maine is the gray oak, *Q. ambigua*, of Michaux, which is a northern oak partaking of the character of both the red and the scarlet oaks. But we have had no means of ascertaining the correctness of this surmise. The most marked trait of the red oak as an ornamental tree is the dull crimson or purplish red color of its leaves in the fall; but as it is much less brilliant than the following, and in no respect a finer tree, the scarlet oak will be preferred.

THE SCARLET OAK. *Q. coccinea.*—This differs from the preceding but little except in its leaves, which are more deeply lobed, more sharply pointed, and have longer petioles. They are smooth and shining on both sides. Their autumn color is a bright scarlet or yellowish red, of uncommon intensity, and at that season it has no superior among trees. It is rather an elegant tree at all times, and one of the cleanest limbed of the oaks in winter. The tendency of its foliage to the extremities of the branches often gives the head too open and straggling an appearance, but this defect can be obviated with good effect on trees from twenty to forty feet high by cutting back the long branches a few times. It flourishes in any good soil, moist or dry

THE·BLACK OAK GROUP.

THE BLACK OAK, *Quercus tinctoria*, becomes a tree of the largest size, but of little value in ornamental grounds. The foliage is very dark, and though glossy, is apt to be scattered about on the long limbs, forming neither rich masses nor picturesque outlines. The whole aspect of the tree, with or without its leaves, is sombre. The foliage comes out late, and falls early. It grows naturally on dry sandy soils.

THE SPANISH OAK, *Q. falcata*, is a southern oak resembling the black oak in its bark, and with leaves somewhat like those of the pin oak and scarlet oak.

THE BLACK JACK OAK, *Q. nigra*, is a dwarf species of no value for decorative planting.

THE MARSH OR PIN OAK. *Q. palustris.*—It has been prettily remarked of this tree that it is *a graceful savage.* A

FIG. 99.

thorny, scraggy tree, armed like a hedge-hog against approach, when growing wild in wet ground, but full of grace with its delicate light foliage when in full leaf in open ground. A multitude of small branches, of great hardness of fibre, radiate at right angles from the main stem, and with their numerous angular branchlets and thorn-like spurs, give the tree the appearance, when bare of leaves, of a prodigious natural hedge-plant. The bark is extremely hard, and darker colored than that of the red oak, but smooth when young. The leaves, the form of which is shown by Fig. 99, are smaller and lighter colored than most oaks. When grown in open ground the lower branches droop to the ground, and the light-green of its fine-cut foliage, the sharpness of its stratified lights and shadows, and the general downward sweep of its branches, altogether make it a pleasing tree ; and, in Loudon's opinion, " the most graceful of the oaks." This, however, is no great compliment, remembering that grace is not a characteristic of the oak family. Our cut gives the usual form of a young pin oak, but does not indicate sufficiently the drooping habit of the lower branches.

WILLOW OAK GROUP

WILLOW OAKS. *Quercus Phellos.*—These are seldom seen north of Philadelphia. There, and southward, they become large trees, whose dark bark and foliage give them a sombre appearance. Leaves very small, lanceolate, smooth edged, and willow-like.

THE LAUREL-LEAVED OAK, *Q. p. laurifolia*, is similar to the foregoing, but with larger leaves. Found principally in the southern States.

THE SHINGLE OAK, *Q. imbricaria*, is a species with smooth-edged, elliptic, pointed, glossy leaves, similar in form to the leaf of the chionanthus. It is a native of the middle States, especially the neighborhood of the Alleghanies, and becomes a tree forty to fifty feet in height. From Michaux' description we infer that it would be a desirable oak to introduce in small grounds.

THE LIVE OAK. *Q. virens.*—Unfortunately this magnificent evergreen of our southern coast is too tender to flourish far north of the Gulf of Mexico. It is a tree of medium height only, but of immense and grand expansion of trunk and branches. A writer in Lippincott's Magazine mentions a specimen on the Habershaw plantation near Savannah, Georgia, which has an extension of one hundred and fifty feet between the extremities of its branches ! · A traveller mentions one at Goose Creek, near Charleston, S. C., the trunk of which measures forty-five feet in circumference close to the ground, eighteen and a half feet in its smallest part, with *a branch which measured twelve and a half feet in girt!* It is one of the grandest trees of the continent, as well as the most valuable of all for ship-timber.

FOREIGN OAKS.

THE BRITISH OAK. *Q. pedunculata* and *Q. sessiflora.*—These varieties of the white oak group are so nearly the same as our white oak, that it is not necessary to describe them separately. But some odd varieties have come into existence, among which are the following :

THE MOCCAS OAK, *Q. p. pendula*, is a variety of the British oak, as pendulous as the weeping willow ; and of course a great curiosity. It is said there are none of this sort in this country. An extraordinary fact, considering that full grown trees of it seventy-five feet high exist in England, and that, according to Loudon, it generally comes true from seed. If grafts can be procured, they may be put into the tops of our common white oaks.

THE UPRIGHT OAK. *Q. p. fastigiata.*—A tree of extremely fastigiate habit, the most so of any of the oaks, but much less slender than the Lombardy poplar, with which it is sometimes compared. Though a native of the Pyrenées, it is hardy at Rochester, N. Y., and makes about the same annual growth as our white oak. The leaves and branches are small and numerous.

THE MOSSY-CUPPED TURKEY OAKS. *Q. cerris.*—The variety of what are called Turkey oaks in England is large, and some of the most beautiful specimens of oaks grown during this century are of one or another variety of this species. Fig. 100 illustrates the common form of the young tree, and the leaf. It is distinguished from the British oak (which it resembles more than any other) by longer, straighter, and more upright branches, and more rapid growth. Judging by the specimens to be seen in this country, we do not perceive any striking peculiarity or beauty that should cause them to be preferred, in pleasure-grounds, to many of our native oaks.

FIG. 100.

There is an English variety, the *Q. c. pendula*, the branches of which "not only droop to the ground, but, after touching it, creep along the surface to some distance like those of the *sophora japonica pendula*" (Loudon). It grows to thirty or forty feet in height.

There are also variegated-leaved varieties, but of little value.

THE JAPAN PURPLE OAK. *Q. alba atro-purpurea japonica.*—Our attention has recently been called to this new tree from Japan. It promises to be the most brilliant member of the oak family. In the nursery of Parsons & Co., at Flushing, L. I., the little trees had as bright and clear a purple tint in September (1867), as the purple beech shows in May and June. It was considered quite hardy.

Such trees as this purple oak, the Moccas oak, and the weeping Turkey oak, can readily be grafted on our white oaks, so that persons having young and thrifty trees may, with care and persisteney through a term of years, secure samples of these curious oaks, and produce novel effects of foliage and form on the same tree. The work must, however, be done year by year, so as not to give the stock a maimed expression, or injure its health.

THE HOLLY OAKS. *Quercus virens.*—These are mostly evergreens, natives of Southern Europe and Asia, near the sea. They will not bear our winters, though they can with care be grown in some parts of England.

THE ELM. *Ulmus.*

The Elm family embraces many species, mostly large trees. Our indigenous weeping elm, *Ulmus americana*, is, however, so much better known in this country than any other, and has so long borne, and deserved, the crown and title of "queen of American trees," that it is always the species uppermost in the mind when Americans speak of the elm. Yet in England and Continental Europe the Dutch, English, and Scotch elms have not been supplanted by it.

THE AMERICAN WEEPING OR WHITE ELM. *Ulmus americana* — A full grown luxuriant weeping elm is certainly the queen, as the oak is the king, among deciduous trees. Its grace is feminine. Its outstretching arms droop with motherly grace to shelter and caress with their mantle of verdure the human broods that nestle under them. It is also a grand tree, well characterized by Dr. Holmes as

"A forest waving on a single stem."

Few trees are more lofty in their native woods, and none spread with more luxuriant amplitude in rich alluvial fields. The roots around the base of the trunk rise from the ground with peculiar picturesqueness to brace it against the winds. Its long branches, curving symmetrically upwards and outwards, describe the segment of a circle till they bend at maturity almost to the earth with their verdant tips.

That master of happy characterization, the Rev. Henry Ward Beecher, in "Norwood," makes the following beautiful allusions to the weeping elm :—"No town can fail of beauty, though its walks were gutters, and its houses hovels, if venerable trees make magnificent colonnades along its streets. Of all trees, no other unites, in the same degree, majesty and beauty, grace and grandeur, as the American elm. Known from north to south, through a range of twelve hundred miles, and from the Atlantic to the head-waters which flow into the western side of the Mississippi, yet, in New England the elm is found in its greatest size and beauty, fully justifying Michaux' commendation of it to European cultivators, as 'the most magnificent vegetable of the temperate zone.'" * * *
"Their towering trunks, whose massiveness well symbolizes Puritan inflexibility; their overarching tops, facile, wind-borne and elastic, hint the endless plasticity and adaptableness of this people ; and both united, form a type of all true manhood, broad at the root, firm in the trunk, and yielding at the top, yet returning again after every impulse into position and symmetry. What if they were sheered away from village and farm-house? Who would know the land? Farm-houses that now stop the tourist and the artist, would stand forth bare and homely; and villages that coquette with beauty through green leaves, would shine white and ghastly as sepulchres. Let any one imagine Conway or Lancaster without elms! Or Hadley, Hatfield, Northampton, or Springfield! New Haven without elms would be like Jupiter without a beard, or a lion shaved of his mane !"

The weeping elm grows with great rapidity, and where uninjured by insects, or lack of moisture in the soil, is picturesque and beautiful in every stage of its growth. No other tree, when young, throws out its arms so free and wild, and assumes so great a variety of forms. Figs. 63 and 76 are two sketches from nature of young weeping elms, illustrative of this characteristic. Very fine specimens of this elm may be seen at the west, which have attained a majestic height in the forest, and then had their environing trees gradually cut from around them. At first they are little more than columnar stems, with a parasol-like tuft of foliage at the top ; but as they are gradually exposed on all sides to the sun the head widens rapidly, the tall trunk covers itself from root to branch with a picturesque small spray peculiar to this elm, the outer branches of the top begin to droop and fall like spray from a fountain, until the whole tree assumes a loftier grace than belongs to its lower and broader-crowned sisters of the eastern valleys.   Fig. 101 is a sketch of a *young* forest elm that is beginning to develop the changes just described.   Unfortunately, however, such forest-grown trees, if more than forty or fifty years old, usually fall victims of the first summer tornado that finds them in its track.

For the formation of wide avenues the elm, in congenial soil, has no equal among trees.   But it should never be planted in narrow streets, nor nearer than forty feet asunder in wide ones.   Its great size and breadth of head should also cause it to be sparingly planted in or near small grounds, if a variety of shrubs or small trees are desired.

The roots of the white elm feed quite near the surface, so that surface manuring in autumn is a wonderful stimulant to its growth.   Large street trees are often seriously injured in old villages by the gradual accumulation of gravel and broken stone incident to annual road improvements, until the feeding roots are so covered that they cease to have any rich surface to feed in.   In other places noble old trees are being literally starved to death, while the good people who walk under them are wondering why their elms do not look as well as formerly.   Streets much travelled are continually enriched by droppings, and where the soil is not covered by water-proof pavements, there is little danger of trees in such streets suffering from this cause.   But many instances have come under our observation of elms in villages and cities that languish for want of fresh food and good soil. Half the diseases that now attack old elm trees are the result of the weakened vigor caused by lack of good fresh soil or manure on their roots, which should be put on over the whole area that is covered by the branches. A moist surface soil is most congenial to the elm.

THE RED OR SLIPPERY ELM. *Ulmus rubra,* or *fulva.*—This native elm is so overshadowed by the superior size and beauty of the weeping elm, that it is rarely planted or seen in open ground. It is a tree of a more straggling open head, somewhat similar in form, with out-arching branches, but with much larger and sparser leaves, and without the pendulous spray of the former. It becomes a tree from fifty to sixty feet high, or about two-thirds the size of the white elm. It is of no value for small grounds.

THE WAHOO ELM. *Ulmus alata.*—This species may be known by its two longitudinal ridges of cork-like bark on all its twigs and branches, though the white elm and the Dutch elm occasionally have varieties that closely resemble it in this respect. It makes a pleasing tree of medium size, and grows rapidly. Found wild in Virginia and southward.

The foregoing are American species.

The following are among the most valued of the great variety of European elms grown in England. Loudon remarks that "the elm is remarkable for the aptitude of the different species to vary from seed ; so much so that it is extremely difficult to say, in this genus, which are species and which are varieties, or even to what species the varieties belong. To us it appears that there are only two sorts which are truly distinct, viz : *U. campestris* (the English elm) and *U. montana* (the Scotch elm)." He classes the American elms as of the same species with the Scotch, *U. montana.*

THE ENGLISH ELM. *Ulmus campestris.*—The finest trees of this species we have seen in this country are on the Boston Common, where, in grandeur of branching, majesty of trunk, and healthfulness of foliage, they are certainly superior to the white elms growing side by side with them. But it must be remembered

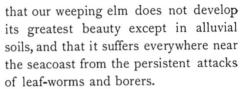

Fig. 102.

that our weeping elm does not develop its greatest beauty except in alluvial soils, and that it suffers everywhere near the seacoast from the persistent attacks of leaf-worms and borers.

The English elm differs materially from our weeping elm in leaves, trunk, and manner of branching. The leaves are smaller, more regularly and sharply cut, and darker; and the bark is also much darker colored. In the ramification of the branches it is peculiar. The first divergence usually occurs at ten to twelve feet above the ground; and these branches, instead of ascending and forming a sharp angle with the trunk, like those of our weeping elm, strike out unevenly, nearly at right angles with the trunk, and with age maintain their superior importance to the branches that diverge above them, notwithstanding the tree usually maintains a central trunk to a considerable height. This projection of massive low-growing branches, as shown in the accompanying sketch, Fig. 102, gives the English elm a much grander expression when seen from below than our white elm, the branches of which are apt to diverge with such even-sized multiplicity that none of them are of great size; and one is not fully impressed with their grandeur until standing at such a distance from the tree that the great verdant arc which the branches describe can be seen as a whole. This is not always the case, as many old white elms ramify into a few great branches; but if one will find contiguous avenues of the English and the American elm, the different effect upon the eye of the forms above alluded to, will be found very striking. Another peculiarity that increases this difference of expression is the tufty habit of the English elm, which forms little masses of leaves at the knots and intersections of old branches, adding by the contrast of their young twigs and verdure a greater apparent massiveness to the branches they grow upon. Though this elm is marked by a greater weight of lower branches than our native favorite, it does not usually spread so broadly. After insuring the strength of its lower arms, the trunk keeps on upwards, and forms a squarish oblong head.

In size the English elm, as recorded by reliable authorities, exceeds any specimens of the American elms we have heard of. In Warwickshire, at Combe Abbey, thirty years ago, stood a tree two hundred years old, one hundred and fifty feet high, seventy-four feet across its branches, with a trunk nine and a half feet in diameter! In Gloucestershire, at Doddington Park, was one ninety feet high, *one hundred and forty-nine feet across its branches,* and seven feet in diameter of trunk. In fact a height and breadth of from ninety to one hundred feet is a common thing in the parks of England, and there are many specimens from one hundred to one hundred and twenty-five feet in height.

Fig. 103.

The growth of the tree is quite rapid, fully equal in that respect to our own white elm; but its growth is so much more compact, filling-in as it rises, instead of sending out the long, curved, and rambling annual shoots peculiar to the latter, that it has not the appearance of growing so rapidly. The comparative growth of the English, the Scotch, and the American elms, may be seen to great advantage near the Mall in the New York Central Park. Fig. 103 illustrates the form and style of an English elm, fifteen years after planting.

As an ornamental tree the English elm partakes of the character of the oaks in its branching; but in the massing of its foliage, and the play of lights and shadows on its head, it occupies a place midway between the dense-leaved and sharply-stratified character of the beech, and the nobler breaks of the oak and chestnut. Gilpin, in analyzing its picturesque qualities, observes: " As a picturesque tree the elm has not so distinct a character as the oak or ash. It partakes so much of the oak, that when it is rough and old it may easily, at a little distance, be mistaken for one. * * * This defect, however, appears chiefly in the skeleton of the elm; in full foliage its character is more marked. No tree is better adapted to receive grand masses of light. In this respect it is superior to both the oak and the ash. Nor is its foliage, shadowing as it is, of the heavy kind. Its leaves are small, and this gives it a natural lightness; it commonly hangs loosely, and is, in general, very picturesque. The elm naturally grows upright, and when it meets with a soil it loves, rises higher than the generality of trees, and, after it has assumed the dignity and hoary roughness of age, few of its forest brethren excel it in grandeur and beauty." The blossoms of this species are of a dark crimson color, and on old trees are sometimes so abundant as to enrich the just-budding verdure of the tree with peculiar beauty.

THE ENGLISH CORK-BARK ELM. *Ulmus suberosa.*—This is a marked variety of the *U. campestris*, with its young branches very corky. The leaves are rough on both sides, more rounded, and two or three times as large as the normal size of the leaves of that species, and in this respect resembles our red elm.

THE DUTCH CORK-BARK ELM. *Ulmus major.*—This variety has still larger leaves and more corky bark than the preceding, and a more spreading habit of growth. It is not considered so healthy as the English elm.

THE PURPLE-LEAVED ELM. *Ulmus purpurea.*—This is a compact, upright grower, with quite small leaves, of a dull purple color. A variety of the English elm.

THE SCOTCH OR WYCH ELM. *Ulmus montana.*—This resembles more our great American elm than any other British species, but it is still very distinct in many respects. Singularly enough, this tree so hardy, vigorous, and beautiful, and so long valued in Scotland and England, is yet but little known in this country. It is one of the most valuable of trees for avenues; beautiful in any situation, and picturesque from its youth upwards. Loudon says of it: " The trunk is so bold and picturesque in form; the limbs and branches are so free and graceful in their growth; and the foliage is so rich without being clumpy as a whole, and the head is so finely massed and yet so well broken, as to render it one of the noblest of park trees; and when it grows wild amid the rocky scenery of its native Scotland, there is no tree which produces so great or so pleasing a variety of character." From the little we have seen of the Scotch elm we are inclined to believe it to be the most interesting foreign variety of the elm. The young trees of this variety in the New York Central Park are certainly the most beautiful of the elms there.

The Scotch elm forms a much more spreading tree than the English, has a squarer form than our white elm, and fills in more massily with foliage. Without being quite so picturesque in outline, in its earlier growth, it certainly displays finer contrasts, and larger masses of light and shadow. The leaves strongly resemble those of our white elm. There are some remarkably pendulous varieties, but the tree does not ordinarily show this quality when young. With age, however, it becomes a characteristic, but not to such a degree as in our native weeping elm; and the more rugged development of its branches adds to the apparent difference. In dimensions it grows to equal the largest oaks. The varieties of the Scotch elm are numerous, and vary in their character to an extraordinary degree; some of them being as pendulous as a weeping beech, and others fastigiate and cup-like. The following are the most note-worthy ·

THE WEEPING SCOTCH ELM. *U. m. pendula.*—This is the most erratic and interesting variety, and takes the same place among elms that the weeping beech does in its family. It assumes a great variety of forms; sometimes branching in a fan-like manner, sometimes marked by a persistent horizontal tendency, and occasionally shooting perpendicularly downwards; but always uneven or one-sided, and picturesque. Like the weeping beech, in the first few years of its growth it is sometimes picturesque to deformity; but it soon outgrows this stage of its eccentricity. The foliage is dark and abundant, and it becomes a large tree.

THE EXETER OR FORD'S ELM. *U. m. fastigiata.*—Noted for its very fastigiate growth and cup-like form. The leaves are twisted, enfolding one side of the shoots, very harsh and dark-colored, and retain their color longer than most others. It is a peculiar looking tree, of smaller size, as well as much more compact growth, than the species. Probably more curious than pleasing.

THE SMOOTH-LEAVED WYCH ELM. *U. m. glabra.*—This is a variety resembling our white elm in form, but not so broadly spreading, and with smoother and smaller leaves. Of no superior value except to complete collections of elms. What are known as the Huntington, Downton, and Chichester elms, each of some English local fame, are varieties of this sort, and would not probably have any sufficiently marked character to recommend them to us.

THE SCAMSTON ELM. *Ulmus m. glabra.*—This is a comparatively new variety of weeping elm, and differs materially from the pendulous Scotch elm, before described; and from all the pendulous forms of our native elms. The characteristic that distinguishes it is a compact overlaying of its branches upon each other, and their uniform downward tendency. Instead of a picturesque outline, it therefore forms a broad low top, quite similar, but on a much larger scale, to that of the Kilmarnock willow. It is of rank growth, often making shoots of a zigzag character from six to ten feet long in a season. The leaves are very large, irregular, dark, and glossy, and clothe the branches superbly. Sargent, in his Supplement to Downing's Landscape Gardening, thus alludes to it: "When grafted as it should be, fifteen to twenty feet high, the branches make a curvilinear droop to the ground with a growth so regular and symmetrical as to give the whole tree the appearance of a gigantic arbor regularly trained and trimmed, and, by making an arched opening on one side, it can be well used for this purpose; the thick umbrageous character of the leaves producing the most agreeable and dense shade." It is a valuable addition to our stock of gardenesque trees, such as are adapted to artificial treatment for special purposes. Thrifty young elm trees of the common sorts, if in locations where such a grand arbor as the kind Mr. Sargent has above suggested would be useful, may be grafted all over the top with the Scamston elm, and changed quickly into a deep shady bower of novel beauty. In our Chapter XIV, on Artificial Adaptations of Trees and Shrubs, are some suggestions on this subject, to which in this connection the reader's attention is invited.

THE CAMPERDOWN ELM so nearly resembles the Scamston, that some persons consider them the same. Sargent believes them different, and notes that the former has a growth a little more open than the latter. From the fact that pretty good observers mistake one for the other, we may infer that the difference is not material.

THE BEECH. *Fagus.*

> " * * * who shall grave, as was the wont
> Of simple pastoral ages, on the rind
> Of my smooth beeches, some beloved name?"
> BRYANT.

The beech is one of the grandest forest trees of both Europe and America. On both continents vast tracts of land are covered with it, to the exclusion of other trees, which cannot thrive in the dense shade it creates. Its smooth gray bark, never furrowing with age, but spotted in old trees with horizontal belts or patches of light-gray, makes a beech tree trunk an attractive and cheerful object among other trees, as well as a convenient surface on which to carve or write. Attaining great size, and forming deep shadows, it is, nevertheless, at all times a cleanly, cheerful-looking tree ; and in winter the great number and light color of its radiating branches and abundant spray is a pleasant characteristic.

The play of light and shade in the foliage of the beech is peculiar. The lights are sharply-defined, and thin ; and the shadows proportionally strong, and disposed horizontally in layers or strata, like those of the pine and spruce families, notwithstanding the branches, when bare of leaves, radiate at acute rather than right angles from the trunk.

The form of the tree is usually ovate, but with more variety of outline in different specimens than is found among maples or horse-chestnuts, varying from oblate to conical forms, with sky outlines occasionally quite broken and spirited.

The leaves expand later than the maples and horse-chestnuts, and earlier than those of the oak or hickory. They are small, oval-accuminate, serrated, thin, wavy, dark, and glossy, and so thickly set on the branches, that its shade is the darkest of all the forest trees. They have the same fault, however, as those of the white oak, of remaining on the tree, dead and dry, during the winter and spring. This quality, though it makes the beech less desirable as a lawn tree, when it mars the tender verdure of spring grass by dropping its second crop of dead leaves, is, nevertheless, rather an interesting feature in winter,—the gathering of snow upon the dead foliage often producing most picturesque effects. We agree with Downing "that a deciduous tree should as certainly drop its leaves at the approach of cold weather, as an evergreen should retain them," and offer this mitigating beauty as a partial apology for the one bad habit of the family.

The roots of the beech grow close under the surface of the ground, and in old forests the radiation of their huge gnarled masses around the base of the trunk, is most picturesque. The poet Gray thus happily describes them :—

> "There, at the foot of yonder nodding beech,
> *That wreathes its old fantastic roots so high,*
> His listless length at noontide he would stretch, •
> And pore upon the brook that babbled by."

In the famous old beech forest of the Hague in Belgium, this curious ramification of the great roots is one of the most interesting features of the place ; and in the wonderfully.picturesque old forest of Fontainebleau, the grand old beech trees that wreathe their roots among the rocks which they seem to love, add greatly to the air of weird antiquity that pervades this ancient hunting-ground of the French kings.

The wild species of the beech are not numerous ; but the varieties of the European beech, *Fagus sylvaticus,* introduced by cultivators and tree-fanciers are some of the most peculiar of trees.

THE AMERICAN WHITE BEECH. *Fagus americana.*—This, the loftiest and most common native species, together with its companion the red beech, *F. ferruginea,* which forms a lower and more

massive head, represent so entirely all the qualities that characterize the common beech tree of Europe, *Fagus sylvatica*, that the
above general remarks on the beech apply equally to all. The
American white beech occasionally attains a height of one hundred
feet, but eighty feet is the more common altitude. This size is exceeded by the finest specimens in England and on the Continent.
Loudon mentions a beech at Kinwell, growing in a pure sand, one
hundred and five feet high, with a head one hundred and twenty-
three feet in diameter. The great beech in Studley Park is one
hundred and fourteen feet high, and upwards of one hundred and
thirty feet in diameter of head.

The rate of growth of the white beech, when young, is about
the same as that of the sugar maple, but its growth is somewhat
more rapid after it has attained middle size, say thirty feet in
height ; and it is not unusual to see specimens growing with much
greater rapidity from the beginning. Loudon mentions one only
fourteen years planted, forty feet high and thirty-two feet diameter
of head. Though the beech adapts itself readily to a great variety
of soils, it attains the greatest size on those with a humid surface,
and a porous and calcareous subsoil. And it will grow to great
size in the crevices of rocks contiguous to moisture. Few trees
vary more in form. While in some groves of English trees, as
among the "Ashridge beeches" (Loudon's Encyclopædia Britan-
nica, p. 1977), the Queen beech is seventy-four feet high, without
a branch, and then forms a tufted head one hundred and ten
feet in height; another specimen is mentioned only thirty-six feet
high, with a trunk fourteen feet in circumference, five feet from the
ground, and a head ninety-five feet in diameter !

The leaves of the beech are said to be less liable to attacks of
insects, or to be eaten by cattle, than any other tree.

THE WEEPING BEECH. *F. sylvaticus pendula.*—We consider
this the most curious tree of our zone, and one that will commend
itself more and more as it becomes known. The original tree
stands in the park of Baron de Man, at Beersel, Belgium.* The

---

* P. J. Berckmans, in Gardeners' Monthly, June, 1869.

Fig. 104.

trunk is three and a half to four feet in diameter, and grows in a
twisted form to a height of twelve to fifteen feet, with an appearance as if an immense weight were pressing it down.   The
branches cover an area nearly a hundred feet in diameter.   Its
history is curious.   Some sixty years ago the baron's gardener was
planting an avenue of beech trees, and the baron, observing a very
crooked specimen, directed to have it thrown out; but the gardener planted it in a corner of the grounds little visited, where it
grew to be one of the most beautiful and singular freaks of sylvan
nature.

The illustration, Fig. 104, at the head of this page, is a portrait
of the weeping beech growing on the grounds of the Parsons nursery at Flushing, and is probably the finest in this country.   It is

impossible for any engraving to do justice to the eccentric luxuriance of this tree. It is the very embodiment of all the odd freaks of growth that make trees picturesque, and the vigorous healthfulness of foliage that makes them beautiful. This tree is but twenty-five years old, forty-five feet high, and fifty feet across the greatest spread of its branches. There is a weeping beech growing in the grounds of John A. Kendrick in Newton, Mass., which has a certain symmetry of proportion, notwithstanding all its erratic tendencies. It was planted in 1834, and is now fifty feet high. From the ground to the top the trunk is straight, and the branches, which directly incline downwards, are thrown off with perfect symmetry. Branches, starting out twenty-six feet high, droop and trail upon the ground.* This, however, is not the usual habit of the tree, which commonly begins its growth in a great variety of tortuous directions; so that cultivators who have never seen well-grown specimens are apt to ask what there can be about that ungainly straggler to recommend it for an ornamental tree. We have seen its leading stem grow so as to tie itself up into a knot, and then start upward as if it quite enjoyed sitting on itself.

The growth of the tree indicates great vitality, and it will doubtless become one of the largest, as well as the most curious, of lawn trees. Its fine masses of pendant boughs, and glossy, wavy leaves, do not fairly hide the occasional uncouthness of its branches until the tree has been five or six years planted. Of course the richer and deeper the soil, the more speedily its best characteristics will be developed.

THE PURPLE-LEAVED BEECH. *F. purpurea.*—This singularly tinted tree is a sport from the common white beech, found in a German forest, and is one of the finest of tree-novelties. In the spring its opening leaves and twigs have a bright purple color, approaching to crimson. As the growth continues, the color changes to a dull purplish-green less pleasing, but still of a character to attract attention throughout the season. The form is perhaps a little more symmetrically ovate than the common beech, and the tree does not attain

---

* Gardeners' Monthly, June, 1867.

so great size, but has the same dense, glossy foliage, and in consequence of its rare color may be designated as one of the best trees for even a small collection. There is much difference in the brightness and duration of the purple color, in different specimens of the purple beech, and planters should select trees from the nursery rows at midsummer to be more certain of their character

THE COPPER-COLORED BEECH, *F. cuprea,* is a sub-variety of the purple beech, the young shoots of which are of a darker and duller color. "It makes a splendid appearance in the sunshine, and when the leaves are greatly ruffled with the wind ; but in a state of repose, and on a cloudy day, it can hardly be distinguished from the common green-leaved beech."

THE VARIEGATED-LEAVED BEECHES, *F. variegata,* and others are pretty and peculiar when the leaves first appear, but at midsummer the variegation of the leaves, as far as it is apparent, only serves to give them an unhealthy appearance.

THE FERN-LEAVED AND CUT-LEAVED BEECHES. *F. heterophylla* and *F. lacimata.*—The peculiarity of these varieties is in the fern-like delicacy of their growing foliage, the young spray of which pushes out from the preceding year's growth like filaments or tendrils, giving the tree an exquisitely delicate sky-outline. Their foliage is of a lighter tone than that of any of the other beeches. H. W. Sargent, in his Supplement to Downing's Landscape Gardening, thus describes the former: "The fern-leaved beech is a great favorite with us, and we hardly know a prettier or more attractive tree, or one less known or planted. If we could plant but half a dozen trees, this would certainly be one of the first. It has the close round habit of the beech, with a pleasing green and glaucous color, and the most tiny and delicate foliage, the persistency of which would make it very desirable for topiary work, as it bears the shears better than any deciduous tree we know of." Loudon thinks it "more curious than beautiful." We have seen some of the best specimens in this country, and can hardly concur with Mr. Sargent in ranking it as one of the most interesting half dozen trees, but it is certainly one of the most delicately beautiful in out-line when in its growing state.

THE RED BEECH. *F. ferruginea.*—This native species, according to Michaux, "bears a greater resemblance to that of Europe than to the kindred American species : it equals the white beech in diameter, but not in height ; and as it ramifies nearer the earth, and is more numerously divided, it has a more massive summit, and the appearance of more tufted foliage. Its leaves are equally brilliant, a little larger and thicker, and have longer teeth." The trunk has a greater proportion of reddish or heart wood, than the white beech ; hence its name.

The following remarks by Loudon on the general characteristics of the beech family are in his habitual fine vein of discrimination :

"*As an ornamental tree* for the park and lawn, especially near the mansion, the beech has many important advantages. Though its head is more compact and lumpish than that of the oak, the elm, or the ash, yet its lower branches hang down to the ground in more pliant and graceful forms than those of any of these trees. The points of these branches turn up with a curve, which though not picturesque, has a character of its own, which will be found generally pleasing. The leaves are beautiful in every period of their existence ; nothing can be finer than their transparent deli-cacy, when expanding, and for some weeks afterwards. In summer their smooth texture, and their deep, yet lively green, are highly gratifying to the eye ; and the warmth of their umber tint, when they hang on the trees during the winter season, as contrasted with the deep and solemn green of pines and firs, has a rich, striking, and most agreeable effect in landscape." *Arboretum Britannicum,* page 1965.

Although not altogether *apropos* in a descriptive work, we cannot close with the beech without quoting for the reader the poet Campbell's exquisite lines, entitled "The Beech Tree's Petition."

> "Oh, leave this barren spot to me !
> Spare, woodman, spare the beechen tree !
> Though bud and flowret never grow
> My dark, unwarming shade below :

Nor summer bud perfume the dew
Of rosy blush. or yellow hue :
Nor fruits of autumn, blossom born,
My green and glossy leaves adorn ;
Nor murmuring tribes from me derive
The ambrosial amber of the hive ;
Yet leave this barren spot to me :
Spare, woodman, spare the beechen tree !

Thrice twenty summers I have seen
The sky grow bright, the forest green ,
And many a wintry wind have stood
In bloomless, fruitless solitude,
Since childhood, in my pleasant bower,
First spent its sweet and sportive hour ;
Since youthful lovers in my shade
Their vows of truth and rapture made,
And on my trunks' surviving frame
Carved many a long-forgotten name.
Oh ! by the sighs of gentle sound,
First breathed upon this sacred ground ;
By all that love has whispered there,
Or beauty heard with ravished ear :
As love's own altar, honor me :
Spare, woodman, spare the beechen tree

THE AMERICAN CHESTNUT-TREE. *Castanea americana.*

This, our common native chestnut, is one of the glories of the rocky hill-sides and pastures of New England, and well known throughout the northern States, and on the mountains of the southern States. It is a tree of great size, grand character, and rapid growth. In form, when mature, it resembles the white oak, but assumes its grand air much younger. Fig. 105, is a portrait of a chestnut about fifty years old, and exhibits the general character of the tree at that age. Afterwards it increases more rapidly in the size of its trunk and branches than in height or lateral extension, and requires about a hundred years to attain its noblest development ; while the white oak does not exhibit its grandest character in less than twice that time. In its early growth it is a little rounder, and more formal, than the white oak ; but develops so much more rapidly that, at middle age (fifty), it is more " oak-like " than the oak itself, of the same age. The chestnut is particularly attached to rocky situations, or loose gravelly

Fig. 105.

soils, and attains its best proportions in such places. Loudon remarks of the European chestnut, *Castanea vesca* (of which the
American is classed as a variety only), "It will not thrive in
stiff tenacious soil ; and in a rich loam its timber, and even its
poles and hoops, are brittle and good for nothing. In loamy soils
at the bottom of mountains, and in loam incumbent on clay, it
attains a large size, and in so short a time, that, according to Sang,
wherever the chestnut is planted in its proper soil and situation, it
will outgrow any other tree in the same length of time, except perhaps the larch, the willow, and some of the poplars. According
to Bosc it will not thrive in calcareous soil, but those lying over
granite, gneiss, and schistus, and which are composed of the debris
of these rocks, appear particularly suitable for it. It thrives well
among rocks where there is apparently very little soil, insinuating
itself among their fissures and chinks, and attaining a large size."
"Wherever I have seen chestnut trees," observes the same author,
"and I have seen them in a great many different localities, *they
were never on soils or on surfaces fit for the production of corn.*
On mountains in France, Switzerland, and Italy, the chestnut
begins where the corn leaves off ; and in climates suitable for
corn, the tree is only found on rocky or flinty soils."

The above observations concerning the European sweet chestnut, though in the main applicable to our own chestnut, are not entirely so; for we have seen some of the largest trees of the species in the neighborhood of Philadelphia, in soils which, if not alluvial, were at least of a character to bear grain. Still, these soils may be composed in part of the debris of the very rocks which the close observer above quoted has mentioned as essential to the growth of the tree. Michaux found the finest chestnut trees of the United States on the mountain slopes of the Carolinas.

The chestnut is remarkable for its longevity and the immense size its trunk attains. On the Blight place in Germantown, near Philadelphia, are some grand specimens. One old trunk, the top of which is a ruin, is nine feet in diameter, with a horizontal branch, at six feet from the ground, three feet in diameter! The "elephant chestnut" of the Hartshorn forest, Neversink Highlands, New York harbor, is a grand specimen, said to be five hundred years old. In the grounds of Moses Brown, School Lane, Germantown, Pa., is an immense chestnut, formed of three trunks, grown into one at the base, which measures nearly ten feet in diameter one way, and upwards of five feet the other. Its height is about ninety feet, and its branches cover an area nearly one hundred feet in diameter; yet Mr. Brown informed us that the tree is probably not more than one hundred years old! At Newton Centre, Mass., on the Rice estate, is one of the grandest chestnuts in New England; height nearly eighty feet, spread of limbs ninety-three feet, and girth of trunk at the base twenty-five feet.

But the greatest of our American chestnuts are small in trunk compared with some of the famous old specimens of the same species in Europe and Asia. In England there are larger trees than our own, notwithstanding the nuts do not ripen so well there. The Studley Park chestnut, twenty-one years ago, was one hundred and twelve feet high, seven and a half feet in diameter of trunk, and ninety-one and a half feet across its branches; and at Croft Castle, in Herefordshire, there is one eighty feet high, one hundred and twelve feet across its branches, and eight and a half feet diameter of trunk. The trunks of chestnut trees continue to expand for centuries after the tops are falling with decay. The knotted base of the old Tortsworth chestnut (supposed to date back to the time of the occupation of Britain by the Romans), is fifty-two feet in circumference at five feet from the ground! It was so large as to be called the "Great Chestnut of Tortsworth" as early as A. D. 1135. The most noted chestnut trees in the world are the venerable trunks on Mount Etna, where the living shells of what are supposed once to have been solid trees, measure from sixty-four to one hundred and eighty feet in circumference near the root!

The chestnut was the favorite tree of the great master of the picturesque in landscape painting, Salvator Rosa, and flourished in the mountains of Calabria, where he painted. For decorative planting a noted English author, already quoted (Bosc), thus speaks of it:—"As an ornamental tree, the chestnut ought to be placed before the oak. Its beautiful leaves, which are never attacked by insects, and which hang on the trees till very late in autumn, mass better than those of the oak, and give more shade. An old chestnut standing alone produces a superb effect."

The leaves of the chestnut expand immediately after those of the horse-chestnut and maple, and a little earlier than those of the oak. They are from six to nine inches long, two to three inches wide, pointed, with scolloped edges, and of a warm green color. The flowers appear in July, when most trees have done blooming, and though not interesting or showy in themselves, the mass of them, mingling their yellowish white with the leaves, or rather projecting beyond the leaves, on the crown of the tree, fringe it with a rich golden color which is very effective, especially where relieved on a hill-side against the darker foliage of other trees. The foliage of this species of chestnut is rarely so dense and luxuriant as that of the horse-chestnuts or the sugar maple, but it divides at an earlier age into nobler masses. Everybody knows the fruit or nut; but everybody does not know what a great prickly burr encases it while growing, and, unluckily for the pleasure-grounds where a chestnut grows, falls with it, and endangers the feet of unwary children or the bodies of summer loungers in its shade. Yet these burrs add much to the beauty of the foliage by forming tufts of lighter green in summer, and by their golden-brown color about the time they are ready to fall

Some curious new varieties are mentioned by H. W. .Sargent in his supplement to Downing's Landscape Gardening, the cut-leaved, and two varieties of variegated-leaved, but it is doubtful if they have been known long enough to decide on their merits or demerits. It is said that the best trees are grown from the nut, without transplanting, the tap-root being essential to the best development of the tree.

THE DWARF CHESTNUT OR CHINQUAPIN. *Castanea pumila.*— Similar to the foregoing, except that it is smaller in all its parts, and does not bear so cold a climate. It does best in a cool, moist, rich soil, and forms a tree from ten to thirty-five feet high, according to its location—"a pretty round-headed miniature chestnut tree." (Meehan)

THE SPANISH CHESTNUT. *C. Vesca.*—A stately tree of grand character, supposed to have been indigenous in Asia Minor, but domesticated in the warmer portions of Europe since the earlier periods of Roman history. It cannot with us be considered entirely hardy north of Washington. In general appearance it closely resembles our native chestnut, but the leaves are not quite so large. During the ages it has been in cultivation in Europe, great numbers of varieties have been found with nuts quite superior to the original sorts, and these are called by the French *marrons*, to distinguish them from the common chestnuts, or *chataignes*, "the latter being to the former what the crab is to the apple." Those who plant the chestnut in Europe select their sorts as Americans choose varieties of apples. The best nuts form an article of commerce, to eat when boiled, and are among the most popular relishes of the poorer classes of France,—a handful of hot *marrons* being the most common present of the French rustic to his sweetheart when they stroll together near the booths where the nuts are roasted. In the south of France and north of Italy, chestnuts are harvested in great quantities, and used in many ways as a substitute for wheat flour and potatoes.

FIG. 106.

The European Horse-chestnut.

THE HORSE-CHESTNUT. *Æsculus* and *Pavia.*

Under this head may be classed the species known as European horse-chestnuts, the American varieties known as buckeyes, and the smooth-fruited horse-chestnuts, the latter being botanically designated as *Pavias;* though the differences between them and the European horse-chestnuts do not seem to warrant so distinctive a separation. We shall treat them all as varieties of horse-chestnuts.

THE EUROPEAN OR COMMON WHITE-FLOWERING HORSE-CHEST-NUT. *Æ. hippocastanum.*—The native country of this tree is somewhat in doubt. It has been known in Europe for three centuries, and it is thought can be traced from the mountains of Thibet. The species was first brought to England in 1550 ; but it was

FIG. 107.

22

a rare tree as late as a century ago in most parts of Europe, though now so universally planted that no tree is more common in avenues and parks. Parkinson, in 1629, says: "Our Christian world had first a knowledge of it from Constantinople." To know that a tree so hardy and well adapted to our country was originally from a region where the winters are milder than our own, is a pleasant encouragement to the introduction and acclimation of new discoveries from semi-tropical regions.

The horse-chestnut, when young, is a tree of formal and uninteresting outline; but as it increases in age its dense foliage breaks into fine masses, and grows more and more beautiful until it becomes a grand old tree. It has an erect trunk, an ovate form when young, and squarish oval at maturity,—the height of the head usually exceeding its breadth.

Each leaf is composed of five or seven leaflets, which radiate from the petiole like parts of a fan. In color they are among the purest of greens, without gloss. The growth of the leaves is very rapid, both shoots and leaves being sometimes perfected in three weeks after the bursting of the bud. Thus the horse-chestnut, though it does not begin to burst its buds earlier than many other trees, is in magnificent foliage while they are yet in embryo development. Following immediately this splendid bursting into leaf, its blossoms glow in great spikes like giant hyacinths set in the green young foliage, and lifted upon a tree stem to form a colossal bouquet. In May and June, in leaf and blossom, no hardy tree equals it in beauty. In autumn, however, it drops its leaves early, and is entirely disrobed when many other trees are putting on their most gorgeous colors. The maples and some other trees are much finer at the season's close, but in its flowering season the horse-chestnut is incomparably superior to all its rivals.

The horse-chestnut should never be crowded. It is one of the most perfect of single lawn trees after the first ten or fifteen years' growth. If a yard is large enough to accommodate but one full tree, it should have few rivals for the place.

For an avenue of street trees it has no superior; but, like the sugar maple, it makes a very dark shadow, and should not be planted closely in rows, nor very near to the windows of a residence. For *wide* avenues its more formal character and narrower

FIG. 108.

head make it quite inferior to our weeping elm, but it has the advantage of that sylvan queen of being less liable to injury by worms.

The rate of growth of the European horse-chestnut is about the same as that of the sugar maple, and half that of the weeping or white elm. Our native sorts, the buckeyes, are of slower growth and smaller size. In England there are trees from eighty to one hundred feet high, and others of equal diameter of head, but in general it is somewhat inferior in size at maturity to the great oaks and chestnuts; sixty feet in height, and fifty feet diameter, being about its average development at maturity. The vignette, Fig. 106, represents the common form of a full-grown tree, Fig. 107 its leaves, and Fig. 108 the form of a thrifty tree of twelve years' growth.

THE DOUBLE WHITE-FLOWERING HORSE-CHESTNUT, *Æ. h. flore plena*, is a superb variety, with double flowers, in larger spikes than those of the common sort, and set with equal or greater abundance on the tree. It is in full bloom in June, two weeks later than the common sort. The form of the tree is higher in proportion to its diameter than the latter, the height being nearly double the breadth, and more square in outline. Ellwanger and Barry, at Rochester, have a noble young specimen about forty feet high, which, in the blossoming season, is like a verdant tower spangled all over with hyacinthine bouquets. It is in all respects an exquisite lawn tree, and one of the thriftiest of the species.

THE RED-FLOWERING HORSE-CHESTNUT. *Æ. h. rubicunda.*— This tree is of less vigorous growth than the preceding, and of more globular form. It blooms at the same time, and the high color of its flowers makes it one of the most showy of trees in the blossoming season.

THE SCARLET-FLOWERING HORSE-CHESTNUT, *Æ. h. coccinea,* is a variety of the *rubicunda,* said to have more brilliantly colored flowers. Sargent mentions it as the most striking floral tree of the season. It blooms when quite young.

THE VARIEGATED-LEAVED HORSE-CHESTNUT, *Æ. h. aurea,* is a variety little commended ; the variegation not remaining a bright and healthy color throughout the season, though it gives the tree a pleasing warm tone in the spring.

THE CUT-LEAVED HORSE-CHESTNUT, *Æ. h. lacianata,* is remarkable solely for the very curious shred-like character of its leaves.

THE DWARF DOUBLE-FLOWERING HORSE-CHESTNUT, *Æ. h. nana flore plena,* is a variety with large leaves and compact head, which is said to grow only eight to ten feet high, and promises to be an interesting shrub.

THE BIG, OR OHIO BUCKEYE, OR YELLOW HORSE-CHESTNUT. *Pavia flava* or *Æsculus flava.*—This fine native tree in some portions of the west is the special herald of summer. Its sudden and early bursting into full leaf makes it, in spring, the most observed of trees, being even earlier than the European sort. It is found wild on the banks of most western streams, and there, among forest trees, it sometimes attains a height of sixty to eighty feet. In open ground its form is very rigid, and it forms a globular head from twenty to forty feet in height. Fig. 109 is a specimen of the buckeye growing in an English park. Both the blossom spikes and the blossoms are smaller than on the European species, and of a greenish yellow color that renders them less conspicuous. The leaves drop long before those of most other trees ; even before those of the European horse-chest-

FIG. 109.

nuts, so that the tree has less value on this account than the imported sorts. It is in fact inferior in nearly every element of beauty. The name Buckeye is supposed to have been given by western hunters to the beautiful nuts of this species in consequence of a fancied resemblance to a buck's eye. Some varieties, crosses probably between the different species, have been originated in English gardens and nurseries that are interesting, and will be mentioned hereafter.

THE SMALL BUCKEYE, OR AMERICAN RED-FLOWERED HORSE-CHESTNUT. *Æsculus pavia (Pavia rubra).*—This is a small tree with more slender branches and leaves than the Ohio buckeye, and dull reddish-colored flowers. It grows wild in Virginia and North Carolina on the mountains. Height from ten to twenty feet. Blossoms in May and June. There is a trailing variety (*P. rubra humilis*), which is insignificant on its own roots, but makes a pretty weeping tree if grafted on the branches of upright varieties. There are several other dwarf varieties of this red-flowered *Pavia* which are being grown in our best nurseries, but whether their peculiarities are sufficiently distinct to make them valuable· is yet to be determined. All the dwarf or small horse-chestnuts or *Pavias* should be encouraged to branch pretty close to the ground.

THE TWO-COLORED PAVIA, *P. discolor*, is a straggling low shrub with beautiful flowers in May, which continue to expand for a long time. It is admirably suited to make picturesque small trees by grafting on other stocks.

THE LONG-FRUITED HORSE-CHESTNUT. *Pavia macrocarpa.*—Loudon describes this as follows· "This variety appears to us intermediate between some variety of the *Æ. hippocastanum* and *Pavia rubra*. The leaves are large, smooth on the upper surface, and shining. The flowers are nearly as large as those of the common horse-chestnut, and of a pale red color mixed with yellow. The branches are spreading and loose ; and the whole tree has an open graceful appearance, quite different from that compactness of form and rigidity of branches which belong to the tree species and varieties both of *Æsculus* and *Pavia*. This sort can scarcely be said to be in cultivation in the nurseries, notwithstanding its claims to a place in every collection of ornamental trees." *

THE DWARF WHITE-FLOWERING HORSE-CHESTNUT. *P. macrostachia.*—This superb spreading shrub was first brought prominently before the public in this country by H. W. Sargent, in his Appendix to Downing's Landscape Gardening, where it is enthusiastically described, and admirably pictured. He thus mentions a specimen in his own grounds. "Our best plant at Wodenethe, twelve years old, is sixty feet in circumference and about eight feet high, and has, at the time we write, between three and four hundred racemes of flowers, the feathery lightness of which, and the fine umbrageous character of the leaves, render it a most striking and attractive object." It comes into bloom late in June, and continues blooming a long time.

THE CALIFORNIA BUCKEYE, *Æsculus californica*, is described in the Pacific Railroad Survey as a low, spreading shrub or tree, eight to twenty feet high; "flowers rose-colored, racemes about six inches long, from spring to midsummer.

The following general remarks on the dwarf varieties are from Loudon's Trees and Shrubs of Great Britain, page 134: "The most valuable varieties of both *Æsculus* and *Pavia* are best perpetuated by budding or grafting, and collectors ought always to see that the plants they purchase have been worked. *Pavia rubra* as a tree, *P. discolor* either as a shrub or grafted standard high, and *P. macrostachia* as a shrub, ought to be in every collection, whether small or large.† *Pavia humilis*, when grafted standard high on the common horse-chestnut, forms an ornament at once singular and beautiful. As the horse-chestnut is found on most plantations

---

* Arboretum Britannicum, p. 473.

† This remark probably applies the word "small" to parks of five to ten acres. Of course it would be absurd to recommend that every owner of a half acre or acre, devoted to decorative planting, in this country, should attempt to have a specimen of every fine variety; *unless he intends to use his entire ground to make a complete collection of some one species of tree or shrub only.*

those who are curious in the species and varieties might graft them in the upper branches of old trees, or young trees might be headed down and one kind grafted on each."

THE MAPLE. *Acer.*

The universal popularity of the maples is a marked proof of their great merits. Among the very earliest to expand into full leaf in the spring, unsurpassed in profusion of foliage and depth of shade in summer, glowing with brilliant colors in autumn, and finally dropping their leaves clean and dry to spangle the lawn with the bright colors of a painter's palette—surely no other family of trees can boast a greater array of merits. Add to these that it is a healthy family, subject to fewer diseases or noxious insects than most others, that the different species are adapted to nearly all soils, and are mostly of that moderate size and compact form that renders them more appropriate than trees of grosser growth to be placed in cultivated small grounds, and the fact of their great popularity is fully accounted for. As to their faults, excepting only their too great uniformity of outline, we confess having failed to discover any. The following species and varieties, however, have many marked differences, some of them being much less valuable than others. At the risk of too frequent repetition, we will here again call attention to the fact, that persons having a collection of native maples on their grounds, whether of one or more species, may obtain a great variety of maple foliage in a short time by grafting the rarer or more curious varieties upon them.

THE SUGAR MAPLE. *Acer saccharinum.*—We begin with this favorite indigenous species, because we believe it, all things considered, the most valuable ornamental tree of all the maples. It is, happily, too well known and appreciated in this country to need have attention called to its beauties. Its form at maturity, when grown in open ground, is ovate, rather higher than its breadth, and remarkable for its compactness and the profuse growth of leaves in all parts of its head. Its lights and shadows are peculiar, being broken into a great number of small masses, strongly defined against each other ; that is to say, the lights being very bright and warm, and the shadows quite decided, and yet softly shaded into each other. The disposition of the shadows is rather lateral, but not in strata, as on the beech. The head of the tree is remarkable for its *sunny expression ;* the parts of the foliage which reflect the light being in excess of the parts in shadow. But it lacks for this reason the grander, because broader and bolder shadows that give superior dignity and variety of expression to the oak, the chestnut, and the hickory. The branches are very numerous, and radiate with tolerably equal divergence at an angle of about forty-five degrees from the trunk. The bark is light-colored, and the tree has a cheerful tone when leafless.

In streets they should rarely be planted nearer than twenty-five feet from each other, and thirty feet apart is better.

The average yearly growth of the sugar maple is about fifteen inches. It is most at home in a gravelly soil, and where such soils are rich and well drained it grows rapidly, while in stiff clay, or ill-drained sandy ground, the growth is slow. In ten years after planting it usually grows to about twenty or twenty-five feet in height, and fifteen feet across its top. Height at maturity from fifty to seventy feet.

The Black or Rock Maple, *Acer nigrum,* is a variety of the sugar maple, with darker and less deeply-lobed leaves, more globular form, and lesser growth.

The White or Silver-leaved Maple. *Acer eriocarpum.—* This native maple, so common on the banks of western streams, has become, perhaps, too great a favorite for street planting. Its growth is very rapid, being nearly double that of the sugar maple. Its form is much looser and more spreading, becoming at maturity an irregularly square-headed tree; the foliage is smaller, less dense, of a lighter green on the upper surface, and the under surface a downy white, which peculiarity gives the tree its name. The stems of the leaves being small and slender, the foliage, as the long branches sway in the wind, is ruffled so as to contrast the white and the green surfaces of the leaves with a sparkling pleasant effect. It is a tree for large grounds and wide streets, and must have ample room. Forty feet is the least distance apart that silver maples should be planted in streets, and no more than they will completely fill in twenty years. The head of the silver maple does not break into good masses of light and shade until it is old, and in the mean time the projection of its numerous spreading branches scatter the light on a great number of small points, and develop no broad, deep, or well-defined shadows.

The silver maple is not quite so early in leaf as the sugar maple; the leaves are not of so beautiful a green, nor so generous in quantity, nor so warm in their manner of reflecting the sunlight, nor so brilliant in autumn. As a lawn tree for the class of grounds treated of in this work, it cannot be considered so desirable as many others; the great size it quickly attains requiring a space for its perfect development that may be more interestingly filled with trees of smaller size. Of course this objection will not apply so forcibly to places where one or more acres is devoted to lawn, nor to places where the proprietor wants but few trees, and those quickly, nor to those who will make a specialty of the maple family alone.

RED-FLOWERING OR SCARLET MAPLE (RED-BUD MAPLE). *Acer rubrum.*—The three names all characterize the spring and autumn peculiarities of the tree. It is covered with small red buds, which open before the expansion of the leaves in spring; and the brilliancy of its scarlet leaves in autumn makes it then one of the most conspicuous of trees, and constitutes a distinguishing beauty, which would, alone, make it a desirable tree. It flourishes best in a soil much richer than that which suits the sugar maple, and attains its greatest size in ground where its roots can reach the moisture of a stream. There are specimens on streams near Philadelphia seventy to eighty feet high, with a proportional amplitude of lateral growth, touching the meadow on one side and the stream upon which they grow upon the other with the graceful droop of their lower branches. On rich uplands it has a compacter growth and darker foliage, and becomes a round-headed tree of about forty feet in height and breadth. The character of its foliage is midway between that of the sugar maple and the silver maple, but its growth is not more rapid than the former. In cool moist soils it should be preferred to the sugar maple. Meehan remarks that though "found in swamps and morasses, it will thrive in any soil or situation." We have observed that its foliage acquires a depth of green, and a glossiness in very rich warm soils that give it quite a different expression from its ordinary appearance when growing wild.

There is a variety advertised in some nurseries as the *Acer colchicum rubrum,* said to be marked by the unusually deep purplish red color of its young foliage

The Moosewood or Striped-barked Maple. *Acer striatum.*— This is a very peculiar small native tree, found principally in the sheltered valleys of northern mountains, in shady places, where it grows sometimes singly, but oftener in groups or stools composed of many strong thrifty sprouts, which, from their straightness and lightness, are used for impromptu fishing rods. The bark is very smooth, and of a dark-green color, marked with stripes lighter and darker than the general color, on wood several years old, and of a warm yellowish or reddish-green hue on the fresh growth. Its leaves are quite peculiar in form, light-green, without any gloss on the upper surface, and of a grayish-green with strongly marked ribs on the under surface, and very finely serrated. The buds and leaves when beginning to unfold are rose-colored, and "it is one of the first trees to announce the spring." It attains a height of twenty to thirty feet, and forms an umbrella-shaped top of slow growth after the first half dozen years. The seeds are grouped in pairs on long peduncles, and in August when ripe are of a dull rose-color, very abundant, showy, and beautiful. We have nowhere seen it so abundant as on Mount Desert Island, in Maine, where, in sheltered valleys between abrupt granite hills, it forms a part of every copse-wood. We believe it will be found a tree of such peculiar habit as to be interesting among other maples, and worth much more attention than it has received from planters. Its small size at maturity, and quick growth in its earlier years, recommend it to persons forming a collection of maples for a small place.

THE SPIKE-FLOWERED OR MOUNTAIN MAPLE, *Acer spicatum*, is another dwarf American species, native of the Alleghany Mountains, and valued in England for its autumn beauty, caused by the rose-color of its large pendulous spikes of winged seeds. Height fifteen to thirty feet. Growth rapid when young.

THE SYCAMORE MAPLE. *Acer pseudo platanus.*—A large, handsome tree, native of Europe, of more rapid upright growth than our sugar maple. The bark of its young wood is ash-colored and remarkably smooth. The foliage has the same cleanly luxuriance that distinguishes our sugar maple, and the leaves are a little larger. In England it becomes a tree of the largest size in sixty or seventy years, and its trunk attains a great size in proportion to its age. There are specimens there nearly a hundred feet high, and six to nine feet diameter of trunk. We do not know of any great trees of it in this country. Loudon says that it will grow on exposed situations, and especially on the seacoast, and maintain its erect position against the sea-breeze better than most other trees, and that it is especially adapted to plant around houses located on bleak hills, as it rarely shows any one-sidedness of growth in consequence of the action of the winds. The four following varieties of the sycamore maple are all valuable:

THE GUELDER-ROSE-LEAVED MAPLE, *A. p. opulifolium*, is a smaller, globular, dense-leaved variety, native of the mountains of France and Spain. A small tree.

THE PURPLE-LEAVED MAPLE. *A. p. purpurea.*—The leaves are purplish beneath, and the stalks of a bright dark-red. The foliage is vigorous and healthy. "The tree has a very fine appearance when the leaves are slightly ruffled by the wind, alternately appearing clothed in purple and pale green. In spring, when the leaves first expand, the purple bloom is not obvious ; but when they become matured it is very distinct" (*Arboretum Britannicum*). A large tree, every way desirable.

THE WHITE VARIEGATED-LEAVED MAPLE. *A. p. alba variegata.*—The silver-striped leaved of some nurseries. This is considered the most ornamental of all the variegated-leaved maples, especially in the spring when the leaves first expand. Small specimens that are growing in this country fully confirm this estimate of its beauty. Its variegation is not uniform on the leaves, but here and there an entire twig has white leaves, and single leaves mottled with white appear occasionally among the green leaves, so that the effect is pleasing, and does not convey the impression of diseased foliage. A large tree.

THE YELLOW-VARIEGATED OR GOLD-LEAVED MAPLE, *A. p. flava variegata* (and *aurea,* of different nurserymen). A healthy variety with some of its leaves a pure light yellow, and occasionally mottled. An exceedingly beautiful warm toned, and healthy variety, that makes a charming contrast with the purple-leaved maple, and in the spring is certainly one of the finest of trees.

THE NORWAY MAPLE. *Acer platanoides.*—This species has a more vigorous growth than the sugar maple, and a similar formality of contour. Its leaves are also similar, but larger and thicker, and not so profusely set upon the twigs. The head is also somewhat rounder, and the young wood stouter; but an observer not critical in trees might easily mistake it for the sugar maple. The difference in the rapidity of their growth is not so great as was formerly supposed. The bark on the young shoots is green, afterwards a brownish red, dotted with white points. The buds are large and red in autumn, and grow to a darker red in winter. The leaves in autumn turn sometimes to a fine yellow, and at others to a brilliant red, and are always well colored.

THE CUT-LEAVED OR EAGLE'S CLAW MAPLE, *Acer p. laciniatum,* is a variety of the Norway maple, with very deeply-lobed and sharp-pointed leaves,—a mere leaf curiosity in a collection of maples.

LOBEL'S MAPLE, *A. p. lobelii,* is an Italian variety of medium size, with smaller and more obtuse leaves of a pea-green color, which hang late in the fall.

THE SHRED-LEAVED MAPLE, *Acer dissectum,* is a new Japan variety, with leaves divided down to the base into nine or ten lobes, that hang almost like separate leaves. Its foliage in the nursery is profuse, and a vivid glossy green; but of its more mature development we cannot speak.

THE GREAT-LEAVED MAPLE. *Acer macrophyllum.*—In the valley of the Columbia river this is described as one of the grandest and most beautiful trees of the country, attaining a height of from forty to ninety feet, and of a graceful spreading form. We have heard of no specimen of much size in the older States. It is reported tender at Rochester in Ellwanger and Barry's nursery when first planted, but likely to be hardy when deeply rooted. The leaves resemble those of the sugar maple in form, but are triple the size.

ENGLISH FIELD MAPLE. *Acer campes-tris.*—"This is a beautiful compact, round-headed tree, or rather bush, rarely exceeding twenty or twenty-five feet in height, and if allowed to assume its natural shape, quite as broad as high. This tree, which is one of the most ornamental of the maples, is very rarely to be met with ; though common, we believe, in our best nurseries. It is a tree, above all others of its kind, suited to small lawns, where it should stand alone, or on the outside of loose gardenesque groups, where it is accessible on all sides ; since the character of its growth is so regular and formal

FIG. 110.

(in shape of a bee-hive), that it does not harmonize with wild or picturesque plantations, but is peculiarly adapted to the neighborhood of the house, or to the more formal trees, like the horse-chestnut and linden. The finest specimens we recollect to have seen is at the late Mr. Downing's, which is nearly full grown; a specimen at Wodenethe, about fifteen feet high, and nearly as wide, is extremely beautiful. The largest specimens in England are at Kew, fifty years planted, twenty-six feet high ; at Milbury Park, one hundred years planted, thirty-eight feet high. It should never be trimmed up ; on the contrary, if by accident the lower limbs are injured or lost, the tree should be severely headed back to encourage new growth from the ground."—H. W. SARGENT. Fig. 110 represents a thrifty young tree of this species.

Montpelier Maple. *Acer monspessulanum.*—In size and general appearance much resembles the preceding, though distinct in the form of its leaves, which are three, instead of five-lobed.

Round-leaved Maple. *Acer circinatum.*—A native of the Pacific slope north of latitude 43°. From twenty to forty feet in height. Loudon describes it thus: "Branches slender, pendulous and crooked, often taking root, etc. * * * * This is a very marked and beautiful species."

The Neapolitan Maple, *Acer obtusatum*, is a large variety, native of the hills of southern Europe. Probably inferior to our common native sorts, but worthy of a trial by professional tree growers.

The Tartarian Maple, *Acer tartaricum*, a low deciduous tree, native of Tartary. Height twenty to thirty feet. Said to thrive in a moist soil, and to be the earliest maple in leaf.

It will be seen that, of the maples, the silver-leaved maple, the sycamore, and the *macrophyllum*, are the most rapid in growth and largest; the Norway, sugar and scarlet maples, and Neapolitan, next smaller; and the English field maple, the Montpelier maple, the round-leaved, the Tartarian, and the Moosewood, the smallest. It would require about an acre of ground to contain specimen trees of the maple family alone. If one could have the nerve to reject all other trees from the plantation, what a beautiful family circle it would be!

THE WALNUTS. *Juglans.*

The family of walnuts, as far as we propose to allude to them, include what are known as English walnuts, our own black walnut, and butternut, and the sub-family of the hickories and the pecan nut, *Carya.* They are all large trees, with pinnate leaves and edible nuts.

THE EUROPEAN WALNUT OR MADEIRA NUT, *Juglans regia,* is a tree somewhat resembling our butternut in its general appearance, but it is loftier and larger, and has fewer leaflets to the leaf— generally three or four pairs and an odd one. It comes into leaf rather late, and drops its leaves early. Though greatly valued in England and the Continent for its beauty as well as for its nuts, its want of hardiness in the Northern States, and lack of any peculiar beauty at the South, has prevented its culture to any great extent in this country. South of Philadelphia it may be grown with safety. Like the black walnut, its shade is injurious to vegetation.

THE BLACK WALNUT. *Juglans nigra.*—A tree of great size, held in high estimation of late years for the dark color and the value of its wood for cabinet purposes. In western forests its average height at maturity is about seventy feet, but specimens are not unfrequent one hundred feet high, with trunks from four to five feet in diameter. Its bark is very dark and deeply furrowed. In open ground it becomes not only a tree of majestic size but of marked beauty, from the light color and softly blended masses of its long pinnate leaves, each leaf having from thirteen to seventeen leaflets. The tree spreads grandly with age, and for park purposes would be worthy of an extended description; but as there is something in the emanations from its leaves and roots injurious to trees near it, and to grass under it, this fault, and its great size, unfit it for use in suburban grounds, and make further description needless.

THE BUTTERNUT. *Juglans cinerea.*—This is a much lower species than the preceding, with lighter colored wood, grayish bark, and an oblate form like that of the apple tree. With or without its leaves, the tree has a cleanly domestic expression. In the color and form of its leaves it resembles the ailantus more than any other native tree, but its outline is more formal, and the foliage is thrown out with less picturesqueness than that of the ailantus. Full-grown trees in open ground rarely exceed fifty feet in height and sixty feet diameter of head. Its odor is less powerful and its presence less injurious to vegetation than that of the black walnut.

A HICKORY TREE IN THE GROUNDS OF SYLVANUS PURDY, ESQ., RYE, N. Y.

THE HICKORY. *Carya.*

The great difficulty of transplanting the hickory, in consequence of its remarkable tap-root, which "strikes for the centre" with a vigor and singleness of purpose peculiar to it, has made the family less popular for home or street embellishment than it deserves to be.   The young trees have scarcely any surface roots that enable them to take a new hold in the soil quickly, like elms and maples, when they are transplanted.

The hickories are noble in their expression in every stage of their growth. All of the species become large trees, with a height considerably greater than their breadth, and a squarish form. The foliage breaks into fine masses while the tree is yet young, and all the characteristics of its head afterwards give it rank midway between the grand trees of which the white oak is a type, and massy-foliaged trees like the horse-chestnuts and the maples, which are less picturesque in outline and less boldly broken in lights and shadows. Its branches are clean, strong, and supple ; not frittered in monotonous radiating lines, but rather given to irregularities. Its leafage is more luxuriant than that of the oak, and makes a deeper shade. The tree is little troubled by insects, except those which may be quickly and effectually dislodged, like the summer caterpillar, which sometimes attacks the leaves.

Hickories are always favorites with children. Their elastic limbs never snap treacherously, and the boys may climb upon them or hang from their tips with little fear of a scolding for breaking the trees ; and in autumn enjoy the sport of scrambling for the earliest nuts, and hearing them rattle through the branches after a hard frost. Bryant thus alludes to the squirrel's sports upon them ·

> * * * " Swaying to the sudden breeze, ye fling
> Your nuts to earth, aud the brisk squirrel comes
> To gather them, and barks with childish glee,
> And scampers with them to his hollow oak.''

It may be passing beyond a description of the tree to suggest also the pleasant nibbles—nuts, apples, and cider—by the winter's fire and the cheerful central lamp!

The hickory has two marked faults when compared with certain favored trees. Its leaves come out quite late in the spring ; not later, however, than those of the oak and ash. The leaf-buds begin to break later than those of the oak, but when once started they burst into full expansion more rapidly. In autumn the leaves drop with the first hard frost, falling dry and clean, easy to gather, or quick to be blown away ; but the shells from which the nuts drop out as they fall, are troublesome in a lawn ; not easy to mow over or to rake out.

The leaves of some varieties turn to a dull yellow color before they fall, but pleasing autumn tints are not common among them.

23

The different species of the hickory vary from one another less in their appearance, as they grow old, than most other trees. While young the differences are more marked, but when the trees are from thirty to fifty years old, all have the same general characteristics of forms and shadows when seen from a distance.—the variations in their bark being the most marked difference between them.

The following are the principal varieties—all natives of our country:

THE SHELL-BARK HICKORY. *Carya alba.*—This species is not

FIG. 111.

excelled in beauty of leaf or form by any of the others, and excels them all in the quality of its nut, the toughness and value of its wood in the arts, and its superiority over all other woods for fuel. But though hard and heavy, and strong beyond other timber, no wood rots quicker when exposed to moisture. When young the bark is smooth ; but after the wood is from twelve to fifteen years old it is generally distinguished from the other hickories by its singularly scaly, or laminate outer bark, which, on old trees, frequently drops off in broad pieces from two to four feet in length, and from one-eighth to a quarter of an inch in thickness, or may be pulled off readily without injury to the tree. This bark is of a cinnamon-brown color on the inside, is full of oil, and valued above all other kindlings for the quick, bright, hot fire it makes.

The tree grows rapidly, and when young the leaves are very large ; each leaf being composed of five leaflets (rarely seven), those of the terminal triplet being usually from five to seven inches long, but much larger in thrifty young trees, and smaller in old trees. Their color is a deep glossy green—darker than most trees. The nuts are whiter and thinner shelled than those of other species, and about an inch in longest diameter ; but there is much difference, as in fruit trees, between different trees of the same species, in the size and quality of the nut. All things considered this is decidedly the most valuable of the hickories. On page 352 we give a good portrait of the finest hickory of this species we know of in this country, growing on the farm of Sylvanus Purdy, Esq., in Rye, N. Y., near the village of Mamaroneck. It is about eighty feet high, ninety feet across the spread of its branches, and has borne fourteen bushels of shelled nuts in one season! The upright growth on the left is a part of the tree which has taken a new upright direction.

THE THICK-SHELLED-NUT HICKORY. *C. sulcata* and *C. tomentosa maxima.*—This is the tree which bears the large oblong nut of commerce, and the thickness of its shell suggests the name. Its bark is somewhat scaly, but in thicker and narrower sections than that of the shell-bark hickory, and not so easy to detach from the tree; it is also much rougher on young trees. The leaves are the largest of any of the hickories. Each leaf is composed of from seven to nine leaflets. The nuts are squarish-oblong, from one and a quarter to two inches in length, with thick yellowish-white shells, but fine flavored. As an ornamental tree it has the same characteristics as the preceding. Nuttall and Michaux describe what is popularly known as the thick-shelled hickory in two species, both of which we give in connection with the popular name for both.

THE PIG-NUT HICKORY. *C. porcina.*—This species is distinguished by its smaller leaves and fruit; the latter not being marketable, though good food for hogs, who crunch and eat the shell and meat together. Its bark when quite young is smooth, and then resembles the shell-bark hickory; but about the age when the latter begins to show its laminate character, the former breaks into fine hard shallow furrows, and is not at all disposed to laminate. Its branches are rather more numerous and straighter than the other hickories; but with age its foliage breaks into the same forms, and is as fine as any of the others. Its leaves are usually formed of seven leaflets, smaller and slenderer than the preceding species. The foliage is also rather lighter colored, and the aspect of the tree when young is less robust. It grows most naturally in moist ground, and there becomes a lofty tree.

THE BITTER-NUT HICKORY, AND THE WATER BITTER-NUT HICKORY, *C. amara* and *C. aquatica,* are similar to the foregoing, the latter having still smaller and more numerous leaflets, numbering from nine to eleven on each leaf.

The *C. microcarpa* is a variety closely resembling the shell-bark hickory in its leaves, which, though smaller, are composed of five leaflets, and in its small thin-shelled nut ; but its bark is like that of the thick-shelled hickory. It is abundant in the forests of New Jersey and Pennsylvania.

THE PECAN-NUT, *C. olivæformis*, is not found much north of the Ohio river valley ; south, it becomes a large and beautiful tree. Its nuts are long, pointed, and thin-shelled, and considered by some persons the most delicate of all the hickories. We do not consider them any better than those of the shell-bark hickory. The tree resembles the water bitter-nut hickory, with thirteen to fifteen leaflets to the leaf.

THE ASH. *Fraxinus.*

The ash is a common forest tree all over the United States, but its varieties are less interesting than those of many other species. In the forest the trees are lofty, with straight stems and slender limbs. In open ground they are generally round-headed or ovate, of tolerably abundant foliage, but late in leaf, and less pleasing in color than many other trees. It is also noted for exhausting the soil to such an extent as to injure the lawn under its branches.

THE WHITE ASH. *F. americana.*—This is the finest and loftiest of the family. It has a straight trunk, occasionally rising in the forest to one hundred feet, with light-colored or gray bark, latticed into ridges and deep furrows. The branches are clean, straight, numerous, and rarely large, and issue from the trunk at an acute angle.

It is a refined, but not a majestic tree, without its leaves. In leaf it is occasionally a superb tree, symmetrically globular or ovate, with abundant foliage, of a dull or bluish-green color. The head does not break into fine masses until the tree is old. In autumn

the leaves change to a deep brownish-purple, and it is then, in contrast with the brighter colors of the maples and other gay-leaved
autumn trees, a valuable addition to the landscape. It requires a
deep, warm, dry soil. No soil is considered poor or cold on which
the white ash grows abundantly, while the black ash is equally
noted for being at home in wet ground. We have known large
trees of the white ash much injured by excessive cold; and infer
that it will not be a good tree to plant in exposed situations at the
north, though usually considered a perfectly hardy tree.

THE BLACK ASH. *F. sambucifolia.*—A tree of medium size;
from fifty to sixty feet high in the forests, and forty to fifty feet in
open ground. Its bark is darker and less deeply furrowed than
that of the white ash, and its limbs are less regular in their growth.
The foliage is brighter colored, and in damp, open ground, quite as
abundant. Its autumn foliage has no beauty, and as it comes late
in leaf, this variety has no special value for ornamental planting.

The other varieties of native ash are the *F. pubescens*, downy
ash; the *F. quadrangulata*, blue ash; the *F. juglandiflora*, green
ash; the *F. caroliniana*, Carolina ash; and the *F. platycarpa*, broad-
fruited ash. The green ash is a large tree with brighter-colored
leaves than the other varieties. The characteristics of the others,
in open ground, we are not familiar with. A few of the foreign
varieties of ash are more interesting for small grounds.

THE ASH TREES OF ENGLAND are mostly of the species known
as the *Fraxinus excelsior*, which is so nearly the same as our white
ash that a description of one will apply to the other. The following are varieties of the *F. excelsior*.

THE WEEPING ASH, *Fraxinus excelsior pendula*, is occasionally
a beautiful tree, with a decidedly picturesque and rambling as well
as pendulous habit; but fine specimens are not common in this
country. It needs an unusually warm, rich, and deeply-drained
soil. We remember one in the old Garden of Plants in Paris, the
trunk of which formed the central support of a large summer-house,
with branches falling over the thatched roof on all sides, and
draping it to the ground with their foliage. It is always grafted on

some erect variety of ash, from seven to ten feet above the ground,
and becomes a tree of considerable size, and usually of more
breadth than height.   It is inferior in beauty to the following weeping variety of the ash.

THE GOLDEN ASH, *F. aurea,* AND THE WEEPING GOLDEN
ASH, *F. aurea pendula,* are warmly commended by Sargent, the
latter as "quite as hardy, and a great improvement on the old
weeping ash."

THE AUCUBA-LEAVED ASH, *F. aucubafolia,* is a variegated-leaved
variety that is quite striking in the spring and early summer, when
the yellow spots on its leaves give it the appearance of a tree in
flower.   It is apt to lose its beauty in the heat of summer.

THE GOLD-SPOTTED-LEAVED ASH, *F. punctata,* is another variegated-leaved variety, considered by some superior in the brightness
of its colors to the foregoing.

THE VARIEGATED WILLOW-LEAVED, *F. salicifolia variegata,* has
brightly-marked white and green leaves in the spring, which, however, turn to a dirty brown in the summer.

There are many new varieties in the great nurseries, that
are not yet sufficiently grown to enable one to judge of their
merits.

THE ASH-LEAVED NEGUNDO, ASH-LEAVED MAPLE, AND BOX
ELDER. *Negundo fraxinifolium. Acer negundo.*—This pretty na-

FIG. 112.

tive tree, found growing on the
mountains of the middle States,
is one of the small trees well
adapted to small grounds, and still
but little known.   It is allied to
both the maple and the ash families, having seeds like the former,
and pinnate leaves, as shown by
our Fig. 112, like the latter ; or
more still like those of the elder
family.   The leaves are composed
of five leaflets on a long petiole,
and are of a bluish or pale-green

color. The branches spring close to the ground, and form a low, loose, wide-spreading head. The seeds are borne conspicuously in autumn, and add much to the beauty of the tree. The leaves die off a rich yellow. Naked young wood smooth and pea-green, with long spaces between the buds. Usual height and breadth about twenty feet. The tree grows rapidly, and is not long-lived.

THE CURLED ASH-LEAVED NEGUNDO, *N. crispum*, is principally marked by curled leaves, and has no superior beauty.

THE POPLAR. *Populus.*

The poplars are all remarkable for a more or less tremulous motion of their leaves. All are rapid growers, some species exceeding all other native trees in this quality. We have seen a cottonwood, *Populus canadensis*, spring from the seed and attain a height of sixty feet in twenty years.

The smaller species, such as the aspen, are short-lived trees, and their greatest beauty is attained young. A moist, warm soil suits them best.

The species of poplar are very numerous, and we shall describe only a few which have the most distinct character, or which, from their abundant distribution, should be known. All have catkins or blossoms which appear in the spring before the leaves, many of them with cottony attachments. They are not ornamental, and are often annoying, while floating in the air, or scattered on the ground.

The following are the most prominent among the poplars :

THE AMERICAN ASPEN. *P. tremula trepida.*—This is the American type of that trembling sensitiveness to every breath of air which has made its English prototype the theme of a thousand poetic similes. Its small heart-shaped leaves, vibrating on slender petioles, seem to be ever in a buzz of excitement. No tree in the forest comes earlier into leaf, although the buckeye displays greater massiveness of early foliage. The exquisitely-delicate green of its first leaves is one of the most charming sights of the spring, while all through the summer their murmuring vibrations never cease

to be interesting.   As the foliage is not dense, the tree is not desirable to plant for shade, but should be placed where it will be
conspicuous in the spring, with a back-ground of heavier foliage in
summer and autumn.

The aspen sheds its leaves early, but they often turn a pleasing
yellow before they fall that renders them quite ornamental.   The
growth is rapid in good soils, giving the tree a pyramidal form
when young, and a symmetrically irregular outline at maturity.   It
rarely exceeds forty feet in height.   The branches and twigs have
a grayish hue, and the older bark is spotted with black.   The outer
branches are slightly pendulous as the tree grows old

The ENGLISH ASPEN, *P. tremula,* is very much like the preceding, but comes into leaf a few days later, and is not so pretty a
tree.

The WEEPING ENGLISH ASPEN, *P. t. pendula,* is a variety that
has long been known in England, and has been grown for a few
years in this country; but we have seen no well-grown specimens,
and cannot, therefore, describe it.

The AMERICAN TOOTH-LEAVED POPLAR, OR LARGE ASPEN,
P. grandidenta, is a variety with larger, rounder, and more scolloped
leaves, and stronger growth, which comes into leaf much later than
the first described aspen, and is less pleasing in all respects.   An
irregularly round-headed tree, from forty to fifty feet in height, and
short-lived.

The WEEPING POPLAR, *P. g. pendula,* is a variety of the preceding species that has recently been much praised.   It is probably an interesting and picturesque tree, and to be preferred in
planting to the common forms of the species.

The COTTONWOOD OR CANADIAN POPLAR.   *P. canadensis.*—
This, we believe, is the largest of the family, often attaining one
hundred feet in height.   It forms entire forests in portions of the
west, some of which are known as cottonwood swamps, though the
soil in which they grow is always warm rich land when drained.
Its growth is the most rapid and coarse when young of any of the

poplars—a character that unsuits it for small grounds, and adapts it to large spaces where it is desirable to have a quick, lofty growth of trees. For some reason, however, the best English gardeners prefer the black Italian poplar for the same purpose—a variety or species supposed to be a cross between this species and the black poplar of Europe.

This tree has been appropriately named cottonwood from the quantity of cotton enveloping its seeds, which in May becomes detached and floats in the air in such quantities where the tree abounds as to be a great nuisance at that season.

In its early growth the cottonwood is simply rank, upright, and uninteresting; but after it has reached fifty or sixty feet in height, its branches begin to bend gracefully, the foliage breaks into fine rounded masses, and it spreads into a park tree of noble proportions. It should never be planted near dwellings or in streets.

The Black Poplar, *P. nigra*, of England, is said to resemble our cottonwood in most respects.

The Black Italian Poplar. *P. monilifera.*—It is in doubt whether this is, or is not, a native of America. The fact that neither of the indefatigable Michaux found it wild in America, and that its characteristics unite those of the cottonwood and some of the European poplars, makes it probable that it is a hybrid between them. In form and vigor of growth it is like the cottonwood. An English specimen is recorded as having attained the height of ninety feet twenty-five years after planting! This in Worcestershire. At the Syon Park, England, there is a tree of this species one hundred and two feet high, and about one hundred feet in breadth of head.

The Balm of Gilead Poplar. *Populus candicans.*—This is a tree of great vigor of growth, with large conspicuous buds covered with balsamic gum. The leaves are nearly heart-shaped, from five to eight inches long, glossy on the upper surface, and downy beneath. The form of the head when young is pyramidal, more compact than that of the cottonwood, and becomes a spreading tree of less height. The leaves appear two weeks later than those of our native aspen.

THE BALSAM-BEARING POPLAR OR TACAMAHAC. *P. balsami-fera.*—Curiously enough, though we have lived in the States where this tree is said to be indigenous, we do not know that we have ever seen it. Loudon thus describes it : "The balsam poplar, in the climate of London, is the very first tree that comes into leaf; its foliage is of a rich gamboge yellow, and so fragrant as in moist evenings to perfume the surrounding air. The tree is remarkably hardy, but, unless in the vicinity of water, it seldom attains a large size in England, or is of great duration."

It is very distinct from the Balm of Gilead poplar—having smaller and much narrower leaves, of ovate-acuminate form. It grows from fifty to eighty feet in height.

THE WHITE OR SILVER POPLAR, OR SILVER ABELE TREE. *P. alba. P. alba canescens.*—This European or Asiatic species has been deservedly the most popular tree of the poplar family for the past twenty years. Contrary to our early impressions of it, it improves on acquaintance. It is the most spreading of poplars, of the largest size, exceedingly rapid growth, and, as far as we have observed, quite healthy. Its leaves are of a deep bright-green color on the upper surface, and have a white down on the under side, which, instead of disappearing as the season advances, as is the case on most leaves of this kind, seems to grow whiter, and in the summer and autumn breezes the tree glows as with myriads of great quivering white blossoms.

The silver poplar comes into leaf later than the maples and earlier than the oaks, and holds its leaves later than any of the other poplars. In fact, it is in its glory in September and early in October. It has but one serious fault to prevent its being one of the most desirable wide-street or large-lawn trees, viz., its tendency to sucker or sprout from the root. On a lawn kept properly mowed, this tendency would not be very annoying, but in or near cultivated ground, or where the sprouts are once allowed to get a good start, they are quite troublesome. The dead leaves, too, are disposed to absorb dampness from the ground and rot where they lie. They should, therefore, be raked and put on the compost heap as soon as they have fallen.

The form of the silver poplar is irregularly squarish, its foliage abundant and massy, and its branches light-colored, and of an ashy-green hue, smooth, and cheerful-looking in winter. It grows luxuriantly in almost any good moist soil, and becomes a spreading tree of great size in less time than any healthy tree we know of. Cuttings from this tree take root freely, and make good trees; but it is usually grown from suckers. It is said to be a longer-lived tree than others of its species. For *wide* avenues, or to stand out on a lawn, it is a superb tree, especially where the subsoil is a rich moist clay. But it takes up too much room to be suitable on any small grounds. We know of no tree that will so quickly make a noble shade for pasture fields.

THE LOMBARDY POPLAR. *P. fastigiata.*—This model of a syl-van sentinel is one of the most peculiar of trees; having the least diameter of head in proportion to its height of any tree known. This slender form has made it most useful in landscape gardening; its spiry top being employed to form a central point in groups of trees, a back-ground relief to level-lined architecture, or to break, with its exceptional erectness, the more monotonous outlines of other trees. When first introduced into this country the rage for it was so great that town streets, and country roads, and farm-house yards, were everywhere filled with them; but familiarity has bred contempt. It has been found that, though a tree of most original and picturesque character, it is not comparable to our native trees in variety of beauty, in usefulness as a shade tree, in cleanliness, or in healthfulness. Worms on the foliage, and borers in the wood, love the tree and kill it. It has become so unhealthy that it is not safe to plant one near the house, where its dirty fallen leaves would be annoying even were it a healthy tree free from worms. But its club-like form, and the vertical shadow lines of its foliage, are so unique, and contrast so picturesquely now and then with round-headed groups of trees, that we must still use it, away from the house, in ornamental plantations. And it may be that the plagues which have infested it will diminish, and yet leave the Lombardy poplar with its normal beauty. In Italy, and in England, it is one of the loftiest of trees, attaining a height of from one hundred to one hundred and fifty feet. There is a noble old specimen north of the Casino, in the New York Central Park, which exhibits all the beauties and faults of the species.

There are many other species and varieties of poplars which are not distinguished by peculiarities or merits that make it desirable to enumerate them.

THE WHITEWOOD OR TULIP TREE. *Liriodendron tulipifera.*

A tree of lofty stature, straight and erect trunk, and exceeding beauty of foliage. In its early growth the beauty of its leaves,

FIG. 113.

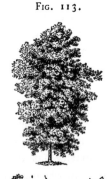

which are of singular form, their unusual purity of color and perfect texture, and the smooth and symmetric growth of the trunk and branches, all combine to form an elegant tree. Yet its head does not usually break into such dense masses of verdure as those of the maples, the horse-chestnuts, and the hickories. Fig. 113 shows a remarkably pretty specimen of a whitewood, about twenty years old, and gives the forms of the leaves, flowers, and seed-vessels. As it becomes an old tree, the branches bend in downward sweep, rising at their extremities, and tending somewhat to unequal lengths, form an outline at once irregular and symmetrical, lofty and graceful. The play of light and shade among the openings of its boughs is similar in expression to that which Loudon (as quoted on page 385) has characterized in describing the foliage of the European plane tree ; though that of the whitewood forms into somewhat more rounded masses. The leaves burst their buds about a week later than those of the sugar maple. They are from five to eight inches in width, and of a peculiarly square form, as will be seen from the above cut. In texture and color they are of that perfect type that leaves nothing to be desired ; and in autumn they turn to a yellow color almost as pure as their summer green, and then fall with those of the maple, strewing the ground with beautiful color. The flowers appear in June, of the size and form of tulips, a greenish-yellow color outside, and orange and yellow within. As the blossoms are upright, or nearly so, their brightest colors are not seen from below, so that the flowers are less showy as usually seen on the tree, than their size and warmth of color when examined separately would lead one to suppose. If one could look down upon the top of the tree, when in full bloom, it would be a superb sight. The seed-vessels which succeed the blossoms are in the form of a cone about two inches in length. After the leaves fall the cones open and drop their seeds, but remain for many weeks upon the tree, their yellowish-brown hue giving them a resemblance to blossoms.

As a timber-tree the whitewood is remarkable above all other deciduous trees east of the Rocky Mountains, for the straightness, length, and size of its trunk. The author has seen a piece of whitewood timber grown in the valley of the Maumee *which squared forty-eight by fifty-four inches, and sixty feet long;* and trees are not uncommon which have one hundred feet in length of straight timber. Indeed, the trunk of a forest grown whitewood is one of the noblest of sylvan sights ; towering erectly without a branch like the redwood of California, to a great height. The bark is of a light color and soft texture, and divided into deep and lattice-like ridges and furrows, much like that of the white ash.

Singularly enough, the whitewood seems to be the only tree of the species ; and though allied in traits to the numerous magnolia family on one side, and the more numerous poplar family on the other, it stands the unique representative of its family.

The whitewood is not tenacious of life when transplanted ; and we advise persons who wish to grow them to choose nursery grown trees of small size in preference to large ones. The oftener they have been transplanted the better. Trees from the woods are very sure to die when planted in open ground.

THE MAGNOLIA. *Magnolia.*

The magnolias are suggestive of all the voluptuous luxuriance of tropical vegetation.   Rapid growth, immense leaves, great blossoms powerfully odorous, all combine to create an impression of trees at home in a warmer zone than that of our northern States. All the large species are, however, natives of our country, and it is believed that with intelligent care the finest of them, excepting only the evergreen magnolia, (*grandiflora*) may be domesticated and grown to their full size as far north as the southern borders of the great lakes, where the altitude does not exceed seven hundred feet above the sea.

The cucumber magnolia (*M. acuminata*) grows to great size in forests at the west end of Lake Erie and in New Jersey, but entirely disappears in the forests a little further north.   Latitude 42° may therefore be considered about its northern limit, and that of the magnolia family.

Michaux speaks of the umbrella magnolia, *M. tripetela*, being found in the northern part of the State of New York; but our eminent botanist, Gray, in his official report of the botanical survey of that State discredits this statement, having failed to find it except near the Pennsylvania border.   It is found in greatest abundance in the upper portions of the Carolinas, Tennessee, and Georgia.

The great-leaved magnolia, *M. macrophylla*, was not found by Michaux except in North Carolina and Tennessee ; the evergreen magnolia, *M. grandiflora*, always further south; while the swamp magnolia, *M. glauca*, is indigenous from Massachusetts to Louisiana.

From these diversities of native *habitats* it may be safe to infer that most of the magnolia family may be domesticated on our lawns in the middle States, and in the northern States south of the great lakes, and probably in that part of Canada between Lake Ontario and the Detroit River.

Some species, which have been introduced from China and Japan, are quite as hardy as the hardiest natives ; and crosses between these and our indigenous species have been made which are valuable additions to our small trees. We believe that by crossing the species still further, very interesting hybrids and varieties may be produced.

The cucumber magnolia being the strongest and hardiest species, is used as a stock upon which

* * "to graft the gentler graces"

of more delicate and beautiful sorts. Prof. J. P. Kirtland, of Cleveland, Ohio, whose very intelligent experience and success in growing fine magnolias near their most northerly line, entitles his opinion to great weight, insists that all the magnolias, which will grow in the northern States at all, should be grafted or budded on the *acuminata* stock. He says: "Employed for this purpose, it imparts vigor to the weak, hardiness to the more tender, and by its profuse supply of sap forces them into abnormal production of flowers, improved in size and perfection, as well as numbers." He describes the effect of grafting the swamp magnolia *(glauca)*— which is but a large shrub on its own roots—on a seedling *acuminata*. The *glauca* grafted on the latter had become a broad, fine tree, twenty-one feet high, while the former, from which the bud was taken, in the same soil, and of the same age, was "an old and decrepit shrub, unworthy of attention." * While the Professor's advice is of great value, it indicates but one of many precautions which must be taken in the northern States to succeed in growing fine specimens of magnolias ; for, unless we can have them luxuriantly healthy, it is not well to have our grounds encumbered with them. A thrifty hickory is better than a scrawny magnolia ; and other blossoms, on healthy trees, will more than compensate for the absence of flowers that grow on a tree which shows by its whole air that it is pining for a more genial home. Those who will grow fine magnolia trees north of Philadelphia must see to it that *all* the conditions necessary to their health and growth are complied with. One of these conditions, which will apply to all the magnolias, is that they be planted where they will be protected from high winds, especially north and west winds ; for which purpose plantations of

---

* American Journal of Horticulture, March, 1867.

such evergreens as the pines and Norway spruce are best adapted; and they must have a deep, warm, moist soil, in which their roots can revel below the reach of the frost.   Most of them need all the sun they can get on their tops, *but their roots must be cool and shaded*—a condition easily maintained by a well-kept lawn and their own shadows, if they are encouraged to grow low.

The bark of all the magnolias is favorite food for rabbits. Where practicable the stems near the ground should be bound with lath at the beginning of winter, and then covered with matting or straw as high as possible.   Of course the ground around the stems should also be thoroughly mulched a little further than the roots extend.

The peculiar habits and needs of the different species will be noted in their descriptions, which follow:

THE EVERGREEN-MAGNOLIA OR BIG LAUREL.   *Magnolia grandiflora.*   (*Laurier tulipier* or tulip laurel of the French.)—We begin with a description of this, the most tender of all the magnolias, because its fame is world-wide, as the acknowledged and worthy head of a royal family.   Michaux, in his great work, the Sylva Americana, published nearly fifty years ago by the French government, says of it: "Of all the trees of North America, east of the Mississippi, the big laurel is the most remarkable for the majesty of its form, the magnificence of its foliage, and the beauty of its flowers.   It is first seen in the lower part of North Carolina, near the river Neuse, in latitude 35°; proceeding from this point, it is found in the maritime parts of the southern States,   *   *   *   and as far up the Mississippi as Natchez, 300 miles above New Orleans.   The French of Louisiana call it *Laurier tulipier*.   It grows only in cool and shady places, where the soil, composed of brown mould, is loose, deep, and fertile."

Bartram (the great tree-hunter of the last century, whose superb collection south of Philadelphia, known as Bartram Garden, is now an illy cared-for wild-wood) speaks of it as forming "a perfect cone, placed on a straight clean trunk, resembling a beautiful column; and, from its dark-green foliage, silvered over with milk-white flowers, it is seen at a great distance."

The finest specimens known of this species reach one hundred feet in height; but sixty feet is about the usual altitude. The leaves vary from nine to twelve inches in length, and from three to four or more inches in breadth; they are always smooth and shining, and entire on the edges. The flowers appear in May, and the tree keeps on blooming through the season. They are white, produced on the summit of the last year's shoots, and are from six to eight inches in diameter. Their odor is powerfully fragrant, and when too near or too abundant oppressively so.

The evergreen magnolia flourishes in the botanical gardens and parks of south France and Italy, where it has been introduced; but not with the luxuriance that marks its growth on the bottom lands of the Gulf States. In England it is cultivated on walls and in hot-houses. It is decidedly a tender tree, and is not likely to repay any attempts to domesticate it north of Washington.

THE CUCUMBER MAGNOLIA, *M. acuminata*, is a native of most of the States of our Union, and grows in western forests to a majestic size. Its trunk is straight, and the branches symmetrically disposed around the main stem. Growing in open ground, it assumes an ovate-conical form. The leaves are oval-acuminate, from six to ten inches long, and four to seven broad, and of a bluish green color. They drop early, turning to a dirty yellow before they fall. The foliage is massy and abundant in soils which are deep, warm, and moist; but in poor or dry ground the branches are not well covered, the leaves have a pale, sickly green color, and the whole aspect of the tree is coarse, and every way inferior in massiveness and color of foliage to the maples, hickories, and horse-chestnuts. The flowers, which have many petals, have the form, and more than double the size of a common tulip, and appear in June; are of a pale-yellow color, varying to white and bluish-white, and slightly fragrant. The fruit is about three inches long, resembling when unripe a green cucumber,—hence the name of the tree,—rose-colored, and ornamental when ripe.

Michaux observes that the situations peculiarly adapted to its growth are the declivities of mountains, narrow valleys, and the banks of torrents, where the atmosphere is constantly moist, and

24

where the soil is deep and fertile. Such facts render it apparent
that it is a tree unsuited to those open sites and gravelly soils at
the north where the sugar maples and the common chestnut are
most beautiful.   It seems to us too gross a tree for small grounds.
The following species is a more pleasing tree·

THE HEART-LEAVED MAGNOLIA. *M. cordata.*—We have seen
in northern grounds more healthy-looking trees of this variety than
of any other.   Doctor Kirtland thinks it may be only a variety of
the *M. acuminata;* but, whether a variety or a species, it is quite
distinct in leaves, flowers, and *style.*   It is a smaller and handsomer
tree in all respects.   Though a native of the Carolinas and Georgia,
where it is found principally on the uplands and mountains, it is
quite hardy in the Central Park, New York, and fine specimens
are growing in private grounds near the Sound and on the Hudson
River.   Downing says of it : "It blooms in the gardens very young
and very abundantly, often producing two crops in a season."   The
flowers appear in June and July, and occasionally afterwards till
frosts.   They are yellow, streaked with red, and from three to four
inches in diameter.   The leaves are smaller, rounder, darker, and
more glossy than those of the *acuminata,* and are disposed to be
wavy, which gives a finer play of light upon them.   The form of
the tree is a true ovate.   The foliage is more abundant, and breaks
into more pleasing masses than that of the larger-leaved magnolias. ' It also keeps a tree-form naturally, while some of the latter
are apt to throw up several stems from the heart near the ground.

In ordinary lawn exposures, this species, we think, will prove
only less interesting than the *Magnolia macrophylla,* on which,
as well as on the *M. tripetela* and *M. auriculata,* the individual
leaves and flowers are so magnificent, that the contours of the
trees themselves, however ungaiply, and the breaks of light and
shade in their heads, are forgotten while observing their remarkable details.   This heart-leaved magnolia exhibits less striking
features, and forms a beautiful connecting-link between the great-
leaved magnolias and our exuberantly-foliaged northern trees,
which are distinguished by the abundance rather than the size of
their leaves.

THE UMBRELLA MAGNOLIA. *M. tripetela.*—A species that seems always in doubt whether to be a shrub or a tree. Fig. 114 shows, not its most common, but its best form, at about ten years of age. It grows rapidly to a huge bush or small tree thirty feet in height. If allowed to send up shoots at will, it is pretty sure to have half a dozen rival stems, and then it is an ungainly great-leaved, and great-blossomed bush. By using care, however, in the selection of a stocky *low* tree from the nursery, encouraging it to branch low, and not allowing any suckers to spring from near the ground, it can be forced to make the pretty tree-form shown in our cut, though this is not as low-branched as it is desirable to make them.

FIG. 114.

The leaves are of great size, often from eighteen inches to two feet long on young trees, and seven or eight inches broad, oval, and pointed at both ends. They are disposed to grow in tufts at the extremities of the limbs, so that the interior branches are bare. This peculiarity suggested the name of Umbrella Magnolia; but the general form of the tree is such as to make the title utterly inappropriate; but it is now too well established to change.

In the latitude of New York this tree is generally in bloom from May to July, and isolated blossoms occasionally appear throughout the season; the flowers are white, from six to eight inches in diameter, cup-shaped, and have an unpleasant odor. The fruit is conical, five or six inches long, of a beautiful pink color, forming quite an ornamental feature of the tree.

Loudon says of this tree :—"In Britain the tree sends up various shoots from the root to replace the stems, which are seldom of long duration." This is also its peculiarity in this country. Though it has been more generally planted than any other half-hardy magnolia, it is in all respects inferior to the *Magnolia machrophylla*, which it most nearly resembles; and to the *M. cordata* and the *M. soulangeana*, from which it differs widely.

The Large-leaved or Michaux' Magnolia.   *M. macro-*

Fig. 115.

phylla.—This species has the most superb leaves of any tree we know of in the temperate zone, being from twenty to thirty-five inches in length, with a width equal to about one-third their length.   It is a native of the mountainous regions of the Carolinas, and was first discovered by the elder Michaux, in 1789, near Lincolntown, in North Carolina.   He remarks, " Extensive researches made in quest of it, in the upper part of the southern States, and east of the Alleghanies, have been unsuccessful.   In Tennessee it is found sparingly at intervals of forty or fifty miles.   It appears to delight in cool sheltered situations where the soil is deep and fertile, where it is constantly attended by the *M. tripetela.*'

This species has less tendency to sucker than the *tripetela*, and becomes a broad oak-like tree, in form, from twenty-five to forty feet high, and equal diameter.   In Parsons' specimen grounds at Flushing, L. I., there is a magnificent specimen with a trunk fifteen inches in diameter, and a head thirty-five feet in height and forty feet in diameter, and truly the most superb tree of its size we have ever seen.   Its branches almost meet the ground, and when the wind plays with its great leaves their white under surfaces light the tree like a mass of immense white blossoms.   This is one of the striking beauties of the tree, and one that is quite as effective on small as large trees.   Fig 115 shows the characteristic form of the tree in from seven to ten years after planting, and also represents the proportional size of the leaves and the blossom.   The leaves are heart-shaped at the base, and increase in width so that they are widest two-thirds of their length towards the point.   The flowers, which appear in June and July, are of immense size, sometimes eight to ten inches in width, white, with purple spots near the centre, and pleasantly fragrant.   Fruit shaped like a cucumber, bright rose-color when ripe, and about four inches long.   The bark is whitish and smooth, so that it can be distinguished from the *M. tripetela* in the winter by this feature. Young plants are said to grow slow until well established, but after they are well rooted the annual growth is from fifteen to thirty inches. It will bear a dryer soil than the *M. acuminata*, but depth, richness, and a surface protected from the sun are indispensable. It would give us great pleasure to have this noble species named after its discoverer— Michaux. It was at one time so known in Europe, and we have inserted this name as a synonym, in hopes that it may yet be adopted. Nearly all the magnolias being remarkable for their large leaves, the title of large-leaved has not a very specific signification.

BARTRAM'S MAGNOLIA.* *M. auriculata.*—The ear-leaved magnolia of Loudon and the nursery catalogues. This sort was discovered by that great tree-enthusiast, Bartram, in the mountainous regions of the Carolinas, three hundred miles from the sea. Michaux says, "I have nowhere found it so abundant as on the steepest part of the lofty mountains of North Carolina, particularly those which are called by the inhabitants Great Father Mountains, and Black and Iron Mountains." "The soil of these mountains is deep, brown, and of an excellent quality, * * * and the atmosphere in such situations, is continually charged with moisture."

It is found in but few regions.

Bartram thus describes it as seen wild. "This tree (or perhaps rather shrub) rises eighteen to thirty feet in height. There are usually many stems from a root, which lean a little, or slightly diverge from each other, in this respect imitating the *Magnolia tripetela;* the crooked wreathing branches arising and subdividing from the main stem without order or uniformity. Their extremities turn upwards, producing a very large roseaceous, perfectly white double flower, which is of a most fragrant scent. This fine flower sits in the centre of a radius of very large leaves, which are of a

---

* We have taken the liberty of re-naming this species in honor of the discoverer, with the hope that the feelings which dictate the innovation will be shared by American tree-cultivators.

singular figure, somewhat lanceolate, broad towards their extremities, terminating with an acuminate point, and backwards
they attenuate and become very narrow towards their bases, terminating in two long narrow ears, or lappels, one on each side of
the insertion of the petiole."

The fruit is quite similar to that of the *M. tripetela.* As this
variety is not equal to the *M. macrophhlla* in size or beauty of leaf
and flower, or in symmetry as a tree, it will be found desirable only
in a collection where magnolias are made a specialty. It is probably less hardy than the *macrophylla* or *tripetela,* but we are not
aware that this has been tested.

THE PYRAMIDAL MAGNOLIA, *M. pyramidata,* supposed to be a
variety of the above, is a much more symmetrical and pyramidal
tree, with smaller leaves, and more tree-like form. It is found on
the banks of the Altamaha river, in Georgia. We are not aware
whether it has been tested at the north.

THE SWAMP MAGNOLIA, *M. glauca,* grows wild in swamps as far
north as Massachusetts, and is found in abundance from New Jersey
to Virginia. "It is rather a large bush than a tree; with shining,
green, laurel-like leaves, four or five inches long, somewhat mealy
and glaucous beneath. The blossoms, about three inches broad,
are snowy white, and so fragrant that where they abound in swamps
their perfume is often perceptible for a quarter of a mile" (Downing). If Dr. Kirtland's success in growing this variety on the *M.
acuminata* can become general, we have in this little tree one of
the best ornaments of our lawns. It is a scrawny bush grown in
dry open ground on its own roots, but does pretty well in a partial
shade and deep moist soil.

The foregoing are all natives of our own country. The following are natives of China and Japan, or hybrids between those and
our own species, which have originated in British gardens. The
remarks as to protection and care which have been made of magnolias in general, apply to all these. They are about as hardy as
the native magnolias.

THE CHINESE WHITE MAGNOLIA. *M. conspicua.*—A beautiful small tree when in congenial soil, but quite often of scanty foliage in northern grounds. Its peculiar quality is the earliest of its great white blossoms, which appear in April before the leaves, and, according to Meehan, "combine the fragrance of the lily with the beauty of the rose." Yet the rose and the lily have this great advantage :—that their blossoms are nestled or environed in green leaves, while the blossoms of this magnolia appear in daring nakedness on the bare twigs of April. On warm spring days the appearance of such noble fragrant flowers is like a breath of the tropics after one has passed an iceberg at sea; but when, after being invited to burst their buds, and expand by the first warm days of spring, they are often startled and chilled by the still whiter snows that occasionally fall in April, and seen from the windows of a fire-warmed room when chilly east winds drive all one's nature-loving fever back to the heart, instead of admiration they then inspire a kind of pity, and our kindliest wish is that they might be back in their warmer homes, where no snows could pale their whiteness, nor chilly winds drink their fragrance. In short, there is something unnatural in the sight of blossoms unsurrounded with the tender green of opening or expanded leaves; and although we cannot but admire and be grateful for such bloom as the Chinese white magnolia gives us, we are not disposed to consider this pre-maturity of its blossoms as a desirable quality of trees or shrubs, and would value this one higher if the blossoms were to appear after, instead of before the expansion of the leaves.

FIG. 116.

Figure 116 shows the characteristic form of the tree five or six years after planting, and the form of the leaves and blossoms. It becomes a neat small tree from ten to fifteen feet in height. The flowers are from three to four inches in diameter, and appear in March, April, or May, according to the season or the latitude.

This species, when grown as a tree, is usually grafted on the

M. acuminata; but by grafting on the *M. purpurea*, it is converted into a low shrub, suitable for growing in pots, and forcing, under glass, into winter bloom. It should have a well-drained, porous, warm soil. Having no leaves of its own during its blooming season, it is the more desirable to place it near evergreens, against whose dark foliage its blossoms will be pleasingly relieved, and whose height and foliage may shield it from winds.

Fig. 117.

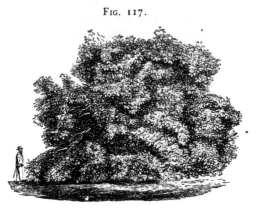

PARSONS' MAGNOLIA SOULANGEANA.

Soulange's Magnolia, *M. Soulangeana*, is a magnificent hybrid between the *M. conspicua* and *M. purpurea*, and more showy and vigorous than either. Fig. 117 is an imperfect representation of a superb specimen growing in the specimen grounds of the Parsons nursery at Flushing, L. I.; in appearance a huge spreading shrub of large glossy foliage, but in size a tree, with a trunk fifteen inches in diameter, the head forty feet in breadth, and thirty feet high. It blooms in May. Its immense flowers begin to appear while it is in the nursery rows, and when larger it rivals the horse-chestnut in the splendor of its inflorescence. The two trees being in bloom at the same time, present the widest difference in the character of their flowers. Those of the magnolia are borne singly, are irregularly cup-shaped, from four to six inches in diameter, white, tinged with purple, and somewhat fragrant. The tree has the abundant masses of glossy leaves that distinguish the *M. purpurea;* but instead of being like that species a low shrub, requiring shade and the coolness of other vegetation near it to protect and develop its best character, this species will grow to large size in open ground (if the soil be deep, rich, and shaded), and the noble massing of its foliage is excelled by no other tree. The leaves are quite small compared with our American species of magnolia; but though less showy separately, they break into finer masses.

From all the information we have, it seems to us that this is the most valuable of all the foreign magnolias, and quite as hardy as any of the family. At Rochester, N. Y., though less luxuriant in its development than near New York and Philadelphia, it bears the winter with no protection.

The *Magnolia speciosa* differs principally from the *M. Soulangeana* in being of more upright habit, and blooming ten days later.

THE PURPLE-FLOWERED MAGNOLIA. *M. purpurea.*—A low. spreading shrub, from four to eight feet high, and greater proportional breadth, noted for the fine masses of its very glossy deep-green leaves. These are from five to six inches long, widest in the middle, pointed at both ends, with wavy edges, and very glossy. Color, a pure dark-green. Flowers in April and May in profusion, and many scattered blossoms again in August and later; form, cup-shaped, three or four inches in diameter; color, purple, shading into white. Almost hardy in the climate of New York, and does well where protected from wind and sun *on the roots*, as it requires a moist, cool soil. One of the richest foliaged of shrubs for a shady border.

The *Magnolia gracilis*, is a smaller variety of the *M. purpurea*, with darker-colored flowers.

THOMPSON'S MAGNOLIA, *M. Thompsoniana*, is reputed to be a cross between the *M. glauca* and the *M. tripetela*, and is considered sufficiently distinct to be desirable in a collection. It blooms in June, several weeks later than the *M. Soulangeana.*

A deep, porous, moist soil, not cold, but shaded from the direct rays of the sun, is the most essential requisite in growing beautiful magnolias.   If the reader remembers what is contained in Chapter XVIII, on growing half-hardy trees, and will follow its suggestions, there need be little fear of failure in growing this tropical family of great-leaved trees in most portions of the northern States.

THE BIRCH. *Betula.*

The lightness, grace, and delicacy of some of the birch family, in bark, branching, and foliage, is proverbial ; and yet, within a few years, new varieties have been introduced that fairly surpass the acknowledged charms of the older members.

Contrary to our ordinary habit of naming the best native varieties first, we shall begin with that most exquisite of modern sylvan belles—

THE CUT-LEAVED WEEPING BIRCH. *B. lacianata pendula.*— Wherever known, this tree stands the ac-

FIG. 118.

knowledged queen of all the airy graces with which lightsome trees coquette with the sky and the summer air.   It lacks no charm essential to its rank.   Erect, slender, tall, it gains height only to bend its silvery spray with a caressing grace on every side.   Like our magnificent weeping elm, but lighter, smaller, and brighter in all its features, it rapidly lifts its head among its compeers till it over-tops them, and then spreads its branches, drooping and subdividing into the most delicate silvery branchlets, whose pensile grace is only equalled by those of the weeping willow.   Fig 118 illustrates its common form about ten years after planting.

We regret being unable to present an engraving that will suggest the airy grace of this tree.   No engraving could do it justice.   Like the palm tree of the tropics, it must be seen in motion, swaying in the lightest breeze, its leaves trembling in the heated summer air, its white bark glistening through the bright foliage and sparkling in the sun, to enable one to form a true impression of its character. Professor Wilson in his "Isle of Palms" thus alludes to a birch tree:

> "————on the green slope
> Of a romantic glade, we sate us down,
> Amid the fragrance of the yellow broom;
> While o'er our heads *the weeping birch tree streamed*
> *Its branches, arching like a fountain shower.*"

This birch is one of the most rapid growers among ornamental trees, attaining a height of thirty feet in ten years.

THE EUROPEAN WEEPING BIRCH. *B. pendula.*—This is the old weeping variety of the birch, and nearly all the encomiums of the preceding newer variety will apply to this, which would be perfect— "were t' other dear charmer away." The former is a little more delicate and decided in each of the peculiarities that make them both beautiful. Both of them are of more vigorous habit than our own very pretty white or mountain birch. They will probably grow sixty to seventy feet high, with a breadth of head somewhat less. The engraving of the preceding variety illustrates also the usual form of the common weeping birch when from thirty to forty feet high; which height they are likely to attain in ten or twelve years after planting.

THE EUROPEAN WHITE BIRCH. *B. alba,* (Fig. 119.)—This is the common wild birch of the continent, from which the above beautiful varieties have sprung. It forms a tree somewhat larger than our own white or mountain birch, which in most respects it resembles.

FIG. 119.

THE AMERICAN BIRCHES. — We quote Downing's excellent descriptions entire.

"The American sorts, and particularly the black birch, start into leaf very early in the spring, and their tender green is agreeable to the eye at that season; while the swelling buds and young foliage in many kinds give out a delicious, though faint perfume. Even the blossoms which hang like brown tassels from the droop-ing branches, are interesting to the lover of nature.

> "'The fragrant birch above him hung,
>   Her tassels in the sky,
> And many a vernal blossom sprung,
>   And nodded careless by.'—BRYANT.

"Nothing can well be prettier, seen from the windows of the drawing-room, than a large group of trees, whose depth and dis-tance is made up by the heavy and deep masses of the ash, oak, and maple ; and the portions nearest to the eye on the lawn ter-minated by a few birches, with their sparkling white stems and delicate, airy, drooping foliage. Our white birch, being a small tree, is very handsome in such situations, and offers the most pleas-ing variety to the eye, when seen in connection with other foliage. Several kinds, as the yellow and the black birches, are really stately trees and form fine groups by themselves. Indeed, most beautiful and varied masses might be formed by collecting together all the different kinds, with their characteristic barks, branches, and foliage.

"As an additional recommendation, many of these trees grow on the thinnest and most indifferent soils, whether moist or dry ; and in cold bleak and exposed situations, as well as in warm and sheltered places."

We shall enumerate the different kinds as follows ·

FIG. 120.

"THE CANOE BIRCH OR PAPER BIRCH, *B. papyracea* or *Boleau a canot* of the French Cana-dians, is, according to Michaux, most common in the forests of the eastern States, north of latitude 43°, and in the Canadas. There it attains its largest size, sometimes seventy feet in height and three in diameter. Its branches are slender, flexible, covered with a shining brown bark, dotted with white ; and on trees of mode-rate size, the bark is a brilliant white ; it is often used for roofing houses, for the manufacture of baskets, boxes, etc., besides its most important use for canoes, as already mentioned. The leaves, borne on petioles four or five lines long, are of a middling size, oval, unequally denticulated, smooth, and of a dark green color." Fig. 120 represents a young tree of this species.

"THE WHITE BIRCH, *B. populifolia*, is a tree of much smaller size, generally from twenty to thirty-five feet in height. It is found in New York and the other middle States, as well as at the north. The trunk, like the foregoing, is covered with silvery bark; the branches are slender, and generally drooping when the tree attains considerable size. The leaves are smooth on both surfaces, heart-shaped at the base, very acuminate, and doubly and irregularly toothed. The petioles are slightly twisted, and the leaves are almost as tremulous as those of the aspen. It is a beautiful small tree for ornamental planting."

"THE COMMON BLACK OR SWEET BIRCH. *B. lenta.*—This is the sort most generally known by the name of the birch, and is widely diffused over the middle and southern States. In color and appearance the bark much resembles that of the cherry tree: on old trees, at the close of winter, it is frequently detached in transverse portions, in the form of hard ligneous plates, six or eight inches broad. The leaves, for a fortnight after their appearance, are covered with a thick silvery down which disappears soon after. They are about two inches long, serrate, heart-shaped at the base, acuminate at the summit, and of a pleasing tint and fine texture."

"THE YELLOW BIRCH, *B. lutea*, grows most plentifully in Nova Scotia, Maine, and New Brunswick, on cool rich soils, where it is a tree of the largest size. It is remarkable for the color and arrangement of its outer bark, which is of a brilliant golden-yellow, and is frequently seen divided into fine strips rolled backward at the ends, but attached in the middle. The leaves are about three and a half inches long, two and a half broad, ovate, acuminate, and bordered with sharp irregular teeth. It is a beautiful tree, with a trunk of nearly uniform diameter, straight and destitute of branches for thirty or forty feet."

"THE RED BIRCH (*B. rubra*) belongs chiefly to the south, being scarcely ever seen north of Virginia. It prefers the moist soil of river banks, where it reaches a noble height. It takes its name from the cinnamon or reddish color of the outer bark on young trees. When old it becomes rough, furrowed, and greenish. The leaves are light-green on the upper surface, whitish beneath, very pointed at the end, and terminated at the base in an acute angle. The twigs are long, flexible, and pendulous ; and the limbs of a brown color, spotted with white."

A full collection of birch trees would form a very interesting arboricultural specialty for a suburban place, especially where the ground surfaces are irregular or rocky

THE LINDEN OR BASSWOOD. *Tillia.*

The linden, famous in Germany as the shade tree of her most celebrated avenues—there taking the same rank that our elm does among us—is inferior to some of our native trees in many essential qualities. It forms an oval, symmetrical head, and the branches, which are smooth and regular, droop with a fine curve from the lower part of the trunk, and, rising again at their extremities, form a graceful sweep most pleasing for an open lawn tree. Indeed, were it not that its leaves are inviting to certain worms, who make silk from them, and then suspend themselves in myriads from the tree, its abundant foliage and graceful form would especially commend it for park use. The flowers appear in June and July, and hang in loose, pale yellow clusters, and are fragrant. Some of the species or varieties are said to be deliciously perfumed. The leaves vary from a true heart-shape to an acutely pointed heart-shape ; are of a pleasing light-green color, and smooth, but not glossy, turning yellow in September, and are among the earliest to drop. The variety of lindens is not large.

THE AMERICAN LINDEN OR BASSWOOD, *T. americana,* is mainly described in the above description of the genus. It is the most robust of the species. . The leaves are from four to five inches in diameter, acute heart-shaped, and pale green. The growth is rapid.

THE BROAD-LEAVED LINDEN, *T. macrophylla*, is a new variety of the basswood, interesting from the exceeding size and luxuriance of its foliage.

THE EUROPEAN LINDEN, *T. europa*, differs from the American in having smaller, darker, and less pointed leaves, and in the more globular form of its head.

THE GRAPE-LEAVED LINDEN. *T. vitifolia.*—This is a new and charming variety. The leaves, which are deeply-lobed like those of some varieties of grape, are also large, more glossy, and of a brighter green than any other variety of linden. The tree is of vigorous habit. Young wood bright red.

THE RED-BARKED LINDEN, *T. rubra*, and the GOLDEN-BARKED, *T. aurea*, the former with red and the latter with yellow branches, are considered "peculiarly beautiful in winter, when a few of them, mingled with other deciduous trees, make a pleasing variety of coloring in the absence of ' foliage." Fig. 121 shows a young tree.

FIG. 121.

THE WHITE LINDEN, *T. alba*, is a native variety, with the under side of its leaves downy, giving the foliage a grayish hue, and with finer flowers and lighter-colored bark.

THE WEEPING WHITE LINDEN. *T. pendula.*—Mr. Sargent says of it: "Of very pendulous habit, and the under part of the leaf very silvery. We esteem this one of the most, if not the most, ornamental of the lindens." Its pendulous habit is confined almost entirely to the tops of the branches and the growing wood.

THE WHITE-LEAVED EUROPEAN LINDEN has a peculiar whitish gray tone of foliage that makes it a striking tree to introduce occasionally as a contrast or foil for the more healthy greens. A robust tree.

THE FERN-LEAVED LINDEN, *T. lacianata*, is curious on account of its shredded leaves. Of its habit of growth as it matures we cannot speak.

All these beautiful or curious varieties may be readily grafted or budded on our basswood, so that persons having one or more trees of the latter may, without marring the general contour of the tree, test and compare the varied foliage of the different varieties. of linden. ·

THE PLANE-TREE. *Platanus.*

THE SYCAMORE OR AMERICAN PLANE TREE. *P. occidentalis.*— There are but two species of the plane tree, and these differ considerably in their characters. One of them is our native sycamore or buttonwood, well known by its smooth and scaly gray bark, which, detaching itself in laminate pieces, reveals a whiter bark beneath, and gives the trunk and branches a spotted or spangled appearance. Occasionally the older bark scales entirely from some of the branches, leaving them nearly as white as those of the white birch. It is one of the largest and most rapid in growth of American forest trees, and, previous to the discovery of the great trees. of California and Oregon, its trunk was the most colossal vegetation familiar to Americans. One has been cut measuring forty-seven feet in circumference; and there was formerly a tree at Jefferson, Cayuga County, N. Y., with a hollow interior fifteen feet in diameter two feet from the ground! The enormous expansion of the trunk is one of its peculiarities, exceeding that of any other tree east of the Rocky Mountains. This characteristic disposes it to become hollow, yet to increase healthily, on its trunk shell like the curious old chestnuts of Mount Ætna. The leaves are double the size, and resemble in outline those of the sugar maple, but are thinner, of a lighter green, have more strongly-marked ribs, and are rarely glossy.

Notwithstanding the grand character of the sycamore, it is little esteemed of late years for decorative purposes. Aside from the fact that it is too large and rank a tree for small places, its diseases have done much to discourage its planting. · The wood is subject to the attacks of a borer, and the leaves are favorite food for worms to such an extent that few sycamores are seen which are not every summer denuded of half their foliage by these pests. The leaves also expand late, drop early, and are apt to rot where they drop. For these reasons it is less desirable than many other trees for streets or pleasure grounds.

THE ORIENTAL PLANE TREE. *P. orientalis.*—This species resembles our maples almost as much as it does its brother the sycamore. It is hardy, and in many respects more valuable for decorative planting than the American species. Whether the following analysis of its character, which we quote from Loudon, is verified by its growth in this country, we have not had the means of judging, but it seems likely to form a connecting link between our compact and slower-growing maples and the loose rank growth of the sycamore. The passage quoted, however, is given quite as much for the purpose of presenting a fine analysis of the characteristics of trees as to call attention to the particular merits of the tree under consideration :

" Pliny affirms that there is no tree whatsoever that defends us so well from the heat of the sun in summer, or that admits it more kindly in winter. Both properties result from the large size of its leaves. In summer these present horizontal imbricated masses, which, while they are favorable to the passage of the breeze, yet exclude both the sun and rain ; while, as the distance at which the branches and twigs of trees are from one another, is always proportionate to the size of the leaves, hence the tree in winter is more than usually open to the sun's rays. As an ornamental tree, no one which attains so large a size has a finer appearance, standing singly, or in small groups, upon a lawn, where there is room to allow its lower branches, which stretch themselves horizontally to a considerable distance, to bend gracefully toward the ground, and turn up at their extremities. The peculiar characteristic of the tree, indeed, is the combination which it presents of majesty and gracefulness; an expression which is produced by the massive and yet open and varied character of its head, the bending of its branches, and their feathering to the ground. In this respect it

25

is greatly superior to the lime (linden) tree, which comes nearest to it in the general character of the head, but which forms a much more compact and lumpish mass of foliage in summer, and, in winter, is so crowded with branches and spray, as to prevent in a great measure the sun from penetrating through them. The head of the plane tree, during sunshine, often abounds in what painters call flickering lights; the consequence of the branches of the head separating themselves into what may be called horizontal undulating strata, or, as it is termed in artistical phraseology, horizontal tuft-ing, easily put in motion by the wind, and through openings in which the rays of the sun penetrate and strike on the foliage below. The tree, from its mild and gentle expression, its useful-ness for shade in summer, and for admitting the sun in winter, is peculiarly adapted for pleasure-grounds, and, where there is room, for planting near houses and buildings.

"A light deep free soil, moist, but not wet at bottom, is that on which the oriental plane tree thrives best; and the situation should be sheltered, but not shaded or crowded by other trees. It will scarcely grow on strong clays and on elevated exposed places; nor will it thrive in places where the lime tree does not prosper." . It is one of the latest trees to come into full leaf, but the foliage is less subject to the ravages of insects than that of the sycamore.

THE WILLOW. *Salix.*

The willow family embraces an immense number of species and varieties. Loudon describes nearly two hundred. They are of all sizes and forms, from creeping plants a few inches in height, up to the magnificent weeping willow. The branches are uniformly slen-der and flexible, so that some varieties form the chief staple for bas-ket-making. Their growth is generally rapid and upright, the weep-ing varieties being exceptional. The white willow, *S. alba,* and the common weeping willow, *S. babylonica,* become large trees in a few years. All the willows grow in moist soils, but the healthiest and most durable trees are grown in a warm well-drained soil, where water can be reached by the roots at no great distance from the tree.

FIG. 122.

A WEEPING WILLOW ON STRATFORD AVENUE, EAST BRIDGEPORT, CONN.

THE WEEPING WILLOW, *Salix babylonica,* is by far the most beautiful of this great family, and its wonderful combination of charms are too common to be fully appreciated. It strikes root from cuttings as readily as a currant twig, and then grows with great rapidity, becoming a tree of irregularly-rounded masses fifty to sixty feet high and broad within twelve or fifteen years after planting

The weeping willow is the type of pensile trees. In their first growth the branches aim bravely upward, but the slender suhsi diary branches soon give up all struggle with the laws of gravity,

and resign 'themselves to their fall with a graceful *abandon* that
is bewitching.   The trunk and great branches become ruggedly
massive as the tree reaches maturity, and their deeply-furrowed
bark contrasts finely with the delicacy of the spray.   The weird
movement of its drooping plumes of foliage, as they wave slowly in
the slightest summer wind, is unequalled except by the more stately
and exquisite palm of the tropics; the full beauty of which can
never be understood by those who have never seen the grace of its
stately motion.   But our willow is one of the grandest, as well as
most graceful, vegetables of the temperate zone, and barely.yields
to the oak and the elm in majesty of proportion.   Fig. 122 is a
noble specimen spanning the old Stratford road in East Bridgeport, Conn., growing in a dry, well-drained soil, near the river or
bay.   It comes into leaf with the aspen and the buckeye, and
holds its leaves later than any other large deciduous tree; often
exhibiting a noble mass of verdure when the chestnuts and the
hickories, and even the maples, are quite bare of leaves.

There is no good reason why this tree should be principally
associated with graveyards.   It is a sunny, cheerful tree, full of
glorious vitality, and always beautiful, though it may have faults
that unsuit it for some places.   These are brittleness of limbs,
tendency to decay soon after it attains large size, and the habit of
its small leaves, when they fall, to settle into the grass and rot
there, making it troublesome to keep the grass clean under them.
The leaves are also attractive to the same caterpillar that weaves
dirty webs in most fruit trees, but by timely attention in cutting
out and destroying these nests this nuisance may be abated.   Such
faults make the weeping willow unsuitable for planting near a
residence or as a street tree.   It must be remembered that it
quickly becomes a tree of great size, and should not be planted
where it will not have room for expansion, or where the extension
of its branches will injure and overtop other valuable trees or
shrubs.   Nor should it be planted in any considerable number
together.   All trees of a highly distinctive character should be
introduced sparingly.   The weeping willow and the Lombardy
poplar represent two opposite extremes of individuality.   If used
in the proper places they serve by their very unusual forms to

enliven or vary the more common tree outlines more perfectly than most other trees.

THE RING WILLOW. *Salix annularis.*—This is only a variety of the weeping willow, curious on account of the leaf curling in the form of a ring. Portions of these trees occasionally return to the natural form of leaf, so that the simple form and the curled leaf are both growing on the same tree. It does not make so beautiful a large tree as the common sort, and is scarcely worth planting.

THE GOLDEN WILLOW. *Salix vitellina.*—A tree but little smaller than the weeping willow, with similar leaves and tone of foliage, but without its perfectly pendulous habit. Its peculiarity, and one which makes it a marked, and often a beautiful tree, is the golden color of its young wood. When the tree is clothed with leaves, the yellow twigs seen through them give additional warmth of tone to their color, and when bare of leaves makes a bright and cheerful winter tree. It is irregularly round-headed in outline, and less broad in proportion than the weeping willow. The lights and shades in its head are softly blended, and the lightness and warm color of its foliage contrast well with trees having dark foliage or abrupt shadows. There is a beautiful specimen on the west side of the Mall in the New York Central Park.

THE WHITE WILLOW, *Salix alba*, and the RUSSELL OR BEDFORD WILLOW, *S. Russelliana*, are both English varieties long domesticated in this country. They become large trees with great rapidity —attaining a height of sixty or seventy feet in thirty years. With the exception of the color of the bark they have the same general characteristics as the golden willow.

THE GLOSSY-LEAVED WILLOW, *S. lucida*, is a native shrub of considerable beauty, described by Gray in the Natural History of New York as " a shrub eight to fifteen feet high, with shining yellowish-brown bark. Buds yellowish, smooth. Leaves three to five inches long, and an inch or more in width, rather obtuse when young, but tapering at maturity to a long slender point, and rather acute at the base. A very handsome willow."

There are hundreds of varieties of wild willows in wet places, most of which would not be valuable in pleasure grounds. The following are some of the dwarf varieties that are sold in our nurseries, and are quite as popular as their merits warrant.

THE ROSEMARY-LEAVED WILLOW, *S. rosemarifolia,* grafted standard high, is a small globular-headed tree, with branches radiating regularly from the centre. Foliage a dull grayish-green. Adapted for cutting into a formal outline, but inferior to hundreds of other shrubs and trees for that purpose. Of little value.

THE GOAT WILLOW, *S. caprea,* in several varieties, with variegated leaves, are curious, but not of much value.

THE KILMARNOCK WILLOW is the finest of the dwarf willows, and quite distinct in appearance from the others. It is grafted from four to seven feet high on the *S. caprea,* and forms, without trimming, a perfect umbrella head, with tips growing always toward the ground. It is so neat in form, and thrifty, that though only recently introduced in the country, it is to be seen in nearly every village yard. It is desirable to obtain specimens budded not less than seven feet from the ground.

THE NEW AMERICAN OR FOUNTAIN WILLOW, *S. americana pendula,* is another so-called dwarf variety, which, when budded standard high on an upright stock, is remarkable for the horizontality of its growth and pendulous branches, which hang like those of the old weeping willow. It covers a large area, and should not be planted on the supposition that being a dwarf it needs but little space, for in lateral extension it is no dwarf at all.

THE LOCUSTS OR ACACIAS.

THE BLACK OR YELLOW LOCUST. *Robinia pseud-acacia.—Were it a healthy tree* we would place this in the front rank of ornamental trees of the second class in size. In delicacy, grace, and luxuriance of foliage and purity of color, it has, when in health, no superior, blending lightness of spray and massiveness of shadows to a degree seldom equalled. The blossoms, too, in abundant racemes in May and June, white and very fragrant, are worthy of the foliage. But a healthy locust tree is rarely seen, especially after the first ten years' growth. Almost everywhere the borer, a pestilent worm, chooses the trunk of this tree for his home, and its scantier foliage, dead limbs, and general look of seedy gentility, show too quickly the result. It has also some faults even in health that warn us not to fall too much in love with it. The branches break easily in summer winds the roots sucker badly, the leaves are late to expand, and the tree even without the attacks of the borer is short-lived.

The *R. p-a bessoniana* is a variety of strong growth, which is thornless, and regarded by some nurserymen as the finest of the family of acacias.

There are several other varieties ; one with light-pink flowers, but with no other marked differences as ornamental trees.

THE GUMMY ACACIA. *Robinia viscosa* or *glutinosa.*—This is a smaller species than the preceding, and grows mostly in the southern States, but is hardy as far north as Albany, N. Y. It blooms a month later than the *pseud-acacia*, and the flowers are of a pale pink color, without fragrance. In foliage it closely resembles the common sort. The bark exudes a gummy substance, from which characteristic has arisen its botanical name. The shorter and more compact growth of this species, its beautiful foliage and pretty bloom, make it one of the most desirable of the acacias for small places.

THE ROSE ACACIA, *R. hispida rosea*, is a trailing straggling shrub rather than tree. The foliage is much like that of the common locust, but its young wood is covered with mossy soft brown prickles. Its flowers, in rosy racemes about four inches long, appear in June, in great abundance, and continue blossoming more or less through the summer. The *R. h. macrophylla* is a variety with larger leaves, and without prickles on the young wood. There are few more superb bloomers among shrubs than the rose acacia, but its habit of growth is so straggling and tortuous that it needs much care to keep it in a form suitable in polished grounds. It is recommended to have a single stem tied to a strong cedar post six or eight feet high (which should be permanent), with a wire parasol-like frame fixed to the top to support the branches and allow them to fall on all sides from it. Thus trained there is no more exquisite flowering-shrub. The post alone will, if care is taken to keep the stem tied to it so as not to injure the bark, be sufficient to keep the tree in good shape.

THE THREE-THORNED ACACIA OR HONEY LOCUST. *Gleditschia.* —A large and curious native of our forests, armed at all points with enormous compound thorns which grow even through the old bark of the trunk as well as on the branches, and arm all parts of the tree in the most formidable manner. Downing gives the tree high rank for ornamental purposes. We have seen much of it, in favorable circumstances, and although it exceeds the *Robinias* in the flaky lightness of its foliage, and in picturesqueness of outline, it is inferior to them in every other respect, and is a desirable tree only for the merits just named, which make it suitable as a picturesque condiment among trees of heavy outlines. Like the beech, though its branches form angles of about 45° with the main stem when the tree is young, the exterior foliage is disposed in horizontal strata, recalling by their appearance pictures of old cedars of Lebanon. Old trees especially, with their tabular tops, are remarkable for this appearance. The thorns of the honey locust which occasionally die out and drop off, are dangerous, as they lie concealed in the grass, to the feet of those who walk under them; and this fact is an objection to the tree where there are children. In blossom the tree is less showy than the common locusts. The seed pods which succeed the blossoms are from five to nine inches long; and though the seeds ripen early in autumn, the pods themselves remain dry and hard upon the tree through the winter, and sometimes for more than a year, and are unsightly.

There are some Chinese species or varieties, *G. sinensis*, whose characteristics are not sufficiently known to describe. Loudon mentions the *G. s. purpurea* as "a small tree of compact upright growth, very suitable for gardens of limited extent." The *G. s. incrmis* is a small sort without thorns, said to be suitable for small grounds.

FIG. 123.

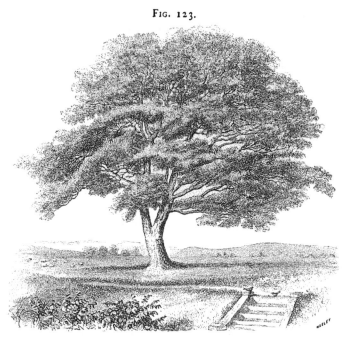

THE SOPHORA. *Sophora.*

THE JAPAN SOPHORA. *Sophora japonica.*—Considering the delicacy of its foliage, its purity and depth of color, and the hardiness of the tree, it is curious that so few fine specimens of this tree are yet to be seen in this country. Fig. 123 is the portrait of a full-grown tree in the Syon Park, England. We have heard of no large specimens in this country. The tree here shown * was fifty-seven feet high, eighty-four feet wide across its branches, and four and one-half feet diameter of trunk. This size is probably its greatest, as nearly all the trees growing in that famous park attain unusual dimensions. The foliage of the sophora closely resembles that of the common locust, but is a little darker. The young wood

* From Loudon's Arboretum Britannicum, Vol. V, p. 76.

is dark green. The tree is believed to be hardy, and, as far as we can learn, is not subject to the attacks of the borer which destroys our locust trees. Loudon says of it: "None of the arboreous leguminacæ are equal to this tree in beauty of foliage and bark. Its flowers (which are cream-colored and appear in August), when they are produced, are also in large terminal-compound spikes, and very conspicuous, though smaller than those of the *Robinia viscosa.* One remarkable property in the sophora is, that the very hottest and driest seasons do not pale the foliage, or cause it to drop off." The peculiar tone of its foliage is a deep velvety green, that is unequalled by any deciduous tree we know of. It requires a thoroughly drained soil. The leaves are among the last to surrender to autumn frosts, and turn to a yellowish-green before they fall. The bark exhales a strong odor when cut, and is said to produce colic on those who are engaged in pruning the tree.

THE WEEPING JAPAN SOPHORA, *S. j. pendula,* is the finest of small pendulous trees when grafted ·on a thrifty stock at a height

FIG. 124.

of seven to twelve feet from the ground. Its young branches are green and somewhat angular or crooked, so that in winter the tree has a knotted and curious look. Its deep velvety-green color, delicately formed acacia-like foliage, and the bold breaks of light and shade in its head, altogether make so rich an effect as to attract the attention of all observers. It is, at the same time, symmetrical and picturesque, while the Kilmarnock willow is mo-notonously symmetrical or lumpish. It seems to be difficult to propagate this variety. Specimens well started, standard height, still command a high price at the nurseries. Fig. 124 is a representation of the prettiest specimen of the weeping Japan sophora we have seen, growing in the deep rich sandy loam of Parsons' specimen grounds at Flushing, L. I. It is grafted but seven feet from the ground, and the branches, spreading first with irregular horizontality, finally droop till they meet the ground, form-ing a perfect and deeply-shaded bower. The tree covers an area about sixteen feet in diameter, and is of equal height. The en-graving might naturally be mistaken for a weeping willow, while the tree itself, by the deeper green of its foliage, and the marked difference in the position of its leaves, is at once distinguishable from a willow, with which, indeed, it would form a pleasing contrast in all but its form, and the common, though differing delicacy of their foliage.

We consider this a hardy tree; but, if one would quickly realize its full dower of beauty, it must have unusual care. First, *very deep drainage* is essential to its health. Second, a young tree, which is budded or grafted from seven to ten feet high, having no side limbs and foliage to strengthen its trunk while the artificial head is form-ing, must be supported a few years by short stakes, and protected both in summer and winter from the sun and the cold by matting bound around the trunk, and thorough mulching over the roots. The deep drainage, after five years' growth, will have invited the roots down to soil which is never frozen, and then, if the tree has had a healthy growth, further precautions may not be needed. The matting should be taken off the trunk early every spring and fall, and renewed for both summer and winter protection.

Sophora heptaphylla.—A Chinese shrub, six feet high, with yel-low flowers in October. Leaves with seven leaflets. Little known.

THE VIRGILIA. *Virgilia lutea.*

Downing remarked more than twenty years ago that this fine tree was still very rare in our ornamental plantations, and the observation is as true now as then. Mr. Thomas Meehan, of Ger-mantown, Pa., informs us that the tree is one of the most difficult to get established; and this, not because of its want of hardiness, for when once well established, it does not seem to suffer from cold in the most exposed location at Philadelphia, nor in ordinary exposure at Rochester, N. Y. It is said to be simply not tenacious of life when young, or perhaps unusually fastidious in soils. On the other hand, a planter in Rochester tells us that he has no more difficulty in making it grow than with any other tree.

The virgilia forms a compact head usually heavier on one side than the other ; and somewhat resembles the horse-chestnut, though its foliage is of finer texture, and its leaves mass in short horizontal layers, forming sharper lights and shadows. These shadows are as sharply defined as those of the beech tree, but not so thin, nor so regular. The color of the foliage is remarkable for its purity. The leaves are compound, and a little larger than those of the shell-bark hickory, with from five to eleven alternate, ovate, pointed leaflets. The leaves expand with the hickory, and keep the purity of their color till frosts, when they turn to a warm yellow.

The flowers appear about the middle of May in large white racemes or clusters of pea-shaped blossoms six to eight inches long, and cover the tree, so that it is then one of the most charming of all trees. It commences to bloom young, and develops its beauty from the start. The bark is so smooth that this feature alone would attract attention to the tree, and suggest the conclusion which all its other traits confirm, that it is one of the most polished and elegant of lawn trees. It will show to best advantage if planted northward from the point from which it is to be seen most, so that its southern side will be towards the observer, and its northern and western sides can be shielded from wind by evergreens. A dry, deeply-drained, porous soil is essential ; and also full exposure to the sun, and some protection from wind.

At the residence of Miss Price, Manheim street, Germantown, Pa., the tree mentioned by Michaux forty years ago as a fine specimen at that time, is still a hale tree, sixty feet high, and extends its branches over about seventy feet, mostly on one side of the trunk, the other side being shaded and confined by large pines and a lofty cucumber tree that overtops it. It is remarked by those familiar with the tree that there seems an irresistible tendency of the virgilia to grow principally on one side, even when fully exposed on all sides to the sun. The place where this virgilia grows is completely exposed to the deepest freezing of the soil ; as the street, which passes within twenty feet of its trunk, has been cut down four feet below the level of the ground about the tree, the latter being supported by a wall on the street line. The extension of this tree is over the road, which is also on the south side.

In the old Bartram garden, south of Philadelphia (now the residence of A. M. Eastwick, Esq.), is a beautiful specimen of the virgilia. It is thirty feet high, thirty-five feet in diameter of head, with a trunk fifteen inches thick. This tree grows principally on the west side; and in September, when the author saw it, was a superb mass of foliage. In size the virgilia is inferior to the horse-chestnut, and when young not so compact, but with age it bears more resemblance to that tree than to any other species, though they are readily distinguished from each other by the sharper shadow-lines of the virgilia, and the finer quality and different character of the leaves.

THE KENTUCKY COFFEE-TREE. *Gymnocladus canadensis.*

This curious tree is a sort of combination of the peculiarities of many trees. In its stubby cane-like young branches, and doubly-compound leaves, it resembles the large shrub or small tree called Hercules club; in the massing and breaks of its foliage it resembles a fine black or yellow locust, though its leaves are not so delicate; while in outline it is like the black walnut, but with a heavier and more rounded or oval contour. Its young branches are so cane-like, and without any indication of buds, that the tree in winter has the appearance of being dead. The bark of the trunk is also extremely rough, and curiously broken transversely. The leaves on young trees are three feet long, and twenty inches wide, but much smaller on mature trees. Each main leaf stalk bears from four to seven pairs of compound leaves, each of which is composed of from six to eight pairs of leaflets, so that each main petiole, or leaf-stem, may bear from forty-eight to one hundred and seventy-four leaflets! The leaflets are of a bluish green, and the general tone of the tree is not among the most lively greens. The blossoms are borne in short spikes from May to July. The leaves come out late, and drop early, turning yellow before they fall. The male and female blossoms of this species are borne on separate trees. It becomes a tree of secondary size, from fifty to sixty feet in height. The early growth is more rapid than that of the sugar maple, but is about the same in their later stages.

THE AILANTUS. *Ailantus.*

This exotic, so popular thirty years ago, is certainly now "in bad odor." Its rank growth when young, its luxuriant and graceful compound leaves, from three to six feet in length, and the fact of its novelty, both in growth and name, when introduced from China (the latter being no less a title than the "*tree of heaven*"—a title erroneously given, but piously adhered to by those who were selling them), altogether caused it to be planted to an extent that its character, on a better acquaintance, does not warrant. It had the additional misfortune to be mostly planted as a street tree in cities ; just where its great fault is most felt, and its beauties least appreciated. This fault is the unpleasant odor of its blossoms, which, to a few persons, is reputed poisonous.

It is a quality which should place it under ban for street planting, but not one of sufficient gravity to require us to banish it from parts of pleasure-grounds at a little distance from streets and residences. The odor of new-mown hay, and even of roses and strawberries, is nauseating and productive of fevers to a few unfortunately organized persons ; but such exceptional facts do not prove them to be poisonous. The odor of the flowers of the ailantus is disagreeable to almost every one, but it lasts but a short time ; and if the tree can be planted at a respectful distance from walks and windows, it does not seem to us a sufficient cause to abandon the cultivation of so beautiful and peculiar a tree.

The exceedingly rapid growth of the ailantus when quite young, sometimes making canes in a single season from ten to fifteen feet long, would be a merit, *if this wood could be kept from winter-killing.* But this very rank growth is generally killed back in winter. Such a growth being excessive, it is evident that the tree will start more hardily in dry poor soils ; for which, in fact, it is admirably adapted. But it is only during the first five years after planting that care must be taken to keep down its vigor. When deeply rooted the rate of growth is slower, and as it becomes a spreading tree, its beauty is greatly heightened by having a rich surface soil.

The ailantus forms a low, square, broad head. There are no full grown trees in this country, but we believe it will attain a height and breadth of about sixty feet in the climate of Philadelphia, and somewhat less north.

There are many features of the ailantus that give it a rare and peculiar beauty, admirably suited to add to the variety of colors and forms in groups of trees. We have no tree that can take its place; none with such immense compound leaves, which alone give the tree an unique character ; and they are thrust out boldly from the tree, thus showing their character to the best advantage. Their color is also of that thrifty yellowish-green, rare among our native trees, and therefore more needed in contrast with them. The flowers, in large terminal panicles, of a yellowish-green color, appear in May and June, and cover the tree with a feathery flowering that is very pleasing to the eye, however unpleasant in odor. In autumn these blossoms are changed to great masses of yellow and orange-brown seed-clusters that add greatly to beauty of the tree, and heighten the individuality of its expression. The leaves when touched by the cold occasionally turn a fine yellow, but drop quickly. The bark of the young wood is of a golden hue, and that of the trunk quite dark colored.

THE LIQUIDAMBER OR SWEET GUM. *Liquidamber.*

This is a great favorite in English parks, was warmly commended by Downing twenty years ago, and is widely distributed in its wild state throughout our country ; yet to this day it is almost unknown to a majority of suburban planters. The tree bears a general resemblance in form and foliage to the sugar maple, and grows to about the same size ; but when young has a more pointed top and conical form ; the leaves, however, are more star-like, thicker in texture, more deeply lobed, as shown on Fig. 125, and glossier than the leaves of the maple.

FIG. 125.

This engraving is a portrait of a fine specimen about forty years old, growing in the grounds of T. S. Shepherd, Esq., at Orienta, near Mamaroneck, N. Y. It was transplanted to its present location from an adjoining field when the trunk was nearly twelve inches in diameter, and has become a luxuriant tree again. During the summer the tree may be easily mistaken for an unusually dark and glossy-leaved sugar maple, but is distinguished from it not only by the peculiarities of its leaves, already mentioned, but by the curious appearance of its secondary branches to which the bark is attached in corky ridges as on the cork-barked elm, giving the branches a more rugged appearance.

The tree is found from New Hampshire to the Isthmus of Darien ; but it is only at the south that a characteristic which gives the tree its name is observed. A fragrant gum there exudes from its bark, which resembles liquidamber, and the tree was so named by the Spanish naturalist who first described it.

Downing's enthusiastic description of this tree is so good that we transcribe it for the reader.

"We hardly know a more beautiful tree than the liquidamber in every stage of its growth, and during every season of the year. Its outline is not picturesque or graceful, but simply beautiful ; * * * it is, therefore, a highly pleasing round-headed or tapering tree, which unites and harmonizes well with almost any other in composition ; but the chief beauty lies in the foliage. During the whole of the summer months it preserves unsoiled that dark glossy freshness which is so delightful to the eye ; while the singular, regularly palmate form of the leaves readily distinguishes it from the common trees of a plantation. But in autumn it assumes its gayest livery, and is decked in colors almost too bright and vivid for foliage, forming one of the most brilliant objects in American scenery at that season of the year. The prevailing tint of the foliage is then a deep purplish red, unlike any symptom of decay, and quite as rich as are commonly seen in the darker blossoms of a dutch parterre. This is sometimes varied by a shade deeper or lighter, and occasionally an orange tint is assumed. When planted in the neighborhood of our fine maples, ashes, and other trees remarkable for their autumnal coloring, the effect in a warm dry autumn is almost magical."

Loudon says of it: "When bruised, the leaves are fragrant at all seasons; but in the spring, when they are at first unfolding after a warm shower, the surrounding air is filled with their refreshing odor."

The liquidamber does best in a moist soil and sheltered situation. Though less beautiful in dry gravelly soils than the sugar maple, its form, and leaves, and autumn colors, ally it to the maple family, and it should be planted where trees of that species are made a specialty. We will add one trait of its autumn color that is not included in Downing's excellent description—its peculiar *golden bronze tone*, caused by the mingling of green, yellow and red leaves in its head. This tone is, at the first glance, less brilliant than the colors of the scarlet maple and scarlet oak; but as the eye rests upon the tree it seems to drink deeper and deeper of the colors until the tree fairly seems to glow with a fascination remotely allied to the effect produced by gazing at the clouds and sky of a gorgeous sunset.

THE TUPELO OR PEPERIDGE TREE. *Nyssa.*

There are several species of the tupelo. The common one in the northern States is the *Nyssa biflora*, or twin-flowered, known in some regions as the sour gum. It is usually found in wet ground, and when grown in swampy places is a conical, rigid, gloomy tree. Its branches are in level strata around a centre stem like those of the firs, and have the same hard, thorny ramification of twigs that characterizes the pin oak. Its top in the forest usually turns to one side after the tree is from thirty to forty

26

feet high.   In swampy ground we have seen trees from sixty to seventy feet high, and covered to the base with wiry branches. The trunk rarely exceeds eighteen inches in diameter.

FIG. 126.

In *warm* rich and moist soils the tupelo changes its character and becomes a wide-spreading small tree, still retaining its tendency to a conical form in some degree.   Fig. 126 is a characteristic form of the tupelo, being the portrait of a tree about thirty years old, grown on a common dry upland, but does not do justice to the clearness of its shadows.   On rich ground it spreads more, and takes the form of a small cedar of Lebanon.

The leaves of the tupelo are about three inches long, pointed-oval, thick, uncommonly glossy, and of a dark green.   They appear late in the spring, and fall early ; but before they fall their color is unsurpassed in purity and brilliancy by that of any other tree, varying from a fiery scarlet to a deep crimson.   It is an essential tree in any group designed to exhibit the brilliancy of autumn foliage, and a pleasing lawn tree at all times when in leaf.   When out of leaf its dark bark and angular twigginess is not pleasing.   The tree is easily transplanted, and will grow in any moist soil, but improves like most other trees in proportion as the soil is deep and rich.

The other varieties of the tupelo are the *N. grandidenta*, or tooth-leaved, a large tree of the southern States ; the *N. candicans*, or Ogeechee lime tree, a southern tree also, of smaller size ; and the *N. sylvatica*, or black gum—none of them notable for their beauty.

THE CHERRY TREE.   *Cerasus.*

The edible fruit-trees of the cherry family are divided into two classes, viz : the *C. sylvestris*, or wild black-fruited, and *C. vulgaris ;* the latter embracing all the Kentish, morello, and sour red cherries ; and it is supposed that all the finer varieties of cherries have sprung from these parents. Our native wild cherry, with black fruit, is the *Cerasus virginiana.*

There is no fruit-bearing tree so essential to a suburban home as the cherry-tree. Climbing into its branches to eat cherries is one of the pleasantest of June enjoyments for young or old. ⸱ Half the pleasure of eating cherries is in plucking them where they hang. Some large fruits may be bought more economically than they can be raised on suburban lots, but cherries are emphatically the fruit-trees of village homes.

The number of varieties in cultivation for their fruit are listed by hundreds in the nursery catalogues. We shall attempt no enumeration of these, but simply give the names of a few standard sorts, and describe more fully only such as are particularly known as ornamental trees.

The following varieties, ripening pretty nearly in the order named, are among the best for fruit : Baumann's May, a rank upright grower, forming a conical tree ; the early purple Guigne, a globular tree with small and numerous branches ; Knight's early black, a strong grower, rather spreading ; the black tartarian, of strong fastigiate growth ; the Mayduke, globular and compact ; Elton, pyramidal ; Downer's late, rather compact ; Downton, pyramidal ; late Duke, similar to Mayduke in form. Nearly all the best-fruited sorts form handsome trees, though many of them in the western States are more tender and liable to disease than wildings. The reader is referred to fruit-books for a selection of cherries suited to special localities. All the fine cherries seem to do much better on gravelly and clayey soils than in a light sandy loam, or rich alluvium, and should never be forced into rapid growth for the first five years after planting. In rich soils their growth is so rapid, when young, as to engender diseases before they are full grown, especially where there is not good subsoil drainage.

The following, known as bird cherries, are planted solely for ornament :

THE EUROPEAN BIRD CHERRY, *Cerasus padus*, is considered by many one of the most ornamental of small shrubby trees. That excellent horticultural authority, Thomas Meehan, of Germantown,

Pa., says of it: "For a single specimen on a lawn, it is not excelled. Its habit is good, and its flowering abundant." The leaves
are rather narrower and thinner than those of the common cherry.
The flowers are white, in racemes from two to five inches long, and
appear in May. The fruit, ripe in August, is black, austere, and
poisonous, but showy, from the abundant racemes that cover the
tree. The growth when young is rapid, somewhat straggling, and
is improved by clipping. Form at maturity, oblate. Height
twenty to thirty feet.

The *Cerasus padus bracteosa* is a variety of the above, especially
recommended in England on account of its larger racemes of pendulous flowers and fruit.

THE MEHALEB CHERRY, *C. mehaleb,* has a large glossy leaf,
rapid growth, and symmetric form, giving promise of great beauty
when young, but as it comes to full size the foliage becomes
meagre, and the mass of branches conspicuous, making it a tree of
little beauty. It forms a round head, twenty to thirty feet high.

THE AMERICAN WILD CHERRY, *C. virginiana (serotina ?)* grows
wild all over our country. It is a large tree, and one of considera
ble beauty at every age. The bark and berries are used in spirits
to make infusions that are considered medicinal. It is a companion for the birches in the lightness or slenderness and partial
pendulousness of its outer spray, but the opposite of that family in
the color of its bark and leaves ; the young wood being very dark,
purplish, and the leaves also dark, but glossy. The characteristic
form of the tree is squarish-oval, the height greater than the
breadth, and gracefully irregular in outline. When well grown, in
rich soil, the dark luxuriance of its shining foliage contrasts well
with such trees as the birches, the catalpa, or the kolreuteria.

THE EVER-FLOWERING WEEPING CHERRY. *C. semperflorens.*—
One of the prettiest of small weeping trees. Grafted on the proper
stock, it becomes a square-headed tree ten feet high, flowering and
fruiting all summer. The flowers are white, and like those of the
common cherry.

THE DWARF WEEPING CHERRY. *C. pumila pendula.*—This is one of the most exquisite of little garden pets. Everything about it is in miniature. The leaves and blossoms, both of extreme delicacy, hang in matted masses differently from

FIG. 127.

the spray of most weeping trees. Fig. 127 is a sketch of a young specimen in the grounds of Ellwanger & Barry at Rochester. It ought not to be called a tree ; for though it is grafted on a single stem of another sort, and therefore maintains a tree form, its size is rather that of a green-house tub-plant. The growth is very slow, and it is said to be difficult to propagate. It should not be grafted more than four or five feet high. Under favorable circumstances it may become a miniature tree six or eight feet in height, and equal diameter.

THE LAUREL CHERRY-TREES, OR PORTUGAL LAURELS, *Cerasus lusitanica* and *C. laurocerasus,* are half-hardy evergreens, greatly esteemed in the south of Europe and the warmer parts of England. They have been found too tender to thrive in the N. Y. Central Park.

THE CAROLINA BIRD CHERRY-TREE, *C. caroliniana,* is another evergreen shrubby tree, indigenous in the Gulf States and in the West India islands, and one of the most superb ornamental shrubs of those regions, but too tender to thrive in the middle or northern States.

THE GINKGO OR SALISBURIA TREE. *Salisburia adiantifolia.*

A native of Japan, remarkable for uniting in its leaves the peculiarities of the pine family with those of deciduous trees. Its leaves are like a tuft of the needle leaves of the pine, flattened out and united together in a fan-like form. They are small, peculiarly clean, sharp-cut, and of a light clear green color. The bark is whitish and fibry, like the surfaces of old pine shingles. The branches incline upward at an angle of 45° with the trunk, are straight, not very numerous, and the foliage is most abundant near their extremities.

The beauty of the tree can be greatly heightened by occasional cutting back. It is a tree to plant near the house, or a walk, where its singular and pretty leaves can be seen readily. The seed is a nut, which is boiled, and valued for eating. A rich sandy soil, with dry subsoil, suits it best. There are specimens in this country from seventy to eighty feet high. In Japan specimens have been seen grown to the height of eighty to one hundred feet, with trunks from six to twelve feet in diameter. One is mentioned by a traveller the trunk of which measured forty feet in circumference !

THE LARGE-LEAVED SALISBURIA. *S. adiantifolia macrophylla.* —This is a new French variety, which has much larger leaves than the species, and divided in two, three, or five lobes, and these again with undulated edges. Probably well worth the price its novelty will command among tree enthusiasts.

THE VARIEGATED SALISBURIA. *S. a. variegata.*—"This variety differs from the ordinary form by its leaves being variegated and striped with yellow." It is recommended on high English authority as a desirable variety.

THE SCOTCH LARCH. *Larix Europæa.*

A tree which has been almost as much over-valued for ornamental purposes within the past twenty years, as the *Morus multicaulis* was for silk-growing fifteen years before. Downing's warm praise doubtless did much to create a demand for it; and the great facility with which it is grown in nurseries made it profitable for nurserymen to echo its praises. If Downing's careful qualification of its praise could always have accompanied his encomiums on its merits, and been intelligently appreciated, little harm would have been done. He says: "Like all highly expressive and characteristic trees, much more care is necessary in introducing the larch into artificial scenery judiciously, than round-headed trees. If planted in abundance it becomes monotonous from the similitude of its form in different specimens; it should therefore be introduced sparingly, and always for some special purpose. This purpose may be either to give spirit to a group of other trees, to strengthen the already picturesque character of a scene, or to give life and variety to one naturally tame and uninteresting."

Fortunately we have many other trees—evergreens too—which are much better adapted to the uses suggested by Mr. Downing than the larch. The Norway spruce is equally picturesque, and at the same time a more beautiful tree. It carries all its foliage through the winter months, sustaining with its verdure great laminate masses of snow to contrast with the green of its drooping branches, while such meagre foliage as the larch carries through the summer months is lost even before it is touched by autumn frosts and wind, and in winter it stands among its family of pines the one naked branched tree which has been robbed of all its beauty.

When the larch puts forth its leaves in the spring, the exquisite tender green of the foliage is very charming, at a time when the evergreens have scarcely burst their buds, and only the aspen, the white birch, the buckeyes and willows, have become beautiful with verdure; but in another month the Norway spruce surpasses it in every element of beauty and picturesqueness.

THE EUROPEAN WEEPING LARCH, *L. e. pendula*, is a very curious and valuable picturesque small tree. It requires to be grafted at from six to twelve feet from the ground, and when well established it is as odd and graceful in its way as anything we have seen. Sargent mentions that it is both difficult to propagate and to transplant. It is irregularly spreading or flat-headed, rather than conical like its prototype, and addicted to eccentricities of form.

THE SIKKIM LARCH, *L. Griffithiana*, is, we believe, a native of China, and is described by Dr. Hooker as "an inelegant, sprawling branched tree, with the branches standing out awkwardly, and often drooping suddenly." All of which goes to show that it is a tree of very odd habit. If it is also well clothed with leaves, its deformities of branching may be converted into picturesque beauty. In autumn its foliage is said to change to a bright red color. These qualities certainly excite curiosity to know more of this species.

. THE AMERICAN LARCH TAMARAC OR HACMATAC, *L. americana*, grows in swamps in nearly all the northern States, where it is a tall, meagre-foliaged, conical tree. When planted in gardens it looks very much like the Scotch larch, but requires a damper and cooler soil.

THE CATALPA. *Catalpa syringafolia.*

This is a native of our southern States; a tree of extremely rapid growth when young, and noticeable for the great size of its heart-shaped leaves, and their soft yellowish-green color. It forms a spreading, flat-headed tree, of medium size. Fig. 128 is a portrait of a noble specimen growing in the pleasure-ground of Alfred Cope, Esq., on Fisher's Lane, Germantown, Pa. It is fifty feet high, and seventy feet across the spread of its branches. The catalpa usually grows more compactly than this specimen. Its blossoms appear in June and July, and are borne in large loose panicles, projecting from the golden green of the young leaves, and by their size, abundance, and rich color, make a superb display. They are as beautiful when seen singly as they are showy in the mass, and also have an agreeable perfume. Color white, flecked inside with orange and purple.

The young wood, which is of a yellowish color, is strong, smooth, cane-like, and stubby; and the ramification of the branches is irregular, open, and spreading. Though planted largely in the northern States, and considered hardy, its beauty would be more uniform, and we should oftener see fine specimens, if, when first planted, it were regarded as half-hardy, and cared for accordingly. In the first place, it should never be planted in rich soil, because the growth which results is so rank that it is liable to be killed back the following winter. The next season it will send up still ranker suckers from the stump, which, in their effort to make up for lost time, are likely to grow late and be nipped again by the succeeding winter. The young trunk of the tree, by this repeated

FIG. 128.

A CATALPA TREE ON THE GROUNDS OF ALFRED COPE, ESQ., GERMANTOWN, PA.

killing back, becomes crooked, the wood less healthy, and the roots are weakened for the want of a top proportioned to their development. A dry deeply-drained soil is necessary to start the tree healthily ; and we advise always mulching under young trees in the fall, and bandaging the trunks with straw, until the rank growth of their early years is over. When once the tree is well established it does not make the rampant growth that endangers its health and gives it so tropical an air in its nursery state ; and may then be considered hardy and the soil enriched to promote its growth. When healthily grown, and exposed to the sun on all sides, its large leaves, tropical growth, and the warm tone of its foliage, make it one of the finest of middle-sized lawn trees, and one that contrasts well with trees of smaller leaves and darker color.

Some dwarf varieties of the catalpa have been found in Asia, which bid fair to be charming acquisitions to our stock of small trees or shrubs. The following are now growing in this country ·

FIG. 129.

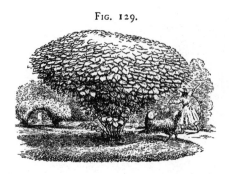

THE INDIAN CATALPA. *C. himalayensis (C. umbraculifera ?).*— Fig. 129 represents a specimen of this species also growing in the grounds of Mr. Alfred Cope, Germantown, Pa. It is seven or eight feet high, and about ten feet broad. ·The crown is like a roof of leaves, laid with the precision of pointed slate, and the play of light on its golden-green head is beautiful. The leaves are about the size of those of the common catalpa. Though formal in its outline, it is at the same time of so unusual a form and style, that its novelty, or oddity, allies it to trees of picturesque expres sion. Judging by this specimen, we would suppose that this vari ety will never be much more than a great shrub, perhaps from ten to twenty feet high. It seems to be hardy in the neighborhood of Philadelphia, and, with thorough protection, will probably succeed as far north as the southern shores of the great lakes. It is well adapted, wherever it proves hardy, to form natural arbors or gate way arches.

THE CATALPA KEMPFERI is similar to the above, except that it has smaller leaves and growth in all respects, and the foliage a little darker. The flowers resemble those of our native catalpa. Mr. Meehan considers it one of the best of trees for the same pur poses suggested in the closing paragraph of the preceding descrip tion. Quite hardy near Philadelphia.

THE CATALPA BANGEI is still more dwarfish, being a shrub, three to five feet high. The flowers are in clusters a foot long. What has been said about protection for our native catalpa at the north, applies with still more force to these imported sorts. We believe that in a deep dry warm soil they will prove hardy in the northern States, *if protected until their roots have had time to become established below the ordinary freezing of the earth.* Yet we would not omit late autumn mulching and some covering for the tops until they are so large that it cannot conveniently be done.

FIG. 130.

THE SASSAFRAS. *Laurus sassafras.*

This is the only quite hardy species of the beautiful laurel family, so highly prized for their abundant glossy foliage in the southern States, (there known as bay trees); and interesting as the only representative in the northern States of the noble laurel or bay, whose leaves have always been symbols of victory, and endless themes for poetical allusions. It is also allied by family ties to those two most aromatic trees, the camphor tree of Japan, and the cinnamon tree of Ceylon, both of which are species of laurel. Though the sassafras grows wild all over the country wherever the soil is rich and warm, in our woods, and by road-sides, it is certainly the most neglected, considering the rare beauty of its foliage, of all our native trees. Its qualities are peculiarly those which adapt it to the embellishment of small pleasure-grounds. The most aromatic tree of the woods, it is also one of the most suggestive, by its umbelliferous form and sunny expression, of the warmth of those southern climates in which the other members of the laurel family flourish. Though it never becomes more than a middle-sized tree, the deep furrows of its warm brown bark, the angular ruggedness of its branches, and the flattened form and horizontal shadows of its head, give it an air of age and dignity unusual in trees of its size; while the pure color, abundance, and fine-cut outline of its leaves, add a refined expression during its period of foliage. The young wood is smooth, and of a beautiful green color. The leaves come late, and drop with the first frosts, but their autumn colors are among the purest, and occasionally the most brilliant: oftenest a bright lemon yellow, but not

Fig. 131.

seldom spangled with red, and sometimes an entire mass of soft crimson. The leaves vary in form on the same tree, as will be seen by the engraving, Fig. 131, some being entire and pointed-elliptical in form, and others three and two-lobed. They are from four to six inches long, of smooth outline, soft texture, and warm green color. The foliage breaks into softly-rounded horizontal layers, drooping on the exterior to catch and reflect the sun, so that they present to the eye broader and warmer masses of light than most trees of similar size. Grown thriftily, in open grounds, the sassafras is one of the most, if not the most, elegant small tree of the north. Fig. 130 gives a tolerable idea of the sassafras as a mature tree, but is less umbrella-formed than the usual type. Figs. 57 and 58, page 260, show some characteristic forms of the sassafras, grown in woods, and in open ground. But no engraving will do justice to the pleasing lights and soft outline of the tree, which carries a sweet smile in the sun that must be observed to be appreciated. It is especially radiant when the setting sun gilds its top. All trees are in fact most beautiful in such a light, but the crown of the sassafras is pre-eminently so.

The tree requires a deep, warm, rich soil, and will do itself no credit in any other. Woodsmen know that soil to be excellent where groves of sassafras abound. In the woods it sometimes reaches an altitude of fifty feet, but in open ground forty feet height and breadth, and two feet diameter of trunk, is about its greatest size. The annual growth after it reaches a height of ten feet is about one foot a year. Its earlier growth is rapid. Cattle and hogs are exceedingly fond of rubbing against the fragrant bark, and young trees must be protected from possible danger from this cause more carefully, and for a longer time than most trees.

The Benzoin Laurel or Benjamin Tree. *Laurus benzoin.* —A deciduous shrub or tree, native of Virginia. Leaves from four to six inches long, like the unlobed leaves of the sassafras. It grows in an exposed location on the brow of a hill in the New York Central Park, and is there ten feet high, with abundant glossy foliage. It will become a tree from fifteen to twenty feet high. One of the finest large shrubs in the Park.

Loudon says of it: " In British gardens it forms rather a tender peat-earth shrub, handsome from its large leaves, but seldom thriving, except where the soil is kept moist, and the situation sheltered." It may not be safe to recommend it for trial in the northern States to any but very careful cultivators, notwithstanding its success in the Central Park.

THE PAULOWNIA. *Paulownia imperialis.*

A Japanese tree introduced into France in 1837, and into this country about ten years later. The enormous size of its leaves, which sometimes measure nearly two feet in length and eighteen inches in diameter, and its rank growth, occasionally making canes from eight to twelve feet long in a single season, were qualities so

Fig. 132.

striking that the tree became famous and in great demand immediately after its introduction. A large proportion, however, of those
which have been planted north of New York during the last twenty
years are either dead, or annually shortened back by our severe
winters, presenting the appearance of decrepit or damaged trees. A
few good specimens have survived, proving the possibility of acclimating the tree in the northern States. Fine specimens may be seen
in the New York Central Park, where, with the excellent judgment
characteristic of the management of that ground, these trees seem
to have had no check in their healthy growth, and they stand in the
most open and exposed localities. The early growth of the tree is
very much like that of the catalpa and ailantus, and if planted in
rich soils the leaves and canes are immense. All such growth
should be carefully guarded against by planting the tree in a poor,
well-drained soil. An excessively rank development during the
first years after planting will generally prove the death-warrant of
the tree in all the northern States, while if a moderate growth can
be obtained, and the top and roots be protected for a number of

years in winter, until the roots permeate largely below the reach of frost, there is little doubt that paulownias of noble size may be grown as far north as around the shores of Lake Erie. Yet we would not omit mulching at any age of the tree.

The form of the paulownia is squarish-oblate. Fig. 132 represents a specimen growing in Mount Moriah Cemetery, near Philadelphia, and is a good illustration of the usual character of the tree. The sketch was made in September, at which time the upright spikes of seed-vessels on the tree were conspicuous and ornamental. The trunk of this specimen is sixteen inches in diameter, its height thirty feet, and the branches cover a space fifty feet in diameter. There is a much larger but less perfect specimen in the home-grounds of S. B. Parsons, Esq., at Flushing, L. I.; and perhaps still finer ones elsewhere which we have not seen. The branches of the paulownia are few in number, long and strong, diverge right-angularly, are disposed to spread laterally, and invariably turn upwards at their extremities. The bark is rather smooth on young trees, dark colored, and furrows with age. The leaves are pointed heart-shaped, a very dark green color, without gloss, and, on old trees, from ten to fifteen inches in length. They appear late in the spring, but retain themselves well upon the tree until hard frosts. The blossoms are formed in large upright panicles on the extremities of the shoots, are silghtly fragrant, and appear early in May. They are trumpet-shaped, and of a purplish color.

THE MULBERRY. *Morus.*

The mulberry is one of those species of trees with rapid succulent growth, and large leaves, which are apt to become spasmodically popular, from the readiness with which these qualities are appreciated; and then to "fall from grace" with a reaction against them disproportioned to their faults. The speculative rage for the *Morus multicaulis*, a variety of the white mulberry, which became one of the wildest manias on record nearly forty years ago, is now almost forgotten; and forms one of the curious facts in the history of speculations associated with the great South Sea scheme, the tulip mania, and numerous later instances to show the lengths to which enthusiasm may carry a whole community when united in pursuit of a supposed quick means of realizing large profits. The silk of all the world is made from the leaves of the mulberry. The *Morus multicaulis*, it was claimed, was the best variety to feed to silk-worms. It was zealously inculcated that silk-worms, and silk, could be produced with great profit in this country. As food for the worm must be grown before the silk could be made, it followed that those who would profit by the production of silk at home must hasten to provide themselves with plants of the *Morus multicaulis!* The result was one of the most amusing and profitless speculations of this century. It is hoped, however, now that the national enter-prise has stretched an iron band across the continent, and put us into close connection with Japan and China, that we will profit by the more patient skill, and the long experience of their people, and induce them to develop on our soil this profitable branch of in-dustry, unrepelled by social or race prejudices, or the spirit of caste which is apt to be arrayed against them.

One characteristic of the mulberry tree is a profusion of foliage, which, being borne on broad low-branching trees, makes a deep shade. It bears a sweet berry-like fruit from three-fourths of an inch to an inch and a half in length, and of the diameter of the common long blackberry, which it resembles in appearance. The fruit of some varieties is delicious. When ripe it is apt to strew the ground below the tree, and form a great attraction for bees and flies. This fact, together with another, that the leaves are favorite food for other worms besides the exotic silkworm, has prevented the best species of mulberry from attaining that popularity for or-namental planting, which their quick growth, domestic character, deep verdure, and dense shade would naturally give them. They are truly fruit-trees, and very beautiful ones. It is surprising how rarely their fruit is offered in our markets, some of the sorts being superior in flavor to the blackberry, and ripening with it, and during a period of a month or more after blackberries are gone. The tree is long-lived, and we have no doubt will yet make pro-fitable orchards in some parts of the country. Poultry are par-ticularly fond of the berries, and in the back court-yards of old

French chateaux the black mulberry was always planted for their benefit. The leaves are particularly agreeable to cattle, as well as to silkworms.

The species of mulberry are not numerous, but the varieties are almost innumerable, though their differences are of little consequence in decorative planting.

THE AMERICAN RED MUL-BERRY TREE, *Morus rubra,* is sometimes called the Pennsylvania mulberry. This is quite the largest and finest ornamental tree of the genus. In the forest it sometimes grows to seventy feet in height, but in open ground assumes a low-spreading form of umbelliferous character, as indicated by

FIG. 133.

Fig. 133, which is a portrait of a good specimen at twenty-five or thirty years of age. The leaves are quite large, nearly equal to those of the catalpa, generally heart-shaped, but often with two or three lobes, as shown by Fig. 134, of a dark-green color, thick texture, and rough surface. The fruit is

FIG. 134.

deep red, oblong, and of good flavor. The trunk of the tree has deeply-furrowed bark, with a tinge of green in its color, and the main branches have a rugged ramification like those of the oak. The leaves make their appearance late in the spring, but, like those of the horse-chestnut, develop with great luxuriance as soon as they burst the bud, and then remain on the tree till killed by hard frosts. They are not considered of any value for the silkworm.

As an ornamental tree this mulberry is one of the most domestic in expression, luxuriant in foliage, and noble in the distribution of its lights and shadows among our medium-sized trees. That it is a fruit-bearing tree is something against its tidiness, but its fruit will assuredly pay for the extra care required to keep the ground or lawn under it in cleanly condition. It does best in a

27

strong soil, and somewhat sheltered location, though it may be considered hardy in most parts of the northern States. Though not truly within the scope of this work, we feel it a duty to call attention to a fact which is not well known in many parts of the country, viz: that the wood of this species is almost as durable as that of the black or yellow locust. Its growth is rapid.

THE WHITE MULBERRY. *Morus alba.*—The varieties of this species are very numerous, and their leaves form the staple food for the silkworm, the *Morus multicaulis* being one of them. Their fruit is red and black, as well as white, although the species is characterized as white-fruited. The leaves resemble those of the red mulberry in form (see Fig. 134), but are smaller, more pointed, and less often lobed, though very variable in this respect, lighter-colored, and more glossy. The tree is of a more shrubby character, of slenderer though rapid growth, and should be allowed to branch low; otherwise its tendency to suckers will be increased. Loudon mentions that it is not able to endure great extremes of heat or cold. There are specimens of the white mulberry in the New York Central Park, with luxuriant and glossy leaves, among the most beautiful to be seen there.

The *Morus multicaulis* has larger and thinner leaves than the parent species, and black fruit. It is also more tender, and forms rather a luxuriant bush than a tree.

THE DANDELO MULBERRY, *M. morettiana*, is another variety, the leaves of which are held in great esteem in France as food for silkworms, and the silk made from it is said to exceed any other in fineness and glossiness. The leaf itself is very beautiful, being thin, large, perfectly flat, deep green, and glossy on both surfaces. Less hardy than the preceding.

There are scores of other varieties, but none that are at the same time hardy and peculiar enough to be interesting. All the white mulberry trees do best in a dry, sandy, or gravelly soil, and a protected situation, and grow occasionally to considerable size; from thirty to forty-five feet in height and about equal breadth.

DOWNING'S EVER-BEARING MULBERRY should, perhaps, be classed as a variety of the *M. alba.* It is a fine rapid-growing tree, and bears delicious fruit from the middle of July till autumn. It is not perfectly hardy in a colder climate than that of New York City, though planted with more or less success all over the northern States. It becomes a beautiful tree where not killed back in winter.

THE BLACK MULBERRY. *Morus nigra.*—This is supposed to be a native of Asia, but has been so long known in Europe as to be thought by some indigenous there. It is a low rugged-branched tree, with yellowish-brown bark, broad heart-shaped leaves, unequally serrated, and very rough. The fruit is large, dark purple, and excellent. The tree is a slow grower, and forms a broad low head. Pliny makes the following curious allusion to this tree : "Of all the cultivated trees, the mulberry is the last that buds, which it never does till the cold weather is past; and it is therefore called the wisest of trees. But, when it begins to put forth buds, it despatches the business in one night, and that with so much force that their breaking forth may be evidently heard." Loudon says that in England the fruit is generally eaten at the dessert; and it is considered of a cooling aperient nature ; that it forms an agreeable sweetmeat, and that, mixed with fresh cider, it makes a strong and agreeable wine. Where fine fruit is an object, it derives the same benefit from culture and manuring as the apple. It is a tree of great durability, but the slowest grower of the mulberries. In time, however, it attains a great breadth ; the finest specimens in England being from thirty to forty feet high, with tops varying from forty to seventy feet in breadth.

THE PAPER MULBERRY. *Broussonetia.*—A rapid-growing small tree from China and Japan, which was formerly much planted in the middle States for avenues ; but its popularity seems to have waned with its novelty. It is certainly an interesting small tree. Few trees develop their beauties more quickly, yet it is not quite hardy, and is addicted to throwing up suckers. Though not a true mulberry, it is always associated with them from its great resemblance to the *Morus* family. The leaves assume a great variety of forms, being heart-shaped, two-lobed, and

FIG. 135.

three-lobed, all on the same stem, as shown by Fig. 135. They are smaller than those of the true mulberry, of a bluish-green color, and somewhat downy or hoary on the surface. The tree quickly forms a neat umbrella-shaped top, from twelve to twenty feet high, and grows in the neighborhood of Philadelphia to the height of forty to fifty feet. From the rapidity of its growth it is adapted to make verdant masses for screens, and has been used with good effect for this purpose in the New York Central Park, where it seems to be hardy.

Fig. 136.

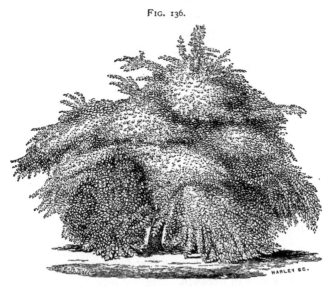

AN OSAGE ORANGE IN THE OLD BARTRAM GARDEN.

THE OSAGE ORANGE. *Maclura.*

This tree, much used of late years for farm and garden hedges, when grown singly, is one of the most remarkable of small trees. Its glossy orange-like foliage is so brilliant, and its erratic luxuriance of growth so extraordinary, that it is difficult to realize that plants of the same tree can be confined within the formal limits of a narrow hedge.

The Osage orange is a native of Missouri and Arkansas, and it is fair to infer that the latitude of those States furnish a climate the most congenial to it. It there becomes a tree from thirty to sixty feet in height and of equal breadth. Hedges formed with it have proved hardy as far north as Albany—perhaps further north. It may prove less hardy as a tree than in clipped hedges, but on the banks of the Hudson, near Albany, it is little injured by the winters, and does equally well on the south shores of the great lakes.

The growth of an Osage orange tree, in a deep rich soil, is quite peculiar. It first sends out a multitude of shoots vertically, horizontally, and at all angles and curves between. Its inherent vitality is so great that it seems scarcely to have room enough upon each preceding year's growth to push out the new growth that struggles to expand its foliage. As the plant attains the dignity of a tree-form, or at least of a distinct trunk, its different parts seem to have various impulses; one branch having shoots nearly all tending upwards, another with shoots crossing each other, with a variety of curves reminding one of the intersections of fireworks projectiles, and another with its rank-growths all tending downward as humbly as those of the Scamston elm.

Fig. 136 is a portrait of a magnificent specimen crowded in an obscure corner of the old Bartram garden on the Schuylkill River, south of Philadelphia. It is about thirty feet high, and from fifty to sixty feet across the spread of its branches, with a trunk twenty inches in diameter one foot from the ground. H. W. Sargent, Esq., mentions a tree growing in the grounds of Dr. Edmondston, near Baltimore, which, when twenty-four years old, measured one hundred and sixty-five feet in circumference—"the limbs lying about with a profusion of growth positively wonderful, and covered with fruit."

The leaves are single, alternate, in form something like those of the lilac, but considerably more pointed and more glossy. They are tardy in the spring, but remain late on the trees in autumn. The flowers are inconspicuous. The fruit is about the size and color of a large ripe orange, perhaps less bright, very showy on the tree, but of no use for eating. Ripe in October.

As the male and female blossoms are borne on different trees, no fruit will be produced except on the trees with pistillate blos-

soms in the neighborhood of staminate trees.   But the beauty of
the tree itself is sufficient, though it have neither flowers nor fruit.
The short strong thorns which make a part of its value as a hedge
plant, are not liable to drop off like those of the honey locust,
until they are blunted by age, and then, from their small size, drop
into the lawn where they are harmless.

It is recommended, when the tree is young, to cut back its
leading shoots one-third or one-half for several years, to prevent
the head from sprawling to one side or the other before the roots
and trunk have sufficient strength to maintain a vertical position.

In a deep, good soil, the Osage orange will become a spreading
tree about twenty-five feet high, and thirty feet broad, in ten years
after planting.

Nurserymen dislike to grow the Osage orange except for hedge
plants, because, after the plants have made one year's growth, their
vigor is so rampant that they become unmanageable in nursery
rows.   Purchasers must therefore buy hedge-plants to set out for
trees ; and their growth will be all the better for the necessity of
choosing small plants.

THE JAPAN OSAGE ORANGE.   *Maclura tricuspidata.*—A new
orange of the *Maclura* family has recently been introduced from
France, which is described as a shrubby bush, very branchy and
thorny, with shining, leathery, three-lobed leaves.

THE KOLREUTERIA.   *Kolreuteria paniculata.*

This is a hardy tree, native of the north of China, introduced
into England in 1763, long cultivated in the United States, and
yet but little known.   It forms a low, umbelliferous head.   The
leaves are pinnate, composed of from five to eleven leaflets of small
size and oak-like shape.   The foliage grows mostly on the outer
ends of the branches, so that the tree when full grown is quite bare
of leaves on the inside, but a thick mass of feathery and very warm-
toned foliage on the crown.   The flowers are yellow, very showy
being borne in long terminal panicles in July.   The leaves turn to

a deep yellow before they fall. The seed is contained in greenish white capsules, and quite showy by its abundance. At Germantown, near Philadelphia, are specimens twenty-five feet high and forty feet diameter of head, which have been planted thirty years.

We know of no tree which, without being variegated, has such decidedly yellowish-green foliage; and this quality, together with the airy delicacy of its leafy outline, its brilliant flowers, and autumn color, combine to make it one of the most desirable trees for even a small collection; and especially beautiful where its low golden top can be seen projecting from a mass of dark-foliaged trees. It becomes quite hardy, though the tops of its branches may be killed back in winter in our northern States when first planted. With protection a few years after planting it will establish itself beyond the need of more. When young its growth does not indicate the form it finally assumes, and is not so pleasing as at maturity.

THE NETTLE TREE. *Celtis.*

"Handsome, much branched, deciduous trees, natives of Europe and North America, varying in size and foliage, but all bearing fruit which is edible, and though small, is remarkably sweet, and said to be very wholesome. Some of the species are very ornamental, particularly *C. crassifolia*, the branches of which assume the character of a fan ; and *C. occidentalis*, the branches of which droop like a parasol. The leaves of almost all the species drop off almost simultaneously, and thus occasion very little trouble to the gardener in sweeping them up." They are also remarkably free from the attacks of insects.

THE WESTERN NETTLE TREE, *C. occidentalis*, is known in some sections as the sugar-berry, and is indigenous from Canada to North Carolina. The branches are numerous and slender, radiating at no great distance from the ground in a horizontal direction, and incline downwards at their extremities. Leaves about the size and form of those of the apple tree, but more pointed and lighter colored; being a bright shining green. They hang late on the tree, turning to a bright yellow, and then drop simultaneously. Fruit small, oval, purplish, ripe in October. Height in the woods thirty to fifty feet, in open ground about the size of the apple tree.

THE THICK-LEAVED CELTIS OR HACKBERRY. *C. crassifolia.*— Michaux mentions this as " one of the finest trees which compose the dusky forests of the Ohio," where it sometimes attains the height of eighty feet, with a very small trunk in proportion to its height. Bark reddish-brown. Young branches downy. It is not frequently found in either the northern or southern States, but principally on the valleys of rivers in the middle States. The leaves are six inches long, three or four inches broad, oval-acuminate, serrated thick, and rough. Flowers small, white, in May. Fruit the size of a large cherry-stone, purple or black, ripe in Octo ber. There is a specimen of this species near the West-town board ing school, Westchester, Pa., with almost the size and grandeur of a full grown spreading white oak.

THE PERSIMMON. *Dyospyrus virginiana.*

The persimmon, or Virginia date plum, is a medium-sized open-headed tree, with foliage of unusual beauty. The leaves are single, alternate, from four to six inches long, smooth-edged, polished as those of the orange, and much larger. The fruit is the size of a crab-apple, red, and noted for its bitterness when immature. The tree is rarely found north of the latitude of New York, and cannot be considered quite hardy north of Philadelphia. The greatest beauty of its foliage develops still farther south.

THE EUROPEAN DATE PLUM, *Dyospyrus lotis,* is a beautiful tree common in the south of Europe, but quite tender.

THE ALDER. *Alnus.*

Most of the species grow in wet places. Downing does not con· sider our native alders worthy of much attention. Sargent, however, says of the common swamp alder, *Alnus glauca:* "We hardly know a more charming plant in winter, when covered with its bright scarlet berries, especially when placed against hemlocks or other evergreens." Loudon says of it: "This is one of the most beautiful trees of the genus." From these differences of opinion, among persons of such eminent taste, may we not infer that, though beautiful, as Mr. Sargent claims, in winter, its beauty at other seasons is not sufficient to give it marked value compared with other trees of similar size and better qualities? We have seen them principally as bushes growing in swampy places by the road-side, where they form dense globular shrubs, with glossy foliage, somewhat sombre. Most of the alders are addicted to damp ground.

The foreign species are held in higher esteem than our own. The following are the most esteemed varieties:

THE COMMON ENGLISH ALDER, *A. glutinoso*, has many varieties.

FIG. 137.

THE CUT-LEAVED ALDER, *A. laciniata* is one of the finest. Fig. 137 is a portrait of a fine English specimen. It becomes a spreading pyramidal tree from fifty to sixty feet high. The foliage is fern-like.

THE IMPERIAL CUT-LEAVED ALDER, *A. laciniata*, is another variety, said to be of still more vigorous habit.

THE GOLDEN ALDER, *A. glutinoso aurea*, is a sport of the common alder, of brilliant and singular foliage, and highly recommended in England and France.

THE HEART-LEAVED ALDER, *A. cordifolia*, Sargent alludes to as "a large tree, native of Calabria, with large, deep-green, shining leaves, rather broad, heart-shaped," which grows rapidly, and which he has found hardy at Fishkill, on the Hudson. Loudon says of it: "A large, handsome, round-headed tree. Height from fifteen to twenty feet. It grows with rapidity in a dry soil, and is one of the most interesting ornamental trees that have of late years been introduced." By *large* Loudon evidently means large among alders, as the dimensions given rank it with the smallest class of trees.

Gilpin, whose works on landscape gardening are of high authority in England, considers the alder among the most picturesque of aquatic trees.; while Loudon, in general remarks on this family, says : " As an ornamental tree, much cannot be said in favor of the alder."

THE APPLE TREE. *Pyrus malus.*

FIG. 138.

For its beauty alone we here treat of the apple tree—one of those admirable families of trees whose members are not less beautiful because they feed our stomachs as well as please the eye. We are apt to forget how often Nature bounteously covers with beauty the productions which minister most to our necessities. The bread-fruit, the palm, the banana, and the cocoa of the tropics, all bear witness to the unity of the greatest beauty and the greatest utility ; while the nut-trees, and the fruit-trees of the north, with their fine foliage, fragrant blossoms, and savory fruit, teach the same lesson in our temperate zone. We have seen the *Magnolia soulangeana*, with its immense blossoms, and the finest horse-chestnuts, like bountiful mountains of bouquets, blooming at the same time, and near old apple trees ; and gazing on all their florescent splendor, have doubted which, *if all of them were equally novelties*, would be awarded the palm for the greatest beauty of bloom. The flowers of the magnolia and the horse-chestnut are more showy ; but how inferior in delicacy and fragrance ! Each twig of the apple tree, with its clusters of buds and blossoms, bedded in nests of bright opening leaves, is, in itself, an exquisite wild bouquet.

The apple tree comes early into leaf, and its foliage is dark, glossy, and abundant. Its low, spreading form has a *home* expression ; and, for a tree of no great size, there is something grand in the wide extension of the branches of old trees, casting shadows sometimes from forty to sixty feet in diameter ; and we have seen

sound trunks three feet in diameter. Fig. 139 is a portrait of a
remarkable apple tree growing in a
low pasture-field on the flats of
Mamaroneck, N. Y., but little· above
the level of high tide. Its top is
sixty feet in diameter, and thirty feet
high. The vignettes of Chapters VIII
and XVI, and the cut at the end of

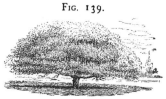

FIG. 139.

Chapter II, illustrate some of the home-pictures to which apple
trees contribute a principal charm.

In its early growth the apple tree has only the beauty of thrift
and blossoms. It is then too round and even, in the ramification
of its branches, to have much play of light and shade in the breaks
of its foliage. Only the old trees develop noble horizontal branches
and massive shadows ; and it is for such that we ask the most loving protection. From the time the tree is out of bloom till the
fruit begins to color, it is certainly inferior to some of the maples, the
horse-chestnut, the hickories, and many other trees, in wealth of
verdure, variety of outline, and contrast of light and shade. But
then what a crown it bears a few months later, of golden or ruddy
fruit, beautiful as blossoms ! The apple tree need never be dis-
carded from the decorated grounds of any one who will keep his
lawn closely shaven, and clean of falling fruit. Without such care
the wind-falls and worm-falls of fruit will soon breed corruption in
the grass, and new crops of insects to attack the fruit the following
season. The beauty and usefulness of a thrifty old tree is well
worth this care.

Notwithstanding we place so high a value on *old* apple trees for
home-grounds, we would not, on quite small grounds, plant them
for ornament ; since it is only after the tree has been growing from
twenty to forty years that it assumes its most pleasing expression.
Other trees will develop beauty much more rapidly. For fruit, except on large lots, the cherry, the pear, the grape, and the different
berry shrubs yield far more value, in proportion to the room they
occupy. Apples are always cheaper to buy than the smaller fruits,
and the trees take up so much room, that we would only plant
them on lots where the ground devoted to orchard is a half acre or

more. But where full grown trees are already on the ground they should be treated like "company," whether they stand in the front, flank, or rear, of the house, or the house-site.

Most of the apples noted for their excellence are borne on trees that are handsome to the eye, so that in naming a small list for places where there is room·for them, the character of the fruit, and its successive maturity, is alone considered. The following is a list of twelve summer and autumn sorts. Yellow Harvest, Sweet Bough, Early Joe, Red Astrachan (for its beauty and for cooking), Gravenstein, American Summer Pearmain, Summer Queen, Autumn Bough, Porter, Jersey Sweeting, Maiden's Blush, Fall Pippin.

Those who have space to plant orchards for winter apples, will find works on orchard fruits, adapted to their wants.

THE CRAB-APPLE. *Pyrus malus acerba.*—All the crab-apples are noted for the beauty and the exquisite fragrance of their blossoms, which exceed in size those of the

FIG. 140.

common apple tree. Their forms are similar, but smaller and lower, being from twelve to sixteen feet in height, and somewhat greater breadth at maturity. The young wood of the wild European and American varieties is thorny, crooked, and hard, so that the tree can be used for hedges. Growing in a rich soil, and preserved from the attacks of the borer, the crab-apple tree becomes a massy-foliaged low tree, whose lower boughs nearly rest on the ground at their extremities.

THE AMERICAN OR SWEET-SCENTED CRAB, *P. m. coronaria,* is a finer variety than the wildings of Europe, having more fragrant blossoms, which cover the tree in May. The foliage is said also to remain on the tree longer. The fruit is round, about an inch in diameter, a pure green color, and of a pungent acidity that has made the phrase "as sour as a crab" a by-word in the language. The leaves when touched by the frost have an odor of violets. Its bark is rough and scaly.

THE SIBERIAN CRAB, *P. m. prunifolia,* has smoother, lighter-colored twigs and bark than our wilding, a more graceful growth, and less abundant and less fragrant bloom ; but its clusters of small yellow fruit add greatly to the beauty of the tree in September. There is a variety with pink-colored fruit.

THE CHINESE DOUBLE-FLOWERING CRAB, *P. spectabilis,* is the finest of all the crab-trees for ornamental planting. Its blossoms are semi-double, very large, nearly two inches in diameter, of a rose-color when expanded, but a beautiful deep red in the bud. The fruit is yellow, when ripe, and the size of a cherry. The tree attains a larger size than most of the crab-apple trees. It is an upright grower, when young, but with age its branches spread and bend until it becomes a graceful drooping-boughed tree. Height and breadth of top from twenty to thirty feet.

THE PEAR TREE. *Pyrus.*

"Ye have no history. I ask in vain
Who planted on the slope this lofty group
Of ancient pear trees, that with springtime burst
Into such breadth of bloom. One bears a scar
Where the quick lightning scored its trunk, yet still
It feels the breath of spring, and every May
Is white with blossoms. Who it was that laid
Their infant roots in earth, and tenderly
Cherished the delicate sprays, I ask in vain,
Yet bless the unknown hand to which I owe
This annual festival of bees, these songs
Of birds within their leafy screens, these shouts
Of joy from children gathering up the fruit
Shaken in August from the willing boughs."

BRYANT.

The pear is so elegant a tree, that, even if it bore no fruit, it would rank high for decorative planting. The lovely green of its bursting leaves, which are among the earliest to expand, must be familiar to all who have ever observed trees ; while its floods of clustered white blossoms make it like a snowy pyramid. Later in the season its glossy foliage is surpassed by very few forest trees ;

while its fruit is one of the most luscious of our zone. Most varieties of pears assume a distinctly pyramidal form, with an irregular and rather hedge-like ramification of branches and spurs as the trees grow old. Without its leaves it is a rough and rather unpleasing tree. In size it is of the second or third class, frequently attaining a height of forty to fifty feet, and a diameter of head of thirty feet. Its flowers are pure white, in clusters, fragrant, and cover the tree profusely in April or May. Unlike the peach tree, the pear tree if not grown too luxuriantly when quite young is a hardy and long-lived tree. If planters would wait till their trees are in full bearing before manuring or otherwise forcing a strong growth of wood, few pear trees would die young. Old trees generally get too few, and young trees too many of such favors. It grows well in any soil which is warm and well drained, but needs to be grown in cultivated ground, otherwise the tree soon assumes a stunted and mossy appearance and the fruit will be quite inferior.

For garden culture pears have been much grown on quince roots, which make dwarf trees. Some varieties bear more and better fruit when thus dwarfed. These dwarf pear trees are exceedingly interesting in every stage of their growth, and both for their beauty and their quick fruiting, merit some of the popularity they have attained. Still, we would recommend planters not to rely on their dwarf, but rather on their standard trees for a permanent supply of pears. The former should be regarded more as temporary investments, or perhaps as garden pets, the beauty of whose growth and early productiveness will serve to make us forget to be impatient of the later productiveness of the standards. But the latter are by far the most profitable in the end, and many of the very best varieties bear almost as quickly on their own roots as upon quince roots.

The Louise Bonne de Jersey, Duchesse d'Angouleme, White Doyenne or Virgalieu, Vicar of Wakefield, and Pound pear (for baking), are varieties desirable to grow on quince. The following is a good list of ten summer and autumn sorts on their own stocks for permanent trees, with the proportional number of each, recommended for a collection of twenty trees, viz.: one Madelaine, one Bloodgood, one Rostiezer, one Dearborn's seedling, four Bartletts, one Flemish beauty, one Beurre Bosc, four Seckels, one Virgalieu, one Sheldon, one Beurre Diel, one Dix, one Lawrence, and two Pound pears for cooking. For a collection of ten standards we would name one Madelaine, one Bloodgood, one Dearborn's seedling, four Bartletts, one Flemish beauty, two Seckels. The variety of fine autumn pears is however so large, that with the exception of the Bartletts and Seckels which are indispensable in the proportions named, numerous other varieties of equal value may be substituted.

THE MOUNTAIN ASH. *Pyrus sorbus.*

The European Mountain Ash, *P. aucuparia,* and the American, *P. americana,* are both among the most common of small ornamental trees, planted principally for the beauty in autumn of their large drooping clusters of bright red fruit, which remain a long time on the tree, and produce a brilliant effect. The foliage is composed of pinnate leaves, forming a delicate spray, but of dull color, and not disposed to form pleasing masses of light and shade. The tree is compactly ovate when young, but becomes round-headed with age. The European variety has the brighter-colored fruit, and is rather more desirable. They become trees from thirty to forty feet high, and nearly equal diameter. The following are interesting varieties:

The Weeping Mountain Ash, *P. pendula,* is a variety of the *P. aucuparia,* of rapid growth, and decidedly pendulous or trailing habit. The flowers, leaves, and fruit, are like the preceding. It is apt to be bald on the crown, showing too plainly the bent framework of its branches; but in other respects is a desirable lawn tree. It is grafted high on some of the upright varieties.

The Oak-leaved Mountain Ash, *P. pinnatifida,* is quite distinct from the *aucuparia* in its general appearance, and in the character of its leaves, though it assumes nearly the same outline. The leaves are simple, instead of compound, and deeply-lobed; a bright pure green on the upper surface, and quite downy beneath. At a little distance its solid mass of foliage gives the impression of a maple rather than a mountain ash. It is in full leaf as early as the horse-chestnut, and holds its leaves and color late.   In bloom and fruit it closely resembles the preceding varieties of the mountain ash, but in the color of its foliage, and the breaks of light and shadow on its surface, it is a much finer tree.   Height and breadth from twenty to thirty feet.   There is a weeping variety of this species, which we have not seen, but which is reputed to be interesting ; also a large-leaved variety.

THE DWARF-PROFUSE-FLOWERING MOUNTAIN ASH, *P. nana floribunda*, is a variety of the oak-leaved mountain ash, but the leaves have returned to the primal form of the species, being compound, quite delicate, and acacia-like.   It is grafted on other stocks from four to six feet high.   The blossoms, in small and abundant white clusters, appear in May.   In blossom, foliage, and bright-red fruit, it is equally pretty.

There are many other varieties named in nursery catalogues, but the above are the most noteworthy.

FIG. 141.

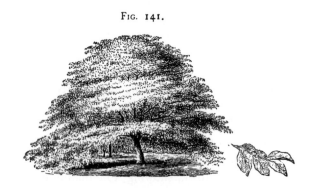

THE DOGWOOD.   *Cornus.*

The dogwood family are numerous and vary widely from each other in their characteristics.   They form low suckering shrubs and whip-plants on the borders of streams and in wet ground, and in other places low trees, most of which are indigenous from Canada to the Gulf of Mexico.   The most common, and the most showy in blossom, if not in leaf, is the following :

THE WHITE-FLOWERING DOGWOOD, *Cornus florida.* Fig. 141 is a portrait of a remarkably fine specimen, on the grounds of E. B. Gardett, Esq., of Germantown, Pa. It is about sixteen feet in height, thirty feet across the longest spread of its branches, and ten inches in diameter of trunk. In the woods it often reaches the height of twenty to thirty feet, and is generally found wild on or near the banks of streams. It is remarkable for the size and showiness of its white blossoms, which make their appearance in April, before the leaves, and cover the tree like immense snow-flakes. They are from two to three inches in diameter. The leaves are in opposite pairs, and vary in color on different trees and localities from a light grayish-green to dark-green, those which are light-colored being rougher in surface; glossiness being usually associated with the darker color. The prevailing tone, however, is a light green early in the season, becoming somewhat darker and more glossy at the close. The tree is too common to be fully appreciated. Those who have been familiar with it only in the woods, can form but a poor idea of its beauty when grown in rich deep soils and open exposures. In such places it assumes an umbrella form, and is not only superb in its April crown of white blossoms, and its massy head of summer leaves, but in autumn, its foliage turning to a deep red, makes the tree a brilliant companion of the varied-hued maples, the golden sassafras, the scarlet oak, and the glowing bronze of the liquidamber. Besides being of an umbrella form in outline, this dogwood is peculiar in the sharp stratification of the lights and shadows of its foliage. The fruit is scarlet, but quite small.

We advise planters who intend to give this tree an open place on the lawn, to obtain their trees of *small size* from a good nursery instead of taking trees from the woods, as the latter rarely grow well, or become so well-formed trees. To develop the great beauty of the dogwood it is absolutely necessary that the soil be well drained, deep, cool, and rich.

Nurserymen in obtaining seed of this variety to propagate, should endeavor to take it only from those trees which are observable for the purity and abundance of their summer foliage, and its brilliancy in autumn. It is a tendency of most gay autumn-tinted

28

trees to lose their brightness under high culture and rapid growth, and it is therefore necessary to guard against this tendency by horticultural discrimination.

THE MALE DOGWOOD OR CORNELIAN CHERRY. *Cornus mas.*— This tree, though a native of Europe, closely resembles the *Cornus florida*, except in its flowers and fruit, and that it forms a still smaller tree. The flowers are insignificant, and appear in March or April. The beautiful cornelian-colored fruit, the size of a small acorn, is one of the attractions of the tree. This is ripe from September to November, and hangs long on the branches. The tree is long-lived and improves with age.

THE WHITE-FRUITED OR RED-TWIGGED DOGWOOD, *C. alba*, of Loudon, *C. stolonifera* of Michaux and Central Park. Accustomed from childhood to see this dogwood in the copses of wet alluvial soils, and to associate its brilliant-colored sprouts principally with the whips used in school chastisements, it has surprised us to see how beautiful a shrub it makes in rich open ground. There are few more pleasing shrubs in the Central Park, where it forms broadly-spreading bushes from six to ten feet high. The leaves are of a glossy green, thin, four to six inches long, and superior in brightness of tone to any of the dogwoods. They turn to yellow and red in autumn. The flowers are white, small, in large clusters, and appear from May to July. The fruit is white, and ripe in September. The young wood is of a brilliant light red, with a slight bloom upon it. This feature makes it a pretty winter shrub, where its wood can be seen against the snow. This is the shrub often sold at the nurseries as *Cornus sanguinea*—a very appropriate title, but one which had been given by botanists to a longer known European variety, on account of the deep red of its decaying leaves.

THE SILKY DOGWOOD, *Cornus sericea* of Loudon, *C. lanuginoso* of Michaux. A spreading shrub of large size, resembling the *Cornus florida* in its foliage, but less tree-like in form. Flowers white, in June and July. Fruit bright blue, ripe in October. Leaves in autumn a rusty brown, sometimes crimson; petioles a bright pink.

Naked young wood brown and green. Size, ten to fifteen feet in height, and greater diameter.

THE PANICLED-FLOWERED DOGWOOD, *C. paniculata*, is a tree or shrub of more upright growth, with a profusion of white flowers in July and August, and purplish young wood. Height, fifteen to twenty feet. On account of its compactness it is considered one of the best for small grounds.

THE ROUND-LEAVED DOGWOOD. *Cornus cercinata.*—A species noted for its large circular wavy leaves, which are downy on the under side, and for its rough warted branches. Flowers small, white, in June and July. Fruit white when ripe, in October. Young wood slightly tinged with red. Height five to ten feet.

THE VARIEGATED-LEAVED DOGWOOD, *Cornus mascula variegata*, is a pretty variation, with leaves striped or blotched with white, interesting to persons who fancy trees which sport in this manner, and considered one of the most desirable variegated-leaved shrubs in cultivation.

THE SIBERIAN GOLDEN VARIEGATED-LEAVED DOGWOOD, *C. aurea variegata*, has a yellow stripe on its leaves, and bark striped with red and yellow. The latter is quite curious.

All the foregoing varieties have their leaves in opposite pairs. The following has alternate leaves:

THE ALTERNATE-LEAVED DOGWOOD. *Cornus alternifolia.*—We are not familiar with this variety in cultivation. Loudon thus speaks of it: "This species is easily known from every other, even at a distance, by the horizontal, umbelliferous character assumed by the branches, which are dichotomous, with clusters of leaves at the joints, and the general color is a lively green. The leaves are generally alternate, but not unfrequently opposite. Flowers white, May to July. Fruit purple, ripe in October. Decaying leaves reddish-yellow. Naked young wood greenish or reddish brown." It seems doubtful if Loudon were familiar with the horizontally umbelliferous character of our *Cornus florida*, or he would not have thought of making this trait a distinguishing one of the *Cornus alternifolia ;* it is a characteristic of all the arboreous dogwoods.

THE JUDAS, OR RED-BUD TREE.   *Cercis canadensis.*

FIG. 142.

A beautiful little tree, native of our forests in most parts of the country. When grown in open ground, its head spreads broad and low in parasol form. It is covered the last of April, or early in May, before the leaves expand, with a profusion of very small pink blossoms, that are showy by their abundance, and have given the tree the name of red-bud, by which, when growing wild, it is usually known. When grown with full exposure to the sun, in rich soil, the leaves are from five to seven inches in diameter, a perfect heart-shape, of a pure green color and glossy surface on the upper side, and grayish-green beneath, forming a mass of most cleanly and elegant foliage. The leaves are quite free from the attacks of insects. A cultivated tree in rich ground differs so much from the same sort growing in the woods, that it is scarcely recognizable as the same ; changing from a straggling small-leaved, thin-foliaged, scrawny little tree, to one of the most luxuriant of low-spreading trees. The engraving, Fig. 142, is a portrait characteristic of the appearance of the tree when young ; the specimen from which it was drawn having been planted but six years. As it increases in age the head becomes more oblate and distinctly parasol-like. The seeds of the tree are contained in bean-like pods from four to six inches long, which hang on the tree through the winter. Height, at maturity, from twelve to eighteen feet ; breadth of head twenty to thirty feet.

THE ENGLISH JUDAS-TREE, *Cercis siliquastrum,* is quite similar to the above, the leaves being a little smaller and the flowers darker. The latter "have an agreeable acid taste, and are mixed in salads, or fried in batter as fritters."

THE HALESIA, SNOWDROP, OR SILVER-BELL TREE.
Halesia tetraptera.

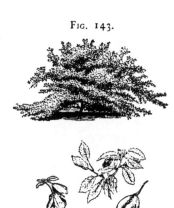

Fig. 143.

Low-spreading trees, blossoming in April and May, with a profusion of pure white pendant flowers resembling those of the snowdrop. They are about five-eighths of an inch in length, and hang in clusters on the last year's wood.

Fig. 143 gives a good idea of the form and style of a tree of this species fifteen or twenty years old, and of the forms of the leaves, flowers, and seed capsules. The latter are shown one-fifth the natural size, and the leaves one-twelfth. During the autumn, or last part of the summer, the head is covered with the four-winged seeds or capsules that distinguish the tree at that season. The leaves are about the size of those of the syringa, of a fine healthy color, without gloss, and, when the tree is thrifty and mature, mass well. There is a fine old specimen in the New York Central Park, near one of the walks to the Ramble, that is about fifteen feet high and more than thirty feet across the spread of its branches, which rest upon the ground. There is a large specimen on the grounds of Miss —— Price, near Germantown, Pa., which, though badly shaded by other trees, has a trunk sixteen inches in diameter, top twenty-five feet high, and is fifty feet across the greatest extension of its branches! There are higher trees of this species in England, but none on record of so great diameter.

THE TWO-WINGED FRUITED HALESIA OR SNOWDROP, *H. diptera*, is a smaller tree, with larger leaves and flowers, and less hardy than the preceding; otherwise closely resembles it.

THORN TREES. *Cratægus.*

Mostly low, flat-headed trees. Though some of the prettiest
varieties of the tree-thorns in the world are growing wild in all the
States, they are so common, and their varieties so numerous, that

FIG. 144.

they have been little valued and rarely
grown in nurseries or pleasure grounds.
The English hawthorn, of which so
much has been said and sung, is inferior in foliage to some of our native varieties, and but little superior in flowers or fruit. The varieties of native
thorn trees are almost as numerous
as apples in a nursery catalogue, and our descriptions must be
limited to a few species and varieties, at the risk of leaving un-
noticed many of conspicuous beauty. Nearly all of them are
observable for the sharpness of their thorns, their abundant clusters
of blossoms in May, their dense growth and low-spreading forms.
On most varieties the foliage masses in horizontal and rather thin
stratifications, especially in the *crus-galli* members of the family.
The fruit is generally red, varying from the size of a pea to that of
a cherry. The larger sorts have a perfumed and quite agreeable
flavor, and are known as thorn-apples. The abundance of the
fruit gives a ruddy tone to the trees in August and September, and
a few sorts are planted in England for the beauty of the fruit alone.

All the species may be clipped into good hedges, but some varieties of the *crus-galli* are the best adapted for that purpose.

The blossoms and fruit are borne in clusters, the former generally white, and the latter red, though there are varieties with bright-
colored blossoms, and yellow, green, and black fruit. The time
of their flowering varies in the different sorts from March to July,
but most varieties bloom about the last of May, and ripen their
fruit in September.

Whether we look at their blossoms, their glossy leaves, their
dense low growth, the clearly marked lights and shadows of their
foliage, their facility for trimming into hedges or other artificial

forms, or the number of differing varieties, we find them equally adapted to beautify small grounds. No one family of trees furnishes so many pretty specimen *small* trees for a lawn ; ranging in size from the smallest shrubs to middle-sized trees—some of them almost evergreen. All the species require a dry, rich soil ; in which their annual growth for the first ten years will be from one to two feet a year.

THE COCKSPUR THORN, *C. crus-galli,* Fig. 145, is the most interesting of indigenous species. All its varieties will assume a distinct tree-form, though some of them are but shrubs in size. The breadth of their heads is usually greater than their height, and their forms vary from globular to squarish-oblate. Their greatest height and breadth is about thirty feet, but usually not more than from twelve to twenty feet. This species is distinguished by thicker and glossier leaves, more entire in outline than the other sorts ; being more or less serrate, but not lobed. The thorns are single, long, and very sharp. At maturity the branches, which are numerous, have a horizontal direction, and the lights and shadows are

FIG. 145.

in thin, sharply defined, and generally level lines like those of the beech tree. We have seen wild groves of these thorns, in western openings, which by the aid of sheep had become exquisite bits of park scenery. The sheep had fed on their sweet leaves as high as they could reach from beneath, so that the under sides of the trees were as level as the pasture below them. Above this level line the trees spread in stratified lines of foliage entirely in harmony with the polished and artificial cut of their bases. Their broad heads, so close to the lawn, and yet with a clearly defined space above it, make shadows of great depth, which bring the lights around them into bright relief.

The most peculiar varieties are the *C. c. splendens,* noted for the abundance and brilliant glossiness of its leaves ; the plum-leaved

FIG. 146.

thorn, *C. c. prunifolia*, for short broad leaves, fastigiate habit and showy red autumn foliage; the *C. c. pyracanthafolia* and the *C. c. salicifloia*, or willow-leaved, are curiously low and broad little trees; and the *C. c. nana* is the smallest dwarf of all. Fig. 146 shows the form of the willow-leaved variety; which is one of the prettiest of all the thorn trees, and is especially noted for the level spread of its top.

THE TWIN HAWTHORN.

THE HAWTHORNS. *Cratægus oxycantha.*—We quote the following from Loudon's *Arboretum Britannicum :* " The common hawthorn, in its wild state, is a shrub or small tree with a smooth bark, and very hard wood. The rate of growth when the plant is young, and in a good soil and climate, is from one foot to two or three feet a year for the first three or four years; afterwards its growth is slower, till it has attained the height of twelve or fifteen feet, when its shoots are produced chiefly in a lateral direction, tending to increase the width of the head of the tree, rather than its height. In a wild state it is commonly found as

a large dense bush; but, pruned by accident or design to a single stem, it forms one of the most beautiful and durable trees of the third rank that can be planted—interesting and valuable for its sweet-scented flowers in May, and for its fruit in autumn, which supplies food for some of the smaller birds during part of the winter. In hedges the hawthorn does not flower and fruit abundantly when closely and frequently clipped; but when the hedges are only cut at the sides, so as to be kept within bounds, and the summits are left untouched, they flower and fruit as freely as when trained as separate trees. The plant lives a century or two, and there are examples of it between forty and fifty feet in height, with trunks three feet in diameter at one foot from the ground." It will not flourish in a wet, cold, or thin soil.

The hawthorn may either be used as stocks for, or may be grafted upon, not only all the other thorns, but upon apple and pear trees. As an ornamental hedge-plant it is inferior in beauty in this country to the arbor-vitæ and hemlock, except in its blossoming time, and in strength to resist animals to the Osage orange.

Sir Uvedale Price, one of the most distinguished of English writers on landscape gardening, especially recommends the hawthorn to be used as a filling-in for a plantation of larger trees: "As trees are frequently planted thick at first, with the intention of thinning them afterwards; *and as this operation is almost always neglected, no more large trees ought to be planted than are intended finally to remain;* and the interstices should be filled up with hawthorns and other low shrubs and trees." The growth of the tree is more rambling than that of our best native thorns, and its outer branches, intercurving, and well covered either with flowers or leaves, often convey the impression of trees composed of garlands, blossoms, and leaves. The flowers are borne in greater profusion than on our American thorn-trees, and sport into a variety of colors. Fig. 147 is a portrait of a pair of hawthorns in the grounds of Ellwanger & Barry, at Rochester, which, in their blooming season, are remarkably pretty; the one on the right being a mass of double white blossoms, and the one on the left nearly as crowded with pink blossoms, and their branches cross and interlace, so that the colors mingle in the centre. There can be no prettier deciduous gateway arch than may be made by planting a white-flowering hawthorn on one side, and some of the pink or scarlet varieties on the other, for the purpose of weaving their branches together overhead, and then clipping to perfect the arch, but not so closely on the outside as to mar the graceful freedom of outline that is one of the pleasing features of the hawthorn. Fig. 37, on page 108, illustrates the mode of treatment here suggested.

The following are a few of the numerous varieties of the haw thorn:

The *C. oxycantha pendula,* a charming little pendulous branched tree. Flowers white.

The *C. o. rosea* has rose-colored flowers in great abundance. May.

The *C. o. punicea* has dark-red flowers in May, brilliant, like clusters of verbenas.

The *C. o. punicea flore plena* has double flowers, less brightly colored.

The *C. o. multiplex* has double white flowers, which die off a beautiful pink. They are borne in great profusion, and last a long

FIG. 149.

time. It has an unusually dark glossy leaf, of the form shown in Fig. 149, and thrives in par-

tial shade. One of the best.

The *C. o. lucida* is a variety distinguished by its vigorous habit and the unusual thickness and glossiness of its leaves. Flowers white. There are varieties with variegated leaves, but they are not of healthy growth, and therefore not worth planting.

The *C. o. stricta* is an upright-growing variety, almost as fastigiate as the Lombardy poplar, and forms a pretty contrast to some of the flat-headed cockspur thorns. All these varieties may be grafted on any of our wild thorns, and they sometimes succeed on mountain ash, pear, and quince stocks.

THE SCARLET-FRUITED THORN. *Cratægus coccinea.*—Under this botanical head are grouped many of those varieties or species commonly known as wild-thorn apple trees. The leaves are irregularly heart-shaped, more or less lobed, and acutely serrated. The flowers are white, except in a few varieties, the fruit is larger than that of the hawthorn or cockspur species, and the growth is more free and vigorous. The fruit has a most agreeable perfume and flavor, but differs in quality and size on different trees almost as much as cultivated apples ; and in autumn is ornamental by reason of its bright red color. Though the trees have the same characteristic of low breadth as the other species, they have a less artificial or gardenesque kind of beauty than the cockspur thorns, and the foliage masses in larger divisions of light and shade.

FIG. 150.

Fig. 144, page 438, shows a fine specimen of this family, drawn from nature on Mount Desert Island, Maine, which is about fifteen feet high and twenty-five feet in breadth. Fig. 150 represents another and larger form that some varieties assume at the west. There are hundreds of varieties of this species. The following are believed to be the most interesting:

THE DOUBLE-SCARLET THORN. *C. coccinea flore plena.*—This is a new variety, and said to excel all the others in beauty. Its flowers are unusually large, of a deep crimson color, with a scarlet shade, and very double. Foliage luxuriant and glossy.

THE DOTTED-FRUITED THORN, *C. c. punctata aurea*, has yellow fruit, and grows to greater size than many other varieties.

THE TANSY-LEAVED THORN. *C. tenacetifolia celsiana.*—A vigorous growing tree of fastigiate habit, and unusual size and beauty of foliage and fruit. Fig. 151 shows the leaf. The fruit is yellow.

FIG. 151.

THE FIERY THORN OR BURNING BUSH. *Cratægus pyracantha.*—An evergreen or sub-evergreen shrub, of dense growth, with very small leaves, which turn brown but do not drop off in winter. Four to six feet in height. Flowers white, in May. Fruit red, hanging a long time on the tree, and by its brightness suggesting the name of fiery thorn. Parsons considers it the best of the thorns for low hedges. Its spines are very numerous and sharp. Hardy near New York. Height six to twelve feet.

THE MEDLAR. *Mespilus (cratægus).*—This is a species nearly allied in all respects to the thorn family. The fruit is larger than that of our largest thorn apples, and pleasantly flavored when in a state of incipient decay. The Dutch medlar is the variety of largest fruit, and Smith's medlar, *M. grandiflora,* has the most showy flowers. The trees when old assume picturesque low forms, and are well covered with glossy foliage. Height fifteen to twenty feet.

THE BUCKTHORN. *Rhamnus catharticus.*—An upright shrubby tree, of European origin, which, a few years since, was greatly commended as a hedge plant. It has not proved of great value, being inferior both in beauty and density to our native cockspur thorns, and to the Osage orange. Its foliage is much like that of the common privet—a dull dark green. It has no marked beauty of any kind.

THE BROAD-LEAVED BUCKTHORN, *R. latifolius,* is said to be very much finer than the foregoing. The shrub and its leaves being much larger and brighter colored.

THE PEACH-TREE. *Persica.*

The peach-tree runs through three stages of existence with remarkable rapidity. When from three to six years old, there are few more beautiful small trees. Its finely cut vivid green foliage and symmetrical form make it a beautiful small tree. But, after a few crops, the growth of the top becomes straggling, and at the end of six to ten years its dead twigs, broken limbs, and general "lopsidedness," mark it a decrepit tree. This is the usual history of the tree in sandy soils. In stiff rich clays it grows slower and lasts longer. But it is a fruit tree which should be kept out of sight as much as possible from' the ornamental part of one's grounds. Peach trees should be planted about twenty feet apart in orchards ; but in fruit gardens we recommend planting them in rows with standard pears (where the latter are not nearer to each other than twenty feet), and by keeping them well headed back, they may not be in the way of the pear trees for ten of twelve years, and then may be cut away to let the pear trees occupy the whole space.

The greatest enemy of the peach-tree is a white grub, which infests the neck of the tree at its intersection with the ground, and sometimes the crotches higher up. No tree should be planted which has had these pests in them. Their presence may be known by an exudation of gum. In trees already planted they can only be got out by carefully cleaning away the gum, and probing and cutting with a knife until the worms are all out. A small conical mound of unleached ashes should then be put around the trunk of each tree, first removing the earth near the trunk down to the divergence of the main roots. Examinations for these worms should be made every April and July, and a fresh cone of ashes should be made around the collar of the tree at these times.

The peach tree is not entirely hardy, as its blossom-buds are frequently killed in winter by sudden changes and excessive cold, and the blossoms by frosts in the spring when they have expanded. A fruit so pre-eminently delicious, and easy to grow, will richly repay the care required to guard against these winter calamities. Experience has proved that banking with earth around the trunk, and mulching as far as the roots extend, aids the tree materially to resist the damaging effects of sudden changes ; acting like a warm blanket on animals. An additional and efficient protection for the blossom-buds and tender wood may be made by planting a strong red cedar-post, twelve feet long, four feet deep, in the spot where the tree is to be planted. In November, when the tree is old enough to bear fruit, the branches which are nearest to each other should be drawn together carefully, and bound with straw, like nurserymen's bundles. The several bundles of branches should then be brought as closely together as may be without breaking them, and all securely tied to the central post. Figs. 53, 54, 55, on page 273, show the manner of protection suggested. Without some strong fixture to which to secure these bundles, the weight of ice and snôw upon them in winter, and the action of the wind, would break the trees to pieces. A substitute for such a centre-post could be effected by driving three or four high strong stakes around the tree, and lashing the bundled branches by intersecting cords from one stake to another, so that the winds could not break them. Planting a cedar-post with the tree is, however, the best and simplest way of providing for this mode of winter protection. Trees that are loaded with vigorous blossom-buds when winter is entirely over, will very rarely have so many of the blossoms killed by frosts during the blossoming as to materially injure the crop.

The following ten varieties will afford a succession of the best fruit through the peach season: Haine's Early, large early York, George the IV., Crawford's early Melocoton, Morris White, Oldmixon freestone, Yellow rare-ripe, Nivette, Red-cheek Melocoton, Crawford's late Melocoton.

THE APRICOT. *Armeniaca vulgaris.*

A native of Asiatic mountains in the temperate zone. In addition to the value of its fruit, the apricot has the merit of being the earliest fruit-tree in flower. Its buds, before they expand, show a brilliant scarlet, and, when fully expanded early in April, are white, tinged with pink. The leaves resemble in form those of the apple tree, but are more wavy and glossy, and perhaps darker colored. The bark is also dark, like that of the plum tree. The growth of the tree is rapid, and it assumes more quickly than other trees, in proportion to size, a broad massive appearance. This quality of its form gives it an expression similar to that of old apple trees at a much earlier age than the latter acquire the same expression. It is, therefore, one of the most ornamental of fruit trees, not only by its luxuriant growth, when first planted, in which respect the peach is quite its equal, but by the substantial strength and durability of its spreading branches, and the permanence of its form, in which the peach tree is sadly deficient.

For fruit the varieties known as Dubois' Golden Peach, Moorpark, and Breda, are highly esteemed, and the latter is noted for the beauty of its leaves and growth. The apricot, having a smooth skin like the plum, is also subject to the attacks of the curculio, but not to so great an extent; and the objections to having plum trees on a lawn, will apply with less force to the apricot, while its superior dignity of form as a low tree will entitle it to room that ought not to be given to the former. The common apricot grows to nearly the same dimensions as the apple tree.

THE SIBERIAN APRICOT, *A. siberica*, is a smaller variety than the above, bearing about the same relation to it that the crab does to the apple tree. Formerly much cultivated in England for its very early blossoms, but of less value in most respects than the cultivated sorts.

THE PLUM TREE. *Prunus.*

Although the fruit-bearing plum trees are occasionally very pretty, they have not such beauty as to recommend their cultivation for ornament alone. And as the fruit is more uncertain in most parts of the country than that of other fruit trees, in consequence of the ravages of the insect curculio, which punctures the green fruit, causing it to drop prematurely, and thus not only destroys the crop, but covers the ground under the tree by the falling of the unripe and decaying fruit. Other fruit trees will yield a better return for the space they occupy and the attention they require.

THE CHINESE DOUBLE-FLOWERING PLUM. *Prunus sinensis.*— A small shrub but recently introduced into this country, which has already become a great favorite, and will probably prove superior to the old flowering almond, blooming at the same time, in April and May. Flowers semi-double, red above, and white underneath, profusely covering the branches.

THE AMERICAN HORNBEAM. *Carpinus americana.*

A small tree with wiry branches and dark-colored bark, resembling the beech somewhat in its mode of growth, but thinner in foliage and more irregular in form. Height fifteen to twenty-five feet. It has been recommended to plant for screens, but we have perceived no peculiar beauty or advantage it has for that purpose ; but it occasionally develops into a pretty isolated tree, of airy outline.

THE ENGLISH HORNBEAM, *C. betula,* is a larger tree than ours, with the same general character.

THE IRON-WOOD OR HOP HORNBEAM, *Ostrya virginica,* is a small native tree, remarkable for the extreme hardness and weight of its wood, but of no peculiar beauty. It grows slowly, and forms a compact little tree, with small dark leaves. Its bark is known at a glance by the extreme fineness of its furrows. Height fifteen to twenty-five feet.

THE LABURNUM. *Cytissus.*

In England and Scotland few small trees are more planted in ornamental grounds than the laburnum ; but our climate does not seem to suit them, so that although long cultivated in the older parts of the country, a fine specimen is rarely seen.

THE COMMON LABURNUM OR GOLDEN CHAIN, *C. laburnum,* is a low tree or big bush from twenty to thirty feet high, of irregular outline. The flowers are in pendant racemes six inches long, of a bright yellow color, and appear in May. The leaves are alternate, and composed of three oval-acute leaflets two to three inches in length. Young wood green. Decaying leaves yellow. The seeds are contained in pendulous pods.

THE WEEPING LABURNUM, *C. l. pendula,* of this species, is not sufficiently hardy and vigorous to be desirable.

THE SCOTCH LABURNUM, *C. alpina*, is considered a hardier and finer species than the preceding, but is closely allied to it in most respects. "The shape of the head is irregular and picturesque; its foliage is of a smooth shining and beautiful green; and it is not liable to be preyed on by insects. Though the laburnum will grow in a very indifferent soil, it requires a deep fertile sandy loam to attain a large size. As the tree puts out few horizontal roots, and has rather a spreading head, when it grows rapidly it is apt to be blown aside by high winds."—(Loudon.) The flowers of this species appear later than the preceding.

THE WEEPING SCOTCH LABURNUM, *C. a. pendula*, is highly valued for its beauty and gracefulness in England, but does not succeed so well in this country, at least in the northern States.

All the laburnums may be regarded as not quite hardy in the northern States, though rarely killed outright by the cold.

THE AMELANCHIER. *Amelanchier vulgaris.*

A low tree, with early and numerous small flowers, which cover it with white bloom about the middle of April. In very warm springs the blossoms appear the last of March, a month before the mass of the fruit trees are in bloom. The leaves resemble those of the pear tree, appear about the same time, and change to a bright yellow in autumn. The fruit is black, about the size of a currant, and of pleasant flavor. This variety is a native of Europe.

THE CANADIAN AMELANCHIER OR SNOWY MESPILUS. *A. botry apium.*—This American species is known in northern woods as the June berry and wild pear. It becomes a taller tree than the foregoing—from thirty to forty feet high in the woods—fastigiate, with long, slender, dark-colored shoots, and dark bark. In leaf and flower it strongly resembles the preceding. The fruit is a dark purple color, ripe the last of July, and very agreeable to the taste. We have not seen this tree of mature growth in open ground, and cannot therefore speak of its character as an ornamental tree when out of blossom.

29

THE FLOWERY AMELANCHIER. *A. florida.*—An upright shrub or tree from ten to twenty feet in height. Flowers white, larger and later than the preceding. May.

THE TAMARISK. *Tamarix.*

These are straggling, upright, sub-evergreen shrubs, resembling asparagus plants in foliage, and grow in stools; that is to say, they send up many sprouts from the intersection of the trunk and root.

The French tamarisk, *T. gallica*, the German, *T. germanica*, and the African, *T. africana*, are all growing well in the New York Central Park, though killed back occasionally in part. Loudon speaks of them as well adapted to thrive under sea-breezes, and that they require to be planted in close proximity to water, and in a deep free soil. The exceeding delicacy of their foliage attracts attention among larger-leaved shrubs, but they are of too careless and unsymmetrical growth to be used except to break the monotony of commoner forms. The flowers are in large loose spikes, of a delicate pink color, and, though small separately, are showy ; and the bloom continues most of the season. Height and breadth ten to twenty feet. In the Central Park the French variety makes the best appearance. We have seen a few fine specimens growing in tree form in city yards, and their great singularity of foliage renders them very attractive when they can be grown in this way.

THE WYCH HAZEL. *Hamamelis.*

This tree is rarely seen in cultivated grounds. It has something of the style of foliage of a beech, though the leaves are quite different in form, being obovate, larger, and broader, with wavy edges and darker color. The tree has the curious trait of blossoming profusely just before the falling of its leaves, and the flowers continue on the tree through the winter. They are of a rich yellow color, and very showy in the mass. We have not seen the Wych hazel developed in open ground, but from specimens growing by the road-side at Mount Desert Island, Maine, would suppose it to be a peculiarly umbrageous and elegant small tree. Height twenty ·to thirty feet.

THE ANDROMEDA OR SORREL TREE. *Andromeda arborea* (*Lyonia arborea* of Loudon).

This is one of the prettiest additions to our stock of small ·ornamental trees. Although a native of the States from Pennsylvania to Florida, it is scarcely yet known in most home- grounds. In the southern States it be- comes from forty to sixty feet high; in England ten tó twenty feet; probably twenty to forty feet in the latitude of New York. It forms an umbrella-shaped top with tapering branches. Fig. 152 repre- sents its common form from six to eight

F G. 152.

years after planting. The leaves resemble those of the common elder in form, color, and abundance. The flowers, are in large terminal panicles of many racemes, white, in June and July, and cover the head of the tree in plumy profusion. The panicles of seeds that succeed them also attract attention by the novelty of ·their appearance, and their great abundance. The foliage turns to a fine crimson in October. The name "sorrel tree" is given to it in consequence of the pleasant acidity of its leaves. Away from the mild climate of the seaboard, in the northern States, it should be treated as a half-hardy tree.

THE SUMACH. *Rhus.*

The species of this family vary so widely that some of them would not be supposed to have any relationship to the others if judged by their general appearance. The purple fringe tree, for instance, with its single clean-cut leaves, and rounded head, is the very opposite in most respects of the long compound serrate-leaved and scraggy little sumach of the fields; and the vine well known as the poison ivy, *Rhus toxicodendron,* which wreaths walls and trunks of trees with its glossy foliage, differs as widely from both. The following is by far the most valuable of the family for embellishment;

THE PURPLE FRINGE TREE OR VENETIAN SUMACH. *Rhus cotinus.*—This forms either a large shrub or small tree of finely rounded outline. The leaves are pretty

FIG. 153

to examine separately on account of their peculiar fineness of texture, their pure bright color, and their cleanly-cut oval form ; and they are borne in such healthy abundance on every part of the branches, and break into so finely rounded masses, that it is very elegant even without the peculiar flowering which gives its name. The flowers when they first appear in June, are a pale green color, with a delicate shade of purple, in large delicately divided panicles projected beyond the leaves, and borne so profusely that they seem like masses of down almost covering the shrub, and revealing in their openings the bright green foliage below. These blossoms become more purplish as they remain on the tree, and finally change to dry masses of delicate seed-vessels, which are partly overgrown by the summer growth of leaves. The latter hang on till heavy frosts, and occasionally turn to a fine reddish-yellow. Both as a bush and as a tree it is beautiful, curious, and desirable.. There are specimens near Philadelphia with trunks eight inches in diameter three feet from the ground, and tops twenty feet high and broad. Fig. 153 shows the common form, and appearance when in flower, of a tree or bush five or six years planted. It requires a dry warm soil.

·THE TREE SUMACH, *Rhus typhina,* a low, irregularly branched, flat-topped, spreading tree or shrub, with compound leaves from two to three feet long, composed of from eleven to nineteen leaflets. The leaves drop very early after changing to a warm yellow or purplish-red. This is occasionally a picturesque tree ; its peculiarly level head and warm-toned ailantus-like leaves showing to best advantage when growing quite alone. The flowers appear in July and August in large spikes above the foilage, of a dark-purple color on male trees, and greenish-yellow and purple on the female, and are followed by purplish seeds ripe in October. The leaves fall early, and change to yellow, red, and purple before they fall. Height from ten to twenty feet, with nearly equal breadth of top.

THE GUM COPAL SUMACH. *Rhus copallina.*—This is the common suckering species of the fields which grows to the height of three to seven feet, bearing beautiful pinnate leaves and compact spikes of flowers and seeds together, which are of a bright-red color, covered with a sticky light-purple bloom which has a most pungent and agreeable acidity. The leaves turn to a brilliant crimson in autumn and fall early. Its suckering habit unfits it for pleasure grounds.

There are many other species, but of no value for ornament.

THE POISON IVY, *Rhus toxicodendron,* will be mentioned with vines.

THE CHIONANTHUS. *Chionanthus.*

Also known by the names Snow-flower, and Virginia Fringe-tree. Fig. 154 illustrates the best form of the *Chionanthus virginica.* It is one of the most elegant little trees, when in bloom in May and June, that can grace a lawn. The flowers, like snow-white filaments, hang in loose racemes about four inches long all over the tree. Its glossy leaves resemble those of the magnolia family, or perhaps more the unlobed leaves of the sassafras, but thicker and larger. Height from ten to thirty feet, according to soil and climate. Loudon says it requires to be grown in a moist soil and sheltered situation. We have seen beautiful specimens in open ground in Hartford, Conn., and it does well at Flushing, L. I.; but is too tender for Rochester, N. Y. Wherever it can be made to endure the winter without injury, and can be shielded from winds, it will be

FIG. 154.

found one of the choicest little trees to plant near dwellings.   But
as it belongs to a family of trees which are generally tender, it will
be well to avoid planting it where its hardiness will be severely
tested ; and to maintain its beauty and health in the middle and
northern States, it must certainly be well protected by mulching
the ground thoroughly over the roots, binding its stem, and bundling its top with straw or evergreens every autumn.

The varieties *C. v. latifolia*, *C. v. angustifolia*, and *C. v. mari-
tima*, are little known in northern nurseries or pleasure grounds.
The latter forms a full-foliaged shrub seven to nine feet high in a
protected situation in Parson's nursery at Flushing, L. I.   Its leaves
are from five to seven inches long, three to four broad, thick as
velvet, of a deep green color, and of a waxen glossiness.   Its name
implies its love of the seaside.   We are not aware whether it has
been tried in the interior.

THE SHEPHERDIA.   *Shepherdia.*

THE BUFFALO BERRY, *S. argentea*, is a small tree, native of the
banks of the Missouri river, where it becomes a tree from twelve
to eighteen feet in height, and is known by the several names of
Buffalo-berry, rabbit-berry, and beef-suet tree.   Flowers yellow, in
April and May ; berries scarlet, about the size of the red currant,
of fine flavor, and "form one continued cluster on every branch."

THE PAW-PAW.   *Anona triloba.*

A small tree, native of the valley of the Ohio, and of the States
southward, that bears a yellow oval fruit two or three inches long,
which is insipid, but eatable.   Flowers purple, one inch in diameter.   The leaves are smooth-edged, of soft texture, wavy, and the
form of the shell-bark hickory leaf, elongated.   Bark very smooth,
and of a silver-gray color.   It is grown in a protected situation in
the Central Park, but cannot be considered quite hardy north of
Washington and Cincinnati.   It requires a very rich soil.

CHAPTER IV

SHRUBS are distinguished from trees by having many stems issuing near the surface of the ground from a common root, instead of having all their branches and foliage supported on a single stem. Among the descriptions of trees in the preceding chapter are embraced many dwarf and shrubby sorts that should rank as shrubs; such, for instance, as the dwarf white-flowering horse-chestnut, the purple magnolia, etc., which have been described with trees in order not to separate families, as explained in our remarks on the classification of trees and shrubs in Chapter II. of Part II.

Before proceeding with descriptions, we desire again to call the reader's attention to the fact, that *shrubs which are the most commonly known, and the cheapest, are generally the finest, or at least have the greatest number of desirable qualities.* Now, what are the most essential qualities of shrubs for home embellishment? Before answering this we must demand what kind of a place is to be embellished; whether large or small, isolated or connected with others; whether it is to be laid out on a geometric plan, in a gardenesque manner, or with more simple groupings in miniature "landscape-gardening" style ; and whether the shrubs are to be used in masses, or for single specimens.   All these considerations will render one or another shrub more desirable according to its size and form ; and size and form will, therefore, be the qualities that must *first* be considered.   But, aside from the question of size alone, there are certain general qualities that will apply to all shrubs to make them always more or less desirable in well-kept places.   The most essential is, that the foliage be so luxuriant on all parts as to cover the branches.   Next, that the leaves come out early, and retain a good color till hard frosts.   Third, that the flowers be conspicuous, of pure colors, and fragrant.   Fourth, that, while preserving a shrubby character, they be free from a suckering habit, by which the ground or lawn for some distance around the collar of the stems is annually incumbered by sprouts from the roots.   Shrubs which have stems uniting like the branches of a tree in a common heart or trunk, provided they cover the ground in a shrubby manner, are likely to be more graceful, and certainly neater and more gardenesque than those which throw up suckers far from the centre stems ; but there are some, like the flowering currant, for instance, which have this bad quality, and are yet indispensable for their many other good features.

Now, if we bear in mind these most essential qualities, and look over any good list of shrubs, to select a half dozen of the best, it will be found that our most common materials, such as the lilacs, bush-honeysuckles, syringas, snow-balls, deutzias, and weigelas, are the ones which approximate most nearly to perfect shrubs ; and we shall find it difficult to select another half dozen, no matter what expense we are willing to incur, that equal the six species in beauty of form, foliage, or bloom ; though single shrubs may be named that will excel some of them in many qualities.

Enthusiastic amateurs, as well as professional gardeners and nurserymen, hail with delight every change and shade of change from old forms, not because the new things are any more beautiful than the old, but simply because they are novelties ; and from much the same impulse that we prefer new books to old ones, without stopping to compare closely their intrinsic merits.   Men who are constantly studying trees and shrubs, learn to observe with infinite pleasure all the little variations of form and shade that can be discovered in them, and appear to place a higher value on a single quality which distinguishes a new plant from all others, than on any combination of merits in the old. We say *appear* to do so; but, in fact, the eyes of such lovers of trees and shrubs are like the ears of highly cultivated musicians, who do not love pure and simple sounds the less because they listen with more rapt and delighted attention to the intricate play of new chords and harmonies that may be interwoven with the simple body of the music. The beauty with which we have become quite familiar, like the warmth of sunlight, is felt without being observed; but what is uncommon in nature or art creates a sensation of excitement, and if it is a thing of beauty, becomes an æsthetic stimulus. But the love of intricate melodies, peculiar to highly cultivated musicians, cannot be ingrafted suddenly upon the greater number who love simple music; nor can the taste of the cultured amateur in trees and shrubs be shared by the great mass of persons who admire sylvan nature only in a rudimentary way.

It will be seen, therefore, that several classes of persons and tastes must be provided for. First, those who appreciate only the most prominent and simple forms of vegetable beauty; second, those (a much smaller number) who have passed the first stage of observation, and whose eyes have become educated to take in and appreciate a greater number of features or peculiarities at once— who have become connoisseurs or *dilettanti* in natural objects; third, those who may be named the artist-eyed class, who value sylvan features not so much for any of their beauties in detail, as for those relations of forms and play of lights and shades and colors which group into what we call pictures. The last class is the one which soonest learns to handle trees and shrubs, so as to make homes beautiful. For the first class it would be absurd to describe numerous varieties of each species of tree or shrub when one or two would answer perfectly their wants; but to satisfy the second class, respectful mention must be made of much that is new and rare. It is by the enthusiasm of just such persons as compose the second class that most of the beautiful trees and shrubs, now common, but once rare or unknown, have been introduced; some from far countries, and more from the wilds of our own country. When, therefore, in the following or the preceding descriptions, there is more warmth of praise of some tree or shrub that is little known than of some of the beautiful well-known sorts, it must be remembered that we are writing partly for a class who are disposed to follow St. Paul's injunction ; — "prove all things ; hold fast that which is good."

The growth of shrubs *singly* to develop the greatest beauty and size they can be made to attain, will produce results that few persons, even among those familiar with shrubs, are aware of. How few of those who have seen tartarian honeysuckles all their lives, have ever seen one standing out alone in a rich soil, ten feet high and fifteen feet in diameter of head, and arching to the lawn like a miniature Connecticut valley elm ; yet this would be a common size and form if this shrub were planted and kept with the intention of developing its greatest beauty. The common snow-ball viburnum can be grown much larger, probably sixteen feet high, and of much greater breadth of branches ; the latter bending to the ground with a graceful sweep that the early growth of the shrub does not promise. The little red-fruited St. Peterswort or Indian currant, known in some localities as the red waxberry, which is usually tucked in among other shrubs as not important enough to stand alone, forms one of the most symmetrical and graceful of low shrubs when grown as a single specimen. In short, among all our commonly cultivated and well-known shrubs, one is rarely found which has had a fair chance to develop all its beauty.

The difference between a forest grown oak, and the spreading oak of an old park is well known, but the fact that the same difference obtains between shrubs grown in the mass or grown singly is not generally understood.

There is much difference in the value of nursery plants for growing good specimen shrubs, depending on the nature of their roots, and the stockiness of the stems. Seedlings generally make the best roots, but as the choicest varieties of most fine shrubs do not come true from seed, the nurserymen propagate them principally by cuttings and layers, and the commoner varieties by suckers. Cuttings generally have roots spreading pretty equally on all sides,

but suckers and layers are apt to be more imperfect in this respect.
Fig. 155, *b*, represents a common stool of
suckers and their roots, which may be
divided to make several plants, each with a
root. The single stems, rooted all around,
like the one marked *a*, are much better
plants than those with roots on one side
only as shown at *c*. It will be seen at a glance that the

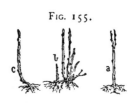

FIG. 155.

latter are much more likely to make lop-sided shrubs. Where
it is desired to confine a shrub to a single stem, a plant rooted
like the one at *a* is indispensable; but for those shrubs which
sucker and sprout so inveterately that they cannot be confined
to a single heart or trunk, plants like those shown at *b* and *c*
will answer as well. In the former case all the buds that can be
seen that would be below the line of ground surface after planting should be carefully cut out. The top should then be encouraged
to branch *low*, otherwise suckers will spring from the roots in spite
of all attempt to keep them back. It is a common mistake of
those who experiment to make tree-like shrubs, to trim up the stems
from the first. This at once lessens the vigor of the stem just
where it needs to be strengthened. To grow a shrub on a single
trunk, strong low branches must be encouraged, and these, resting
upon and shading the ground around the stem will usually lessen
the tendency to suckers, which is worse in many-stemmed and
"trimmed-up" shrubs. The advantage of a central trunk for
some shrubs is not in the sight of tall bare stems which at once
destroy the shrubby effect which shrubs are planted to produce,
but rather for their greater neatness of appearance, ease of culture,
and finer shadows under their drooping branches, than are ever
seen under sucker-environed shrubs. These remarks of course apply
only to those shrubs which show some aptitude for an arboreous
habit. To attempt to grow currants, spireas, and other shrubs, in a
tree form, will be time and labor thrown away.

F:G. 156.

THE LILAC. *Syringa.*

The lilac among shrubs in this country is like the maple among trees, the most common and the most indispensable. Many home yards are made incongruous medleys of expensive novelties in flowers and shrubs which might have been more nobly adorned with masses of well-selected lilacs alone. The home of our poet Longfellow, in Cambridge,. Mass., is a fine example of the simple beauty of such groups ; a few masses of lilacs and some ancient elms being all its sylvan decoration.

The lilac is indigenous in Persia and the valley of the Danube. Some of the species grow to the height of twenty feet. The common white, *S. alba,* and purple, *S. vulgaris,* and their varieties, are stout upright growing shrubs, usually higher than their breadth. They may easily be trained into tree-form if care is taken to plant single stems with well-balanced roots, encouraging them to branch low, and pruning all suckers away as soon as they appear. All the lilacs tend to the bush form, and except where fine single specimens are desired for their novelty, it is not advisable to meddle with this tendency, but rather to encourage it by heading back at the top, so as to keep the bottom of the bush from growing scantyfoliaged and " scrawny." The lilac may be grafted on the white ash.

The Persian lilacs, *S. persica* (called by some Siberian lilacs), have smaller leaves, darker colored blossoms, and slenderer branches than the common lilac. We have seen a specimen in

Rochester, N. Y., twelve feet high and sixteen feet or more in diameter, drooping on all sides to the ground with the weight of its blossoms. This, however, is an unusual size.

The lilac is usually propagated from suckers, which it produces in great abundance, but better trees or shrubs can probably be produced by budding or grafting the best varieties upon seedling plants.

There are several varieties of the common and of the Persian lilacs of distinct character. A few that are cordially recommended will be named somewhat in the order of their size, beginning with the largest. The list embraces but a selection from the large number of varieties on the nursery catalogues.

THE COMMON WHITE LILAC, *Syringa alba*, is not surpassed by any other white variety in size or beauty of foliage; but as its growth is upright, and it has a tendency to get bare of leaves at the bottom, we recommend that it be generally cultivated in tree-form. Flowers white, beginning to end of May. Height twelve to twenty feet.

THE GIANT LILAC. *S. gigantea.*—A very rank upright grower, with the largest leaves and spikes of flowers of any of the species. It blooms in May. Flowers a dark reddish purple, in spikes from nine to twelve inches long, and eight inches broad. Its leaves retain a pure color later in autumn than the other lilacs. Height twelve to twenty feet.

CHARLES XTH. *S. carola.*—One of the best to grow in tree-form. The foliage and blossoms are both darker colored and larger than that of the common lilac, *S. vulgaris*, and the growth a little coarser. Height ten to fifteen feet.

EMODI LILAC. *S. emodi.*—A Himalayan variety. Foliage large, and among the most glossy of the lilacs. The leaves are more pointed than any other variety. Habit erect, but not so stiff as many others, and good for a tree-form. Flowers the darkest purple, lavender-scented, and very fragrant. Height ten to twelve feet. There are good specimens of this in the New York Central Park.

The *S. cærulea superba* is a fine blue-flowered variety, originated by Ellwanger & Barry, of Rochester, N. Y.

THE COMMON PURPLE LILAC. *S. vulgaris.*—This is almost too well known to need description. Fig. 157 gives its character-

FIG. 157.

istic habit in four to six years after planting, and Fig. 156 shows the noble development it makes when allowed ample room for extension in a rich soil. Its blossoms are the standard lilac color, and when the blossoms of the other purple-flowered lilacs are described as more or less purple, the comparison is always with this one. Height ten to twelve feet.

THE BEAUTIFUL LILAC. *S. speciosa.*—This is one of the smallest bushes among the lilacs, of short stout growth, and robust appearance. It forms a compact bush, from five to eight feet in height. Flowers large, in compact spikes, of a purplish-red color. One of the best in every respect.

THE JOSIKA LILAC. *S. josikea.*—Also called the chionanthus leaved lilac, from the strong resemblance its leaves bear to those of the chionanthus. It is quite different in foliage and general appearance from the other lilacs. A native of Transylvania, growing in shady places near the water. Leaves of a waxy appearance and wavy surface. An upright grower, and will probably bear to be grown as a tree. It holds its foliage of good color quite late in the fall, and blooms one month later than other lilacs. Flowers deep purple in June. Height ten to twelve feet.

The following old sorts are still the most valuable of the small-leaved species variously known as Persian, Chinese, or Siberian lilacs. Their growth is more slender and less rigid than the preceding.

THE PERSIAN WHITE LILAC. *S. persica alba.*—This forms a large spreading shrub. whose branches with age bend with a fine curve so that their tips touch the ground when loaded with blossoms. Flowers a delicate lavender-white in May.

THE COMMON PERSIAN LILAC. *S. persica.*—Same as preceding, except that its flowers are a dark lilac color. The spikes of flowers are larger than those of the common large-leaved lilac, and looser. Though the growth of this species is every way more delicate than the common lilac, it forms at maturity a broader bush.

THE ROTHMAGENSIS LILAC. *S. rothmagensis.*—This is probably thè finest of all the lilacs. It is a cross between the *S. vulgaris* and *S. persica*, originated in Rouen, France, more than seventy years ago. In leaves, flowers, and graceful habit, it most resembles its Persian parent, but is more robust ; and in the size of its panicles of flowers exceeds any of its relatives. These sometimes grow from ten to sixteen inches long, and bend the branches to the ground with their abundance. They are a little later than those of the 'common lilac. May and beginning of June.

In making a collection of six lilacs only, in addition to the common purple, the following might be selected : *S. alba, S. emodi, S. cærulea superba, S. josikea, S. rothmagensis,* and *S. persica alba.*

THE HONEYSUCKLE. *Lonicera.*

The honeysuckle family is divided into two classes, viz : those of a twining character, or vines, and those of a shrubby character. The latter are here referred to. Fig. 158 gives the characteristic form of a well grown honeysuckle bush from six to eight feet high and broad. Some varieties spread more in proportion to their height ; all are noted for

FIG. 158.

the small size and delicacy of their leaves, which cover the branches profusely. Their flowers are small, but very pretty and abundant.

THE RED TARTARIAN HONEYSUCKLE. *L. tartarica.*—Old and common, it still takes a front rank among ornamental shrubs ; and were we to have but one shrub, or but one species of shrub, we would probably choose the honeysuckle. No shrub is earlier in leaf, and the delicacy of its foliage, its pure color, and graceful luxuriance of growth, would, without the flowers, make this species one of the most desirable ; but with its delicate. perfumed, pink bloom in May, it becomes altogether a perfect shrub. When young its form is rather fastigiate, but in a few years it begins to spread outward, and at maturity, in rich open ground, it becomes a superb spreading mass, much broader than its height, with branches bending on all sides to the lawn. One may have seen honeysuckle bushes a lifetime in shrubbery borders, or neglected in the grass, without knowing how graceful an object it is when growing in rich ground, quite alone, with the breadth and grace of its maturity. The honeysuckle holds its leaves late in the fall, and occasionally they are brightly colored before they drop. The berries in autumn are yellow or pink, and ornamental.

THE WHITE TARTARIAN HONEYSUCKLE. *L. t. alba.*—This variety is of stronger growth than the preceding, becomes a higher bush, and may with care be made into a low tree. The flowers and fruit are both white. The foliage is a little larger and paler than the red tartarian, and the bush does not become so graceful with age.

THE PINK-FLOWERING HONEYSUCKLE. *L. t. grandifolia.*—The most vigorous grower, and the most showy bloomer of the species. In habit of growth it is more like the white-flowering honeysuckle, but attains still larger size, sometimes twelve to fifteen feet high, and may easily be grown as a tree if forced to one stem and allowed to branch near the ground. Flowers in May, bright red, striped with white. Fruit red.

THE AUTUMN HONEYSUCKLE. *L. t. fragrantissima.*—A low and spreading variety four to six feet high. Flowers in October and November, small, not abundant, but exceedingly fragrant. The foliage is larger than that of most of the honeysuckles, of a deep green color, and sub-evergreen.

THE BLUE-BERRIED HONEYSUCKLE. *L. cœrulea.*—A small upright growing shrub, three to four feet high. Flowers greenish yellow, in June; inconspicuous ; berries blue. Foliage very abundant and of a beautiful green.

There are many other varieties, but not of such marked character as to be interesting except in an arboretum.

THE SYRINGA. *Philadelphus.*

This old, vigorous, and graceful shrub is still one of the finest, grown singly or in masses ; and though surpassed in profusion of

bloom by the lilacs and other shrubs, and in delicacy by the deutzias, its masses of foliage when out of bloom are not surpassed by
any. The variety of syringas is not large, and the common sort,
first named below, is still unsurpassed in fragrance of flowers and
beauty of foliage by the newer sorts.

THE COMMON SYRINGA. *P. vulgaris.*—This forms a shrub
from eight to ten feet high, and spreads at maturity like the head
of an elm. It is early in leaf; the foliage is luxuriant and breaks
into fine masses; the flowers in May and June are white, single,
about the size of an apple-blossom, and noted for their fragrance.

THE DOUBLE-FLOWERING. *P. flore plena.*—This forms a smaller
bush than the above, has semi-double flowers at the same time;
also fragrant.

ZEYHER'S SYRINGA, *P. zeyheri*, is noted for the size it attains,
forming a spreading bush twelve to fifteen feet high, with larger and
less abundant flowers than the preceding, and but slightly fragrant.

GORDON'S SYRINGA. *P. Gordonii.* — A large round-headed
shrub eight to ten feet high, blooming a month or more later than
the other sorts. Flowers large, white, and scentless. Its slender
side-shoots give it the appearance of a weeping habit. Foliage a
bright green.

THE SHOWY-FLOWERED SYRINGA. *P. speciosa* or *grandiflora.*—
A large bending-branched shrub, ten to fourteen feet high, bearing
large white scentless flowers in June.

THE DWARF SYRINGA. *P. nana.*—But two to three feet high,
and grows like a cabbage with in-curved branches. A shy bloomer,
but a pretty shrub. When syringa bushes make too long and rambling growth, they are improved by heading back.

THE VIBURNUMS. *Viburnum.*

This family of shrubs embraces a few evergreens, but is
best known through its popular representative, the showy snow-
ball viburnum, or guelder rose, *V. opulus.* The foliage varies
widely in the different species. The evergreen species is known as
the laurustinus, *V. tinus laurifolia*, and has laurel-like leaves, thick

and glossy, and in England is considered one of the most ornamental of evergreen shrubs, "the foliage tufting in beautiful masses, and covered with a profusion of white flowers which commence expanding in November, and continue flowering till April or May." From the fact that this species is not grown in our best nurseries, we infer that it is too tender to be grown in the northern States, though a common garden-shrub in the south of England. It forms a compact shrub from eight to ten feet high. Native of the south of Europe and north of Africa. The *viburnum, awefuki,* or *japonicum,* is a beautiful new Japanese evergreen variety which, it was formerly supposed, would prove hardy; and the *V. sinensis,* a Chinese evergreen sort, was once reported entirely hardy in England. We have not heard from either of them in this country.

SNOW-BALL VIBURNUM. *Viburnum opulus.*—The snow-ball, or guelder rose, is a shrub so common, and so showy when in bloom, that few, even of towns-people, are unfamiliar with it. Its magnificent balls of white flowers, from two to four inches in diameter, appear about the first of June, when the lilac has done blooming, and for showiness have no equals in their time. The bush is large, massy, and though coarse in foliage, spreads broadly and gracefully as it grows old. They may be grown in symmetrical tree-form, branching and bending on all sides to the lawn with a wealth of "snow-balls" exceedingly showy. Either as a bush or tree, it requires, at maturity, ten to twelve feet space for its perfect development; and it sometimes attains a height and breadth of fifteen feet. The leaves in autumn assume bright warm colors.

THE VARIEGATED-LEAVED, *V. o. foliis variegati,* has leaves variegated with white and yellow.

THE DOUBLE-FLOWERING, *V. o. flore plena,* flowers double, but no more showy than the common sort.

THE DWARFS, *V. o. nana* and *V. pygmœa,* are very diminutive varieties.

THE HIGH-BUSH CRANBERRY, *V. o. oxycoccus,* a large coarse shrub or small tree, bearing a fruit that is eatable, and with leaves larger and less deeply lobed than the common snow-ball. Its flowers are less showy, and a month later. Its fruit resembles the cranberry, and may be used in the same way.

The Lantana Viburnum, *V. lantanoides.*—The under-sides of the leaves and branches covered with a white down. Flowers abundant; May and June. Decaying leaves a deep red. Loudon says that when grown on a single stem, it becomes a handsome, durable small tree from twelve to fifteen feet in height. A very rapid grower.

The American Lantana Viburnum, *V. lantanoides.*—Similar to the above. Flowers in May, and holds its foliage very late.

The Cotinus-leaved Viburnum, *V. cotinifolium*, has foliage covered with gray down on both surfaces. Flowers small, bell-shaped, tinted with pink, and in large clusters, in April and May. A variety rare in our nurseries.

The Japan Viburnum, *V. plicatum*, is a vigorous, hardy variety, with rough dark-purple tinted leaves, and balls of flowers slightly tinted with rose color.

The Great-leaved Viburnum, *V. machrophyllum*, is a variety with very large leaves, said to have "immense clusters of flowers, greatly more showy than the old sort."

The Maple-leaved Viburnum, *V. acerifolium*, is a pretty native shrub from four to six feet high, with umbellate clusters of white flowers, less showy than those of the common snow-ball.

The Pliant-branched Viburnum, *V. lentago*, an indigenous variety that forms a robust shrub, or low tree, from six to ten feet high, bearing large umbrels of small white flowers in July. Decaying leaves purple, red and yellow. Naked young wood yellowish and reddish-green. Fruit black, in September.

The Plum-tree-leaved Viburnum. *V. prunifolium.*—The foliage of this variety resembles that of both the pear and the plum tree, and is less luxuriant than many other varieties. It flowers profusely in May and June. Fruit dark blue; ripe in September. Height eight to ten feet. Growth rather thin and straggling.

The Pear-tree-leaved Viburnum, *V. pyrifolium*, resembles the preceding, but of less straggling growth. Fruit black; September.

The Tooth-leaved Viburnum or Arrow-wood, *V. dentatum*

—-This variety has poplar-shaped leaves, of a light clear green color ; globular clusters of small white flowers in June and July; and small, round, dark-blue fruit. Height four to six feet. It is a lively-toned, well-leaved shrub, in the New York Central Park.

THE DOWNY VIBURNUM, *V. pubescens.*—A downy-leaved south ern shrub. Height three feet. Flowers white ; June and July.

FIG. 159.

FIG. 159.

THE WEIGELA.   *Weigela.*

This noble shrub, which was introduced from Japan as late as 1843, has already found a place in most home-grounds from Maine to California. Its robust habit, profuse bloom, and easy culture, have combined to rank it in popular estimation with those dear old shrubs the lilacs and the honevsuckles. The foliage is, how-ever, less smooth and elegant, and more allied to that of the syrin-gas and deutzias ; and like these shrubs, the bushes as they grow old break into fine masses of light and shade. Most of the weige-las are erect when young, but form graceful, bending, wide-spread-ing bushes when old, where they have room for expansion. The varieties are increasing rapidly in number, and though June and

FIG. 160.

July are their natural blooming season at the north, sporting plants are being propagated which will add greatly to the length of their blooming time and the variety of their colors. The following are among the best sorts :

THE ROSE WEIGELA. *W. rosea.*—The original species. Fig. 159 shows the characteristic form of a bush four or five years planted, and Fig. 160 the leaves. It will be seen that the latter vary greatly in appearance. The upright twig shows the growth and appearance of the leaves on the top of the bush, and the horizontal twigs their appearance on the lower branches, which are shaded. Placing the two side by side, it is difficult to believe that they are from the same bush, so entirely do they differ in all respects. The leaves growing in partial shade are of finer texture and more glossy than those on the top, but the finest formed bushes are grown in the most open locations. The leaves appear a little later than those of the lilac, are of a warm-toned green, keep their color well through the summer, hang on till late, and turn to a purplish-red before they fall. 'Buds a bright red; flowers quite large, bell-shaped; pink; June or July. Height and breadth from seven to ten feet.

THE DESBOIS WEIGELA. *W. Desboisii.*—Of ranker growth than the preceding. Foliage dark, rough, and coarse, but showy. Form more upright than the *W. rosea;* may probably be grown as a low tree. Flowers blood red and abundant. June and July. One of the most showy of shrubs. Height eight to twelve feet.

THE LOVELY WEIGELA. *W. amabilis.*—This is the largest of the weigelas, and is looser and more spreading in its habit than the others. Foliage large and coarse. Flowers a deep red, in June, and then flowering freely again in September. This can also be grown to advantage on a single stem in tree-form. Height twelve to fifteen feet.

THE WHITE-FLOWERED WEIGELA, *W. hortensis nivea*, is a new variety, with large white flowers, borne in profusion in June and July, and retain their pure color a long time. Growth vigorous and spreading. Leaves light green, large, and deeply veined. Height six to eight feet.

THE VARIEGATED-LEAVED WEIGELA. *W. variegata.*—Somewhat dwarfish compared with the others, and spreading. Leaves mottled with yellow, so as to make a good contrast among dark-leaved shrubs. Flowers pink, in June and July. Height four to six feet.

There are some other fine varieties, but the above will give the species a good representation.

THE DEUTZIA. *Deutzia.*

Another species of beautiful flowering shrubs for which we are indebted to Japan. It belongs to the same family as the common syringa, is similar in growth and foliage, but its style of bloom is more graceful. The different varieties are among the most charming late acquisitions to shrubberies, and already take rank with lilacs, honeysuckles, and weigelas. The leaves are simple, serrated, and opposite, about the size of syringa leaves, of coarse surface, and without gloss; they appear later than those of the lilac, or about with the *Weigela rosea,* which the deutzias also resemble in growth, though a little less spreading. The flowers, in most varieties, pure white, appear in June, in pendulous little panicles or racemes from two to four inches in length. Either on or off the bush they are very graceful.

THE ROUGH-LEAVED DEUTZIA, *D. scabra,* is the variety most largely disseminated, and the coarsest and most robust grower. It becomes a spreading bush from eight to twelve feet in height and breadth.

THE CRENATE-LEAVED DEUTZIA, *D. crenata,* differs principally from the foregoing in having a less rank and more graceful habit.

THE DOUBLE WHITE-FLOWERING CRENATE DEUTZIA, *D. crenata flore plena,* differs in having double flowers in greater abundance.

THE PINK-FLOWERING DOUBLE DEUTZIA, *D. rubra flore plena,* is similar to the preceding in habit of growth, and the most beautiful of all in bloom. This, and the double-white, are the finest large sorts, and should be planted near together, where the colors will be contrasted during their profuse blossoming.

THE GRACEFUL DEUTZIA. *D. gracilis.*—This is the smallest variety and the greatest favorite. It is equally at home in the green-house or in open ground, as it is readily forced into winter bloom. Its flowers are white, in slender little racemes, in June. On the bush, in bouquets, or wreathed with other flowers, the blossoms of the *Deutzia gracilis* are equally graceful. We remember no church decoration so charming as the wreathing and bordering of the pulpit and altar of a chapel in Brookline, Mass., decorated almost exclusively with the pendant racemes of this variety mingled with green leaves. The form of the shrub, when young, is rather stiffly upright, but in time it spreads into a graceful little bush, from three to four feet in height and breadth.

THE ALTHEA. *Hibiscus syriacus.*

Fig. 161 shows the common form of the althea, which is usually quite fastigiate, broadest at the top, and often bare of leaves below ; but it oftenest forms 'a head on a bundle of stems growing from the trunk near the ground, rather than with so tree-like a trunk as the illustration shows. It is one of the longest known and commonest of garden shrubs, and forms a good centre for a group of lower shrubs, and is

Fig. 161.

useful in belts of shrubbery where its high top and showy blossoms may be seen over the tops of more graceful and lower shrubs in front. Blooming in August and September when most shrubs are done flowering, and with flowers of large size and many colors, it will always be found quite useful and showy in pleasure-grounds, though the flowers are of coarse texture, and not fragrant. They are from three to four inches in diameter, both single and double. Purple is the prevailing color, but nearly all the bright colors are represented by the finest varieties. The leaves appear later than those of most shrubs, but are of a pleasing green color. The althea has been considerably used for hedges, but its lateness in spring renders it less desirable than the privet and many other deciduous shrubs ; and its inferiority to some of the evergreens for this pur pose is manifest. The following are some of the best varieties :

The Single and the Double White, Double Red, Double Blue Pheasant-eyed, White-striped, the *elegantissima*, and the Variegated-leaved. The latter is one of the finest of variegated-leaved shrubs. Some of the most showy varieties of the althea are not quite hardy in the coldest parts of our country, and to insure their greatest beauty in summer must be planted in sheltered situations, or protected by mulching and bundling.

THE DWARF ALMOND. *Amygdalus nana.*

" Blossoms of the almond trees,
April's gifts to April's bees."

A small shrub of the nut-bearing almond family, bearing in March or April an abundance of small double rose-like flowers, closely set upon the twigs, before the appearance of the leaf. The latter is similar to the leaf of the peach tree. Height from two to six feet. It is not perfectly hardy, and to grow and bloom to the best advantage at the north, it should have a dry warm soil, the ground around it mulched in the fall, the annual growth partly cut back every summer, and the suckers allowed to renew the bush by fresh wood. It is one of the most common of early flowering spring shrubs, but rarely makes a handsome bush when out of bloom.

There is a variety, *A. pumila alba*, with white flowers; also a Siberian variety described as follows:

A. n. siberica. "An upright shrub, about six feet high, with wand-like shoots, clothed with fine long, willow-like, glossy, serrate leaves; on account of which, and its upright habit of growth, different from all the other varieties, it is valuable" (Loudon). Flowers rather larger than the common sort.

The dwarf almonds may be budded on the common peach or plum tree stocks.

THE AMORPHA, OR BASTARD INDIGO. *Amorpha.*

A family of large spreading shrubs, from six to eight feet high, natives of our continent. The leaves are compound, with many pairs of small leaflets, resembling those of the locusts. The flowers are disposed in long spikes or panicles on the tops of the branches, and though "small separately, and imperfect in form, are yet rich from their number, and their colors of purple and violet spangled with a golden yellow. The plants are not of long duration; and are liable to be broken by wind; for which reason they ought always to be planted in a sheltered situation. They produce an abundance of suckers, from which, and from cuttings, they are readily propagated." The following are some of the varieties ·

Amorpha fruticosa.—The shrubby amorpha or wild indigo. A native of Carolina and Florida. Height nine to twelve feet. Flowers a dark bluish-purple, in June and July.

A. glabra.—The glabrous amorpha. A low shrub three to six feet high. Flowers bluish-purple in July and August.

A. nana.—The dwarf amorpha. Native of Missouri. Height one to two feet. Flowers purple, fragrant.

A. fragrans. The sweet amorpha. A hairy shrub. Height seven to eight feet. Flowers dark purple. June and July.

A. croceolanata.—Saffron woolly amorpha. Plant covered with short soft hairs. Racemes branched. Height three to five feet. Flowers purple or purplish-blue. July and August.

A. canescens. — White haired amorpha. Height three feet. Flowers dark blue. July and August.

THE DECIDUOUS ANDROMEDAS. *Lyonia (Andromeda).*

The andromedas have been represented in the chapter on trees by the larger deciduous species ; and in the chapter on evergreen trees and shrubs, the evergreen species will be mentioned.

The following are the shrubby deciduous species :

The *L. racemosa.*—A graceful shrub growing wild in southern swamps, bearing short racemes of small, white, fragrant, jar-shaped flowers, in June and July. Height three to four feet.

The *L. mariana* is a dwarf species found wild from New England to Florida, and bears pretty little racemes of small white flowers, tinged with pink, from May to August.

The *L. paniculata*, is a Canadian species three to four feet high, little known. The *L. salicifolia* or willow-leaved, is distinguished for fine glossy foliage. The *L. frondosa, L. multiflora, L. capreafolia,* are small shrubs, whose qualities in cultivated grounds are not well known.

THE ARALIA. *Aralia.*

Otherwise known as the angelica tree and Hercules club. The stout, club-like, and prickly annual canes of this curious shrub make the latter name not inappropriate. It has a partly perennial character, the canes usually dying to near the ground, like the raspberry, at the end of the year, and renewing themselves annually. These grow quickly to the height of eight to twelve feet, and bear immense doubly-compound leaves which form into an umbrella-like head of picturesque luxuriance. We have seen it established as a tree, with a trunk six or seven inches in diameter; and grown in this way, it has an unusually distinctive character; but it does not often make for itself a good trunk, and is oftener not quite a tree, nor yet a shrub. Flowers in large, loose panicles, greenish-white, in August and September.. Height ten to twenty feet.

There is a Japanese species, *A. japonica*, that is smaller, and has not, it is believed, been introduced in American gardens.

THE AZALEA. *Azalea.*

A deciduous shrub of the rhododendron family, natives of both hemispheres. The species vary in height from six inches to fifteen feet. The following are a few of them:

Azalea pontica, a native of the eastern borders of the Mediterranean. Height four to six feet. Flowers yellow; in May and June. "There are a great number of varieties of this species in the gardens, differing principally in the color of their flowers and the hue of their leaves. The flowers of the species are of a fine bright yellow; but those of the varieties are of all shades, from yellow to copper or orange color; and they are sometimes of a pure white, or of white striped with yellow and red. Besides, as this species seeds freely, and is easily cross-fecundated with the North American species, an immense number of varieties of it have been originated in British and Continental gardens" (Loudon). Some of these varieties may be found in the catalogues of our principal nurseries.

Azalea nudiflora.—Upright American honeysuckle ; natives of hilly or mountainous parts of the United States. Leaves lanceo-late-oblong, nearly smooth, and green on both surfaces. Flowers scarlet, pink, white, striped, variegated, red, and purple ; and disposed in terminal clustered racemes, appearing before the leaves ; April to June. Height three to four feet. The wild varieties are numerous, and have been superseded in cultivation by new varieties.

Azalea viscosum. Flowers produced in terminal clusters ; leafy and hairy ; white and sweet-scented ; June, July and August. The varieties and hybrids produced by cultivation from this species, are as numerous as those of the preceding species. Height two to fifteen feet.

Azalea speciosa.—The showy azalea. Flowers scarlet ; June and July. Height two to six feet. A native of our country.

Azalea arborescens.—The tree-like azalea. Height ten to fifteen feet. Flowers rose-colored ; June and July. Leaves glossy on both sides ; long oval, with obtuse end. Pursh, a distinguished botanist, says it forms, with its elegant foliage and large, abundant, rose-colored flowers, the finest ornamental shrub he knows.

The following is a list of a few *hardy*-bedding azaleas, recommended by Mr. J. R. Strumpe, of the Parsons' nursery at Flushing, one of the most skillful cultivators of the azalea and the rhododendron in this country :

A. parmicellata stellata, straw-color and salmon. *A. elegantissima,* pink ; late. *A. calendulacea flamula,* scarlet. *A. calendulacea coc cinea,* orange scarlet. *A. visocephalum,* white and very fragrant. *A. coccinea,* scarlet. *A. bicolor,* orange, yellow and white ; superb. *A. ne plus ultra.*

These are mostly hybrids, produced by skillful cultivation. A soil composed largely of leaf mould, with the roots somewhat protected from the sun, is considered desirable for the azalea. It is a species of shrub that requires much attention, and not noted for the abundance of its foliage when out of bloom. Those who have green-houses find the azalea one of the most available of bedding-out shrubs, but with common culture it is not so valuable.

THE BUDDLÉA. *Buddiea.*

Some varieties of this Chilian shrub have been tried in open ground near New York, and the *Buddlea Lindleyana* is advertised by some of our leading nursery-men. The genus is not considered hardy in England, and is not likely to be in the northern States.

THE GLOBE-FLOWERED BUDDLEA, *B. globosa*, in Chili, is a large spreading shrub, twelve to fifteen feet high, with small balls of bright yellow flowers and long lanceolate opposite leaves, growing at right angles with their twigs, to which they are attached.

THE BUTTONWOOD. *Cephalanthus.*

This is not our American plane tree, or sycamore, which is sometimes called the buttonwood tree, but a compact, glossy-leaved shrub, indigenous throughout the States on the borders of swamps and in wet shady places. For such places it is one of the best shrubs, forming a globular bush, well covered with thick glossy leaves. The flowers are yellowish-white, and appear in globular clusters, about one inch in diameter, in July and August. Height four to six feet. In dry sunny exposures the foliage is rusty, less abundant, and less glossy.

THE BERBERRY. *Berberis.*

A spreading, many-stemmed, deciduous prickly shrub; the habit of growth being much like that of a gooseberry bush. Height from four to ten feet. Leaves small, very glossy, obovate, serrate, with hairy edges; flowers yellow; May and June. Berries red; ripe in September. Grown in England for its fruit. It is a long-lived shrub, and sometimes grows into a small tree.

THE COMMON BERBERRY. *B. vulgaris.*—When well grown, in a warm soil, it forms a very pretty shrub. Its short racemes of small yellow flowers, in May, though not showy, are pretty. When growing alone, or on the border of a mass of shrubs, its branches, with age, bend gracefully to the ground, though for some years after it is planted the habit is erect.

THE PURPLE BERBERRY. *B. atropurpurea.*—This is a variety of the common berberry, with leaves and young twigs of a pure purple color. A beautiful and indispensable shrub in every collection, on this account, as well as for its gracefully spreading habit Flowers like the preceding. A spreading bush, five to seven feet broad and high, ordinarily, but may be grown much larger.

THE CALYCANTHUS, OR SWEET-SCENTED SHRUB.
Calycanthus floridus.

A spreading bush, native of the southern States, with fragrant flowers and camphor-scented wood. The flowers, produced from May to August, are small and inconspicuous, but of a peculiar and delicious perfume. Color, a deep dull purple. The leaves are dull in color. At the south it is a handsome shrub, but is not so well worth planting in the northern States, except for the peculiarity of the perfume. It does best in a rich, warm, sandy soil, and a shady place. The *C. glaucus* is a variety very similar to the above, with glossier leaves, and less odorous but brighter-colored flowers. Height at the south six to eight feet. The *C. prunifolius* is a variety highly recommended for its good habit and fragrance.

THE CARAGANA. *Caragana.*

An Asiatic species of *leguminaceæ*, mostly shrubs. The following are the best known ·

THE SIBERIAN PEA-TREE. *Caragana arborescens.*—A fastigiate shrubby tree, with numerous yellow twigs and very small pinnate leaves of the same character as those of the acacias, but much smaller and of a rare golden-green color. Flowers small, yellow, in April or May. Seeds borne in pods, ripe in August. A tree of marked beauty in early summer, by the contrast it presents with shrubs of dark and less delicate foliage. Height ten to eighteen feet.

The *Caragana frutescens* is a more shrubby species of the same, growing six to ten feet high; also noted for the yellowish hue of its leaves.

The *Caragana grandiflora.*—A pretty, quite low shrub, with the same characteristics of foliage as the preceding. Height two to four feet. Flowers yellow, an inch long, in June and July. Pods brown, ripe in September.

THE CHINESE CARAGANA, *C. chamlagu*, is a low spreading shrub, two to four feet high, with branches at first upright and then decumbent. Grafted on the *C. arborescens* it forms, according to Loudon, "a singularly picturesque pendulous tree; beautiful not only when it is in leaf or in flower, but from the graceful lines formed by its branches, even in the midst of winter, when, they are completely stripped of their leaves." Flowers yellow, or reddish yellow, in May and June.

THE CALOPHACA. *Calophaca.*

This is another species of *leguminaceæ* from Russia and Siberia, with extremely small acacia-like leaves. composed of many leaflets, and racemes of yellow blossoms, on long upright stalks. It bears a reddish pod in August, which is ornamental. It is recommended to graft this species on the laburnum, as it forms a shrub only two to four feet high on its own roots. Flowers in June.

THE CHIMONANTHUS, OR WINTER FLOWER.
Chimonanthus fragrans.

A half-hardy shrub, from Japan, producing yellow and purple flowers, an inch or more in diameter, of great fragrance, from November to March; hence its name of winter flower. It flourishes in the south of England, and will probably thrive on the Atlantic and Gulf slopes south of Washington. It is considered one of the choicest acquisitions to English gardens, as its flowers can be gathered fresh daily through the winter, to decorate and perfume the drawing-room. Those who have cold grape-houses at the north may grow the shrub in tubs, to be kept in the open air during the summer and under glass in winter. Height six to eight feet. It can be trained to walls or *espaliers*. The name so nearly resembles chionanthus that it is sometimes erroneously supposed to be the same.

CEANOTHUS, OR RED ROOT. *Ceanothus.*

THE AMERICAN CEANOTHUS OR NEW JERSEY TEA-PLANT, *C. americanus*, is a wild-wood shrub from three to four feet high, well covered with small racemes of white flowers from June to August. The leaves were used during the American Revolution as a substitute for tea.

C. thyssiflorus is a sub-evergreen shrub of Upper California, which there becomes a small tree bearing bright blue flowers from May to November. In English gardens it is an esteemed flowering shrub.

C. velutinus, is another sub-evergreen species, native of the lower hills of Oregon, where it sometimes covers their declivities with almost impenetrable thickets. Height three to eight feet; flowers white.

THE CHASTE TREE. *Vitex.*

The chaste tree of our nurseries is the *V. agnus castus*. A deciduous shrub, native of South Europe. The leaf is composed of five to seven slender leaflets joined at a common centre like those of the *Pavia* family. They are aromatic, but not agreeably so. Flowers in September, small, bluish-white, rarely reddish-white, in loose terminal panicles, from seven to fifteen inches in length, and of an agreeable odor. Height eight to ten feet. The *V. a. latifolia* is a variety with broader and shorter leaflets, and flowers always blue. The cut-leaved chaste tree, *V. incisa*, is a newer

Chinese species that blooms profusely from July to September. Height four to five feet. The India chaste tree, *V. arborea*, is the largest species, and has broader and paler leaves. Flowers pur plish, in July and August. Height thirty feet. Half-hardy. All the family require a dry soil.

THE CLETHRA. *Clethra.*

Fig. 162.

This shrub, though indigenous in our woods, has been brought into notice in the New York Central Park, more than ever before. There are specimens there of several varieties. Fig. 162 represents one of them.

THE ALDER-LEAVED, *C. alnifolia*, forms a dense low shrub, covered in July with a mass of white flowers in racemes or spikes, and in September with a load of seeds that are showy, and rather ornamental. It also blooms a little for the second time in September. Hardy. Leaves abundant, light-colored, and without gloss. Height three to four feet, and greater breadth. A native of swamps.

THE FRAGRANT CLETHRAS grow by many divaricating sprouts or suckers, into a broad mass of coarse light-colored foliage. A specimen in the Central Park is eight feet high, ten feet in diameter, and, in September, one of the best single masses of shrub foliage.

THE DOWNY CLETHRA, *C. tomentosa*, differs principally in having the underside of the leaves covered with white down.

THE LARGE CLETHRA, *C. acuminata*, is a large shrub or low tree, with flowers like the first-named sort. A native of the high mountains of the Carolinas.

COLUTEA, OR BLADDER SENNA. *Colutea arborescens.*

A quick-growing straggling shrub, with delicate acacia-like leaves, of a warm light color. Its flowers are small and yellow, in July and August. Its fruit-pods are like little bladders, and explode with pressure. *A good shrub for the interior of masses of shrubbery.* Height twelve to fourteen feet. *C. cruenta* is a smaller variety, with reddish flowers. *C. media* is near the size of the first, with orange flowers. They require cutting back, to prevent the bottom parts from becoming bare of leaves, unless placed behind masses of lower shrubs. The *C. arborescens* can, with care, be made into a pretty tree.

THE FLOWERING CURRANT. *Ribes.*

The several varieties of flowering currants are graceful shrubs of slender growth
and small leaves ; with less weight of foliage
than characterize the lilacs, syringas, and
bush-honeysuckles, but so early in leaf and
flower, and pleasing in form, that they are
apt to grow in favor where well known.

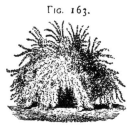

Fig. 163.

There is a grace in the drooping—almost trailing—habit of the lower growth of old bushes when allowed free expansion on all sides, that adapts them for the borders of groups. Height and breadth five to eight feet.

THE MISSOURI CURRANT. *Ribes aureum.*—This blooms in April, as the leaves are beginning to expand. The blossoms are yellow, small, in racemes from one to two inches long, and fragrant. Covering the slender branches, bending to the lawn, these early flowers mingled with opening leaves have a pretty effect, and the shrubs cover pleasingly with delicate yellowish-green glossy foliage after the flowers are gone.

THE RED-FLOWERING CURRANT, *R. sanguineum*, is much more showy in bloom. Its flowers are a deep rose-color, small like the preceding, but the racemes a little longer, and it blooms even earlier. There are many varieties, hybrids between this and the *R. aureum.* The following is generally considered the finest:

GORDON'S FLOWERING CURRANT, *R. Gordoni*, has both crimson and yellow flowers ; it blooms profusely, and somewhat later than

31

the preceding, and is of vigorous growth and very graceful habit at maturity.

THE DOUBLE CRIMSON, *R. sanguinea flore plena*, is a new variety, said to be more showy in flower.

The *R. s. glutinosum* is a variety with pink flowers and earliest of all in leaf. The foliage of all these shrubs falls early, but turns to brilliant crimson and yellow colors before it falls.

THE FUSCHIA GOOSEBERRY, *Ribes speciosum*, is necessary to complete the variety. Its shining leaves and vivid crimson blossoms, like miniature fuschias, and its lesser size, make it an appropriate border companion for the preceding sorts. Flowers in May and June. It can be budded on any of the currants.

All these varieties of *Ribes* are natives of the valley of the Columbia, or California.

Many of the old high-bush gooseberries are beautiful shrubs in the spring and summer, but most of them drop their leaves so early in the fall that it is a serious objection to their use.

THE WHITE CYTISSUS, OR PORTUGAL BROOM.
Cytissus alba.

A half-hardy shrub, allied to the laburnums. A native of the south of Europe. Growth rapid, fastigiate, and composed of a great number of green upright shoots. Flowers white, in May, like very small pea-blossoms, and very sweet. " Placed by itself on a lawn, it forms a singularly ornamental plant, even when not in flower, by the varied disposition and tufting of its twiggy thread-like branches. When in flower it is one of the finest ornaments of the garden. Trained to a single stem, its effect is increased ; and grafted on the laburnum, a common practice about Paris, it forms a remarkable combination of beauty and singularity " (Loudon). Height from ten to twenty feet.

THE FLESH-COLORED CYTISSUS. *C. a. incarnata.*—This is a dwarf variety of the above which blooms profusely, and is probably the most desirable of the species. The varieties of broom are very numerous, but not of sufficient value to enumerate.

THE COTONEASTER. *Cotoneaster.*

Shrubs, deciduous and evergreen, from four to twenty feet high. The leaves of some varieties resemble the quince leaf, and others the leaves of the purple fringe tree. Mostly half-hardy.

THE COMMON COTONEASTER. *C. vulgaris.*—A shrub three to five feet high. Flowers small, white, slightly tinged with pink, in April and May. Fruit red or black, ripe in July and August. Of little value.

THE FRIGID COTONEASTER. *C. frigida.*—This is a native of the high mountains of Nepal, in Asia, and becomes under cultivation a tree from fifteen to twenty feet in height. It is sub-evergreen in England, but deciduous in this country. Leaves pointed-elliptical, smooth on the upper side, woolly on the under side, when young, and from three to five inches long. Flowers small, white, in terminal panicles, produced in great abundance in April and May. Fruit crimson or bright red, of the size of a small currant, and remains a long time on the tree—sometimes all winter. The growth is quite rapid when young, and in three or four years from the seed it bears flowers and fruit. "As the fruit, with the greater part of the leaves, remains on all winter, the tree makes a splendid appearance at that season" (Loudon). Quite hardy in England, but only half-hardy in our northern States. It may be grafted on the hawthorn.

THE DOWNY COTONEASTER OR DOWNY NEPAL. *C. affinis.*—This is a more commonly cultivated variety of the above, and differs only in its broader and shorter leaves. Both resemble thrifty pyramidal dwarf pear trees, with larger and thicker leaves.

THE POINTED-LEAVED COTONEASTER OR THE MANY-LEAVED COTONEASTER, *C. acuminata* and *C. numularia*, has smaller and rounder leaves, a more spreading habit, and less abundant bloom. It is grafted by some of our nurserymen on the mountain ash.

THE LOOSE-FLOWERED COTONEASTER, *C. laxiflora*, is a variety with pink flowers borne in loose racemes in April.

There are some dwarf evergreen varieties which are mentioned in the chapter on evergreen trees and shrubs.

THE DAPHNE. *Daphne.*

Low shrubs, both deciduous and evergreen, growing in shady places.

THE MEZEREON PINK. *Daphne mezerium.*—A low, fastigiate, deciduous shrub, valued for the earliness of its very bright red blossoms, which are formed upon the branches in March and April before the leaves appear. They are about a half inch in diameter. The berries are red and ripe in September. In a deep loam and open exposure it becomes a shrub four to six feet high, and of equal breadth. The berries and leaves are both poisonous if eaten. There is a white-flowered variety, *D. m. flore alba;* a purple-leaved, *D. van Houtti;* and an autumn bloomer, *D. m. autumnale.* The latter blooms in November and December, and has larger leaves and a more spreading habit than the common mezereon.

There are numerous species of Daphne, but no others of known value except the *Daphne cneorum,* which is mentioned among evergreens.

THE ELDER. *Sambucus.*

THE COMMON ELDER, *S. canadensis.*—This is the Canadian elder of the English. A large spreading bush from seven to ten feet high, and of greater breadth ; with a flattened umbrella-shaped top. Its compound leaves are composed of nine leaflets, of a light green color, and glossy on the upper surface. The flowers are small, white, and in large flat clusters, in July. The fruit, about the size of the currant, is bluish-black, good to eat, and excellent for wine ; ripe in September. The spreading form, handsome compound glossy leaves, and showy fruit of our wild elder, sometimes make it a shrub of considerable beauty

THE BLACK-FRUITED ELDER. *S. nigra.*—This is the common elder of the English, and a native of Europe. It grows as a tree rapidly when young, but remains stationary after the tree has attained twenty or thirty feet in height, and equal breadth. The leaves are pinnate, of five leaflets, smooth, and of a deep green color. The flowers, of a pleasing cream color, are small, but in large flat clusters, in June. When in bloom the tree is showy; and it has a pleasing appearance at other times. The berries are purplish-black, ripe in September, and valuable, like those of our native sort, for making wine. A wine is also made from the flowers.

THE MOUNTAIN ELDER, *S. racemosa,* is a shrub from ten to twelve feet in height, "a native of the middle and south of Europe, and Siberia, on the mountains, where it forms a large shrub, or low tree, growing from ten to twelve feet high" (Loudon). It is remarkable for the color of its panicles of fruit, which are a brilliant scarlet, and considered by some the most beautiful of wild fruits. The leaves are composed of five leaflets, of a pale green color, and smooth. Flowers a whitish-green. Why is it not cultivated in our nurseries?

THE VARIEGATED-LEAVED ELDER. *S. variegata.*—This is one of the most showy of variegated-leaved shrubs. The growth is strong and healthy, the leaves are mottled with a clear yellow, and preserve their bright color throughout the season.

THE EUONYMUS. *Euonymus.*

Shrubs, or small trees, popularly known by the names strawberry tree, spindle tree, and burning bush. Different species of the euonymus are indigenous in America, Europe and Asia. There are several varieties of decided beauty. The name burning-bush, given to both the common European and American euonymus, well describes them as seen at a distance when covered with their pendant crimson or scarlet seed-capsules in October and later; and especially when seen in the thickets of a forest. They are all of easy culture, hold their leaves longer than many other shrubs, and turn to fine colors in autumn.

THE AMERICAN EUONYMUS, *E. americana,* forms a pretty little umbrella-shaped tree, from six to ten feet high, with pretty green striped bark, and dark glossy leaves, somewhat resembling those of the dogwood family. It is a pleasing tree or shrub without its fruit, though it is for the beauty given it in autumn and winter by its brilliant and curious seed-vessels, that it is usually planted. The flowers are a greenish-yellow, in May and June, and inconspicuous. The seed is enclosed in a capsule, which opens like a chestnut burr, showing a glowing crimson lining, from which the white and scarlet seeds are suspended by delicate threads, and remain a long time on the tree—sometimes all winter—and when contrasted with the snow around them, render the tree singularly brilliant.

THE PURPLE-FLOWERED EUONYMUS, *E. atropurpureum*, is another native variety, distinguished by its purple flowers in June and July, and its narrower leaves.

THE EUROPEAN EUONYMUS. *E. europæus.*—This species has a smaller leaf than our own, and, we think, is not so handsome; but the difference is slight in all respects. It becomes a tree of larger size, sometimes attaining a height of thirty feet.

THE BROAD-LEAVED EUONYMUS. *E. latifolius.*—This is the most beautiful in foliage of the family, with leaves considerably larger than the others, quite abundant, and of a fine glossy green; the fruit is also larger, and of a deep red color, more showy in quantity, but not so brilliant in color as the American sort. The decaying leaves turn to a fine purplish-red, and the naked branches are of a pleasing reddish-green. It forms a tree from ten to twenty feet high. One of the finest of shrubby trees.

The *Euonymus radicans* is a new variety from Japan, recommended by Thomas Meehan, Esq., as a tree of striking beauty.

There are several new variegated-leaved varieties from Japan, and some dwarf species, the beauty and hardiness of which have not yet been sufficiently proved to call for special notice.

THE ELÆAGNUS, OLEASTER, OR WILD OLIVE.
Elæagnus

THE GARDEN ELÆAGNUS OR OLEASTER. *Elæagnus hortensis.*—This is an old English garden shrub, a native of southern Europe. It is noted for the silvery whiteness of its foliage, and, on this account, is often selected to plant where it is desired to attract attention to a particular point, or to create variety with other trees. Flowers in May, quite small, pale yellow, and fragrant. Fruit reddish-brown ; insipid. Height fifteen to twenty feet. Half-hardy.

THE MISSOURI SILVER-TREE. *E. argentea.*—A fastigiate small tree, with whitish-colored small leaves, and rather a pendulous disposition of its spray. A fine specimen is growing near the Seventh Avenue entrance to the Central Park, in an exposed locality, which, in September, 1868, was fifteen feet high and eight feet broad ; and was quite showy by reason of the whiteness of its foliage and its graceful growth. Flowers small, yellow, in July and August. Fruit about the size of a small cherry ; the flesh dry and mealy, but eatable.

THE JAPAN OLEASTER, *E. japonica,* and the small-flowered *E. paniflorus,* are shrubs noted for their whitish foliage.

THE FOTHERGILLA. *Fothergilla alnifolia.*

A dense-foliaged, low, and very spreading native shrub, which thrives only in partial shade and moisture, and requires some protection at the north. Leaves obovate, bluntly serrated, and downy beneath. Flowers small, white, in terminal spikes, sweet-scented and appear before the leaves in April and May.

THE FORSYTHIA. *Forsythia viridissima.*

A large spreading shrub, of brilliant green foliage, and straggling willow-like sprouts and growth. Its luxuriance, the earliness of its bright small yellow flowers, and the fact that it is a comparatively new thing, has given this shrub a reputation that it may not sustain. It is a little tender north of New York, and when young and growing rapidly the summer growth should be headed back, about the first of October, one-half its length. At the west end of Lake Erie it kills back winters in consequence of continuing its growth too late in autumn. Its leaves hang on late in the fall almost with the persistency of an evergreen. Height and breadth

seven to ten feet.   It does not, at the north, grow into a good form
to stand alone, and should, therefore, be grown among other shrubs.

THE HAZEL AND FILBERT. *Corylus.*

Our common bush hazel can hardly be unknown to any persons
in this country; as it grows wild in all sections, forming copses from
four to seven feet high in new clearings and by the sides of fences,
wherever the ground is warm and rich.   Its nut is the most delicate of all native nuts, and quite equal in flavor, though inferior in
size, to the Spanish filbert.   Where squirrels abound it is difficult
to preserve the nuts, as the nimble animals usually gather them the
moment they are fit, and lay them by for winter use ; while to pluck
them before the husk is brown injures their flavor and plumpness.
The bushes in foliage resemble young elms so closely that they are
frequently dug for them.   The green-fringed husk of the nut is
quite ornamental, and, if rare, would be considered a great curiosity.   As it is, we would prefer the hazel bush, as an ornamental
copse, to quite a number of foreign shrubs grown in our nurseries.
It does best in masses, and in the dry rich soil of cultivated grounds
it would, doubtless, give a grateful return of vigorous growth and
picturesque fruit, to repay all extra attentions.   Some of the petti-
est examples of shrubbery vistas we have ever seen were on cow-
paths (followed when a boy) winding between clumps of luxuriant
hazel, and among exquisite little thorn trees, elegantly trimmed by
browsing sheep and cattle :—not "tangled wild-woods" either—but
with velvet lawn, and all the rounded and cultivated beauty essential to the neighborhood of a dwelling-house.

The following are varieties of hazels and filberts : *Corylus americana* is the common American hazel-nut above described.   *C.
avellana* is the common European hazel or filbert.   The varieties
of this are numerous ; some of them are cultivated for their beauty
alone, and others for their superior nuts.

THE PURPLE-LEAVED FILBERT, *C. a. purpurea,* has leaves of a
dark red or purple, and is one of the most showy of colored-leaved
shrubs.   Its sporting character is so vigorous that it is said to im-

part its color to the leaves of the stock on which it is grafted! It might be grafted or budded on strong canes of our native hazel.

The *C. a. crispa* is one of the finest filberts, and also remarkable for the length and showiness of its fringed nut-husks. The *C. a. tennis*, *C. a. tubulosa*, *C. a. barcelonensis*, are all fine large varieties of filberts, and somewhat larger shrubs than our native hazel.

THE CONSTANTINOPLE HAZEL, *C. colurna*, is the largest of the species, making a tree fifty to sixty feet high.

THE HYDRANGEA. *Hydrangea.*

Herbaceous shrubs, mostly natives of this country, some of which have globular masses of white and pink-white flowers, and generally fine masses of large, rather heart-shaped leaves, of a pleasing light-green color. Generally half-hardy.

THE GARDEN HYDRANGEA. *H. hortensis.*—This is the common bushy plant grown in boxes and seen in or near almost every New England village porch. It is well worthy of its popularity. Few plants better repay attention. It forms a globular bush, from two to four feet in diameter, densely furnished with large leaves, and covered all summer with light pink blossoms, in massy clusters, frequently six inches in diameter. The flowers change their color in an unusual manner with the treatment they receive, sometimes changing to blue and purple; a mixture of a few iron-filings with the soil producing the former color. It is best to grow it in boxes, to be wintered in dry cellars, as it is too tender to be trusted in the open ground in the northern States. It is one of the most beautiful outdoor box-plants, of easy culture, and as it does best in the shade, is peculiarly adapted to positions near walks in the shadows of trees. It requires rich, warm, and always moist soil.

THE SILVER-STRIPED LEAVED, and the GOLDEN-STRIPED LEAVED HYDRANGEAS, have only the peculiarities which their names import.

THE OAK-LEAVED HYDRANGEA. *H. quercifolia.*—A hardier shrub than the *hortensis*, and more woody; of bushy habit. It becomes a massive-looking shrub, six feet high. The leaves are large, rough, lobed like an oak, and hairy or downy beneath. The flowers, which are white, and about one and a half inches in diameter, are borne in clusters from four to six inches long, from June to September. It requires a sheltered situation, and a moist soil. In autumn the leaves turn to a fine deep-red color.

THE HEART-LEAVED HYDRANGEA, *H. cordata*, has large foliage and small flowers : the tree-like, *H. arborescens*, is a native of Pennsylvania and Virginia ; the bush, leaf, and flower being smaller than the preceding : the snowy-leaved, or hoary-leaved, *H. canescens*, is a low shrub of the southern States, with flowers larger than the preceding, and leaves white and velvety beneath. The *involucrata* is said to be a hardy and unusually erect variety.

THE JAPAN HYDRANGEA. *H. deutziafolia* (*H. paniculata grandiflora*).—This variety, but recently introduced into this country, bids fair to be quite the most valuable of the hydrangeas. It seems to be hardy in the Central Park, with straw protection in winter, and there forms magnificent masses of fine leaves and flowers, blooming profusely from the first of August until frosts. The leaves are large, abundant, and of a dark bright glossy green color. The flowers are larger than those of the old box-hydrangea, of a creamy-white color, and waxy texture. They grow in immense spikes six inches or more long, and of equal breadth, and turn to a purplish-pink color as the season advances. Height and breadth of bush from three to five feet.

THE HYPERICUM, OR ST. JOHNSWORT. *Hypericum.*

Low sub-evergreen shrubs suitable for shady places. The varieties *H. prolificum* and *H. kalmianum* are broad, compact, low shrubs, two to three feet high, with small elliptical leaves, and corymbs of small yellow flowers in July and August, and are highly valued (especially the latter) for their neat compact growth and the warm tone of the foliage. The *H. calycinum* is an evergreen trailing species with much larger leaves and flowers, the latter of a bright-golden color, which is greatly esteemed for planting among rocks and trees in very shady places. The root creeps and stoles so that the plant extends itself rapidly over the surface.

THE JASMINE. *Jasminum.*

The name jasmine has been so interwoven with poetical associations that it carries with it an aroma of literature as well as of flowers. It is time-honored as one of the emblems of bridal adornment, the blossoms being used to deck the hair. Moore alludes to this custom in the oriental story of Lalla Rookh :

> " And brides as delicate and fair
> As the white jasmine flowers they wear,
> Hath Yemen, in her blissful clime."

Cowper describes both the leaves and blossoms in the following lines •

> " The deep dark green of whose unvarnished leaf
> Makes more conspicuous and illumes the more,
> The bright profusion of her scattered stars."

The family embraces vines, shrubs, and trees, evergreen and deciduous ; some of them hot-house plants, most of them half-hardy vines, and a few hardy ones. The fragrance of their blossoms is their most charming trait. Most of the species will not bear the winters in our country. Their most beautiful use is for covering low walls or arbors in protected situations.

THE COMMON JASMINE, *J. officinale*, may be grown as a shrub, but is really a noble climber in congenial climates ; as in its native wilds in Asia, Georgia, and the mountains of Caucasus, it grows forty to fifty feet in height, and attains similar dimensions in our southern States. Its young wood is of a fine deep-green color, and being quite abundant, gives the vine in winter the appearance of an evergreen plant. Leaves pinnate, five to seven leaflets. Flowers white, in June, July, and August, and exceedingly fragrant. This jasmine requires winter protection in the northern States.

The *Jasmine nudiflorum* is a sort recently introduced ; with fragrant yellow blossoms from May to October. Mr. Meehan recommends that it " be trained to a stiff stake and pruned twice a year ; it then grows very compact, and will support itself after the stake rots away, and makes one of the prettiest shrubbery bushes imaginable." Requires protection in winter.

These are the only jasmines sufficiently hardy to be recommended for out-door culture.

THE JASMINE OF GOA, *J. odoratissimum*, is a yellow-flowered green-house variety, native of Madeira, of exquisite fragrance; to which the charming lines of Moore apply—

> "'Twas midnight :—through the lattice, wreathed
> With woodbine, many a perfume breathed,
> From plants that wake when others sleep,
> From timid jasmine buds, that keep
> Their odor to themselves all day,
> But, when the sunlight dies away,
> Let the delicious secret out
> To every breeze that roams about."

It may be kept through the winter in a pit or green-house, and planted out as a pot-shrub in summer, in corners near windows, or other places where its evening fragrance can be best enjoyed.

Loudon relates an extraordinary fact concerning the jasmine, viz: "When it is desired to turn a green-leaved jasmine into a variegated one, a single bud of either the silver-leaved, or the golden-leaved, inserted in it, will communicate its variegation to every part of the plant, even to suckers thrown up by the roots!"

THE JAPAN KERRIA, OR GLOBE FLOWER.
Kerria japonica.

A low shrub bearing yellow flowers from March to June, and sometimes all summer. Leaves deeply and unequally serrated. The bark of the twigs is a fine green color. The double-flowered variety, *K. j. flore plena*, is not quite hardy. Height three to five feet.

THE PŒONY. *Pæonia.*

THE TREE-PŒONY, *P. moutan*, is among the most showy of low garden shrubs, and in dry soils sufficiently hardy to be planted throughout the States; though considerable protection in the northern States improves its size and beauty. It attains a height of from five to eight feet in ten years, if properly taken care of. The two most common varieties are the Chinese double-blush, *P. banksii*, with pale, rose-colored flowers, from four to six inches in diameter, very double and fragrant, and much the finest of all; and the poppy-flowered, *P. papaveracea*, with pale, blush flowers, less double than the preceding. A large number of varieties are produced in the nurseries, some of which may be improvements on the parent species. They range through many colors, from white and variegated, to bright red, violet and purple. The following are a few of the best:

P. alba variegata, white petals, purplish centre, very double.

P. gumpperii, "bright rosy pink, very large and full; plant vigorous; one of the very best in all respects." (E. & B.)

P. kochlerii, dark rose-color; very large and vigorous.

P. maxima plena, rosy carmine, very double and compact.

P. rosea superba plena, dark rosy violet.

P. schultzii, carmine, shaded with rosy lilac; fine form, and fragrant.

P. incarnata flore plena, pure white, with violet centre; fragrant.

THE PRIVET. *Ligustrum.*

THE COMMON PRIVET, *Ligustrum vulgaris*, is one of the commonest of old garden shrubs, and has been greatly valued for deciduous hedges, for which its fastigiate form, ready growth from cuttings, its twiggy and healthy habit, well adapt it. The leaves are small, appear early, and hang so late that in England it is called a sub-evergreen. The flowers are small, white, on terminal spikes, which cover the shrub in June and July. Berries a dark purple. Growing as a shrub, it forms a globular bush of rather dull green color, and from seven to ten feet high. No shrub bears clipping better, or is more easily shaped into hedges, screens, or other desirable forms. Yet, for such purposes, it does not seem to us so desirable as the fine arbor-vitæs and the hemlock. It has, however, the valuable quality of flourishing in the shade and drip of trees. It needs a strong soil.

THE EVERGREEN ITALIAN PRIVET, *L. sempivirens,* is an improved variety, more valuable where hardy.

THE GOLD-STRIPED AND SILVER-STRIPED PRIVETS, *L. foleis aureis* and *argenteis,* are considered by some "pretty and desirable mingled with the common privet."

THE OVAL-LEAVED PRIVET, *L. ovalifolium,* is a variety with larger leaves and stronger growth than the common, which we have seen formed into a superb hedge ten feet high, at the residence of Alfred Cope, Esq., Germantown, Pa.

There are numerous varieties named from small differences in forms of leaves and fruit, which it is not necessary to enumerate.

THE WAXY-LEAVED PRIVET, *L. lucidum,* is a species recently introduced, and now growing with great beauty in the Central Park. It is a native of China, where it forms a low sub-evergreen tree, twenty feet in height. The leaves are much larger, brighter-colored, and more glossy than those of the common privet. *L. l. floribundum* is its finest variety.

THE SPIKE-FLOWERED PRIVET, *L. spicatum,* is a tender species from Nepal, with large pointed elliptic leaves, and larger spikes of flowers ; six to eight feet high.

THE CALIFORNIA PRIVET, *L. californica.*—This species, recently introduced, has a leaf of such remarkable beauty, that, if the shrub proves hardy, it will be very popular and in great demand. The leaf is considerably larger than that of the common privet, of a very dark waxy-green on the upper surface, a purplish tinge about the edges, and the under surface pea-green. The growth of young plants is about the same as that of the common privet, but from the greater size of the leaves, their thicker texture, and brilliant glossiness, they have a ranker appearance. The leaves have a peculiar veining, that adds to their beauty. Mr. J. R. Strumpe, of the Parsons' nursery, believes that it will prove hardy. What size it attains in California we have not learned. We fear that the thick waxy foliage of this beautiful species indicates a tropical nature that may not be acclimated in most parts of the northern States.

PTELEA OR SHRUBBY TREFOIL. *Ptelea trifoliata.*

This is a thin wild shrub, which can be trained into a miniature tree six to ten feet high. Leaves of three ovate acute leaflets, on long stalks; they turn to a clear yellow in autumn. Fruit winged, and in clusters, like those of the *Halesia tetraptera*, Fig. 143.

THE QUINCE. *Cydonia.*

THE COMMON ORANGE QUINCE, *Cydonia vulgaris*, is sometimes one of the prettiest of shrubby trees. But it is so commonly seen crowded into some corner of the garden, or neglected grassy ground, that the idea of its being classed with favor among ornamental trees for small grounds will seem to some persons almost ludicrous. Yet we have seen young quince trees loaded with large white blossoms, slightly tinged

FIG. 164.

with pink, standing near masses of the finest varieties of lilacs, and in full view of blossoming magnolias, horse-chestnuts, and apple trees, and though lowly and shrubby compared with them, it was yet not inferior to any in the beautiful profusion of its bloom, and the pleasing setting that its polished young leaves make for their flowers. Fig. 164 is a sketch of a pretty young quince tree of this sort. When grown in the moist rich ground which it requires, the foliage is always fine, and its low broad form is well adapted to gardenesque grounds. Its great golden fruit in autumn is among the most showy of fruits while hanging on the tree, as well as the most fragrant of native conserves. It grows quickly to the height of six or eight feet, and afterwards gains more in breadth than height, so that in ten or twelve years it forms a tree about eight or ten feet high, and twelve or fifteen feet diameter of head. It is best grown with a single stem, and allowed to branch about two feet above the ground. If all suckers are kept down, the head will usually grow to a good form without pruning. The branches are of crooked, rambling growth, and the tree is not a pleasing one in winter. The common orange quince is the best variety. It grows readily from cuttings.

THE CHINA QUINCE TREE. *C. sinensis.*—This differs from the preceding in having serrated instead of smooth-edged leaves, and rose-colored flowers. Its fruit is green, egg-shaped, and of little value.

THE JAPAN QUINCE. *C. Japonica.*—This variety is almost too well known to need description. Unlike its fruit-bearing relative, the *C. vulgaris*, this later importation has been planted as it deserves to be. It is a low straggling thorny bush, and grows from five to eight feet in height and breadth. Its large bright-scarlet flowers are the earliest showy blossoms of the shrubbery; appearing with those of the red-bud and the white-flowered dogwood. On thrifty bushes which have been well cut back, the blossoms cover the branches with a blaze of bloom. Its leaves are a glossy-green, appear early, and keep their color late. A rich soil, moist or dry, is essential to it. When growing thriftily its straggling shoots should be headed back twice a year, in June and October, to thicken its foliage and bring the flower-buds, which are formed at the base of the annual growth, on the outside of the bush at the blooming season.

Among the sub-varieties of Japan quince are the following: The *C. j. umbellicata*, flowers a brilliant rose-color. Fruit orange-colored and very showy. It forms a large shrub, and is considered by some growers the finest variety. The Blush Japan quince, *C. j. alba*, large pale-blush flowers; the Double-Flowering Scarlet, *C. j. flore plena*; the Dark Crimson, *C. j. atrosanguinea*; the Orange Scarlet, *C. j. aurantiaca*; and the *mallardie*, with white flowers and rosy crimson centre. Nearly all are distinguished by what their names imply.

Were the Japan quince not somewhat difficult to propagate, it would be a most desirable low hedge-plant. Its thorns are decidedly quick to repel aggression, its leaves are bright and glossy from early spring to late in autumn, and its blossoms are unequalled in brilliancy, in their season, by any other hedge-plant.

THE ROSE. *Rosa.*

Fig. 165.

Du Hamel observes that "Nature appears scarcely to have placed any limit between the different species of the rose ; and, if it is already very difficult to define the wild species, which have not yet been modified by culture, it is almost impossible to refer to their original type the numerous varieties which culture has made in the flowers of species already so nearly resembling each other." To the ordinary amateur the great number of divisions among cultivated roses into classes and sub-classes, by which professional florists endeavor to facilitate a knowledge of the different sorts of roses, sometimes serves rather to make the confusion worse confounded. The distinctions which seem simple enough, and quite necessary to professional florists, who have examples of all sorts constantly before their eyes, is a bewildering mass of floral lore, quite embarrassing to the amateurs for whom one or two dozen of the best varieties of roses will do as well as a thousand. The author of a recent horticultural work, after enumerating we know not how many classes of roses, closes the chapter by condensing the results of his experience into a "select list" of upwards of two hundred varieties! A generosity scarcely exceeded by the nursery catalogues.

A plan now adopted by many nurserymen, and recommended by Francis Parkman in his excellent treatise entitled "The Book of Roses," is to arrange roses in two great divisions, viz: the first division embracing all roses, whether hardy or tender, which bloom in June, and not afterwards; the second division embracing all which bloom more than once in a season.

32

Division I.—Hardy June Roses.

Under this head are the following sub-divisions or classes given nearly in the order commonly adopted in late nursery catalogues.

Class I. Hybrid China Roses.—These are the hardy crosses which long cultivation has produced between the European June roses of various families and the true China roses. They are mostly free growers, with long flexible shoots; many of them well adapted for pillars or trellises, though of less rank growth than the wild climbers. The fine old crimson rose, known as George the Fourth, is one of the finest of this class. The following six are among the most desirable varieties. Those marked with a (*P*) are the tallest growers, and may be used for post-roses. The descriptions refer to the flowers.

    1. *Bizarre de la China.*—Crimson purple, globular and double.

    2. *Charles Duval.*—Deep rose, large, and well formed.

    3. *Chenedolle* (*P*).—Brilliant light crimson, large, double, and fragrant.

    4. *George the Fourth* (*P*).—Deep velvety crimson, and dark glossy foliage.

    5. *La Tourterelle* (*P*).—Dove colored, and well formed.

    6. *Madame Plantier.*—Pure white, blooms in great clusters. The best white.

Class II. Hybrid Provence, Damask, and French Roses.— The old cabbage or hundred-leaved rose is the type of the Provence roses, which are noted for fragrance and globular forms. The damask roses are of shades from white to the deepest crimson. Those which of late years are known as French or Gallican roses are of stiff erect growth, and the foliage is rough and hard, and of a lighter green than other roses. On the other hand, the miniature roses long known as Burgundy roses, and noted for their dwarf habit, in all respects are also hybrids of this class. The following half dozen are among the choicest of all these sorts, but do not include the Burgundys:

1. *Blanche Fleur.*—Pure white, very double, in clusters, early and profuse. Low bush.

2. *Double Margined Hep.*—Creamy white, edged with purplish-red; very large.

3. *Double White Sweet Briar.*—Pale blush, nearly white, very sweet.

4. *George Vibert.*—Striped red and white.

5. *Madame Hardy.*—White, full, and large.

6. *Rivers Superb Tuscany.*—Velvety crimson.

CLASS III. MOSS ROSES.—Six choice varieties are subjoined.

1. *Common Blush.*—Light pink, large; grows freely, and blooms profusely.

2. *Baron de Wassenaer.*—Bright pink, large; flowers in clusters. Vigorous.

3. *Countess of Murinais.*—White, large, and double; in clusters. Vigorous.

4. *Crested Province.* — Rose-colored; calyx curiously moss-fringed.

5. *Lanei.* Rosy crimson, tinted with purple, large and full.

6. *Princess Adelaide.*—Light rose, very large. Growth very vigorous, and adapted to be grown as a post-rose.

CLASS IV. CLIMBING ROSES.—This class embraces the PRAIRIE, BOURSAULT, and AYRSHIRE roses, which are hardy; and the MULTIFLORA and EVERGREEN roses, which require protection in the northern and middle States.

THE PRAIRIE ROSES, so called, are supposed to be hybrids between the common wild single-flowered pale-pink climbing rose of our woods, and old garden varieties. But there is little resemblance between what are now known as prairie roses and this parent from which they claim descent. The wild variety blooms later than any of the others, and is always single. The *Queen of the Prairies* is a very double rose, light red, and a vigorous grower. The *Baltimore Belle* is a blush white, very double, and a profuse bloomer, but not quite hardy in exposed situations. These are the best varieties of the prairie roses.

THE BOURSAULT is the common long smooth-branched climber, with reddish wood, few thorns, and semi-double crimson flowers in clusters. One of the most vigorous growers and profuse bloomers. The new variety, known as the *Blush Boursault*, is more showy.

THE AYRSHIRE ROSES are varieties of the wild field roses of England and Scotland, and have a slenderer but not shorter growth than the vigorous American climbers, and creep or trail rather more than our natives. *Bennett's Seedling*, which has a pure white flower, and the *Queen of Ayrshire*, a dark purplish-crimson flower, are the best sorts. They are best adapted to cover fences, chains, low trellises, or banks of earth, their natural habit being like that of the trailing blackberry, to keep close to the ground.

THE MULTIFLORA ROSES are seedlings from China roses, and require protection at the north. The *De la Grifferaie* and *Eugéne Gréville*, or *Seven Sisters*, are varieties advertised in northern nurseries; the former with rosy purple flowers, and the latter with flowers varying from blush to crimson. The latter is nearly hardy.

THE EVERGREEN ROSES, not being perfectly hardy, do not fairly come into this division, but as they are June roses, they do not belong with the second division, and are therefore referred to here. They are natives of the borders of the Mediterranean, and in the wild state single. Beautiful double varieties are now grown, but principally in green-houses. The *Felicité Perpetueé* is one of the best, and may be grown at the north with slight protection.

CLASS V. YELLOW AUSTRIAN ROSES.—This class has few varieties, and is represented by what are generally known as the *Persian Yellow* and *Harrison's Yellow*, beautiful double yellow roses, growing on tall delicate-leaved, and not very robust, bushes; and by the single yellow rose, known as the *Austrian Yellow*, which has a still more delicate or weakly growth. These roses are among the earliest to bloom. The single roses are noted for their disagreeable odor.

CLASS VI. WILD BUSH ROSES.—In the opening remarks on the rose a few of these have been referred to. As they are little grown in nurseries, and inferior to cultivated sorts, it is needless to enumer--

ate them; and though they form very pleasing clumps when growing wild, it is not certain that they could be made so beautiful even for that purpose alone as selected cultivated sorts. What are known as the Scotch roses are valuable only for the extreme earliness of their flowers. Their growth is slender, stiff, and very thorny, and they send up innumerable suckers. The flowers are small, semi-double, and numerous.

DIVISION II.—HYBRID PERPETUAL ROSES WHICH BLOOM MORE THAN ONCE EACH SEASON.

This division embraces classes of roses that differ widely in many respects. Some flower but twice, others are in almost constant bloom till late in autumn. Some are quite hardy, others half hardy, others, among the Noisette, China, and tea roses, are tender house-plants, though many of these may be wintered out with careful protection. The China and tea roses are the original perpetuals, and all the other classes have been created by hybridizing with one or another of the numerous species of June roses, and "breeding in-and-in" with these crosses to produce all the varieties now in cultivation. All are hybrid perpetuals; but those which show some resemblance to the families with which they are crossed are separated into classes as follows:

CLASS I. PERPETUAL MOSS ROSES.—The name signifies their character. The following are good sorts, but are not so mossy as the parent species, blooming in June

1. *Alfred de Dalmas*, light blush, in clusters; blooms freely.
2. *Eugénie Guinoiseau*, deep cherry; large, and quite mossy.
3. *Madame Edward Ory*, rosy carmine, large; not vigorous.
4. *Pompone*, dark crimson; blooms freely in autumn.
5. *Perpetual White*, white; large clusters of buds and flowers.
6. *Salet*, bright rose; quite mossy; a free grower and bloomer.

CLASS II. HYBRID PERPETUALS OR REMONTANTS.—Though all the roses of this division are really hybrid perpetuals, our nurserymen have classified certain hardy sorts under this title, which is retained on that account, to conform to usage. The class embraces crosses between a great number of species, the varieties differing greatly in vigor of growth and foliage, and in the character of their flowers. Some bloom but twice, others show only an occasional blossom after June, and some bloom constantly. The fine old *Madame Laffay*, and the magnificent newer *General Jacqueminot*, belong to this class. The following selection of eleven are among the finest

1. *Baron Prevost.*—Deep rose, large and full; a very vigorous grower, abundant bloomer, and perfectly hardy.

2. *Caroline de Sansal.*—Clear delicate light blush, very large and full; foliage luxuriant and growth vigorous.

3. *General Washington.*—Brilliant red, very large; "superb in autumn."

4. *General Jacqueminot.*—Crimson to scarlet, velvety, and of great size. Every way superb.

5. *Madame Laffay.*—Rosy crimson, large, and full.

6. *Madame Boutin.*—Cherry rose, large, and full; foliage very fine.

7. *Louise Darzens.*—Pure white, medium size; blooms in clusters, and constantly.

8. *Madame Alfred de Rougemont.*—Pure white, large, and a profuse bloomer.

9. *Duc de Cazes.*—Purplish crimson.

10. *John Hopper.*—Deep rose, large, and full.

11. *Mrs. Elliott* (P.).—Rosy purple, large, full, and sweet. Suitable for a post-rose.

CLASS III. BOURBON ROSES.—A race of which Parkman remarks—"Of sweeter savor in horticulture than in history." They are not quite hardy, and have less vigor of growth than the preceding class, but are mostly rich in glossy foliage, of stronger growth than the tea and Noisette roses, and sufficiently robust to remain out throughout the winter with proper protection. Growth from two to six feet. The following eight are favorite varieties:

1. *Duchess de Thuringen.*—Light blush, free bloomer; vigorous.

2. *Hermosa.*—Flesh color, large, and full, blooms profusely. Good grower.

3. *George Peabody.*—Dark velvety crimson.

4. *Sir Joseph Paxton.*—Bright rose, shaded with crimson large and full. Growth very vigorous.

5. *Souvenir de la Malmaison.*—Pale flesh; very large and full. Once considered the most 'splendid rose of its class.

6. *Souvenir de l'Exposition.*—Dark crimson; free bloomer.

7. *Marquise Balbiano.*—Bright rose, in clusters; fragrant.

8. *Piérre de St. Cyr* (P.).—Pale rose, large and full.

CLASS IV. NOISETTE, TEA, AND CHINA ROSES.—Of these the Noisettes and the tea-roses are the stronger growers, some of them forming quite fine bushes of secondary size. The foliage is smooth and fine, and the flowers of the Noisettes are borne in clusters. All are tender, but many of them may be left in the ground through the winter if skillfully covered in the fall. The tea roses are noted for the delicacy of their colors, and their delicious fragrance. The China (or Bengal) roses are the most delicate in growth, and the least hardy; and require to be removed to a green-house, plant-room, or cellar, after the first strong frosts.

The following is a select list of good varieties of Noisette and tea roses:

1. *Aimée Vibert.*—Pure white, small cupped flowers, in clusters. Bush small and low. One of the hardiest.

2. *Caroline Marniésse.*—White, with creamy centre, small perfect flowers, and a profuse bloomer.

3. *Solfaterre.*—Saffron-yellow, fragrant and fine.

4. *Céline Forester.*—Pale yellow, large, full and hardy.

5. *Isabella Gray.*—The deepest yellow.

6. *Jane Hardy.* Golden yellow, very double, free bloomer, and rich foliage.

7. *Lamarque.*—Pale lemon-yellow, very large flowers.

8. *Maréchal Niel.*—Deep yellow, very large, full, and fragrant. New, and of distinguished beauty.

Tea-scented Roses.—Eight choice varieties :

1. *Bougére.*—Deep, rosy bronze, large. Vigorous plant.

2. *Fleur de Cypress.* — Bright rose, shaded with salmon. Strong grower and free bloomer.

3. *Glory of Dijon.*—Yellow, shaded with salmon ; large and full. Growth vigorous.

4. *Général Tartas.*—Deep rose, large and double.

5. *Madame de Vatry.*—Deep rose, shaded with crimson. " The darkest tea rose."

6. *Pauline Plantier.*—White, tinged with yellow

7. *Triumph de Rens.*—Rosy salmon, very large ; free grower and bloomer.

8. *Safrano.*—Buff and rose, one of the hardiest.

China Roses.—The following is a list of eight good varieties :

1. *Agrippina.*—Deep velvety crimson, small. Growth delicate, but blooms profusely.

2. *Archduke Charles.*—Pale rose, changing to crimson ; very large and full.

3. *Eugéne Beauharnais.*—Amaranth, large and full.

4. *Impératrice Eugénie.*—Clear rose, shaded with salmon ; large and sweet.

5. *Louis Philippe.*—Dark crimson, blush centre ; large.

6. *Sanguinea.*—Deep crimson, small, but a profuse and constant bloomer.

7. *Mrs. Bosanquet.*—Flesh-color, large and double.

8. *Clara Sylvain.*—Pure white.

The foregoing lists embrace a very small number out of hundreds which may be named by rose-growers that are nearly or quite as fine, and are chosen only to facilitate a selection by persons not familiar with varieties. The best manner of arranging and growing rose-bushes depends very much on one's means and space. Where one can have but few, single plants in a walk border give the most pleasure, and these may be either in the natural bush form, or in tree form. The delicate China and tea roses must necessarily be in shrub form, in order to be protected or removed in winter; and the smooth-leaved hardier hybrid China, either June, or perpetual, in tree form. With stout, thrifty stocks, it requires but little time, if one understands budding roses, to produce low rose trees, like the one shown in Fig. 165; and as these take up less room on the ground, and present a more gardenesque appearance, it is much the best mode of showing a variety of roses in a limited space, especially bordering straight walks; as a number of different varieties may be grown on the same stem. Another beautiful mode of making good rose-standards for the centres of beds, is to bud upon a strong stock all the way up, or on its side branches, so as to make a cone or tower of foliage supported on one stem, but composed of several hardy varieties budded into it, and displaying their foliage and flowers from the bottom to the top. As such cones, or rose-towers, may easily be bound up, and protected in winter with straw or evergreen boughs, the finest half-hardy roses may be used on them. Where there is a good breadth of lawn, a variety of roses, massed in beds, will have the best effect.

To produce fine roses, a deeply-drained soil, enriched to the highest degree, and manured annually, is essential. Those who wish to make a specialty of the rose, should procure Parkman's Book of Roses.

PLATE NO. XXXI.

The accompanying plate shows a variety of forms for rose-beds, some of which may be adapted to almost any place which has a lawn. We will suggest, briefly, the roses that will produce a good effect grouped in these beds:

BED, FIG. I.—This may have a fine tree-rose in the centre, budded with such hybrid perpetuals as any of the list in Division II, Class II, so that the head shall be a great bouquet of many-colored roses. At 2, 3, 4, and 5, plant from the same list those which will make the best variety of colors in the group, and keep well-rounded bushy forms. The four should be kept equal in height, not exceeding three feet, and the tree-rose should be grafted, or budded, about three or four feet from the ground. The first season, or until the bushes planted at the four figures meet, small half-hardy monthly roses from Class IV may be planted in the bays of the bed, such as the *Aimée Vibert*, *Jane Hardy*, *Fleur de Cypress*, and *Général Tartas*. Or the bed may be completely filled between the larger plants first named with the old China roses from the last list of Class IV.

BED, FIG. 2, is an odd form, occasionally suitable for the intersection of two walks. This one is intended to be on a walk circling near the inner or longest side of the bed, and to be planted with bush roses from Division II, as follows: at 1, *Baron Prevost;* at 4, *Général Jacqueminot*, with *Caroline de Sansal* on one side at 3, and *Madame Bouton* on the other at 5; the *Louise Darzens* at 6, and the *Duc de Cazes* at 2. The bushes at 1 and 4 should be of stronger growth than the others, so that the outline of foliage will rise from the ends to the centre of the bed.

BED, FIG. 3.—This is a very large bed, designed for a post, pillar, or trellis in the centre. At 1 and 2, plant *Queen of the Prairies* and *Baltimore Belle*, which bloom in June only, and at the opposite sides of the post (no figures on the plan) the *Baron Prevost* and *Caroline de Sansal*. At 11, 12, 13, 14, 15, 16, 17, and 18, we would have a circle of strong-stemmed tree roses, grafted and budded with hardy varieties of perpetual and hardy Bourbon roses from Classes II and III of Division II. Between these, in the same circle, tea or China roses should be sunk in pots, so that all the ground may be covered with a mass of rose foliage. At 7, 8, 9, and 10, plant from the classes last mentioned the most robust sorts, to be grown as bushes; and at the ends 3, 4, 5, 6, plant Nos. 4, 5, 6, and 7, from the select list of Bourbon roses. When these roses are full-grown, they should cover the bed completely; but until they do, the spaces may be filled with choice spreading cluster-flowered roses of the Noisette, tea, and China classes.

BED, FIG. 4.—The circle is ordinarily the best form for a rose-bed. This one is represented eight feet in diameter, which is perhaps too large for the number of plants in it, unless they be sorts of pretty bushy growth. The centre should have either a very strong rose tree, or a bush of sufficient vigor to rise above the roses that are planted around it. The tree, if well headed out, will be best. The surrounding circle of eight plants we would make Nos. 1, 2, 3, 4, 5, 6, 8, and 10, of our select list of hybrid perpetual roses. Or two sets of bushes may be planted around the central rose-tree ; say four, consisting of Nos. 1, 2, 4, and 8 of the list just mentioned, planted equidistant two feet from the centre, with a circle of twelve or sixteen Noisette, tea or China roses around them. The first-named list will, however, fill the bed completely in two or three years. If a pillar, and climbing roses, should be preferred to the tree-rose for a centre, the *Queen of the Prairies* and *Baltimore Belle* may be used.

BED, FIG. 5.—This bed is supposed to be near a walk on its longest side, and to have a row of chioce hybrid perpetual or Bourbon roses in the middle of the part parallel with the walk ; and at 3 and 4, in the centre, a low post for some perpetual pillar roses, like *Mrs. Elliott* and *Piérre de St. Cyr.*

BED, FIG. 6.—This is a pretty form for a large bed, and very simple to lay out, being on a hexagonal plan, where the distance of each circle from the centre may measure the distance from one plant to another in that circle. The centre is to have a post, for, say the *Baltimore Belle* and *Queen of the Prairies* for June bloom, and *Mrs. Elliott* and *Piérre de St. Cyr* for autumn flowers. In the circle three feet from the centre are places for six hybrid perpetual or Bourbon roses of strong growth ; and on the outside, four feet from the centre and five feet apart, six smaller and bushy varieties of the Noisette, tea, or China varieties. In the latter places (marked 9 to 14 inclusive), three sorts of the smaller and delicate roses last named may be planted, instead of one, so that each little mass or projection of the bed will form a group of low rose-bushes with flowers of contrasting colors.

BED, FIG. 7.—This should have a high compact bush in the centre, or post-roses, on a short support entirely concealed by the foliage. The *Mrs. Elliott* and *Caroline de Sansal* side by side, and kept together either with a hoop or with the post just suggested, would make a beautiful centre-bush ; and for the three ends of the bed strong plants of the Bourbon roses, *Hermosa, Sir Joseph Paxton,* and *Souvénir de l'Exposition,* which will represent flesh color, bright rose, and deep crimson. If a pure white rose is desired in the place of one of these, take *Louise Darzens* or *Madame Alfred de Rougemont;* and for a yellow rose, *Maréchal Neil.* These end bushes should be managed so that they will be pretty nearly equal in size, and about three or four feet high, while the centre one should be two feet higher. The first year the bed between these plants may be filled with trailing flowers; but if the roses have done well the first year, they should cover the bed thereafter.

BED, FIG. 8.—A bed of this form may be appropriately filled out of any of the lists we have named, but perpetual roses are preferable, and we suggest for the centre at 1, the *Caroline de Sansal;* at 2, *Celine Forestier* or *Jane Hardy;* at 3, *Aimée Vibert;* at 4, *Maréchal Neil;* at 5, *Caroline Marniesse.* This will give blush-flowers in the centre, golden-yellow on each side, and white at the ends. Another selection of more decided colors may be for the centre, *General Jacqueminot,* deep crimson; at 2, *Hermosa,* flesh color; at 3, *Caroline Marniésse,* white; at 4, *Madame Boutin,* cherry-rose; at 5, *Jane Hardy* or *Maréchal Neil,* golden-yellow. This will shade the bed from deep crimson to white on one side and to the richest yellow on the other.

BED, FIG. 9.—This is a great bed, appropriate only where there is ample lawn room, and if skillfully managed is large enough to constitute a very respectable rose-garden. An inspection will show it to be arranged on an octagonal plan, with roses in straight lines from the centre, and in decreasing distances apart towards the outside. This arrangement enables the cultivator to get at all the roses conveniently from the lawn, which is deeply scolloped into the bed between its projecting lines. The lawn might perhaps run to points towards the centre, and thus expose less soil to view between the lines of rose-bushes. This bed should have a substantial post or pillar in the centre, ten or twelve feet high, and at the foot of it two prairie roses, and two of the rankest climbing perpetual roses, say the *Caroline de Sansal* and *Mrs. Elliott.* Four feet from the centre of the post, at 5, 6, 7, 8, 9, 10, 11, and 12, permanent stakes about five feet high should be set, and on each side of them pairs of strong growing roses from the hybrid perpetual list; making sixteen plants of eight varieties. Each radiating line beyond these might approximate to one tone of color, so that whatever colors are placed at 5 and 6 may have somewhat similar shades at 13, 13, and 14, 14, of smaller growing sorts. At from 13 to 20 inclusive, next to the above, selections of the bushiest growers may be made from Classes I, II, and III of Division II. The outside figures of the same numbers represent the most vigorous roses from Classes III or IV of the same division. Outside of these, near the lawn, each of the eight projecting parts of the bed may have seven China and tea roses bedded out in the spring, and removed in the fall. Or by making the projecting parts of the beds narrower, these may be dispensed with. The number of roses indicated to fill this bed is as follows : For the centre four ; for the first circle sixteen ;. for the second circle eight ; for the third eight ; and around each of the outside ends of the lines seven pot-roses. The bed, therefore, would require thirty-six permanent roots, and fifty-six pot-plants ; but the latter may be dispensed with. As no large bed like this should be laid out except by those who are either well versed in roses, or who employ good gardeners, it is not necessary to name the roses for each place in it.

BED, FIG. 10, is too simple to require a selection named in detail. A bed of that size we would recommend to crowd full of noisette, tea, and China roses, the largest in the centre, although only three places are figured ; three bushes being enough to fill it if the largest kinds are selected.

BED, FIG. 11, is a bed supposed to be near a walk on its straight side, for a compact mass of low-growing Noisette, tea, and China roses from Class IV.

THE CANADA RHODORA. *Rhodora canadensis.*

A little mountain shrub, growing in wet places, and noticeable for the extreme earliness of its pale purple flowers, which bloom in terminal clusters, before the leaves expand, in April and May. Height two to three feet. A pretty companion for the flowering almond and the Japan quince.

THE SPIRÆA. *Spiræa.*

It is a curious fact that this native shrub, growing wild in num-berless varieties all over the country, has but recently attracted great attention as a garden shrub.   Few families of shrubs vary so widely in their forms, leaves, and flowers as the spiræa, and the species and varieties recently brought into notice are so numerous that we shall make no attempt to name them.   The following list of a dozen sorts it is believed will embrace the best characteristics of the family, beginning with the smaller varieties·

Spiræa callosa alba.—A low, broad, compact bush, two to three feet high.   Flowers a dull white, in corymbs three inches in diame-ter, from May to October and November.   Foliage dense, and a light green color.   A French seedling from the following:

Spiræa floribunda.—A low spreading bush, two to three feet high.   Flowers in spikes, white, changing to pale red ; July and August.   Foliage light green, and looks well after the flowering is over.

Spiræa callosa fortunii.—An upright grower, apt to get bare of leaves at the bottom, so as to need cutting back occasionally. Height three to four feet.   Flowers, in superb panicles, four to six inches in diameter, of a bright red color ; June to October.   Fo-liage opens a dull red color, and changes to purplish-green.

Spiræa oximea. — A compact bush, spreading considerably around the root by suckers.   Height three to four feet.   Flowers in large terminal spikes, from June to October ; color bright rose to deep red.   Foliage light green.

Spiræa trilobata.—A very broad, oblate-headed, low shrub, with branches spreading horizontally, and bearing flat clusters of white flowers in May.   When out of bloom it is a massy-foliaged low bush of pleasing color and form.   Height three to four feet, and much greater breadth, forming a broad flat head when growing alone.

Spiræa thunbergia.—This is a variety of the willow-leaved spi-ræas, with light very small willowy leaves and white blossoms, about the end of April.   Noticeable for the extreme delicacy of its foliage spray.

Spiræa Reevesi flore plena. — A shrub of very graceful spreading growth. The branches, on old bushes, assume a curved form, their tips touching the ground. Flowers white, very double ; May and June. Foliage deep green, and not glossy. Height four to six feet, with a greater breadth. Fig. 166 shows the characteristic form of this variety.

FIG. 166.

Spiræa Van Houtti.—A graceful spreading shrub, with deep rose-colored flowers in June. Height six feet.

Spiræa prunifolia.—One of the most common and most beautiful, but apt to be undervalued, when first planted, on account of its apparently stiff and twiggy habit, and many suckers ; but when it becomes an old bush, it has quite another appearance. Then its long slender branches arch gracefully towards the lawn, and its small and very glossy oval leaves form pleasing masses of foliage of a fine dark green in summer, and a rich purple or crimson in autumn. Flowers white, in May and June. Height six to eight feet, and very broad at maturity if allowed room for expansion.

Spiræa billardi.—A strong upright grower, in form like the althea. Flowers red, in long terminal spikes ; in bloom from June to October. Foliage light green. Height six to eight feet. It should be planted behind low full-foliaged shrubs, as it becomes bare near the ground.

THE GOLDEN SNOWBALL SPIRÆA. *S. opulifolia aurea.*—This variety forms a great round bush, ten to twelve feet high. Flowers white, in June. Foliage a yellowish-green, abundant and massy.

WHITE BEAM-LEAVED SPIRÆA. *S. ariæfolia.*—A strong upright grower, native of Vancouver's Island, distinguished for the great size and fragrance of its spikes of flowers, which are sometimes from twelve to fifteen inches in length. They are a yellowish-white color, and appear in July. Height ten to twelve feet.

The *Spiræa japonica (?)*—This is a compact dwarf, with a compound leaf of many leaflets, and long spikes of flowers projected beyond the foliage. Height one to two feet.

THE STUARTIA. *Stuartia.*

THE STUARTIA. *S. Pentagynia.*—A splendid native shrub, from seven to twelve feet high, found wild in the mountains of the middle and southern States ; long known, but only recently much planted in this country. Its flowers, of a creamy white, from three to four inches in diameter, appear in July and August. It is not quite hardy in the northern States, and requires a sheltered situation, and about the same protection as a chionanthus. It is a noble-flowering shrub, and well worth the care required to grow it. It does best in a deep, moist, sandy loam, and a shady spot. The foliage resembles that of the dogwood, and in autumn turns to a dark reddish purple. There is a noble bush-tree of this species in open ground at Parsons' nurseries at Flushing, ten feet high, and sixteen feet in diameter.

THE VIRGINIA STUARTIA, *S. virginica*, resembles the preceding in general appearance, but is a smaller bush, and not quite so hardy. It is a fine shrub when out of blossom, and very showy during its blooming season, which is the same as the preceding.

Both these varieties, where they can be well grown, are superb acquisitions to shrubberies. They are reported not hardy at Rochester, but do well at Flushing, L. I. Their very late period of bloom, and their great showiness when in flower, will render them favorites wherever the climate is such that they can be grown with certainty.

THE STAPHYLIA. *Staphylia.*

THE BLADDER-NUT TREE. *Staphylia trifolia.*—A shrub or small tree, indigenous in moist places from Canada to South Carolina. It sends out an abundance of suckers from the base of the stem ; but if these are rubbed off as they appear, it forms a handsome low tree. Flowers small, whitish, in May and June. Leaf formed of three acuminate serrate leaflets. Nuts in a bladdery capsule, white ; ripe in October. Height six to twelve feet.

The Pinnate-leaved Staphylia or Bladder-nut Tree. *S. pinnata.*—A European species long known in shrubberies. Leaves with five small leaflets. More vigorous in habit than the preceding, and of such singular appearance, when loaded in autumn with its seed-capsules, as to be cultivated principally for that peculiarity. Like the preceding, it is a smooth-branching shrub, throwing up many side-suckers. Naked young wood, greenish, with green buds. Flowers same as the preceding sort. Height six to twelve feet.

THE ST. PETERSWORT, OR WAXBERRY.
Symphoricarpus.

Some of this very pretty class of little shrubs are also known as the snowberries. All of them are nearly related to the tartarian honeysuckles. Low native shrubs, with small flowers of several colors, and small waxen berries, which hang on through a part of the winter.

The White-berried, or Common Waxberry, *S. racemosas,* is a bushy shrub, with small rose-colored flowers, from July to September, and white, oval berries, about a half inch in length. The berries, hanging in ropes on the branches, are quite ornamental, and much used for large winter bouquets.

The Red-berried Waxberry, *S. vulgaris,* has very small leaves, flowers, and fruit, but the leaves appear early, and hang quite late, and the shrub forms one of the most perfect of miniature trees when growing quite alone ; with a breadth double its height, but with side-branches projected as boldly, and falling gracefully as those of a low, broad, weeping elm ; and all within the compass of three feet in height, and four or five feet in breadth. Flowers small, red and yellow, in August and September. Fruit purple ; ripe in December.

33

CHAPTER V.

EVERGREEN TREES AND SHRUBS.

HAVING in the chapter on the Characteristics of Trees, pages 294 and 295, treated of the relative value of evergreen and deciduous trees for home embellishment, the reader is referred to those observations as embodying a comparison of the beauties and advantages of the two classes.

In the descriptions which follow, it has been the aim to group families of evergreens under popular names that will give the best suggestion of the general characteristics of the group, and under one popular name, sometimes to class several distinct but allied genera, giving at the same time the several botanical names which are thus, for the convenience of readers little versed in such matters, grouped together : and following the botanical nomenclature and arrangement, as far as any is attempted, of George Gordon, A. L. S., of England, as given in his work on the *Coniferæ*, entitled "THE PINETUM."

THE PINES. *Pinus.*

The hardy pines of the temperate zone will be grouped in three divisions: First, those which are indigenous on the Atlantic slope of the United States; second, those which are indigenous on the Pacific slope of the United States, including a few from the highlands of Mexico; third, those which are indigenous in Europe and Asia. The latter division embraces a larger number than the others of species which have proved desirable for embellishment; and from the fact that the most valuable of these have been in cultivation for many centuries, and developed many interesting varieties, they are rendered additionally interesting.

Pine trees are generally distinguished from other families of evergreens by the greater length of their needle leaves, and the fact of their being grouped in two's, three's, and five's, issuing from a common sheath. Botanists classify them, in part, by the number of leaves to the sheath.

PINES OF THE UNITED STATES ON THE ATLANTIC SLOPE.

THE WHITE PINE. *Pinus strobus.*—Though in one kind of beauty or another, separately considered, the white pine may be excelled by many other trees, we know of no hardy evergreen of the temperate zone that unites so many elements of beauty, picturesqueness and utility, as this noble native of our own forests. In grandeur of elevation, and in the beauty of its columnar trunk, regarded merely as a forest tree, it ranks among trees east of the Rocky Mountains as the red-wood or big-tree (*sequoia*) and Douglass spruce of California among the more colossal trees of the Pacific slope. The white pine forests of Maine, New York, and the northwestern States, furnish our country with more than half of all the wood used in its buildings. It is recorded on high authority that trees have been cut in Maine measuring upwards of two hundred feet in height. Frigate main-masts one hundred and eight feet in length have been made of single pieces of its timber. The fact that this tree is of such vast use in the arts has caused it to be

Fig. 168

A WHITE PINE GROWING ON " MONTGOMERY PLACE," BARRYTOWN, N. Y.

regarded as merely a timber tree ; the idea of beauty being falsely
dis-associated with things of great utility.   The value of its timber
has also deprived the country of nearly all the grand specimens
which doubtless grew here and there in open ground a century ago,
but are now very rare.   New England owes a debt of gratitude
to the impecunious quality of its elms, which have consequently
been left to enrich her villages with their beauty. We had travelled
for years through the northern States, and looked in vain to find a
single full grown white pine which had developed from youth to
maturity in open ground!   Fig. 168 is a portrait of one of a very
few that we have since seen.   It is a magnificent specimen, ninety
feet across the spread of its lower branches, and of equal height,
found on the old Livingston estate, known as "Montgomery place,"
the residence of Mrs. C. L. Barton, near Barrytown on the Hudson.
An engraving cannot do justice to the softly shaded tuftings of its.

fine masses of verdure, its deep shadows, or the wing-like expansion of its massive lower branches. The vertical growth on the left which shows like a distinct small tree behind it is really a sprout, issuing from a great horizontal limb forty feet from the trunk like a perfectly formed distinct tree, and twenty-five feet in height! In an open field near the Delaware water gap in Pennsylvania is a white pine but fifty feet high, with an oblate top like a park oak, its branches radiating at about fifteen feet from the ground, and covering a space nearly seventy feet in diameter, and forming a head of softly-rounded masses of foliage as dense as those of the sugar maple.

A pine tree recently cut in Columbia County, Pennsylvania, had its trunk sawed into nine logs, whose united lengths were one hundred and thirty-six feet ; the smallest log being eleven inches in diameter at the top! Allowing four feet for the height of the stump, this would make one hundred and forty feet in height of heavy timber in the trunk. The branching above this part of the trunk must have made the tree from one hundred and sixty to one hundred and eighty feet in height as it stood. Imagine a tree with such inherent vigor expanding in an open park, and it does not seem unreasonable to believe that it might attain dimensions not inferior to the historic grandeur of the cedars of Lebanon.

Though the white pine attains such colossal height, and occasionally great breadth, it is not so far unsuited to the requirements of small grounds as might be inferred. It is a manageable tree. When its main stem attains a height of from twelve to twenty feet it can be cut back, to make a more spreading tree. Its foliage is much more massive, and the lights and shadows bolder and more varied when thus treated. If it is desired to strengthen the spreading branches decidedly, it may be necessary to cut out two or three years' growth of the "leader," so that one of the side branches will not turn up too readily to make itself a leader. If it is necessary to keep the tree within a moderate compass, it can be safely pruned of half its growth every year—say in June or July—and the rich density of its foliage will be increased by the process. This pruning should be done with some irregularity ;—cutting-in some branches deeper than others, to prevent the formation of a smoothly globular head ; which form, not being in harmony with the nature of the tree, would do injustice to its beauty. To reduce its size and add to the luxuriance of its foliage without varying too much from its native form, and materially changing its expression, will be a pleasant study for the amateur gardener. Not only, however, is the tree capable of being improved in form and foliage by judicious pruning, but it is so far docile to the hand of art that it may be reduced even to hedge-limits, and will bear the shears or the pruning-knife to shape it into other artificial forms of embellishment.

Those who have seen the white pine as exposed in its native forests, a bare and lofty black-barked trunk, with a monotonous uniformity of meagre-foliaged branches in level whorls towards its summit only, can with difficulty realize the graceful spreading luxuriance of the tree in rich sandy open ground. The foliage is a warm light-green, often with a bluish tinge. The leaves, five in a sheath, are from three to four inches long, slender, straight, soft to the touch, and delicately fragrant. They fall at the end of their second summer, so that each summer the tree is clothed with two years' foliage, while in winter it has only the preceding summer's leaves. The cones are from four to six inches long, curved, cucumber-shaped, and drooping. The bark is dark, smooth on young trees, and grows rough and darker with age.

High winds are the greatest enemy of the white pine. Its wood is not so tough as that of most deciduous trees. In winter the foliage catches and holds the snow, which sometimes breaks the branches by its weight alone, but oftener by the assistance of the wind when they are thus loaded. Trees grown from the beginning in places fully exposed to the wind will be more likely to resist such strains, and become strong old trees, than those which have grown up in sheltered places, or in too rich a soil.

A warm, sandy soil, with a clay substratum, is the one in which this pine is most at home, and its rate of growth (at the top) in such soils, is about three feet a year. In stiff clays, or in cold or "clammy" soils, it does poorly, and has but little beauty. But by deep drainage even these may be changed, so as to allow the white pine to develop handsomely.

There are a few very pretty dwarf varieties, as follows :

THE PIGMY WHITE PINE. *P. strobus nana.*—An exceedingly diminutive curiosity, having a broad, flattened form, and maturing at the height of one to two feet.

THE DWARF WHITE PINE, *P. s. pumila.*—A globular, bushy diminutive sort, with all the characteristics of the white pine, except that the annual growth is so short that it becomes an evergreen shrub only, from six to ten feet in height and breadth.

THE COMPACT WHITE PINE, *P. s. compacta,* is so similar to the above, that the difference is not material when they are young; but this one is said to exceed it in size at maturity. It is, un doubtedly, the finest dwarf form of the species, and, we think, of the whole pine family. The foliage is not diminished in size, but only the woody growth. Height and breadth, *probably,* from ten to fifteen feet at maturity. The annual growth is from two to five inches. The common white pine, if cut back annually from the beginning, would present nearly the same appearance.

THE SNOW OR SILVER PINE. *P. nivea.*—A lofty tree, quite similar to the white pine, and supposed to be a variety of it; but the leaves are somewhat shorter, and more gray or "silvery" below. Of little value, as distinguished from the white pine.

THE RIGID PITCH OR POND PINE. *P. rigida (P. serotina).*— Leaves in three's, three to four inches long. Cones ovate-oblong, in three's or four's, much shorter than the leaves, their scales ter minated by a rough, thorny point.

An irregularly-branched, rough-barked tree, with coarse, warm, green foliage, not very dense, and rather tufted, and borne principally on the outside of the tree. The branches are not numerous, and radiate so as to form, when growing in open ground, a broad oblate or flattened head, the lower branches bending down at their extremities. Seen at a distance, a well-grown tree is pleasing by virtue of the warmth of its green color, and its umbelliferous head; but a ragged-limbed, rude tree, when seen near by. The bark is a warm brown color, broken irregularly into large patches, like the markings of a turtle's back. Found principally away from the sea-coast, from Canada to Virginia, generally in poor, sandy soils. Height forty to seventy feet.

THE RED PINE. *P. rubra (P. resinosa).* Leaves in two's, four to five inches long, straight, stiff, yellowish-green, thickly set on the shoots, compressed and collected in bunches at the extremities of the branches. Branches rather naked, straight, open, and reddish brown. Very similar to the above in most respects.

THE TABLE MOUNTAIN PINE. *P. pungens.*—This species was described by Michaux more than forty years ago as one of the rarest and most peculiar of American pines; yet it is little known away from the high mountains of the Carolinas and East Tennessee, in which region alone it is found. There can be little doubt of its hardiness in most parts of our country. A tree of more irregular and spreading growth than is common to American pines; color of foliage a light yellowish-green; leaves in two's, resembling those of the Scotch fir; "cones top-shaped, rather large, light yellowish-brown, three and a half inches long, generally in whorls around the stem and top branches, pointing horizontally, and remaining on the tree for years" (Gordon). Old trees are said to exhibit a tabular form of top. It is strange that this tree is still almost unknown in nurseries and home-grounds. It seems to have peculiarities of form and color to make it valuable. Height forty to fifty feet.

SHORT-LEAVED YELLOW OR SPRUCE PINE. *P. mitis.*—This variety is found all along the coast from Connecticut to the Gulf of Mexico, generally associated with the Jersey scrub pine on light poor soils. Height fifty to ninety feet. "The branches are spreading on the lower part of the trunk, but become less divergent as they approach the top of the tree, where they are bent towards the body so as to form a summit regularly pyramidal, but not spacious in proportion to the dimension of the trunk." This narrow conical form of head has given rise to the name of spruce pine. Josiah Hoopes, in his Book of Evergreens, mentions the changeable color of its leaves, "softly merging from a bright bluish-green to the darkest hue in alternate changes of light and shade," as a pleasing feature.

THE LONG-LEAVED YELLOW, OR GEORGIA PITCH PINE. *P.*

australis.—This is the great timber tree of the southern forests and pine barrens in the Carolinas and the Gulf States, and is not hardy north of Richmond. It grows to sixty or seventy feet in height, with a slender trunk. The leaves are from eight inches to a foot or more in length, in three's, of a beautiful brilliant green, and collected in bunches at the extremities of the branches. This pine is put to more varied uses than any other. Its timber is close and heavy, and valuable both for house and ship-building. Its sap is the raw turpentine of commerce (from which the spirits of turpentine is distilled), and is gathered in the same manner as that from the sugar maple. Tar is made from the dead wood, which has the curious property, as the wood decays, of absorbing from it year after year all the resinous matter ; so that the heart-wood, already filled with resinous juice, becomes surcharged to such a degree as to double its weight in a year, and continues to draw from the sap-wood till the latter rots off. Pine-knots, which are so largely used for torches and fires at the south are the butts of small branches from which the sap-wood has rotted off, leaving them full of rosin.

P. australis excelsa is a variety from the northwest coast of America, which has proved hardy in north Germany, and ought to be tried in our northern States.

THE LOBLOLLY PINE. *P. tæda.*—This tree is peculiar to the sand-barrens of the southern States, and is the first tree to occupy grounds exhausted by cultivation. It rises to the height of eighty feet with a clear stem of forty or fifty feet without a branch, and above, a wide-spreading head. Not hardy, and of no value north of Virginia.

THE JERSEY SCRUB PINE. *P. inops.*—A low tree of rough and straggling growth, a native of New Jersey. Not desirable as an ornamental tree.

BANKS', OR GRAY PINE. *P. banksiana.*—A dwarf variety from the north of Canada, which does not seem to refine with cultivation, and is described by Sargent as "a stunted scrubby straggling bush." Loudon, however, considered it quite interesting on account of its curious manner of growth, and another writer (Richardson) describes it as a "handsome tree, with long spread-

ing flexible branches." An odd and picturesque, but not handsome, low tree.

AMERICAN PINES OF THE PACIFIC SLOPE.

Among the wonders of vegetation on the Pacific slope, the
variety of pines is not the least remarkable. From the maritime
slopes, to the heights near perpetual snow, the species vary from
colossal trees, to bushes; but the giant forms predominate, and a
coarse open growth is a peculiarity of most of them. It is probable that most of those which prove hardy in the Atlantic northern
States will be barred by the grossness of their features from use in
decorative pleasure-grounds, except as novelties or curiosities.

BENTHAM'S PINE. *P. Benthamiana.* — This giant pine is
indigenous on the coast mountains of California near the bay of
Monterey, and on some of the mountains bordering the valley of
the Sacramento river, where it occupies the greatest elevations.
Its growth is rank, regularly pyramidal, the branches numerous,
spreading, and irregular, and the leaves of great length. Though
tested but a few years on the Atlantic slope, it has generally proved
hardy. But the success of well cared-for young plants, a few years,
is no proof of their continued health in our climate. Besides, its
rank loose growth may show it unfit for suburban planting, even if
it proves (which we doubt) hardy enough.

PARRY'S PINE, *P. Parryana*, resembles the preceding, but has
more slender branches, and its cones are remarkable for their bright
glossy yellow color, and their freedom from resinous matter. Said
to be as hardy as the *Benthamiana*.

BALFOUR'S PINE. *P. Balfouriana.*—A species found in northern
California, between the Shasta and Scott's valley, at an elevation
of five to eight thousand feet, growing on volcanic debris; said
by Gordon to be quite hardy and very distinct. This author
describes the branches as slender and flexible. Of its beauty or

want of it we know nothing, and have not heard of it in planted grounds.

COULTER'S OR SABINE'S PINE. *P. Coulterii* (*P. Sabiana, P. macrocarpa*).—This species is usually found associated with the *P. Benthamiana,* but on lower elevations. It is a lofty tree, with slender branches and very long foliage borne near the extremities of the limbs. Not a pleasing tree.

CALIFORNIA MOUNTAIN PINE. *P. monticola.*—A species closely resembling the white pine of the eastern States, and therefore of little value in a collection where the latter is growing.

AMERICAN CEMBRAN, OR CONTORTED-BRANCHED PINE. *P. flexilis.*—A tree of very slow growth, indigenous on the mountains of northern Mexico and California, at elevations of from seven to fourteen thousand feet above the sea. It varies in size from a tree from sixty to eighty feet high near Sante Fe, to a low flat-top shrub, only a few feet in height, and "so compact that a man may walk upon it," where found at its greatest altitude above the sea. It forms a tree of oval outline like the European cembran pine, the lower branches horizontal, the upper ones ascending, and both large and somewhat tortuous, but very flexible; whence its name. The foliage is said to resemble most that of our white pine, but the leaves are shorter and stouter, and the branching more irregular. Supposed to be quite hardy. Desirable for great collections.

FREMONT'S PINE. *P. Fremontiana.*—A small, nut-bearing tree, found in the upper elevations of the Sierra Nevada range, from five to seven thousand feet above the level of the sea. It has many and slender, spreading branches, which are fragrant when bruised. It is a very slow grower. Whether hardy and of beauty enough to give it value east of the Rocky Mountains is yet a matter of experiment. Height twenty feet.

HARTWEG'S PINE. *P. Hartwegii.*—"A handsome tree growing from forty to fifty feet high, with a dense compact head of a fine dark green " (Gordon).   Found in Mexico at elevations nine thousand feet above the sea. · Half-hardy, *perhaps* hardy.

PINON, OR NUT PINE.   *P. edulis.*—A small-sized, short-leaved mountain pine of California, which promises to be hardy, and may prove interesting.   Height twenty-five to forty feet.

THE HEAVY WOODED PINE. · *P. ponderosa.* — A California tree of great size, and coarse, rapid growth.   Branches in regular whorls, but twisted and tortuous, rising from the trunk at an angle less than a right angle, drooping towards the middle and rising at the ends.   They are quite large and rope-like, and not being well concealed by leaves, except near the extremities, give the tree the appearance of a very bony frame illy clothed.   It proves perfectly hardy at Rochester, where Ellwanger & Barry have a fine specimen thirty feet high and twenty feet in diameter across the branches. It is a curious, but far from a handsome tree.

JEFFREY'S PINE.   *P. Jeffreyana.*—One of the lofty pines of northern California, where it attains a height of one hundred and fifty feet.   Not yet thoroughly tested on the Atlantic slope.   Young specimens look like a cross between the Austrian and Pyrenean pines.   The leaves are longer and warmer toned than those of the Austrian pine.

LAMBERT'S PINE..   *P. Lambertiana.*—This is · another of the lofty trees of California.   It resembles our white pine so much that common observers would suppose it the same.   We have seen no quality that should cause it to be recommended for planting ; our white pine being its equal or superior in all respects.

THE MEXICAN FOUNTAIN PINE.   *Pinus patula.*—H. W. Sargent says of this : " Of all the pines which we have seen, this is beyond measure the most graceful and charming, not only in its growth and habit, but in the nature, softness, and color of its leaves.   It resembles a beautiful, delicate green fountain of spun glass, and has a parti-color like shot silk, which catches the sunlight almost like a kaleidoscope. The leaves resemble the silk of maize, being as soft and delicate and not unlike it in color." Al-though it grows on the mountains of Mexico at the height of eight thousand to nine thousand five hundred feet above the level of the sea, Mr. Sargent dares not trust his beautiful specimen in open ground in winter, and is satisfied that it is not suited to bear our winters, deeming it "quite beautiful enough for pot-culture to sat-isfy anybody."

PINCE'S MEXICAN WILLOW PINE. *P. pinceana.*—This is another of the Mexican mountain pines, found on the same elevations as the preceding, on a road leading to the City of Mexico. It is de scribed as "a very handsome tree, with long weeping branches like those of the weeping willow, and easily distinguished from all other Mexican pines on that account."—(Gordon.) There is no proba-bility of its proving hardy in this country, but it may be grown in boxes by those having conservatories to winter it in, and serve to give variety to a pinetum in the open air in summer. It grows to sixty feet in height in its native places.

THE CHILI PINE. *Araucaria imbricata.*—This is not a true pine, but is classed with them because the name by which it is widely known implies that it is a pine. One of the most curious of all trees; the branches growing like tortuous canes, covered with large pointed green scales for leaves. The color of the foliage is the purest of deep greens. If it could be grown successfully in open ground we know of no evergreen that, as a curiosity, would be more desirable. Of the thousands of trees planted about twenty years ago, and since, very few are living; but we do not yet aban-don the hope of seeing it acclimatized in the middle States. A few careful cultivators have succeeded in growing it. There are good trees in Baltimore and Washington, but it has failed at Newport, Flushing, and Cincinnati. If seed could be procured from the most southerly limit of its growth in Patagonia, and from the most exposed specimens, it could, perhaps, be made to sport into hardy varieties in this country. The seeds have been obtained principally from near Concepcion, in latitude 37°, near the sea.

There is no snow there in winter, and the summers are about as hot as our own. We have seen the fuschia growing wild there; but the araucaria is found growing in large quantities six degrees further south; how much farther still we do not know. The Indians say that it grows only on the Pacific slope of the Andes.

PINES OF EUROPE AND ASIA.

THE AUSTRIAN PINE. *Pinus austriaca.*—A native of southern Europe, there holding the same rank in size and in value of timber as our white pine. This tree is a type of a perfect color in evergreen foliage. By this we do not mean to convey the impression that any one shade of color, however pleasing, is desirable for all trees, but only this: that there is a happy medium between the wide diversities in color that Nature charms us with, and this medium is a measure or standard of color by which we rank one tree as light colored, because lighter than the medium, and another dark, because darker than the medium. Thus all diversities of color are described by some ideal standard. The color of this pine is so clear and pure that it seems to be such a standard. There is a liveliness, purity, and depth in its green not surpassed by any tree we know of; forming a marked contrast in this respect to the rather grayish-green of the Scotch pine, and the lighter green of the white pine. It is, however, a stiffer, coarser, and more robust tree in its growth than either of them. Its young wood is remarkably rough; the branches issue in whorls almost right-angularly from the main stem, describing a slight upward curve, and on thrifty young trees the spaces between them, and their coarse character, give the tree a rude appearance when seen too closely. When young the tree has the usual conical or pyramidal character of the pines, but after it reaches middle size the top begins to round out somewhat, and at maturity it becomes rather a round-headed tree, sometimes even flat-topped when old.

The leaves of the Austrian pine are from three to five inches long, two (occasionally three) in a sheath, rigid, slender, and with prickly points. The buds are large, very long, and of a whitish color; by which feature alone this species can be distinguished at a considerable distance in the fall and spring. The annual growth in strong soils is about three feet a year.

Josiah Hoopes, in his valuable Book of Evergreens, observes that "where the soil is retentive of moisture, and consequently becomes sour and soddened, he has seen this species succeeding moderately well, while the white pine, planted in the same situation, died outright." This remark gives the key to the use of the two species—the white pine being the most beautiful of hardy pines in sandy or well-drained loams, and the Austrian pine equally superior in compacter soils. Both should be fully exposed on all sides to the sun to develop their best beauty.

There is much difference among seedling Austrian pines in their mode of growth, some being much longer jointed and more rigid than others. A nurseryman skilled in observing such things can often select trees that will display most of the beauties and none of the conspicuous coarse growth of the usual form. In Ellwanger & Barry's specimen ground at Rochester, is a seedling of theirs, of such spreading habit and short growth at the top that, but for the brightness of its color, it might easily be mistaken by its form for a large dwarf mountain pine, though the masses of its long leaves are finer than the latter ever forms. The variety is worth propagating from, and we suggest that, as the species is a German tree, the variety take the name of the Ellwanger Austrian pine. It is a much better form for ordinary home-grounds than the usual type; but the latter, by heading back its long shoots when too gross, will present a similar appearance.

There is a variegated-leaved variety not yet, we believe, grown in this country.

THE SCOTCH PINE. *Pinus sylvestris.*—The Scotch pine is indigenous throughout middle and northern Europe, and takes the same rank among pine trees in Great Britain as the oak among deciduous trees. It is the most useful for timber, and adapts itself to a greater variety of park uses than any other. Its spreading habit, sometimes so free in outline, and well broken by shadows as to rank among grand trees, and in other localities developing into smoothly-rounded and symmetrical beauty, gives it an expression more in harmony with deciduous trees than most evergreens, while in mountain regions it develops the highest degree of picturesqueness. Its form is generally rounded rather thàn pyramidal; the branches radiate more irregularly, and are not so straight and formal in their disposition as those of the white and Austrian pines, and the foliage therefore breaks into less stratified and more oaklike masses. For this reason, on young trees, the foliage appears to be more dense than that of the white pine.

The dull color of its foliage is the one thing that prevents the Scotch pine from being the most popular of evergreens; for it unites every other good quality for planting. This color varies from a grayish to a bluish green, not at all pleasing in itself. The leaves are in two's, from one and a half inches to two and a half inches long, twisted, rigid, standing out all around the branches. Cones ovate-conical, from two to three inches long.

Whether the following variety of the Scotch pine, so highly commended, has been cultivated in our nurseries, we do not know; but have supposed all the American stock of this tree to be of the common sort above described.

THE RED-WOOD SCOTCH, OR HIGHLAND PINE. *P. s. horizontalis.*—This variety is distinguished by the horizontal and drooping character of its branches, which tend downward close to the trunk; by the lighter and brighter bluish-green color of its leaves, and less rugged bark. Sir Walter Scott urged this as the *true* Scotch pine, or at least the variety which develops the noble and picturesque forms that have given the species its high rank, and that the common sort "is an inferior variety, a mean looking tree, but very prolific of seed, on which account the nursery gardeners are enabled to raise it in vast quantities." The highland pine bears comparatively few seeds; and the seed gatherers, who are only paid by the quantity, naturally collect only from trees the most prolific in cones.

No finely-formed trees of either variety can be produced which do not grow from the start in open ground, exposed on all sides to the sun and wind. When "drawn up" by the shade or contiguity of other trees, it speedily forms a lank, ill-branched stem, and rarely recovers that sturdy dignity of form which it naturally assumes in an open exposure.

THE PIGMY SCOTCH OR KNEE PINE. *P. s. nana.*—A broad spreading dwarf that rarely exceeds three feet in height, and is very stunted in branches and leaves.

THE VARIEGATED SCOTCH PINE, *P. s. variegata,* differs from the ordinary form only in having pale straw-colored leaves mingled among those of the usual color.

THE PERSIAN SCOTCH PINE. *P. s. latifolia.*—A robust variety attaining great size on the mountains of Persia, which has longer and broader leaves than any other variety.

THE SILVERY SCOTCH PINE. *P. s. argentea.*—A large tree from east of the Black sea, with leaves and cones both marked with a silvery hue.

THE MUGHO PINE. *Pinus mugho.*—A dwarf species with numerous ascending branches thickly covered with foliage resembling that of the Scotch pine, but of a better and warmer color. It is indigenous on the mountains from the Pyrenees to the Austrian Alps, and forms a compact, rather fastigiate, shrubby tree, from ten to thirty feet in height. This species is often confounded with the mountain pine, *P. pumilio,* which indeed it greatly resembles ; but differs in having shorter leaves, and a more compact and tree-like growth. The branches of the *P. pumilio* spread more upon the ground, though they rise at their extremities on all parts of the tree to a nearly vertical direction. There are many distinct varieties of the mugho pine, varying in size from the knee pine, *P. mugho nana,* which rarely grows much higher than the knee, to the Austrian marsh mugho, *P. m. uliginosa,* which forms a pyramidal small tree. The common variety, of good nurseries, is the best, and forms a very pleasing miniature specimen of a pine tree. The foliage has a warm or yellowish-green tone in the spring. A great variety of forms of this species may be seen in the New York Central Park, usually from four to eight feet high. It is one of the most pleasing of shrubby evergreens for small grounds.

There is a tree in the specimen grounds of Messrs. Parsons & Co., at Flushing—which is shown by Fig. 169—that is probably one

34

of the larger forms of mugho pine, but is entered on their catalogue simply as *Pinus uncinata erecta.* It has the deepest pure green color we have ever seen in an evergreen, and as there grown, in rich, cultivated ground, there is a velvety depth in the shadings of its foliage that we have never seen surpassed. May this not be the

FIG. 169.

P. m. uliginosa of Gordon? The specimen which is given in the engraving is about eighteen feet high, and bids fair to greatly exceed this height at maturity. How much of the beauty of this specimen depends on the unusual fertility of the soil in which it grows, and how much on the innate character of the species, we cannot tell. Possibly in a common soil, the richness of its dark verdure might change to sombreness.

THE MOUNTAIN PINE. *Pinus pumilio.*—Described by Gordon as follows: "Leaves in two's, curved, short, stiff, thickly set on the branches, from two to two-and-a-half inches long, etc. Branches turned upwards and very numerous, forming a dense bush, with the bottom branches creeping on the ground, but growing in favorable situations, into a small tree twenty or thirty feet high, with a gray and rather smoothish bark." " At great elevations on the mountains it becomes merely a spreading bush creeping along the ground." The largest specimens we have seen are about twelve feet high and twenty feet in diameter, and are well described by the above quotation. This and the mugho pines are often confounded from the fact of being about equally dwarfish. The mugho has a more compact form and a warmer green color.

THE SWISS STONE PINE. *Pinus cembra.*—A tree of very compact, erect, ovate-conical form, dark foliage, and slow growth. On account of its formality of out-line it has been much employed in gardening. Fig. 170 illustrates its characteristic form. It retains its lower branches and foliage to a considerable age. The greatest peculiarity of its foliage is the dense mass of globular tufts of leaves which compose the entire surface of the tree. Its rate of growth is from six inches to one foot per year, and it grows to thirty or forty feet in height.

FIG. 170.

PYRENEAN PINE. *Pinus pyreneaca (P. monspelliensis, P. his panica).*—Leaves two in a sheath, from five to seven inches long, fine, stiff, straight, thickly-set on the branches, of a clear green color. Cones two and a half inches long, conical-oblong, smooth, light yellow color, at right angles to the branches. " Branches stout, of an orange color, numerous, regular, spreading in all direc- tions around the stem, and well furnished with laterals " (Gordon).

A large, wide-spreading tree, native of the most elevated forests of the Pyrenees.

It is extraordinary that a tree so distinct and beautiful, and seemingly hardy as this, should be almost unknown in this country. The largest tree of the species we have seen is growing in the specimen grounds of Parsons & Co., Flushing, L. I. It is now thirty feet high, and so far assumes about the same form as a very spreading white pine. But its leaves are much longer than those of the white, Scotch, or Austrian pines, and quite as long as those

of the exquisite plume-like tufts of the more delicate *Pinus excelsa.*
Judging by the Parsons specimen, it is a more beautiful lawn tree
than either the white, Scotch, or the Austrian pines, less rough-
branched and formal than the Austrian, of a more pleasing green
than the Scotch, and more massy-foliaged than the white.   In its
general appearance it bears the same relation to the Austrian pine
that the *Pinus excelsa* does to the white pine; that is to say, it is
proportionally of more free and graceful foliage.*   It has proved
quite hardy in H. W. Sargent's place at Fishkill, on the Hudson.

THE BHOTAN PINE.   *P. excelsa.*—Leaves in five's, five to seven
inches long, slender, loose, and pendulous, like plumes.   Cones
cylindrical, larger than the leaves, and pendulous.   Color of foliage
a light green.

This queen of the pines is a native of the southerly slopes of
the Himalayas, in latitudes 27° to 35°, and at elevations of from
five thousand to twelve thousand feet above the sea ; where it attains a height of one hundred and fifty feet, and forms in open
exposures a broad pyramidal mass.   A traveller in the Himalayas
says : "It is remarkable for its drooping branches, whence it is
frequently called the 'weeping fir.'"   There are yet no specimens
in this country large enough to indicate with certainty what the
habit of a full-grown tree will be, but the exquisite bending plumes,
formed by each annual growth of leaves, which gleam with a silvery
light as they are moved by the wind, are alone enough to entitle it
to the name of the weeping pine, were it not a misnomer to apply
the term "weeping" to a tree so radiant with sunny cheerfulness.
As far as we can judge by the specimens now growing in this
country, this pine spreads more in proportion to its height than the
white pine—more like the Scotch—and retains a strength of growth
in its lower horizontal branches, that gives promise of a nobler

* Since the above was written, the large trees in Parsons' specimen grounds at Flushing have
died, while small trees in their nurseries are uninjured.   Mr. J. R. Strumpe, the very skillful
propagator of that establishment, and a careful observer, does not consider the misfortune as
conclusive of the lack of hardiness of this species, as our own native white pines occasionally
die in the same way from some unseen cause ; but it is certainly suggestive that our climate
may not be adapted to it.   These specimens had been grown with great luxuriance in a rich
deep soil.   Perhaps excessive feeding had something to do with their premature death.

form of park tree than any evergreen that will grow in this country. We believe the finest specimen in this country is in the Parsons nursery at Flushing, L. I. It is now about forty feet across the spread of its branches, which almost rest upon the ground. The form is rather globular than pyramidal; the height not being equal to the breadth. Most other specimens are broad ovate-pyramidal. Trees not more than twelve years planted in the New York Central Park, are now upwards of twenty feet high, about the same diameter of branches, and perfect in every way. It does well at Rochester, N. Y., for six or eight years after planting, and then gives indications of weakness and disease.

An impression gains ground that this pine is not quite hardy in the northern States. It is not possible to speak with certainty on this point. It is hardy to resist cold, but it seems to be weak, and to develop disease in the summer. The tree not being a native of our country, may not adapt itself to our varied soils or climates so readily as natives. But we still hope that, with care, when young, it may be rooted in most parts of this country, so as to grow healthily.

The following remarks by H. W. Sargent in his Appendix to Downing's Landscape Gardening, are interesting: "It is universally returned to us as hardy from all parts of the country, though sometimes suffering from sun in summer. Near Boston this is the case, and at Natchez, where plants have to be shaded from the summer sun. Mr. Barry writes from Rochester it is hardy there, but will not make an old tree. Our own trees at Wodenethe, sixteen and eighteen feet high, certainly suffer from sun, and not cold. The winter of 1855 and 1856, which destroyed some and damaged many other white pines here, and even road-side cedars, produced no effect upon this tree, which was entirely unprotected and uninjured; and yet, often in midsummer, it will become ruptured in its leading shoots, and die back. This may be on the principle of the frozen sap-blight in fruit-trees, where the damage done in winter does not develop the injury before the succeeding summer; but we are more inclined to believe that the tree, if planted in rich holes, overgrows, and a sort of apoplexy supervenes. We form this theory from observing that, where a great growth has taken place, and the leading

shoot is three or four feet long, and extremely succulent, this rupture is most often the result when the sun being hot, activity of
circulation is excessive. When, however, the exuberance of
growth is checked by poor, thin soil, the tree grows enough,
and seems to mature its wood—at any rate sufficient to with-
stand what might be called determination of sap to the head;
so that, in future, we shall always plant *excelsas* in poor soil."

It is some years since the above was written. Mr. Sargent's
finest trees of this species are now in a precarious condition. He
has stated the symptoms of their decline, but there seems to be
something in the inherent organism of the tree to produce these
results, which will not be fully counteracted by the treatment
recommended. The fact that Parsons & Co.'s superb tree —
probably the finest in this country—is growing healthily (thus far)
in a soil rich enough to produce the most luxuriant growth, tends to
prove that the rank growth is not the invariable cause of the decay
of these trees. This tree is growing in a position exposed on all
sides to wind and sun. We have seen the commonly cultivated
varieties of cherry, like the black tartarian and the yellow Spanish,
growing in different soils in the same town; in one, always forming
short well-ripened wood, and growing into healthy trees; and in
the other, growing excessively, and developing early disease and
decay. A well-drained stiff clay produces the healthy trees; and
a warm sandy surface soil, with a springy subsoil, produces a
plethora of growth, rupture of the bark, exudation of gum, and
all the symptoms of a diseased condition. If a tree that succeeds
so generally in the northern States as the cherry, is liable to the
peculiar form of disease that distinguishes the Bhotan pine, it is a
reason to be hopeful that the best soil and exposure for the latter
may be determined, so as to give assurance of growing it to maturity
in some localities. We would follow Mr. Sargent's suggestions
implicitly as far as relates to starting the tree in a poor surface
soil, but we would leave it exposed on all sides to the sun and
wind from the beginning, and seek to harden its growth *by giving it
deep root in a rich dry subsoil.*

But it must be remembered that the Bhotan pine is a native of
the latitude of the northern shore of the Gulf of Mexico; and it is

not likely that our northern sun can be too much for it, unless some preceding cause exists for abnormal sensibility to heat. The tree is found at an elevation of from six to ten thousand feet above the level of the sea, and "prefers the more open and cheerful aspects of the mountains." Such an elevation even in the tropical latitude of 27° to 29° insures a comparatively temperate summer climate and severe winters, but does not diminish greatly the blistering power of the sun's rays, as those know who have travelled on the glacier heights of the Alps. We cannot therefore believe that full exposure to the sun will of itself be found prejudicial to the health of the Bhotan pine, but think it much more likely that the source of its weakness in this country is simply a density of air quite different from that breathed by the tree at an elevation of six and ten thousand feet above the sea ; and this alone may produce what Mr. Sargent terms "a determination of sap to the head "—or vegetable apoplexy. It will therefore be a simple matter for patient experimenters to determine to what extent the Bhotan pine may be acclimated in the United States.

We believe that much may be done by selecting seed from trees that exhibit the greatest vigor in localities the most exposed to sun, wind, and cold, at the lowest elevation where the tree flourishes. It is quite probable that most of the seed imported into England has been obtained from the great trees of the valley-forests nearest to the English stations. With seed from the most weather-tried trees, it seems reasonable to suppose that a hardier stock of this pine may be grown, and from among the progeny of such seed some specimens of sufficient hardiness to insure their healthy growth in the United States. We have not heard whether any experiments have been tried in grafting the *P. excelsa* on different pine stocks to learn the effect, if any, on the subsequent growth. By grafting scions from the same tree on the roots respectively of the white, the Austrian, and the Scotch pines, it may readily be ascertained whether anything can be gained in that direction. If the *P. excelsa* scion will take readily on the Austrian pine stock, very beautiful effects may be produced by cutting off the leader of the latter from eight to twelve feet above the ground, and inserting grafts of the former, without marring the side branches of the stock. The

silvery foliage of the Bhotan pine springing from the dark cushion
of foliage the Austrian pine would throw around it, would make a
beautiful effect.

THE CORSICAN PINE. *P. laricio.*—A lofty tree of the most
rapid growth and regularly pyramidal form. Though a native of
the high lands adjacent to the Mediterranean, it is also found on
the mountains of Caucasus, and it is considered hardy with us.
Hoopes (Book of Evergreens) says of it: "For lawn-planting the
Corsican pine is one of the most beautiful and available trees we
have, and is almost invariably an attractive object in a collection.
As it is a native of warm climates, many persons suppose it will
prove too tender for this section (Westchester, near Philadelphia);
but so far as we have been able to ascertain, it has given entire
satisfaction. The long wavy leaves are of a bright green color, and
the perfect shape of the tree has always produced a favorable
impression with us, and we wish it were more extensively known "
It is not quite hardy at Rochester. H. W. Sargent says of it:
" It is quite as hardy as the Austrian all over the country, having
somewhat the same robust habit, only a less vivid green." Its
growth is rather more loose and open than that of the Austrian
pine—the space between the whorls of its branches being much
greater, and, taken altogether, it is a less pleasing tree.

The *P. l. caramanica* is a variety of the Corsican pine, of less
size, and lower, rounder, and more bushy form ; a distinct and
valuable variety.

The *P. l. pygmœa* is an extremely dwarf variety, whose branches
trail along the ground, and bear short rigid curled leaves (Hoopes).
Will probably be useful for grafting on other pines.

CALABRIAN PINE. *P. bruttia.*—Leaves in two's, rarely three's,
about nine inches long, slender, glabrous, wavy, light green.

A lofty tree from the mountains of Calabria, where it grows from
four to five thousand feet above the level of the sea ; of spreading
umbelliferous form, and fine color. The length of its leaves is one
of its interesting features. Sargent and Hoopes both speak of it
as having proved hardy ; the former at Fishkill, N. Y., and the

latter at Westchester, Pa. It is said to develop a straggling habit in this country, and its beauty as a tree is more doubtful than its hardiness. Probably suited to regions south of Washington.

THE ITALIAN CLUSTER PINE. *P. pinaster.*—This tree, famous for its gardenesque effect in Italian scenery, has not proved hardy in the northern States. Though frequently grown for many years in open ground, it always succumbs to the climate before it arrives at maturity. It flourishes best on the shores of the Mediterranean Sea, where it rises to the height of sixty to seventy feet, and forms a peculiarly flattened tabular top, often represented in pictures of Italian scenery.

THE ITALIAN STONE PINE. *P. pinea.*—This tree resembles the preceding, but is of lower stature and more globular form. We have not heard whether it has been acclimatized in the southern States, but it is certainly too tender for the northern. There are many varieties in Europe, some of which attain dimensions equal to the cluster pine.

THE CHINESE LACE-BARK PINE. *P. bungeana.*—A middle-sized tree found in the extreme north of China, which is much grown in pots on the island of Chusan. From the fact that it has been chosen for that kind of petting and dwarfing, it may be inferred that it has some interesting peculiarities. Reported perfectly hardy.

COREAN SEACOAST PINE. *P. koraiensis.*—A dwarf species growing near the sea on the peninsula of Corea, in China, and in Japanese gardens, where it rarely exceeds twelve or fourteen feet in height. From the fact that it is valued in Chinese and Japanese gardens, and reported quite hardy, it is probably a handsome tree, and should be tested by large collectors.

THE SPRUCE FIRS. *Abies.*

For the reader not familiar with botany, the general distinction between the pines proper, and the firs, is, that the latter generally have shorter leaves attached all round the twigs, or occasionally on two sides, and the trees are more uniformly conical in form. This meagre mention of their differences can, of course, convey no valuable idea of the obvious diversity of characteristics which they present to the eye.

The firs are subdivided into two great classes, the *Abies*, or spruce firs, and the *Piceas*, or silver firs.

Gordon, author of "The Pinetum," describes the *Abies* botanically, as follows: "Leaves solitary, four-sided, and scattered all round the shoots, or flat, and more or less in two rows laterally. Flowers, male and female on the same plant, but separate. Cones *pendant*, solitary, and terminal, with thin persistent scales."

THE WHITE SPRUCE FIR. *Abies alba.*—This is a light-colored thin-foliaged tree with horizontal branches; growing wild in the northern border of our country, in the Canadas, and north to the Arctic Sea. Height fifty feet; diameter of the trunk seldom more than eighteen inches. "The bark is lighter colored than that of any other spruce; the leaves are also less numerous, longer, more pointed, at a more open angle with the branches, and of a pale bluish-green" (Loudon). Cones pendulous, one and three-quarters to four inches long, and five-eighths to six-eighths broad. We are not certain of having seen this variety fairly grown in open ground. There is much confusion existing between this and the intermediate varieties of the black and red spruces. The white spruce has probably not had a fair trial in cultivated grounds. Growing wild it is certainly a thin, meagre-foliaged tree, decidedly inferior to the black spruce or the Norway spruce. Grown thriftily in open ground, perhaps it may develop some beauty. There are two pretty dwarfs of this species: the *Abies alba nana*, which forms a dense spreading bush three or four feet high; and the hedge-hog white spruce, *Abies alba minima*, which is much smaller—almost too small to be useful.

The Black and Red Spruces. *Abies nigra. A. rubra.* — These beautiful natives of our northern border have been under a cloud, or rather in the shadow of a great foreign rival. The beautiful imported Norway spruce has so many good qualities, in addition to the prestige of being a *foreign* tree, that no native of only equal merit can vie with it in popularity. Yet our black spruce, which more than any other resembles the Norway spruce, is in some respects a finer tree. The latter is the more graceful in the first ten years of its growth, but afterwards the droop of its branches is sometimes saggy rather than graceful. The black spruce is more sturdy looking in its outline, and its branches which have a more upright direction at first, afterwards bear themselves in nearly horizontal, but not drooping masses, having apparently more strength than those of the Norway. This alone gives it an expression that, as far as it goes, makes it a superior tree. Fig. 171 is a portrait of a specimen growing wild on Mt. Desert Island, on the coast of Maine, and gives a very correct idea of the character of the tree. Its rate of growth is.from two to three feet a year in good soils, or about the same as that of the Norway spruce ; but it does not eventually become so lofty a tree, eighty feet being its maximum height. The author, in the spring of 1847, planted a Norway spruce and a black spruce of the bluish-green sort contiguous to each other, in a warm sandy loam. Both trees proved to be superb representatives of their species. The former is now (1870) about fifty feet in height, and the latter forty-five feet, and each covers an area of thirty feet in diameter ; their lower branches resting upon the ground. But the black spruce, if the wood and foliage of both could be weighed entire, would be found the heavier of the two. The horizontal branches of the latter have the appearance of bending with the weight of their foliage, while those of the Norway spruce decline so directly from the trunk as to convey the idea of a sag, rather than

Fig. 171.

a bend.   We do not wish to abuse this graceful peculiarity of the
imported tree, but only to call attention by a comparison, to the
decided and neglected merits of the native fir.

Michaux considers the red spruce only a variety and not a
distinct species.   Other authorities differ with him, but until the
matter is decided we prefer to describe them under one head.   The
foliage variations are certainly quite marked, and from these alone
there would be an equal propriety in calling one variety the blue
spruce, and another the golden spruce ; for among hundreds of trees
of this species growing side by side, two colors are as distinct as if
they were of two species.   The trees of the bluish cast have leaves
a little longer, and arranged around the twigs with more open
divergence than the yellowish-green variety.   Young trees of the
blue foliage seem more dense and vigorous than the yellowish-
green sort, but at maturity they have not gained much in growth
on the latter.   Though the twigs of the yellow-green sort are stiffer
and its leaves smaller, the branches of old trees have a way of
bending downwards at their extremities, so that their foliage takes
the light in finer masses than the blue sort, and at a distance,
especially near sunset, an old tree of the latter variety has a warmth
of tone that gives it a most pleasing expression.

THE WEEPING BLACK SPRUCE.   *A. nigra pendula.*—A variety
that exhibits a very pretty pendulous habit on its outer growth.
We do not know whether this and the weeping black spruce, described among the varieties of the Norway spruce, may not be the
same.

THE NORWAY SPRUCE FIR.   *Abies excelsa.*—This universally
popular fir is the great timber-tree of northern Europe, rising in its
native forests, and in the parks of England, to the height of one
hundred and fifty feet.   It is so healthy, thrifty, and graceful when
young, and adapts itself to so great a variety of soils and climates,
that no native tree on our own continent is so universally planted for
embellishment.   And certainly, among evergreens, none better
deserves to be ; for though our white pine has a grander character,
and the hemlock more delicately beautiful foliage, more time is
required to develop their forms and characters.   The Norway

spruce is a graceful mass of drooping foliage from youth to age, but perhaps there is no period when its graces are more conspicuous, and its faults less so, than when it has been planted from fifteen to twenty years. After that age it begins to exhibit, little by little, the dark interior colors and saggy droop of boughs that give it, to a slight degree, a sombre and monotonous expression, reminding one of the dripping moss-hung trees of evergreen swamps. In June and July, when the growing twigs are in a succulent state, and bending by their own weight, their velvety masses of verdure produce a more exquisite effect than those of any deciduous tree we know of, and very few evergreens equal the Norway spruce in this species of grace ; though most of the *Abies* and *Picea* family are peculiarly beautiful during the growing season from the same cause.

There is a great difference of growth among Norway spruce trees, and a skillful judge of trees will be able to select from the nursery those which are likely to develop the greatest luxuriance of foliage and grace of form ; or, at least those which will develop the greatest beauty during fifteen or twenty years. After that age it sometimes happens that trees of the stiffer and more meagre foliage while young, form heads as dense and well broken by light and shadow as those which have been more beautiful in their early growth.

In Chapter XIV will be found some suggestions on artificial adaptations of trees, some of which will apply to the Norway spruce.

Some interesting dwarfs and sports of this species are peculiarly adapted to small grounds. The following are some of them :

THE PIGMY FIR. *Abies excelsa pygmæa.*—This diminutive variety is perhaps the smallest of firs, not exceeding one foot in height, but growing more laterally. Its foliage is minute, of a light green or golden tinge. Hardy.

THE DWARF BLACK SPRUCE. *Abies e. nigra pumila.*—This is a little larger than the preceding, and grows from two to three feet in height and three to four feet in breadth. Foliage dark colored.

CLANBRASIL'S DWARF SPRUCE. *A. e. clanbrassiliana.*—This is a little larger than the preceding, attaining a height of from two to four feet, and about equal breadth. It is considered less healthy in its growth than some of the other dwarfs.   At Ellwanger & Barry's nursery, in Rochester, a specimen was shown us which, after grow- ing as a dwarf for some years, at last started up more ambitiously, and having elected a leader, proceeded to grow at the same rate as ordinary Norway firs, and was, when seen, twelve feet high!   Mr.´ Edward Dagge, the foreman of the ornamental department of that great nursery, thinks that many of the dwarf firs are so in conse- quence of the inferior vigor of these varieties being distributed among an infinitude of twigs ; and that when one of the vertical branches is favored by accident or design, so as to make it a leader, it will bring the tree back, in a considerable degree, towards the normal form and habit of the species.

GREGORY'S DWARF FIR.   *Abies e. gregoriana.*—This is a dwarf of recent introduction, and, considered as an evergreen shrub, is the most valuable for garden embellishment of any of the dwarf spruces.   It will probably grow from three to five feet high, and four to eight feet broad ; has a compact yet not rigid growth, and the foliage is a pure healthy green.   We cordially recommend it.

THE CONICAL NORWAY SPRUCE FIR.   *A. e. conica (stricta ?).*— A variety of slow growth and very compactly conical form.   It will probably make a tree twenty to forty feet high, of formal outline. The *Abies elegans* is much like it, but has stiffer and more meagre foliage.

THE COMPACT NORWAY SPRUCE FIR, *A. e. compacta,* resembles the preceding in form, but has a little more freedom of growth.   It is simply an unusually compact tree, with the normal habits of the species in most respects, but of less vigorous growth.

THE TORTUOUS COMPACT SPRUCE FIR, *A. e. tortuosa compacta,* is a dwarfish and more spreading tree than the preceding, with young branches curiously twisted.   It promises to be an interesting tree.

THE INVERTED-BRANCHED SPRUCE FIR, *Abies e. inverta,* Fig. 172, is the most curious and the prettiest of all the sports of the Norway spruce.   The branches turn so naturally towards the earth, that it is absolutely necessary, as with the weeping beech, to tie its leader to a stake or stiff twig, to gain the height necessary to ex- hibit the charming oddity of its growth.   When it is thus trained,

the side branches fall directly downwards, and
with their rich covering of foliage drape the
stem as a robe falls around the person. The
growth is vigorous, and the leaves are longer,
larger, and of a brighter green than the average of the spruces. This, and Wales' new
drooping Norway spruce, and the *Picea pectinata pendula*, their counterpart in another family, are the three most charming novelties
among the hardy evergreens · suited to the
decoration of small places. As the leading stem should be tied in
a vertical position while it is growing and succulent, it must be
handled carefully to avoid breaking it off; the jointure to the preceding year's wood being very weak at that season.

FIG. 172.

WALES' DROOPING NORWAY SPRUCE FIR. *A. e.* —— ?—This
is a new variety, recently brought into notice by William Wales, of
Dorchester, Mass., which has the same habit of growth as the *A. e.
inverta.* Judging by a photograph of a single specimen, it seems
to maintain a more erect leader than that variety, and to have the
same draping of branches drooping closely around the central stem.
Whether its foliage is so fine in color we do not know. It will
probably be adapted to all the positions where the former is appropriate. Having been brought to notice since the body of this work
was written, no allusion has been made to it in descriptions of
plans in Part I; but it may be considered a candidate for any
place where the weeping Norway spruce *(inverta)*, or the weeping
silver fir *(Picea p. pendula)*, have been recommended. When quite
young it does not give an indication of its final form, and must
have its leader kept in a vertical position to give an early development of its peculiarity. It will probably grow to the full height
of the species.

THE WEEPING N. SPRUCE FIR. *A. e. pendula.*—This is a variety longer known, but not so curious as the preceding. Its branches
droop in a graceful curve, rather than by direct inversion. It is
not, by any means, a dwarf variety, but its form is such that it takes
less room laterally than the common sort; but it is less remarkable
in its drooping habit than the two preceding sorts.

THE PYRAMIDAL SPRUCE FIR.   *A. e. pyramidata.*—A vigorous growing variety, with more fastigiate growth than any other, and also noticeable for the reddish color of its strong young wood.

THE ALATA SPRUCE FIR, *Abies e. alata,* is a variety with heavier and longer leaves, coarser branches, and ranker growth than the common Norway

THE DEFORMED SPRUCE FIR.   *A. e. monstrosa.*—This is simply a tortuous branched and almost leafless monstrosity, of much vigor and no beauty.   It somewhat resembles in growth the Chili auracaria, but is much more rambling.

THE FINEDON VARIEGATED SPRUCE FIR.   *A. e. finedonensis.*— A new English sport of the Norway spruce, remarkable for the yellow color of the upper sides of its leaves and shoots when they first appear, which afterwards change to a light green.   If healthy it may prove an interesting variety.

THE ORIENTAL SPRUCE FIR.   *Abies orientalis.*—A careless observer would mistake this species for an unusually dense, rigid, small-leaved, Norway spruce.   When small it looks like an inferior and dwarfish tree of that species.   But as it attains the height of fifteen to twenty feet, the multiplicity of its twigs gives the tree a superior density of foliage which its early growth does not promise ; and when a large tree, its dark-green masses break into strong and irregular lights and shades, and it is then easily distinguished from the Norway spruce, by a greater solidity of character, or, to speak more specifically, by the less distinctly marked separation of its horizontal branches.   A native of the coast of the Black Sea, and the neighboring mountains, and quite hardy.   It does not grow to so great a size as the Norway spruce ; seventy to eighty feet being its maximum height.

MENZIES SPRUCE FIR.   *Abies menziesii.*—A native of northern California, the Shasta region, and the island of Sitchka.   On a casual glance, this tree resembles the bluish variety of our native black spruce ; but with closer observation, it is seen to be very distinct from all the common spruces.   Gordon describes it as follows : "Leaves solitary, thickly scattered in every direction round the branches, twisted at the base, narrow, rigid, linear, sharp-pointed, in-curved, silvery below, and vivid-green above, three-fourths of an inch long, and soon falling off after the first season, leaving the branches very naked, warted, and with a jointed appearance. Buds ovate-pointed, and covered with resin. Cones three inches long, one to one-and-a-quarter inches broad, pendulous, cylindrical, blunt-pointed, and with the scales loose, and not compact." * * "The young twigs are slender, and of a yellowish-brown color. The tree grows to the height of sixty or seventy feet, with a pyramidal, thickly-branched head, and a silvery appearance." It prefers the alluvial soils on the banks of rivers, in shady places. All authorities concur in this, that it flourishes best in moist soils and air, and that in very dry places and seasons it loses a part of its leaves in the summer, and then presents the appearance of a tree being killed by drought. Yet we have seen specimens growing in deep garden loam, and densely clothed with bright foliage, giving no indication of the premature falling of the leaves mentioned by Gordon, and confirmed by most of our own authorities. The form of the tree is compact and stiffly pyramidal, but less stratified in the disposition of its branches than the balsam fir. It may be considered almost hardy as to cold, but nearly worthless in many locations by reason of its burnt and denuded appearance in the sun.

One quality in the *Abies menziesii* deserves attention. Its leaves are stiff and pointed, like the sharpest needles ; and as they are very numerous, and point so as to prick in every direction, and the growth is dense and compact, it would seem a formidable evergreen hedge-tree for a fence against men and animals. Its tendency to lose its leaves in summer will, however, condemn its use, unless it shall be found to thrive without this fault in damp shady places.

THE HIMALAYAN OR MORINDA SPRUCE FIR. *Abies Smithiana, A. morinda.*—This is the most graceful of all the *Abies*, and in its contour and foliage takes a rank midway between the Norway spruce and the hemlock. When introduced about twenty years ago it was supposed to be quite hardy, and its novelty and beauty

35

created great enthusiasm among tree-growers. But out of tens of thousands which have been imported and planted, there are probably not a hundred fine specimens in the country. Some are scorched by the summer sun, and others cut down by the cold of winter. Sargent thinks it may be acclimated in well-drained, gravelly soils, and partial shade. We do not believe in the shade, except for the soil in which it grows. Ellwanger & Barry, at Rochester, many years since, imported thousands of plants, and out of all, but one proved hardy. That one is now twelve or fourteen feet high, feathered beautifully to the ground, and grows in a deep, warm loam, exposed on all sides to the sun and wind, though in a kind of shallow valley. They inform us that *all the trees grafted from this stock on the roots of the Norway spruce, have proved hardy.* We have faith to believe, that if care is used to get seed from the hardiest specimens growing in the most exposed localities where they are indigenous, and grafted if necessary on our native spruces, we may yet grow large trees of them. It is not improbable that the seed usually obtained in India is from the most beautiful specimens growing in favored locations nearest to the English settlements, rather than from the more rugged and exposed trees. However this may be, whoever plants it in the northern States, must do so with the hope of growing it to large size, qualified by the risk of losing it at any time.

In its native country, the Himalayan spruce attains great size. A specimen has been measured one hundred and sixty-five feet in height, and another twenty feet in the circumference of the trunk. These are the maximum measurements. It grows on the spurs of the Himalaya mountains, on elevations from seven thousand to eleven thousand feet above the sea, and is said to be found usually higher up than the Deodar cedar. It might be supposed that it would suffer more from the density of the air on the low levels of our own great American plain than from the cold alone, though this theory is contradicted by its success in England!

The Japanese have named this tree the Tiger's-tail fir, on account of the long pendulous branchlets on old trees resembling the tail of a tiger.

DOUGLASS' SPRUCE FIR. *Abies Douglassi.*—This is one of the

·great trees of California and Oregon, where, in rich valleys, it grows to a height of 'one hundred and fifty to two hundred feet, with a trunk from five to ten feet in diameter. In appearance it strongly resembles our common balsam fir, but all its parts are on a larger scale. Downing mentions a specimen seen at Dropmore, England, which had been planted twenty-one years, and which was then sixty-two feet high; of which he wrote: "It resembles most the Norway spruce as one occasionally sees the finest form of that tree, having that graceful, downward sweep of the branches, and feathering out quite down to the turf; but it is altogether more airy in form, and of a richer and darker green color. At this size it is the symbol of stately elegance." Doubtless the Dropmore specimen was an uncommonly beautiful one. A portrait of 'this fir, grown to full size, given in the Pacific R. R. Survey, has much of the formal, sombre air, of our old balsam firs. Hoopes (Westchester, Pa.), considers this much hardier than the Himalayan spruce, and less liable to be scorched by the summer sun; but does not think it quite hardy. Sargent (at Fishkill, on the Hudson) says: "Plants with us, in low damp ground, suffer occasionally in color if not in loss of leaves; while those grown in the shade, or on an exposed hill-side in poor, slaty soil, succeed admirably."

THE YEW-LEAVED DOUGLASS SPRUCE FIR. *Abies D. taxifolia.*— This is a variety with much longer leaves, and lesser growth, distinguished also by the very level stratification of its branches. Probably not hardier than the above.

PATTON'S GIANT CALIFORNIA FIR. *Abies Pattonii.*—A native of California and Oregon, discovered by Lewis and Clarke, of which specimens are known growing to the height of three hundred feet, and trunks forty-two feet in circumference! Scarcely known yet in our collections, though reported hardy in England.

THE HEMLOCK FIR. *Abies canadensis.*—This common native tree is certainly the most graceful, beautiful, and available of all evergreens for the embellishment of small places. Hardy as an oak, delicate and airy in outline as the grasses of a winter bouquet, soft to the touch, fragrant, yet forming deep masses of verdure

FIG. 173.

with a color that cannot be improved—what more can we say for a tree? Fig. 173 is a portrait of a full-grown hemlock in Studley Park, England. Fig. 174 suggests the general appearance of a well-grown hemlock at ten years after planting. Fig. 175 bears a strong resemblance to a middle-aged and picturesque specimen formerly growing on the edge of the rocky cliff below Niagara Falls. The three will give a fair idea of the varieties of form that hemlocks assume from youth to age. When quite young, however, they are apt to grow with a lighter, looser, and more open growth than any of these cuts indicate ; and for half a dozen years, by cutting back one-half the annual growth every spring, a richer weight of verdure is produced.

The hemlock loves a warm humid soil, and does not develop all its beauty in thin light sandy loams, where the white pine luxuriates. In a congenial soil the foliage is equally fine in sun or shade, and where it is grown so that its branches overarch a walk or road, no tree that we know of shows so fine a verdure on its inner or shadowed surfaces. Yet, notwithstanding the cheerful

purity of color which distinguishes a young hemlock tree,
it assumes with age a sombre
tone. This expression, however, is rarely acquired before
it is thirty to forty years old,
and may readily be counteracted by planting the Chinese
wistaria, Virginia creeper, or
trumpet creeper at its root.
These will speedily intermingle the rich drapery of their
lighter-colored foliage, and fall
like pendants from the highest boughs of the tree.

Fig. 174.

The following are varieties of our native hemlock·

LARGE-LEAVED HEMLOCK. *A. c. macrophylla.*—This is distinguished in the nursery by larger leaves and denser growth than the
common hemlock, but whether it will exhibit peculiarities to render
it worthy a distinct name is a question to be determined by longer
cultivation.

THE SLENDER-DWARF HEMLOCK. *A. c. microphylla,* or *A. e.
gracilis.*—A small-leaved, slender-branched, very dwarf variety that
looks thin and uninteresting when young, but may possibly have
some value at maturity.

PARSONS' DWARF HEM
LOCK. *Abies c. Parsoni.*—
This is a very pretty dwarf,
noticeable for the symmetrical out-curve of its slender
branches.

SARGENT'S HEMLOCK.
Abies c. Sargenti.—This bids
fair to be one of the most
curious and interesting additions to our stock of gardenesque evergreens—bear-
.ing the same relation to the

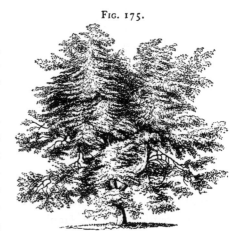

Fig. 175.

common hemlock that the weeping beech does to the common beech
It is of an eccentric rambling nature, but well clothed with verdure
Grown without training it will probably be a broad, irregular, flat-
headed tree or great bush, with an overlaying of downward growing
branches like that of the Scamston elm. By grafting it well up
on other trees, or by tying its leader to a stick or stake, we believe
it will be one of the prettiest and most picturesque of evergreens.
The best effect will be produced when grafted well up on an
ordinary hemlock stem. The tree was brought into notice by H.
W. Sargent, Esq., who found it growing wild on Fishkill mountain.

The Japan Hemlock Spruce. *Abies tsuga.*—This species,
which is a great favorite in Japanese gardens, seems scarcely known
yet in this country. On the mountains near Yeddo it is a lofty
tree, while in gardens it is grown in pots and boxes to any size
that the gardeners desire. There is also a variety that is dwarf by
nature.

The California Hemlock. *Abies mertensiana. Abies canadensis taxifolia.*—This is described in Gordon's Pinetum as " A handsome, bushy, round-headed tree, growing from one hundred to one
hundred and fifty feet high, and from four to six feet in diameter,
with a straight round stem, etc. It is quite hardy, and resembles in
general appearance the hemlock spruce." * * " It is found in
Oregon and Northern California, where it constitutes one-half the
timber in the neighborhood." Probably only a grosser variety of
our native hemlock.

THE SILVER FIRS. *Picea.*

The difference between the spruce fir family and the silver firs,
aside from their botanical traits, may be briefly mentioned as
follows :

The silver firs have a more rigid horizontality of branches, and
the stratification of their foliage is usually more marked and formal.
In general outlines the two families differ but little, but the rigidity

of the branching in silver firs gives them a more monotonous and less picturesque expression at maturity. In general tone of color there is little difference ; but the leaves of the *Piceas*, when seen from below, show more or less white, yellowish-white, or gray lines, which fact gave rise to the name Silver Firs. This peculiarity, however, makes little display, except to persons walking under, or looking up to them. Nearly all the species at maturity are sombre and formal trees ; but there is much difference between them in this respect, and some of them have a pleasing, warm green tone. The family embraces trees of all sizes, from three feet to three hundred feet in height. All which we are about to describe are hardy, or nearly so.

THE BALSAM FIR. *Picea balsamea.*—This native tree of our northern States is the best known, the most popular, and the least valuable of the tribe. As seen in the nursery, with its soft and pleasing green leaves, healthy growth, and agreeable fragrance, it is not singular that its infantile beauties have made it the universal favorite with all novices in planting. But it is like one of those pretty little girls who surprises us in a few years by the suddenness of her transition to prim and glum old maidenhood. It not only does not grow old gracefully, but shows its unpleasant features so soon after it is out of the nursery, that it is a wonder it has so long held place in good society. Compared with scores of other ever-green trees, it is not worth planting. Rigid in outline, and in its mode of branching, and becoming year by year darker in foliage, scarcely ten years pass, in many cases, before its stiff and gloomy expression suggests that its room is better than its company. Height forty to fifty feet. Rate of growth about one foot and a half to two feet a year.

FRASER'S SILVER FIR, *Picea Fraseri*, is a smaller variety of the balsam fir, with shorter and more thickly-set leaves ; found on the mountains of Pennsylvania and North Carolina, and of the same general character as the preceding.

THE HUDSON'S BAY SILVER FIR. *Picea Hudsonica.*—This is one of the finest of dwarf evergreens, growing not more than four or five feet high, and of great proportional breadth. The growth is as dense as that of a clipped hedge, and the foliage is a dark, velvety shade of green. A pleasing companion for the dwarf silver fir, *Picea p. compacta.* A native of the northern parts of our continent.

THE EUROPEAN SILVER FIR. *Picea pectinata.*—A much nobler tree than our native balsam fir, though it has some of the same faults in a modified degree. The foliage is warmer-toned, longer, and more silvery on the under side, and the growth somewhat stronger. The disposition of the branches is even more in horizontal layers than those of the balsam fir, and when quite young, this character gives it the same formality of shadow lines ; but these being still more decided, in connection with the warmer-toned foliage, the tree has a more distinctive character. It finally, however, acquires a sombre expression, but does not arrive at that state until it is from thirty to forty years old. When grown in strong soils, it is apt to lose its leader while young by excessive cold. This is not so great a misfortune as many persons suppose. It is very easy to select some of the little twigs the following spring from the buds around the base of the leader, and make leaders of them. The check in the growth of, the upright stem may tend to make the foliage at the bottom more dense and beautiful. There are many beautiful varieties of the silver fir, among which are the following·

THE WEEPING SILVER FIR. *P. p. pendula.*—This is an exquisite tree when carefully trained to a stake until from six to ten feet high. It is peculiar in form, and the foliage is quite bright-colored. The specimen in Parsons & Co.'s ground at Flushing is a very embodiment of graceful, slender elegance. By the smooth, downward sweep of its branches, it is relieved of the formality of stratification and outline peculiar to the family, and retains all the soft beauty of their foliage. It is a twin beauty with the pendulous Norway spruce *(inverta).*

THE UPRIGHT SILVER FIR. *P. p. fastigiata. (P. p. metensis).* —A German garden variety, of more erect fastigiate habit than any other, and is said to resemble the Lombardy poplar in outline.

The Pyramidal Silver Fir. *P. p. pyramidata.*—Another German variety, a little less fastigiate than the preceding, with a pendulous tendency in the smaller shoots.

The Tortuous Silver Fir. *P. p. tortuosa.*—A German variety, with crooked and tortuous branches and branchlets.

The Oblate Dwarf Silver Fir. *P p. compacta. (P. p. nana?)*—This is a charming, very low dwarf variety; so broad and low, that we have ventured to add to its title the word *oblate* to make the name more characteristic of the form, which is in breadth nearly double its height. The color is a very warm, almost golden, green. Height from two to three feet.

Fig. 176.

The Cilician Silver Fir. *Picea cilicica (P. leioclada).*—This is a very distinct, and very beautiful species, from the mountains of Asia Minor. Gordon describes it as "a handsome tree of a pyramidal shape, thickly furnished with vertical branches to the ground, and growing fifty feet high, and three feet in diameter." The branches are thickly set on the stems, and the branchlets are much more irregular and intermingled than those of the common silver fir. A fine specimen, growing in the grounds of Parsons & Co. at Flushing, L. I., has a form and expression such as one might imagine from a cross between the sturdy Cephalonian fir and the graceful Himalayan spruce. It seems to us that it will make a tree of more graceful outline and varied shadows than the old silver fir; but its mature character, as an ornamental tree, and its hardiness, cannot yet be determined.

The Cephalonian Fir. *Picea Cephalonica.*—This hardy and sturdy-looking evergreen takes a somewhat similar rank among the *Piceas* that our native black spruce does among the *Abies*. Its leaves stand at right angles and rigidly all around the branches, instead of being disposed in lines on the sides of the twigs only; and the branches, though numerous, and in tiers, on the main stem, have branchlets in every direction, instead of being in level lines, as in other silver firs. When young the trees have a round-ish-pyramidal form, with compact and solid masses of foliage, which, on account of the spiney character of the leaves, is un-pleasant to push against or handle. We have, therefore, else-where suggested the use of this tree for garden hedges. The color of the foliage is a bluish-green on top, and grayish-green beneath.

NORDMANN'S SILVER FIR. *Picea nordmaniana.* — This is quite the finest of the silver firs which have been growing long enough in this country to give a fair impression of their qualities. Its superiority in beauty to the common European silver fir consists mainly in the denser and larger masses into which its foliage forms; the horizontal divisions being somewhat less rigid, and more rounded in outline, and its lights and shadows less thinly stratified. The leaves are soft to the touch, do not prick on handling, are set at an angle of 45° with the twigs, and have a lively warm green color, unsurpassed by any large evergreen; in length they are about the same as those of the European silver fir, but they curve upwards at the ends, giving to the branchlets the appearance of being much more thickly foliaged. The young shoots are quite smooth and glossy. A native of the mountains around the Black Sea, and there grows to the height of one hundred feet. It is not unlikely that with age it will develop more of the monotonous formality of expression which distinguishes our own balsam fir, but its warmer-toned foliage must always be in its favor. Trees of fifteen to twenty years' growth in this country are certainly more pleasing in all respects than any other large species of the *Picea* family. It is quite hardy.

THE NOBLE SILVER FIR. *Picea nobilis.*—Though this is one of the immense trees of Oregon and northern California, where it attains a height of two hundred feet, its growth when young is much more compact and full-foliaged than most of the trees from the Pacific slope, having rather the appearance of a vigorous dwarf tree than of a scion of a lofty family. The leaves are about the length of those of the balsam fir, and so thickly set on the twigs that the latter can scarcely be seen. The upper side of the leaf is a dark green, the under side lined with white, giving the foliage a bluish-gray tone. The growth is slow and compact when young, and the tree has been found quite hardy in the eastern States. Mr. Downing, writing from England, described the specimens seen there as the most majestic of evergreens. The best specimens we have seen spread upon the ground with more breadth than height. Probably they had not yet reached the age of most rapid upward growth. When larger the branches are in whorls, disposing the foliage into strata, so that it lies in masses, says a recent writer, "almost as level as Utrecht velvet."

This, after the *P. nordmaniana*, is doubtless the most valuable of the newer evergreens of the *Picea* family.

THE GREAT SILVER FIR. *Picea grandis.*—This is another of the giant trees of the Pacific slope. It bears a striking resemblance to the common European silver fir, but has rather longer and, perhaps, lighter-colored leaves. The branches are regularly disposed in whorls, and the foliage lies in thin layers. We believe its growth will prove too rank and monotonously symmetrical to become a valuable tree for small grounds.

PARSONS' SILVER FIR. *Picea grandis Parsonii.*—This is supposed to be a sport of the *Picea grandis*, originating in the grounds of Messrs. Parsons & Co., of Flushing, N. Y. It is certainly the most exquisite *young* tree of the silver fir type that we have seen; exceeding all others in the length of its leaves, and the soft shadings of their warm-toned layers. It bears a similar relationship to other *Piceas* that the exquisite Bhotan pine does to the pines. The new twigs are small and yellowish-brown; older wood, slate-colored. The trunk enlarges rapidly near the base like a cypress.

LOW'S SILVER FIR. *Picea lowiana (P. lasciocarpa).*—This fine species differs from the common silver fir and the *Picea grandis* principally in the greater length of its leaves, which are arranged on the sides of the twigs in two level lines as flatly as if they had all been ironed out; and also in their paler color, the more slender character of the branches, and the fact that the latter are "not glossy like those of the true *grandis* when young."—(Gordon.)

THE LOVELY SILVER FIR.   *Picea amabilis.*—This is also one of the trees of California and Oregon, growing there occasionally to the height of two hundred and fifty feet.   It has longer leaves than any other tree of the family (except Parsons' silver fir, which most resembles it), being from one and a half to two inches in length, arranged in rows on the sides of the twigs, and of a bluish-green tone.   Young twigs a light brown ; older bark greenish-gray.   The smaller twigs are less regular in their horizontal direction than those of the *P. grandis* and *P. Parsonii,* and the foliage is therefore not quite so thin and regular in stratification.   One of the most beautiful of the silver firs.   Its hardiness is not determined.

THE SIBERIAN SILVER FIR.   *Picea pichta.*—This is one of the most valuable of the European firs recently introduced, on account of its medium size and dense foliage.   The latter is of the balsam fir type, but the leaves are nearly double the size.   They are soft to the touch ; the young wood is short and thick, but bends yieldingly in the hand, resembling in this respect the beautiful *P. nordmaniana,* from which it differs in having darker foliage, denser and shorter growth, and still greater pliability of young wood, which is of a grayish hue.   The shade of color is peculiarly deep and rich in young trees.   Whether it may not become a sombre tree with age is a question.   It is advisable to plant it where its deep green color will be contrasted with trees or shrubs of a light warm tone. A native of the mountains of Siberia.   It will probably make a tree of about the height of our balsam fir, but broader, better filled in with foliage, and less sharply conical.   Our opinion of this tree has been formed principally from one specimen, which is now about twelve feet high.

THE JAPAN SILVER FIR.   *Picea firma.*—A species recently introduced, which has a strong resemblance to the common silver fir at a little distance, but is distinguished on a closer approach by its shorter and stiffer leaves, thickly set on the sides of the twigs, and terminating in two sharp points. The general expression of a tree of six or eight feet in height is rather rigid and uninteresting.

THE PINSAPO FIR. *Picea pinsapo.*—A native of the mountains of Spain, regarded as hardy by Sargent at Fishkill on the Hudson, and as of doubtful hardiness, according to Hoopes, in the neighborhood of Philadelphia. The leaves are about the length of those of the Norway spruce, borne all around the twigs, sharp-pointed, and rather dark colored. Branches and branchlets very numerous, the former in whorls. Probably of no peculiar value as an ornamental tree.

There is a variegated variety with some of the young shoots and leaves of a pale yellow color.

THE UPRIGHT INDIAN SILVER FIR. *Picea pindrow.*
WEBB'S PURPLE-CONED SILVER FIR. *P. Webbiana.*

These are similar trees, both from the Himalayas, where they attain great size and beauty ; but, so far, they have proved unsuited to our climate. Some cultivators believe that hardy specimens will yet be found from which to propagate, as in the case of Ellwanger & Barry's Himalayan spruce. When we can know something good of them by their growth on our own soil, there will be time to describe them.

THE CEDARS AND JUNIPERS. *Cedrus* and *Juniperus.*

Under this common head we shall describe the two botanical families. *Cedrus* and *Juniperus;* many of the junipers being popularly known as cedars. The true cedars are natives of Asia, and include the renowned Cedar of Lebanon, and its more valuable brother, the Deodar cedar. Of the junipers there are species on both continents ;—the native red cedar being the best known American representative of the family.

THE RED CEDAR, *Juniperus virginiana,* is noted above all American trees for the durability of its heart wood, which is remarkably fragrant, and of a dark red color ; making it pleasing to the senses as well as valuable in the arts. It grows from thirty to forty feet in height, and assumes a variety of forms in different soils and parts of the country. On the banks of the Hudson River, and streams farther north, it is usually a compactly conical tree ; at the west and south, it grows in more irregularly-pyramidal forms, with much freer and more open branching. "The red cedar varies exceedingly from seed ; some are low and spreading, and others tall and fastigiate ; some bearing male blossoms, and others female ones. The foliage in some is of a very light hue ; in others it is glaucus, and in some a very dark green."—(Loudon.)

The red cedar just falls short of being one of the most beautiful of evergreens. When grown in rich, deep soil, it assumes an irregular and spirited outline. While young, in such soils, the length of its side branches, which take a horizontal direction near the ground, give it the appearance of a free-growing evergreen shrub, of a less formal character than any other evergreen we have. In gracefulness of growth it is only excelled by the hemlock, and it exceeds that tree in the diversity of its forms. The foliage in spring and summer varies greatly in color on different trees, from a bluish to a yellowish green. On old trees the sunny side often exhibits great warmth of tone, and a soft blending of strong lights and shades on the rounded details of its contour. But in winter, though called an evergreen, its foliage turns to a dull brown that is rarely pleasing ; and occasionally it is tinged with this color in excessively hot, dry weather. This winter color, however, is thrown off with the returning warmth of spring, and the foliage resumes its natural green some weeks before the new growth shows itself.

The elder Michaux made a mistake, in which Downing followed him, of supposing that the red cedar flourished best near tide-water ; and that in the western States "it is confined to spots where the calcareous rock shows itself naked, or is so thinly covered with mould as to forbid the vegetation of other trees" (Michaux). Certainly it seems greatly at home in a soil not far removed from limestone rock, but it is most luxuriant in deep, alluvial soils above such rock. On the islands in the west end of Lake Erie, on the shores of Sandusky Bay, and on the banks of the Maumee river, we have seen noble native growths of the red cedar. On Kelley's Island there were formerly trees with trunks thirty inches in diameter. It is also found of large size in the valley of the Ohio.

THE WEEPING RED CEDAR. *J. virginiana pendula (J. viridissima pendula).*—This variety is distinguished by more slender branches, of which the young twigs and growing wood are pendulous. It has a free, loose, irregularly conical growth, that promises, *on rich soils*, to make it a spirited old tree. The foliage is of a decidedly yellowish tone of green. It seems likely to prove the most interesting of the red cedars.

THE GLAUCOUS RED CEDAR. *J. virginiana glauca (J. cinerescens ?).*—This is simply a variety of the common cedar, with decidedly bluish-green and abundant foliage, in pleasing contrast with the warm green of the preceding variety.

THE COMPACT RED CEDAR, *J. v. pyramidalis*, is a variety described as having an unusually fastigiate habit.

THE VARIEGATED RED CEDAR. *J. v. variegata.*—Of this we know nothing more than that its foliage is said to be "deeply variegated with a golden yellow."

The above, we believe, are the most noted varieties of our red cedar which have been honored with names, and all become medium-sized trees.

THE WHITE CEDAR, well known as a swamp timber tree, is classed by botanists with the cypress family as *Cupressus thyoides*, under which head it may be found.

THE ENGLISH JUNIPER. *J. communis vulgaris.* FIG. 177. —This is a spreading, shrubby bush, usually from three to ten feet high, and generally of little beauty, though it sports occasionally into pleasing forms.

THE SWEDISH JUNIPER, *J. suecica*, a slenderly ·conical little tree, as shown by Fig. 177, in which pe- ·culiarity it is only excelled by the Irish juniper. It is one of the most available slender evergreens for small places, growing to the height of ten to thirty feet, and in diameter about one-fourth its height.

THE DWARF SWEDISH JUNIPER, *J. s. nana*, is like its prototype in foliage, but forms only a very diminutive low bush.

FIG. 178.

THE IRISH JUNIPER. *J. hibernica.*—Fig. 178. This is, we believe, the most slender and fastigiate of all evergreens; and is therefore peculiarly useful on small places, where, while occupying a miminum of space, it is conspicuous by its height; and by its vertical growth breaks with pleasant contrasts, when not too frequently repeated, the level lines of lawns and terraces. The foliage is somewhat darker than that of the Swedish juniper. It suffers occasionally from the sun in summer, and where practicable should not be planted where there will be a reflection of southerly light upon it. Though generally considered hardy, it is advisable to mulch over the roots, and bundle the top every winter in the interior, north of the latitude of New York. This may not be necessary to insure its life, but adds so much to the brightness of the foliage in the spring that it should be practiced if for that reason alone; but should also be done to save it from real danger in unusually severe winters. The slenderness of its form makes it very easy to bind with straw. There is a variety of this tree, the *J. robusta*, that is said to be more uniformly healthy and vigorous than the common sort.

THE CAUCASIAN JUNIPER, *J. oblonga*, is a straggling bush with slender drooping branchlets. Height five or six feet. Quite hardy, but probably inferior in all respects to the following ·

THE OBLONG WEEPING JUNIPER. *J. oblonga pendula.*—A Japanese variety, considered by competent observers who have been well acquainted with its growth since it was introduced into this country, about fifteen years ago, to be the most interesting of all the Junipers. Its form is what the name implies. The pendulousness is in its small twigs only. Color of foliage a warm light-green. Breadth about two-thirds the height, which at maturity is about twenty feet. Sargent writes that it is with difficulty transplanted, and recovers slowly afterward; but when fairly started succeeds admirably. Parsons & Co., at Flushing, have beautiful specimens. It requires care and protection while young from summer's sun as well as winter's cold. Hoopes in his Book of Evergreens states that it may be grafted upon the red cedar. If it is durable and thrifty as a graft upon that stock, its beauty may be rendered quickly available by grafting it not too high on strong young trees of this common sort.

The Chinese Juniper. *J. sinensis.*—This was highly commended six years ago, but is now considered by most planters who have tried it to be almost worthless.

The Canadian Juniper, *J. canadensis.* The Savin, *J. sabina,* and the Alpine Juniper, *J. alpina,* are low, broadly spreading shrubs, that take up a great deal of room that may be much more prettily occupied by other things.

The Dense Indian Junipers, *J. densa, J. repanda densa,* and *J. recurva densa,* are so well confused that we do not know if the three botanical names are of different varieties or the same thing. The species is from the Bhotan or Nepaul country in Asia. A small plant seen at Parsons & Co.'s was the most perfect little thing of the Juniper family seen there, having a velvety compactness of foliage unequalled by any other. The name given to it at the nursery is the *J. repanda densa.* Hoopes does not consider these Junipers quite hardy. Sargent makes them hardy at Fishkill. We have faith in the one just mentioned merely by reason of its very healthy and hardy appearance. Height and breadth three to six feet. (?)

The Scale-leaved Juniper, *J. squamata,* has become one of the most popular of the family since the publication of the excellent engraving in Sargent's Supplement to Downing's Landscape Gardening, of a specimen growing in the grounds of R. S. Fields, N. J. After seeing the engraving we think most persons will be disappointed in the tree (or rather bush) itself. It certainly makes a fine broad mound of the peculiar foliage of the Junipers, but it is

36

scarcely more than a mound for quite a number of years, though it eventually assumes a pyramidal form. Where one has room for shrubs of much breadth and little height, the *squamata* is one of the best. The foliage presents a roughly broken surface and a prickly appearance when the plants are young, but with age becomes dense, and smoother in outline, and then breaks well into light and shade.

THE CREEPING OR PROSTRATE JUNIPER. *J. repens* (*J. prostrata, J. recumbens*).—This is a true evergreen creeper which spreads in every direction, and covers the ground with a deep velvety mat of dark green foliage. It forms a rich carpet for rocks which have but little soil upon them, and does best in partial shade. There are fine specimens in the Central Park. Height from six inches to two feet. Hoopes mentions that the *aphis* or plant lice are particularly injurious to this species, and sometimes kill them in one season. He recommends sprinkling the plants frequently with hot (?) tobacco water until the insects are destroyed.

THE INCENSE OR SACRED JUNIPER. *J. religiosa.*—This becomes a large tree in its native Nepaul. Sargent considers it hardy at Fishkill, but makes no mention of it as a beautiful or especially desirable sort. It is simply on trial.

THE CEDAR OF LEBANON. *Cedrus libani.*—The interesting religious associations of this tree, its great size and grand lateral expansion of head, so much more noble in this respect than most of our northern evergreens, and the fact that some of the most beautiful specimens in the world are those which have been planted in England within the last two hundred years, have all tended to make every planter desire a Cedar of Lebanon in his collection. Yet it is by no means one of the most beautiful evergreens when young. Both in contour and branch-lines it is rigidly formal during the first fifty years of its growth, the outline being conical-ovate, and the branching rather horizontal; and it develops the peculiar tabular expansion of its top and grand lateral sweep of branches only as it approaches a century or more of growth. The foliage in general appearance resembles that of the Juniper family.

It cannot be considered hardy north of Philadelphia, although there are a few fine specimens near the city of New York. It will probably become a grand tree in the upper table lands and mountains of the southern States.

There is a new variety recently brought out in England with slenderer and more pendulous branches, and named botanically the *C. l. pendula.*

THE DEODAR CEDAR, *Cedrus deodora,* belongs to the same family as the Cedar of Lebanon, and has many of the same characteristics at maturity, but when young is far more graceful in its branching and spray. It resembles the hemlock in its branching, but its foliage is not so soft to the touch, nor so pleasing in color, being a bluish or grayish green. Those who have seen it in its native localities on the mountains of northern Hindostan, describe it as a tree of colossal dimensions, uniting gracefulness and grandeur beyond all other evergreens. It is found in the same regions where the Bhotan pine is indigenous, near latitude 30° north, at elevations from six to twelve thousand feet above the sea. It has been pretty well tried in this country, and has not proved hardy in the northern States. Sargent mentions that its habit of making a late autumnal growth, makes it peculiarly liable to injury in winter, and that it is quite *unreliable.* He believed they would do best on the northerly side of hills or other protection from too much sun, and in soils that are deep, poor, and dry; while Mr. Meehan, of Philadelphia, reports that all deodars on wet low soils are uninjured, while those on dry are killed outright. It is not unlikely that specimens may be made to grow to large size as far north as Lake Ontario, but such successes will probably be exceptional. Trees which never attain large size may, if but half-hardy, be protected at every age, but those which are planted for their ultimate greatness should be of sorts that will not be endangered by extremes of heat or cold after they become too large to protect. The deodar *when young* is not so beautiful as the hemlock. We need not therefore feel sad over our failure to domesticate it.

THE SILVERY DEODAR CEDAR. *C. d. argentea.*—This is a variegated variety of extraordinary beauty, of which we have only seen small plants in Parsons & Co.'s nurseries. The foliage is so silvery, that it is fairly brilliant. Probably not hardier than the species, but considered as an evergreen shrub, to be protected regularly, it commends itself to the attention of collectors.

THE JAPAN CEDAR. *Cryptomeria japonica.*—This is an exquisitely graceful tree when young, and so peculiar in the form and droop of its foliage, that it is quite unfortunate it cannot be grown as an open ground tree in the northern States. It is decidedly tender. At Newport, and near Philadelphia, a few specimens have survived the winter uninjured, but they are exceptional. Southward of Washington it is comparatively safe. Sargent recommends that it be grown at the north in tubs, to be wintered in a cool, dry cellar or green-house, and placed where wanted on the lawn in summer, burying the tubs in the ground, so that the tree will seem to belong there. In its native country it is a great tree.

The *Cryptomeria elegans.*—This is a very peculiar smaller species, with foliage in general appearance between that of the red cedar and common asparagus, dense, of a light green color, and somewhat drooping. Small plants survive the winters in open ground at Rochester *with protection.*

THE ARBOR-VITÆ FAMILY. *Thuja. Biota. Thuiopsis.*

Under the three botanical divisions above given, the different species of arbor-vitæ are grouped. They are all conical or pyramidal trees, or fastigiate shrubs, remarkable for the flattened appearance of their leaves and branchlets, which in most varieties appear as if they had been pressed.

FIG. 179.

THE AMERICAN ARBOR-VITÆ. *Thuja occidentalis.*—This beautiful native tree, frequently called the white cedar, is now well known everywhere in this country. It grows wild in most of the eastern and middle States, but in greatest abundance on the banks of the Hudson, forming a conical tree, branched to the ground, and from twenty to forty feet high. Even without clipping, it grows in a form almost perfect for high hedge screens, and bears the shears so well, that it may easily be kept to the height of three or four feet. It is beautiful in any form it is made to assume. The foliage has a bright green tone, which is slightly browned by the cold in winter. Fig. 179 is the usual form of specimens growing on exposed hill-sides.

PARSONS' ARBOR-VITÆ. *Thuja occidentalis compacta.*—This is a beautiful sport of the native sort, of a golden-green tone, and globular form, nearly as broad as high. The warmth and brightness of its color are conspicuous. Its growth is slower, broader, and more compact, than the American or Siberian.

HOVEY'S ARBOR-VITÆ. *Thuja occidentalis hoveyii.*—A pretty seedling of the common arbor-vitæ, of dwarf habit, globular form, and warm green color.

THE SIBERIAN ARBOR-VITÆ. *Thuja siberica.* — This most beautiful tree of the family has come among us in such a mysterious way, that even our indefatigable amateur arboriculturist, H. W. Sargent, does not seem sure of its origin or relationship. It greatly resembles the American arbor-vitæ in all its good qualities, but has a more velvety tone of color, is broader in proportion to its height, and probably a lower tree or bush at maturity; perfectly hardy, always beautiful, and regarded either as an evergreen shrub or small tree, unites more good qualities for common use than any other we know of. Josiah Hoopes, in his Book of Evergreens, claims it as a variety of the American arbor-vitæ.

THE TARTARIAN ARBOR-VITÆ. *Biota tartarica (B. pyramidalis).*—It is doubtful if it offers features distinct enough to distinguish it at sight from the varieties of the American and the Siberian arbor-vitæs. Form compact, pyramidal; foliage dark; hardy.

THE AMERICAN GOLDEN ARBOR-VITÆ. *Thuja occidentalis aurea.*—A seedling brought to notice by H. W. Sargent, Esq., which he describes as having its new growth very distinctly yellow, the old foliage of a bright, clear green, both blending to form a most pleasing little tree, or shrub, and perfectly hardy.

THE GLOBE ARBOR-VITÆ. *Thuja globosa.*—This is a pretty dwarf shrub, very round and compact, and quite a favorite in the neighborhood of Philadelphia ; three to five feet high.

THE TOM THUMB ARBOR-VITÆ. *Thuja minima ?*—A roundish or oblate dwarf, of compact habit, which originated in the nurseries of Ellwanger & Barry, Rochester, N. Y., and is highly recommended by them. Height three to four feet.

THE NOOTKA SOUND ARBOR-VITÆ. *Thuja plicata.*—This is a native of the Pacific slope, and differs from the indigenous arborvitæ of the eastern States in the more vertical and flatter arrangement of its foliage plaits, and its shorter and stouter young wood. Very like the Siberian in the color of its leaves, but less rich in the massing of its foliage: quite hardy.

THE GIGANTIC ARBOR-VITÆ. *Thuja gigantea.*—A tree of the largest size, growing on the banks of the Columbia river, where it grows upwards of one hundred feet in height. It is said to develop into " a fine, umbrella-shaped top, and picturesque head." This form is unusual among evergreens, and so desirable, that, if it proves a characteristic of the tree, it must become popular for that reason alone. Hoopes, however, believes that it will not prove hardy, though it has not been tested long enough to determine this point fully.

THE CHINESE ARBOR-VITÆ. *Biota orientalis.*—This is a little beauty when quite young, and marked by a warmer-toned green, and a finer quality of foliage, than the common American. It is also less regular in outline, and the foliage breaks apart into masses rather vertically. Unfortunately it has not proved hardy, and is so often injured by winter and summer, that instead of growing more beautiful as it approaches maturity, it becomes less comely, and after a half dozen years trial is generally pronounced scrawny. There is a tree in the Bartram garden south of Philadelphia, growing in a good exposure, which is twenty feet high, nearly as broad, and with a trunk ten inches in diameter ; but it is decidedly a meagre-foliaged tree.

THE WEEPING ARBOR-VITÆ. *Biota (Thuja) pendula.*—This is said to be a native of China, growing wild there ; also said to be a seedling originated in an English nursery. Both statements may be true ; as it is not impossible that the foreign seeds may have been planted accidentally. Hoopes is quite confident that it is a seedling sport of the Chinese arbor-vitæ. It is a hardy tree of oblong form, with all its smaller branches quite pendulous, and regarded by those who have had it a long time as one of the most pleasing of the arbor-vitæs ;—perhaps, considering its peculiar weeping habit, the most interesting of all for a single specimen on a small place. Its beauty is heightened by winter protection.

THE GOLDEN ARBOR-VITÆ. *Biota o. aurea.*—This exquisite little tree or rather shrub is a variety of the Chinese, and though not perfectly hardy, is more so than its parent. Its rare shade of green is truly golden, and its compact growth, pretty ovate form, and dwarf habit, combine to make it one of the most indispensable of evergreen shrubs. It is too easily protected in winter to make its slight tenderness a bar to its cultivation in all parts of the country. Height three to five feet.

THE VARIEGATED GOLDEN ARBOR-VITÆ. *B. o. aurea variegata.* —A variety originated in France. We have not seen it, and will quote Hoopes' observations concerning it. " In our opinion it is the most distinct and beautiful of the variegated conifers. The rich golden-yellow is so exquisitely shaded and mellowed down to pure white, and again so prettily tipped with pink, as to cause the most inveterate hater of these oddities to respect it." In reply to Dr. Siebold's assertion that these variations are but results of disease, and must therefore be of weaker habit than normal plants, he remarks : " Practice certainly, in many instances, refutes this theory, for we frequently find the variegated forms even more hardy than the parent in its perfect state. A case in point is this variety, for it has proven itself less liable to injury from excessive cold weather, or sudden changes, than the species. It also stands our hot summers remarkably well. We also find the variegated yews to be more hardy than their parent." There is another variegated variety called the *elegantissima*, on which the ends only of the branches are marked with a warm yellow.

THE PYGMY ARBOR-VITÆ, *Biota o. pygmæa*, is the smallest of all the species, and of a rich dark-green color.

SIEBOLD'S ARBOR-VITÆ. *Biota o. nana.*—A round compact dwarf of a bright green color.

THE NEPAL ARBOR-VITÆ. *B. gracilis* (*B. nepalensis*).—Form about the same as that of the American arbor-vitæ. Foliage more delicate, and of a darker green. Quite hardy. The specimen from which we formed our opinion of this species was in Parsons' specimen ground at Flushing. Hoopes describes it as having a light-green color; the one we observed (in the month of September) was darker than either the American or the Siberian, which were growing near by.

THE BROAD-LEAVED ARBOR-VITÆ. *Thuiopsis dolobrata.*—A new variety from Japan of strong growth. The branches are fastigiate, but drooping at their extremities and forming rather an open head. The foliage is a dark-green above and gray or "silvery" beneath. It is a very popular tree in China and Japan, where it reaches a height of forty to fifty feet, and is also much esteemed in England; but has not been cultivated long enough among us to test its hardiness. It is said to do best in shaded places and moist soil.

THE CYPRESS FAMILY.
Cupressus, Taxodium, Glypto-strobus, Retinispora.

The evergreen species of cypress, famous in old British and Continental grounds for their cemeterial associations, their slow growth, great longevity and final size, are the types of the *true* cypresses or *cupressus* of the botanists Our native swamp white cedar, and some of the evergreen cypresses of California are classed under the same botanical head. The American deciduous cypress is named by botanists, *Taxodium ;* and the new deciduous species from China are classed separately under the name *Glypto-strobus.* Another class known as Japan cypresses are classed, botanically, under the title *Retinispora.*

Fig. 180.

EVERGREEN-WALK IN PARSONS' NURSERY, FLUSHING, L. I.

THE COMMON (BRITISH) EVERGREEN CYPRESS. *Cupressus sempervirens.*—A tree with dark foliage and fastigiate habit, resembling in mode of growth the Lombardy poplar, though not quite so slender. This tree, so generally grown throughout England and middle Europe, is found utterly unsuited to our middle States. Sargent seems to have given up hope of acclimating any of the numerous English and Continental varieties. We shall, therefore, make no mention of them. The species which now give promise of hardiness, in the middle and southern States at least, are the new varieties from the Pacific slope. These are: the Lawson cypress, *C. Lawsoniana*, and the Nootka Sound cypress, *C. nootkaensis*, more generally known by the botanical name, *Thuiopsis borealis.*

THE LAWSON CYPRESS. *Cupressus Lawsoniana.*—This tree when young looks like a cross between a hemlock and a thrifty red cedar, with a dash of arbor-vitæ blood, but is more airy and thrifty in growth than any of these trees. Its main stem rises with a very decided leadership, throwing off numerous branches nearly at right-angles, and at irregular distances around it. Those which are near the base, taking a more upright direction as they grow in length, at last become almost vertical, and surround the centre stem so as to give the appearance of circles of smaller trees around the parent tree. The top growths of the main-stem, and of all the surrounding branches, bend with the same plumy grace as those of the hemlock; but their growth being more rapid, this peculiar grace is a more marked feature of the tree. The growth of the leader is so rapid that it seems to lift itself out of and above the group of environing branches that form a dense mass below, so that all its gracefully curving branchlets are very conspicuous. The tree shown on the left of the vignette, page 569, is one of Parsons' specimens of this sort. The color of the foliage is about the same as that of the American arbor-vitæ—perhaps not quite so bright. The young wood has a reddish-brown color, and smooth bark. Concerning the hardiness of this tree, accounts vary. At Parsons & Co.'s grounds in Flushing are very beautiful specimens sixteen feet high, in open ground, that do not seem to have been touched by the cold at any time. Mr. Sargent considers it hardy at his place at Fishkill, on the Hudson. Hoopes thinks it promises to be hardy near Philadelphia. Yet we have seen specimens from eight to ten feet high in a protected situation in the grounds of Thos. S. Shepherd, Esq., of "Edgewater," on the shore of Long Island Sound, near Mamaroneck, N. Y., badly injured by the winter of 1867 and '68, which was not unusually severe. This may, perhaps, be attributed to their growth in too rich a border where they were stimulated into a strong late fall growth. Hoopes mentions the necessity of avoiding this. At Rochester the hardiness of this species is considered doubtful. We would advise to take the benefit of the doubt, by testing it everywhere in the United States. It grows to the height of one hundred feet in northern California.

The *C. l. erec'a* is a new English variety of exceedingly slender and compact habit, and the *C. l. gracilis* is another of a different type, said to be more graceful even than the common form. These seem likely to be the best adapted to small grounds.

THE NOOTKA SOUND CYPRESS. *Cupressus nootkaensis, Thuiop-sis borealis.*—This strongly resembles the Lawson cypress, but is more compact and less graceful; about midway in general appearance between it and a Siberian arbor-vitæ. The form at the bottom is globular in young trees, and the top conical. The lower branches are not disposed to rest on the ground, like those of the hemlock, Norway spruce, or even so much as those of the Siberian arbor-vitæ, but curve upwards more decidedly. The foliage resembles that of the Siberian arbor-vitæ, dark, but bright. Young wood a dark purplish-brown. Growth more rapid than that of the arbor-vitæs, but less than the Lawson cypress. When young it closely resembles the latter, but may be readily distinguished by handling the foliage, which is prickly, while Lawson's is soft to the touch. The tree grows to great size northward of the Columbia river, and has proved hardy, as far as we can learn, in all the States.

THE WHITE CEDAR CYPRESS. *Cupressus thyoides (Chamæcy-paris).*—We have never seen this native species in cultivation, from which we infer that it does not do well out of its native swamps. Hoopes, however, mentions having seen very beautiful trees of it, and one very perfect hedge; and Emerson, in his "Trees of Massachusetts," speaks of it as "this graceful and beautiful tree." As it grows naturally in wet places, it is probable that it will develop its beauty only in soil that is cool and moist.

THE GOLDEN CYPRESS OR CEDAR. *C. variegata.*—This, Sargent thinks simply a beautiful variety of the white cedar, one that is highly valued in England among variegated trees, and believed to be hardy here.

THE FRAGRANT CYPRESS, OR OREGON CEDAR. *C. fragrans.*—This tree is described in the proceedings of the California Academy of Natural Science as follows: "This species bears the nearest resemblance to *Cupressus Lawsoniana*, but differs from it most strikingly in the brighter green of its foliage, and its far denser branchlets ; also in the leaves being narrower, much more angular, and sharper-pointed ; * * * it is also a tree of larger proportions in all respects." It grows to the height of one hundred and fifty feet, with a trunk six feet in diameter. When growing singly, it assumes a columnar form, with long, slender, pendulous branches. It has not, we believe, yet been tested in the eastern States.

THE CHINESE WEEPING DECIDUOUS CYPRESS. *Glypto-strobus sinensis pendula (Taxodium sinensis pendula).*—Though this belongs to a species of the *conifers*, which are deciduous, they are in

FIG. 181.

all other respects so allied in appearance with the evergreens, as usually to be classed with them. This variety in the neighborhood of New York is certainly the most beautiful and hardy of all the deciduous cypresses. Fig. 181 shows the form of the fine specimens in Parsons & Co.'s grounds at Flushing ; but no engraving can render the soft, downy tuftings of the foliage, or the warmth of its light green color.

—— " Her sunny locks
Hang on her temples like a golden fleece.''

The tree in its whole appearance is so distinct from all the trees generally cultivated in this country, that it is certainly one of the most desirable novelties among trees. We have seen it only in autumn, at which time the weeping character of the foliage is not marked, and the outline is distinctly formal. The pendulousness is only in the curl and droop of the young foliage, the branches radiating quite rigidly. It is known in China as the water pine, and found principally in the maritime districts. It is undoubtedly hardy in the neighborhood of New York and Philadelphia, and at Sargent's place at Fishkill on the Hudson. Whether it will succeed as well in the same latitude in the interior is doubtful ; but that it is hardy enough to plant in most of the States, with a little protection, there is good reason to believe.

Parsons & Co.'s superb specimens, which are now about twenty feet high, are in a deep, warm, sandy loam, and fully exposed in every way. The tree grows from twenty to thirty feet high, and casts its lower limbs as it rises ; so that at maturity its form is like that of a common pear tree, or somewhat more slender.

THE DECIDUOUS OR SWAMP CYPRESS. *Taxodium distichum.*— This is the lofty and moss-hung tree of the gloomy maritime swamps of Virginia and the Carolinas, but becomes a stately tree of some beauty in open grounds near the sea south of Philadelphia ; and there are many fine specimens around New York, some even in quite dry localities in the Central Park ; but it is quite inferior to the preceding in all respects for private grounds. The foliage is of fern-like delicacy, of a light green color, but rather thin. The trunk increases rapidly in size near the bottom ; the lower branches die out as the tree gains in height, and the top forms a conical pyramid, supported loftily at maturity on a straight and rapidly-tapering trunk. In the Bartram garden, south of Philadelphia, is a tree, planted by John Bartram in 1749, which is now one hundred and twenty-five feet high, with a trunk twenty-eight feet in circumference at the base, growing healthily, and to all appearance rapidly. It is of course unsuited to small grounds.

JAPAN CYPRESSES. *Retinispora.*—This new botanical family in general appearance resemble the junipers, and the arbor-vitæs, as much as the cypress. The following have been in cultivation in this country long enough to be pretty well tested.

THE HEATH-LIKE CYPRESS. *Retinispora ericoides.*—The first small plants which were sent out from the nurseries in this country attracted universal attention by the density and moss-like delicacy of the foliage, its clear green, and the pretty pink tinge it often wears. But it has generally been voted nearly worthless on account of a tendency to die by branches, and to lose its leaves. Our summer and winter climate seem alike uncongenial to it, and it has not, as far as we can learn, proved a perfectly healthy tree anywhere in this country.

THE JAPAN CYPRESS, *Retinispora obtusa*, is reported hardy at

Flushing. In Japan, on the mountains of the island of Nippon, it is a grand forest tree, from seventy to one hundred feet high, with a straight trunk from three to five feet in diameter. Its Japanese name signifies "tree of the sun." The plants in the nursery have a free, spreading growth, like red cedars, growing in strong soils, with foliage resembling that of the arbor-vitæs. The massy character of the foliage, and the free spreading growth, so rare among the arbor-vitæs, suggest that this tree, if its hardiness is established, is likely to take a conspicuous place among popular evergreens. The leaves have a warm green color, which they are said to retain throughout the winter. The twigs have a reddish color.

THE GOLDEN RETINISPORA. *R. pisifera aurea.*—A smaller and slenderer tree than the preceding, also from Japan, just introduced, and said to be "promising." Sargent marks it for us as "one of the most beautiful of trees," and all those who have it on trial agree in considering it uncommonly beautiful and probably hardy.

THE YEW FAMILY.
Taxus, Cephalotaxus, Torreya, and *Podocarpus.*

Whatever legendary and poetical interests are associated with the yews of the mother country, seem unlikely to be maintained in the United States. The islands of Britain have a climate peculiarly adapted to this tree. They there become trees with massive trunks and noble heads. Though quite a number of species are sufficiently hardy for general cultivation with us, and are among the most interesting of small evergreens, they cannot equal their prototypes in England, nor their rivals among those species for which our climate is best suited. There are specimens in England eight hundred years old, with trunks eight feet in diameter. The yews are of slow growth, but great duration, and generally noted for dark and dense foliage, resembling that of the firs, but the leaves are longer and thicker. A deep, moist, clayey soil, and partial shade, suit the tree best. The foliage loses the purity of its green, and becomes rusty when fully exposed to our summer sun.

THE ENGLISH YEW. *Taxus baccata.*—This is the parent species of most English varieties. A bushy tree, of compact growth, ovate-conical form, and dark foliage. It is considered hardy at Newport and New York, but not in the interior in the same latitude. It should be planted only in sheltered situations, protected from wind and excessive sunlight. The rate of growth is from six inches to one foot a year.

THE ERECT YEW. *Taxus b. erecta (stricta).*—This is a variety of the above, of exceedingly dark foliage, and fastigiate habit. Form ovate-conical. It is hardier than the parent, and better adapted to culture here. Fig. 42, page 141, is a group showing a pair of these trees behind a golden arbor-vitæ. The golden green of the arbor-vitæ contrasts finely with the very deep green of the yews, and the unusual fineness and verticality of the shadow-lines in the latter, is a peculiarity of this variety.

THE GOLDEN YEW. *Taxus baccata aurea (variegata).*—This is an exquisite little shrub or tree; the leaves being touched with yellow just enough to give a golden-green tinge to its color. Certainly one of the prettiest of dwarf trees for small grounds. Form irregularly conical or ovate. Hardier than the common yew.

THE VARIEGATED-LEAVED YEW. *Taxus elegantissima.*—Quite similar to the above—the leaves being variegated sometimes with white, and again with yellow tips or lines. Hardy near New York, and almost hardy at Rochester. Form about the same as that of the golden arbor-vitæ shown in Fig. 42.

THE IRISH YEW. *T. hibernica.*—One of the slenderest of the yews, but not considered hardy even at Flushing, L. I.

THE FLATTENED YEW. *T. adpressa.*—A low spreading shrub of very dark fine foliage, and pretty, red berries. For shady places.

DOVASTON'S WEEPING YEW. *T. Dovastoni.*—This is considered very beautiful in England, its growth being decidedly pendulous. Sargent, in Downing's Landscape Gardening, alluded to it as hardy with him at Fishkill; but he now marks it "tender"

HEATH-LEAVED YEW. *T. ericoides.*—Sargent speaks of this as a very pretty slender variety with minute foliage quite distinctive, and hardy with him in 1861. He now marks it *very hardy.* This is not the same as *Cypress ericoides* already described.

THE AMERICAN YEW, *T. canadensis,* is a spreading savin-like shrub that grows as if around the bottom of a bowl. Of no value.

THE CLUSTER-FLOWERED YEWS.   *Cephalotaxus.* —These are modern additions to the family of yews introduced from China and Japan, that promise to be more hardy than the English yew, and to bear our sun without injury. Those we have seen are many-branched, wide-spreading shrubs with long thick leaves.

THE PLUM-FRUITED YEW.   *Cephalotaxus drupacæ (Podocarpus drupacea; Taxus japonica).*—Growing in the north of China, it is described as a compact evergreen tree, from twenty to thirty feet high, found wild on the mountains, and cultivated in the gardens. " The leaves are arranged in two rows, laterally along the branches, regularly opposite, rather close, leathery, stiff linear, slightly curved or falcate, bluntly tapering to a short acute spiney point * * from three-quarters to one and one-fourth inches long, of a deep glossy green above," etc. (Gordon). Branches straight, stiff, and spread ing ; branchlets in two flat lateral rows, short and numerous. Believed to be hardy at New York and Fishkill.

FORTUNE'S CEPHALOTAXUS.   *C. fortunii mascula, C. of femina.* —These are male and female plants, both of which are known by the above popular name, but the *femina* is said to be less hardy than the *mascula.* We consider this one of the prettiest evergreen acquisitions of late years. In its early growth it forms a spreading shrub or bushy tree with many branches and branchlets, the latter of a light green color that contrast prettily with the pure deep green of the long stiff leaves, which are about two inches in length. The branchlets are generally described as drooping at the ends, but the specimens we have seen had not that character. Parsons & Co.'s best specimen is about seven feet high, and eight or nine feet in diameter, and of such peculiar appearance as to attract at once any observer of shrubs and trees. In China it is found from forty to sixty feet high, and the branches are represented to droop gracefully. So far we can only regard it in this country as a promising evergreen shrub which has proved hardy around New York, but which should be insured by adequate winter protec-

tion. Ellwanger & Barry do not think it will prove hardy at Rochester.

The female variety has lighter colored foliage than the other,
and bears coral-colored oval berries as large as acorns.

HARRINGTON'S YEW. *Cephalotaxus pedunculata (Taxus Har-
ringtonia).*—" A handsome small evergreen tree, growing from
twenty to twenty-five feet high, with numerous spreading branches,
mostly in whorls around the· stem ; found abundantly in Japan,
cultivated in gardens under the name of Junkaja " (Gordon).
Hardly known yet in this country.

SIEBOLD'S SPREADING YEW, *Cephalotaxus umbraculifera,* is
another species from the northern parts of China, noted there for
the horizontal extension of its branches. Not tested yet in ·this
country.

THE PODOCARPUS YEWS.—This is a large branch of the family
of yews which have been discovered within the last thirty years in
China, Japan, and other parts of Asia, and South America. Most
of them are tender, even in England ; but there is reason to hope
that a few will prove hardy in our northern States. But lately
introduced in American collections, and now
on trial.

FIG. 182.

THE JAPAN PODOCARPUS.—*Podocarpus japonica.*—Gordon describes this species as follows : " Leaves alternate, flat, linear lanceolate,
elongated, obtuse· pointed, thick, leathery and
stiff ; from four to eight inches long, and about
half an inch wide, with an elevated rib almost
acute along the upper surface, but rounded
on the under one, and tapering into a long,
slender point at the apex, and into a short,
stout foot-stalk at the base." The color of the foliage is the dark
est of greens ; but the very unusual size of its leathery leaves gives
it a marked appearance among evergreens, that, with its pretty
erect habit, will doubtless make it popular wherever hardy. It is
considered so at Flushing, L. I., and at Fishkill, N. Y. ; but we
have heard nothing from it in other places. Parsons' specimen,

37

Fig. 182, has not near so long or large leaves as Gordon describes (May it not be the *P. chinensis ?*).

There is a variegated variety, originated in some European garden, under the name of the *Podocarpus j. elegantissima*, which has pale yellow leaves when they first expand, but change afterwards to the normal color.

THE CHINESE PODOCARPUS. *P. chinensis.*—Gordon's description of this corresponds in general to the foregoing, and with Parsons' specimen of the *P. japonica.*

THE COREAN PODOCARPUS, *P. koraiana*, is another similar fastigiate bush from China, reputed hardy in England, but not fully tested here.

THE NUBIGEAN PODOCARPUS, *P. nubigæna*, from the province of Valdivia, in Chili, is reputed one of the most beautiful. Sargent supposes that the latitude and climate of southern Chili, where this tree is found, is a strong reason for believing that it will prove hardy with us. Having been there, we can state from personal knowledge, that the coast, further south than Valdivia, on the Pacific slope of the mountains, has a climate modified by the ocean and air currents from the Pacific, so that there is never anything like severe winter there, though a vast amount of cold rains fall in winter on the coast; and on the mountains the same moisture falls in snow: but it is only by crossing to the east side of the Andes, or several hundred miles south of Valdivia, or Chiloe, that winters of extreme cold like our own are experienced.

THE TORREYAN YEWS. *Torreyas.*—This is another botanical branch of the yew family, to which large additions have been made by the discoveries of botanists in China, Japan, and our Pacific slope. The name has been given in honor of Dr. Torrey, one of America's most indefatigable botanists, who was most prominent in bringing it into notice. The wood and foliage of most of the species emit a bad odor when bruised, and are therefore called stinking yews. The only variety which bids fair to prove hardy in the northern States is the following, a native of Florida:

THE YEW-LEAVED TORREYA. *T. taxifolia.*—This has proved hardy at Mr. Sargent's place at Fishkill, on the Hudson. He says

·of it: "This one of our greatest accessions in the middle States, being now perfectly hardy with us, and very distinctive. It is a handsome, pyramidal tree, with numerous spreading branches, growing from forty to fifty feet high, found in the middle and northern parts of Florida, where it is commonly known by the inhabitants as stinking cedar, and wild nutmeg. Our best specimen is about eight feet high, very dense, showing nothing but foliage, like a thrifty arbor-vitæ, and remarkable, particularly in winter, for the star-like appearance of the extreme tips of its shoots."

THE SEQUOIA. *Sequoia.*

This name has been given to those giant trees of California, popularly known as the redwood, and the big-tree of California, the latter being formerly named by botanists *Washingtonia* and *Wellingtonia.*

THE BIG-TREE OF CALIFORNIA. *Sequoia gigantea (Washingtonia, Wellingtonia).*—The size of this giant among giants may be imagined by the fact, that through the hollow of one of the felled trees, a man on horseback rode seventy-five feet, and came out through a knot-hole in the side, without dismounting! Trees three hundred feet high are known, and one has been measured, with a circumference of one hundred and six feet, four feet from the ground.

At Rochester, in the specimen grounds of Ellwanger & Barry, are fine healthy specimens, from ten to sixteen feet high, that do not seem to be injured in winter. In form they are as conical as the balsam fir; in foliage resemble the arbor-vitæs. The branches are numerous, straight, evenly and irregularly distributed from the trunk, quite horizontal, and small in proportion to the size of the trunk. The bark is of a light cinnamon color. The tree shows early a tendency to cast its lower branches. The trunk swells to great size at the base in proportion to the height of the tree, and diminishes regularly and rapidly above, like the cypress. Annual growth at the top from two to three feet. The foliage is mostly 'on the exterior of the tree, so that the stem and branches are plainly seen through it. It is not a beautiful tree, and deserves to be cultivated in ordinary grounds only as a curious souvenir of its mighty family on the Pacific slope. Hoopes does not consider the tree entirely hardy ; but we believe its hardiness is now pretty generally conceded. It is unreliable in transplanting, and should be bought in pots or boxes.

THE CALIFORNIA REDWOOD. *Sequoia sempervirens.*—This and the preceding being almost equally famous for size, and both brought to notice about the same time, are often confounded. Sargent makes the following description of their differences :—" the foliage of the *Sequoia sempervirens* being flat, two-rowed and dark-green, while that of the *Washingtonia (S. gigantea)* is needle-shaped, spirally alternate, and on the branchlets very close and regularly imbricated like an arbor-vitæ, besides being a light or yellowish-green." It has been found too tender to succeed in the northern States, but may grow healthily south of Washington.

THE LAURELS. *Laurus.*

THE NOBLE LAUREL OR SWEET BAY. *Laurus nobilis.*—This is a noble evergreen tree " or rather enormous shrub, sometimes growing to the height of sixty feet, but always displaying a tendency to throw up suckers ; and rarely, if ever, assuming a tree-like character " (Loudon). It is a native of the south of Europe and north of Africa. It was a favorite tree with the poets of mythology, and several of the Greek gods and goddesses were intimately associated with its poetical legends. At what period of history its leaves became emblems of victory is not known, but the Romans used them on all occasions where bravery and success were to be symbolized.

The noble laurel is considered hardy in and near London, but does not attain a great luxuriance north of it. It will probably be liable to winter-kill north of South Carolina and the Gulf States, though in favored locations it may thrive as far north as Richmond, Va. It has a thick aromatic leaf, smaller and more slender than:

that of the sassafras, about four inches long and one inch wide. Where hardy it is considered a superb tree for massive hedges.

THE CAROLINA LAUREL OR RED BAY. *Laurel carolinensis.*— An evergreen tree, indigenous from Virginia to Louisiana, and similar in character, in most respects, to the noble laurel above described. It forms a crooked trunk with few and irregular branches, and only becomes luxuriant in the low wet lands of the Gulf border, where it reaches a height of from fifty to seventy feet. It is less hardy than the *Laurus nobilis.*

THE CATESBY LAUREL. *L. catesbiana.*—This is a low evergreen shrub from five to ten feet high, growing on the sea-coast of Georgia and the Carolinas. It has smaller and slenderer leaves than the foregoing. How tender we do not know.

THE PORTUGAL LAUREL. *Cerasus lusitanica.*—An evergreen tree of the cherry family, native of Portugal and the Canary islands, where it becomes a huge bushy tree from thirty to sixty feet high. In the south of England it is considered hardy, and one of the most prized of gardenesque evergreens. It there ripens its seeds perfectly without protection, though in Paris it is treated as but half hardy. It grows in the form of a broad pyramidal bush, with dense foliage and branches diverging regularly from an erect stem. The leaves are from four to six inches long, slender, alternate, thick, glossy, and a very pure green color. Flowers in small racemes in June. Berries dark-purple. Rate of growth about one foot per year. Loudon remarks that the tree grows well in any soil that is very dry and poor, or very wet! Many specimens growing in England are remarkable for their low spreading forms. In Oxfordshire, at Blenheim, is a tree, or bush rather, seventeen feet high and one hundred feet in diameter! The common form of head is a diameter one-half greater than the height. In the latitude of New York its cultivation is impracticable.

THE GORDONIA. *Gordonia.*

THE LOBLOLLY BAY, *Gordonia lasianthus*, is one of the splendid flowering trees of the southern States, where it is sub-evergreen, and grows in moist cool soils from thirty to eighty feet in height.   At the north it can only be grown as a tub-shrub to be wintered under glass.   The leaves are similar to those of the rhododendron family.   Flowers single, white, four inches in diameter, and fragrant.

THE PUBESCENT GORDONIA, *G. pubescens,* is a smaller deciduous species, becoming a tree from thirty to fifty feet high in the Gulf States, and diminishing to a shrub farther north.   A little more hardy than the preceding, but unsuited to open-ground planting north of the Carolinas.   Its large white flowers appear from May to August, and are exceedingly fragrant.   It does best in a cool moist soil and sheltered situation.

THE HOLLY.   *Ilex.*

The hollies are mostly evergreens, and embrace species of all sizes from small shrubs to large trees ; and are natives of both continents.   They grow slowly and live long.   The name holly is supposed to be a corruption of holy, and the branches are always used in England to decorate dwellings and churches during the holydays of Christmas.   The species thrive better than most trees in the shade and smoke of cities.

THE EUROPEAN HOLLY.   *Ilex aquifolium.* — In the British islands this holly forms a very compact conical tree twenty to thirty feet high.   Its leaves are glossy, deeply scolloped, and armed with many sharp points or spines.   It bears clipping well, forms the most impenetrable of hedges in the moist mild climate of England, and is more free from the attacks of insects than other hedge trees ; but it endures neither the winters or summers of our middle and northern States.   South of Washington, in shady situations, it sometimes develops its beauty.   The varieties of this holly are very numerous, and vary much from each other ; and it is observed of the variegated-leaved sorts that they are quite as healthy in their appearance as the normal form.   The most marked varieties are the smooth-edge-leaved, *I. a. marginatum,* having pointed-oval leaves with smooth edges, without prickles, thick and leathery ; the hedge-hog holly, *I. a. ferox*, with leaves crowded with spines and rolled at the edges ; the white-edge-leaved, *I. a. alba marginatum*, and the yellow-edge-leaved, *I. a. aurea-marginatum.*

THE AMERICAN HOLLY, *Ilex opaca*, is a beautiful conical ever green tree, similar in appearance to the European sort, and some what hardier, but not fully at home north of Washington, though grown with some success all over the country. In South Carolina it becomes a tree from sixty to eighty feet in height : in the middle States half that size, and at the north still less. The leaves are thick, tough, and very glossy, scolloped and armed with spines on their edges. Most specimens we have seen growing in open ground at the north are not' sufficiently covered with foliage to conceal the hard stiff ramification of the branches, which present an appearance similar to the pin oak. But if these were cut back to thicken the growth, the tree could doubtless be made to develop much of the beauty that has made the European holly a favorite for hedges ; the leaves of the American species having the same kind of glossiness. At the north it should be treated as a half-hardy shrub, and when clipped to promote a dense growth, the pruning should be done with a knife between the leaves, as the latter when cut have rusty edges that mar the cleanly character of the foliage. A deep, rich, cool soil, and rather a shady place, are essential to its handsome growth.

MAHONIA, OR ASH-BERRY. *Mahonia.*

These are mostly natives of the valley of the Columbia river, and the finest low evergreen shrubs we have. The leaves are thick and glossy like those of the holly, with scolloped and prickly edges. Though pretty hardy, they are often injured by cold in winter. If not planted where living evergreens protect them in winter, they should be well covered with evergreen boughs. Their growth is so low and bushy that this can easily be done.

THE HOLLY-LEAVED MAHONIA, *M. aquifolium*, is the best known variety. It forms a low broad bush covered with deep green glossy leaves, many of which in winter and spring are spangled with deep crimson or purple, and sometimes yellow, or mingled green and deep purple. Flowers small, yellow; April and May. It grows to the height of five to seven feet in its native wilds; and ten feet in England. Probably five feet in height and five to eight in breadth is about its maximum size in our northern States. "In its native country it grows in rich vegetable soil, among rocks, or in woods, where it forms a thick and rich undergrowth." It grows better in partial shade than in an unprotected exposure.

The *Mahonia fascularis* is similar to the *aquifolium*, but has narrower and more deeply toothed leaves, which are lighter colored, and the plant is more tender. The *Mahonia nervosa* is a dwarf border-plant whose stem rises but a few inches from the ground, but the compound leaves of which are from one to two feet in length. A pretty and showy low plant. The *M. repens*, or creeping-rooted mahonia, resembles the *aquifolium*, but has a more oval leaf, and is a lower and less robust plant.

JAPAN MAHONIA. *M. japonica?*—This variety has not long been grown in this country, but it is considered the hardiest of the family, and probably the most showy.

THE ARBUTUS. *Arbutus.*

A half hardy species of shrub or tree, mostly evergreens, and natives of countries with mild winters. The *A. unido*, variety *rubra*, is considered by Loudon the most ornamental variety of that species. It takes the form of a bush or tree, according to the care given it, and becomes in the south of England from twenty to thirty feet high. Evergreen. Flowers reddish, in drooping racemes; September and December; fruit scarlet, hanging with the last blossoms. The *A. hybrida milleri* is a variety with more showy leaves and pink flowers. The Arbutus andrachne, *A. andrachne*, is distinguished by smaller and glossier leaves without serratures. Flowers greenish-white, in March and April. Not quite hardy in London. The tall arbutus, *A. procera*, is a variety from the north-west coast of North America, with large serrate leaves, forming a tree from ten to twenty feet high.

THE MADRONA of the Mexicans, or *Arbutus menziesii*, is described in the report of the Pacific Railroad survey as follows· " A small tree twenty-five to thirty feet high, twelve inches diameter at the base. Found on the Willamette, Oregon, and ranges north of the Columbia, and is there called the laurel. The large, thick, and shining leaves, the smooth and colored bark, give this tree a tropical look, recalling the *Magnolia grandiflora* in its general aspect. The berries are red and resemble morello cherries. When ripe they are quite ornamental, and, together with the rich foliage, flowers, and colored bark, renders it one of the handsomest trees I saw." It seems as if this ought to be hardy in our middle States, but we have not heard that it has been acclimated on this side the Rocky Mountains. It is described by a recent writer as the most beauti ful small tree of the Pacific slope.

THE BOXWOOD. *Buxus.*

This beautiful family of evergreens includes small trees as well as shrubs, but is best known by the shrubby boxwood used in old gardens to form borders for walks. There is no other evergreen so dwarfish, delicate, and beautiful, and which is so facile under the shears or the pruning-knife to shape into any desired form of verdant sculpture, for which its size adapts it. The dwarf-box is used for edgings, and the larger sorts, called tree-box, are only varieties of the same species, distinguished as follows :

THE EVERGREEN TREE-BOX, *Buxus sempervirens*, is a native of many parts of Europe, found in a natural state as an under-growth among other trees. It becomes a tree from twelve to twenty feet in height, growing very slowly, and attaining great age. When grown without clipping, it does not form so dense a surface of foliage as the dwarf-box exhibits, and the greatest beauty is therefore obtained by keeping it within less than the maximum dimensions. Grown in open, sunny situations, the foliage is a warm, yellowish-green color ; but in partial shade, and in the cool, deep soils, which are most congenial to the species, the color is a deep, glossy green.

THE VARIEGATED-LEAVED BOX-TREES, *B s. argentea* and *B. s. aurea,* are, as their names imply, simply marked with white or yellow-edged leaves. In the shade these markings are inconspicuous, and in the full. sun they have not a healthy appearance, so that, on the whole, they are of less value than the un-variegated sorts. There is a variegated-leaved boxwood tree in the old Bartram garden, south of Philadelphia, which is eighteen feet in height, twenty feet in breadth, with a trunk ten inches in diameter, the form resembling that of a common apple tree, but with light, pendulous spray, and delicate foliage, making altogether a very charming small tree. It is probably about a hundred years old.

THE DWARF OR GARDEN BOXWOOD, *B. s. suffruticosa,* is usually seen from six to eighteen inches in height, but grows to a massive bush if allowed time for expansion. There is a specimen in the grounds of Miss Price, at Germantown, Pa., eight feet in height and twelve feet in greatest extension, that is an exquisite mound of the richest verdure from the lawn to its crown. No other evergreen shrubs form so naturally into smoothly-rounded surfaces, or present such a velvety tone of foliage, as old dwarf box-woods. They rarely attain their full size, or best tone of color, except where partially shaded, and are not quite hardy away from the sea-coast north of Philadelphia, though grown with partial success in all the northern States, and in Upper Canada. Edgings are made with cuttings of one year's growth, and should be protected at the north in winter for many years after they are set. June is the best time for trimming them. The dwarf-box forms an exquisite little shrub when grown alone, and is planted less than it deserves to be.

THE RHODODENDRONS. *Rhododendron.*

Rhododendrons are indigenous on both continents. They form shrubs from one to ten feet in height, the breadth ordinarily about equal to the height, with thick, glossy, smooth-edged leaves, of a slender elliptical form, three to five inches long. Their flowers are borne in terminal clusters close to the leaves, the separate flowers varying from one inch to two inches in diameter, and the clusters from two to six inches. The colors range from pure white to pink, yellow, lilac, crimson, and deep purple, and their variegations. Period of bloom about one month, varying in time on different varieties from May to August, but mainly in June and July.

The following are the principal species from which the varieties now in cultivation have sprung; but the various products of hybridization have so far surpassed the originals in beauty and hardiness, that the latter are of little importance practically, except to the growers of new seedling varieties, and to show what the gardener's skill can effect:

THE PONTIC RHODODENDRON, *R. ponticum,* is a native of Armenia, in Asia Minor, and in England becomes a spreading bush from six to fifteen feet high, and of greater breadth. It does best in shade, and cool, moist or tenacious soils; and is not hardy in our northern States. Flowers in June, of a purplish color.

THE AMERICAN RHODODENDRON, *R. maximum,* is almost a tree, but of a straggling, open growth. It is oftenest found wild in shady, moist, rocky ground, contiguous to the humid atmosphere of running streams, where it grows ten to fifteen feet high, and blossoms from June to August. Flowers a pale red color. Found from Canada to the Gulf States. There is a wild native variety with larger leaves, which attains greater size, and bears purple flowers in May and June, known as the *R. m. purpureum.*

THE CATAWBA RHODODENDRON. *R. catawbaensis.*—This is a native of the mountains from Virginia to Georgia, and forms a lower and more compact bush than the preceding; and, though not indigenous so far north, is yet the parent of varieties that are the hardiest and most beautiful in the northern States. Its leaves are the handsomest, and hybrids from it bear full exposure to the sun in common soils better than most others.

THE DOTTED-LEAVED RHODODENDRON, *R. punctatum,* is another wild variety of the south, with pink flowers.

THE GOLDEN-FLOWERED RHODODENDRON, *R. crysanthemum,* is a very dwarf variety, with yellow flowers; found in Siberia and Kamtschatka.

THE CAUCASIAN RHODODENDRON, *R. caucasicum,* is a dwarf sort, which grows only a foot in height on its native mountains.

With the above sorts to work upon, British and Continental gardeners have originated thousands of seedlings of all colors and qualities, large bushes and small, tender green-house varieties, and hardy sorts, that bear full exposure to the sun in summer and the cold in winter, and well adapted to common use everywhere. Of the latter the following is a choice list of varieties recommended by J. R. Strumpe, Esq., of Flushing, one of the most skillful American cultivators of rhododendrons. These have all been tested in open ground for many years, and are recommended for combining good foliage with fine flowers.

R. album candidissima.—A dwarf bush.—The best white-flowered variety.

R. album elegans.—Tree-like habit ; blush-white flowers.

R. album grandiflorum.—A large bush ; foliage handsome ; flowers white.

R. bicolor.—Tall straggling grower.   Rose-colored flowers.

R. blandyanum.—Bushy and dwarf.   Flowers bright cherry.

R. blandum.—Bush middle size.   Flowers lilac-white ; late.

R. everestianum.—Dwarf, round bush.   Rosy-lilac with yellow centre.

R. gloriosum.—Handsome tree-like form.   Large blush clusters.

R. grandiflorum.—One of the most prolific bloomers.   Rose to crimson.

R. purpureum elegans.—Dwarf, bushy.   Large trusses of purple flowers.

R. Leeii purpureum.—Lee's dark purple.   Middle size, bushy. The best dark purple.

R. roseum elegans.—Low and bushy.   Best dwarf with rose flowers.

R. speciosum.—Large bush.   Flowers light-pink, and late.

It has usually been recommended to form a peculiar soil for the rhododendrons, to resemble that where they are found wild ; but the best cultivators are now repudiating that idea, as far as relates to the hardy hybrids from the *catawbaensis,* and recommend deep culture in ordinary garden loams containing some clay.

THE KALMIA. *Kalmia.*

This evergreen shrub, also known as the American or mountain laurel, in its wild state is smaller than the rhododendrons, and is found from Canada to the Gulf States in rocky, shady, and moist places, such as suit that shrub. It has not been hybridized and improved by culture to near so great an extent as the rhododendrons, and the natives of the woods being difficult to grow into thrifty shrubs in common soils and exposures, have not been much used for embellishment. The indigenous varieties are

THE BROAD-LEAVED KALMIA. *K. latifolia.*—Height three to six feet. Leaves thick, glossy (in the shade) long and slender. Flowers in clusters, in June and July, white to red.

THE NARROW-LEAVED KALMIA. *K. angustifolia.*—Known as sheep laurel. A dwarf shrub with clusters of red flowers, in June Two feet high.

THE GLAUCOUS-LEAVED KALMIA. *K. glauca.* — An upright shrub two feet high, bearing red flowers in May.

All these species are charming shrubs where growing in congenial soil, shade, and moisture, but do not develop much beauty in open situations and with common culture.

EVERGREEN BERBERRIES.

Some evergreen species have been introduced into England which are esteemed. The following may be adapted to this country:

DARWIN'S EVERGREEN BERBERRY. *B. Darwini.*—Described (in England) as "a thoroughly hardy evergreen, with neat shining dark-green foliage, and in the spring covered with deep orange-colored flowers." It is on trial in our nurseries; also the *B. neuberti.* Loudon mentions the sweet-fruited evergreen berberry, *B. dulcis,* which grows in the neighborhood of the Straits of Magellan, as "an elegant evergreen bush," five feet or more in height; also some Asiatic varieties which are not yet in cultivation in our nurseries, and probably not of sufficient merit to warrant their culture.

THE ANDROMEDAS.   *Andromeda* (*Leucothœ* of Loudon).

Low evergreen, or sub-evergreen, shrubs; mostly natives of the southern States, some of which have come into notice at the north within a few years, and prove valuable acquisitions in the middle States.

FIG. 183.

The *Andromeda floribunda*, Fig. 183, is the most charming dwarf evergreen shrub we have. It grows well in the Central Park, and in private gardens near New York; but is extremely difficult to propagate, and therefore scarce, and high-priced. It forms a very compact oblate shrub, two to three feet high, and much broader. The leaves resemble those of the privet in color, size, and form. Flowers in May and June, small, white, in spikes or racemes three to five inches long, projected beyond the leaves. An exquisite shrub while in bloom, and of conspicuous neatness of form and foliage throughout the season.

The *A. axillaris* is a dense-leaved compact spreading shrub, three feet high. Flourishes in the Central Park, New York. Flowers small, in white spikes, in May and June. The leaves turn a brilliant reddish-purple in autumn.

The *A. catesbeii* or shiny-leaved, is a pretty variety with glossy leaves which turn to a brilliant reddish-purple in autumn. Size same as preceding.

A. spinulosa is a low variety, evergreen, native of Canada, which we have not seen in cultivation; said to resemble the preceding.

THE COTONEASTER.   *Cotoneaster.*

The Small-leaved Cotoneaster, *C. microphylla*, and the Round-leaved, *C. rotundifolia*, are prostrate evergreen shrubs, adapted to creep on rock-work or walls. Loudon says of the former: "It is exceedingly hardy" (in England), "and forms a fine plant on rock-work or on a lawn where it has room to extend itself. A plant at High Close, of about ten years' growth, was six feet high, and forms a dense bush twenty-one feet in diameter. Grafted standard high on the thorn or any of its cogeners, this shrub forms a singular and beautiful evergreen drooping tree ; or it will cover a naked wall nearly as rapidly as ivy." Flowers white in May and June. Berries bright-scarlet, ripe in August, and remaining on all winter. Not hardy at Rochester.

THE AUCUBA. *Aucuba japonica.*

An evergreen shrub from Japan, six to ten feet high. The leaves are pale-green, spotted with yellow. It is one of the most ornamental of variegated-leaved shrubs in England, but requires protection in our northern States, and is not classed as more than half-hardy at Rochester. It is in some locations healthy and beautiful, but not usually so north of Philadelphia, nor anywhere so fine as in England.

THE JAPAN EUONYMUS. *Euonymus japonicus.*

Evergreen or sub-evergreen trees and shrubs of many and widely differing characters, which are not hardy north of New York, and which have not been tested sufficiently to enable cultivators to judge them well. Among them are many variegated-leaved varieties.

THE DAPHNE CNEORUM.

An evergreen dwarf shrub or trailing plant of great beauty, which has become very popular during the short time it has been in cultivation in this country. It is a native of the mountains of Switzerland, growing naturally in moist soils and sheltered places. The flowers are a bright pink color, in April, and again in September. As a shrub it should be grafted on stocks of the *Daphne laureola.* Height one to two feet. Hardy.

FIG. 184.

CHAPTER VI.

VINES AND CREEPERS.

NO one needs to be reminded of the beauty of vines and creepers. Many of the most vigorous and beautiful vines in the world are indigenous in our woods, in all the States; growing on the loftiest trees, and clothing even their summits with the waving streamers of their foliage. The different sorts of vines may be distinguished as creepers, twiners, climbers, and trailers. The creepers are those which throw out little roots from their stems as they climb, by which they attach themselves to the bark of trees and rough walls, like the Virginia creeper and English ivy. Twiners, honeysuckles for instance, rise by winding round and round objects with which they come in contact. Climbers rise by having tendrils which lay hold of twigs of trees, or fix themselves in crevices, and support the vine till its large arms have wreathed themselves upon some other support—grape-vines, for instance—or without tendrils, by the mere force of their growth overlying the branches of trees and finding support by hanging over them, like the wild roses. Trailers are those which prefer to creep upon the ground like the low vine blackberry.

THE VIRGINIA CREEPER. *Ampelopsis virginiana.*—Often called the American ivy, though it has little resemblance to the true ivy except in its power of adhesion to the bark of trees, and to walls, and in the fact that it forms an equally luxuriant mass of foliage upon them. The leaf is composed of five irregularly serrate leaflets, radiating from a common point of intersection. These are often, but not always, quite glossy on the upper surface. The vine is furnished with tendrils which flatten out against the tree or wall with which they come in contact, and become auxiliary roots, attaching themselves firmly wherever they can find adequate support. Roots also break out from the stem of the vine where it comes in contact with such objects. The growth of the Virginia creeper is very rapid. We have seen the vines streaming from the parapet of a church tower seventy feet high, within eight years after being planted. On stone, or unpainted common brick, it forms a thick mass of graceful verdure, covering every part, and pushing out its young shoots in airy profusion from the body of the foliage. It is by far the finest of vines in this country for covering walls where it can take root, or for covering tree trunks ; but on brick walls that are ordinarily smooth it needs some fastening in addition to that which its own rootlets give it, to prevent the wind, which takes strong hold of its waving branches, from detaching the entire vine. In autumn the foliage turns to the brilliant crimson or purplish-crimson that landscape painters rarely fail to make a conspicuous feature in representations of American autumn scenery. The vine is found wild everywhere in the States, and grows readily from layers or cuttings. The flowers are greenish-purple, and inconspicuous ; fruit a purple berry, in large flat clusters.

38

THE PEPPER-VINE. *Ampelopsis bipinnati.* — A variety with compound pinnate leaves, of lesser growth than the preceding, and not so close a creeper.

THE AKEBIA. *Akebia quinata.*—A vine of delicate appearance, recently introduced, which has proved thrifty and hardy; and covers whatever it climbs upon so well with foliage that it is already quite a favorite. Flowers in clusters, bluish-violet, sweet-scented; in May and June.

THE BIRTHWORT. *Aristolochia.*—This is a twiner and climber. It is therefore unsuited for walls ; but its great heart-shaped leaves, from seven to twelve inches in diameter, borne with tropical luxuriance, make the finest exhibition of massy foliage for covering isolated artificial constructions of anything we know of. It is found wild in the middle States, and climbs to the tops of lofty trees. The flowers are the shape of a syphon or hook, of a yellowish-brown color, borne in May and June. It requires a deep rich dry soil.

THE COMMON TRUMPET CREEPER. *Bignonia (Tecoma) radicans.*—This is a true creeper, with long pinnate leaves composed of seven to eleven leaflets. It adheres to the bark of trees and to walls with the same tenacity as the Virginia creeper, and its growth is equally vigorous, but its vigor tends more to the top, so that the trunk and large branches become bare as it grows old. The leaves appear late in the spring, and are not brilliant in autumn. Its magnificent trumpet-shaped flowers are from three to four inches in length, borne in clusters in August and September, and of a brilliant orange color. It is a superb vine to grow on old evergreen trees that are not in themselves pleasing.

THE LARGE-FLOWERED TRUMPET CREEPER. *Bignonia (Tecoma) grandiflora.*—This is a Chinese variety with much larger, more open, and equally brilliant flowers of similar color, and with similar foliage to the trumpet creeper, but not quite so vigorous and hardy. Flowers pendant, in large clusters, in July and August.

THE DARK RED TRUMPET CREEPER, *B. (T.) atrosanguinea,* is

:a variety originated in France, distinguished by the crimson purple color of the flowers.

THE YELLOW-FLOWERED TRUMPET CREEPER, *B. (T.) flava speciosa*, is a variety with flowers colored as its name imports.

THE BITTER SWEET. *Celastrus scandens.*—A twining, wiry-wooded vine, with handsome, glossy, pointed leaves. It twines so tightly around the stems of young trees as frequently to kill them. Flowers in June, violet color, and inconspicuous. The berries are red, and showy in autumn, when they burst open, and display orange-colored capsules; but they are poisonous. Height fifteen to thirty feet. Of little value for culture.

THE CISSUS. *Cissus.*—A running vine, resembling the Virginia creeper in its general appearance, but not of equal beauty. There is a variegated-leaved variety, *quinquefolia variegata*.

CLEMATIS OR VIRGIN'S BOWER. *Clematis.*—The species are very numerous; some natives of Europe, and others of our own country. All are twining, of slender, irregular growth, delicate foliage, and marked fragrance of blossoms. They require artificial support, and are adapted to cover arbors, bowers, and low trees, or to be trained on verandas, but not to creep on tree-trunks, or to decorate walls. The petioles of the leaves serve as tendrils. There are many charming varieties in the south, not hardy at the north, and scores of hybrids and varieties have been originated.

THE EUROPEAN SWEET-SCENTED CLEMATIS, *C. flamula*, has compound leaves, with very narrow leaflets. The flowers are quite small, white, borne from July to October, and exceedingly fragrant. Extent of mature vines from fifteen to thirty feet.

THE WHITE-VINE CLEMATIS, *C. vitalba*, is a stronger-wooded vine than the preceding, with broader leaves, greenish white, inconspicuous flowers, and the distinguishing peculiarity of seeds around which grow long silky tufts or tassels of a greenish white color, forming a feathery mass of beautiful effect in August and September, when covering roofs, low trees, or arbors. These tufts have given the names of "old man's beard" to this species. The vine quickly grows bare of foliage towards the bottom, and displays all its beauty late in the season, and at the summit, where the fresh growth rests in masses. A useful vine to cover unsightly roofs.

THE AMERICAN WHITE CLEMATIS. *C. virginica.*—Similar in appearance to the preceding, but with more profuse and conspicuous white flowers, in August, and less showy seed plumes.

THE VINE-BOWER CLEMATIS. *C. viticella.*—This is a more showy species, bearing much larger flowers than the preceding sorts, of various colors, blooming from June or July to October, and two inches or more in diameter. Varieties.—The *C. viticella venosa* has rich purple-colored flowers, touched with crimson, and blooms profusely from June to October : considered the best. The *C. v. flora plena* has double flowers of the same color. The *C. v. cerulea* has blue flowers, quite large.

THE SHOWY-FLOWERED CLEMATIS. *C. Florida.*—A Japanese species, with flowers white, blue, and purple, two to three inches in diameter, from June to September. Growth slender, and not quite hardy.

THE LARGE AZURE-FLOWERED, *C. azurea grandiflora*, is a Chinese species, not long introduced, with flowers larger than the native or European sorts. The *C. cerulea*, of the same species, bears the finest blue flower. Both are hardy, and pretty, woody vines.

The *C. Sophia*, a Japanese variety with very large lilac blossoms ; and the *C. Helena*, another with very large white blossoms, are both elegant vines, but require protection in winter.

HONEYSUCKLES. *Lonicera.*—These most cherished vines have been gathered from all parts of the world, and the species hybridized and improved until their beautiful varieties are so numerous, that, like the roses, they are almost innumerable, and a description of them would fill a small volume. The best varieties are the most suitable of all vine decorations for verandas and porches. We shall merely mention a few sorts.

THE WOODBINE HONEYSUCKLE. *L. periclymenum.*—A native of Europe. One of the most showy in its flowers, which are red outside and buff within ; June and July ; berries deep red.

THE LATE RED HONEYSUCKLE, *L. p. serotinum*, is simply a late variety with darker flowers, and very showy during its blooming.

THE DUTCH HONEYSUCKLE, *L. p. belgicum*, differs from the first only in being more shrubby.

THE YELLOW-FLOWERED HONEYSUCKLE, *P. flava*, is a native of our States, half hardy, with large ovate leaves nearly joined at the base, and bright yellow flowers in June and July.

THE TRUMPET HONEYSUCKLES. *L. sempervirens.*—Indigenous, and sub-evergreen at the south. Flowers scarlet, and borne throughout the summer season after May. The *H. s. superba* and *H. s. Browni* are superior varieties.

THE CHINESE OR JAPAN MONTHLY HONEYSUCKLES. *L. japonica.*—Sub-evergreen, and not quite hardy; but of robust growth, densely clothed with leaves, constantly in bloom and deliciously fragrant, and of course universally popular. Protection is so easily given them that their slight unhardiness is a small objection to their use. The varieties are very numerous. Among them is the GOLD-VEINED-LEAVED sort, *L. j. folies aurea reticulata*, the leaves of which are exquisitely veined with gold lines, each leaf as pretty as a blossom, making it one of the most interesting to plant in porches or verandas among the darker leaved sorts. A moderate grower.

THE EVERGREEN IVY. *Hedera.*

"Creeping where no light is seen,
A rare old plant is the ivy green."

"The common evergreen ivy is a rooting climber; but when these roots are opposed by a hard substance which they cannot penetrate, they dilate and attach themselves to it, by close pressure on the rough particles of its surface." Unless, however, the surface presents some crevices into which roots can penetrate a little, the plant cannot sustain itself on a wall by the mere adhesion of its root-mouths against it; in other words, it cannot sustain itself on a *hard* and smooth stone surface. In this respect it is neither stronger nor weaker than our Virginia creeper. The evergreen ivy can hardly be said to have become domesticated in this country. Our summers are too hot and dry, and our winters too cold for it; and it rarely clothes lofty walls with such masses of verdure as in the British islands. In cities, on north walls, and sheltered corners of church towers and buttresses, it occasionally mounts and covers them, suggesting the beauty for which it is renowned in the moist mild climate of England; but these instances are exceptional in the northern States.

It is believed that all the varieties of the ivy may be grown as shrubs, and become quite valuable on account of the unusual purity of color of their evergreen foliage throughout the year. By planting an elm-post, say four feet above the surface of the ground, and ivies at the foot of it, they will cling to the post, and can be protected upon it for a few years in winter with straw. After they are well rooted, and form a mass several feet in thickness around the post, they will not need further protection in most parts of the northern States. No vine we have is so well adapted to cover the trunks of old dead trees which have had their tops cut off.

The varieties do not vary widely. THE ENGLISH IVY is known as *H. vulgaris*. The IRISH IVY, *H. canarienses*, has a leaf a little larger. This is the variety most planted in this country, and usually considered the hardiest. Then there are the GOLD-STRIPED, *H. foleis aureis*, the SILVER-STRIPED, *H. foleis argenteis*, the GIANT-LEAVED, *H. ragneriana*, and numerous others with some mark of difference from the normal form.

THE POISON IVY, *Rhus toxicodendron*, is also a beautiful native creeping shrub with fine glossy leaves, but the plant is a fearful poison to some persons, and should not be allowed to grow in settled neighborhoods. It may be readily distinguished from the Virginia creeper when in leaf by its three instead of five leaflets, and by their smooth edges; the Virginia creeper having strongly serrate leaves. Its wood is somewhat stronger and more stubby than that of the latter, and when the vine is attached to trees it sends out stiff shoots like branches, which do not fall gracefully like those of the Virginia creeper.

THE GRAPE-VINE. *Vitis.*—No intelligent person needs to be reminded that grape-vines are among the most beautiful as well as valuable of climbers. There is much difference in the habitual healthiness of different varieties which bear good fruit. The Clinton and the Concord are probably the most healthy and productive vines in the northern States when left to grow naturally; and their fruit, though not of the best for table use, makes a fine wine when carefully made and kept long enough. The Isabella, Catawba, Diana, Delaware, and a host of newer sorts, all do well in the middle States, but require more care than the two first named. In the southern States other varieties are more esteemed We believe that all our native vines are usually trimmed too much, and their healthfulness impaired by it; and that if their roots have a deep dry soil their tops may be allowed to cover a great space.

THE PERIPLOCA. *Periploca græca.*—A shrub from France, also known as the Virginia silk-vine, which is a vigorous twining vine, with large clean-cut, glossy, wavy leaves. The flowers are small, of a rich velvety brown; in July and August. Their odor is said to be unwholesome to those long exposed to it, and the vine should not therefore be planted on porches or near to windows.

CLIMBING ROSES.—See roses in Chapter V, Part II.

THE PERIWINKLE, OR RUNNING MYRTLE. *Vinca.*—A trailing evergreen that covers the ground rapidly, and is adapted to make a deep mat of verdure in shady places under trees where grass will not grow. It bears blue flowers which appear constantly from March to September.

THE WISTARIA. *Glycine. Wistaria.*—Twining vines of great vigor, indigenous in our country, and in Asia; with compound pinnate leaves, and long racemes of blue or lilac flowers.

THE AMERICAN, OR SHRUBBY WISTARIA. *W. (G.) frutescens.*— A free-grower, indigenous in the middle and southern States. Leaves composed of nine to thirteen leaflets. Flowers bluish-purple in shouldered racemes about six inches long, and borne from July to September.

THE CHINESE WISTARIA. *W. (G.) sinensis.* — This most vigorous of twining vines was introduced from China to England in

1816, but was little known in this country until within thirty years. There is no twining vine that will mount so rapidly, or that will cover so great a space. Planted at the foot of a lightning-rod it has been seen to mount to the top of a five-story house within four years after planting. Mr. Fortune, the great botanist, gives the following account of a famous vine which be saw in a Japanese city:—"On our way (May 20th) we called at Nanka Nobu to see a large specimen of *Glycine (Wistaria) sinensis* which was one of the lions in this part of the country. It was evidently of great age. It (the trunk) measured at three feet from the ground, seven feet in circumference, and covered a space of trellis-work 60 × 102 feet. The trellis was about eight feet in height, and many thousands of the long racemes of glycine hung down nearly half way to the ground. One of them which I measured was three feet six inches in length! The thousands of long drooping lilac racemes had a most extraordinary and brilliant appearance." On page 244 some wistaria vines, in Germantown, Pa., are mentioned, which have covered the head of a lofty hemlock tree, and almost hid it from sight under their own more luxuriant growth. If the vine has an opportunity to keep on growing vertically, it soon loses its foliage towards the bottom. It should therefore have a place for horizontal expansion in order to exhibit its greatest beauty, unless wanted to cover tree-tops. The foliage is composed of long pinnate leaves of many leaflets. The flowers appear in May and June, and again in August. They are borne in great abundance in long loose pendulous racemes from eight inches to several feet in length, and are mostly of a pale-blue or lilac color.

THE CHINESE WHITE WISTARIA, *W. (G.) sinensis alba,* is a recently imported variety with white flowers ; otherwise resembling the preceding.

The *W. brachybotria* is a variety with shorter racemes of more fragrant light-blue flowers. The *W. brachybotria rubra* is a variety with reddish-purple flowers. The *W. magnifica* is a new variety with lilac blossoms, believed to be a cross between the Chinese wistaria and the American species ; the *W. frutescens alba* is a white-flowered seedling of the latter.

APPENDIX.

—◆—

THE following tables are prepared merely to facilitate selections of trees and shrubs on the basis of size and growth alone. Deciduous trees are arranged by classes in three tables, as follows · First, DECIDUOUS TREES OF THE LARGEST CLASS. Second, DECIDUOUS OF SECONDARY SIZE. Third, DECIDUOUS TREES OF THE SMALLEST CLASS. The usual growth, under good culture, at twelve years from the seed, is approximated; and the ordinary height and breadth the tree attains at maturity, in the latitude of New-York City. Evergreen trees and shrubs are divided into three similar classes, except that evergreen shrubs are included with the smallest evergreen trees. Deciduous shrubs form a separate class, with their development indicated at *six* years after planting such plants as are usually received from nurseries; and also at maturity. These estimates of size are all based on a supposed good soil and culture; and for specimens having an open exposure. The trees are classed as of the first, second, or third class, in size, on the basis of their entire weight. The Lombardy poplar, for instance, by height belongs to trees of the first class, but by breadth ranks with the smallest: it is therefore put between the two extremes in the second class.

When trees are budded or grafted on other stocks, as many weeping trees are, the age of the stock is included in the age for which estimates of size are given. But as such "worked" trees are grafted at quite different heights on stocks of the same age, it must be understood that the estimates here given are for trees grafted in the manner most common in the great nurseries. Trees marked with a star * are those generally grafted on other stocks.

It must not be inferred that these tables embrace all the trees described in the preceding work. Most of the leading species are represented by one or more out of many varieties. The species and varieties which are not included in the tables will be found at once by referring to the INDEX.

DECIDUOUS TREES OF THE LARGEST CLASS.

Page.	Popular Name.	Botanical Name.	Usual Size 12 Years from Seed.		Usual Size at Maturity.	
			Height.	Breadth.	Height.	Breadth
304	The White Oak.............	*Quercus alba*..............	20 ft.	12 ft	80 ft.	80 ft.
307	" Swamp White Oak......	*Q. tomentosa*...........	20	12	80	70
308	" Burr Oak.........	*Q. macrocarpa*...........	20	12	70	60
310	" Chestnut Oak.........	*Q. prinus palustris*........	25	15	80	60
310	" Rock Chestnut Oak.....	*Q. p. monticola*...........	20	15	50	60
312	" Scarlet Oak...........	*Q. coccinea*........ ...·...	25	15	70	60
313	" Pin Oak.................	*Q. palustris*...............	20	15	70	60
315	" Turkey Oak	*Q. cerris*.................	20	15	70	60
316	" American White Elm...	*Ulmus americana*.........	30	25	70	80
319	" English Elm...........	*U. campestris*...........	30	20	80	70
322	" Scotch Elm...........	*U. montana:*..............	25	20	70	70
326	" American White Beech..	*Fagus americana*.........	25	15	80	70
331	" American Red Beech....	*F. ferruginea*...........	20	15	60	70
327	" Weeping Beech.	*F. sylvaticus pendula*.....	25	15	70	70
332	" American Chestnut......	*Castanea americana*..... .	25	20	80	80
344	" White or Silver Maple...	*Acer eriocarpum*...........	30	25	70	70
347	" Sycamore Maple	*Acer pseudo platanus*......	25	16	80	70
348	" Norway Maple..	*Acer plat anoides*...........	20	16	70	60
349	" Great-leaved Maple.....	*Acer macrophyllum*........	30	25	70	70
351	" Black Walnut..........	*Juglans nigra*.............	30	20	80	70
354	" Shellbark Hickory......	*Carya alba*..............	25	16	80	60
356	" White Ash	*Fraxinus americana*......	25	16	80	60
360	" Cottonwood....	*Populus canadensis*........	40	20	80	70
362	" Silver-leaved Poplar.....	*Populus alba canescens*....	35	25	70	70
364	" Whitewood or Tulip-tree.	*Liriodendron tulipifera*....	30	16	80	70
369	" Cucumber Magnolia....	*Magnolia acuminata*.......	30	16	80	60
384	" Sycamore	*Platanus occidentalis*......	35	25	80	80
385	" Oriental Plane-tree	*Platanus orientalis*........	30	20	80	80
387	" Weeping Willow........	*Salix babylonica*...........	40	40	60	60
389	" Golden Willow.......	*Salix vitellina*............	35	30	60	50
405	" Ginkgo, or Salisburia....	*Salisburia adiantifolia*.....	30	16	80	60
406	" Large-leaved Salisburia..	*Salisburia macrophylla*...	30	16	80	60
406	" Variegated Salisburia...	*Salisburia variegata*.......	?	?	?	?
406	" Scotch Larch..........	*Larix europæa*......... ...	35	20	80	50

DECIDUOUS TREES OF SECONDARY SIZE.

Page	Popular Name.	Botanical Name.	Usual Size 12 Years from Seed.		Usual Size at Maturity.	
			Height.	Breadth.	Height.	Breadth.
314	The Shingle Oak............	*Quercus imbricaria*........	20 ft.	10 ft.	40 ft.	40 ft.
315	" Upright Oak	*Q. fastigiata*...............	20	10	70	35
323	" Weeping Scotch Elm ...	*Ulmus montana pendula*...	20	20	60	60
324	" Scamston Elm...........	*U. m. glabra*...............	15	20	40	60
329	" Purple-leaved Beech....	*Fagus purpurea*............	20	15	60	60
330	" Copper-leaved Beech....	*Fagus cuprea*...............	20	15	60	60
330	" Fern-leaved Beech......	*Fagus heterophylla*........	20	15	50	50
337	" Horsechestnut	*Æsculus hippocastanum*....	20	15	60	50
339	" Double White-flowering.	*Æ. h. flore plena*..........	20	12	60	40
339	" Red-flowering H. C. ...	*Æ. h. rubicunda*...........	16	12	50	40
340	" Scarlet-flowering H. C...	*Æ. h. coccinea*.............	16	12	50	40
340	" Big Buckeye of Ohio.. .	*Æ. (pavia) flava*...........	16	12	40	40
341	" Long-fruited H. C.....	*Æ. macrocarpa (pavia m.).*	16	16	40	40
343	" Sugar Maple...........	*Acer saccharinum*.........	20	12	60	50
344	" Black or Rock Maple ...	*Acer nigram*..............	16	12	50	50
345	" Scarlet Maple	*Acer rubrum*..............	20	12	50	50
347	" Purple-leaved Maple....	*Acer p. p. purpurea*.......	20	16	60	60.
347	" White variegated-leaved Maple....... }	*Acer p. p. alba variegata*...	16	12	50	50
348	" Yellow variegated-leaved Maple....... }	*Acer p. p. flava (aurea) variegata* .... }	16	12	50?	50?'
348	" Eagle's-claw Maple.....	*Acer p. lacianatum*........	16	12	50?	50?'
348	" Lobel's Maple.........	*Acer p. lobelii*...........	16	12	40	40
348	" Shred-leaved Maple.....	*Acer dissectum*	20	12	50?	50?'
350	" Round-leaved Maple....	*Acer circinatum*...........	12	12	40?	40?'
351	" Butternut	*Juglans cinerea*...........	20	16	40	40
360	" Weeping English Aspen.	*Populus tremula pendula..*	16	20	30	40
360	" Weeping Amer. Poplar.	*Pop., grandidenta pendula*	16	20	30	40
363	" Lombardy Poplar......	*Populus fastigiata*........	40	10	80	20
370	" Heart-leaved Magnolia..	*Magnolia cordata*.........	20	12	40	30
372	" Great-leaved Magnolia....	*Magnolia macrophylla*.....	20	12	30	30
378	" Cut-leaved Weeping Birch .... }	*Betula lacianata pendula*...	30	20	60	50.
379	" Old Weeping Birch.....	*Betula pendula*	30	20	60	50
380	" Paper or Canoe Birch...	*Betula papyracea*	30	20	60	40
381	" Yellow Birch ..,.......	*Betula lutea*.............	30	20	70	40
382	" American Linden.......	*Tillia americana*.........	20	16	70	50
383	" European Linden.......	*Tillia europæ*.............	20	16	60	50
383	" Broad-leaved Linden....	*Tillia macrophylla*...	20	16	60	60
383	" Grape-leaved Linden....	*Tillia vitifolia*..........	20	16	?	?
383	" Red-barked Linden.....	*Tillia rubra*.............	20	16	?	?
383	" White Weeping Linden..	*Tillia pendula*...........	20	16	?	?
390	" Locust, Black or Yellow.	*Robinia pseud-acacia* ..,....	25	20	60	40
393	" Japan Sophora	*Sophora japonica*..........	20	16	45	40
395	" Virgilia	*Virgilia lutea*.............	25	16	45	40
397	" Kentucky Coffee-tree....	*Gymnocladus canadensis*...	25	20	50	40
398	" Ailantus.............	*Ailantus*	25	25	40	50
399	" Liquidamber	*Liquidamber*	25	16	60	40.
401	" Tupelo	*Nyssa biflora*............	20	16	50	40
402	" Cherry................	*Cerasus*.................	25	16	30	30
408	" Catalpa	*Catalpa syringafolia*......	25	30	50	70.
411	" Sassafras....	*Laurus sassafras*.........	20	16	40	40
413	" Paulownia ..	*Paulownia imperialis*......	20	20	40	60.
417	" Am. Red Mulberry.....	*Morus rubra*............	20	20	40	50.
418	" Downing Mulberry......	*Morus*	20	20	30	30
419	" Paper Mulberry........	*Broussonetia*.............	20	20	30	40.
420	" Osage Orange	*Maclura auriantica*........	25	30	40	60.
423	" Western Nettle-tree.....	*Celtis occidentalis*.........	20	20	30	30
424	" Nettle-tree, Hackberry..	*Celtis crassifolia*........	30	20	50	50.
424	" Paw-paw........		25	16	40	40.
425	" Cut-leaved Alder	*Alnus lacianata*	20	16	45	45
426	" Apple-tree...........	*Pyrus malus*............	20	16	30	40
429	" Pear-tree	*Pyrus*	20	16	40	30.
446	" Apricot	*Armeniaca vulgaris*.......	16	16	30	40
454	". Persimmon	*Dyospyros virginiaca*	20	16	40	40.

DECIDUOUS TREES OF THE SMALLEST CLASS.

Page	Popular Name.	Botanical Name.	Usual Size 12 Years from Seed.		Usual Size at Maturity.	
			Height.	Breadth.	Height.	Breadth.
336	The Dwarf Chestnut........	*Castanea pumila*...........	10 ft.	10 ft.	25 ft.	25 ft..
341	" Small Buckeye.........	*Æ. pavia rubra*...........	12	10	20	20
342	" California Buckeye......	*Æ. californica*............	12	12	20	20
346	" Striped-bark Maple.....	*Acer striatum*.............	20	16	25	30
347	" Guelder Rose-leaf Maple	*Acer p. opulifolium*........	12	10	30	30
347	" Spike-flowered Maple...	*Acer spicatum*.............	12	10	25	20
349	" English Field Maple....	*Acer campestris*...........	15	12	25	20
350	" Tartarian Maple........	*Acer tataricum*...........	15	10	25	20
357	" Weeping Ash..........	*Fraxinus excelsior pendula.*	15	15	30	30
358	" Golden Ash............	*Fraxinus aurea*..........	20	12	40	30
358	" Weeping Golden Ash...	*Fraxinus aurea pendula*...	15	15	30	30
358	" Ash-leaved Negundo....	*Negundo fraxinafolium*...	15	12	20	20.
359	" American Aspen	*Populus tremula trepida*...	25	16	40	30.
371	" Umbrella Magnolia.....	*Magnolia tripetela*........	20	16	20	20
374	" Swamp Magnolia.......	*M. glauca*...............*	10	10	15	15
375	" Chinese White Magnolia	*M. conspicua*.............	15	10	20	20
376	" Soulange Magnolia.....	*M. soulangeana*...........	15	15	20	30
381	" American White Birch...	*Betula populifolia*.........	20	10	35	30.
390	" Kilmarnock Willow.....	*S. caprea pendula*........*	8	10	10	15.
390	" Amer. Fountain Willow.	*Salix americana pendula..*	10	10	12	20
391	" Gummy Acacia........	*Robinia viscosa*...........	16	16	20	20.
394	" Weeping Japan Sophora	*Sophora japonica pendula.*	12	10	20	20.
403	" European Bird Cherry..	*Cerasus padus*............	15	12	25	25.
404	" Everflowering Weeping } Cherry .... }	*Cerasus semperflorens*......	10	10	15	15.
405	" Dwarf Weeping Cherry..	*Cerasus pumila pendula*...*	6	5	8	8
407	" Weeping Larch.........	*Larix pendula* ....*	10	15	20	30.
410	" Indian Catalpa.........	*Catalpa himalayensis*......	10	12	12	16
410	" Kempfer Catalpa.......	*Catalpa kempferi*.........	8	10	10	14
413	" Benzoin Laurel........	*Laurus benzoin*...........	12	10	16	16.
422	" Kolreuteria...........	*Kolreuteria paniculata*.....	16	12	20	40
423	" Western Nettle-tree.....	*Celtis occidentalis*..........	16	16	25	25.
428	" Crab Apple...........	*Pyrus malus coronaria.* ..	12	10	15	20.
429	" Siberian Crab..........	*Pyrus malus prunifolia....*	12	10	15	20
429	" Chinese Double-flower- } ing Crab.......... }	*Pyrus spectabilis*.........	12	10	20	30
431	" European Mountain Ash	*Pyrus sorbus aucuparia....*	15	10	25	25.
431	" European Weeping } Mountain Ash..... }	*Pyrus sorbus pendula.....*	10	15	15	20
431	" Oak-leaved Moun. Ash	*Pyrus sorbus pinatifida (quercifolia)*...........	20	12	30	30.
432	" Dwarf profuse-flower- } ing Mountain Ash. }	*Pyrus nana floribunda*.....	8	8	12	12
432	" White-flowered Dogwood	*Cornus florida*.............	12	12	16	30
434	" Cornelian Cherry.......	*Cornus mas*...............	10	8	14	16
436	" Judas or Red-bud.......	*Cercis canadensis*..........	12	12	20	30
437	" Halesia or Silver-bell....	*Halesia tetraptera*	12	12	20	30
438	" Thorn-trees............	*Crataegus.*	12	10	16	25
440	" Hawthorn.............	*Crataegus oxycantha*.......	12	10	20	25
448	" American Hornbeam....	*Carpinus americana*.......	16	10	30	20.
449	" Scotch Laburnum.......	*Cytissus alpina*............	16	10	16	16
449	" Amelanchier...........	*Amelanchia vulgaris*......	16	10	25	20
450	" Tamarisk.........:....	*Tamarix*.................	16	10	18	18
450	" Wych Hazel............	*Hamamelis*.......	16	10	25	20
451	" Tree Andromeda........	*Andromeda arborea*.......	12	9	30	30
451	" Tree Sumach..........	*Rhus typhina*.............	12	9	16	16
452	" Purple Fringe-tree.....	*Rhus cotinus*.............	10	8	20	20
453	" Chionanthus..........	*Chionanthus virginica*.....	12	8	20	12
474	" Hercules Club...	*Aralia spinosa.*	15	10	16	16
477	" Siberian Pea-tree	*Caragana arborescens..*	15	10	18	12
484	" European Elder........	*Sambucus nigra*...........	12	8	15	20

* Trees marked with a star are usually grafted on other stocks.

HARDY EVERGREEN TREES OF THE LARGEST SIZE.

Page	Popular Name.	Botanical Name.	Usual Size 12 Years from Seed.		Usual Size at Maturity.	
			Height.	Breadth.	Height.	Breadth.
515	The White Pine	*Pinus strobus*	25 ft.	16 ft.	90 ft.	60 ft.
524	" Jeffrey's Pine	" *jeffreyana*	25	16	100	60
526	" Austrian Pine	" *austriaca*	25	16	80	60
527	" Scotch Pine	" *sylvestris*	25	16	70	60
531	" Pyrenean	" *pyreneaca*	20	16	70	60
539	" Black or Red Spruce Fir	*Abies nigra* (*rubra*)	20	14	70	50
540	" Norway Spruce Fir	" *excelsa*	25	14	90	50
544	" Oriental Spruce Fir	" *orientalis*	20	14	70	50
547	" Hemlock Spruce Fir	" *canadensis*	20	14	70	50
552	" European Silver Fir	*Picea pectinata*	20	15	80	40
553	" Cephalonian Fir	" *cephalonica*	18	15	60	60
554	" Nordmann's Silver Fir	" *nordmaniana*	18	15	80	60
554	" Noble Silver Fir	" *nobilis*	10	12	150	80
571	" Nootka Sound Cypress	*Cupressus nootkaensis*	12	7	80	60
579	" "Big-tree" of California	*Sequoia gigantea*	16	10	150	70

EVERGREEN TREES OF SECONDARY SIZE.

Those marked P may require protection in some parts of the Northern States.

Page	Popular Name.	Botanical Name.				
531	The Swiss Stone Pine	*Pinus cembra*	10 ft.	5 ft.	40 ft.	20 ft.
540	" Weeping Black Spruce	*Abies nigra pendula*	12	10	?	?
542	" Conical Norway Spruce	" *excelsa conica*	12	6	30	15
542	" Inverted-branched Spruce	" " *inverta*	15	6	50	20
549	" Sargent Hemlock	" *canadensis sargenti*	10	10	30	40
552	" Weeping Silver Fir	*Picea pectinata pendula*	15	6	50	20
552	" Upright Silver Fir	" " *fastigiata*	20	8	50	20
556	" Siberian Silver Fir	" *pichta*	12	8	40	20
557	" Red Cedar	*Juniperus virginiana*	16	6 to 12	40	20
573	" Japan Cypress (P)	*Retinispora obtusa*	16	10	50	40
578	" Yew-leaved Torreya (P)	*Torreya taxifolia*	12	8	30	20
583	" American Holly (P)	*Ilex opaca*	10	7	30	20

EVERGREEN SMALL TREES AND SHRUBS.

Page	Popular Name.	Botanical Name.				
519	The Compact White Pine	*Pinus strobus compacta*	5 ft.	5 ft.	12 ft.	12 ft.
529	" Mugho Pine	" *mugho*	6	5	12	12
530	" Mountain Pine	" *pumilio*	6	7	12	18
541	" Pigmy Spruce	*Abies excelsa pygmæa*	1	2	2	4
541	" Dwarf Black Spruce	" " *nigra pumila*	3	4	5	6
542	" Gregory's Dwarf Spruce	" " *gregoriana*	3	4	5	8
551	" Hudson's Bay Silver Fir	*Picea hudsonica*	4	5	?	?
553	" Oblate Dwarf Silver Fir	" *pectinata compacta*	3	4	4	7
559	" Swedish Juniper (P)	*Juniperus suecica*	10	3	18	8
560	" Irish Juniper (P)	" *hibernica*	10	2	18	6
560	"Oblong Weeping Juniper(P)	" *oblonga pendula*	10	5	20	15
561	" Scale-leaved Juniper	" *squamata*	5	10	15	20
564	" American Arbor Vitæ	*Thuja occidentalis*	15	8	20	10
565	" Parsons's Arbor Vitæ	" *o. compacta*	8	8	12	12
565	" Am. Golden Arbor Vitæ	" *o. aurea*	12	6	20	10
565	" Siberian Arbor Vitæ	" *siberica*	12	8	20	12
567	" Weeping Arbor Vitæ (P)	*Biota pendula*	10	6	15	10
567	" Golden Arbor Vitæ (P)	" *orientalis aurea*	6	5	8	6
575	" Erect Yew (P)	*Taxus baccata erecta*	10	5	15	8
575	" Golden Yew (P)	" *baccata aurea*	5	4	10	8
576	" Fortune's Cephalotaxus(P)	*Cephalotaxus fortunii*	8	9	20	20
577	" Japan Podocarpus (P)	*Podocarpus japonica*	12	6	?	?
583	" Holly-leaved Mahonia	*Mahonia aquifolium*	5	7	5	8
585	" Tree Box	*Buxus sempervirens arborea*	5	5	18	18
586	" Dwarf Garden Box (P)	" *suffruticosa*	1½	1½	8	8
586	" Rhododendron	*Rhododendron*	4 to 12	4 to 12	4 to 16	4 to 16
590	" Dwarf Andromeda (P)	*Andromeda floribunda*	2	4	3	6
591	" Daphne Cneorum	*Daphne cneorum*	2	2	3	3

COMMON DECIDUOUS SHRUBS.

In estimating the usual size six years after planting, it is supposed that the plants when set out are of the sizes usually obtained from nurseries.

Page	Popular Name.	Botanical Name.	Size at 6 years.		Size at Maturity.	
			Height.	Breadth.	Height.	Breadth.
340	The Dwarf Double-fl. Horse-Chestnut...	*Æsculas nana fl. pl.*........	6 ft.	4 ft.	10 ft.	7 ft..
341	" Two-col. Horse-Chestnut.	*Æ. pavia discolor*.........*			10	10
342	" Dwf. White-fl. "	*Æ. p. macrostachia*.......			12	20
377	" Purple-flowered Magnolia	*Magnolia purpurea*........	6	6	6	10
391	" Rose Acacia.............	*Robinia hespida rosea*.....*	8	8	10	12
434	" Red-twigged Dogwood...	*Cornus stolonifera*..........	7	7	8	12
447	" Chinese Double-fl. Plum.	*Prunus sinensis*.............	?	?	?	?
461	" Common White Lilac....	*Syringa alba*...	9	5	15	10
462	" Common Purple Lilac...	" *vulgaris*..........	7	4	10	8
462	" Persian Lilac............	" *persica*.............	5	5	8	10
463	" Rothmagensis Lilac.....	" *rothmagensis*......	6	6	8	10
463	" Bush Honeysuckles.....	*Lonicera tartarica*..........	4 to8	4 to6	6to10	8 to12
464	" Syringas..	*Philadelphus*................	7	7	8	12
466	" Snow-ball Viburnum.....	*Viburnum opulus*..........	7	7	10	15
466	" Dwarf "	" *o. nana*..........	4	4	6	6
467	" Japan "	" *plicatum*........	7	7	?	?
467	" Great-leaved "	" *macrophyllum*..	7	7	10	15
468	" Rose Weigela...........	*Weigela rosea*............	7	7	1	15
469	" Lovely Weigela...	" *amabilis*	8	10	18	15
469	" White-flowered Weigela...	" *nivea*..........	4	6	7	10·
470	" Rough leaved Deutzia...	*Deutzia scabra*...........	8	8	10	15
470	" Double White Deutzia...	" *crenata fl.-pl.*......	6	6	8	10
470	" Pink "	" *rubra fl.-pl.*.......	6	6	8	10·
470	" Graceful "	" *gracilis*........	4	4	5	8
471	" Altheas.................	*Hibiscus*...................	7	4	10	8
472	" Dwarf Almond..........	*Amygdalus nana*..........	3	3	4	4
476	" Berberries....	*Berberis*	6	6	7	10·
477	" Calycanthus..............	*Calycanthus*	4	4	7	7
480	" Clethras............	*Clethra*	5	5	7	10
480	" Bladder Senna..........	*Colutea arborescens*........	9	5	10	7
481	" Yellow-flowering Currant..	*Ribes aureum*.........	6	8	7	10
481	" Red-flowering "	" *sanguineum*...........	6	8	7	10·
481	" Gordon's flowering "	" *gordoni*...............	6	8	7	10
482	" Foschia Gooseberry...	" *speciosum*.............	3	3	4	5
484	" American Elder.........	*Sambucus canadensis*.......	8	8	10	15
485	" Variegated-leaf Elder....	" *variegata*.........	8	8	10	15
485	" American Euonymus.....	*Euonymus americana*......	8	5	10	10·
486	" Broad-leaf "	" *latifolius*........	10	6	15	15
487	" Forsythia	*Forsythia viridissima*......	7	7	8	10
488	" Purple-leaf Filbert.......	*Corylus purpurea*...........	7	7	8	10
489	" Oak-leaved Hydrangea...	*Hydrangea quercifolia*.....	5	5	6	8
490	" Japan Hydrangea........	" *deutziafolia*....	5	5	6	8
492	" Tree Pœony.......	*Pæony moutan*..............	4	4	6	8
493	" Common Privet.........	*Ligustrum vulgaris*........	8	5	10	10
496	" Japan Quince............	*Cydonia japonica*..........	4	4	5	7
497	" Roses...........	*Rosa*	1 to7	1 to5	1 to7	1 to7
510	" Spireas.................	*Spirea*....................	2 to8	3 to8	3 to10	3 to12·
512	" Stuartia................	*Stuartia pentagynia*.......	6	5	10	16
513	" Waxberries.............	*Symphoricarpus*...........	3	4	4	6

INDEX.

39

Lightning Source UK Ltd.
Milton Keynes UK
UKHW02n1207120218
317657UK00006B/1160/P